The Development of Education in Canada

JARVIS COLLEGIATE INSTITUTE, TORONTO, ONT.

In the centre of the facing page is shown the present-day Jarvis Collegiate (1922) surrounded by buildings that successively housed the establishment during the preceding 115 years.

1807   *The Home District School: a small, low, stone building attached to the frame house of the Reverend Dr. Okill Stuart who taught there.*

1816   *"The Old Blue School", so called because of its blue-painted exterior: a two-storeyed frame structure.*

1829   *The old Grammar School: for a short time amalgamated with Upper Canada College and re-established separately in 1834.*

1864   *Toronto Grammar School, Dalhousie Street, north of Gould Street.*

1871   *Toronto High School, Jarvis Street. From 1869 to 1871, classes were held in King's College, Queen's Park while arrangements were being made for this building.*

1922   *Jarvis Street Collegiate Institute, Jarvis Street at Wellesley.*

578

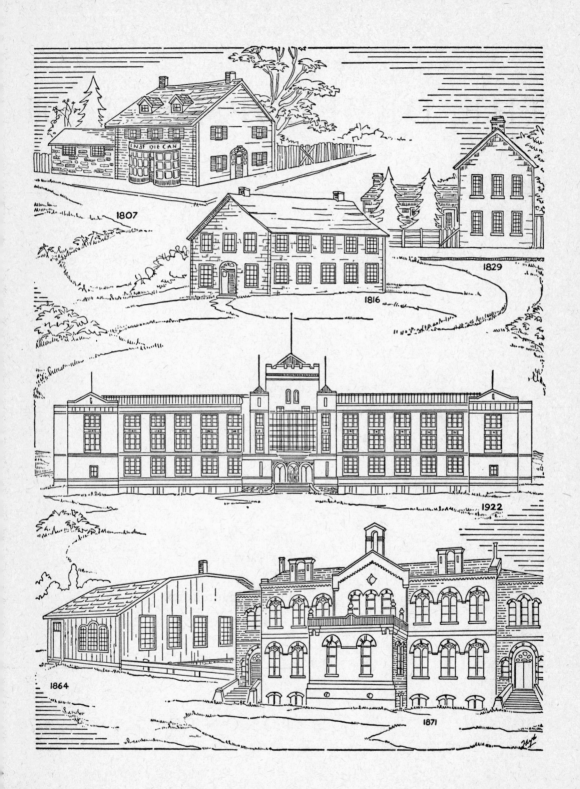

THE DEVELOPMENT OF

Illustrated by
Fay Edwards
and
Priscilla Hutchings

TORONTO   1957

EDUCATION IN CANADA

Charles E. Phillips

Professor of Education
Ontario College of Education
University of Toronto

W. J. GAGE AND COMPANY LIMITED

578

Printed and Bound in Canada
By W. J. Gage & Co., Limited

Contents

Foreword

"We are the workers of a new dawn . . .
. . . Men who look forward . . ."

"That forward view will reveal to educators of all times the vision of all seekers — the spires of the city of God — that world wherein Truth and Beauty and Justice hold sway. They will not reach it themselves but their pupils will set out towards it with higher hopes and braver hearts because of their Teacher's help."

If as has been said we are witnessing a race between catastrophe and education it should be a revealing experience to have a flashback of the race from the beginning so far as Canada is concerned. This we have in *The Development of Education in Canada*. Sir Percy Nunn once said "We have all got hold of a dream we are trying to convert into reality, that education is not something to be given to the elite of a nation to sunder the classes more than nature has done, but it is something to develop the whole manhood and womanhood of a nation."

Again "A progressive society must adapt its educational system to the idea of change and must learn how to combine flexibility of mind with firmness of purpose."

"The citizen of a democracy must be a man of independent judgment; he must care intensely for freedom; he must respect the individuality of others and therefore be tolerant of opinions in conflict with his own; he must prefer methods of discussion and persuasion to methods of force."

These quotations seem to me to sum up the philosophy of this book.

Education in Canada has waited a long time for an historian and interpreter. Dr. Charles E. Phillips is admirably fitted for this role. He is a product of Canadian institutions; he has had unusual opportunities not only for observing the educational scene in all the Provinces but has shared generously in the shaping of modern programs. He has long been a student of history with special reference to education. His experience as editor of *The School* and later as Executive Secretary of the Canadian Education Association have well fitted him for the task of producing at once an informative, authoritative, and well documented book. Students of education, teachers, trustees, parents — indeed anyone in this country at all interested in knowing how we came to be what we are will find themselves greatly in debt to Dr. Phillips.

I count it an honor and a pleasure to have the privilege of saying a word of welcome to this significant and important work.

G. Fred McNally

Edmonton, 1955.

Preface

One should know what to expect and what not to expect before deciding to read a lengthy book like this. The next four short paragraphs explain its theme.

Two centuries ago schools were provided for children of the people, through religious and charitable agencies, by a few who had the means and the will to support them. The purpose and content of the meagre education offered in these schools were determined, of course, by those who provided it.

Today in Canada the people provide schools for their children and decide, however indirectly, the types of education they want. They do this through public school systems. One purpose now of education under public control is to strengthen the ability of successive generations to decide — in education as in other affairs of life and government — the means and ends of their own lives.

Thus a radical change has occurred both in the control and administration of schools and in the character of education. Obviously the change has been related to economic, political, and other social developments of the last two centuries.

The Development of Education in Canada is an explanation of how this change in education came about. In Parts I and II it gives an account of the origin and early development of education in different parts of Canada. In Parts III and IV it deals topically with various aspects of school administration and of educational thought and practice.

As an exposition of this major change in education the book has certain characteristics which will please some and which need not annoy others if they are forewarned.

The content is almost wholly Canadian. Our country is grown-up enough now to take a nation-wide view of its educational development without perpetual bobbing of heads and Thank you, sir's for every idea we may have borrowed. I have acknowledged our indebtedness briefly in appropriate chapters. If educators of other times and places have been slighted, there are many histories of education elsewhere to do them justice.

The book is written from an uncompromisingly democratic and rather strongly equalitarian point of view. It is concerned with the education of all Canadians, not mainly with outstanding people, as historical works generally are. Its preferred criterion of knowledge and ignorance is not how soon enlightened words were spoken but how many lived enlightened lives.

By any such criterion, of course, the past is likely to suffer in comparison with the present — with regard not only to educational achievement but to nearly everything else. The historian's sympathetic interest in his subject usually nourishes an admiration, if not a nostalgia, for bygone days. But *The Development of Education in Canada* is an account of past developments as leading to the present and as judged by the values of the present. As such it should be agreeable to adults who need no convincing that life in Canada today is the best kind of life we know, who see better people than themselves in the younger generation, and who look to the future for a golden age.

Since there has been no other comprehensive work on the subject, it seemed necessary to weave into the narrative thousands of facts. In topical chapters it was something of a problem to give fair representation to separate developments in ten educationally independent provinces. There was danger of infecting every page with a rash of For example's. To avoid doing this, I have asked the reader to accept a convention: particular statements are local illustrations which imply no denial of similar occurrences elsewhere. As compensation I think I can promise that most of the chapters will not be found heavy going.

But those with no interest in administration are warned against the first few chapters of Part III. Study of administrative developments is valuable and intriguing to the administrator, but wearisome to most of us.

The breadth of the field and the multiplicity of detail give another cause for worry. In spite of every precaution, there are sure to be errors. I hope that they are minor ones and that readers will be charitable to one who has had the temerity to pioneer over such an extensive area.

Readers well-informed about Canada may wonder why it was thought necessary to introduce early chapters with sketchy statements on the size, location, and political development of the region under discussion. The intent is to make the book intelligible to readers in other countries. Other sections on social developments were included for different reasons: because people are educated not only by the school but also by the whole environment, and because social change helps to explain educational change. In all cases content of a more general nature was selected for its pertinence to the educational theme. It is not intended to be a substitute for the more comprehensive and balanced treatment of a general history.

Limits had to be set to the scope of the work. There is only incidental mention of higher education. For later years, the same might be said of private schools, because attention is focussed on education under public control from the time when the provincial systems of education were established. Although an effort has been made to do at least partial justice to French-speaking Canada, it was inevitable in topical chapters that fewer illustrations of developments should be drawn from Quebec because of the distinctive character of education and other exceptional conditions in that province. In spite of necessary omissions and possible failure to be fair to every point of view, there is no intent to be contemptuous of any institution or agency engaged in the work of public education in Canada.

If the book as described is likely to please you, I hope you read and enjoy it.

A comprehensive history of this kind would not be possible if others had not written histories of different aspects of education and histories of education in many different localities. The author is indebted most of all to graduate students in education who engaged in the historical research which is reported in their theses for the master's or doctor's degree. These theses cover considerable ground, but leave much for other students to do, particularly in relation to educational thought and classroom practice. The author is also indebted to others who have published histories of education in some of the provinces of Canada, and, for the more general social background, to Canadian historians and other social scientists. The number whose works were consulted or quoted was so large that acknowledgment by name must be made by referring the reader to the bibliography. Moreover, to spare the reader footnotes and the distraction of hundreds of numerical references in the text, acknowledgment of sources of quotations is made at the end of the book by reference to page and line. For the willing and efficient assistance of librarians and archivists no writer can express adequate appreciation.

Exhausting routine chores at school and at home have left too few Canadian educators with time and energy to write. Thanks to my two bosses — Cliff and Jean — for making this effort possible.

C. E. P.

Toronto, 1957

PART ONE

The French Regime

The period covered in this part extends from 1604 to 1763 — from the first attempt by Frenchmen to settle in Canada to the final cession of Canada to the English by the Treaty of Paris. During the period there were intermittent wars between England and France and continual rivalry for colonial advantage in North America. The two major French settlements were (1) The Quebec Colony and (2) Acadia. The former remained under French government until 1763 except between 1629 and 1632, when it was held by the British; the latter came by treaty under English control in 1713 but the social and educational life of the French settlements was not greatly affected until close to the later date.

CHAPTER I

The Quebec Colony

THE RELIGIOUS AIM · CONVERSION OF INDIANS · EDUCATION IN FRANCE
OCCUPATIONAL INFLUENCES · TOWN LIFE · THE GENTRY · GOVERNMENT
THE CHURCH AND MORALITY · INSTITUTIONS FOR FORMAL EDUCATION
ELEMENTARY SCHOOLS FOR BOYS · SCHOOLS FOR GIRLS · PRACTICAL
EDUCATION · SECONDARY EDUCATION · AN APPRAISAL · SUMMARY

THE history of the Quebec colony began in 1608, when Champlain founded what is now the city of Quebec — the first permanent settlement of the French in Canada. Although explorers and fur traders ranged far inland, the land occupied during the French regime by any considerable number of residents consisted of a narrow strip on each side of the St. Lawrence, extending about 250 miles towards the mouth of the river from Montreal and including the original settlement of Quebec as its capital.

The expansion of the Quebec colony was retarded by internal disorder in France and also by opposition to extensive settlement from those who were anxious only for profits from the fur trade. Not until 1617 did the first farmer begin to clear his land, and in 1628 there were only sixty-five residents in the original settlement at Quebec. More active colonization began in 1634, which was also the year in which a fort was built eighty miles up the St. Lawrence at Three Rivers. In 1642 a party of colonists from France settled ninety miles farther up at Montreal. Between 1659 and 1673, largely because the King of France took over the government from a trading company, some 4000 immigrants arrived. In the later year, when sponsorship of emigration to Canada ceased, the total population was 6705. Before the end of the seventeenth century it was over 15,000. Thereafter it approximately doubled in each of the succeeding thirty-year periods, and it was more than 60,000 when the whole of Canada came under English rule in 1763.

The Religious Aim

To understand education during the French regime, one must keep in mind that the one agency claiming responsibility for the formal instruction of the young was the church. In principle this was true of all countries in the western world at the time, but of New France it was true both in principle and in practice. In the Quebec colony the church used its educational prerogative so exclusively and so zealously that virtually all schools and educational institutions were under direct ecclesiastical control, and most of the intentional work of education, apart from the efforts of parents, was performed by secular priests or members of religious orders. There were, as always, a few exceptions: apparently some immigrants who were unwilling or unable to do manual work took up teaching in rural districts. This practice resulted in an ordinance of 1727 forbidding anyone to teach the young without permission in writing from the bishop. We may therefore assume that in the comparatively few cases where lay teachers were employed — chiefly in country schools for boys — there was close supervision by church authorities. Moreover, there was only one church — the Roman Catholic Church. Huguenots were not permitted to settle in the colony, and there was no alternative creed or form of worship to breach the authority of Rome.

The primary aim of education, therefore, was the aim of the Roman Catholic Church: to ensure the salvation of souls — of as many Indians as could be reached and of all the colonists if possible. In Protestant countries a similar aim appears at times to have been associated rather closely with the more immediate objective of material gain, so that no inconsistency was seen in a greater emphasis on secular subjects, and education preponderantly religious at first later became more utilitarian. But educators in the Quebec colony kept both eyes without misgiving on the spiritual purpose, and gave attention to more worldly and practical content only as a necessity subsidiary to that purpose, or as a supplement when the achievement of the primary purpose was well assured. Any fair exposition and appraisal of education in the Quebec colony must be based in the first instance on an acceptance of this dominating religious objective. Later we may assess the implications of that objective and of related practice with reference to other social and ethical values which many of us today have in mind, but to which the church in the seventeenth and eighteenth century gave no approving thought.

The dramatic theme in the development of education in the Quebec colony is the unremitting struggle of the church to attain its objective against opposing forces in the environment. Our plan, therefore, will be to examine the characteristics of pupils and teachers, the occupational, geographical, and other factors affecting education, the agencies and means of formal education, and the results achieved — all in relation to the objective of the protagonist.

Conversion of Indians

The tireless zeal, self-sacrifice, and heroism of the French missionaries among the Indians of Canada are too impressive to be forgotten. It will be sufficient here to recall the name of Jean de Brébeuf and the total of twenty-nine missionaries who labored among the Hurons between 1615 and 1650 and of whom seven suffered a violent death. Although the Jesuits bore the brunt of missionary work, the Recollets established the first permanent mission in 1615 at Quebec and what may perhaps be called the first schools, that of Brother Pacifique at Three Rivers in 1616 and that of Father Le Caron at Tadoussac in 1618, both for Indian children, of course. The Recollets left the colony in 1629, but returned in 1670. Perhaps even more moving than the work of men in either order was that of the Ursuline nuns, gentle women who in 1639 came to a still harsh land to teach the children of "savages" and, heedless of hardship and danger, to save at least a few immortal souls. As compared with English settlements in New England and elsewhere, New France was remarkable for the amount of missionary effort. No doubt, as Colby suggests, this was partly because the Roman Catholic had no doubts regarding the efficacy of baptism to ensure the salvation of those who died at an early age, or of conversion and the sacraments to benefit those who lived; whereas the Calvinist might think he was wasting part of his time on some who were predestined, according to his unbending doctrine, for another fate.

The Indians were not wholly unpromising pupils. They were credited with good qualities, including generosity and hospitality, fortitude under hardship and suffering, and retentive memories. As James Hannay, a historian of Acadia writing in 1879, points out, their reputation has not been enhanced by having only their enemies as historians; he praises their honesty and their record of having offered no insults to female captives in spite of any injury their vengeance imposed. Their accomplishments may have been few: since they had no true writing, the boy's education was largely concerned with skill in the hunt and valor in war, and the girl was an accomplished bride if she could make snow-shoes, moccasins, pouches, and birch dishes, string wampum beads, and boil the kettle. Their agriculture was limited and their homes were temporary or without the solid gains of permanent settlement and cumulative achievement. But the Indians in Canada, except the Iroquois, who were associated with the English, were for the most part

friendly and helpful to the French. On more than one occasion they saved the lives of colonists who were perishing from hunger and cold. A chief reason for their good disposition may be that the French treated them with greater kindness than did the white men farther south and were primarily and sincerely concerned about their spiritual welfare.

But even zealous workers encountered great difficulties in teaching the Indians. The red men for the most part were hunters constantly on the move, and continuous instruction was rarely possible. When they were in camp they not unnaturally preferred feasting, singing, dancing, jesting, games, or contests to serious instruction from foreigners on their spiritual deficiencies and the means of salvation. They had an animistic religion which sought to gain the favor of good spirits and drive away the bad; and although their belief in an after-life even for animals may have predisposed them to acceptance of Christian doctrine on immortality, their medicine men, trained in the lore of healing and of the supernatural, were jealously opposed to invading rivals who taught another creed and challenged their security.

The new teachers, besides, had a strange language to master. It is said that within five months of their arrival in Quebec in 1639 two of the Ursuline Sisters had prepared themselves to instruct the Indians in their own tongue. For more thorough teaching, however, the Jesuits composed a grammar and a dictionary and translated the catechism. The Jesuits also avoided the Indians' resentment by rejecting only what was irreconcilable with Christianity in pagan customs and beliefs, and by making conversion easier for the Indian learner by developing concepts already in his mind. But for one reason or another instruction of the Indians must have been a laborious and discouraging task, especially in the outposts or far off from

*Madame Champlain teaching Indian children
(from the painting by W. Sherriff Scott)*

We take Indian girls of all ages. It happens that if an Indian, whether a Christian or a Pagan, wishes to commit a breach of duty and carry off some one of his nation to keep her against the law of God, she is committed to us and we teach and protect her till the Reverend Fathers [the Jesuits] come and remove her. Others come and go like birds of passage, and remain only till they become homesick when their parents take them away, lest they die. While we do not give them full liberty in this respect, by humoring them we win them over better by persuasion rather than retaining them by force. Others persevere and we bring them up as French girls. We look after their welfare and they do well. One of them was given to M. Boucher, who was afterwards governor of Three Rivers. But others, who speak French and read and write, return to their parents.[2]

civilization in the Indian villages. In Quebec itself, the chief centre of the colony, the work was made somewhat easier by facilities at hand, since it could be combined to an extent with the teaching of French children. A Jesuit *Relation* of 1642-43 mentions the work of the Ursulines soon after the sisters' arrival:

They are in a place of safety, so far as it is possible in Canada, being located from 80 to 100 paces from the fort of Kebec. They have always had a fairly good number of Savage girls, both permanent and temporary boarders, besides the little French girls; and many Savages, men and women, often come to visit them and to receive some help and instruction.[1]

Marie de l'Incarnation, superior of the Ursulines, wrote in 1668 that the Indian girls often became homesick and had to be allowed to go, but that the sisters persevered with others and tried to bring them up as if they were French girls:

This attempt not only to convert Indian children but to absorb them into the French culture applied to boys as well as to girls. It was encouraged by Louis XIV but was not much more successful than the later attempt of the English to Anglicize the French. The following account by Laval, Bishop of Quebec in the latter part of the seventeenth century, tells about his efforts in this direction and is an interesting revelation of the many difficulties encountered in the education of Indian children:

As the King has notified me that he desires us to attempt to bring up the little Savage children after the French manner of life, in order to civilize them, little by little, I have formed a Seminary, into which I have taken a number of children, from whom, by living with them, the Savages will learn more easily the customs and the language. This enterprise is not without difficulty, on the part of both the children and the parents; the latter have an extraordinary love for their children, and can scarcely make up their minds to be separated from them. Or, if they do permit this, it is very difficult to effect the separation for any length of time, for the reason that ordinarily the families of the Savages do not have many children, as do those of our French people — in which there are generally in this country, 8, 10, 12 and sometimes as many as 15 and 16 children. The Savages, on the contrary usually only two or three; and rarely do they exceed the number of four. As a result, they depend on their children, when they are somewhat advanced in years, for the support of their family. This can only be gained by the Chase, and by other labors for which the parents are no longer fit when their children have the years and ability to help them; to do so at that time, the Law of nature seems to constrain the children by necessity. Nevertheless, we shall spare no pains on our part, to make this blessed undertaking succeed, although its success seems to us very doubtful.[3]

Bishop Laval

Education in France

As we turn to conditions influencing the education of white children, the first factor to be considered is the educational level of those who came as colonists from France. The desire for education, like a northerner's taste for olives, is ordinarily acquired, and even today the parents most anxious to provide a lengthy period of schooling for their children are usually those who in one way or another have acquired considerable education themselves.

Nearly all of the minority who held places of influence in the Quebec colony were, of course, educated men — the secular and regular priests, the officers of the sovereign council of government, the justices of inferior rank, and most of the officers of the army, retired officers, and other gentlemen, including the seigneurs. But what of the merchants, artisans, and laborers, and of the growing number of habitants who established farms on the banks of the St. Lawrence? Perhaps one thing should be said before we consider their origin: the social chasm

between classes in New France was neither as wide nor as deep as in old France; communication and friendly relations were both possible, and the influence of the better educated on the more ignorant might be personal and rather more effective than in the old country.

Two facts should be kept in mind about conditions in France in the sixteenth and seventeenth centuries. First, the mass of the people lived in wretched poverty and were without the means of voicing an effective protest. The king, the nobility, and the gentry, including the lesser nobles and wealthy merchants, generally had no real concern about the ignorance of the common people; they preferred the majority to be illiterate or at least not sufficiently literate to acquire and disseminate subversive ideas. This is true despite the fact that an ordinance of 1560, re-enacted by King Henry IV ten years before the founding of Quebec, required parents under penalty of a fine to send their sons and daughters to school. Laws are of little avail without the will and the means to put them into effect. Barnard adds that the poor themselves were not always anxious to have their children receive an education even when it was offered free of cost.

The second fact, however, is that more was done for the education of the poor in Catholic France in the sixteenth and seventeenth centuries than was done in England up to the end of the eighteenth century. The Roman Catholic Church, stimulated to greater effort by the Protestant Reformation, tried in many ways to provide schools for the poor. In a considerable number of localities throughout the country there were parish, or charity, schools under the direction of the local curé, and the number of these was increasing towards the end of the seventeenth century. In Paris and other large cities and in the north and east of France, excluding Britanny, there were numerous *petites écoles* commonly taught by lay teachers but under the supervision of the Church. Schools of both types were free to the poor although the masters and mistresses of the latter were often obliged to take some fee-paying pupils in order to exist. Hence there was a considerable, if inadequate, provision for elementary education in larger centres of population and in some sections of the country. This more favorable estimate of the number of schools for children of the people is based on the results of research in the latter part of the nineteenth century; it compels at least a modification of the common impression that children of the poor in seventeenth century France were all but destitute of any useful or significant educational advantage.

Gosselin, a historian of education in Quebec, has therefore some reason for insisting that the early settlers in the colony had during their childhood in France at least the opportunity for elementary schooling in the three R's. He points out that a good many of these settlers had come from Normandy or from other provinces in the west and north of France which were well supplied with schools. Whether or not many children did actually receive the benefit of secular instruction is still uncertain. "Except in Scotland and some parts of Germany", wrote William Boyd, "most of the common people got no education at all; and most of those who were relatively more fortunate got their education under the worst possible conditions."[4] Evidently that was not quite true of France in the seventeenth century, where even methods of instruction were sometimes more enlightened than in other countries. According to the statistician Maggiolo, literacy as judged by ability to sign marriage contracts ranged from five to forty-six per cent in the different cantons of France towards the end of the seventeenth century and from eight to seventy-two per cent towards the end of the eighteenth century, with averages of twenty-five per cent and forty per cent respectively. Cubberley estimated that more than half of French men and three-quarters of French women were unable to sign their names at the beginning of the nineteenth century. If we assume that the proportion of literate men and women was relatively high in sections of France from which the colonists came to Quebec in the seventeenth century, it seems probable that about one third of the settlers were literate by this not very exacting criterion.

From another point of view, however, the emigrants to Canada might be regarded as very well educated. Whether they had attended school or not, they had almost certainly been taught the essential prayers, doctrines, and observances of the Roman Catholic Church, and such religious knowledge had almost certainly been reinforced by regular practice. A speaker addressing a conference of teachers in the *petites écoles* of Paris in the seventeenth century warned his hearers that they had been appointed "not only to teach children reading, writing, arithmetic, the church service, and grammar (i.e. the elements of Latin), but also to teach them the catechism and to give them instruction in Christian doctrine."[5] In charity schools the religious content was even more preponderant. Early in the sixteenth century the Council of Chartres had decreed that every parish, if it were possible, should have a free school conducted by a "priest or clerk sufficiently well educated to teach the children the Lord's Prayer, the Creed, and the other things which are contained in the 'Alphabet' (i.e. a primer)."[6] As we shall see later, the religious aim was no less emphasized in schools established by teaching orders, which were growing in number and importance in France at the time. There is every reason to believe that those who had not become literate, no less than those who had, were well prepared by instruction and experience to retain a belief in Catholic doctrine and to be anxious that their children in the new world should receive similar teaching from the priests and other servants of the church.

Occupational Influences

A second consideration affecting the success of educational endeavor was the type of occupation which was to dominate life in the colony. The first continuing North American interest of influential men in France was the fur trade, which was a quick source of high profits. For more than half a century, control over the Quebec colony was exercised by a trading company which discouraged large-scale immigration and the extension of agriculture. During this period and later, adventurous Frenchmen in Canada engaged more or less illicitly in the fur trade as *coureurs de bois*. Setting out by canoe they went to the camps or villages of the Indians far from the white men's settlements. Their life was one which called for courage and hardiness, but it held for them the compensation of freedom from the restraints of church, government, and a restrictive social code. When they returned from the vast forest to the little patch of civilization, they sold at a good profit the furs acquired from the Indians in exchange for cheap gew-gaws from France. They then squandered their surplus money in celebrations shocking to pious and respectable citizens of the town and were off again to the hazardous but uninhibited life of the woods, and to their lady loves or wives and the unlicensed pleasures of the Indian villages. If the church could have found no lay members other than intractable men like these, it could hardly have succeeded in educating new generations to build the solid and devout communities characteristic of the Quebec colony in later years.

Nine years after the founding of Quebec, the first farmer, Louis Hébert, began to clear and dig his land on the site of the Upper Town of Quebec. Shortly thereafter a few farms were established along the north shore of the river. But for a long time the rural population was scattered in small clusters all but isolated from one another, because prior to the building of roads their easiest means of communication was by canoe. Towards the end of the seventeenth century many settlers were disbanded soldiers living out of reach of the government, seldom within sight of a priest, and independent and lawless in behavior. Their chief contact with civilization was through alcohol, which Parkman says was sold in half of the score of houses to be found in the villages of some seigneuries. Among these remote settlers a boy at an early age might be given a gun and allowed to go off into the woods. Sometimes he would make friends among the Indians and forsake what few civilized ways he had acquired for the attractions of Indian life. In any case he was soon beyond the possibility of restraint by his parents, and was ill prepared for the discipline of regular work and family life. The difficulties were explained by Denonville, governor from 1685-1689, as follows:

This, Monseigneur, seems to be the place for rendering you an account of the disorders which prevail not only in the woods, but also in the settlements. They arise from the idleness of young persons, and the great liberty which fathers, mothers and guardians have for a long time given them, or allowed them to assume, of going into the forest under pretence of hunting or trading. This has come to such a pass, that, from the moment a boy can carry a gun, the father cannot restrain him and dares not offend him. You can judge the mischief that follows. These disorders are always greatest in the families of those who are *gentilshommes,* or who through laziness or vanity pass themselves off as such. Having no resource but hunting, they must spend their lives in the woods, where they have no curés to trouble them, and no fathers or guardians to constrain them. I think, Monseigneur, that martial law would suit their case better than any judicial sentence. Monsieur de la Barre [the former governor] suppressed a certain order of knighthood which had sprung up here, but he did not abolish the usages belonging to it. It was thought a fine thing and a good joke to go about naked and tricked out like Indians, not only on carnival days, but on all other days of feasting and debauchery. These practices tend to encourage the disposition of our young men to live like savages, frequent their company, and be forever unruly and lawless like them. I cannot tell you, Monseigneur, how attractive this Indian life is to all our youth. It consists in doing nothing, caring for nothing, following every inclination and getting out of the way of all correction.[7]

Denonville insisted that if the children of settlers were not to remain in ignorance more parishes would have to be established and more curés installed. Even in the early eighteenth century when there were more parishes and priests, there was difficulty in providing schools; children of the dispersed population could not be brought together or reached by a teacher other than the curé, who on Sundays and fête days had enough to do to teach them the catechism when they came to church with their parents. But after the larger wave of immigration in the last third of the seventeenth century, and the growing up of an increasing number of large families, the farms on both sides of the river began to take the arrangement of two rows of elongated dominoes with their long sides touching and with one short end marked by the water's edge. The Swedish naturalist, Peter Kalm, who visited New France in 1749, wrote that even then each church was surrounded by a little village consisting largely of the priest's residence and a school for boys and girls. This cannot be accepted as evidence that there were schools in all districts at a time when universal education and literacy in older countries were regarded as an impossibility by most people and as anything but desirable by not a few. But the conversion to an agricultural economy supplied the church with parishioners who were stable and amenable to discipline. If only a fraction of the children in the rural parishes were given daily instruction in secular subjects at school, and not very much or for very long, the farms were close enough together for the parents and the priest to make sure that all learned the catechism and were in other ways prepared for confirmation. When in 1760 much of the land along the north shore of the river, and some on the south shore, was under cultivation and when three-quarters of the population lived on farms, the church had not only obtained conditions conducive to the success of its educational program but by successfully fostering the growth of an agricultural economy had given proof of accomplishment.

The life of a habitant's family was simple and regular. There was hard work to be done in the fields, not only for the father and older sons, but for the women as well. Nearly everything was made at home — furniture, most clothing, and much of the cloth. The father was a handy-man at all trades. The mother's life was particularly laborious: she did all kinds of household chores with primitive equipment, looked after her many children, and had no store from which to purchase ready-made supplies. But there were diversions. Going to mass on Sundays and holy days was not only an obligation but a social opportunity. Any event like a marriage was made the most of by neighbors and relatives invited to the celebration. Visiting and stopping to chat, singing, dancing, and skating in winter were enjoyed to the full. Those who came to the Quebec colony were struck by the evident happiness of the people, in spite of their comparative poverty. The following observation by Peter Kalm in 1749 suggests that they also took delight in purchasing a little finery and a few luxuries at the high prices prevailing, but we need not believe that they regularly deprived themselves of all good food for this purpose:

The common people in the country seem to be very poor. They have the necessaries of life and but little else. They are content with meals of dry bread and water, bringing all other provisions, such as butter, cheese, flesh, poultry, eggs, etc., to town in order to get money for them, for which they buy clothes and brandy for themselves, and dresses for their women. Notwithstanding their poverty, they are always cheerful and in high spirits.[8]

Town Life - The Gentry

A third factor which had an effect on education was town life, especially of the better-to-do, in Quebec and Montreal. The urban centres grew slowly. In Quebec in 1663 there were about one hundred houses in the lower town close to the river and only a few in the upper town on the heights; by 1712 there were about 2500 inhabitants in all, and by 1763 about 8000. In Montreal and its whole surround-

A habitant family (from a painting by Kornelius Krieghoff)

ing district there were 625 people in 1666, and in the city of Montreal itself about 5,000 people in 1763. Quebec was the more dignified city, especially its upper town, where there were no places of business but only church and educational buildings and the residences of the governor and the gentry. Montreal was a centre of the fur trade. Even in 1763, Three Rivers was only a village of about 600 population.

The social life of the upper classes was enjoyable and lively: it included outings in carriages, sleighs, or canoes, horse-racing, skating, shooting, and parties for cards and dancing. The social gaiety at the governor's residence in Quebec emulated in a small way the glittering court of Versailles. Manners were agreeable and polite, and the wives and daughters of townspeople of any position were said to be superior in manners to those of equal rank in France. Although it is never safe to put much trust in generalities about the fair sex, the intriguing comments of Peter Kalm do show that the graces and wiles of civilization were not lacking in the two towns in the middle of the eighteenth century:

One of the first questions a Canadian lady proposes to a stranger is whether he is married; the next, how he likes the ladies of the country, and whether he thinks them handsomer than those of his own country; and the third, whether he will take one home with him. There are some differences between the ladies of Quebec and those of Montreal. Those of the last place seemed to be generally handsomer than those of the former. Their behavior, likewise, seemed to me to be somewhat too free at Quebec, and of a more becoming modesty at Montreal. The ladies at Quebec, especially the unmarried ones, are not very industrious. A girl of eighteen is reckoned very poorly off if she cannot enumerate at least twenty lovers. These young ladies, especially if of a higher rank, get up at seven and dress till nine, drinking their coffee at the same time. When they are dressed they place themselves near a window that opens into the street, take up some needlework, and sew a stitch now and then; but turn their eyes into the street most of the time. When a young fellow comes in, whether they are acquainted with him or not, they immediately lay aside their work, sit down by him, and begin to chat, laugh, joke, and invent *double-entendres;* and this is reckoned being very witty. In this manner they frequently pass the whole day, leaving their mothers to do all the business in the house.

In Montreal the girls are not quite so volatile, but more industrious. They are always at their needle-work, or doing some necessary business in the house. They are likewise cheerful and content; and nobody can say that they want either wit or charms. Their fault is that they think too well of themselves. However, the daughters of people of all ranks, without exception, go to market and carry home what they have bought. They rise as soon, and go to bed as late, as any of the people in the house. I have been assured that, in general, their fortunes are not considerable, owing to the smallness of the family income and the large number of children. The girls at Montreal are very much displeased that those at Quebec get husbands sooner than they. The reason of this is that many young gentlemen who come over from France with the ships are captivated by the ladies at Quebec, and marry them. But as these gentlemen seldom go up to Montreal, the girls there are not often so happy as those of the former place.[9]

As has already been suggested, the cleavage between the gentry and the common people was not as clear cut as in the old world. Actually there were very few in the colony who could claim truly noble birth, and even they were not of the highest rank. There were only a dozen such among the many seigneurs, or local landlords, many of whom were poor, since the various forms of rent paid by the habitants did not amount to very much in all. Two letters of the governor Denonville to his minister, dated 1685 and 1688, have to do with the plight of penurious gentry and the problem of educating their children:

Before all, Monseigneur, you will permit me to tell you that the nobility of this new country is everything which is most beggarly and to increase their number is to increase the number of "do-nothings" in the place. A new country demands hard-working and industrious people who will handle the hatchet and pickax. The children of our Councillors are no more hard-working, and have as their only recourse the woods where they do some trading, and for the most part make all those disorders which I have had the honor to discuss with you.

I hope in time we shall have succeeded in suppressing the great disorders of our young people or at least in moderating them. However, Monseigneur, it is necessary to help them by giving them the means of relief and livelihood for, in truth, without that there is great fear that the children of our nobility, or of those living as such of whom there are a great number, will become bandits because of having nothing by which to live, not being able to apply themselves to labor on the soil since they are not accustomed to it. In truth, Monseigneur, it is an essential thing for this country to discipline all these young people and to keep them engaged in some companies.[10]

There were many who agreed with Denonville that the economy was unable to support without hardship the increasing extravagance of the upper classes, or of those who wished to be so regarded, especially in the towns. For this extravagance the women were blamed. They were said to be fond to the last degree of dress and show, and their levity and superficiality reached its height in the last years of the French regime. Baron de Lahontan, a traveller, writing towards the end of the seventeenth century, gives a quaint account of the drain on the resources of the male providers:

The Gentlemen that have a Charge of Children, especially Daughters, are oblig'd to be good Husbands, in order to bear the Expence of the magnificent Cloaths with which they are set off; for Pride, Vanity, and Luxury, reign as much in New France as in Old France. In my opinion, 'twould do well, if the King would order Commodities to be rated at a reasonable Price, and prohibit the selling of Gold or Silver Brocades, Fringes, and Ribbands, as well as Points of rich Laces.[11]

One cause of extravagance and a life of gaiety was the sending in of troops to garrison and defend the colony. The first ball in Canada was given in February, 1667, by the officers of the Carignan regiment, soon after their arrival in Quebec. In spite of the piety of the inhabitants there was a deterioration in morals after this date. The soldiers sent by Louis XIV were fresh from the licence and excitement of the Turkish wars. They were ready to obey their officers, but no one else, and were responsible for scenes of violence and dissipation. Whatever may have contributed to their foibles and ostentation, the townspeople gave the church much work to do, including a counterattack against luxury and the provision of education for girls, both of which will be described later.

Government

A fourth influence on education came from two characteristics of government in the colony. The first of these was the close union between church and state. The only powerful members of the governing council were the governor, the intendant, or special agent of the king, and the bishop. There were sometimes rivalry between the governor and the bishop, differences on matter of policy, and dispute on questions of precedence, such as whether school children should salute the bishop before the governor on fête days. But the government did not challenge the authority of the church to decide the nature and content of education.

The second characteristic of government was its paternalism. In the quotation from Lahontan on page 13 it will be noticed that the remedy suggested to improve the lot of hard-pressed gentlemen was price-fixing on luxuries by the king. An appeal to the king was the usual solution proposed for economic problems, and the fixing of prices by the council was common practice.

In the colony power was vested in a council which consisted entirely, except for a short period in the seventeenth century, of the king's appointees and the bishop. Obviously such a government gave no encouragement to political activities among the people, and in this respect there was a rather marked contrast between the dependence of the French colonists and the initiative shown by the English colonists of New England. Nevertheless, the government was not wholly arbitrary: for example, the captains of militia who had considerable power in the localities were appointed only after consultation with the people. Moreover, pioneer life encouraged independence, and submissiveness had its limits even in districts within easy reach of the arm of government. The feudal system of land tenure, which required the habitant to pay trifling dues to the seigneur, was never burdensome, but a higher fee for the transfer of land to other than one's descendants and heirs made for permanent tenancy by a family.

On the whole, one gets the impression of a strong desire for stability, and of contentment that others should play the role of benefactors. Even in this new country begging was so prevalent in the towns that the government found it necessary to limit the practice by issuing licences and also to build almshouses for the relief of the destitute. But the government was not prepared to provide an education that would give the people power to help themselves.

Le gouvernement, d'ailleurs, se gardait de troubler un état de choses qui rendait les colons moins exigeants, moins ambitieux, et par suite plus faciles à conduire.[12]

It left education to the clergy. A reasonable judgment is that the type of government was conducive to docility under teachers who spoke with authority, and that this teaching fostered attitudes favorable to such a government. To the extent that this is true, the government and the partnership between church and government contributed to the achievement of the basic educational aim.

The Church and Morality

A major objective of the church was to counteract social forces responsible for laxity of behavior, particularly in relations between the sexes. Laval, as bishop, denounced the love of finery and the revealing costumes of women, and went so far as to forbid priests to offer the sacrament to those who came to church in low-cut dresses, exposed or covered only with diaphanous material. He also decreed ex-communication for selling, trading, or giving liquor to Indians. His successor to the bishopric watched the morals of his flock with unrelenting vigilance and issued strictures against disapproved practices in relation to balls, dancing, theatrical performances, late dinners, and luxury in dress. Some parish priests and other clergy took up the crusade with such zeal as to cause bitter resentment among laymen of easier habits and disposition, who found themselves under what they considered moral espionage which seemingly made it impossible to do anything in a social way without detection. A similar campaign against luxury and immorality was carried on by the church in France.

Underlying the actions of church and government authorities was apparently a conviction that human beings cannot be trusted without supervision and an ever-present fear of punishment. For example, Marie de l'Incarnation was concerned about the danger to which young girls were exposed if they were left at home with men around while the parents and others were at church. Consistent with the dire threats already mentioned were the severe penalties of the law. Swearing and blasphemy were punishable by increasing fines up to the fourth offence, by an iron collar and subjection to insult and shame for the fifth offence, by the pillory and cutting of the lower lip for the sixth offence, and by having the tongue cut out entirely for subsequent offences and apparent incorrigibility; even more severe penalties were decreed for expressions of disbelief; rewards were offered to informers and a fine could be imposed for failure to inform.

There were direct reflections of these attitudes in education. Until near the end of the seventeenth century dramatic performances were included in the program of the Jesuit college at Quebec: on one occasion of a visit by the governor there was a presentation by students of Corneille's *Le Cid*, which had first been played in Paris ten years before. But such performances at the college were forbidden later by the bishop. Close supervision of conduct and instruction was characteristic of Roman Catholic schools in the Quebec colony as in other places and times. As for the more limited area of morality, which received most stress, there are pertinent paragraphs in the school regulations of the Ursuline order in France, which sent out teachers to Quebec before the middle of the seventeenth century:

A mistress must give her pupils high ideas of the majesty of God and speak often to them of His adorable perfection; she must accustom them often to make acts of faith, hope, and charity, and inspire them with a deep love for Jesus Christ . . . . She will make them fear and avoid any occasion of sin — bad companions, dances, staying up late at night, vanity in dress, etc. She will encourage them to love chastity, modesty, reserve, simplicity in dress, obedience to superiors, respect for those who are consecrated to God. She will forbid them to be curious or to pry into their neighbors' affairs, and will make them love silence. She will inspire them with a horror of scandal and accustom them to speak well of everybody and evil of nobody, to avoid idleness, and to love work. She will forbid them ever to show themselves to anybody — even to their family — without being completely and modestly dressed.[13]

But the chief means of securing observance of the moral code was through teaching that made large families almost inevitable and early marriage desirable. The counsel of the church was reinforced by state action. An edict of 1669 proclaimed rewards and penalties to encourage the marriage of girls before the end of their sixteenth year and boys before the end of their twentieth. Premiums, or small dowries, were also offered with the girls imported for marriage from France, and pressure was put on indentured persons to marry within fifteen days after the expiration of their contract. Bonuses were held out to parents whose families had expanded to ten or twelve living children. From eight to eighteen children was set as the standard of normal expectancy. The doctrines and incentives that supported this plan, although they had the further social purpose of strengthening the colony numerically, may rightly be regarded as an educational program for moral objectives.

Institutions for Formal Education

Before looking separately at different types of formal education, we may glance for an overview at the chronological order in which more important schools made their appearance during the seventeenth century:

1635 *Petite Ecole of the Jesuits, Quebec*. It began as an elementary school with an enrolment of twenty boys. But Latin was introduced in 1636 and the school developed into a college for secondary education by 1655. The elementary school continued in operation.

1642 *School of the Ursulines, Quebec*. This was a boarding and day school for girls. In time it also offered more advanced education.

1659 *School of Marguerite Bourgeoys, Montreal*. At first this was an elementary school for young boys and girls, but from about 1666 it was for girls only.

1663 *Grand Séminaire, Quebec*. This was a seminary for the training of priests.

1666 *School of the Sulpicians, Montreal*. At first an elementary school for boys, it was expanded to include also a seminary for the preparation of priests.

1668 *Petit Séminaire, Quebec*. This was a seminary for boys destined for the priesthood.

1668 *School at St. Joachim*. This school for boys offered training in practical arts and trades.

1694 *School of Brothers Hospitalers, Montreal*. This was a school for boys.

During the eighteenth century, up to 1763, most of these schools continued and many more were established at other places in the country.

It is difficult to classify schools as elementary or secondary in the ordinary way because the church's disapproval of co-education made sex, more often than educational level, the basis of division between schools. Hence an elementary school might take boys and girls if there was no other school in the locality; but a second school would provide separate education for either boys or girls, possibly at more than one level. The classification used here, therefore, will be: elementary schools for boys (with girls possibly tolerated); schools for girls (chiefly elementary but perhaps extending into the secondary level); secondary schools (for boys and young men extending in some cases to the higher education level); and practical education (either in schools for boys or in schools for girls).

The abhorrence of co-education was not, of course, an indigenous development in the Quebec colony but a deep-seated attitude brought over from France. In the address to teachers in Paris already quoted (pp 8-9) is this warning:

Take great care never to have in your schools children of both sexes. There are no longer children, there is no longer innocence. Wickedness has grown to such a pitch that children of five, six or seven years know more about it at the present day than persons of thirty or forty did in the old days.[14]

The contrast of the sophistication of the younger generation with the innocence of the old has a familiar ring. But even the most timid of adults today would hardly admit to so great a fear of free association of the sexes at an early age as is revealed by the following injunction to the Ursuline teacher on the supervision of her pupils in the streets:

She will forbid them to talk, unless it be necessary, to little boys, and will strictly prohibit them from associating with them — and especially laughing, playing, and wantoning with them.[15]

The same nervousness about the association of young men and women is revealed in a letter written by Marie de l'Incarnation, head of the Ursuline Sisters at Quebec:

In this country great pains are taken to educate the French girls, and I can assure you that but for the care exerted by the Ursulines, their salvation would be in constant danger. The reason is that there are so many men. As a consequence, a father and mother, if they do not omit attendance at mass on feast days or Sundays, must leave their children at home with several men to keep them company; and if they have daughters, no matter what their age, they are in evident risk, and therefore must be committed to some place of safety. I must admit, therefore, that girls in this country know much more on dangerous subjects than their sisters in France. Thirty boarders here give us more trouble than sixty in France. Our day pupils give us some anxiety, but we cannot watch over their morals as sedulously as if they were boarders. They are tractable, of good temperament, and firm in following their duty when it is pointed out to them, but as many of them are boarders for a short time, the teacher must instil a great deal of education into them during their limited residence, such as teaching them to read, write, learn their prayers and the code of Christian morals, and all else which it is necessary a girl should know. There are, however, some parents who leave their daughters under our care till they reach an age to enter the world or adopt a religious life.[16]

Elementary Schools for Boys

In refutation of statements that the education of boys was neglected during the French régime, the Abbé Amédée Gosselin devoted many chapters of his history of education to details regarding some thirty-two elementary schools known from records that have been preserved. He also advanced arguments to show that more was probably done than can be proved by direct evidence.

In the town of Quebec the school of the Jesuits, founded in 1635, was supplemented by a school in the lower town in 1699 and by another in the upper town soon after. In parishes of the Quebec district, five elementary schools are known to have been established during the seventeenth century, and seven more by 1750, all in different places. But complete data on the regularity with which the schools were in operation and on the number of pupils in attendance are not, of course, available.

In Montreal, Marguerite Bourgeoys probably began teaching boys as well as girls before the opening of her school in 1659. The elementary education of boys was taken over by the Sulpicians in 1666. This school and others which came under their charge were, like the Jesuit school in Quebec, regularly conducted by teachers selected for ability and zeal. The Brothers Hospitalers opened a school in 1694 at Montreal and several others in parishes of the district. The Sulpicians also conducted schools in country parishes. Altogether, at least eight or ten schools are known to have been established in the Montreal district before 1721. In the district of Three Rivers seven schools were opened between 1652 and 1739.

Such a catalogue has little meaning except to show that there were certainly some schools in operation. Undoubtedly those in Quebec and Montreal, and probably a few in parishes close to these towns, were organized and taught in a manner creditable for the time. But throughout the rest of the countryside, if we are to believe the reports of the Intendant Raudot, there were no regular teachers except where the Sisters of the Congregation had established schools for girls. He wrote in the first decade of the eighteenth century:

The habitants of the country are uneducated, owing to the weakness and mistaken tenderness which fathers and mothers exhibit to their children. In this respect they imitate the Indians. As there are no school-masters the children are always at home, and as they grow up, having never been inured to discipline they develop an unruly and even ferocious disposition, which they vent even on their parents, to whom they show little respect, and on their superiors and the clergy.[17]

As has been suggested, Garneau attributed the limited provision for education to deliberate policy of the government and clergy, who "regarded elementary education as more dangerous than useful," not an uncommon opinion at the time. But there were some resident teachers and some itinerant teachers in the country. There must also have been some teachers and teaching which the church did regard as dangerous, for as early as 1691 the bishop warned his clergy not to permit anyone to act as schoolmaster who had not given proof of orthodox belief and morality. The probability is that school was conducted spasmodically in only some country parishes and that only a minority of country boys received any secular education at all.

The curriculum content was meagre at best — religious education, more or less reading and spelling, still less writing and arithmetic, and, in a few cases, elementary Latin. The method was almost certainly an individual assignment of material to be memorized or practised with little or no previous explanation or subsequent questioning to ensure understanding. Strict discipline was imposed by corporal punishment. There is an interesting passage in a Jesuit *Relation* of 1673, which shows how much more severely French children were treated by their elders than Indian children by theirs:

This year our Hurons observed that, in The School which is kept in their village of notre Dame de foy for the french children, those who are neglectful of Their duties are frequently punished; and they thought that, in order to bring up Their own children properly, it was necessary to chastise them for their faults, as is done with the french children. So the Captain has been in the habit of going around the village from time to time, Calling out aloud that the fathers and mothers are to tell Father Hechon their children's faults, so that he may have them whipped therefore, — The Boys by the french schoolmaster, and The girls by a good matron.[18]

Schools for Girls

Schools for girls in the Quebec colony were conducted by two orders of nuns — the Ursulines with headquarters in Quebec, and the Sisters of the Congregation in Montreal. The Ursulines were an established order in France: the first sisters to come to Quebec arrived in 1639, under Marie de l'Incarnation as superior, and began teaching Indian children within a few months; but from the opening of their convent school in 1642 their chief occupation became the education of French-Canadian girls. The Sisters of the Congregation were founded in Canada by Marguerite Bourgeoys, who first came to the colony in 1653. She established the sisterhood in 1659, although it was not until 1671 that the order received sanction and not until after her death at the end of the century that it had full and final recognition by the church. At Montreal, in the year in which their order was founded, these sisters opened their first school, in a building that had been a stable. From the first they were to all intents and purposes a religious community of teachers. They received a financial endowment from the bishop in 1693.

How many teachers and schools were these orders able to provide? The number of Ursulines listed at Quebec according to the census of 1681 was twenty-two "mothers" and seven "sisters." Twenty-five Sisters of the Congregation in Montreal took their vows in 1698 when the bishop submitted regulations to the community. In addition to their school in Quebec, the Ursulines operated a school in Three Rivers from 1697. The Sisters of the Congregation had half a dozen or more small schools in parishes throughout the colony and schools in Quebec and Three Rivers, all in addition to their school, and subsequently two schools, in Montreal. Even in the town schools the attendance was not large, probably because the school life was short. Marguerite Bourgeoys mentioned the many deaths of children at an early age as a reason that few could be retained at school for long, although she added piously that this gave "good reason for hope, as God had been taking the first fruits." Marie de l'Incarnation said that some girls came to school for only twelve months although others remained for six or seven years. Probably parents who could afford to pay 120 livres* (the annual fee for boarders at the Ursuline school) would prefer to have their daughters live at the convent and continue their education until they were of marriageable age. The census of 1681 listed seventeen French boarders at the Quebec school and ten Indian boarders who must have been kept without charge. Over a period of 100 years, from 1639 to 1740, the records of this school showed the names of more than 1200 boarders from all parts of the country. Day pupils were, of course, more numerous. If one had to make an estimate from scanty data, he might guess that in the early eighteenth century between one-quarter and one-half of the girls in the colony may have attended school for periods ranging from a few months to several years, with an advantage even more than the usual in favor of the towns.

The curriculum in schools for girls, according to Marie de l'Incarnation, included prayers, reading, writing, arithmetic, church doctrine, and moral instruction. Actually the schools did much more for the girls than these subjects would suggest. They were of incalculable value in maintaining purity of speech and gentleness in manner; they saved the vitality of French-Canadian girls from coarseness, and gave them instead a vivacity tempered with reverence and disciplined to courtesy and grace. Even the songs of the colonists that are still preserved are said to owe their softness and beauty of words and music to the good offices of these good sisters in the early days.

A Jesuit record of 1667-68 declared:

The Ursuline Mothers have had so great success in the instruction of the girls who have been confined to them — whether Boarders, or the day-scholars who frequent their Classes — that on visiting the households of Canada, and each house in particular, it is very easy to distinguish, by the Christian education of the children, the mothers who have come out of Ursuline houses from those who have not had the advantage.[19]

Sister Marie had reason for saying that without the instruction given by the nuns the daughters of the colonists might have been worse than savages. How then could Quebec have become a country of civilized men? Although only a few girls could continue their education for long, the Quebec school of the Ursulines did offer more advanced studies for those who could go on. Insofar as they had such ambitions, women had more educational opportunity in the Quebec colony than in English colonies in America; and through the religious orders at least, they had more opportunity for a vocation other than that of housewife or household servant.

Practical Education

Men like Intendant Talon and Bishop Laval realized the need for instruction in practical skills and trades. Talon sent to France for skilled artisans, and secured, among others, teachers of rug-making. Laval, about 1668, opened two schools to give elementary vocational instruction to

---

* A livre was rather more than the daily wage of a laborer in France in the late seventeenth century. It had a still higher value in the Quebec colony.

boys who were inclined more to practical work than to academic study. One of these was at the seminary in Quebec, the other at St. Joachim fifteen miles down the river. Among the trades taught were cabinet-making, carpentry, masonry, roofing, shoemaking, and tailoring; there was also teaching of sculpture, and of painting as both a trade and an art. Laval also had a model farm at Cap Tourmente, near St. Joachim, where boys were given instruction in agriculture. The work of these schools was limited by the difficulty of retaining pupils for long and by shortage of funds; the governor wrote in 1686:

It is not possible to retain for a considerable time children at study if they are not ones who plan to become priests, and the number of these is small among the natives of the country, who are light-headed. In regard to the children whom we had planned to bring up in an establishment to improve their vocation and make them learn some trade, not having this year permission to give a contribution to their pension, our Bishop is not rich enough nor is our seminary to maintain these schools which have been well begun and which will end for lack of funds.[20]

But they were able in a small way to serve a useful purpose during the later seventeenth century at least. Schools for girls gave some training in household skills. Domestic spinning and weaving were first practised at Beaupré, where instruction was also provided for boys in the use of tools. Since the province of Quebec in the present century is noted for ample provision of practical training for boys at an elementary level, it is not unlikely that more was done than was recorded in the teaching of trades and skills in the Quebec colony.

At a higher educational level, courses in mathematics might include work of a practical nature, relating particularly to surveying and hydrography, or the charting of navigable waters. In 1671, Talon had the Jesuit college in Quebec appoint a layman to teach practical subjects of this kind, and after 1707 similar work was carried on by the Jesuit professor of mathematics. A considerable number of pilots, ship-captains, explorers, and surveyors were trained in this way. For a time before the end of the seventeenth century the Jesuits also operated a college in Montreal where mathematics, which included navigation and fortification, was taught to young officers of the army.

Secondary Education

Secondary education nearly everywhere up to fifty or one hundred years ago was a distinctive type of education for the few and not an extension of elementary education for the children of the people. In the Quebec colony the differentiation could apply only to a limited extent. Sons of the upper class were sent to secondary schools for a classical education, but the small population and limited number of schools made it impossible to keep them always apart from the sons of the common people. That this was the case at the lower educational level is suggested by the inclusion of Latin in some local elementary schools for boys and confirmed by the fact that even a boy sent to Quebec at an early age would attend the school of the Jesuits which at first served the whole population of the town. Those who completed the work of the secondary school were likely to be destined for the priesthood, since there was at the time no other profession for which secondary education was necessary and for which one might get preparation in the colony.

The chief providers of secondary education in the Quebec colony, as in many places at the time, were the Jesuits. Their order, the Society of Jesus, founded in 1534, tried to combat heresy through education in two ways: the Jesuits educated themselves to be formidable op-

The Quebec Seminary

ponents in any intellectual argument; they also founded, throughout the world, Catholic schools to give secondary and higher education of a thoroughness and quality to command respect and to compete successfully for attendance against all others. They took no salaries, charged no fees for instruction, and devoted themselves to the education of French-Canadian boys, with the same iron will and unflagging zeal that they displayed in the conversion of the Indians. The Jesuit plan of instruction called for a quasi-military organization of the classroom: it utilized rivalry, demanded precision, and was highly efficient in securing mastery of content.

By 1655 the school of the Jesuits in Quebec had developed into a secondary school, or college, with three instructors in addition to the one for the elementary school; by 1676 the teaching staff numbered six. During the last years of the seventeenth century the average attendance of day scholars and boarders was about 130-140 in all. There was also at that time a Jesuit college in Montreal, but it did not flourish. Before the end of the French regime in Canada, the order had

aroused the antagonism of governments in many countries and its wealth and power caused growing resentment even in the Quebec colony. The buildings of the Jesuits in Quebec were more extensive than all other public buildings combined.

The program at the Quebec college probably did not differ markedly from that of other Jesuit institutions. The course was almost wholly classical and the lectures were delivered in Latin. Students' exercises included disputations in Latin, sometimes in the form of a public debate, and always rigidly confined to the syllogistic method. Discipline was the keynote of the school. The instructors demanded strict observance of rule, inculcated profound reverence for authority, pressed for minute introspection into motives and causes of actions, and maintained a supervision which hardly fell short of espionage. In the early eighteenth century, the superior of the Jesuit order at Quebec could boast that the college, apart from its smaller enrolment, was everything a European college could hope to be: it had a complete program, including classes in grammar, the humanities, rhetoric, mathematics, philosophy, and theology; and the students were reported to be industrious, docile, and capable of great progress in the study of letters and in virtue.

Higher education in the Quebec colony was exclusively training for the priesthood. In 1663 Laval founded the seminary in Quebec. He said:

There shall be educated and trained such young clerics as may appear fit for the service of God. We desire it to be a perpetual school of virtue, and a place of training, whence we may derive pious and capable recruits.[21]

Students in the seminary attended the courses of the Jesuit colleges, where instruction in theology had just been introduced in addition to the classical course. In 1668 Laval founded also a *Petit Séminaire* or junior seminary to give elementary training to boys destined for ecclesiastical life, partly because the church preferred to begin the special preparation of candidates for the priesthood at a very early age, and partly because a beginning in good time was even more advantageous when such candidates were recruited from the Indians. The junior seminary began its work with seven or eight French pupils and six Huron children. Students were under constant supervision and were not permitted to return home even during the summer holidays. At both the *Petit Séminaire* and the Jesuit college the students' work day began at five in the morning and continued until nine in the evening. The qualities which the junior seminary sought to inculcate were humility, obedience, purity, meekness, modesty, simplicity, chastity, charity, and an ardent love of Jesus and His Holy Mother.

In spite of a serious reverse from fires in 1701 and 1705, the Little Seminary grew in strength. The enrolment in 1701-2, apparently after the first fire, was in the neighborhood of one hundred; in 1726 it was only twelve; towards the end of the French regime it was from fifty to sixty. Altogether, between 1668 and 1759, there were 843 registered students: of these, 198 completed their studies, and of these 118 became priests. Laval endowed the Quebec seminary with the lands given to him in Canada, cherished it with affection, and worked unceasingly on its behalf. The seminary became and has remained the corner stone of the Roman Catholic Church in French-speaking Canada. Until a few years after the resignation of Laval as bishop, in 1684, parish curés were appointed by the seminary, which was their headquarters; and although since then they have been appointed by the bishop to reside in the parishes, the seminary has continued to be a spiritual home. After the capture of Quebec by the English in 1759, the seminary took over the work of secondary education and became the successor to the Jesuit college. In Montreal a seminary to train priests for the growing number of parishes was conducted by the Sulpicians from the 1660's.

An Appraisal

Keeping in mind that the objective of education was to ensure the spiritual salvation of the individual through acceptance and observance of the teaching of the Roman Catholic Church, one must credit educational work in the Quebec colony with truly remarkable success. There is no doubt that Quebec became and has remained a stronghold of Catholicism, in which the people, with a minimum of exceptions, are devout in faith and practice. Religion so permeates the life of the people of Quebec that they have an orientation quite foreign to the restless drive of English-speaking North America. Bracq goes so far as to say:

Their angle of vision rests upon an immovably fixed point in the infinite. To use Carlyle's words, in another connection, they lie "at anchour in the stream of time." They completely disregard the universal flux of men and philosophies, the mighty and related currents of life, and the transformation of the vital impulse which moves the world . . . In keeping with this, the great study of men is not initiative, a march onward, and enterprise, but imitation, resignation, and obedience to the priests of God.[22]

Very largely because of the deep hold of their religion, the people of the Quebec colony retained their language and their way of life, as well as their church. The English governors after 1763 soon gave up any serious attempt to convert them.

The only acceptable teachers willing and able to give formal instruction were servants of the church or their employees. Religious and secular instruction went hand in hand. So, compared with the little secular instruction given the children of the people in most other countries, the French-Canadian child's attainment in the three R's, spurred as it was by strong religious motives, seems very good. The same might be said of practical education, and even more pointedly of education in the refinements of living — the latter through the education of girls and through secondary education for boys. It is pointless to argue that more might have attended school if it had been open to anyone to teach as he liked, since private enterprise for profit has never achieved much for the education of the poor, and since there was here no possibility of a publicly controlled system.

Literacy as indicated by the ability to write one's own name is an objective measure of education on which some evidence can be found, although it is incomplete and inconclusive. Gosselin, who searched parish records to test a common belief that girls in the Quebec colony were more often literate than boys, gives figures which suggest that about one-quarter of the women and a higher proportion of the men in some country parishes in the early eighteenth century were able to sign their names. Let us assume that twenty-five per cent of the population in all rural parts were literate by this standard, and that this rural population was about three-quarters of the total. Let us also assume that ninety per cent of the remaining quarter, which would include most of the well educated, could at least sign their names. Then we may hazard a guess that something close to a third of the population could meet this minimum standard of literacy in the eighteenth century, and that, as usual, a higher proportion were able to read a little. Contemporary and modern appraisals have often been less generous. The intendant in 1736 sent the government in France a letter which placed the educational level exceedingly low even for families of superior position:

Toute l'éducation que reçoivent la plupart des enfants d'officiers et des gentilshommes se borne à très peu de chose; à peine savent-ils lire et écrire . . .[23]

Wittke says that the masses of the people remained illiterate, and Colby that the wives of the habitants were almost always so. But if our estimate does not greatly misrepresent the facts, the educational achievement among a scanty population in a new country was as much as could be expected at the time.

If an appraisal of the results of moral education is limited to relations between the sexes (on which emphasis was placed as an objective) it appears that the efforts of the church were quite successful. Bracq says that in the forty years between 1621 and 1661 the records of 664 baptisms of children reveal only one illegitimate birth, an amazing testimony, if it tells the whole truth, since approximately twenty in the same number of children were born out of wedlock three hundred years later in 1941. Yet the policy of early marriage and uninterrupted child-bearing gave little scope for irregularity, and even less chance for tangible evidence of its existence. There were occasional rebels, of course: we are told that one girl who would not observe the strict code of morals escaped in a ship by disguising herself as a boy, and that a married woman who ran off with an outlaw was reported to have sold her children to the Indians. But scandals like these were rare. Family life in the country parishes in the eighteenth century must have presented an almost unbroken pattern of moral conformity; and feminine frailty which provoked the wrath of the church in the cities appears in the writing of the critical observer, Kalm, to be usually no more than frivolity and extravagance. Even Lahontan admits that intrigues were well concealed. If morals in a somewhat broader sense are considered, the church had less reason for satisfaction. Bishop St. Vallier, who succeeded Laval, at first thought the people of good disposition, but later said that most of the young men were demoralized. He had chiefly in mind the prevalence of heavy drinking. Although it is difficult to know what any observer will consider to be over-indulgence in spirits, it is likely that by modern standards the charge was true. But, as Parkman says, excessive consumption of alcohol did not cause a deterioration of the race, for men had large families before dissipation could be responsible for debilitation and death. Among the upper classes towards the end of the French regime there was a splurge of lavish entertaining and luxurious living, encouraged by the corrupt administration of the Intendant Bigot, who brought the poor to the verge of starvation.

This brings us to criteria of evaluation other than those emphasized by the church. Material progress, beyond the immediate needs of subsistence, was not a serious concern of those responsible for education, and it is not surprising that

little was achieved. The Quebec colony was poor from the first, and only slightly less so from the time of Talon. The average habitant had no theoretical knowledge of agriculture and he soon exhausted the soil by routine crops. The distribution and sale of produce was hampered by the lack of roads and convenient markets. Not until 1734 was it possible for a vehicle on wheels to go from Quebec to Montreal. Goods and money were scarce among the majority and even in the middle of the eighteenth century it was still customary for guests invited to dinner to bring their own knives and forks. Whether the people were lazy, as Denonville said, or whether they found too much enjoyment in life to seek escape in never-ending ambition, they did not lift themselves far above the level of poverty in one of the most fertile areas of the new world. They were handicapped, however, by limited opportunities for export trade.

A second criterion, important in the modern world but not included in the educational objectives of the colony, is intellectual progress. This is not the same as the intellectual discipline and knowledge effectively taught in the Jesuit college, but a less controlled advance in unrestricted fields. From the point of view of an outside observer, the Quebec colony remained in this respect woefully deficient. During the whole period of a century and a half not a single printing press was set up for the dissemination of news and ideas, whereas in Massachusetts, one may recall, a press was established within a decade of the founding of that colony. The importation and reading of books, other than religious books of orthodox content, was not encouraged. Although Lahontan was not an impartial or cautious critic, it is safe to conclude that he had grounds for the following complaint against the priests:

They prohibit and burn all books but books of devotion. I cannot think of this tyranny without cursing the indiscreet zeal of the curé of this town. He came to the house where I lived, and, finding some books on my table, presently pounced on the romance of Petronius, which I valued more than my life because it was not mutilated. He tore out almost all of the leaves . . .[24]

Certainly there was very little chance that the minds of the people would be upset or stimulated by new and controversial thought on the printed page. Actually there were no incentives to intellectual brilliance except within the discipline of the church. Not unreasonably, a parish curé would try to direct a bright boy at school into training for the priesthood. When more and more of the clergy were recruited in this way from the sons of the colonists and trained in a seminary at Quebec or Montreal, there was a narrowing of cultural outlook, whatever may have been the compensating advantage of having curés who had a more intimate understanding of the lives of the people from whom they had sprung.

Summary

The Quebec colony provides an excellent example of coordinated educational effort, by direct teaching and by church and governmental action, to achieve a definite and limited objective. To counteract human weakness and social tendencies unfavorable to the religious and moral aim, church and state together set up opposing forces of custom, obligation, law, censorship, and a pattern of life which gave security and happiness. To identify education in such a society merely with formal instruction in school is to disregard, as the church did not, the meaning of Pericles' statement, "The city teaches the man." Such identification would be as wrong as an assumption that the strength of the Catholic religion can be measured by the ability of the priest in the pulpit — an assumption commonly made in the case of some other denominations.

The number, size, and quality of schools established is therefore only one measure of educational effort. The names are known of some thirty elementary schools for boys, including three which offered practical training, of one college for secondary education, of two seminaries, and of some fifteen convent schools for girls. Most of these schools were small. They and some others may have given enough secular instruction to enable about one third of the people to read and write, and to offer classical education and some practical instruction to a very small minority. They also preserved and fostered good speech and manners and other refinements of life.

The broad program of education was most successful in strengthening faith and in giving the people a deep-rooted, ever-present sense of religion. It was markedly successful in controlling overt relations between the sexes, but less so in moderating fashions and manners among those in the towns who had money. It did not succeed as well in reducing drunkenness and boisterous or lawless behavior in some places, but perhaps did about all that could be done under the circumstances and at the time.

The regime achieved a marked growth of population from very small beginnings and might have produced a numerically powerful state if immigration had been strongly encouraged at the start; but since admittance was barred to non-conformists and others who would otherwise have come freely, the colony could probably never have vied with others to the south. The Quebec colony did not produce — and it did not aim to produce — material prosperity and freedom for intellectual advance. It aimed to secure, and did secure, obedience and conformity rather than independence of thought and initiative in action, personal contentment from acceptance of authority rather than impersonal progress from rebellious freedom. Self-determination by the individual or by citizens collectively, except within narrow limits, was not even an issue, let alone a recognized right or a goal.

This unified program of education helped to make a distinctive type of society which did not change as France changed and did not yield to new-world opportunity as other colonies did — a remarkably homogeneous and cohesive society, unique in Canada and perhaps in the western world.

CHAPTER 2

Acadia

EDUCATION OF INDIANS · UPBRINGING OF ACADIAN CHILDREN · UPPER
SOCIAL CLASSES · RELIGIOUS INFLUENCE · SUMMARY

The limits of Acadia were not defined until the end of the
French regime. As used here the term covers parts of what are
now the provinces of Nova Scotia, Prince Edward Island and
New Brunswick.

The first permanent settlers came to Acadia in 1604 and
moved the next year to the meadows in the lovely valley of the
Annapolis River in Nova Scotia. There they established the
colony of Port Royal. The development of the colony was interrupted by destructive wars in America between the English
and French and by rivalry between French leaders. Although
new settlers came in 1632, and again in 1671, the number of
colonists in the whole of Acadia in the latter year was only 500,
the majority of whom lived at Port Royal. Thereafter, in spite
of neglect by an indifferent government in France and further
wars, the population of the French settlements on the peninsula
of Nova Scotia increased to almost 2500 in 1713, when Acadia
came under English rule, and to about 8000 in 1755. In the
latter year when the persistent struggle between England and
France was approaching a crisis, the English for reasons of
security deported all Acadians they could find on the peninsula,
to the number of more than 6000. Farms and houses were destroyed.

Meanwhile other settlements in Acadia had been established. On Ile Royale, the present Cape Breton Island, Louisbourg
was established immediately after the Treaty of 1713. To it
were transferred fishermen and their families from the French

settlement at Placentia in Newfoundland. The population of Louisbourg and other French settlements on Ile Royale increased to over 4000 by the middle of the eighteenth century. Louisbourg was captured by the English in 1745, restored to the French in 1748, and again captured by the English in 1758. The French also settled Ile St. Jean, now Prince Edward Island, where the population increased to over 2000 in 1752 and perhaps to a peak of from 3000 to 4000 shortly after. There were also at least 3000 Acadians in what is now New Brunswick.

Halifax was established in 1749 by the English, who came with a fleet carrying more than 2500 colonists. Additional settlers came to Nova Scotia from the Old World and from New England, and some French-Canadians returned. All French possessions in what is now Canada were ceded to Britain in 1763. Four years later the population of Nova Scotia was 13,374, of whom 1265 were listed as Acadian-French.

The history of Acadia is rich in romance, tragedy, and exciting adventure, but the shifting current of events made any consistent development of education impossible. Provision for formal education was necessarily meagre and spasmodic, and even the unorganized educational forces in society were too short-lived and divergent to develop a definite movement in any one direction. If conditions and events had any dominant educational effect, it was a sense of uncertainty and possible disaster tending towards resignation and little willingness to venture. The one constant was the Roman Catholic Church, but even its effectiveness was repeatedly checked by vicissitudes and calamity.

The mood of the story during the 150 years of the French regime is expressed by the sullen gray rocks on the south shore of Nova Scotia; the keynote of the history of the area was struck during the cold, hard winter of 1604, when thirty-five of the first seventy-nine settlers at the mouth of the St. Croix River perished from disease. No sooner had agriculture been successfully begun in the fertile valley of the Annapolis River than the founder of the colony was compelled to recall these settlers by his loss of the fur trade monopoly in 1607. A new colony was established at Port Royal in 1610, but it was destroyed by the English in 1613. It would take much too long to recount the trials decade by decade of the many settlements in Acadia. They are epitomized in the story of Nicholas Denys, who with dogged determination made effort after effort to establish an economic enterprise, whether in lumbering or farming, only to be cheated out of his property or have it destroyed and to be driven away to another location, until he found obscurity in petty farming and trading in an out of the way place near what is now Bathurst, New Brunswick.

Education of Indians

Efforts were made from the first to teach and convert the Indians. A priest came with the expedition of 1604 but remained for only a short time. Another secular priest, Jesse Fleché, who came with the expedition of 1610, hastily converted and baptized some twenty-five Indians by June of that year. But in the ship that came the following year were two Jesuits, Father Biard and Father Massé, who found to their horror that the so-called converts had no knowledge whatever of Christian doctrine and no intention of discarding their pagan customs.

The Jesuits set about their work with thoroughness and disciplined skill. Father Massé went into the woods with the Indians and lived among them to learn their language. These two Jesuits and a third member of the order who came out the next year assumed a monopoly of missionary endeavour for a while, but came into conflict with the colony's leader. After the destruction of Port Royal by the English in 1613, missionary work lapsed, but was resumed by the Recollets from 1615 until Port Royal was captured again in 1629. Three years later the Company of New France brought about three hundred settlers to La Hève on the south shore of Nova Scotia. With them came three members of the Capuchin order, whose numbers were augmented to eight a few years later, when the colony had been moved to Port Royal, and to twelve by 1643. The Capuchins probably conducted a school for Indians at La Hève and certainly did so in Port Royal. When weather permitted they met the Indians' preference by conducting classes out of doors and had lessons on reading as well as religious instruction. Among adults they probably also had some remedial work to do on the use of the French language, since some of the expressions picked up first by the Indians from the colonists tended to be of the stronger and more colorful variety. The Capuchins were driven out by the English in 1654.

Later missionary work was carried on among the Indians in some districts by Jesuits from Quebec, and around the settlements by parish priests. The conversion of virtually all was not impossible, since the Indians in the coastal regions were friendly Micmacs and since the total number of Indians in Acadia probably was not more than thirty-five hundred at any time. Evidence that the church was able to gain a secure hold may be found in the gathering twice a year of Indians from near and far to the chapel built about 1740 by the Abbé Jean le Loutre at Shubenacadie. Even more striking proof is the difficulty that the English encountered in winning the friendship of the Indians and their failure to convert the Redmen from the Catholic faith to Protestantism.

Schooling for Acadian Children

The nature of the education received by the Acadian children may be surmised from facts and opinions about who the Acadians were and what kind of life they lived. The people were mainly the descendants of those who came from the west coast of France in the 1630's and among whom there were only sixty women. We have been led by sympathetic accounts of the tragedy of their expulsion to think of the Acadians as hard-working, peace-loving people living in an idyllic environment. No doubt they were peace-loving, although the English found them disposed to wrangle about property rights and obstinately determined not to give in completely to the conquerors' demands. No doubt they did work hard when compelled to do so in order to survive, but they had no great reputation for industry. Reports of both English and French administrators agree that the Acadians were lazy and incapable of accomplishing much for themselves. It was said that rather than spread manure for fertilizing they would merely let it accumulate until they were forced to move their barns to another spot. A governor in the middle of the eighteenth century said that their houses were "wretched wooden boxes without conveniences and without ornaments and scarcely containing the most necessary furniture."[1] The inhabitants of Ile St. Jean were described as "poor, miserable, and inoffensive" and incapable of getting a task completed without the constant supervision of an overseer. Even the Bishop of Quebec who made a tour of Acadia in 1686 had tales to tell of "the numerous disorders committed by the miserable outlaws in the woods, who for a long time have lived like the savages without doing anything at all towards the tilling of the soil."[2]

Yet these were the people who built and maintained dykes against the inundation of their farms by the tides in the Bay of Fundy. The adverse opinions may be attributed in part to the prejudice or impatience of their critics. The last of the French governors of Acadia said, "The more I see of this people, the more I think that they are the happiest in the world."[3] It is probably correct to think of them as being less vivacious, less adventurous, and even less enterprising than the people of the Quebec colony, but with the same characteristics of simplicity and piety. They seem to have had the peasant's petty cunning and petty greed, but no great ambition.

The training given to children, apart from religious instruction, was largely a matter of preparation for an adult life of the kind their parents lived. There was a saying among the Acadians that no girl was ready for marriage until she could weave a pair of sheets and that no young man was ready until he could make a pair of wheels. The girl had to be able as a married woman, not only to look after

the food and clothing of her family, but to look after the livestock too, and in the absence of doctors to concoct remedies for either when needed. The young man had to learn from his father, not only the ordinary work of the farm, but all kinds of simple crafts and skills, since he was the handyman who did everything and made everything that could not be left to his wife. Practically nothing could be purchased ready for use, even if one had the money; and if any article or implement needed attention or repair, there was no shop or service station to do the work. The one exception was that the curé was ready to give advice on serious matters when a tutored judgment was needed, or to perform such offices as the drawing up of a will or other documents for which facility in reading and writing was also essential. With so many ordinary practical skills for a young person to learn, and with no insistence that getting on in the world was the first duty of man, it could hardly have been a matter of great regret to parents that few children spent time enough with the curé to be taught to read and write.

As for regular instruction in school there is no record of any systematic teaching of either white or Indian children in the early settlements at Port Royal, and nothing to suggest that schools were ever numerous during the French regime. The Capuchin school at Port Royal had both day pupils and boarders from a distance and taught French pupils as well as Indians; there can hardly have been much class or race prejudice, since all sat side by side on the same benches and since the sons of the governor, D'Aulnay, were among the pupils. About 1642 a certain Madame de Brice was brought out from France and placed in charge of a school at Port Royal. She taught the daughters of the governor and of other settlers, along with ten or twelve Indian children, and continued to act as schoolmistress until

1652. In 1685 the Abbé Petit, curé of Port Royal, had a school for boys taught by a man considered to have special aptitude for the work. In the same year a Sister of the Congregation was sent to Port Royal by the Bishop of Quebec, who found on a visit to Acadia in the following year that she was teaching several to read and some to write; the bishop expressed the hope that she would be able to create a "nursery of teachers" who might spread throughout the country. There was at least one school-house in Port Royal when the English looted the settlement in 1690.

Although there is practically no information about particular schools for more than forty years after this date, there is evidence of persistent efforts by the clergy to establish schools and some proof that the settlements were not entirely destitute of facilities for education. The Recollet Father Patrick René had a school built in Port Royal in 1703 and the convent school at Port Royal also was revived. The rapid progress made in secondary education by two young men expelled to France from the colony at Minas in 1755 is cited by Le Gresley as evidence that elementary instruction must have been given in that colony. The same author points out that the lack of records and the failure to mention schools in such records may easily be explained: many documents were destroyed in Acadian times or lost later, and in any case there was little reason to mention such a commonplace occurrence as the establishment of a school by the clergy when there was much of an unusual nature to tell about the Indians and much to record about seemingly more important events. Many individual priests and lay men and women about whom no record has survived must have at different times and at various places taught the rudiments of a secular education to a few children.

In Louisbourg in 1733 the Sisters of the Congregation opened a school which

Marguerite Bourgeoys, founder of the Congregation of Notre Dame

received financial aid from private sources and shortly after from the government. The first pupils were orphans and destitute children, but later the school attracted daughters of gentlemen, including those of the officers of the garrison. Some of the town pupils and some from distant points lived at the school as boarders. Since there were four or five sisters on the staff of the school, they were able to give both the religious education and the secular instruction usually offered in schools for girls at the elementary level. For a time after the capture of Louisbourg in 1745 the school was closed, and when it opened again in 1748 the sisters were able for a few years to do no more than prepare girls for their first communion. That it was again in full operation when Louisbourg was taken over finally by the British in 1758, we know from a Frenchman who served as a spy for the attackers and wrote commendingly of the work and piety of the sisters.

What proportion of the children born

in Acadia actually did learn to read and write? The authors of three doctoral dissertations on education in Nova Scotia conclude from an examination of petitions sent to the English government at Annapolis by the Acadians that at least half of the petitioners were able to sign their own names. It is argued not unreasonably by Le Gresley that little weight should be given to the less favorable evidence of petitions sent to the English governor or the King of France by Acadians deported to New England; these documents are signed almost as often by crosses as by signatures and almost all the signatures on any one document are in the same hand.

Some attention must also be paid, however, to opinions expressed about the time of the expulsion. Some of these are quite sweeping — to the effect that the Acadians were virtually all illiterate. The opinion expressed by a certain Moses des Derniers, who assisted in the deportation, is more discriminating: "They were altogether ignorant of progress in the arts and sciences. I have known but one of them that could read and write well; some could do so, but imperfectly."[4] This statement suggests a possible interpretation of the more favorable evidence of the earlier documents. Since the ability to write well or even to read well was much less common up to the middle of the nineteenth century than a bare and halting literacy, we may guess that most of those who signed their names had extended themselves to about the limit of their power with the pen. It must be assumed also that those who took the trouble to voice their grievances in any formal way were probably more accomplished than those who did not. A reasonable conclusion is that only a minority of the Acadians could write their own names and decipher the meaning of simple written French and that only a very small minority could read and write with ease.

Upper Social Classes

The upper classes and their children were, of course, in a better position. The chief centre of the nobility and upper classes in the eighteenth century was Louisbourg. During its short and broken history this town had a lucrative fishing industry and conducted a lively trade with New England. Its prosperity supported an élite who had luxuries and advantages not shared by the Acadians at large. There was a social life not quite as lustrous as that of Quebec, but as gay and diverting as circumstances would permit. A ball was a major event in government circles and those who were just below the rank needed for an invitation could attend parties given by wealthy merchants at the same time. During the day the fashionable might promenade on the rampart of the fortress or take a drive; in the evening, or at any hour, they might gossip or play cards. The young ladies of the town had for their education not only the school of the Sisters of the Congregation, but a dancing master as well. It is a reasonable supposition that the sons of the upper classes might begin their classical education in Louisbourg, but for more advanced schooling and further polish they were sent to Quebec or France.

In Louisbourg, and the surrounding area in Ile Royale, flagrant misbehavior brought to light the moral issues on which the broader educational program of the church was centred in the Quebec colony. Louisbourg, of course, was a garrison town. Those responsible for public affairs had difficulty in coping with licentiousness and disorder, including prostitution and heavy drinking. Gambling was a universal pastime among all classes. As for the fishermen, it was said that they were anxious enough for money, but were more inclined to trickery and deceit than to hard work in order to improve their fortunes. Throughout Acadia, however, as in the Quebec colony, heavy family responsibilities suppressed the more glamorous manifestations of irregular behavior between the sexes. Nearly all adults were married and those that had been married for some time had many children and usually little money.

Religious Influence

In Acadia, as in Quebec, although in less degree, the clergy had a strong influence over the lives of the people, not only in moral questions and religious faith, but on political issues as well. The Jesuits were particularly adroit in filling the dual role of priest and politician. One resolute priest, the Abbé Jean le Loutre, all but compelled Acadians to move from the peninsula to French territory in Ile St. Jean or Ile Royale rather than become subjects of Britain. Parish *curés* were largely responsible for the continuing loyalty of the Acadians to France and for their obstinate refusal to submit to all British demands before their expulsion.

New thought and scepticism from eighteenth-century France did not infiltrate into either Quebec or Acadia sufficiently to weaken the power of the church. Since the centre of ecclesiastical authority in New France during the last century of the French regime was at Quebec, control from the top, though strong, did not as closely affect the lives of the people in the eastern colony. In sections under British rule, the barrier of a different language was sufficient to keep most people remote from the Protestantism of the invaders.

Halifax in 1759

Summary

The broken history and lack of political unity in Acadia prevented the consistent development of a comprehensive educational program by the church. Formal instruction for most Acadian children was limited to religious knowledge. A very few schools for the people were established and very few learned to read and write. The sons and daughters of the more privileged classes could acquire something more than the elements in Louisbourg, but for more advanced education they were sent abroad.

The work of the church was effective in converting the Indians and in holding the Acadians to a simple faith and to loyalty to Catholic France. Conditions in Ile Royale were not conducive to steadiness and respectability of life, but in agricultural areas throughout most of Acadia the moral and religious teaching of the church established a pattern of family life from which it was difficult for even the impetuous to escape. Training in the skills necessary for this life on the farm was acquired by the children as they grew up. Not much schooling was needed or provided.

PART TWO

The Beginning of Education
under British Rule

The period covered in this part extends from the British conquest to the setting up of schools by the people and the organization
of public systems of education — roughly from 1763 to 1830. But
the earlier limit must be moved back to the sixteenth century for
Newfoundland, and to the early part of the eighteenth century for
Nova Scotia in order to start from the beginning of English settlement or rule. The later limit is also extended forward to cover early
educational developments of a corresponding nature in parts of the
country that were settled later.

For the most part, the geographical area under discussion is
comprised of the districts settled by 1830 in what are now the six
eastern provinces of Canada. By 1791 there were under British rule
six colonies corresponding to these provinces: Newfoundland, Prince
Edward Island, Nova Scotia, New Brunswick, Lower Canada (now
Quebec), and Upper Canada (now Ontario).

This is a period during which educational policy in these colonies
was determined almost entirely by European tradition as expressed
in English practice. None of the colonies had had time and opportunity under English rule to consolidate its institutions and adapt
them to the American environment. Settlers who came in from New
England had already acquired a different point of view, but other
settlers were still of the old world in their thinking. Moreover, Englishmen of the ruling class had English attitudes and opinions which
determined the type of education they might be prepared to tolerate
or encourage in the new world.

The first chapter of Part II, therefore, gives a short exposition of education in England in the eighteenth century. The next four chapters give accounts of education during the period in Newfoundland, in Nova Scotia, New Brunswick and Prince Edward Island, in Lower Canada, and in Upper Canada. The next chapter is transitional: it deals with a type of school which marked the end of the paternalistic period and demonstrated in some places the possibility of public education for all; and it shows how the administrative machinery of public education was created in eastern Canada. The following chapter describes the prototype of modern schools of the people. The last chapter deals with the later beginnings of education in western Canada.

CHAPTER 3

Education in England in the Eighteenth Century

EDUCATION AND THE CHURCH • KINDS OF SCHOOLS • POOR SCHOOLING
FOR POOR PEOPLE • UPPER CLASS EDUCATION

Education and the Church

As in most of the western world at the time, responsibility for education in eighteenth-century England rested in principle on the parent and on the church. As we shall see, the law required some action by the municipalities, but not enough to make education truly a function of the state or of civic authorities. Well-to-do people might help in some way to provide education for children other than their own, but they did so as a charity or benefaction, not as an obligation of citizenship. The educational opportunities made available to the poor by casual charity were meagre, and the poor were indifferent about making the most of them. It was therefore up to the church to provide schools, to organize philanthropic effort to provide more schools, and to secure the attendance of children. It was also the

right as well as the duty of the church to see that the content of the education was not contrary to orthodox religion. In practice, this responsibility of parent and church meant that the great majority of parents could give their children a little schooling only by accepting what their superiors thought fit to offer. The minority purchased a very different type of education for their own sons and daughters.

Yet the church in England did not maintain as tight a control over education as did the Roman Catholic Church in countries where the latter was supreme. The established Church of England was a national church and its power was thus affected by changes in the religious complexion of government, notably when the succession of the Stuarts was interrupted by the Commonwealth in the seventeenth century. A further loosening of ecclesiastic-

37

al authority came with the engrossing pursuit of commerce and with developments towards political democracy and intellectual freedom. On the whole, the clergy of the Church of England during the past four centuries cannot be accused of taking themselves and their responsibilities for education too seriously. If the church did less to provide schools as it became more tolerant of the educational activities of others, what else could reasonably be expected?

In the seventeenth century the policy of uniformity in religious faith already prescribed by Henry VIII and Elizabeth was extended to cover the whole field of education. In 1604 the church drew up, and parliament enacted, regulations which forbade anyone to teach who had not declared his acceptance of the doctrines of the established church and secured a schoolmaster's licence from the bishop of the diocese. The church defined the duties of a teacher: to give his pupils thorough grounding in the catechism; to take them to church on holy days and to question them later on what they had learned from the sermon; to instruct them on other days by means of texts from Holy Scripture. After the Restoration, an Act of Uniformity of 1662 required all heads of schools and all teachers, even tutors in private homes, to conform to the liturgy of the Church of England; failure to obey meant loss of office and of the right to engage in such work, "as if such person were naturally dead."[1] Later acts defined other restrictions and increased the penalties for violation.

But the laws were not rigorously enforced. Teachers called to account for infringements in the seventeenth century were mostly dog-catchers' victims — too small to be dangerous or troublesome when apprehended. At the beginning of the eighteenth century court decisions exempted lowly teachers of elementary subjects and held that a bishop's licence could be required only for teaching in a grammar school. Even at the secondary level non-conformists were able to operate academies if they could raise the means. In effect, therefore, the restrictions did little more than assure an Anglican tone in the endowed secondary schools and in higher education. Late in the eighteenth century Protestant and Roman Catholic dissenters were given freedom to teach anywhere except in the universities and the great public schools.

All of this explains why gentlemen and adherents of the Church of England in the colonies, whether members of the government, clergymen, or other people of position and influence, tried as a matter of course to Anglicize the populace, partly through Church of England schools, but did not try to enforce extreme measures against persistent opposition.

Kinds of Schools

What were the educational institutions and schools which many of the colonists from England had known or attended? Six institutions provided a modicum of elementary education for children of the people.

APPRENTICESHIP

From the fourteenth to the nineteenth century the education of some children was ensured through apprenticeship. By the terms of the indenture the master undertook not only to look after the moral and religious training of the apprentice, but sometimes to have him taught the three R's as well. Presumably the latter practice was common if the apprentice had not yet attended school. Apprenticeship agreements were ordinarily arranged privately but laws enacted in the reign of Elizabeth made it incumbent on parishes to provide through apprenticeship for the education of children of the poor. The importance of apprenticeship in relation to elementary education was reflected in legislation of 1802, which required employers of "apprenticed" children in cotton mills and cotton factories to provide for their instruction in reading, writing, and arithmetic. Laws of this kind, however, were indifferently obeyed, and the most that can be said is that apprenticeship ensured the literacy and the vocational preparation of children whose parents could pay a rather substantial fee to the master, and of some less fortunate children in the cities whose fees were paid by municipalities or charitable endowments.

PARISH SCHOOLS

From before the time when the Church of England was established as a separate church, conscientious parish priests gave instruction to the children of the poor. The content taught was primarily religious but might be extended to include reading and writing. The priest either instructed the children, or more often, employed a teacher to conduct the school under his supervision. Ardent churchmen and churchwomen would have liked to see schools of this type in operation everywhere. The sponsors of early unsuccessful bills for state support of education at the beginning of the nineteenth century had such parish schools in mind.

CHARITY SCHOOLS

In 1699 Anglican philanthropy was organized to create the Society for the Promotion of Christian Knowledge. This society established charity schools for the education of the poor in the principles of the established church. The schools taught reading, with the addition of writing and counting for boys and of knitting and sewing for girls. But they sought even more earnestly to inculcate religion, gratitude, industry, frugality, and subordination — in short, to make their pupils "loyal church members and to fit them for work in that station of life in which it had pleased their Heavenly Father to place them."[2]

To this end some charity schools, and other self-supporting institutions called schools of industry, taught simple vocational skills. In the charity schools the children were clothed and fed. They were also taken to church, and on the special occasion of a charity sermon, they heard an appeal addressed to the congregation for donations and a reminder that they should be thankful to their benefactors for the blessings so provided. By the middle of the eighteenth century there were about 30,000 children enrolled in charity schools. Founded in 1701, the Society for the Propagation of the Gospel in Foreign Parts, an offshoot of the S.P.C.K., became active in supplying schoolmasters for the colonies.

DAME SCHOOLS

Dame schools were conducted by needy women as private ventures for profit. Those which appealed to the poorer classes were usually little more than child-minding centres. Parents, including those who worked at home or in a factory, sent their offspring to the dwelling of the schoolmistress, or dame. She, for a few pennies a week, tried to teach them to read — not an easy task, since she commonly had no great facility with letters herself and no technique except the use of a switch. She might even have to do other work, like washing or knitting, while the class was present, to eke out a livelihood. Some dame schools, run by genteel ladies and patronized by the middle classes, did give their pupils an education. But the quality of instruction in cheap schools for the laboring poor is epitomized in the remark of one female proprietor: "It's little they pays us, and little we teaches."

An English dame school

COMMON DAY SCHOOLS

Privately run schools for the poor, when conducted by men, were called common day schools. Ordinarily the classroom was simply the room or workshop of the master, who charged a small fee for instructing the children. Although the curriculum was more extensive than that of the dame school, in that writing and arithmetic were more often included, the quality of the teaching was no better. Order was enforced and learning motivated by corporal punishment inflicted by the rod and in some cases by such torments as suspension by the thumbs. Some of the schools were much better than others, but most of those for the poor were very bad.

SUNDAY SCHOOLS

In the last fifteen years of the eighteenth century Sunday schools became suddenly and increasingly popular as a means of instructing children who worked in factories or at other employment on week days. In 1803 there were reported to be 7125 Sunday schools with over 88,000 teachers (mostly voluntary and unpaid) and 840,000 pupils. This phenomenal growth reveals not only the desire of philanthropists to give the poor some education but the even stronger desire of employers and parents to put children to work. The usual hours for a Sunday school were nine to twelve in the morning and one to six in the afternoon. The lengthy day permitted attendance at divine service twice and gave time for instruction in reading, in addition to religious subjects. Amazingly enough, the giving of even this little education to the poor aroused opposition. The Bishop of Rochester in the House of Lords condemned Sunday schools as fostering the views of the French Revolution, and many people agreed that revolt would spread to England if the poor were educated beyond the level in which God had placed them.

Poor Schooling for Poor People

From these brief descriptions of schools it will be seen that elementary education for the poor in eighteenth century England had definite and consistent characteristics. Its purpose was mainly religious: but rather to instil respect for the authority of religion than to assist understanding; rather to justify inequality by attributing it to God than to lend divine strength to the cause of justice. The secular content was meagre and assigned for memorization verbatim. Discipline imposed by punishment was designed to secure obedience. There were not enough good schools teaching enough children to give the means of enlightenment to any dangerous number.

All of this was in keeping with attitudes approved and fostered by privileged people. The more conservative preferred to keep the poor in ignorance, since knowledge might make them rebellious and difficult to manage. The more liberal believed that they might be permitted to read and learn a little if the content was rigidly controlled. Hannah More, a devoted worker in the education of the lower classes, declared: "My plan for instructing the poor is very limited and strict. They learn, of week days, such coarse works as may fit them to be servants. I allow of no writing . . . . To teach the poor to read without providing them with safe books has always appeared to me a dangerous gesture."[3]

Inevitably the children were the ultimate and defenceless victims in this embittering hierarchy of deprivation and control. The poorest parent could assert his superiority over them and in self-righteous safety vent on them the resentment he felt against those he feared. Children were accused of having the devil in them and were whipped on every apparent manifestation to drive the devil out. They were regarded impatiently as partly-grown adults and were put to work at the earliest possible age. Sir Robert Peel, not an illiberal Tory, thought it better to have poor people's children employ-

ed than to see them idle and useless in the streets. They were employed in factories and coal mines, or as chimney sweeps at as early an age as six, and if we are to believe Robert Owen, sometimes at the age of five or four and in one instance at three.

Upper Class Education

Children of the upper classes did not attend the elementary schools provided for the poor. They learned to read and write at home or in some genteel primary school; or the boys might acquire even these rudiments in a secondary school. For the eighteenth century, and for a long time before and after, the term "secondary" has the connotation of education for the gentleman and scholar, and does not indicate a later stage of education following completion of the elementary. Secondary education, also, was all but synonymous with classical education. The great public schools — Eton, Harrow, Winchester, and the others — were patronized by the upper classes. The local grammar schools, also endowed, were attended by sons of minor gentlemen. In both types the subject of first importance for all was Latin, the subject of second importance for many was Greek, and the one other subject worth mentioning was mathematics. This program was preparatory to further study at Oxford and Cambridge, although only a minority went on to university.

These institutions of secondary and higher education were not doing good work in the eighteenth century. Study of the classics had degenerated in the schools to grammatical grind and formal imitation of the prose style and poetic metres of ancient authors. Crude living conditions, harsh, ineffective discipline, and rampant abuses and immorality among students had given the great boarding schools an unsavory reputation. One would

Eton, best known of the great English Public Schools

think that only a hard-crusted, blue-blooded, Anglican Tory could have had no qualms about sending his son to one of them. The universities were said to have granted degrees on the basis of lectures delivered by the students in empty rooms and of answers to casual questions on the pedigree of a racehorse.

These statements, of course, show things at their worst and do not imply that good teaching and sound scholarship had disappeared. But the rapid decline in attendance at Oxford and Cambridge and the fluctuating enrolment at the great public schools give colorless evidence that the deterioration was real. One cause of the deterioration was the very fact that classical education had become the fashion for the upper classes and not simply the discipline of scholars. The drop in university enrolment reflected a decline in the relative importance of land and the landed aristocracy as compared with the growing prosperity of industry, commerce, and the middle class.

Some of the upper classes preferred now to employ a tutor at home and to give their sons further education by travel abroad. Some of the upper middle class, and especially non-conformists, joined together to form proprietary schools, or academies, which offered not only a classical education but some more practical subjects as well. Girls of the privileged classes were given a "useful and orna-

mental" education at home or at school: they were taught reading and writing, enough arithmetic for the keeping of household accounts, drawing, needlework, dancing, a little French, and possibly music and Italian. But care was taken not to lessen feminine attractiveness by making the young ladies capable of displaying knowledge or intelligence which might be disconcerting to men.

On the whole, upper class education gave simply a veneer to distinguish the gentleman or lady from the men and women of the lower orders. The veneer might consist of a smattering of the classics or of other accomplishments. Serious studies in school were the business of scholars and especially of the clergy. The really effective education of the young ladies or gentlemen came from association on equal terms only with members of a clearly marked caste, whose attitudes, manners, speech, and way of life were different from those of the great majority. In the education of all classes there was a common element — emphasis on loyalty to the king and adherence to the church, although many, of course, were non-conformist in religion. But even in this common element there was a difference: at the lower level the stress was on humility and obedience; at the upper level there was consciousness that the learner would someday play an active and less dependent role.

CHAPTER 4

Newfoundland

THE EDUCATIVE ENVIRONMENT · SCHOOLS · SUMMARY

Newfoundland, discovered by Cabot in 1497, began to be used almost immediately as a local base for fishing ships from Europe. England asserted possession of the island in 1583 but did not encourage settlement and actually did not regard the island as a colony until early in the nineteenth century. There were, nevertheless, permanent residents in Newfoundland from early in the sixteenth century: at first a few winter caretakers of fishing equipment; by 1650 upwards of three hundred and fifty families; and by 1800 a year-round population of perhaps twenty thousand. Although fishermen came from several other countries to Newfoundland waters, the supremacy of England was challenged only by France, who claimed possession of much of the island and established bases at a few places on the south coast — notably at Placentia, where there were French inhabitants from 1662 until 1714. The island and its people were almost entirely under British control for the three centuries of the period under discussion — up to the year 1836.

The Educative Environment

In those provinces of Canada whose history under British rule began no earlier than the eighteenth century, characteristically North American influences soon became powerful in education. Free land and freedom of economic enterprise led quickly to social democracy, to successful demands for political responsibility, and to schools controlled by the people. The counter-force of strong authority exercised by a few to protect and foster the interests of minorities did not continue without effective challenge. But in Newfoundland, whose story goes back to the days of the

43

Tudors and Stuarts, the older concepts dominated more completely from the first and up to a later date. It is therefore revealing to examine the educative forces in a society which was in the new world but not of it, especially because for that very reason there is little to tell about the development of that special agency of education, the school. Twelve influences were noteworthy.

LIMITED AIMS OF GOVERNMENT

The sole educational aim of the English government, with respect to Newfoundland, was the training of men for the navy. This educative function of the fishing waters was stressed in the arguments of those who opposed colonization and was mentioned as an objective in legislation of 1698. In the words of Pedley, a nineteenth century historian of Newfoundland:

Its fisheries, so abundant as to afford a compensation for the hardships attendant on toilsome labors amidst the fogs and tempests of these seas, tended to form a race of men to whom the rough work and dangers of the deep were part of a familiar, undreaded experience, and who therefore in times of war might be relied on as the best and stoutest material for manning the wooden walls of Old England.[1]

OBSTACLES TO SETTLEMENT

Settlers in Newfoundland learned to distrust and resent government because governmental policy was opposed not only to their welfare but to their very existence. The purpose of this policy was to secure an immediate and direct advantage from fishing operations in the teeming waters near the island. During Elizabeth's reign the observance of fish days by the English populace was extended on economic, not on religious, grounds. In support of fishermen on the west coast of England and of associated commercial interests, the government imposed staggering handicaps on permanent settlers in Newfoundland, who seemed likely to be in a favorable position to catch and market the fish.

Although serious attempts at colonization were made by Guy and others in a fifty-year period beginning in 1610, they were largely thwarted by those who profited from fishing operations conducted from bases in England. To forestall competition the commercial interests apparently did not stop at encouraging pirates to plunder settlements during the first precarious years of their struggle to survive. The settlers who did remain were plagued for a century and a half by discriminatory regulations from England and by the high-handed behavior of the annual visitors. By a regulation of 1633 the commander of the first ship to enter a harbor in the spring had authority over that harbor for the season. He could and commonly did make things uncomfortable for the settlers, or "planters," as they were called.

DEFICIENCIES OF THE SETTLERS

Educational progress was hampered by an insufficient number of settlers of respectable background, ability, and unity of purpose. A considerable proportion of the settlers in Newfoundland were men from the south and west of England, no different in origin from those who went to colonies farther south. But there were not enough of them. Those who had the positive purpose of building a home in the new world were likely to be dissuaded from choosing Newfoundland by reports of conditions there, even if they could secure transportation. An edict of 1660 forbade the master of a vessel to carry passengers likely to remain on the island. Too often the new settlers were summer visitors who found it convenient to stay in Newfoundland, leaving debts and sometimes a wife and children behind them. It is probable that some of the colonists in the early seventeenth century were unwilling emigrants from England "corralled like so many cattle and sent out to the new settlement."[2] In the eighteenth century Newfoundland became a refuge for thousands of Irish who had been demoralized by want and maddened by oppression. They were different from other settlers in religion and in the nature of their grudge against the English throne. For these and other reasons the settlements were separated by other than geographical barriers, and the few who had educational aspirations for their children were unable to speak in unison and with force.

LEGAL HURDLES

The inability of settlers to acquire a secure stake in the colony left them without that stimulus to learning and advancement. Settlers were forbidden by the regulations of 1670 to cut wood or build within six miles of the sea. They were also restrained from the cultivation and enclosure of land. Although in later years permissions to build were reluctantly granted, the restrictive policy continued. As late as 1798, a governor returning to the island was annoyed to find that the sheriff had made certain concessions and reprimanded him sharply:

Your having suffered Thomas Nevan to put up what you are pleased to call a few sheds, is clearly an infraction of my orders; you will therefore direct him to remove them immediately; which, if not complied with, I desire that you will yourself see this order executed.

You will take good care that Jeremiah Marroty and John Fitzgerald do not erect chimneys to their sheds, or even light fires in them of any kind.

I shall conclude this letter with informing you that if you at any time hereafter presume to disobey my orders, as in the instance above set forth, I will immediately, on the discovery thereof, remove you from your office of sheriff.[3]

Residents had either no legal right whatever to occupy and hold a piece of ground or, at best, a precarious title based on a conditional grant by a previous governor. Consequently the dwellings they erected were of the poorest sort, since a new or capricious governor might order their demolition. This condition of insecurity continued until the nineteenth century.

WARS

War also discouraged building for the future. Between 1689 and 1713 the French destroyed virtually all settlements and left scenes of utter desolation and misery. After the capture and destruction of St. John's in the early winter of 1696, the two hundred and twenty-four homeless, hungry, and shivering survivors were crowded into a small French vessel for transportation back to England. In this one town the houses, shops, fishing establishments, and stores of material had been substantial. The site was re-occupied and new buildings erected, but most of these were burned by the French in 1708. In smaller places the property loss was less in amount, but no less complete. The number of fishing boats fell from 1564 in 1700 to 260 in 1705. Entirely fresh starts had to be made in one place after another. During the Seven Years' War, St. John's and nearby settlements were again captured by the French in 1762.

ISOLATION

Many inhabitants were cut off from any civilizing influences. Fishing as an occupation tended to scatter the settlements among the isolated bays of a long, island coastline. But this inevitable condition was aggravated when settlers went to remote places to escape the constant threat of government and law. There were no roads before 1825. Settlements on the west shore and the northerly part of the east shore, where the French had fishing rights after 1714, were denied assistance and amenities on legal grounds until well on in the nineteenth century. In all remote settlements during the eighteenth century conditions approached the barbaric.

DEGRADATION BY CONTEMPT

The low opinion of the inhabitants held by their rulers and superiors had the effect of keeping them in a deplorable state. The disdain of the government in England for the welfare of the settlements postponed the appointment of a governor until 1729. Even the resident magistrates appointed by the governor were considered by him to be "but meen people," and they were contemptuously disregarded by the visiting admirals, who continued to have inhabitants seized, fined, and whipped at their pleasure. The one supplement to a meagre existence which the authorities seemed to think suitable for the inhabitants was a plentiful supply of cheap rum. Annual imports at the end of the eighteenth century were about fifteen gallons for each adult in the population and the price about a shilling a quart. This beverage in quantity did not help to check violence and disorder or to turn men's minds to thoughts of schools.

EXPLOITATION

Economic practices based on distrust kept the majority poor, improvident, and ignorant. When the Newfoundland fishermen had established themselves in spite of obstacles imposed by commercial interests in England, it was not long before they became the victims of merchants in St. John's. The latter became the favored few who were affluent in the midst of poverty. Under the system of credit that came into general use, the fishermen secured supplies in advance at any price or on any terms the merchant might see fit to impose. If men who would enter into such a bargain may be accused of

recklessness in the first place, the continued operation of the contracts left them utterly without hope or ambition to provide for the future. When the season's catch was absorbed by payment of the debt, they were ready — at first in desperation and later in resignation — to mortgage the next summer's earnings to tide them and their families over the winter. Since there was a risk that some of the debtors would make little effort to pay, or be unable to do so, the merchant felt justified in charging high prices and in making the more energetic and conscientious of his customers pay even more when the default of others threatened to lower his profits. The fishermen could not protest effectively for fear that they might "starve at the approach of every winter." It can hardly be imagined that under such circumstances they could have been concerned about schools.

POVERTY AND PATERNALISM

Paternalism of government sought only to make existing economic conditions more tolerable; it stunted the growth of initiative and power in most people to improve their own lot and educate their children. How a governor attempted to check the injustice of the credit system is illustrated by the following record of a court case in 1781:

Luke Ryan was ordered to attend the court to answer a complaint made against him for selling beef at 1s.3d. per lb., in contradiction to the Governor's order of the 19th of August, which positively directed that no person shall ask more than 1s. per lb. for beef, veal, or mutton.

He appeared, and acknowledged to have gained the hide, offal, and 5 pounds upon the cow he bought on Thursday last, by selling it at the above exorbitant price. He was therefore fined 10 pounds.[4]

Early in the nineteenth century another governor issued an edict that required merchants to state the prices of commodities sold on credit and the prices they were prepared to pay for fish that season. But the essential evils were the constant indebtedness and poverty, which forced the fishermen to barter to their disadvantage instead of selling for money, and these evils continued in remote places on the island up to the present century.

As might be expected there was pauperism as well as poverty. In 1797 a governor urged the establishment of some regular organization for the relief of the destitute, and set an example by subscribing £20 himself.

Yet trade flourished with New England: twenty American vessels visited the island in one year before the end of the seventeenth century, some of them several times; by 1765 this trade had reached a value of half a million dollars annually and was three times that amount at the beginning of the American Revolution. That the people at large in Newfoundland did not acquire the same ability as their southern neighbors to conduct private and public business for themselves must be attributed in part to the more effective paternalism of government in the island.

GRAFT AND CORRUPTION

Inefficiency and corruption in the administration of justice reduced confidence and respect for social institutions. Justice administered by captains and admirals on their summer visits in the old days was rough, ready, and biased against the settlers. In the case of any serious dispute or criminal charge, the only recourse was trial in England. Towards the middle of the eighteenth century resident magistrates were appointed and a court was established in St. John's.

But the magistrates looked after the interests of themselves and their friends by levying exorbitant costs and favoring the merchants in their verdicts. It was said that the expense of the most trifling case was £20 — a crippling sum for any

but the well-to-do. The poor man who had been cheated or robbed kept away from court for fear of losing more. An unfortunate tailor who was charged with the use of improper and abusive language when intoxicated, and who failed to appear in court because of his demented condition, was fined £150 for contempt; his property was attached to pay the amount, which the three magistrates divided among themselves.

About the same time, in the 1780's, the magistrates found another source of income by issuing licences for 108 public houses in St. John's, which had a population of about 1700, for four and a half guineas each, and pocketing half of the fees themselves. By a curious coincidence, a petition signed in 1787 by the chief merchants of St. John's expressed regret at a diminution in the number of public houses and the consequent reduction in strength of the civil power, for all publicans served the magistrates in the capacity of constables.

INTIMIDATION

The notion that good discipline can be imposed and lawlessness checked by threats of dire punishment and exposure of culprits to public view had its usual demoralizing influence. In Newfoundland in the seventeenth and eighteenth centuries, as in other countries, extreme penalties for petty offences lessened the chance of enforcement and encouraged resort to violence. Threats and public punishment were no less commonplace and no less destructive of any nascent ability to determine the right and to act in accordance with an inward decision.

In 1729 the first governor reported that he had erected several pairs of stocks for the punishing of petty criminals. In 1752 a governor ordered the construction of gallows in the most public places of several districts. In 1757 a woman who gave liquor to a seaman and stole his money and buckles was sentenced to be put in the whirligig and then sent out of the country. In the same year, a justice of the peace who struck a married woman of "troublesome and turbulent disposition" was ordered to pay £5 to the husband and to erect at his own expense a cage for the punishment of such women. About 1765 a drunken soldier who stole and killed a lamb escaped the gallows but forfeited all his goods and chattels, was required also to pay the charges of the court, and had his right hand branded with the letter "R". The gallows, the stocks, the lash, and the mark of the brand were constant reminders to the people that they lived in the shadow of vengeance from without; the feeling could hardly have been conducive to an inward urge to self-improvement.

Although these were common practices in other countries too, their negative educational effect was likely to be greater when self-confidence was less for reasons already stated.

BIGOTRY

Religious bigotry did more to suppress those it feared than to elevate those who conformed. The clearest case in point was the treatment of Irish Catholics in the eighteenth century. For a time about 1765 the Irish made up more than half of the resident population. Wretchedly poor and ignorant, they were easy victims of economic and religious persecution. Those who violated the law by surreptitiously giving shelter to a priest and providing a room or building for a public celebration of mass were severely punished — ordinarily by a heavy fine, the burning of the building where mass was said, and deportation. Even those who were convicted of no overt offence were constantly under suspicion as likely to be disorderly, disaffected, and

disloyal. It is little wonder that they frequently learned to deserve the reputation they had acquired.

An important consequence of this religious intolerance, as Rowe points out, was the exclusion from the island of the Roman Catholic teaching orders, which otherwise would have undoubtedly established schools and assumed responsibility for the education of a large proportion of the population. Instead of being permitted instruction, the Irish Catholics were encouraged by merchants and publicans to buy more rum and subject themselves to exploitation by creditors. Their religious persuasion deprived them in practice of any meagre political rights or hopes of legal redress that other poor settlers enjoyed. These disabilities were officially removed when a broad-minded governor in 1784 issued orders that all were to be allowed the free exercise of religious privileges permitted by law. From that time on there was increasing freedom of conscience and of religious practice, although prejudice and bigotry were too firmly rooted to be eradicated immediately.

Results of Oppression

These twelve factors produced conditions of life, the effect of which, in summary, was to impress on the people a sense of helplessness, to encourage escapist outlets of a low order, and to discourage growth in intellectual power and in willingness and ability to take responsibility. A governor, Lord Gambier, did urge changes which would have educated the people for political power:

I am led to apprehend that the present system of policy observed towards this Island is defective, being insufficient for effecting the happiness and good order of the community which is the chief end of all government. This I attribute to the want of a power in the Island for framing laws for its internal regulation, and for raising the sums necessary to promote any measure of public utility by which expense must be incurred. . . . No money can be raised here except by voluntary contribution, and that mode must be always inadequate for the many useful purposes for which it is required . . . . I therefore feel it incumbent on me to propose to your Lordship's consideration the establishment of a Legislative power in Newfoundland similar to that which has been found necessary to the prosperity and good government of other parts of H.M. foreign dominions.[5]

But that was in 1803. Political reform did not come for another thirty years. As for popular enlightenment of a general kind, a newspaper began publication in 1806; but the venture was regarded by the authorities as so dangerous that the publisher had to deposit a bond and submit the contents of the paper to magistrates for perusal and censorship before publication.

Hence a black picture of Newfoundland society, painted by a Recollet priest who accompanied the French forces at the end of the seventeenth century, had some justification in fact:

They have not a single minister of religion in these establishments, though more than twenty of them are larger settlements than Placentia. They do not know what religion they belong to. The greater part of them, born in this country, have never received any instruction, and never make any act of religion, no more than mere savages. Drunkenness and impurity are common and public among them, even among the women. It is impossible to imagine anything more abominable than the life led by the English on these coasts; they are left altogether without the succor of religion and are degenerated into a race almost worst than savages. Crime of the most loathsome nature is quite public among them. . . .[6]

We have the word of a more friendly authority, the Society for the Propagation of the Gospel in Foreign Parts, that in 1703 there was no public exercise of religion in Newfoundland except in St. John's. A report of the same society eighty-seven years later asserted that "the generality are a barbarous, perfidious, and cruel people." Although some settlements were much better than others, Newfoundland as a whole remained until near the end of the eighteenth century a society in which cultural and moral values had failed to develop. A later Methodist superintendent of education declared with only slight exaggeration that when the first missionaries of his church arrived about 1875:

. . . not a school was known in the Island, nor was a single temple raised to the worship of Almighty God. Men who had come from England had never seen a minister since they left their native shore; and those who had been born on the island had never seen one in their lives. The sabbath was unknown; there was none to celebrate marriage, and the marriage vow was little regarded. Oppression, violence, swearing, debauchery, profanity, licentiousness, and every crime that can degrade human nature, sink civilized man to a savage, or even reduce him below the brute, was practised without a check . . .[7]

Schools

It is probable but not certain that a school was conducted in Placentia during the French regime. In 1689 the Bishop of Quebec visited that settlement and apparently took with him a few Franciscans to engage in educational work. But with this possible exception, there appears to have been no formal instruction of children at school anywhere in Newfoundland before 1722. Rowe,[8] on whose recent dissertation the following section is mainly based, says that in that year an Anglican clergyman named Jones opened at Bonavista a school on his own initiative and secured occasional financial aid from the Society for the Propagation of the Gospel in Foreign Parts.

S. P. G.

This society, commonly known as the S.P.G., sent out and paid clergymen and teachers, or gave assistance to those already at work in the colonies. At the beginning in any settlement the clergyman was expected to teach the young himself as a supplementary duty, but he might persuade the society when the need became greater to provide him with a schoolmaster assistant. Education, in the view of the society, was definitely subsidiary to the general religious welfare, as may be seen by the usual allowances paid — seventy pounds to the clergyman and from fifteen to twenty pounds to the schoolmaster. The educational activity of the society expanded in North America from the opening of its first school in New York in 1704, until in 1827 it was employing two hundred teachers. It withdrew from strictly educational work in Newfoundland in 1858. The S.P.G., of course, was a distinctly Anglican organization; its clergy and teachers were members and protagonists of the Church of England.

The second school of the S.P.G. was opened in St. John's in 1744 under a clergyman who had formerly been stationed at Bonavista. Curiously enough one of the reasons given by the clergyman for setting up a school was that "a large number of children attended a Papist one" — a clear indication that a private venture school under a Roman Catholic teacher was already in operation. In 1766 a school was opened at Harbour Grace under a teacher appointed by a clergyman and paid by the S.P.G. Between 1766 and 1824 the society established schools in over twenty settlements. But the operation of these schools was very irregular: by

1800 there were no more than half a dozen schoolmasters and after 1800 no more than fifteen at any one time; in some years there were only two or three; in 1824 there were thirteen listed by name — six with sixty-six pupils or more and seven with thirty pupils or less. The number of days on which school was conducted is also uncertain, but some teachers operated Sunday schools, presumably in addition to week-day schools in nearly all instances.

Obviously the resources of the S.P.G. were not equal to the educational needs of the island. At the end of the eighteenth century the settlements could be counted in hundreds, and access from one to another was too difficult to make it possible for one teacher to serve several at the same time. Nevertheless, as Rowe points out, the S.P.G. made important contributions to education in Newfoundland. The few schools it established were "cultural beacons" in a country which might otherwise have remained in educational darkness. By setting up examples it showed the people the desirability of establishing schools everywhere. The children who were taught to read and write, though few in number, might later teach their own children and others, if they moved to some other part of the island where there was no school. The textbooks and reading material sent out by the society, which in many places were the only printed matter to be found, continued for that very reason to serve an important purpose.

OTHER CHARITY SCHOOLS

During the first decade of the nineteenth century Newfoundland experienced a wave of prosperity which lasted until 1815. Its advent gave rise to movements for social and cultural improvement. One of these movements was the founding in 1802, or possibly a year or two later, of the Society for Improving the Condition of the Poor in St. John's, to which both

Roman Catholics and Protestants contributed support. Among its activities was the operation at first of two Sunday schools, one Roman Catholic and the other Protestant, and later of two week-day charity schools, one for boys and one for girls. By 1809 the charity schools were attended by ninety-one boys and one hundred and two girls. The schools were financed by subscriptions and, for a time, by grants from the British government. They were free to all and undenominational in character. But in the 1830's the society turned over its educational work to the Newfoundland School Society, an affiliate of the Church of England.

BENEVOLENT IRISH SOCIETY

A second charitable organization in St. John's, the Benevolent Irish Society, was founded in 1806 and began twenty years later to engage in educational work. It opened a school in a private house and enrolled one hundred and thirty-six boys and seventy girls. In 1827 the society completed the construction of an orphanage and transferred the school to the new premises, which provided much better accommodation than had hitherto been available for education. The enrolment of pupils in 1828 was nominally six hundred, including orphans in residence and other children of the poor, and the average attendance about three hundred — a not unusual ratio at the time.

The Benevolent Irish Society was supported and governed by both Protestant and Roman Catholic subscribers, and the school was open to children of all denominations. But in reality it was largely, and became wholly, a Roman Catholic institution. Members of the society objected to the use of the school for Catholic religious instruction even when there were no Protestant pupils, but by the 1830's the opposition was overcome and the school came under the direct supervision of the Roman Catholic bishop.

NEWFOUNDLAND SCHOOL SOCIETY

The body which carried on the most extensive educational work in the early nineteenth century was loosely connected with the National Society, which operated in England under the aegis of the established church. (See below, page 118.) The Newfoundland organization, founded in England in 1823, had several changes of name but was most commonly known in its early years as the Newfoundland School Society. Its major aim was "to communicate free instruction to the poor of all denominations," but the teachers were to be members of the Church of England and were to be trained for the work in the Central School of the National Society. The attempt to be fair and impartial by employing only respectable Anglican agents to do non-sectarian work was better understood and appreciated by churchmen than by dissenters in the colony and led to some hard feeling. But the society did excellent work.

By 1828 the Newfoundland School Society had schools in operation at St. John's, Harbour Grace, Carbonear, Petty Harbour, Quidi Vidi, Trinity, and Bonavista, with five hundred and forty-six pupils on the register in day schools. For the year 1827-8 total expenses were £1688, or a little over £3 per pupil enrolled — considerably more than the cost per pupil in National schools in England, as might be expected in a less populous area. Most of the schools were staffed by a husband and wife, and there were altogether twelve teachers — masters and mistresses — who received an aggregate of £833; if this can be interpreted as slightly less than £140 a couple, it was a generous income for an elementary school teacher and his wife. The number of schools continued to increase, and would have multiplied quickly if the resources of the society had not been limited, for their establishment appears to have been

St. John's, Newfoundland, about 1770

well received by the settlers. Indeed, the people profited so quickly from observing a school in operation that they volunteered in two settlements to cut and bring in timber for the construction of a better building and, in one of the two areas, to contribute £100 towards its erection.

Unfortunately the attendance was poorer than it might have been, partly because children were employed at an early age in connection with the fishing and at other work. For this reason six of the seven schools also conducted Sunday schools, at which the aggregate attendance was listed in 1828 as three hundred and seventy-one. Another cause of failure to attend was sheer poverty, since many children were without shoes and sufficient covering to go to schools. The society's remedy was to collect donations of clothing in England and ship them out to the island. Teachers acknowledged these ship-

ments with letters of gratitude, but were sometimes obliged to say that there were many more applicants than garments to distribute and that some children were still obliged to remain at home and without benefit of instruction during the winter. For the benefit of those who had had no opportunity for schooling when young, six of the seven schools in 1828 conducted classes for adults and had altogether three hundred and forty on the roll. These conditions and practices continued until well on in the nineteenth century.

UNORGANIZED SCHOOLING

The more important schools for children of the people were provided by one or the other of these societies. But throughout the settlements educational work of a less organized nature was carried on by clergy and lay men and women. Most of it was voluntary. An educated woman would undertake to give daily lessons in reading and writing to children of her neighbors. In another place a man or a woman would teach in the evening or in a Sunday school. In Fortune Harbor, a northern settlement, the Roman Catholic bishop in 1834 found the people exceptionally well instructed in their religion and virtuous in their ways, thanks to the fathers of three families, who took turns in assembling the whole populace at their respective houses on Sundays and holy days for a religious lecture and devotions.

Another interesting and not uncommon practice is illustrated by the story of the master of a fishing boat who had among his crew an Englishman of some education who was growing old for the work. The master, who had had no schooling when he came out from England in his youth, and who had been compelled to work hard to support a large family, said to his elderly employee: "John, thee canst read. It seems a sad unchristian way for my boys to grow up without learning. Do thee stop ashore and teach the children and I'll pay thee the wages as thof thee went in the boat."[8] Not only was the bargain made, but arrangements were made also to include the children of a neighbor's family.

EDUCATION FOR THE WELL-TO-DO

Children of the socially elite and well-to-do were educated in one of three ways: they might be sent to schools in England or in some other part of North America; they might be given private tuition at home; or they might be sent to schools for young gentlemen or young ladies in Newfoundland when these were established.

An attempt was made in 1799 to establish in St. John's a classical school for boys on the English model under a clergyman of the Church of England. A master named Anspach was brought out from England by the merchants of St. John's, and the school was operated for three years. Although in purpose and curriculum it was essentially a Latin grammar school, the intention was to make this an all-purpose establishment with a primary department and a department for girls. In the absence of any existing endowment, the method of organization, finance, and control was necessarily that of a proprietary school, or academy, for which twenty-five families entered into an agreement to raise the necessary funds. The short duration of the school resulted from disputes among the subscribers, the master, and the resident clergyman of St. John's. At a meeting of the subscribers the original plans were altered so that each subscriber should contribute according to the number of children that he sent for instruction. The resident clergyman and some others had large families and objected. They kept their children away from school and did everything possible to embarrass the master.

The failure of the grammar school in St. John's left the provision of schools for the upper classes to the initiative of private individuals. The probability is that there were schools before 1807 conducted by men or women of education who were willing for a price to undertake the instruction of young gentlemen or ladies. But the records of these schools date only from that year, when the *Royal Gazette* was first published. There were several such schools in the next three decades, the majority of them in St. John's and most of them surviving for only a few years. In addition to the necessary subjects for beginners and the more advanced elementary subjects of grammar and geography, they offered for boys not only the classics but practical subjects like bookkeeping, mensuration, and navigation, and for girls such accomplishments as fancywork, drawing, and painting.

Summary

It is apparent that very little formal education was provided in Newfoundland until the latter part of the eighteenth century. From then until 1836, the end of the period under discussion, organized education for the poor was provided as a charity by school societies financed by people of means in England or on the island. The provision of education for the upper classes was left almost wholly to private initiative, but parents who wished a superior education for their children continued to send them abroad to school. Much voluntary work of an educational kind was carried on by individuals in settlements where no school had been established. It is not possible to estimate the proportion of young people who attained literacy or education beyond this bare minimum. It is clear that there was an educational awakening in the first part of the nineteenth century but that the great majority of the people of Newfoundland were not yet in a position to assume, by their own action, responsibility for the education of their children.

CHAPTER 5

The Maritime Provinces

The period covered in this chapter extends for about a century from the beginning of British rule in Nova Scotia in 1713. The territory, after 1763, was that now occupied by three maritime provinces. For a short period after 1763 the whole area was included in one colony, Nova Scotia; but Prince Edward Island became a separate colony in 1769, and New Brunswick in 1784. In this latter year Cape Breton Island was also separated, but it was reunited with Nova Scotia in 1820.

Up to 1740 there were only a few hundred English-speaking people in the colony. But after the founding of Halifax in 1749 the population was increased rapidly for a time by immigration from Europe and New England. Then in the last quarter of the eighteenth century about thirty thousand Loyalists came from the United States and over twenty thousand remained. By 1806, according to Brown, there were approximately sixty-five thousand people in Nova Scotia, twenty-five hundred in Cape Breton, thirty-five thousand in New Brunswick, and ninety-five hundred in Prince Edward Island.

From 1763, of course, the whole of Canada was British. But communication was so difficult that the maritime area under consideration in this chapter was quite distinct and separate.

Since the period of attendance at school for most people was short at best, the influence on the minds of children and adults of other social institutions, of tradition, and of the environment was correspondingly great. Brief consideration will therefore be given to the origin of the people, to the ruling class and government, to geographical factors, occupations, and customs, and to the churches.

The People

Far from being united and homogeneous, the people were divided by characteristics associated with their national origins. The French-speaking Acadians have already been described. Four other important groups who came to the colony were: Protestants from England and continental Europe; merchants and farmers from New England; Loyalist emigrés from other parts of the United States; and Highland Scots.

England sent out some thousands to the colony in the 1750's, another large wave, including a thousand from Yorkshire in the 1770's, and a fairly steady trickle of individuals and small groups year by year. But the government was equally pleased to have Protestant settlers go to the colony from other European countries. Hence the English-born formed an important nucleus, but not a majority for any length of time, so that the educational ideas and practices imported from England were subject to modification under other pressures.

Merchants and adventurers came from New England when Halifax was founded, and larger numbers came in the early 1760's when representative government had been established and civil liberties were assured. Many of them occupied deserted Acadian farms, and many engaged in trade. The majority were of English stock and were Calvinist in religion. Their stern concepts of moral and religious propriety made life no laughing matter. A girl who failed to conceal a smile during an hour-long sermon might expect a public rebuke from the minister and a painful interview with her father. The man who let slip an expletive addressed to the Devil or mended his fences on Sunday might be forced, if caught, to submit to open censure by the church. The same earnestness of purpose made the New Englander insistent on the establishment of schools. His ancestors in Massachusetts before the middle of the seventeenth century had required local communities by law to make provision for teaching the young to read Holy Scripture and so to ensure the discomfiture of that "old deluder, Satan."

The Loyalists began coming in numbers during the 1780's. Nearly fifty-six hundred sailed from the city of New York to Halifax in ships of a British convoy in 1783. Some eight hundred went from Pennsylvania to New Brunswick, which came to be populated almost wholly by Loyalists. A considerable number intended to settle in Cape Breton Island, although only a few hundred actually came and remained. Fewer still went to Prince Edward Island. But the total number of Loyalists who came to the Maritime Provinces before the end of the century far exceeded the existing population when the influx began. Their influence, therefore, was very great.

Some had been men of substance and power in their home communities, many more were ordinary people, but all were prepared to make their voices heard. They sought such improvements as better roads, political reform in the direction of self-government, and the establishment of schools. Some, notably in New Brunswick, became members of a ruling oligarchy, and many irritated the rest of the population by their presumptions of superior patriotism and loyalty to the British throne. But life in the American environment had educated them away from acceptance of any authority not of their own creation and of dependence on paternalistic charity. Their traditions had disposed them to manage their own affairs, including, when they were ready, the educational agencies to which they entrusted their children.

The first considerable number of Highland Scots arrived in the 1770's, and about twenty-five thousand more came between 1790 and 1830. Those who settled around Pictou were mostly Presbyterian, and those who went to the vicinity of Antigonish and to Cape Breton Island were preponderantly Roman Catholic. They came to escape extreme poverty and were willing to work hard for a poor living on land that held little attraction for others. All retained their clannishness and displayed a fierce family pride unrelated to their paucity of worldly goods. A large proportion of them were illiterate, and nine out of ten spoke Gaelic only. By ordinary standards they were an ignorant people, and not less so because they were versed in the legends and mystical lore of what others might think a primitive society.

Unlike the settlers from colonies to the south and west, they were far from ready to provide for the enlightenment of their children by joint efforts. But their clergy were educated men, and some of them, like Dr. Thomas McCulloch of Pictou, made outstanding contributions to the advancement of education. The Roman Catholic Scots, who had left Scotland partly because of religious oppression, were under educational handicaps in the colony for a time because of restrictions against any activity of their church.

Government and the Ruling Class

At an early stage the government of a British colony usually consisted of a governor representing the king and an appointed council responsible to the government in England. In 1758 Nova Scotia advanced to a second stage of colonial development when it was granted the right to elect a legislative assembly. Prince Edward Island, separated from Nova Scotia in 1769, gained an assembly in 1773; New Brunswick had one from the time of its separation in 1784; but Cape Breton Island was left without one during the period of its separation, 1784-1820. The assembly had little power at first in its struggle against the council, which had both legislative and executive functions, control of the purse, and usually the support of the English government. Nevertheless these early assemblies in the colonies gave valuable education for self-government: by immediately useful experience in making known the aspirations of the people and source of the irregularities in administration; by appointing committees of investigation; and by securing the right to approve estimates and to receive accounts of public expenditure.

On the other hand the councils were supported by people of influence and by others who hoped to gain influence through association with those who had it. In Halifax prosperous merchants became part and parcel of the ruling oligarchy. The associates of the council were often able to secure election to the assembly not only in the capital but sometimes in outside constituencies, partly because men who were hard pressed to make a bare living could not afford to take time from their work for unpaid public service. Hence the government fostered the creation and survival of a social class distinct from the people at large. Members of this class, and those who would have liked to be so regarded, sought an exclusive type of school for the education of their children. They showed less concern about the education of children of ordinary people, except to have schools that would make them amenable, rather than capable of directing the course of society. In this attitude they were in accord with the views of those in the home government who would have liked to see a hereditary aristocracy founded in major colonies as a bulwark of imperial power.

The attitude and actions of government were a much more powerful factor in education for citizenship than was any slight attention to civics in schools. Ruling class distrust of participation by the people in government is illustrated by an extract from a letter of the first governor of New Brunswick, Thomas Carleton. To explain his delay in calling for an election of the assembly he wrote to the Secretary of State:

I think on all accounts it will be best that the American spirit of innovation should not be nursed among the Loyal Refugees by the introduction of acts by the legislature for purposes to which, by the common law and the practice of the best regulated colonies, the crown alone is acknowledged to be competent.[1]

This was written within ten years after the successful revolt of the thirteen colonies to the south against treatment of the same kind. The resentment engendered by such a governor in the minds of some who had come from the seceding colonies spurred them to aggressive political action, but fostered among others a cynical view of government.

This cynicism had already been established in the minds of older colonists by actions based on a discriminating concept of equity, which may be illustrated by the scale of land grants adopted for veterans of the Seven Years' War who settled in New Brunswick. Field officers received 5000 acres, captains 3000, subalterns 2000, non-commissioned officers 200, privates 50. Associated with this scheme of values were practices of favoritism by which army officers and others were able to acquire 100,000 acres or more of the most favorably located land. Although most of this land had to be redistributed when the Loyalists came, such actions of the ruling class disposed the less fortunate majority to get what they could out of government and to have little respect for political administration. A low opinion of the many and partiality in the distribution of benefits or power tend to make the majority the kind of people their detractors consider them to be.

Moreover, educational ambition was discouraged by the policy of the home government in making appointments. It was considered "vain to cultivate the higher branches of learning" when superior positions were almost certain to be filled by men sent out from England, or at best by colonials in high favor with the ruling clique. Great deference was paid to the officer class and to economic status: the uniform was powerful and wealth omnipotent. Earnest young men who might otherwise have sought to improve themselves by study must often have become cynical and have given up.

Geographical and Economic Factors

Agriculture was the mainstay of life in the river valleys. The ground had to be laboriously cleared of trees and the surplus wood and stumps burned; and even bringing in the seed might be heavy toil, for the settler had often to carry it for long distances on his back. When a young man married and moved to new ground, he had the same pioneer labor to perform. The new colonists were not good farmers and were slow to learn. Those who settled on the old Acadian lands lacked the skill of their predecessors in cultivating soil reclaimed from the sea; dykes remained broken for decades and many fields were used for grazing. Until well on in the nineteenth century, the time of all members of the family was occupied with chores and the making of nearly everything that was used on the farm. The men of families living on the coast might also be employed in deep-sea fishing and would then leave the farm work to their women and children. However educative this burden of work may have been in some respects, it did not encourage schooling.

Fishing might be combined with trading, and these occupations led to lumbering and ship-building. Before the end of the eighteenth century there was a lively development of commerce from these related industries. The West Indies and England were the outside markets. Within the colonies even rural areas came to have a local store, which often served also as a bank, a tavern, and a rendezvous for news and gossip. The coming of Loyalists caused the sudden appearance of larger urban centres, of which the outstanding example is Shelburne. Nearly ten thousand people spent the winter of 1783-4 on the site of this town, which soon had a rapid expansion of industry and business, fine residences, and three newspapers. Although Shelburne's prosperity was short-lived, the development of industry and trade did act as an educational stimulant. Trade requires people with some schooling, and creates conditions under which schooling is possible by distributing goods which save work and time and by causing concentrations of population. In 1790 the Bishop of Halifax while in Shelburne found twelve schools with 257 scholars; he estimated

that there were then about 3500 whites and 1160 Negroes in the town, including about 770 children in all.

Halifax, of course, was not only the capital of Nova Scotia but the most important city in the maritime colonies. It sprang suddenly into being in 1749. In the spring of that year there were only trees and rock on the shore of the harbor previously known as Chebucto; before winter there were streets through the forest, 2500 colonists from Europe, 1000 traders and adventurers from New England, many buildings, much activity of all kinds, and plenty of rum. There was even by the next spring a schoolmaster, although not as yet a school. Within two years the population was 6000, and although it fell again to a third of that number shortly after, it had risen to about 8500 at the end of the century. The residents of the city were a mixed lot. Of a total of slightly more than 3000 according to a census of 1767, only 302 were English; about 850 were listed as Irish and about 1350 were described as Americans; there were smaller numbers of Acadians, Scots, Germans, and other people from Europe.

But among the inhabitants of the city were the social aristocracy of Nova Scotia; and the *Halifax Gazette*, the first newspaper published in Canada, gave all classes from 1751 a new motive for learning to read. The seamy side of life, for which the seaport was also noted, was no doubt educative in a different way. Unfortunately, as the home of the privileged and well-to-do, as the seat of government, and as a centre of entertainment for transients, the city did not gain in good repute among the people in other parts of Nova Scotia. The cleavage between Halifax and rural areas, which still exists, created dissension on educational matters. This was not true in the same degree of the chief urban centres in other maritime colonies.

The educational environment differed not only as between town and country but among the four colonies. Nova Scotia proper was the oldest settlement and had the earliest development under English rule. In comparison, Cape Breton Island was seriously handicapped: before the Loyalist migration the English government refused to grant land on the island, and until well on in the nineteenth century discouraged any full-scale development of natural resources in coal for fear of competition with English mines. The separate government created in 1784 served no purpose except to create more governmental jobs and to foster a local spirit which persisted even after the island was reunited politically with Nova Scotia. Although plans were made to send some 3000 Loyalists to the island, it appears that only a few hundred came and remained. The settlers who did come were predominantly Roman Catholic Scots.

In 1767 the territory which later became New Brunswick had only 322 white inhabitants, including 147 Acadian French, 60 Germans, 53 Irish, 25 English and 17 Scots. But in 1784 there were about 16,000 residents, of whom 12,000 were Loyalists, 1500 French, and most of the remainder earlier settlers from New England. Because of the large proportion of people from the older colonies, interest in education was more immediate and general in New Brunswick than in any other of the Maritime colonies, for the Loyalists, even before they left New York, had met to consider the need of securing educational advantages for their children in the country to which they were going.

Prince Edward Island was slower in its development, partly because an aristocratic scheme of tenancy under landlords kept most Loyalists away and discouraged the 600 who came. A survey made in 1764-5 showed only thirty families on the island, wretchedly poor people "living in little cabins or huts in the woods." The landlords were more anxious to establish a separate government and a capital for Prince Edward Island than to expand opportunities for colonists. Some Acadians returned, and settlers came from Scotland in the 1770's and, in greater numbers, at the beginning of the nineteenth century. A census in 1798 showed a population of only 4372, but by 1830 there were 50,000. Prince Edward Island was never wealthy. It experienced the common difficulty of poorer countries in keeping up the supply of currency, which constantly tended to leak away to places where it had greater purchasing value. It was even found necessary to oblige outgoing ships to secure a licence to carry passengers, in order to keep people from drifting away.

Life in Charlottetown and the vicinity appears to have been pleasant in many respects, but a visiting bishop in 1789 found not a church or a schoolhouse on the island, although the population then was between five and six thousand. The first printing press was set up in 1788 and the first post-office established in 1801. In 1814 Lieutenant-Governor Douglas Smith wrote to Lord Bathurst that the state of education was "truly deplorable." The royal instructions had directed that lands be reserved for clergymen and schoolmasters throughout the island, but these had "in no instance yet been appropriated or even marked out."

The Church

Education both in school and out of school was influenced greatly by the preferred position of the Church of England. From 1758 it was the established church in Nova Scotia and as such had the right to control public education. One of its major objectives educationally was to maintain the superiority of the church in the colony, in number of adherents if possible, but certainly in terms of influence and power.

The first education act passed in Nova Scotia, dated 1766, required that a licence be obtained by anyone proposing to conduct a grammar school anywhere in the province, or an elementary school in Halifax county. Although the act did not specifically require formal acceptance of Church of England doctrine as a condition for securing a licence, it may be assumed that the lieutenant-governor would approve, without question, applications from Anglicans only. Thibeau states that in the eighteenth century, there is not an instance to be found of a licence to teach granted to any person other than an employee of the S.P.G.

Protestant non-conformists were free of restriction at a distance from the capital but only with respect to elementary education. This was equivalent to saying that dissenters might provide ordinary instruction for their children, but not schools that offered education preparatory to training for the ministry or to a position of leadership in society.

The act was much more drastic in precluding the possibility that "any popish recusant, papist, or person professing the popish religion" should "be so presumptive as to set up any school within this province." But this disability was removed in Nova Scotia in 1786, except that for some years Roman Catholic schools were forbidden to admit, under the age of fourteen, pupils who had been brought up as Protestants.

Thus the Church of England fought a rearguard action as it retreated from fortified strongholds. In the 1730's and 1740's there had been confident correspondence between governors and their superiors in England about plans to convert the Acadians, and the Lords of Trade and Plantations recommended to the S.P.G. that some of their schoolmasters be able to speak French in order to "advance the true Protestant religion." When this more aggressive project met defeat, reliance was placed on restrictions, which were gradually abandoned under pressure. The last

stronghold of privilege to be defended was in higher education. In 1802 King's College at Windsor received from England a grant and a charter which stated that:

No member of the university shall frequent the Romish Mass or the meeting-houses of Presbyterians, Baptists, or Methodists, or the Conventicles or places of worship of any other dissenters from the Church of England, or where Divine Service shall not be performed according to the liturgy of the Church of England.[2]

But this last restriction simply spurred non-conformists to establish other colleges and to secure public money for their support.

Parish and Charity Schools

In the eighteenth century the most efficient elementary schools were as a rule those provided as a religious charity through the Society for the Propagation of the Gospel in Foreign Parts. Teachers supported by the S.P.G. had to meet certain requirements of character, knowledge, patriotism, and religious conformity, and those sent out from England had also to pass a committee of selection who tested the ability of candidates to teach reading, writing, and the catechism of the Church of England. They were therefore, in a sense, qualified teachers and as such commanded a little respect.

In Nova Scotia the first educational venture of the S.P.G. was to assist in the support of schoolmasters at Annapolis from 1729 to 1738 and at Canso from 1736 to 1743. Then in 1746, when plans were being made for serious colonization, the Society undertook to send out six schoolmasters and to pay each of them a salary of £15 a year in addition to an initial sum of £10 to help defray the cost of getting settled. S.P.G. schools were established at Halifax in 1750 and at

Lunenburg in 1753, and schoolmasters in other places applied for assistance. In various years between 1782 and 1802 there were licensed teachers paid or approved by the S.P.G. in at least eight different places, including Yarmouth, where there were six holders of a licence in 1785. But a school might be conducted in a centre only for a brief period; in 1787 the number of schoolmasters actually employed by the Society was only five. In Cape Breton after 1787 a school at Sydney was conducted at times by a teacher with S.P.G. support. In New Brunswick by 1800 the Society had opened or helped finance schools in fourteen different places, and before withdrawing from educational activity in 1836 it was at one time paying about forty teachers.

Similar in their religious purpose to the week-day schools of the S.P.G. were the Sunday schools established by various teachers and churches. The first of these under the English regime was conducted by the Reverend Richard Watts at Annapolis in 1728, apparently before he received help from the S.P.G. Soon after his arrival from Scotland in 1776, James Davidson opened the first Sunday school in Pictou County; and in a few years the Sunday school movement became as popular in a small way as it did in England. In Halifax in 1783 St. Paul's Anglican Church opened a Sunday school in which needy children were clothed and provided for in other ways. In 1814 the Pictou Sabbath School Society was founded, and by 1827 the society had seventy-seven schools, 198 teachers, and 2335 pupils. Although Sunday schools in Nova Scotia were attended by many children who were working on week-days, the instruction appears to have been almost wholly religious even in the early years.

Education of a kind was also provided in an orphanage at Halifax. It was said that destitute children who "might otherwise have perished or been useless to the public" were "graciously relieved" by admission to this benign institution of 1761. They were kept constantly at such tasks as carding or spinning wool, picking oakum, or weeding, to preserve them from habits of idleness until they could be put out to indentured service at the age of twelve.

Private Venture Schools

For the period under discussion, when organized systems of education had not appeared and the operation of schools was spasmodic, it is not possible to classify teachers or institutions in any clear-cut way. A teacher might sometimes operate a school entirely on his own, and at other times with assistance from a voluntary agency like the S.P.G., or with assurances from a group of parents as in the case of an academy, or in later years with the help of a grant from the government. Nevertheless a large number of schools were on the whole of the private venture type. Although of varying quality and uncertain duration, they performed an important function and were significant also as the true predecessors of the public schools. In America, when the people could not or would not accept education as a benefaction outside their control, they managed to pay a teacher in some way or other until the present system of public finance and administration began to evolve.

The first reference to a private venture school in Nova Scotia appears in a letter addressed to the S.P.G. in 1765. It mentions a teacher named Morrison who had opened a school at Granville and who wished to apply for assistance from the Society. James Davidson, already mentioned, appears to have begun teaching in Pictou County on his own initiative. Among the first schools in Prince Edward Island was that of Alexander Richardson, who held classes in St. John's Coffee

House in Charlottetown about the year 1780. In New Brunswick, David Burpee taught at Magerville in 1778-9 on the understanding that he would receive three shillings eleven pence ha'penny a month per pupil; it was not a lucrative venture since the parents of only seven scholars made the payment, and chiefly in produce at that. Teachers were commonly hired by individuals or small groups in Loyalist settlements, especially in Nova Scotia. But it was hard for the parents of a few large families to pay enough to secure the full-time services of a capable teacher. Unless they were willing and able to get a schoolmaster in the pay of the S.P.G., the one who instructed their children was likely to be a man unfit for regular employment, such as a partly incapacitated veteran of the wars who supported himself by odd jobs, teaching included.

The financial problem and the difficulty of bringing a number of children together in a sparsely settled country resulted in the appearance of many itinerant teachers. These travelling salesmen of learning, attracted by a wandering life and a changing scene, were not likely to have the subdued and steady character sought by the S.P.G. and by later employers of those who teach the young. The itinerant teachers did not feel obliged to set a better example than their fellow-men by abstaining from alcohol and other open indulgences. Unfortunately, too, they sometimes had no qualifications of a positive nature to fit them for teaching. But when they went the rounds as visiting boarders in the settlers' homes, they enlivened the evenings by the fireside and prevented people forgetting about education and the desirability of regular schools.

School buildings erected by the people of a community were exceedingly crude in the early days. Matthews gives the following description of the few such structures in Prince Edward Island:

The first school-houses were little log huts without any floors except the native earth. For a chimney, two logs standing upright in the middle of the room, about three feet apart, served as jambs between which the fire was built to warm the children all around. On the top of these perpendicular logs of about four feet in height, was constructed the cob and clay work; namely, a mixture of mud and ferns between sticks with the ends of each crossing those of the other like the walls of a log house. This formed the funnel aperture to throw off the smoke. Around this primitive and odd fireplace marched the monarch of the birchen rod and sceptre, with as much dignity over his mud floor as ever did Commodore of a large fleet over his quarter deck.[3]

Schools for Special Groups

Because of local differences of language, religion, race, or color, before the appearance of the universal public school no one type of education could be acceptable to all of the people. For example, the German colonists who went from Halifax to Lunenburg in 1753 were determined to maintain their language and Lutheran religion for future generations. A minister of the Church of England named Vincent, supported by grants from the government at Halifax and from the S.P.G., tried at first to conduct a school in English. Failing to persuade the parents to send their children, he secured an S.P.G. grant for a German-speaking schoolmaster. But the people of Lunenburg continued to protest: they claimed to have opened a school on their own initiative and that the Anglican divine had suborned their teacher and broken up their school by requiring that English be the language of instruction. An attempt was made to compromise by using English in the forenoon and German in the afternoon, and requiring attendance in the former as a condition of attendance in the latter; but it was too late. The government in Halifax withdrew its support because Vincent had failed to make progress in Anglicizing the Germans, and the Germans resented efforts to convert their children from the language and religion of their parents. The government made two more efforts to achieve its end: in 1767 it gave Lunenburg a minister, certified as Lutheran, who nevertheless instructed the children in Church of England doctrine; a few years later it was ready again to try the direct method of sending an English-speaking missionary to convert everyone to the use of English. In 1774, the S.P.G. abandoned its mission in Lunenburg, and the language problem was left to be solved in time by the environmental force of an English-speaking majority.

The same difficulties were encountered in attempts to proselytize Roman Catholics of different nationalities. Among the Acadians, the first English school at Annapolis under the Reverend Richard Watts, already mentioned, was supported by the S.P.G. partly for the purpose of Anglicizing the population. The schoolmaster, Jean Baptiste Moreau, who had been sent to Nova Scotia with the S.P.G. clergyman in the year that Halifax was founded, was a former Roman Catholic priest. He was ordained soon after by the Church of England and was sent in 1753 to work as a missionary and schoolmaster among the French at Annapolis. Efforts of this kind met with little success, for the Acadians would listen to no teaching but that of the Roman Catholic Church. They had become accustomed in remote places and while without their own clergy under English rule, to dispense with any formal instruction. The consequence was that at the beginning of the nineteenth century they were mostly illiterate and lacking in any desire for education.

As for schools among Roman Catholics of mixed nationality, there is the example of Sydney in Cape Breton. The population of Sydney was nominally Church of England, but the majority of the island population was composed of Roman Catholic Scots, Irish, and Acadians. After two unaided attempts of individuals to operate schools in Sydney had failed, the S.P.G. in 1795 voted £10 to £15 a year, and the English government in the following year voted £40 a year, for a schoolmaster when a suitable applicant could be found. At first glance it would appear that this was an exceptionally generous provision, compensating for the poverty of the colony. But it applied to one school only, and the intention of the S.P.G. at least was that it should be a Church of England school to serve Anglican townspeople and help to convert the children of others. For years there was wrangling about appointments and payments. At intervals a Roman Catholic taught school and managed by subsequent petitions to collect the government grant. At one time the Roman Catholics threatened to set up another school in opposition when a Protestant teacher was appointed. From 1806 the Anglican minister was paid £60 to supervise the teacher of the school. After the reunion of Cape Breton and Nova Scotia in 1820, Sydney ceased to receive any special governmental subsidy. But the payment of public money to a denominational teacher not of the established church is significant as an early instance of the practice which now prevails in the Maritime Provinces. There, some schools are to all intents and purposes Roman Catholic, although not classified as "separate" in distinction from "public," or vice versa. Apart from this one institution in Sydney, there were in Cape Breton no schools worthy of the name. In 1786 liberty was granted to the considerable French population at Arichat to erect a schoolhouse, but little was done in a regular way to ensure the instruction of children until well on in the nineteenth century.

Soon after the major educational restrictions against Roman Catholics were removed, St. Peter's Church in Halifax opened a free parish school for English-speaking children of that faith. Among rural French-speaking Roman Catholics the most notable work was that of Father Sigogne, who came to the district of Clare in the western part of Nova Scotia at the end of the eighteenth century. He endeavored to provide systematic instruction for children by teaching himself, by appointing catechists to teach under his supervision, and by enlisting the aid of mothers who were able to assist. He also conducted a Sunday school for adults, and gave special instruction to girls and boys whom he brought to his presbytery as resident pupils. In Prince Edward Island at Rustico a school was established around 1816 by the Abbé Beaubien and was taught under his supervision by a young man who knew how to read and write and who had some idea of arithmetic.

Efforts were made to convert and educate the Indians from the time of the first English school at Annapolis. For example, in 1765 an S.P.G. clergyman named Wood reported that he was at work on a Micmac grammar. Le Gresley says that in a supreme effort a clever teacher was brought in from Boston and given ample resources to win over the Indians by any inducements likely to succeed. Apparently this teacher opened a school, offered to feed and board Indian children, tried to make friends with them and their parents, gave them presents — and failed to attract a single pupil. Thibeau is insistent that all attempts at conversion were futile because the Indians were quite unsusceptible to the new creed. He points out that a new approach to assimilation was introduced in 1792, when a bounty was offered to any British subject who married an Indian. The failure of Protestant missionary efforts caused the government ultimately to invite French priests from Quebec to resume educational and religious work among the Indians. In 1786 a society which had formerly operated in New England set up a commission in New Brunswick to engage and pay suitable teachers for civilizing and instructing the natives. The commission opened schools in six places, but in 1794 abandoned all but the one in Sussex, where an attempt was made to teach farming as well as the ordinary elementary subjects. When by 1833 about $140,000 had been spent, the project was abandoned. Hannay wrote in 1909 that no trace was left to show the school ever existed:

The Indians to whom it had undertaken to teach agriculture, the arts of civilization, and the Protestant religion, relapsed at once into barbarism and returned to their ancient faith. There are no Protestant Indians in New Brunswick and there are none which live after the manner of white men.[4]

Only the Roman Catholic religion apparently, could keep its hold on the Indian mind.

A school for Negroes was opened in Halifax in 1788, when a licence was given to Limerick Isaac to teach the "reading and writing of English to the Black people." In the same year the Anglican bishop appointed a Negro as schoolmaster at Tracadie and supplied him with religious tracts. Several other schools were established, for the Negro population was considerable. There were 2000 Negroes among the Loyalists, and although more than half that number left under organized philanthropy for Africa, the remainder were reinforced before the end of the eighteenth century by Maroons from Jamaica. The latter were reported by the governor in 1797 as being constantly at school and learning with "decency and diligence" to read and write.

Schools for the Few

It was inevitable during this early period under English rule that disproportionate attention should be given to schools for a very small percentage of the population. Only the few who had both education and means were certain to demand and get regular schooling for their children. In an aristocratic society, moreover, education was chiefly needed by leaders in government and church. Since there was as yet no thought, let alone the means, of socializing education to provide equal opportunities for all, anything more than a minimum could be made available only to the very small number who had money and leisure.

To avoid confusion, schools for the few may be classified as Latin grammar schools, academies, and private schools, even if particular schools did not always stay in the same category or call themselves by the name of the category to which by their characteristics they belonged. Latin grammar schools in Canada were the same as those in England except that some form of public financing had to take the place of century-old endowments: they taught Latin, mathematics, and Greek as if for university entrance. Academies, like English proprietary schools, were established co-operatively by well-to-do parents in a locality, or by a non-conformist religious denomination, and were not initially or primarily supported by public funds. They taught not only a classical curriculum but usually more practical subjects as well. Private schools were operated at the financial risk of the proprietor: those for the few taught some or all of the subjects offered in grammar schools and academies. Latin grammar schools and private schools ordinarily taught elementary subjects as well, since upper class parents preferred not to send their children to a school for the people; academies, if true to type in all respects, gave instruction only at the secondary level. Latin grammar schools were intended to be for boys only, but might tolerate girls at the elementary level; the other types were for boys or for girls, or for boys and girls in separate departments. Although Latin grammar schools might have free places for able children of poor parents, schools of all three types ordinarily charged substantial fees which only the few could pay.

Latin Grammar Schools

In Nova Scotia the executive council in 1768 submitted to the Lords of Trade and Plantations a plan for a collegiate school. Nothing was done. In 1780 legislation was passed in the province to raise £1500 by lottery to build a public, or Latin grammar school and to provide for its operation by government subsidies of up to £100 for a master and £50 for an usher, or assistant, when needed. The lottery was not a success and no school was established. In 1788 and 1789, however, money was voted to found two Latin grammar schools — the first in Windsor, called Horton Academy, and the second in Halifax, called the Grammar School.

The school at Windsor was opened in a rented house on November 1, 1788, by Bishop Inglis of Halifax. It had an enrolment later in the month of twenty pupils. The plan was to have two departments — an upper department where the classics were taught, and an English department which included arithmetic and practical mathematics in its program. Four hundred pounds had been voted by the legislature for salaries. Fees at the two levels were four pounds and three pounds respectively, and sixteen pounds for boarders. This school became the preparatory division of King's College, and was later called King's College School. In 1802, when there were thirty-three students in classics and mathematics under the instruction of the president, the English department was "laid aside."

The Halifax Grammar School was placed under the direction of trustees appointed by the governor. Its first headmaster was William Cochran, a graduate of Trinity College, Dublin, and, prior to his appointment, professor of classical languages at Columbia University, New York. He had two assistants. In 1790 Cochran became headmaster at Windsor and the Reverend George Wright, another import from New York, succeeded him at a salary of £150 a year, supplemented by the fees of pupils, who were about seventy in number by 1793. The following year a special tax was imposed, in the form of a duty on wine imported into Halifax, to pay the salary of the master and an assistant. Although this type of financing is hardly steady enough for its purpose, all in all a comparatively handsome provision had been made through these two schools for the education of the approximately one hundred young gentlemen enrolled.

In New Brunswick there were petitions and memorials for the establishment of institutions of secondary and higher education as soon as the Loyalists arrived. The governor in a despatch of 1790 indicated that a grammar school had been in operation for a few years, although on a modest basis, since the trustees had "employed such masters only as were to be found on the spot." Revenue for the purpose was obtained from rental of part of the land set aside for a more ambitious "academical establishment" in Fredericton, and this was matched in 1792 by a grant voted by the New Brunswick assembly. The number of pupils in the following year was seventeen, not counting beginners under nine years of age. In 1800 the College of New Brunswick was founded and for the next twenty years it served as the Fredericton grammar school. In 1805 legislation provided for the establishment of a grammar school at Saint John, which had a population of about 3000, nearly four times as large as that of Fredericton. The act provided for a grant of £100 a year for the master, with the somewhat

optimistic limitation that as soon as the income of the school rose to £600 the grant should cease. Fees were to be charged, of course, but the trustees were empowered to extend the benefits of a classical education to a number of free scholars, not exceeding eight. The first of these, admitted in 1806, was Peter James Bowry, the son of a master mariner.

In Prince Edward Island in 1804 land was granted "for the education of the youth in the learned languages, the liberal arts and sciences and all the branches of useful and polite literature." A building was erected in 1819 and classes were begun in 1821.

That the Latin grammar schools were intended primarily for a few people of means and social standing is apparent. They were few in number and attracted only a few pupils. The fees they charged were high enough to exclude the majority. Although not intended to offer primary work, they gave instruction to young children whose parents paid a higher fee than in elementary schools for the majority. In the secondary level they taught subjects far removed from the lives and needs of ordinary people. In short, they did not as a rule recruit pupils from elementary schools, but from a social class. Finally, the grammar schools were essentially Church of England institutions. In the case of the Public Grammar School of Saint John, the president of the board of directors was by law the rector of Trinity Church in that city. The masters had to be members, and were usually clergymen, of the Anglican Church. A chief purpose of the grammar schools was to prepare students for one of the two institutions of higher education, both of which were even more distinctly Church of England in character.

An Academy

In spite of the frequent use of the term "academy," there seem to have been no

Dr. Thomas McCulloch

schools that definitely had all the characteristics of such an institution. But the school founded by Dr. Thomas McCulloch of Pictou was probably of this type in most respects. McCulloch referred to his school as a grammar school, probably because of its classical curriculum; others might regard it as a private school because the initiative and energy of one man were responsible for its existence and success; but since it was not regularly supported by the government or operated for private profit, and since its founder had financial assistance from members of his congregation, it is reasonable to regard the school as an academy even in its earlier years.

Soon after his arrival in Pictou county in 1803, McCulloch was deeply concerned that children were growing up in ignorance and illiteracy. He began teaching in his own house, then built a log school at his own expense, paid for stores, fuel, and other necessities, lent his own

books to the scholars, charged low fees, and encouraged attendance even when parents could not pay. The school awakened a desire for education among the people of Pictou and attracted pupils from distant parts of Nova Scotia and from Prince Edward Island. In January, 1815, when the attendance was between thirty and forty, the schoolhouse and most of the books of the master and scholars were destroyed by fire. Then, at least, whether or not they had subscribed for its support before, people in the neighborhood donated money and rebuilt it. An additional sum of £50 was obtained from a government surplus which had been turned over to local authorities for expenditure on public services.

In 1816 the school became Pictou Academy. Its founder and his supporters were anxious to provide Presbyterians with educational advantages equal to those enjoyed by Anglicans through the grammar schools and King's College. To obtain wider support from the public and the assembly they were willing to make the institution wholly undenominational. But the council, though willing to concede a degree of respectability to the Church of Scotland, would go no further in the recognition of dissenting bodies; it granted permission to found an academy but insisted that the trustees be Anglicans or Presbyterians. By this time the institution was certainly an academy in fact — financed by subscriptions and fees, nonprofit yet self-supporting. In subsequent years, although it had no degree-conferring powers, its work extended through the college level, since graduates were able to pass the examinations of the University of Glasgow. Financial difficulties compelled it to seek and accept government aid and to become the frequent subject of contention between the assembly and the council. When grants were withdrawn, it was forced back to the status of a secondary school.

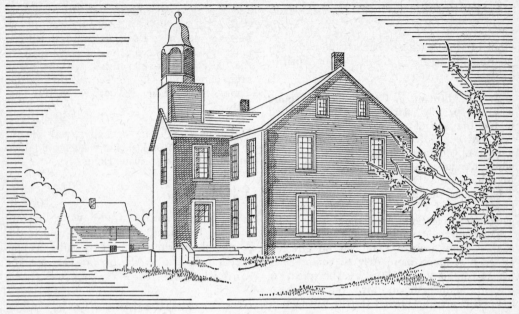

Pictou Academy

Private Schools

These schools appeared in number and variety in more populous centres of the colonies. Since other educational facilities were limited, they could at times appeal successfully, but not as a rule for long, to the restricted clientele of parents able to pay. Sometimes they offered the curriculum of a Latin grammar school, as in the following advertisement in *The Royal Gazette and The New Brunswick Advertiser*:

GRAMMAR SCHOOL

The subscriber hath taken Rooms in a pleasant part of the town of Magerville, where a school is opened for the Education of Boys in the Latin and Greek Languages and will provide them with Board, Lodging, etc., in families near the School.

He also proposes to take a few boys to instruct in English, Writing and Arithmetic. - - - - For terms enquire of Mr. Sower, or

Mr. Ryan, Printers, at St. John, or to the subscriber.

William Jennison
Magerville, 16th April, 1787.[5]

More often they gave equal prominence to elementary skills and to a variety of practical subjects, as did Michael Forrestal, a licensed teacher, who advertised in the *Halifax Gazette* on June 6, 1805:

ENGLISH ACADEMY

By permission of his Excellency, Sir John Wentworth, Baronet, & c. - - - - the subscriber respectfully informs the public, he will open an English Academy, in Halifax, on Monday the 23rd, June next, for the instruction of youth in the following branches of Education viz;

Reading, Writing, English, Grammar, Arithmetic, Book-keeping, Geography, with the use of the Globes; Geometry, Trigonometry, Surveying on a modern and highly improved plan; Navigation, Gnomonics, Natural Philosophy, Astronomy, Elocution, Composition, & c.

Public Examinations will be held half-yearly.[6]

One of the earliest advertisements, appearing in the *Halifax Gazette* for April 6, 1752, offered every type of subject:

At the Academy in Grafton Street. Young men are speedily instructed & well grounded in the true art of spelling by rules short & easy but expressive & comprehensible to almost the youngest capacity. They are likewise taught reading writing arithmetic, French, Latin & Dancing, Algebra, Geometry Trigonometry both plain and spherical the mensuration of Planes and Solids Surveying, gauging Navigation Astronomy taught by Trigonometry or without any at all by a method more concise than can be effected by Trig, & much more easy to comprehend by an ordinary capacity, as the great & learned Mathematician Mr. Whiston hath testified & may be proved for the satisfaction of any who doubt by me Henry Merton.
N.B. Young ladies as well as Gents taught dancing every Wed. & Sat. afternoon.[7]

Probably the versatile Mr. Merton taught all these things himself. His list of offerings is an early example of the variegated curriculum characteristic of American academies and private schools of similar purpose. They appealed less to the established aristocracy than to those who made money in business, as many did in the first boom years at Halifax. Shelburne in 1790, before its collapse, had twelve private schools. The newer clientele was less restricted and exclusive, and private schools often conducted classes in the evening for ambitious young men who had gone to work at an early age. The advertisement below appeared in the *Nova Scotia Chronicle and Weekly Advertiser* for October 10-17, 1769:

At the House of Mr. LEWIS BELOUD
There is to commence immediately

A NIGHT SCHOOL

Where Youth will be carefully taught & instructed in Reading, Writing, Arithmetick,

and the principal Branches of the Mathematics, together with Bookeeping in all its Parts, according to the most approv'd Method now in Use; Any who are inclined to learn the chief or particular Branch of the aforesaid, may expect it on the most reasonable Terms; and their Favours gratefully acknowledged by

L. BELOUD.

N.B. Any Gentleman or Lady, who chooses to learn French or Dancing shall be attended on; in Schooll or private Hours.[8]

Schools for Girls

In larger centres there were private schools for daughters of the well-to-do. A school offering elementary subjects advertised in the *Nova Scotia Gazette* for April 23, 1801:

FEMALE EDUCATION

James Bowen, Schoolmaster, at the next corner house, to the westward of Mr. Noonan's (Sign of the Bunch of Grapes) respectfully acquaints the public that he has commenced the Tuition of Young Ladies in Reading, Writing, Arithmetic and Accompts, from the hours of 12 'till 2 (the useful days of attendance) and having engaged a Person every way qualified to assist him in the duties of the School, flatters himself by their united exertions and assiduity of giving satisfaction to the Parents who are pleased to intrust him with the Education of their Children.[9]

More exclusive and expensive, no doubt, was the boarding school of the Misses Cunningham, who announced in the *Nova Scotia Royal Gazette* for June 5, 1811, their removal to a commodious house in Windsor

where they can accommodate a great number of young Ladies and will continue to pay every possible attention to the health, morals, manners and education of those confided to them: Reading, Writing, English Grammar, Arithmetic, and all kinds of Needle-work, carefully taught. Terms for Board, Lodging, Washing and Tuition: For Children under

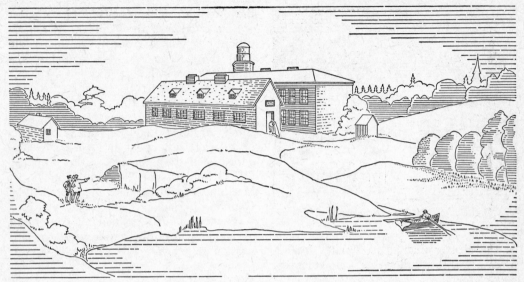

King's College, Nova Scotia

ten years, 35£. per annum, for Ladies above that age, 40£.[10]

The curricula of these two schools were plain and drab in comparison with the instruction in feminine arts offered elsewhere, as will appear in a later chapter. But, as we saw in another advertisement, a young lady in Halifax could find instruction in French or dancing. At the beginning of the nineteenth century there were teachers of music also.

Higher Education

For a very few young men prepared in grammar schools or private schools, two institutions for higher education were established. King's College was founded in 1789 by an act of the Nova Scotia legislature, built at Windsor during the next few years with assistance to the extent of £4500 from the British government, and supported by an annual grant of £400 from the government of Nova Scotia, which had also voted £500 for the purchase of buildings. In 1802 the college secured a royal charter and a further

grant from the British government of £1000 a year. Although these sums are not large by modern standards, they exceeded governmental expenditure on schools for the people as greatly as grants for popular education now exceed subsidies to universities. Most of the financial assistance to education from the public purse went to the grammar school at Halifax and the grammar school and college at Windsor, where in 1795 the students numbered approximately thirty.

There were two chief reasons for making the necessary outlay to establish a college. The first was put forth by a Halifax committee of the S.P.G. in 1787:

to prevent as early as may be, the Youth of this Country (now panting after Knowledge) from rushing into the various Seminaries, already established in the United States of America, by which means their attachment to their native Country may be in Danger of being weakened, and principles imbued unfriendly to the British Constitution.[11]

The second was to strengthen the position of the Church of England: it was required

The College of New Brunswick, 1795

by the charter that all candidates for admission to the college, not to mention faculty members, should subscribe to the thirty-nine articles of the established church.

In New Brunswick an endowment of land for an institution of higher education was set aside in 1785 and trustees were appointed to administer the endowment. About 1793 the trustees purchased an acre lot with a house considered suitable for a college building. In 1800 the College of New Brunswick was established and members of a corporation were appointed. The provincial charter of the college required that the president be a clergyman and the faculty members communicants of the Church of England. Although for this reason it was not in favor with the assembly, and although it was able to do only the work of a superior grammar school, its legislative grant increased from £100 in 1792 to £600 in 1823. Negotiations were then begun for a royal charter and financial aid from the British government. Against the wishes of the Archbishop of Canterbury and the Bishop of Nova Scotia, the royal charter was drawn up without a proviso that candidates for degrees should subscribe to the tenets of the Church of England, but the council, chancellor, president, and faculty had all to profess

the Anglican faith. In 1827 the charter was granted and the name of the institution changed to King's College. From 1829 the college received annual grants of £1100 from the government of Nova Scotia and £1000 from revenues formerly claimed by the British government. But in spite of this substantial support, says Fitch, it failed to attract many students or to exert any great influence over the educational development of the province. Only a minority of the population in the Maritime Provinces were members of the Church of England, and few new converts were gained by making conformity or acquiescence the requirement for admission to educational privilege.

State Assistance

When money was scarce and the ruling classes were cautious about educating the majority, it is not strange that state support of schools for the people should have been chiefly in the form of land, which was plentiful, and that the land should be allotted through the S.P.G. An agreement was made in 1749 between the Lord Commissioners for Trade and Plantations and the S.P.G. that in townships about to be settled 400 acres should be set aside for the support of a clergyman and 200 acres for a schoolmaster. During the period of active settlement between 1759 and 1785, 12,000 acres in 31 townships were set aside for school purposes and further grants of crown lands were made in ensuing years. In accordance with the original agreement it was the practice for all such lands to be used for the furtherance of educational work under the Church of England, since only licensed teachers could benefit from them. The government also voted money grants year by year to teachers in some places — to a total amount as high as £440 in the latter part of the century.

The slow development in Prince Edward Island illustrates the difficulty of getting a government to make any adequate provision for schools. There was an item of £50 for the salary of a schoolmaster in the estimates of 1777, but these estimates were prepared in England by a government that had voted £3000 for the civil establishment of the island. In 1790 the governor and the assembly agreed on "the expediency of entering upon some methods for the erecting and maintenance of schools." But in 1798 legislation passed by the assembly to raise money for this very purpose was rejected by the council. Similar bills in 1801 were defeated in committee, and a bill of 1803 for the encouragement of schoolmasters was left for future consideration. In 1817 a bill for promoting education and encouraging schools throughout the island was passed by the assembly but thrown out by the council. The first successful legislation to provide state assistance of local effort was passed in 1825.

In New Brunswick, as in Nova Scotia and Prince Edward Island, land was set aside for the support of schoolmasters, who, by the Royal Instructions, had to be licensed by the Lord Bishop of London. Earlier than in the other colonies, money was voted to provide for local schools in an organized way. The first attempt of the assembly to secure an appropriation was defeated by the council in 1793. But in 1802 an Act for Aiding and Encouraging Parish Schools set up a grant of £420, the equivalent of £10 for each parish, to be apportioned by the county

justices of the general sessions in such manner as they thought best to maintain existing schools or induce the establishment of others. In 1805 legislation which set up a grammar school in Saint John also provided for superior elementary schools of the movable type throughout the colony. The sum of £375 was voted for distribution by the justices, at the rate of £25 for each schoolmaster, to operate a school for a year in one parish after another in rotation. The schools were to instruct young people of both sexes in the English language, writing, and arithmetic — a modest program, but suggestive nevertheless of more than a pupil might have obtained from attendance for two or three sessions at a humbler school, since writing and arithmetic were introduced at a later stage than reading and spelling. The act continued in force until 1816.

It might appear from the New Brunswick legislation of 1805 that there was no real distinction between the grammar schools and the higher elementary schools, since the latter could not be set up in Saint John or Fredericton, the two centres where grammar schools were established. But this limitation was probably included in the act as a concession to local jealousy of the two large towns, which would otherwise have secured a double portion of government funds. There would have been no real duplication of educational services if a superior elementary school for ordinary people had been provided in addition to a classical school for the few.

Summary

In the Maritime Provinces in the early period of British rule the Church of England made efforts to provide education — efforts that were inadequate and not always welcome. The government did a little to help the church and a little to hinder the non conformists. The schools of the S.P.G. and a very few Latin grammar schools were the major contributions of church and state. There were, however, enough people who attached a value to schooling and who were capable of acting on their own initiative to encourage the establishment of other institutions — private schools and academies. Early in the nineteenth century the government began to offer some assistance to local communities. Further developments in this early period will be covered in Chapters 8 and 9.

CHAPTER 6

Lower Canada

The Quebec colony and territory to the west, which came under British rule in 1763, were divided in 1791 into two political units — Lower Canada and Upper Canada, corresponding respectively to the present provinces of Quebec and Ontario. They were, and are, quite different in language, religion, and other social institutions. This chapter covers the early educational history of Lower Canada under the English regime from 1763 to 1829. It was a period of difficult readjustment for French-speaking Canadians and a formative period for English-speaking Canadians. The year 1829 is a useful point of reference because in that year the first legislative provision was made for elected local boards.

Politics and Education

FRENCH AND ENGLISH

Political, social, and educational history in Lower Canada during this period all centre in one issue. What adjustment was to be made between a small minority claiming rights by conquest and a large majority asserting their right to the continuance of established ways of living wholly at variance with those of the minority? Although the question was not answered to the satisfaction of either side, justice rather than might prevailed, at

75

least to the extent that the question remained open. In contrast with what a ruthless victor might have tried, British rule from the first, both in legislation and in practice, showed remarkable consideration for French-Canadian institutions. In 1774 the Quebec Act guaranteed the free exercise of the Roman Catholic religion, retained French law in civil cases, and left the seigniorial system in places where it was already established. In return the French-Canadian clergy, the seigneurs, and the populace under their influence showed equally remarkable loyalty to the new regime against attack from without by propaganda and by military operations in 1774-78 and in 1812-15. Internal dissension continued, but so did the new colony.

The French-Canadians of Lower Canada increased in number from about 60,000 in 1763 to about 434,000 in 1837. In their attitudes and manner of life they remained as they were. They clung tenaciously to their religion, their language, and their agricultural economy. The constitutional act of 1791 helped them to maintain their identity by giving Lower Canada a government of its own. At the same time the introduction of an assembly gave them an opportunity to express their views and later to acquire the abilities for democratic government. They would have preferred to be left to themselves, but adapted themselves reluctantly with as little change as possible to the strange ways of foreigners in power.

The native French nobility and clergy — as distinguished from their French-Canadian counterparts — had, of course, departed for France.

The French-speaking Canadians, except for their numerical superiority, were at a severe disadvantage. They had been defeated in war, with the concomitant dislocation of their economic and social life. Having never been distinguished for exuberant commercial and intellectual activity, they had now sunk to a state of lethargy. Although noteworthy above people of other countries for religious and moral observance, they were now left with an inadequate number of clergy; even in the first decade of the nineteenth century there were only eighty priests for a Roman Catholic population of two hundred thousand. The English-speaking invaders considered the French-speaking Canadians shrewd, hardy, active, graceful in manners, temperate in conduct and happy in domestic relations; but they also thought them backward, lacking in enterprise, excitable, and credulous to the point of accepting as implicit truth "the many arrant falsehoods and atrocious lies" circulating among them.

Yet some British statesmen had a sympathetic admiration for the tenacity with which the French-speaking Canadians adhered to their institutions: Lord Grenville, for example, in the debate on the act of 1791 said that such loyal attachment to customs and law deserved a better word than prejudice. But others were not as generous and understanding. Although they comprised three-quarters of the population, the French-speaking majority held only one-quarter of the public positions and sometimes only one-third of the twenty-seven seats in the legislative council. The first truly French-Canadian newspaper, *Le Canadien,* was suppressed early in the nineteenth century by the high-handed and reactionary governor, Sir James Craig, who is credited by Lower with being "one of the founders of French-Canadian nationalism".[1]

The English-speaking people increased from the time of the conquest to about 10,000 by 1791 and about 166,000 by 1837. Since most of them lived in Montreal and Quebec and in a limited number of counties, throughout most of the province they were an exceedingly small minority. The first English-speaking arrivals in the cities were mostly enterprising traders and occupants of posts in the administration — in the eyes of the French-Canadians just avaricious exploiters, and described even by the English governor as ignorant and rapacious bullies, trying to trample on a brave people. From about 1793 for some twenty-five years, numerous settlers came northward across the border from Vermont and New Hampshire into what are called the Eastern Townships. These New Englanders were not as a rule Loyalists, but farmers seeking better land and merchants who followed them. They were of Puritan background, accustomed to regard a local school as a first necessity. Loyalists went as pioneer settlers to counties west of the Richelieu River and north of the border of New York State. They were joined before 1824 by numerous immigrants from the British Isles, many of them Scots and Irish.

GROUNDS FOR CONTENTION

The grounds for contention among the people of Lower Canada were numerous. As in the Maritimes and in Upper Canada, an assembly, representative of the people, battled towards responsible government against the oligarchy in the council. But representatives of the English-speaking minority in the assembly could and did defeat the purposes of the French-speaking majority by their greater influence with the council and the lieutenant-governor. Thus differences of national origin, language, and religion complicated and overshadowed the contest for democracy.

The division between the two peoples was intensified by diverse economic interests: most of the French-speaking people were farmers and preferred that expenses of government be defrayed by taxes on imports; whereas English-speaking people, concerned directly or indirectly with trade, had less objection to taxation on land.

Although the French-Canadians learned to engage effectively in political activities, many did not welcome or trust the institution of an assembly, which they regarded as a form of governmental machinery invented by commercial interests to further their own designs, as do some advocates of authoritarian government today. Many influential French-Canadians believed they would have had more hope of securing what they wanted for their people from aristocratic English governors if the raucous voice of business had had no parliamentary trumpet.

Some English-speaking people, of course, were confident at first that the others would adopt their language and possibly, with a little assistance, a Protestant faith. The French-Canadians disappointed them by obstinately clinging to the belief that their own institutions were superior, their language preferable, and their church the one repository of religious truth. The first governor, Murray, ordered the *Te Deum* sung in all churches in praise to God for the victory accorded to British arms, but its educative effect on the French-speaking congregations left much to be achieved by more reasonable measures.

OPPOSING VIEWS

French-Canadian accounts of education in this period seem to other readers more like polemics against the English than a record of events. They tell how Quebec was deprived of educational advantages by the departure of educators, including all professors of the Jesuit college, to France, and by the indifference or worse of the new government towards their intellectual welfare. The Jesuit college was occupied by troops and the students were turned away. The government confiscated the Jesuit estates and turned a deaf ear to petitions that they be used

The Ursuline monastery at Quebec

for the support of Roman Catholic education. It took away the property of the Recollets and so compelled them to abandon their educational institutions in Montreal and Three Rivers. Until 1786 it forbade religious societies, including the teaching orders, to recruit new members, and even after that date would not allow the bishops to import priests from France as professors. The royal instructions to the first governor in 1763, repeated verbatim in 1768, made the intention of these acts clear:

And to the end that the Church of England may be established in Principle and Practice, and that the said Inhabitants may by Degrees be induced to embrace the Protestant Religion, and their children be brought up in the Principles of it . . . all possible Encouragement shall be given to the erecting of Protestant Schools . . .[2]

For the same purpose, goes the argument, nothing was done until the end of this period to encourage the establishment of the only schools acceptable to the majority — Roman Catholic schools.

From the point of view of English-speaking Canadians, however, the government had been tolerant and conciliatory in granting religious freedom and in permitting most French-Catholic schools to operate without interference. The Recollets continued or resumed their teaching in villages of rural parishes, as did the Ursulines in Quebec and Three Rivers and the Sisters of the Congregation in Montreal and in rural parishes. There was nothing to hinder the establishment of schools by the Roman Catholic clergy or laity, or the use of French as the language of instruction. True, there had been the usual stipulation that schoolmasters be licensed by the Anglican bishop, but this had been modified in 1787 by an instruction to Lord Dorchester that a certificate from the Bishop of Nova Scotia was to be required only in the case of masters of schools intended for members of the Church of England.

As for failure to take more positive action, it was not the conviction of ruling classes at the time that all the people should be educated, and not the practice of governments to finance schools for all; and the policy of the British government in Lower Canada was neither discriminatory nor different from the policy of the British government elsewhere. Moreover, when proposals were made to establish schools and educational institutions for all without religious bias, leaders of the French-Catholic majority refused to co-operate and insisted on exclusive control. Principal Dawson of McGill University and the Protestant Normal School made the following statement in 1864 regarding recommendations of a committee of the council in 1789:

. . . it shows that from the very first the English colonists desired to erect a public school and university system, as distinguished from the purely sectarian and ecclesiastical methods advocated by the religious leaders of the French inhabitants . . . They also show a strong desire to meet the views of the Roman Catholic clergy, by avoiding all interference with their seminaries or schools, or the religious education of their people, and by permitting them to educate their own people in separate schools.

Had this wise scheme been carried into effect immediately and with vigor, the whole future history of Lower Canada might have been different, not only educationally but politically; and a great impulse would have been given to the industrial progress of the people.[3]

The truth of the last sentence would hardly be disputed by the French-Canadians, who nevertheless would deny that the difference would have been for the good or that industrial progress was for them a primary consideration.

Legislative Efforts toward Harmony

In 1789 the aforementioned committee of the council appointed by the governor-general recommended the immediate erection, in every district, of free parish or village schools to give instruction in the 3 R's, and in the central or county town of each district a superior school to teach grammar, languages, advanced arithmetic, book-keeping, and applied mathematics, including navigation, surveying, and gauging. The committee was so far in advance of the times in its thinking that it advocated a legislative enactment to require that each parish be assessed to support the schools of a district. For the teaching of the liberal arts and sciences it recommended the establishment of a "collegiate institute." This college was to be non-denominational in that no Christian theology was to be taught and in that sectarian characteristics were to be guarded against in its charter. Its board of directors was to consist of the judges, the bishops of the Churches of England and Rome, and twenty other persons — ten Roman Catholics and ten Protestants — appointed by the government.

From the French-Canadian point of view, expressed by a Chief Superintendent of Education in Quebec at the end of the nineteenth century, these recommendations were obviously the attempt of an unsympathetic government to get complete control over education. The "highly enlightened and unbelievably foolish report," as a Protestant historian, Woodley,[4] describes it, was resolutely opposed by the Roman Catholic Bishop of Quebec, who counterattacked by demanding that the Jesuit estates be restored to the support of Catholic education. Nothing at all was done. In subsequent years, laws proposed by English-speaking members of the assembly to establish schools in all parishes were defeated for similar reasons when the full text was read in French.

ACT OF 1801

An act "to establish free schools and to promote the cause of education" was passed in 1801. Curiously enough, there was very little opposition except the distraction of an alternative proposal from a lawyer keenly interested in education, J. F. Perrault; the Roman Catholic bishop and his coadjutor had nothing to say at the time. In accordance with the recommendations made twelve years before, this legislation provided for the establishment of a non-sectarian elementary school in each parish and a model, or superior, school in the chief town of each county.

The plan was reasonable in that the language of instruction was to be the mother tongue and was not unreasonable in leaving religious instruction to priests or ministers. It was advanced in providing for free schools and local support by taxation, although the arrangements for the latter were complicated. But it was made unacceptable to the Roman Catholic Church and to many Protestants by the stipulation that the schools were to be owned and operated by a central authority which was to appoint teachers and control the course of study and the choice of textbooks.

Probably there was no direct threat to the Roman Catholic church in the law itself, since there was an escape in the clause which made it necessary for a locality to ask for a school. But there was great fear of the purpose to which the law might be put. Grounds for such fear had been provided by zealous individuals. A young Loyalist lawyer from New England named Ogden had talked about Anglicizing the French-Canadians by establishing free schools to teach English and enlighten their ignorance. Much more disturbing was the Anglican Bishop Mountain, who had arrived in Quebec to take office in 1793 and who was largely responsible for the legislation passed eight years later. Bishop Mountain had written with approval of "the inducing of the Inhabitants to embrace by degrees the Protestant Religion and to bring up their Children in it, and the establishing of the Church of England in the Province both in principle and practice."[5] He had spoken of the need to "dispel the fixed cloud of bigotry and prejudice" and to "break down the partition wall." He wanted to have elementary schools in each parish — but schools under Protestant teachers offering free instruction.

The Royal Institution

The Act of 1801 was inoperative until 1818, when the central authority was set up under an overpowering title, the Royal Institution for the Advancement of Learning. It consisted of a committee, preponderantly Protestant and under the presidency of the bishop of the Church of England to exercise the functions stipulated in the Act of 1801. From the French-Canadian point of view, the institution was "conceived in an intolerant and proselytizing spirit" and "its real purport, hidden under a pretence of goodwill, was to take away the right of teaching from the Canadians and to establish an educational monopoly . . . for the upkeep of Protestant or neutral schools." Even the chief official of the Protestant educational system early in the present century wondered "how intelligent, educated men could be so unreasonable as to expect success under such management,"[6] although he believed that the charge of proselytizing could not be proved. Mgr. Plessis, the Roman Catholic Bishop of Quebec, ordered his clergy to stand out against the establishment of schools of the Royal Institution in their parishes.

But the Royal Institution hardly deserves such strong condemnation. English-speaking writers have defended it, at least in part. Buller, who prepared a report on education for Lord Durham, pointed out certain liberal provisions in its constitution: schools were to be under the supervision of the clergy of the religion professed by the inhabitants in the locality,

The Royal Institution school at St. Roch des Aulnaies, about 1830

and school visitors named by the corporation were to include one or more of such clergy. Woodley defended the institution as "an honest attempt to solve the educational problems of the province."[7] Finally, in 1953, a French-Canadian historian, Audet, in a doctoral dissertation, proved quite conclusively that in its actual operation the Royal Institution showed itself willing to defer to the interests of the French-speaking and Roman Catholic population.*

It is clear from the records of the Royal Institution that the greatest care was taken to see that French-speaking Roman Catholic teachers of good character and the best available competence were appointed in French-Canadian communities. Not only was the Institution willing to accept the nominations of the parish curé or of the people locally when a teacher was to be appointed, but in one instance

went as far as to remove a teacher that the people had requested, in favor of a Roman Catholic teacher who had been found later. On another occasion, in 1822, the secretary informed an applicant for a position, who had been previously advised to study French, that he would be appointed only if the local school visitors approved of his competence in that language.[8]

In spite of the opposition of the church, about a score of Roman Catholic parishes founded schools under the Act of 1801 either before or after the setting up of the Royal Institution in 1818, and there were eight Institution schools actually being conducted by French-Canadian teachers in 1820. There were always at least a few French names in the list of those appointed as commissioners or visitors, and there would undoubtedly have been many more if the church had not been hostile. The charge made by Desrosiers that the Royal Institution "drew up programmes

* See bibliography no. 6

of study" and "dictated the methods and books to be used"[9] might be difficult to prove. In practice, apparently, the Royal Institution was not concerned about the details of such *interna* of the schools, but only about getting good schools into operation.

Between 1826 and 1829 the Royal Institution showed its willingness to make concessions to the Roman Catholic position by a proposal to set up two committees within the Institution — one Roman Catholic and one Protestant. In a letter of May 2, 1826, the secretary of the Institution explained to the Roman Catholic Bishop of Quebec that "each Committee will have exclusively the internal regulations of the School of its own persuasion, with which the Board will not interfere without the consent of such committees." The Bishop gave his approval to this arrangement, but his coadjutor in Montreal was uncompromisingly opposed — a position which Audet describes as *"assez inexplicable."* On June 11, 1829, the secretary wrote another letter saying that the Board of the Royal Institution had "long been anxious to divest themselves of the charge of Roman Catholic schools."[10] There is little doubt that he was sincere and truthful in this statement. A number of Protestant members of the Institution resigned to make room for Roman Catholic members, but it was necessary to revise the Act of 1801 to make the appointment of the two committees legal.

The legislative council passed a bill for the formation of two committees; but in 1829 the assembly was too much occupied with an educational plan of its own to give the Royal Institution more than routine attention and it did not pass the bill. It is clear that if this reorganization had been successful, it would have created, more than thirty years earlier, the type of divided central authority which has proved workable and satisfactory to the people of Quebec.

But there were grounds for the unpopularity of the Institution. In the early years, when it was able to offer high salaries, the Board imported most of its teachers from England — a policy that has always been irritating to Canadians, although there was some justification at a time when there were few well-educated people in Canada. These teachers did not adapt themselves readily to Canadian ways and acted, no doubt, on the assumption that the inhabitants here should be pleased to have things Canadian compared disparagingly with superior counterparts back home.

The regulation regarding ownership of school property was also a cause of friction. On September 28th, 1820, the Institution found it necessary to publish a notice to school commissioners and others interested "to take the necessary steps for conveying all lots of grounds and buildings" to the Royal Institution. Most of the localities eventually agreed to the transfer but with some reluctance. For reasons like this the Royal Institution was in disfavor even among Protestants, other than Anglicans whose Mecca was across the Atlantic. Few of the Institution's establishments were located in the eastern townships among English-speaking people born on this continent, who preferred to run and manage their own local schools.

Although the Royal Institution has usually been represented as an almost complete failure, the number of its schools increased rapidly in the 1820's to a maximum of 84, with 3140 pupils at the end of the decade. During the following years the number declined — to 63 by 1834, to 37 by 1838, and virtually to the vanishing point by 1841. The Institution had therefore some good work to its credit, although its later decline was more spectacular. Its apparent failure has generally been attributed — and with considerable reason — to the stubborn refusal of the Roman Catholic Church to co-operate. But since the increasing number of schools before 1830 had been established almost wholly for English-speaking people, the subsequent turn in the fortunes of the Institution might, with even more reason, be attributed to a lack of financial resources. For a few years after 1829, the assembly voted the Royal Institution about £2100, a substantial amount, but not enough to permit the same generous allowances to teachers that had prevailed in the earlier years. Then, after 1832, schools of the Royal Institution were simply made eligible to share in grants distributed to schools by the assembly, and the authority of the Institution was undermined. All school grants stopped in 1836 and the Institution found itself in 1838 in possession of the property of 82 schoolhouses in different parishes and townships but with no money to keep them in operation.

If the proposed reorganization had been put into effect in 1829, the star of the Institution would have been in the ascendant. Failure must therefore be attributed primarily to the decision of the assembly in the same year to sponsor schools of its own. The hostility of the people's representatives was not new. As early as 1822 the Institution had experienced difficulty in securing money and had been forced to discharge some teachers and cut the salaries of others. In a letter of June 11, 1829, the secretary stated that the Royal Institution was withdrawing from the Roman Catholic districts and was telling the people there to avail themselves of the grants under the new act passed by the assembly. He was convinced that the latter body would never ratify the legislation for the reorganization of the Institution. The passing of the Act of 1829, therefore, spelled *finis* to the prospects of the Institution among French-speaking people. It also marked the beginning of the end of the Institution's work among English-speaking people — not only because the Institution was un-popular with the assembly but also because that body had rightly interpreted a growing demand for schools under local democratic control.

Local Church Schools

Between 1818 and 1823 a number of bills to establish schools were presented to the assembly, but none of them became law. Buller mentions one which was passed by the assembly, amended and passed by the council, reserved for Royal Assent, and never heard of again. This bill would have provided funds for the establishment of schools under trustees consisting of the clergymen and church wardens of either Roman Catholic or Anglican churches. Two other bills met the same fate and two were rejected by the council.

Then in 1824 the assembly was successful in securing ratification of a bill for the establishment of schools under church control. This legislation had been suggested by the seminary at Quebec. It required no expenditure by government but set up an administrative organization through which financial help from well-to-do citizens could be utilized. The legislation permitted the *fabrique,* or vestry, of a parish church to use one-quarter of its revenue for the operation of a school in a parish of two hundred families, or of two schools in a parish of three hundred families. The fabriques were to have control over the building of a school, the choice of a teacher, the amount of the salary, and the course of study. This was a plan acceptable to the Roman Catholic people and clergy. Its success was limited, however, by the slender resources of the parish, and sometimes by the opposition of prominent parishioners who did not favor expenditures for the purpose and who could argue with some reason that the fabriques had enough to do already. But some fifty to sixty fabrique schools were in operation between 1824 and 1829.

The next year, when grants from the government were available, the number in operation was 68. Later reports of school visitors illustrate the characteristics and varied fortunes of these schools. In the county of Chambly, parish of Longueuil, a stone school building was erected by the fabrique unaided; it had separate accommodation for boys and girls and a residence for a man and his wife to serve as teachers; and the whole property was deeded to the churchwardens. Another fabrique school was built in the parish, but this was united later with the first school to reduce expenses. In one district of the parish of Boucherville a school building was erected but subsequently rented as a family residence to reimburse the owner of the lot and the fabrique which had paid for the building. In another district of the same parish the fabrique built first one school and then a larger school with a separate residence to accommodate girls as boarders. This fabrique received government aid in the 1830's for a while, forfeited this assistance through refusal to submit to all conditions, but continued to operate the school at its own expense.

Act of 1829: Local Authorities

An act of 1829 introduced for the first time schools controlled by representatives of the voting public. In effect a new central authority resulted from the act, since a Committee of the Assembly on Education directed subsequent educational policy of the assembly and suggested amendments to the act which were passed during the next six years. The legislation itself set up as local authorities trustees elected by the people locally. It provided grants to pay half the cost of erecting schoolhouses up to £50 per schoolhouse in Halifax currency. It also provided grants to schoolmasters of £20, plus 10s for each indigent scholar taught gratis.

Religious communities and fabriques were entitled to a share of the benefits under the act, as were subsequently schools set up under the Royal Institution. Owing to the increasingly generous grants offered by the assembly during the next few years, schools grew like mushrooms to the amazing total of something like 1500, although the quality of the teachers and the efficiency of administration left much to be desired. A final amendment to this act in 1835-36 was rejected by the council, which had good reason for its contention that the proposed expenditure was excessive. As a result of this action and the disturbed conditions before and during the Rebellion of 1837, the government grants to schools were cut off entirely.

Roman Catholic Education

SET-BACKS FROM WAR

The educational attainments of the French-Canadian people after the conquest appear to have been very low. In correspondence between the Chief Justice and Bishop Hubert in 1789, estimates of the number of people in each parish who could read or write ranged from half a dozen to from twenty-four to thirty. Even the highest estimate would indicate that less than one in twenty of the rural population of all ages could be described as literate in any degree. This condition may be attributed partly but by no means wholly to the effect of war. Undoubtedly education had received an appalling setback, as Groulx maintains, by the depletion of the resources of teaching communities and in other ways.[11] He points out, for example, that in 1760, at the end of the previous period, there had been 44 *petites écoles* in 112 parishes; and if corroboration of the existence of such facilities is needed we have the remark of an English officer who travelled the road on the north shore of the St. Lawrence between Quebec and Montreal in 1776 and remarked that "every three leagues may be found a kind of small village, consisting of a presbytery, an inn, a school for little children, and some houses."[12]

But one cannot help wondering how regularly the schools had been open, and how well had they been attended, to have left so little result a generation later. After the conquest the Recollets were still teaching in several large villages, sixty Ursuline Sisters were at work in Quebec and Three Rivers, and the Sisters of the Congregation had a dozen rural parish schools for girls in operation in the 1780's. But there was hardly an elementary school worthy of the name for educating boys.[13] The total number engaged in the instruction of the young, including the native clergy who could find the time, was altogether inadequate for the growing population.

EFFORTS FOR IMPROVEMENT

The obvious deficiency of educational resources and the consequent ignorance, to which the English were not slow in calling attention, spurred the French-Canadians to demand assistance from the new authorities. They asked for the maintenance of the teaching orders, for boys' schools in rural areas, for a school at Three Rivers similar to those at Quebec and Montreal, and for other assistance to Roman Catholic education. In particular, they asked in numerous petitions that the revenue from the Jesuit estates be applied to the maintenance of Roman Catholic schools. These revenues were used instead for the support of grammar schools under Church of England auspices, and it was not surprising, as Buller said later, "that the Catholics of Canada should have felt discontented when they saw the great Catholic legacy of their fore-fathers thus converted into a fund for the establish-

ment of a rival church."[14] In 1801 the governor announced that land grants would be made available for education, but the promise was never fulfilled. Only a few parishes were willing to seek and accept money on the terms of the Act of that year.

When there was no help forthcoming for schools under purely Roman Catholic auspices, some laymen and clergy attempted to do what they could by independent action. Zealous laymen who had the resources set up schools and procured teachers or gave instruction themselves. Schools were opened beside churches or even in homes. The most distinguished of these laymen, J. F. Perrault, who was clerk of the courts and sometimes a member of the legislature, gave most of his spare time to educational work. After failing in his efforts to block the establishment of the Royal Institution and to secure school legislation acceptable to the Roman Catholic Church, he used his own money to set up two elementary schools at Quebec. One, which he built at his own expense in the suburb of St. Louis, was large enough to accommodate three hundred scholars. Perrault also organized a Society of Education to enlist voluntary assistance for such work and wrote a *"Manuel pratique,"* or Book of Practical Exercises, for the guidance of teachers.

Another member of the legislature founded two schools — one for boys and one for girls — at St. Eustache, and also published two school manuals. In an early issue of the *Quebec Gazette* — for April 26, 1792 — three teachers named Brunet, Noel, and Paquet announced that they gave free instruction in reading, writing, and arithmetic. As for the clergy and the religious, parish curés, the Sulpicians, the Ursulines, and the Sisters of Charity all founded several schools. As an example, Magnan mentions a classical school at Longue-Pointe established by a Sulpician curé and destined to become the Collège de Montréal. The return of French priests from France to Canada strengthened the inadequate personnel for educational work.

ILLITERACY

In spite of these efforts the educational level of French-speaking Canadians remained appallingly low. Desrosiers states that a rapid recovery was made in the 1820's and that there were nearly 15,000 children in small free schools by 1824. The fabrique school act of 1824 helped only a little by authorizing a plan without providing funds, and the assembly grants from 1829 helped considerably by dispensing money for a period of six years. But there was no solid, steady, cumulative growth in educational resources and attainments over the province as a whole. Most of the schools taught exceedingly little, and many of the teachers were said to be unable to write. Textbooks were poor in quality and few in number. The Abbé Groulx etches in words a sharp and revealing picture of the utter ignorance that prevailed, at least in the earlier decades. In some parishes, according to Daniel Wilkie, a teacher of the time, there were not half a dozen people who could read; many important landlords were unable to sign their names, and men with substantial holdings had to walk four or five miles to get a letter read. Lawyers said they hardly ever encountered a witness, a prisoner, or a petty juryman who knew how to write. Buller found that the great majority of country children could not write at all and that some of the others could do no more than sign their names. Wrote Durham: "It is impossible to exaggerate the want of education among the *habitants;* no means of instruction have been provided for them, and they are almost universally destitute of the qualifications of even reading and writing."[15] Conditions prompted a visitor to the country to say that ". . . there are two ladies in the province, I am told, who read, but both of them are above fifty and they are regarded as prodigies of erudition."[16]

The prevailing ignorance was often a subject for jest. In a petition of 1827 to which 87,000 names were attached, the signatures of 78,000 were made by a mark, and the document provoked witticisms about the "Knights of the Cross." A head of the militia department remarked that the officers under him were "generally very experienced *marksmen.*"

GROWTH OF SECONDARY EDUCATION

Secondary education was also at a low ebb at the beginning of this period. Enrolment at the Jesuit college had begun to fall off many decades before the closing of the institution at the time of the conquest. After 1763 the Petit Seminaire was forced to rely on its own staff for instruction but succeeded immediately in organizing a five-year classical course, with classes in French, English, Latin, Literature, Rhetoric, and some Physics and Chemistry. The complete secondary program in French-speaking Canada, as we shall see later, is an eight-year course beginning with an emphasis on languages and ending with an emphasis on philosophy based on the teachings of St. Thomas Aquinas. This program, which is now preparatory to further study at university, is offered in classical colleges.

In a relatively short time facilities for secondary education were expanded until they were recognized as superior to those of the English-speaking population. In 1774 the Protestants of the district of Quebec were disturbed because the Roman Catholic clergy had re-opened the seminaries in Quebec and Montreal. By 1840 Durham was moved to write: "I know of no people among whom a larger provision exists for the higher kinds of elementary education."[17]

The building erected for the classical college at Nicolet, 1829-1832

A return of colleges and endowed schools in Lower Canada dated 1837 mentions three classical colleges established by 1829 and offering at least part of the secondary program. The College of Nicolet was opened in 1806 and given a Royal Charter in 1821; it was endowed and supported by requests from clergy and successive bishops and had accommodation for 70 boarders. The Seminary or College of St. Hyacinthe, which developed from a Latin school, opened as a college in 1818 and had 66 boarders and 30 day pupils by 1824; it also was supported by an endowment and subsequent contributions from clergy and began to receive state support in 1829. Similarly endowed were the College of Chambly, which opened in 1826, and the College of Ste Anne de la Pocatière, which opened in 1829. Other colleges of the type were operated at least for a time. The salaries in these institutions were very moderate — usually in the neighborhood of £20 a year — and the fees were correspondingly low. The curriculum followed the pattern set by the Petit Seminaire at Quebec, but was not always exclusively classical, for the College of St. Hyacinthe received a grant in the 1830's for a chemical laboratory.

At Montreal in 1773 the Sulpicians founded St. Raphael's College in a building purchased for the purpose by the fabrique of Notre Dame in that city. The staff of this institution was reinforced in the 1790's by eleven Sulpicians who left France after the revolution. Because of their superior resources the colleges at Montreal and Quebec alone were able to offer more advanced work at the beginning of the nineteenth century. They, and later the other colleges, gave the education basic to training for the priesthood, which was also the type of education a French-Canadian of position or substance would desire for his son.

Protestant Education

PETITIONS FOR SCHOOLS

The history of Protestant education also began with petitions. The first of these was signed by 61 residents of Quebec in 1768. It appears that before then a school for English-speaking children had been taught by a master who gave notice of his intention to resign in June and set up a public house. The petitioners asked that he be replaced by a former army sergeant named Fraser, who had been wounded and had forfeited his pension by failure to return home. The government refused to give approval and assistance, but in August of the same year this announcement appeared in the *Quebec Gazette*:

The Government of this Province having considered how necessary, useful, and ornamental the proper Education of Youth is; and being well informed of the Prudence and Capacity of Mr. James Jackson, have properly authorized him publickly to teach Reading and Writing, the English and Latin Languages, Arithmetic vulgar and decimal, Book-keeping according to the true Italian Method of double Entry, Navigation, and other Branches of the Mathematics, in this City: By Virtue of which Authority Mr. Jackson has opened a School in the Jesuits College, on the 22nd Instant.
N.B. He teaches Reading, not by using the common Names of the Alphabet, but by the Sounds which originally they were, at present are, and for the future will be, intended to signify. He also purposes to teach Writing before and after common School Hours.

In Montreal English-speaking residents raised £100 by subscription for a school, procured a master from New York, and engaged an assistant. But since the fees had been set low for the benefit of the poor, they found their funds running out and wrote in 1774 to the government for financial assistance — not as a grant to the teacher, but "for the benefit of the undertaking in general."

A memorial of a more general nature was addressed to Lord Dartmouth, secretary of state for the colonies, on December 31, 1773, by a committee of English citizens in Quebec:

They beg leave to lay before Your Lordship the deplorable State it [the colony] is in for want of Protestant Seminarys and Protestant Schools for the Education and Instruction of Youth. . . . The Children of British Parents must therefore go without or attend these [Roman Catholic Seminaries], For though his Majesty's antient Subjects are willing to contribute to the utmost of their Power to encourage Men of Learning and Ability to come to reside among them, Yet that is insufficient without the aid and assistance of the Government.[18]

It is evident that nothing adequate was being done by the government; in 1789 only four teachers were receiving assistance at a total cost of £200. It is also evident from the various petitions that the people were not asking the government or any other agency to provide schools as a charity but were trying to secure government money to assist their efforts. A typical appeal of 1809 from the inhabitants of the township of Sutton, on the border of Vermont, pointed out the "remoteness of their situation and smallness of their means," urged the governor to extend to them the benefits of the Act of 1801, and gave assurance that they themselves would build a schoolhouse with "convenient apartments" for a schoolmaster. Up to the time of the Royal Institution an increasing number of such appeals poured into the government offices from local communities.

SPORADIC SCHOOLING

Clearly a transition was under way from schools for the people provided from above to schools of the people set up by the people themselves. Schools for English-speaking Protestants were therefore established in considerable number and

The petition of 1768 (Public Archives of Canada)

variety. They are difficult to classify, because parents and teachers might be willing to try various expedients to get a school into operation or to secure some education for their children. Associated with the transition mentioned was the frequent appearance in towns of schools which departed from tradition to offer what the growing middle class were able and ready to pay for — private schools and academies teaching a number of subjects and practical skills, sometimes operating as early morning schools or evening schools, and providing for the instruction of young people of both sexes in useful and recreational accomplishments.

Some early schoolmasters offered free instruction to the poor. The following appeared in an advertisement in the *Quebec Gazette* for March, 1789:

Whereas, from the Hardness of the Times at present in this Country, many young people are deprived of the inestimable blessing of Education, the Subscriber proposes receiving into his School Six Young Lads, viz., three English and three Canadians, and giving them a Genteel Education Gratis.

Obviously there was an attempt here to attract French-Canadians, no doubt for reasons acceptable to the government, since four additional free places were advertised in June, with a rider to the effect that candidates were now to be recommended by justices of the peace and that stress would be placed on the candidates' patriotism.

There is other evidence that the educational efforts of Roman Catholics and Protestants were not wholly separated in the early decades of the English regime. The reader may apply his skill as a detective to the hints and uncertainties in the following record. A notice similar to that just quoted appeared in the *Quebec Gazette* for January, 1792, over the name of Louis Labadie, who, "seeing with pain the profound ignorance that reigns in the country parts," offered to educate gratis a certain number in his school in the parish of Berthier, and asked aid for books and other necessities. The advertiser was a French-Canadian and a Roman Catholic from a district north of the St. Lawrence up the river from Quebec. In March of the same year at a meeting of the Constitutional Club in Quebec the 104 members in attendance decided to help a Mr. Labady by raising a voluntary subscription.

They advised the teacher that while he was occupying the schoolhouse belonging to the parish he should receive only children recommended by the curate and churchwardens into whose hands they were going to put the money. They called attention to the good work being done in a charity school founded by the bishop; and this was two years before Quebec had a bishop of the Church of England. If Labadie and Labady were one and the same person, is it not reasonable to conclude that some English Protestants were willing to contribute to Roman Catholic education under the supervision of a parish curé?

PROGRESS IN SOME LOCALITIES

By 1790, cities and towns were relatively well supplied with schools. The minutes of the Council for 1790 showed twelve Protestant teachers — 6 in Quebec, 4 in Montreal, and 1 each in the intervening towns, Three Rivers and William Henry, now Sorel. These were teachers likely to share in government money for education, which increased from £150 in 1793 to £1856 in 1817, when the Royal Institution took over. There were other city schools which offered elementary education.

In addition to Sunday schools for children there was a rather novel Sunday school for adults advertised in the *Quebec Gazette* for November 7, 1816. By learning to read your Bible, said the sponsors, "you gratify the wishes of your beloved sovereign and render obedience to the command of the Almighty"; the school invited those who had had no opportunity for schooling in their childhood to come every Sunday to a good room supplied with books and there receive free instruction in reading every Sunday. In the nineteenth century there were also large monitorial schools, about which more will be said later. In addition there were private schools which took some poorer children as well as the better-to-do.

In the Eastern Townships elementary schools were provided by the joint initiative of parents. Any building might be used at first, but soon the fathers of families contributed labor, materials, or money to construct a log schoolhouse. They then engaged a teacher who received fees for the children's instruction and his board from one family after another. Naturally the parents and the teacher were anxious to get assistance from the government also, since a grant to the teacher would enable them to educate some children gratis and reduce fees for the others; but the schools were essentially local ventures. By 1800 Stanstead and

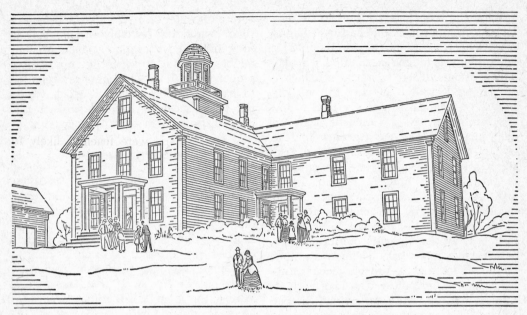

Coaticook Academy, Lower Canada

Hatley counties had each three or four schools, and Barnston one or two. Less populous districts had to resort to itinerant teachers at first but set up schools when fifteen or twenty children could be brought together. By 1821 in two counties, Stanstead and Sheffield, there was a school for every fifty pupils. The conclusion to be reached is that the development in the Eastern Townships was exceptionally good for the time, but it would be a mistake to think that good instruction was regularly available to all children. In the districts of the province further west and north where English-speaking settlers were numerous, progress was similar but somewhat retarded. In 1821 Hull had three schools which taught the three R's to 150 pupils.

SECONDARY EDUCATION

Latin grammar schools with Church of England respectability and regular state support were established in Quebec and Montreal in 1816. The government in England then appointed Rev. Mr. Burrage and Dr. Shakel as masters. In 1811 Bishop Jacob Mountain of Quebec had recommended to the governor "that in proceeding to provide the means of liberal education in this province it would be most advisable to begin by the foundation of a good grammar school." He had suggested a house for the headmaster and his wife and a salary of at least £300 sterling. For an assistant there was to be an apartment and a salary of £150-£200. The bishop recommended accommodation for 50 boarders and a schoolroom for 150 boys. He suggested also that the headmaster should collect fees, restricted for seven years to not more than 35 guineas for each boarder and 15 guineas for each day scholar. The generous provision proposed for this establishment shows clearly that the bishop thought it fitting that the staff of a grammar school should occupy positions of distinction and that the scholars should be the sons of gentlemen well able to pay.

What the schools turned out to be may be seen from a report on the Royal Grammar School at Montreal in 1829. This institution was taught by Alexander Shakel and assistants. There were 35 scholars — 15 paying fees and 20 taught free. The fees were from £8 to £10 for tuition and £30 for board. The government made an allowance of £60 a year currency for the rent of the schoolhouse and £200 a year sterling to the headmaster. The subjects taught were the English, French, Latin, and Greek languages, writing, ancient and modern geography, mathematics and natural philosophy — the last subject "illustrated by experiments performed by an extensive apparatus." There was a note to the effect that a French teacher "attends for teaching those who may wish to employ him" on terms of four guineas per annum. This program was that of a grammar school with exceptional resources, as shown by the addition of science to the curriculum. Making French an extra subject without the same status as the ancient languages was a reflection of the practice in the great public schools of England at the time.

These two "royal grammar schools" came under the management of the Royal Institution shortly after its establishment. The generous stipends to the masters were paid out of the revenues from the Jesuit estates until 1831, when these resources were turned over to the assembly. That body reduced the grants to £100 for each of the two masters — the amount usually paid to grammar school masters in other provinces. The Quebec school remained in operation until 1839 and the Montreal school until 1846.

In addition to these two favored institutions, there were schools of the grammar school type conducted by well-educated clergymen from Britain. In 1804 in Quebec Rev. Daniel Wilkie, a capable Scotsman, opened a private classical school. In several places Church of England clergymen offered instruction to possible candidates for holy orders, and to such other boys or young men as they might be willing to accept as pupils. Consequently in 1829 Chambly was reported to have a grammar school which taught the usual secondary school subjects and gave instruction in divinity as well.

PRIVATE SCHOOLS

For those who had the means there were numerous private schools, some of them undoubtedly more pretentious in their claims than in their performance. In 1776 Mr. Belmont Fortin A.B. arrived in Quebec and offered to teach reading — "not in the vulgar monotony commonly used, but in the same free and natural manner the great Mr. Sheridan[*] teaches;" he was prepared also to instruct in the writing of themes, to enable the learner to discover the finest sentiments in English poets, to refine his concepts of morality as well as his taste, and to give a tolerable knowledge of the classics. Mr. James Tanswell and his son conducted a school in the Bishop's Palace, where, according to an announcement in 1795, young gentlemen might "be educated in all the various Sciences and Languages usually taught in the Public Schools in England, but after such plain and easy Methods as do not require one quarter of the time commonly employed in them." Tanswell senior also offered two courses of twenty-four lectures each — one "to comprehend the whole Theory and Practice" of the French language, the other to embrace "the whole Science of Geography." The school had in addition "a very handsome, pleasant, separate Apartment" in which young ladies might receive "such an Education as they have as yet had no opportunity of receiving in the Schools of this Country."

[*] Thomas Sheridan (1719-1788), father of dramatist Richard Brinsley Sheridan.

Some of the private schools were for boarders. An announcement of a school at Three Rivers in 1784 stated that young gentlemen would be "commodiously and plentifully boarded and expeditiously instructed." No Dotheboys Hall, that establishment! The proprietor of a school announced in 1798 that he would accept only boarders and half-boarders, not day pupils; he took the opportunity of thanking the public for their liberal support for fifteen years but earnestly requested those indebted to him to make immediate payment. Perhaps boarders could be retained as hostages when fees were not paid. Even a modest school for young children and girls might have resident pupils. For example, a Mrs. Crofton in 1775 begged leave to inform the public that she had taken a house in the lower town of Quebec, where she would instruct children in reading and spelling, plain work and marking, and board them if desired.

In the new commercial society the need to work, the urge to get ahead, and some ability to pay for instruction created a clientele for schools in the early morning or evening. The indefatigable Tanswell, who had classes from nine to twelve and from two to five, and lecture courses sometimes in the hours between, was only one of three teachers who advertised evening instruction in Quebec in 1871. There were frequent announcements of the kind in subsequent years. The most usual offerings were French, English, and mathematics — all useful in business. Tanswell taught both English and French at different times, and two other teachers in 1780 advertised their willingness to "attend" pupils before or after school to teach any of several modern languages. In 1807 Mr. Wilkie announced classes for young gentlemen from 6 to 7 a.m. in English grammar and composition, including letter-writing. Instruction in mathematics was offered by a Mr. Reid of Quebec in the evening during the winter of 1871.

Mathematics of a definitely practical nature was offered in 1817 by a Mr. Thom, who announced an evening school for instruction in arithmetic "adapted to the business of the counting-house" and in "those contractions also which are of so much utility in mercantile computations."

Instruction was available in almost everything except science, about which most teachers knew nothing, and history, which anyone could read for himself. A school in Montreal in 1781 added gunnery and fortification to a long list of ordinary subjects. A simple school for young ladies, like one opened by three women in Quebec in 1871, might teach only embroidery, plain-work, spelling and reading; but Agnes Galbraith from Edinburgh opened in July, 1783, an establishment "for boarding and teaching Young Ladies white and coloured Work, Tambour, Embroidery, and Dresden-work." In 1819 Mrs. Boyle, lately arrived from Great Britain, offered to teach clients to read and pronounce French with ease and fluency in twelve lessons by the "logographic" method.

Instruction in social accomplishments was available to both men and women. At the establishments of Mrs. Chillay at Quebec and Mrs. Wadden at Montreal dancing was included in the instructional program, and a master was in attendance two days a week. The barrier between the sexes in education was breached in 1784 by an "academy" which announced instruction for youth of both sexes in the usual branches of education to be given in a "large and commodious room." Ira Weldin announced in 1802 afternoon and evening classes for ladies and gentlemen at his dancing school. In 1818 Mr. Antoine Rod, who had operated a dancing school for seventeen years, offered to go to the lodging of clients to give instruction and promised them that "their friends may be assured of his perfect attention and greatest regulation and decorum." The same year another teacher offered instruction in music and dancing. In January of the previous year the cathedral organist announced his willingness to give music lessons in singing or playing the piano.

CULTURAL DEVELOPMENTS

From all of this it is apparent that social life in the cities of Lower Canada was lively once more and that there were certain extensions of freedom. In 1783 the Quebec Theatre advertised a performance of "High Life Below Stairs," with a promise of music, dancing, and pleasing decorations, and an injunction to patrons not to enter into any parts of the theatre allotted to the performers. In January 1779 there was an announcement that a subscription had been begun for the establishment of a public library: the fees were five pounds to enter and two pounds annually, the books were to be lent out to subscribers, and an assurance was given that "no books contrary to religion or good morals" would be permitted. There was evidently a good market for books: in 1781 James Tanswell offered for sale a large and general assortment that he had imported; in 1817 the advertisement of a long list to be sold at auction suggests that they were then more plentiful. Not everything on the market was as edifying or as clearly indicative of progress: the number of advertisements of pills for various ailments increased noticeably in the second decade of the nineteenth century. But the pace of life was speeding up. Before the end of the period steamboats were sailing regularly between Montreal and Quebec; and the *Gazette,* in which these many announcements appeared, was being published twice a week.

As compared with the French-speaking majority, the English-speaking people were generally literate, although the educational level was so low that instruction in anything beyond the bare elements had the appeal of an exceptional opportunity. From the first there had been at least some interest in higher education. Two hundred people in 1790 sent the governor general a petition in favor of a non-denominational and secular university of the type advocated by the committee which reported the previous year. But nothing was achieved toward the establishment of a university until James McGill bequeathed £10,000 and 46 acres on the outskirts of Montreal for this purpose. The Royal Institution was entrusted with the management of this endowment and procured a charter for a college in 1821. Its establishment was held up by litigation concerning the will until 1829.

Although it is true that the English-speaking majority had some advantages in grants from the government before 1829, the effect of this assistance was limited. The chief beneficiaries were the royal grammar schools, which were of service to only a few. A good many Protestants spurned the grants of the Royal Institution and established their own elementary schools. Other grants to city schools, and to country schools after 1829, were available to people of either language or any denomination.

The Separation

In this chapter there have been several suggestions that the educational cleavage between the French-speaking Roman Catholics and the English-speaking Protestants might have been avoided. It was said that the French-Canadians might have taken advantage of the plan for non-denominational schools put forward in 1789, of the legislation passed in 1801, or of the offers of the Royal Institution. There were probably many other cases like the one mentioned of voluntary cooperation for educational purposes between members of the two groups. What further evidence supports the view that a separation was not inevitable?

Perhaps worth mentioning is the fact that for years the Anglicans of Quebec held their services in a Roman Catholic chapel. Another small point is the approval given by the principal of the seminary of Montreal to at least one school of the Royal Institution — that at Terrebone. Actually, about one-quarter of the commissioners, school visitors, and teachers around 1825 were Roman Catholics. But by far the most impressive evidence is the attendance together of large numbers of Roman Catholic and Protestant children at city schools. Examples of this condition in other places will be given elsewhere, but consider for the moment the evidence of a full, though undated, report on eight schools in Quebec and the vicinity in the early 1830's.

The report shows very definitely that Roman Catholics and Protestants attended the same schools. In the National Monitorial School* 46 of 170 pupils in actual attendance were Roman Catholic. In the British and Canadian Monitorial School, in which one of the three teachers was French-speaking and Roman Catholic, 93 of the 161 pupils were of that faith. In the Church of England infant school two-thirds of the 45 children, and in the British and Canadian infant school four-fifths of the 75 children, were Roman Catholic although the teachers were in both cases English-speaking and Protestant. Only a few Protestants attended the three Roman Catholic schools, of which two were French-speaking and the third was taught by "an indifferent teacher." But of the reputedly Protestant schools, only the Presbyterian institution appears to have been strictly denominational; in it 72 of the 73 pupils were Protestant.

In a report of 1829 schools of the Royal Institution and schools established under the act of that year were described as being "attended indiscriminately by Protestants and Catholics." Might it have been possible to secure the acquiescence of the clergy and the hierarchy in the establishment of more and more state-supported community schools for all? A few of the former deviated from the usual policy of the latter by showing a willingness to co-operate with the government when aid was offered, and the number might have been greater if the government had been quick to support local schools with no stipulations at all regarding religion or language in the regulations. Even as things went, there were two instances of divided opinion in the hierarchy. In 1789 Mgr. Bailly, the coadjutor, supported the move to establish a non-sectarian university, to which the bishop in Quebec was opposed. In the late 1820's Mgr. Plessis, the Bishop of Quebec, approved of the proposed reorganization of the Royal Institution, and in this case the coadjutor refused to agree.

Logically no acceptable compromise could be reached between the two positions. On the one hand was a church claiming to be the custodian of definite revealed truth; on the other were churches insisting on certain practices or beliefs but leaving more or less latitude for the individual to discover truth not precisely defined. Only the latter group were willing to have undenominational or neutral schools. The Church of England moved with considerable reluctance from the former position to the latter.

But what if the government had refused to take sides or even to recognize differences in convictions or faith among the people and had been content merely to help them look after their own affairs, provide schools, and work out their problems? Durham's indictment was that:

The continued negligence of the British government left the mass of the people with-

* See below, pp. 116 ff.

out any of the institutions which would have elevated them in freedom and civilization . . . without education and without the institution of local self-government.[19]

If there had been more encouragement of ability through experience and less upholding of partisan principle, Durham might not have found eighty years after the conquest that: "No common education has served to remove and soften the differences of origin and language."[20]

Just how common schools would have been organized if an attempt had been made to establish them, it was then and is now impossible to say. For that very reason, those who insisted that only one pre-determined way was right made any theoretical solution impossible. In both of the contending groups, leaders of that type were in control.

CHAPTER 7

Upper Canada

Beginning about fifty miles up the river from Montreal, the southern limit of the land comprising Upper Canada extended about five hundred and fifty miles along the north shores of the St. Lawrence River and of Lakes Ontario and Erie westward to the Detroit River. Most of the people settled close to this southern boundary. The period of British rule over this territory began in 1763, and the history of Upper Canada as a separate colony extended from 1791 to 1841.

The latter year has been chosen as the end of the period for this chapter in spite of the fact that schools of the people were recognized in legislation of 1816. Extension of the period to 1841 makes possible a more complete account of educative conditions and educational institutions in an expanding pioneer society. Since many changes occurred in Upper Canada during its first fifty or sixty years of rapid expansion, it will save unnecessary explanations if we assume that statements unqualified as to date are descriptive of conditions about 1830.

Settlement

During the French regime there were no signs in Upper Canada of occupation by white men except fortified outposts and the homes of a few settlers along the banks of the St. Lawrence and Ottawa Rivers in the east and near the Detroit River far to the west. After 1763 the first new residents were disbanded officers and men of the army and large numbers of United Empire Loyalists who came between 1784 and 1800 from New York, Pennsylvania, and other north-eastern states. They were given substantial grants of land along the upper St. Lawrence, near the Bay of Quinte, in the Niagara Peninsula, and along the north shore of the eastern end of Lake Erie. By 1800 the population numbered about 70,000, of whom about half were of Loyalist stock. Among the Loyalists, those not of English descent were frequently Dutch or German, as were many of the later immigrants from the United States between 1800 and 1825, among whom there were numerous Quakers. Some of the first settlers from across the Atlantic were Highland Scots, who came to Glengarry County about 1800, many of them after a brief stay in the United States. Immigrants from England and other parts of the British Isles began to come in great numbers when a depression followed the end of the War of 1812-15. Fewer than 100,000 entered in the two years 1831 and 1832, although by no means all remained. The population reached 150,000 in 1824 and 432,000 in 1840.

People of different origins had different views on schooling and how it was to be provided. The Loyalists and those who came later from the United States were prepared to take some local action themselves to give their children a minimum of education, although they were glad enough to have state assistance. Quite early in the nineteenth century the Scots petitioned the government to have charity schools provided for them. It cannot be said that there was any great eagerness for education, since the Assembly before the War of 1812 showed more anxiety about checking public expenditure on grammar schools for a few than desire to spend money to encourage the establishment of schools for the many. This attitude may be explained partly by the preoccupation of the people with the immediate necessity of making a bare living and partly by the difficulty of obtaining agreement and concerted action among people in scattered and separated areas. For a time co-operative action of the people was also checked by the policy usually followed in the allotment of land, whereby people of different national origins were intermingled. Ultimately this intermingling was a good thing, since it kept extreme peculiarities from taking root in clusters and made it easier in the long run to obtain province-wide agreement on the administration of schools.

The continuing population was predominantly rural. Since the convenience of newcomers was a secondary consideration in the minds of those who allotted the land, the settlements were also remote from one another. Kingston, Niagara, and York (Toronto) were the first centres of any importance, but even in 1830 there were only five places with populations in excess of 1000. The heavy immigration in the 1830's caused towns to expand rapidly: Hamilton for example had 250 inhabitants, four stores, one church, and five taverns in 1829; in 1833 it had 1350 inhabitants, eighteen stores, three churches, and ten taverns. But the town dwellers were the minority; most of the people lived where ready-made goods were scarce and expensive and where home industry had to supply not only food but clothing, furniture, and many other necessities. These conditions retarded the development of education beyond a minimum elementary level: there were too few places with a sufficient number of permanent residents to support secondary schools; furthermore, chores and long hours of manual employment from an early age made prolongation of schooling a burden, a waste of time, or an impossibility.

Travel and Communication

Difficulties of travel and communication prevented one's escape from a local point of view and narrow prejudice. For a long time the preferred mode of transportation was by water. Only canoes were used at first, then freighters of different types propelled by oars and sails, and finally steamships. Steamers appeared on the Great Lakes before 1820 and became numerous after 1830. Although canals were constructed — the Lachine in 1825, the Welland in 1829, and the Rideau in 1832 — travel and transportation of goods remained expensive and slow. The Reverend William Proudfoot in 1833 obtained passage for himself, his wife, and six children in the steamer *Great Britain* from York to Queenston for $13.75, but had to spend $8.00, plus 35 cents on drinks for teamsters, to secure transportation and conveyance in wagons from Queenston to a point above Niagara Falls, which he reached nine and a half hours after his departure from York. But not so long before the same journey would have taken four days by land, and cost much more, for the roads were exceedingly bad except when covered with snow in winter. The traveller by stage-coach was jolted and tossed wildly about in a swaying vehicle which might at any time break down or sink up to the axle in mud. His only comforts were the taverns along the way, of which Proudfoot listed twenty on the Dundas road between York and Hamilton, a distance of less than fifty miles. Just north of muddy York itself, in what is

now the heart of Toronto, a winch, set up permanently to pull wagons slithering in the clay of Yonge Street over the crest of the slope, gave the place the name of Gallow's Hill.

Communication of ideas was hardly less difficult. A letter sent from York to Kingston or London, 160 miles away, cost the recipient ninepence, and from York to Quebec one shilling and sixpence. A letter from Great Britain to York in Upper Canada cost the one who received it more than six shillings — a good day's wages for an ordinary man. Already Canadians, as compared with Americans, were having to pay for an inefficiency only partly excused by geographical handicaps: a correspondent said that the same letter sent via New York instead of Halifax would have cost less than a third as much and would have reached its destination in half the time. For many people post-offices were anything but convenient. For residents of Barrie the nearest post-office was in Newmarket, twenty-five miles away.

NEWSPAPERS AND BOOKS

The first newspaper was the *Upper Canada Gazette,* which began to publish in 1793. The first to rouse the ire of the government by its criticism was the *Upper Canada Guardian,* which appeared in 1807; its editor John Willcox was imprisoned, ostensibly for breach of parliamentary privilege. Newspapers were handicapped by high postage rates and limited circulation. A leading paper, the *Christian Guardian,* had 1600 subscribers in 1830, but others survived on only a few hundred. Although often narrow in vision and abusive in language, the editors who ventured on publication and persisted in their efforts despite all obstacles rendered a valuable service to the province. The newspapers kindled the thoughts of people and turned the light of information against injustice and bigotry in all its forms. Although penurious and shabby in appearance they had the vitality of independence and served not so much those who advertised as those who read. In 1836 there were 38 of them — one a daily and the rest weeklies or monthlies. They were of the highest importance in adult education, and their presses, incidentally, provided the only facilities for printing any material in the province. By 1836, according to an estimate of Bourinot, some 425,000 copies of newspapers circulated yearly among a population of 370,000.

There was not much else to read. Books were scarce and not many people had the means or desire to subscribe to circulating libraries. Bath had a "social library" before 1811. An advertisement in the *Kingston Gazette* of February 24, 1816, announced that from 11 a.m. to 1 p.m. daily in the courthouse a library would be open for distribution of books to subscribers paying thirty shillings a year. Some who could have paid the fee disapproved of books and would have agreed, if they had read Sheridan, with Sir Anthony Absolute's declaration that a circulating library was "an evergreen tree of diabolical knowledge." Mavor, the author of a thin little *English Spelling Book,* said in an introduction that he was aware that the volume might constitute the entire library of the child, and this may often have been the case in Upper Canada. The one book read with regularity in devout homes was the Bible.

Occupations

The chief occupation was farming: exports of wheat rose to 450,000 bushels by 1812; grist mills numbered 250 in 1826 and 435 in 1840; livestock, not plentiful at first, increased from about 140,000 to 350,000 head during the same fourteen years but not as rapidly as the human population. Life on the pioneer farm was laborious. It accustomed the body to toil and compelled the acquisition of manual skills. It gave the head of a new family independence and authority after years of subjection to similar control by his parents — a sudden right to crude self-assertion and obstinate prejudice untempered by intellectual discipline.

Second in occupational importance came lumbering, which by 1834 provided almost two-thirds of the total exports to Great Britain. The number of sawmills increased from about 425 in 1826 to 975 in 1840. Lumbering drove the centre of the fur trade from the St. Lawrence area to the region of Hudson Bay. The new type of work in the woods was somewhat more favorable to the establishment of schools, and the processing industry much more so.

The economy became more diversified. In addition to important products of the farm and forest, including potash made by burning trees felled when the land was cleared, some goods were produced by industries of local importance, including linen and paper mills and iron and steam-engine works. But consumer goods of domestic manufacture were of low quality as compared with imports, and the quantity and variety of all merchandise were exceedingly limited, by modern standards. Nevertheless there was sufficient expansion of industry and trade to make the increase in the number of merchants impressive and to cause concern among those who looked with disapproval on commercial ethics.

A skilled workman — carpenter or mason — could be hired for about 7/6, or $1.50 a day; a laborer for about 2/6 or 3 shillings a day, plus board; a woman servant for 20 shillings a month and board. These wages were low in relation to the cost of most articles, with the exception of ordinary food and drink. The daily wage of a carpenter would buy less tea and sugar than now, but more meat, and very much more whisky. The workman with a shilling a day to spare had not enough to pay for the cheapest seat at a theatre, would have had to save every penny to buy a horse in less than a year, and had reason to think that any good furnishings for a home, a wife, or himself were beyond his means. Under such circumstances it is not surprising that drinking and gambling with men and crude intercourse with women were popular forms of entertainment and escape. The economy provided for the physical needs of ordinary people, but not much more. This condition, and the accepted opinion that only a minority could appreciate the finer things of life, were educationally effective in keeping aesthetic tastes and intellectual activity low.

Leisure and Recreation

Work and recreation were combined in the co-operative "bees" characteristic of a time when money and specialized services were equally hard to find. Neighbors might be assembled for any type of work which could be done more expeditiously by many hands, including stumping, logging, ploughing, hay cutting, corn-husking, sheep-shearing, butchering, and raising a house, barn, or other building. Liquor flowed freely as a rule during and following these activities; after dinner the men engaged in competitive feats of strength, like wrestling, stone-putting, or a tug-of-war, while the women cleaned up; later there might be dancing far into the night. Women had bees for paring and preserving fruit, spinning, quilting — and a chance to gossip. There were many who disapproved of indulgences at these events, and particularly of the heavy drinking among the men. Proudfoot wrote:

And now that the raising is over, I am able to form my own opinion of these bees. From first to last, there have been at this raising the work of 90 men for one day which was at the very least about two thirds more than was necessary. So far as the waste of time is concerned, the house is a very expensive one. Had I had to give them their victuals and drink the raising would have cost an outlay more than a frame house. Many of the people came for the sole purpose of drinking, and never once assisted in lifting a log. Many of them got drunk — There was such a quantity of swearing, and low buffooning that the whole thing was very painful. — Upon the whole I would never again make a bee if I could help it. The work is not so well done as when it is paid for, and if a person treated the folks so as to acquire a reputation in his neighborhood for hospitality, he would actually be at more expense. I am now done with it, and I am very glad.[1]

Nevertheless the bees made social men and women of settlers whose lives might otherwise have been solitary, morose, and even harder than they were.

Most other amusements were of a physical nature. Sports included wrestling, horse-racing, lacrosse, football, handy-ball, cricket, curling, hunting, fishing, and hawking. Sailing, sleigh-riding, snowshoeing, and skating were popular types of recreation. Any special event, like Parade Day, called for celebrations in such forms as horse-racing and bibulous conviviality. Fall fairs were often riotous affairs. The popularity of bull- and bear-baiting and of cock- and dog-fighting showed the callousness to bodily injury or suffering which was reflected in the treatment of children. That actual pleasure was derived from the torment and destruction of living creatures is suggested by an attempt to send a boat-load of animals — buffaloes, bears, foxes, dogs, cats, and geese — over the falls to provide a spectacle that would draw crowds to Niagara.

Gambling for high stakes was common. Because money was scarce, cattle, horses, and produce were wagered, and everything a man had accumulated by years of labor might be thrown away in a desperate effort to recover losses. Chess, billiards, and cards were played for stakes. Fortunately those who bet within their means on races or lotteries were not ruined by heavy taxes and "rake-offs" which make losing certain and reward the exploiters. In Montreal, before the two Canadas were separated, a lottery to build a prison subtracted only about fifteen per cent from the pool and awarded a prize of some sort to one ticket in every three. But gambling under any conditions can hardly be regarded as culturally constructive; it was akin in cause and effect to the rough and tumble of the times.

Visiting, in the absence of commercialized entertainment, meant more to people than now. Hospitality was bounteous. Probably the conversation would have seemed dull and circumscribed to one who had had greater advantages of intellectual stimulation. There was little chance that any in the company had recently read a book, although some would have seen a newspaper and possibly a copy of the *Canadian Magazine*, which was published in Toronto in 1833. When a show came within range of attendance, it was more than likely a circus. In Toronto, where there were enough people with money and with somewhat cultivated taste, amateur and professional actors could be sure of an occasional audience at a play. There, too, was established in 1831, a mechanics' institute, which offered informative lectures and reading material to those who wished to improve their minds. But work and play were both of a predominantly physical nature, and topics of conversation must have been mostly of the same variety.

One hopes that something gracious and aesthetic was achieved in relations between young men and women. They were not without opportunities of being together. After the dance the young man walked or drove with his girl to her home. Sunday gave the best opportunity for courting. There were even "sparking bees," where the group chaperonage was likely

to be sufficient but not suppressive. There was at least a chance for the development of sensitivity and empathy in men who grew up in a coarse environment.

Ethics and Religion

The excesses of the time aroused counter-forces equally extreme. By the 1830's a growing opposition had assumed the proportions of a religious revival. Inevitably, of course, the ethical attack of religion was directed chiefly against prevalent vices which were an open scandal, and practices associated with them. It may, therefore, be a legacy from the pioneer period in Canada that those concerned about the improvement of character in the twentieth century are still preoccupied with negative virtues in a limited field.

Since temperance education is still a lively issue in this country, it may be worth while to add a few more words on the consumption of alcoholic beverages in Upper Canada. In the first two decades their use was almost universal among men, so that the young were virtually taught to believe that the imbibing of alcohol was a natural privilege of the adult male. So well established was the practice that the temperance movement at first sought only to limit a man's daily consumption of spirits to an amount which few would want to exceed today: one pledge said no more than a pint, and a pint of fiery stuff then must have contained nearly as much alcohol as the diluted beverage in a "reputed" quart now sold at thirty times the price. Beer and wine were not included in the pledge of the early days. The distilleries and numerous taverns made liquor easy to buy, and some stores kept an open keg from which customers might help themselves. Drunken men staggered along the roads, caused scenes of disorder and violence, and lay in a stupor exposed to public view. There were cases where not only men but boys drank themselves to an immediate death. With bad examples everywhere to serve as object lessons, many boys turned against the ways of their elders. Since drinking by women was not countenanced, most wives and daughters were also ready to support the temperance movement. Conditions were therefore favorable to acceptance and support of vigorous teaching against the use of alcohol.

In 1840 the bulk of the population was distributed among four large denominations: the Anglicans, the Presbyterians, the Methodists, and the Roman Catholics. There were also other sects. The campaign against risky amusements was conducted mainly by Protestant non-conformist churches. The Quakers set an example against drinking, gambling, horse-racing, card-playing, dancing, and even music. The Methodists, who rapidly became the largest non-conformist group, rivalled the Quakers in the scope of their disapproval and employed strong emotional appeal to corral the sinners. This is a description of a Methodist camp meeting:

The fierce urge of the sermon and the passionate call of the singers stirred the massed audience to a state of indescribable excitement. I have seen people literally fall over each other while the anguished wails of repentant sinners mingled with the voices of the singers and the weird sound of the wind in the tree tops. . . . Warned . . . to prepare for the end of the world . . . one man actually tried to climb a stovepipe on the way to heaven and one woman went raving mad.[2]

The Presbyterians were strict, but not about everything; they were more staid and less offensive to the aristocracy. The Anglicans were less disturbed by social pleasures than by revolt against a comfortable orthodoxy. Although all the sects professed their faith in certain fundamental doctrines of Christianity, and in a basic code regarding relations that should exist between the sexes, there was nothing approaching uniformity in religious or ethical concepts.

Church-going could not be a regular practice until the population increased and roads were improved. The Methodists sent out itinerant preachers in the early days. Even when churches were built, there was less formality than now, for people might come and go during the lengthy service. One gets the impression that religion was more of an outward display than an inward faith, that it was more taken for granted than thought about. Youngsters in school were forever confronted with moral platitudes and melancholy discourses on the gravity of sin; it hardly seems possible that their spirits were thereby permanently depressed. Perhaps their elders, too, could take a spiritual licking and carry on. The voices of righteousness must thunder all the louder when individuals are not encouraged to make moral decisions themselves.

Punishment of crime was severe and demonstrative: forgery was a capital offence, and there were stocks in York until it became Toronto in 1834. The violence of legal punishment was matched occasionally by outbreaks of mob justice which had been known to tar and feather its victim or ride him out on a fence rail.

Yet life in the new world environment caused virtues to grow in a positive way. Canadians acquired a reputation for honesty, even if Proudfoot, as a Presbyterian divine, felt uneasy that this virtue was not an achievement of moral struggle but simply the result of an abundance of food, which reduced a major temptation. In 1851, another observer, the author of *Views of Canada and the Colonists*, wrote that "the large amount of material comfort . . . allows, of course, fewer temptations to commit offences against property."

Government

The government of Upper Canada was of the same type as the government of most of the other colonies. It consisted of a lieutenant-governor, a legislative council appointed by the governor, an executive council similarly appointed and recruited largely from the legislative council, and a legislative assembly elected by male voters who met the property qualifications for the franchise. The usual rivalry between the council and the assembly hampered legislative action, and meagre revenues made it impossible for the government to do very much. The oligarchy, protesting loyalty to the Crown and to the Church of England, reserved public offices and other benefits for a limited group of people, whose members came to be called the "Family Compact." Actually there was some justification for this policy, since the number of educated and capable men was small. But the assembly fought against this restriction of privilege and prepared the people for responsible government, although riotous scenes at open elections, vitriolic speeches and editorials, and the resort to rebellion in 1837 were violent means of education.

Local government was in the hands of magistrates at the quarter sessions, although township meetings were authorized to attend to minor matters like choosing a clerk and an assessor, deciding the height of fences, and carrying out the regulations of the quarter sessions. The larger units for local administration were not the counties, but districts, of which there were eleven before 1830.

To invoke the wrath of society against those who sought popular government, the words of denunciation were "disloyalty" or "republicanism." Methodists were regarded as fellow-travellers because of their link with the American conference; and some living in the province today received in their youth the traditional advice, "Fear God, honor the King, and never trust a Methodist." Some of the old aristocracy were quite frank in saying that what they feared was power for the people.

Although pioneer society was unlike modern society to a marked degree, we should not get the feeling that life then was entirely different. An hour's perusal of old newspapers will show that even the curiosities of early days have a familiar ring in twentieth-century ears. Consider the weekly issues of the *Kingston Chronicle* for 1819. A theatre advertising regularly through the winter and spring offered *Hamlet, She Stoops to Conquer,* and lighter entertainment, and even assured audiences that efforts had been made to keep the building comfortable. From the end of April to the middle of November the steamer *Frontenac* sailed three times a month to York and Niagara, with restrictions on weight of baggage suggestive of the airways; the bay and river steamboat *Charlotte* made shorter trips and more numerous calls. There was a dancing school of sorts. There was even a soda water advertisement which in quaint language extolled the properties of a "cooling, salutary, and delicious beverage"; apparently such drinks were a novelty because the merchant expressed his confidence that "no Lady or Gentleman will conceive it any tax on time, constitution, or propriety occasionally to indulge in the innocent and healthful hilarity inevitably attendant upon a glass of Syrup and Soda Water."

Educational Aims

As might be expected leaders in society expressed views on education which emphasized its value in maintaining the existing order. The first lieutenant-governor, Simcoe, whose most fervent wish was to transfer to Upper Canada and keep intact the institutions of England, sought an endowment of education for the few "that from ourselves may rise up a loyal, and in due progress, a learned clergy."[3] The lieutenant-governor in 1808 approved of the grants given to grammar schools as a method of securing the instruction of youth and "of instilling into their minds principles of Religion and Loyalty."[4] "As morality and religion are the foundation and stability of all good governments," said the Reverend Robert Murray, Superintendent of Education in 1842, "and as these are taught in their purity in the word of God, a portion of the scriptures should be read in the schools."[5] It will be noticed that the social aim was closely linked with religion.

Educational leaders regularly emphasized moral and religious aims. John Strachan, the dominating figure in education during the period, believed that children should be taught "to understand and admire the beneficence of their Creator in the works of His hand, to feel that they are immortal and accountable beings, that Christian virtue is the first distinction among men, and that useful knowledge is the second."[6] Murray, the editor of the widely used *English Reader,* said that his book was "designed to inculcate some of the most important principles of piety and virtue." The Midland District School Society, organized to set up a monitorial school in Kingston, stated that its object was "to promote the educational and moral improvement of the poor." Upper Canada Academy, the predecessor of Victoria College, assured the parents of students that the new institution would pay "strict attention to their morals." Proprietors of private schools vied with one another in assertions that "nothing shall be neglected for health, instruction, religion, and good morals." The lieutenant-governor in 1839 said that, "A system of sound and religious instruction, for the rising generation, ought to be established under every Government. . . ."[7]

Among the ordinary people, however, there was less manifest concern about the loyalty, religious beliefs, or moral behavior of other people's children or their own. "The parents had neither the time nor the inclination to concern themselves about manners,"[8] said David Boyle. The truth is that few were prepared to make sacrifices to do more than a minimum for their children. The Reverend Robert McGill of Niagara wrote in the 1840's, "Notwithstanding all the noise upon the subject, education is not really held in high estimation among us . . . . cheap education is wanted; I have not seen much desire for improvement in quality."[9]

A reasonably accurate estimate of educational aspiration in the "good old days" would be this: A few leaders in church and state, with some little support from their friends at the higher social level, were earnestly concerned about providing secondary education for men who would assist and succeed them; they also sought to give the children of the people an education of a type which would make them acceptable to their superiors. Others of high economic or social status were prepared to give their own children a respectable education as befitted their station, but an increasing number who were prospering in trade favored something more practical than education of the strictly traditional type; most of these people were content to let others, including the poor, look after their own offspring. If we divide the rest of the people into two groups at a higher and a lower level, we shall find among the former the first aspirations for an educated and educative society; here were those who wanted all to learn and to grow in power to direct their learning. The characteristic of the latter group was indifference. Education beyond the barest minimum was despised by many, worn by some as a badge of membership, and regarded by a few as a means of control. But others were beginning to appreciate its coming value. The remarks of a member of the legislature during a debate of 1832 were reported as follows:

> The poor should have such an education as would enable them to rival the rich. He was afraid of that distinction between rich and poor ever taking place in this Province, that had been the ruin of other countries, where the rich often took the advantage of the poor, and the educated of the uneducated. Liberty was on the march, and Education should keep pace with liberty, or we would have anarchy and confusion. But when the people generally were educated, when every man understood his political and civil rights, then we would be a happy country.[10]

Dr. Charles Duncombe in presenting a report on education in 1836 urged that schools be given support sufficient "to interest all classes of the community in endeavouring to avail themselves of them." He pointed out the need in a changing world for changes in "the modes and means of instruction and also in the course and character of the studies pursued. We must look, then," he said, "to the world as it now is, and not as it has been."[11]

Schools for the Few

The primary concern of the oligarchy, of course, was to establish grammar schools and a university for the training of leaders in society. The first step was to procure, in 1797, half a million acres of land as an endowment for this purpose. The land, however, was carelessly selected and was practically valueless at first; in 1800 a large tract of crown land sold for only two and a half cents an acre. In 1827 more than half of the endowment was exchanged for better land, but this was set aside for the support of a university yet to be built and was used in the meantime to finance one superior gram-

mar school, Upper Canada College, established in lieu of a university in 1830.

PRIVATE SCHOOLS

In the early years the only education available to the children of wealthy or cultured people was offered by private schools. Two of the earliest schools were a garrison school at Kingston in 1785 and a school at Fredericksburgh in 1786. The most notable early teacher was the Reverend John Stuart, a United Empire Loyalist, born in Virginia, who opened a school in Quebec in 1781 and moved to Kingston in 1785. There he immediately opened a select classical school, and from 1792, when a school building was erected, he received a regular annual grant of £100 from the government. Farther west, regular schools were established in Dundas in 1788 and in York (Toronto) in 1798.

During the first few decades of the nineteenth century private schools became numerous. Their advertisements have a curious interest. Here is an announcement of a school of the grammar school type in Niagara in 1796:

> The School lately taught by Mr. Richard Cockrel will be opened on Tuesday next, under the direction of the Rev. Mr. Arthur. The pupils will be instructed in Reading according to the most approved method, and English Grammar, Writing and Arithmetic, the Latin and Greek languages, Geography and the Mathematics, to which will be added, if required, an introduction to the other sciences.
>
> If any number of boys offer, and books can be procured, a Latin class will be commenced immediately.[12]

Another school in Niagara offered in 1802 elementary and practical education to boys and girls:

> Mr. and Mrs. Tyler take the liberty of informing the public that on Monday, the 1st of February they will open their School for young people — Men and Ladies.

They will keep a regular day School and night School. Children of each sex, above the age of four years will be received, and the price will be in proportion to the kind of instruction the parents may wish their children to receive.

They will teach in Reading, Writing and Arithmetic; the young ladies will be instructed in all that is necessary for persons of their sex to appear decently and be useful in the world, and of all that concerns housekeeping, either for those who wish to live in town or country.

The situation is healthy and agreeable, and the house suitable for a number of boarders.[13]

An advertisement of a school in Kingston in 1817 gave definite information about the cost of instruction and shows that a privately operated institution was obliged to consult the needs of its clientele by offering various subjects:

Scholars may be instructed at the Academy, in Mr. Henry Baker's red house, Rear street, Kingston, in the following branches of literature at the annexed prices, viz.:

	£	s.	d.
In Orthography, Reading and Writing per quarter .... Or £4 per annum.	1	2	6
English Grammar, Arithmetic and Book-keeping	1	10	0
Composition, Oratory, the Elements of Natural and Civil History, Practical Mathematics, Geography, etc.	2	0	0
Latin, Greek and other classical branches	2	10	0

An evening school will also be taught for the benefit of those who are unable to attend the day school.

A young lady is wanted to instruct the Misses in plain sewing. Enquire at the Academy.[14]

JOHN STRACHAN

An event of the highest importance to education in Upper Canada was the arrival in 1799 of John Strachan, who came over from Scotland to take charge of a

John Strachan

non-existent university and found an almost unbroken forest. In his brief but intensely interesting biography W. Stewart Wallace tells us that Strachan would have returned to Scotland if he had had the money to pay his fare. But of necessity he decided to stay and "mak' the best of it," and that he undoubtedly did. He acquired friends of influence in Kingston, where he quickly saw the light and became a member and a priest of the church of true respectability in the colony. In 1804 he became rector at Cornwall, where he opened a school. Not long after, he married a wealthy widow, moved to York, and became a member of the ruling oligarchy. He advanced in the church to become the first bishop of Toronto and was the dominating figure in education in Upper Canada for at least the first four decades of the nineteenth century.

THE FEW VS. THE MANY

In 1807 the government passed a Public Schools Act which provided for grants of £100 apiece to masters of grammar schools,

Strachan's school, Cornwall, 1803

one in each of the eight districts of the province. Grants had occasionally been made to masters who conducted schools of this type on their own initiative, but this act marked the beginning of regular state support for secondary education. Strachan received a grant while at Cornwall and later as master of the grammar school in York. But the Act had no strong support in the assembly, which tried in 1810 to prevent its provisions from becoming permanent, although without success.

The essential reason for the unpopularity of the grammar schools was, of course, that they served very few people. They were accessible only to those who lived within the town in which they were located and to those who could afford to send their sons away from home to board with the master. Fees were high and the curriculum was of an academic type that had little value to those who were compelled to make a living in occupations other than the professions and the favored positions in government.

One of the most bitter critics of the grammar schools was William Lyon Mackenzie. Their exclusiveness, of which he complained, is revealed by enrolment figures: in eleven schools there were 372 pupils in 1828 and only 311 ten years later; of 280 pupils in 1829 more than half were in elementary subjects — young boys or girls sent because their parents objected to having them attend a common school. In 1819 an amendment to the Act had been passed to provide ten free places in each of the grammar schools for children from the common schools. Candidates for scholarships were to be chosen by lot from nominees of the trustees of the common schools. But although this amendment gave promise of breaking down the distinction between the two types in some places, it did not work out in practice. Even with the remission of fees for tuition, other expenses of attendance were considerable, and a boy whose parents were compelled to make sacrifices was out of place among young gentlemen. Petitions to the lieutenant-governor suggest that the free places had more appeal to genteel mendicants who had more trust in flattery than in fate. Actually, by Strachan's own admission in 1832, not a single grammar school had scholarship pupils from the common schools in attendance.* The same amendment provided for some check on the schools by requiring an annual public examination and an annual report to the lieutenant-governor. But although Strachan reported the grammar schools as "effectively possessing the confidence of the public," he was prepared in 1830 to have the lieutenant-governor appoint Roman Catholic and Presbyterian clergy among the trustees as a measure of expediency to secure the interest of those groups. The schools remained in disfavor with the majority of the people and did not escape censure in Lord Durham's report at the end of the period.

KING'S COLLEGE

Meanwhile Strachan and other zealots were pursuing a project dear to their hearts — the establishment of a university. The watchful Scotsman never missed an opportunity to keep the subject before the minds of the authorities. In 1816 at a public examination of the Home District Grammar School in York, at which Lieutenant-Governor Gore was in attendance, he had the poet laureate of the school recite verses composed for the occasion:

Yet much remains for some aspiring Son,
Whose liberal Soul from that desires renown
Which gains for Wellesley a lasting crown;
Some gen'ral structure in these wilds to rear
When every Art and science may appear.
O happy Gore! this proud distinction woos
Thy quick acceptance, back'd by every Muse,
Those feelings too when joyful fancy knew
When learning's gems first opened to my view
Bid you to thousands smooth the stormy road
Which leads to gracious Science's sweet abode.[15]

In 1827 Strachan secured for the proposed university a more valuable land endowment and a royal charter. Since it was the intention that the institution should be essentially a missionary college of the Church of England, it is not surprising that the Archdeacon of York was designated as the president *ex officio* and that subscription to the Thirty-nine Articles of the Church of England was required of the seven professors, who with the president and the chancellor were to form the council of the college. This religious test aroused the opposition of the assembly and had no support from the British House of Commons or the Colonial office. In 1837 the legislative council agreed reluctantly to a change in the charter which left the presidency open to appointment by the king, and required of the faculty and members of the college council only a declaration of belief in the "authenticity and divine inspiration of the Old and New Testament and in the Doctrine of the Trinity."[16] Under this charter King's College opened in 1843 and was constitutionally sectarian only to the extent that there was an Anglican professorship of theology and no such privilege for any other denomination.

UPPER CANADA COLLEGE

In the meantime, however, from 1829 until the opening of King's College, the Church of England had held a dominating influence in another institution, which served as a temporary university. This was Upper Canada College, a superior grammar school housed in a more pretentious building than the others and having five graduates of Oxford and Cambridge as senior members of its staff. It was designed to be a replica in small scale of an English public school, and as such it offered a classical education to young gentlemen in York and to those from other places whose fathers could afford the heavy expense of board and tuition. Opponents of the grammar schools made Upper Canada College the central

* He himself would have been glad to see them there. Secondary education in Scotland was not socially exclusive.

Upper Canada College in 1829

target of their attack, since it was obviously a creation of the Family Compact in York, maintained for their own advantage by grants of government land and money.

According to William Lyon Mackenzie, Upper Canada College was conducted "on a narrow, bigoted, and sectarian plan." As a supplement to this charge he mentioned that the Home District Grammar School was absorbed for a time by the new institution. It so happens that the vice-principal of Upper Canada College, the Rev. Dr. Thomas Phillips, had been the master of the Home District Grammar School and had reported in 1829 on the program he followed in that school:

Saturday morning all except senior classical students say the church catechism or the collect for the ensuing Sunday and the arithmetic tables. On Saturday before prayers one of the senior pupils reads out of some book on the evidence of the Christian religion. At ten o'clock every morning Scripture reading and prayers; at four afternoon prayers.

It would appear from this that those who objected to Church of England teaching had little reason to lament the passing of the Home District Grammar School, and that if Upper Canada College was even more strongly sectarian there was considerable reason for complaint.

VICTORIA AND QUEEN'S

The prerogatives asserted by the Anglicans in the original charter of King's College and in the operation of Upper Canada College caused other denominations to found colleges of their own. The Methodists decided in 1830 to establish a literary institution or "seminary of learning," of a non-sectarian character. As a result, in 1836, Upper Canada Academy received a royal charter and opened in Cobourg; in 1841 it became Victoria College. The Presbyterians, disappointed in their hope of having a professorship of theology in King's College, secured in 1841 a charter for Queen's College, now Queen's University, at Kingston.

The English Influence

Chiefly because of its later development, and partly because of its distance from the ocean and the convenience of access from New York State, Upper Canada had fewer charity schools of the English type than were found in the older colonies. There were, however, some examples of these older institutions for the education of the people. Apprenticeship is one illustration. An indenture of apprenticeship in Upper Canada stated that Charles Ward, alias McCarty, was apprenticed to Dr. Solomon Jones, to be taught "the mistery (sic) or occupation of agriculture" and that Dr. Jones was "likewise to teach him or cause to be taught, to read Write and Cypher as far as the Rule of Division." Advertisements for apprentices began appearing in the *Upper Canada Gazette* in the first year of its publication — for a blacksmith shop, for a joiner and cabinet maker, for a printing business, and so on.

Another educational institution from England, the infant school, was praised editorially by *The Loyalist* for August 30th and October 18th, 1828; six years later two young women came from the old country to open one such school in London, Upper Canada.

One other English institution, which, as we have seen, spread through the United States and Canada was the Sunday school, which in the first few decades of the nineteenth century taught reading and spelling, although the instruction became wholly religious at a comparatively early date in America. One of the first Sunday schools in Upper Canada was established in Kingston in 1817 for those who "from peculiar circumstances are unable to attend the common school"; it charged fees. The next year an undenominational Sunday school was opened at York in a Methodist church near King and Jordan Streets. Spelling and lesson books were supplied by a Sunday School Society in the United States and supplemented by shingles on which passages from the Bible had been pasted. A few years later Sunday schools were common in the older settlements. During the session of 1823-24 the legislature voted £150 as a yearly grant to purchase books and tracts for Sunday schools in the more remote and indigent areas. Jacob Gander, who was superintendent of a Sunday school near the Niagara River, tried to obtain some of these publications and "prize tickets" by addressing a petition to Lady Sarah Maitland, wife of the lieutenant-governor. The pious superintendent kept a careful record which showed regular attendance by the scholars and by two of his sons and one of his daughters, who were teachers. There were at least two other Sunday schools in the adjoining township. Gander's deferential language in the closing paragraph of his petition gives a suggestion of the attitudes encouraged by his school:

Will your Ladyship pardon me when I make so very bold as to remark, that the honor of your presence for a few minutes some Sunday during the Summer, would very considerably add to the credit of our school.[17]

Schools of the People

The usual type of school for children of the people, however, was the common school — built by the parents, and taught by a teacher whom they engaged. An early example was a school which opened in 1797 in the Township of Charlotteville, County of Norfolk, District of London. A certain William Pitt Gilbert and a companion, travelling by canoe in Lake Erie, were overtaken by a storm and left stranded on an uninhabited stretch of the northern shore. Exhausted and starving, they managed some days later to reach the Charlotteville settlement. There, after three weeks' rest, Gilbert was able to seek employment and offered to conduct a school. Nine residents jointly engaged him and provided temporary accommodation in a small outhouse belonging to one of the number. The thirty or so pupils were lucky, for the teacher had "an easy

An early common school (from a sketch made at Adelaide, Middlesex County, Ontario, in 1845, and now in the John Ross Robertson collection)

and engaging manner of communicating instruction" which commanded their respect, so that "he never found it necessary to chastise, correct, reprimand, admonish, or reprove" any one of them during his three years' stay.[18] Although the teacher and the particular circumstances were exceptional, this illustrates the regular method of establishing a common school.

THE COMMON SCHOOL ACT

In 1816 the government first used the revenues of the province to encourage local initiative of this kind, and schools of the people were given sanction and encouragement. The Common School Act of that year provided that when the people of any community had built a schoolhouse and could undertake to supply it with twenty pupils, they might elect three trustees who should have authority to examine and appoint a teacher. When the teacher had taught for six months, and had received from the trustees a certificate of acceptable service, he was to present this chit to the district treasurer and receive his portion of the public money voted for the purpose. The only qualification demanded of the teach-

er was that he should be a British subject, or have taken the oath of allegiance. The trustees had complete control over their school, although they were required by law to report every three months to a district board appointed by the lieutenant-governor. The act was to be in force for four years only and was passed with some reluctance by the legislative council in return for non-interference by the assembly with the grammar schools. The total grant was £6000, and the amount receivable by a teacher depended on the number of scholars and was in no case to exceed £25, or $100.

The oligarchy's distrust of schools under popular control was expressed four years later, in 1820, by a reduction of the grant from £6000 to £2500. There was the excuse that in some districts considerable sums of money had remained unappropriated and that certain schools could not command a sufficiently numerous or regular attendance to deserve the support. The revenues of the province were limited, and some of the money was misspent by ignorant and inexperienced trustees. There may also have been a feeling that no further concessions should be made to

The first schoolhouse in Waterloo, Ontario, built in 1820

popular opinion after the amendments to the Grammar School Act in 1819. But the chief reason, surely, for reducing the appropriation to schools of the people was associated with a plan to provide a different type of school for children of the people — a school calculated to fulfil more efficiently the aims that the minority regarded as appropriate for the education of children of the majority.

In the next chapter we shall see that the type of school favored by the lieutenant-governor, Sir Peregrine Maitland, and by others of the Family Compact was a monitorial school on the National plan. To secure premises for such a school at York in 1820, the Executive Council and District Board of Education arbitrarily cut off the grant to the common school and appropriated the building in spite of the protests of the trustees and the teacher, whose claims for financial redress were supported in the assembly, sometimes warmly, for fifteen years.

CENTRAL BOARD OF EDUCATION

The governing minority found a means of exerting some little influence on the teaching in common schools through the operation of the Central Board of Educa-

tion. This board, appointed in 1823 by the lieutenant-governor, and presided over by the inevitable Dr. Strachan, was given financial resources by a liberal grant of land. A special grant of £150 annually was "laid out in religious books and tracts for the children of the poor and destitute throughout the province"[19] — a charity more far-sighted than the humanitarian activities of a later period. Many of the books distributed gratis by the board, like Mavor's *Spelling Book*, were of a distinctly Church of England character, and all were imbued with approved sentiments. The Central Board also issued rules for the government of schools, but these could have had little effect, partly because there was no means of checking their observance and partly because the board was in strong disfavor with most of the people and with their representatives in the assembly. The views of this aristocratic central authority were reflected chiefly by Upper Canada College and the Central School at York. The board went out of existence in 1833.

UPS AND DOWNS

The operation of the Act of 1820 terminated in 1824, but legislation in that year renewed without time limit its niggardly and discouraging policy. From one point of view some of the clauses enacted in 1824 were desirable. The application of the grants was extended to cover the education of Indians. The qualifications of teachers were subject to check by the requirement that they secure a certificate from a member of the District Board. Money was voted, as has been mentioned, for the purchase of books and tracts to be distributed by the district boards to Sunday schools. But all of these clauses, combined with the inadequacy of the common school grant, gave no encouragement to the development of schools of the people. They made an inroad on the common school fund by broadening its purposes without adding to its resources. They caused teachers to be screened by appointees of the lieutenant-governor, whose social and religious attitudes were likely to be in accordance with those of the oligarchy. They gave further money only for purposes which, however, commendable, were those of the government rather than those of the people themselves.

For eleven years thereafter the schools of the people struggled along with insufficient support. The teacher had to eke out the pittance received from the government with what he could collect from the rate-bills or fees imposed on the parents. In the meantime members and committees of the legislature showed how educational development was being held back. More than one proposed bill of an enlightened character was introduced, but without avail, since existing practice had not been designed to bring people to the point where they would support an efficient system of schools under popular control. In 1835 the assembly passed a bill to provide for a general system of education, including local scholarships to pay living and tuition expenses of selected students at grammar schools; but the legislative council rejected the measure.

In the same year, however, the amount of the grant to the common schools was increased by £5650, with the stimulating proviso that the District Board could not pay out the allotted amount of public money to a teacher unless the local trustees had ensured provision of at least twice as much for his support. Since the population had more than doubled between 1824 and 1835, the supplementary appropriation did little more than restore the financial support of the earlier date. But it checked the relapse and gave enough to encourage local initiative.

A report of a commission on education showed that in 1838 there were 651 common schools attended by 14,776 pupils in ten of the fourteen districts of the province. Since the remaining districts contained about one-third of the total population, it may be assumed that the total number of pupils was 20,000. From the public funds these schools received the former permanent provision, which had increased only to £3500, plus the augmentation of 1835, so that the total grant was £9150. The commission considered this amount "inadequate to the wants of the province," and recommended that an additional £15,000 be raised by taxation.

As a final commentary on the state of education in Upper Canada at the end of the pioneer period, we may note that the amount of public money expended on the total of 311 pupils reported to be attending the grammar schools was £1400 — an average of about $18.00 a pupil, as compared with less than $2.00 per pupil in the common schools. The disproportionate expenditure in the interests of a few was actually much greater because of the income derived from land endowments used for the support of institutions in York for the benefit or purposes of the Family Compact.

Developments in Upper Canada and other provinces up to 1840 are summarized at the end of the following chapter.

CHAPTER 8

The Transition to Public
Control of Education

MONITORIAL SCHOOLS: ORGANIZATION IN ENGLAND · TEACHING METHODS
ESTABLISHMENT IN NORTH AMERICA · PROGRESS IN THE MARITIMES · IN
LOWER CANADA · IN UPPER CANADA · NON-DENOMINATIONAL CHARACTER
END OF PATERNALISM

THE BEGINNING OF PUBLIC EDUCATION: RECOGNITION OF STATE RESPONSIBILITY
STATE RECOGNITION OF COMMUNITY INITIATIVE · REPRESENTATIVE LOCAL
AUTHORITY · COMMUNITY RESPONSIBILITY · ESTABLISHING AN ACCEPTABLE
CENTRAL AUTHORITY · STATE OF PUBLIC EDUCATION · SUMMARY

This chapter refers to the older part of what is now Canada
from the Atlantic to the western boundary of Ontario. The first
section gives an account of the monitorial school movement,
which marks the transition in urban centres from philanthropic
to public provision of education. The second section surveys
legislation which introduced public support and control of education and summarizes briefly the state of education in the
fourth decade of the nineteenth century.

MONITORIAL SCHOOLS - THE LAST MAJOR EFFORT OF PHILANTHROPY

At the beginning of the nineteenth century in England, and a few years later in Canada, schools of a novel type were greeted with enthusiasm by men and women who were anxious to find some cheap and practical method of giving a little education to the growing hordes of children in cities and towns. The unique advantage of these schools was that hundreds of pupils could be given instruction under a single master, and consequently at little cost. This was accomplished by having superior and senior pupils act as teaching monitors. The novelty was not in the idea, which was centuries old, but in its application. The organization and operation of the school was systematized to a degree which would do credit to any factory, and efficient mass production in education was the result.

Organization in England

As with many types of educational venture that appealed for public support, religious competition stimulated enterprise; but by attacks, by counter-attacks, and by duplication of resources it wasted much of the effort expended. One inventor of a monitorial system in England was Joseph Lancaster, a Quaker, who provided for religious instruction of a non-denominational character most likely to be acceptable to Protestant dissenters. The other inventor was Andrew Bell, a clergyman of the Church of England, who included the catechism in religious content and insisted upon practices and materials of Anglican hue. Schools were established by rival societies: the British and Foreign School Society, which employed the system of Lancaster; and the National Society

for the Education of the Poor in the Principles of the Church of England, which, needless to say, adopted the system of Bell. The two systems, which for simplicity may be identified as the Lancastrian and the National, were essentially alike educationally, although the two founders made much of superficial differences. Both used a large room to accommodate a large number of pupils, who were divided by grade level into several classes. Both used rivalry as a stimulus to effort and as a substitute for corporal punishment. In Lancastrian schools the seats and writing desks occupied the centre of the room, and the stations for oral instruction were located around the walls; in the National schools these arrangements were reversed.

Teaching Methods

Since the most that could be expected of monitors was following instructions to the letter, the teaching was necessarily mechanical; and the response and movements of pupils had also to be carefully regulated to avoid chaos among the one hundred to a thousand pupils at different levels of attainment. "A place for everything, and everything in its place," was one of the Lancastrian mottoes; and the place for a hat, to give one example, was on the pupil's back, where it was held suspended by a string. Bell kept a "paidometer," or "boy measurer," in which everything to the pupil's credit or discredit was recorded.

Actually the precision in routine was pleasing to average pupils, and the more intelligent were relieved of boredom by competition for prizes and by appointment

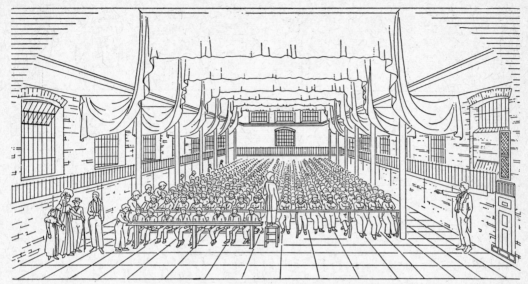

A British monitorial school of the Lancastrian type

as monitors. Although monitorial schools rightly fell into disrepute by the 1840's, when Pestalozzian ideas were beginning to take hold, the systems of Bell and Lancaster had much to commend them in contrast with practices in most other schools in the earlier decades. One of the improvements they introduced was the use of dictation in spelling, which in ordinary schools had been an oral exercise. An extract from a manual for Lancastrian schools on the teaching of writing and spelling shows in operation the slow-moving mechanism of the monitorial system:

When the children are seated the monitor of each class takes a small lesson board in his hand, called a battledore, and at the command of the general monitor, the eighth class monitor stands on the form at the head of his class, and spells a word aloud, adding a simple definition. He is followed by the seventh, sixth, fifth, and fourth class monitors to the lowest. The words thus dictated, are written by the boys. As soon as the monitor has given out his word, he and his inspectors pass down the class, and inspect the writing, pointing out errors, which the boys are re-

quired to correct. They continue to do so, till the general monitor says, "Dictate another word." The eighth class monitor then recommences, followed by the other monitors; and so on, till six words have been written, when the slates are full.

The general monitor then says, "Hands! — Down!" "Clean! — Slates!" "Hands! — Down!" The boys are then prepared to resume their writing, and other words are dictated. About two minutes should be allowed for the writing and correction of one word; so that the slates should be cleaned every quarter of an hour. Less than this time does not allow of the care necessary to improvement, and more often induces idleness.[1]

Yet the monitorial system was the "progressive" educational method of the time and was regarded as going far in the direction of making instruction interesting and appealing to the scholars. The routine in a Canadian monitorial school at the beginning of the day is described in a report on the Madras (National) school in Saint John:

There were generally some two hundred boys in attendance who were taught by about a dozen teachers chosen from their own

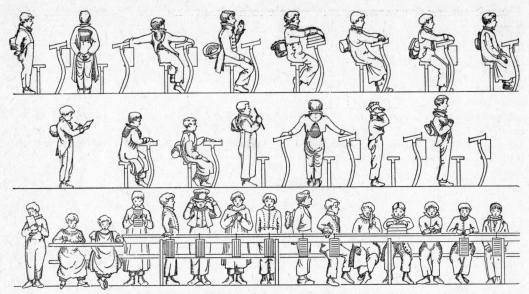

Positions to be taken by a pupil in response to commands in a Lancastrian school
(from an engraving in Lancaster's Manual)

ranks by the master as being the most promising and intelligent pupils. Over the teachers an usher was placed, also appointed by the master, whose duties were analogous to those of a sergeant major in the army — namely to exercise general supervision under direction of his superior. Promptly at the hour for opening, the usher mounted the platform. In the absence of the more modern school bell, a stamp of his foot commanded silence and the attention of the school. A moment later his hand was raised as the signal for prayers; the boys knelt with hands folded whilst the usher repeated sentence by sentence the words of the Lord's Prayer, the boys all repeating each sentence after he had pronounced it.[2]

There was no recess either in the morning or afternoon, since movement to stations and other precision exercises were thought sufficient to relieve the monotony of study.

Establishment in the Colonies

In British North American colonies National schools were established after 1815 in capital cities or towns and in some other larger centres of population. They were initiated or supported by the S.P.G., the S.P.C.K., the National Society, the bishops and clergy of the Church of England, and by the governors and councils. The first step towards the establishment of a Lancastrian school was usually taken by one enthusiastic individual, who might then go to England for financial support. To supervise the operation of the school and to extend the blessing of the monitorial system to other places, a local committee or society was usually formed. Applications for grants-in-aid were made by the legislatures, usually with success. Many of the schools continued in active operation through the third and fourth decades of the nineteenth century.

The larger schools, in which the monitorial system was fully employed, usually had enrolments of from one hundred to five hundred pupils and an attendance at any one time of about half the number enrolled. Whenever possible, a building was constructed to provide a large classroom, commonly about thirty-five feet by seventy feet, and sometimes with a second storey or other separate accommodation for girls. School was kept open throughout the whole year, with only short vacation periods. Partly for this reason and partly because they had had specialized training, the masters of monitorial schools were better paid than other teachers of elementary schools for the people. In some schools, mistresses were employed to teach the girls.

The schools were intended primarily for the poor, and in nearly all cases the pupils were the children of ordinary people. Fees were usually low, and a considerable and increasing number of pupils were taught without charge. School life ranged from a few months to two or three years at most. In some cases however — notably in Halifax — families "of the highest respectability" were sufficiently impressed by the schools to send their children. Governor Smythe in New Brunswick sent his son to the monitorial Central School in Saint John. Although the usual curriculum went no further than the three R's, and possibly sewing for girls, the Halifax National School offered grammar, geography, and French to those who had the aspiration and the means to remain at school longer as fee-paying pupils. These and other characteristics of the monitorial schools will be revealed in the brief accounts that follow of the development of the movement in the various colonies. A full account of the monitorial school development in Canada is given by Spragge, on whose dissertation this section is partly based.

Progress in the Maritimes

In Halifax a Lancastrian school was established in 1815 and given a legislative grant of £200. The next year a teacher was brought from England to establish a National school. For this a building was constructed in 1818 at a cost of over £1900,

more than £1000 of which was raised by subscription. It was attended immediately by 250 boys, and by 150 girls under a woman teacher, and by 1821 had given instruction to 881 children. In 1820 a third monitorial school was established in Halifax by the Roman Catholics under a teacher who had received instruction from the master of the National School. Other schools of the National type were set up in five other towns of Nova Scotia.

In New Brunswick there was an extensive development of National schools, or Madras schools, as they were called. This began with the opening of a school in Saint John in 1818. Shortly after, a building was erected with funds raised by subscription and by the help of a grant from the legislature. The governor was enthusiastic about the project and formed a Madras Board, for which a royal charter was secured in 1819. The next year the Madras Board was paying grants to six other schools, and in 1824 to thirty-nine schools in all. The enrolment in these schools at that time was 4736 and the daily attendance something less than 2000.

The Saint John school with an attendance of close to 200, and some other schools, were undoubtedly of the monitorial type in fact as well as name; but it is doubtful whether the rest were "National" except in the sense of being Church of England. MacNaughton says that one who visited the schools in 1822 found them to be monitorial in name only, and that a committee of the assembly reported a few years later that the Madras schools in rural areas were failures. The schools were supported by the Madras Board, by legislative grants which were fixed at £700 for some years after 1825, by voluntary subscriptions, and by grants from the National Society and the S.P.G. The grants of the latter organization amounted in 1827 to £400, which was distributed among twenty teachers working under the supervision of parish clergymen — an arrangement

The Halifax National School, built in 1818; this building now houses the Nova Scotia College of Art

which suggests that at least half of the thirty-nine schools were to all intents and purposes the same as those sponsored by the S.P.G. before the National system became the fashion.

In Prince Edward Island a National school, called Kent College School, was built in Charlottetown in 1820. The following year it began its work under a Mr. James Breading, who kept his connection with the school until he became a priest of the Church of England in 1839.

In Lower Canada

In the *Quebec Gazette* for August 30, 1810, there appeared an account of a school in New York conducted on the Lancastrian plan. Two years later a teacher of Montreal named Engell, in petitioning the government for a grant or pension, made the claim that he had kept school on a plan similar to the one pursued by Mr. Lancaster and that he had first used it in 1786, twelve years before Mr. Lancaster's epoch-making discovery. About the same time the Reverend Thaddeus Osgood, a minister of views too liberal to escape suspicion, became ex-

cited about the possibility of the Lancastrian system and went off to England from Quebec to collect money. In this he was quite successful, and the Quebec Free School opened in 1814 with an enrolment of 250 boys. A committee for the Advancement of the Education of the Poor in the City of Quebec sought aid from the legislature for the support of this school and the establishment of others. But although the assembly seemed to be favorably disposed to the Lancastrian system, the disapproval of the Anglican and the Roman Catholic bishops caused the governor to withdraw his support and the committee was forced to close the school in 1817.

Church of England organizations in Lower Canada had now been stirred to action. A Diocesan committee of the S.P.C.K. was formed in Quebec in 1818, and a National school was opened a year later in that city. A special building was erected in 1824 with two schoolrooms measuring thirty feet by forty-two feet each, and thereafter the enrolment was in the neighborhood of 200 until 1840. A similar development took place in Montreal, where a National Free School was opened in 1819 and moved to a new building in 1823; there the actual attendance increased rapidly to 300 and remained at about that figure until the 1840's.

In Montreal, in 1822, a British and Canadian School Society opened a school on the Lancastrian plan. This was very successful and had about the same enrolment as the National school. In the following year a branch of the same society at Quebec opened a school, which also continued in operation with about the same attendance as the local National school. There were other Lancastrian societies and schools. In 1826 Osgood again raised money in England and founded there a Central Auxiliary Society for Promoting Education and Industry in Canada, but it was unsuccessful in its educational efforts among Roman Catholic Indians and suspended operations a few years later. The two schools in Quebec built before 1830 and maintained for some years by J. F. Perrault were of the monitorial type.

Between 1829 and 1832 the great Lancaster himself was in the city of Montreal. With characteristic modesty he announced his presence to the public in a printed pamphlet entitled *The Gazette of Education:*

A petition in the handwriting of Joseph Lancaster
(Public Archives of Canada)

Twenty Egyptians are now in Joseph's House in London, being sent there by the Pacha of Egypt to learn the Lancasterian System of Education. In the meantime, Joseph, himself is now, not on the banks of the Nile, but of the River St. Lawrence, making two ears of corn for mental bread grow where only one grew before.[3]

With the aid of a parliamentary grant of two hundred pounds, voted on the motion of Louis Joseph Papineau, he demonstrated and publicized his methods until as usual he ran into personal difficulties.

Of the Lancastrian schools in Lower Canada one of the most important was the Roman Catholic school founded in Quebec in 1822 by the Educational Society of that city. The attendance at this school increased from 254 in 1827 to 490 in 1840. There were smaller schools of similar societies in Three Rivers and Berthier, and schools reported as monitorial at Portneuf, Cap Santé, and elsewhere. The method was in such high favor that some teachers who had few pupils expressed their disappointment at not being able to follow the pedagogical fashion. Other teachers used the monitorial system at least to the extent of having advanced pupils hear the lessons of slower learners.

The monitorial schools in Lower Canada were assisted by government grants both for operation and for new buildings. The first grant was given in 1823 to the Educational Society of Quebec, which also received £683 of the £2783 granted to nine different societies or schools in 1829. In later years these grants were not restricted to organizations operating schools of a strictly monitorial type: for example in three years between 1832 and 1836, the Ursulines at Quebec received £1750 and the Ursulines at Three Rivers £600. Equal grants were not made to monitorial schools of different types: in 1835-36 the Roman Catholic school at Quebec received £560, the Lancastrian schools at Quebec and Montreal £400 each, and the National schools at Montreal and Quebec slightly over £222 each. It is clear from this that the Church of England no longer held a privileged position in education.

In Upper Canada

In the large and sparsely settled province of Upper Canada, conditions were not favorable to the establishment of monitorial schools. In 1815, at Kingston, the Midland District School Society was created with the intention of opening a Lancastrian school, which was in operation as such for ten months after November 1817 in a building erected by the subscribers on a lot which had been granted for the purpose. But the lieutenant-governor on a visit to Kingston made his influence felt; a new teacher was employed, a grant from the S.P.G. accepted, and a National School Society formed. The National school appears to have been carried on for a few years in the 1820's, and a Lancastrian school again for some months about 1827, but the monitorial system did not take permanent hold as it did in the cities of Lower Canada.

Only one monitorial school in Upper Canada had a long and continuous history, the National School at York. It was a creation of Lieutenant-Governor Maitland and his council, who looked upon elementary education as one means of preserving the English and Anglican characteristics of the province. In 1820, grants to common schools were reduced, as we have seen, and the Central School at York was opened under the direction of a master, Joseph Spragge, who had been sent out from England. The building was one that had been erected two years before on what is now the northwest corner of Jarvis and Adelaide Streets, but since the classroom was designed for ordinary teaching it was only twenty and one-half by twenty-eight feet in size. Nevertheless the enrolment at the school increased from less than 100 when it was founded to about 400 when it was closed in 1844. Before 1830 it had two masters and a mistress. It received from the government financial support generous by comparison with that given to other elementary schools — £240 in 1828 and £365 in 1837 — much to the annoyance of those who opposed any special subsidies to Church of England activities.

It was, of course, the intention of the oligarchy in Upper Canada to establish National schools throughout the province. Authorization was obtained from the British government to use part of the university land grant for the purpose and the Central Board of Education was favorably disposed toward the project. But in spite of all efforts no more than four or five schools on the National plan were ever established in Upper Canada, and only one of these, the Central School at York, was of any importance.

Interdenominational Character

The records of attendance at monitorial schools throw interesting light on a question much under discussion today. Apparently it was quite common for the Roman Catholics to attend the same school as Protestants, and this is true both of the Church of England National schools and of the non-denominational Lancastrian schools. At the Halifax National School over 150 Roman Catholic children had been in attendance before 1821. At the National School in York in Upper Canada the attendance of Roman Catholic children in the 1830's was sufficient to cause a noticeable drop in enrolment when a Roman Catholic school was built. In Lower Canada the proportion of Roman Catholic children in Protestant monitorial schools was quite high. At the Lancastrian

Central School,

ESTABLISHED AT YORK.

His Excellency the Lieutenant Governor being desirous to extend the course of Instruction at the Central School so as to embrace all the branches usually comprehended in a good English Education, has directed that it be opened on the 25th instant under a new and improved system of Management.

BOYS SCHOOL.

FIRST DEPARTMENT,

Joseph Spragge, Master.—*English Reading, Writing and Arithmetic, on the principles of Bell and Lancaster.*

SECOND DEPARTMENT,

J. T. Wilson, Master.—*English Reading, Writing, Arithmetic, English Grammar, Book Keeping and Elements of Geography.*

GIRLS SCHOOL.

Rebecca Sylvester, Mistress.—*English Reading, Writing, Arithmetic, and Sewing.*

The Scholars shall pay one Dollar per Quarter for instruction, provided that no family be required to pay for more than two Children at the same time whatever be the number attending.

Such Parents as wish to pay for the Education of their Children at this low rate, have merely to signify to one of the Masters, or Mistress, their intention to send them regularly, in as neat and decent order as their circumstances will permit.

The President and Secretary of the Board of Education will attend, at the Office, on Friday of each week, at 12 o'clock, for the purpose of giving Free Tickets of admission to the Children of Parents who are unable to pay for their Instruction.

York, 19th January, 1830.

A contemporary notice (Public Archives of Canada)

School in Montreal, the attendance figures for years following 1822 show that nearly one-half of the children were Roman Catholic and that there were twice as many Roman Catholics as members of any other denomination. At the National School in Montreal, of the 1000 or more children who attended between 1819 and 1826, no less than 426 were Roman Catholic and only 392 were Anglican, in spite of the fact that this was essentially a Church of England school. Among the pupils attending the British and Canadian School of Lancastrian type at Quebec, Anglicans were more numerous at first but Roman Catholics became the major group when the school was moved from the Upper Town to the Lower Town.

End of Philanthropic Control

In English-speaking Canada, the monitorial school movement was the last important attempt of philanthropic minorities to provide schools for the people as a benefaction or charity. By 1840, or shortly after, schools *for* the people had become, nearly everywhere, schools *of* the people, built and controlled by the people themselves. But to such an extent had the monitorial system caught the fancy of well-known people, that it was advocated with confidence where its unsuitability should have been apparent. Apparently Lord Selkirk thought it might be used with success even in a first school for the Red River settlements. He wrote in 1813 to his agent:

K. McRae is well acquainted with the improved methods which have been introduced with such wonderful effect by Joseph Lancaster and he could in a few weeks organize a school on his plan, if you could pick from among the settlers a steady young man of a cool temper to be employed as their schoolmaster.[4]

A last stronghold of the method was the province of New Brunswick. There the "Thirty-fifth Report on the State of the Madras School" stated as late as 1854: "Long experience has shown that the monitorial system is admirably adapted to economise the time of both Masters and Scholars, and to impart life, energy, and accuracy to the whole course of Instruction." By then, however, there were only seven Madras schools in operation, and the school at Saint John was teaching not only the three R's and the catechism and chief truths of religion, but also geography and history. A method designed to secure memorization of cut-and-dried material had reached the end of its usefulness when the latter subjects were introduced.

THE BEGINNING OF PUBLIC EDUCATION

That education for all children should be provided and controlled by the people was a revolutionary concept in the early nineteenth century. It was not suddenly accepted and applied. On the contrary, the people were compelled by circumstances to do a little and then to acquire by experience the willingness and determination to do more. Action was not taken on principle; the principle was realized in action.

Nevertheless it is possible in retrospect to identify five steps by which publicly controlled education was established. It proved necessary during the first half of the nineteenth century:

(1) to secure recognition of state responsibility;

(2) to have the state recognize community initiative;

(3) to establish a representative local authority;

(4) to overcome extreme dependence and independence and to encourage community responsibility;

(5) to establish an acceptable central authority.

Obviously this process was quite unlike the establishment of state authority in highly centralized systems of education. Although Ryerson in Upper Canada was accused of introducing Prussian despotism, he rightly pointed out that local control of the schools rested with the people. The five steps in the Canadian development will be discussed in order.

(1) Recognition of State Responsibility

The only institutions recognized as having responsibility for education, apart from the individual family, were the church and philanthropic or charitable organizations associated usually with one or more of the religious denominations. In English-speaking Canada no one of these institutions was acceptable to all the people. But in the eighteenth and early nineteenth centuries, governments in the colonies, as in England, recognized the responsibility of religious and charitable organizations by giving them grants-in-aid. Had this policy been maintained, the establishment of public education would have been delayed. Hence the first significant step in the new direction was the regular provision by legislation of state grants paid directly to the schools or to their teachers or trustees.

This step was more easily taken in connection with the grammar schools, in which the privileged and governing minority had a special interest. We have seen that in Upper Canada grants of £100 each were provided in 1807 for the masters of grammar schools, one in each of the eight districts of the province. In Nova Scotia, where two grammar schools had been supported from public funds since the eighteenth century, the Grammar School Act of 1811 made regular provision for grants of £150 each to grammar schools in ten counties or districts. In New Brunswick, where aid for three grammar schools had also been previously given, grants of £100 each were provided for schools in each of five other counties by legislation of 1816.

For elementary schools New Brunswick introduced a grant of £10 to each parish in 1802 and grants of no more than £20 to each school by legislation of 1816. Nova Scotia made similar provision for a grant of no more than £25 to a school by an Act of 1811. It may be observed, incidentally,

that in these two provinces grants for elementary schools and grants for grammar schools outside the major towns were established together — in 1811 in Nova Scotia, and in 1816 in New Brunswick. In Upper Canada grants to common schools were introduced nine years after the appearance of grants to grammar schools — that is, in 1816, when an amount not exceeding £25 was made available to the teacher of an elementary school. The two types of education were more sharply distinguished in the western province.

Newfoundland must be regarded as a special case because of the persistence of Church responsibility. In 1836, however, three years after the establishment of a legislative assembly, an education act was passed to provide a grant of £2100, most of which was to be distributed through nine district boards. This established only in part the principle of state responsibility, since a denominational system evolved and became fixed in 1874, when the grants were apportioned to the various religious denominations according to population. Because of this unique development, no further reference to Newfoundland will be made in the present section. A separate account of developments in that province will be given in a later chapter.

The province of Quebec is also exceptional. The recognition of state responsibility had not the same significance for the French-Canadian people, since the Roman Catholic Church was for them no less universally acceptable and no less comprehensive and non-partisan than the state. Grants introduced in 1829 were of importance, however, because they were voted by the assembly and marked a recognition of the responsibility of that body in educational finance; for obvious reasons the assembly was more acceptable to the Roman Catholic population than the English-speaking Protestant oligarchy or its creation, the Royal Institution for the Advancement of Learning. But the dema-

Petition for a school, 1830 (Public Archives of Canada)

goguery and the secular control over education associated with the assembly's largesse did not please the church. What might have happened is mere speculation since the veto of the council and the rebellion of 1837 cut short the educational activities of the assembly.

Only this first step towards public responsibility was taken in connection with the grammar schools in the early nineteenth century. Reference will be made, therefore, almost exclusively to common schools in the sections immediately following.

(2) State Recognition of Community Initiative

Before grants were voted to common schools it had already become the practice in many localities for the people themselves to take the initiative in building or providing a school and obtaining the services of a teacher. The Common School Acts of 1811 in Nova Scotia and of 1816 in New Brunswick and Ontario marked state recognition of this practice by voting assistance from the public treasury. To illustrate: a committee of the legislature in Upper Canada reporting before the passing of the Act of 1816, said with reference to the establishment of common schools that "the people have shown among themselves a laudable zeal in this particular which ought to be aided." It is important to note that the state did not itself take the initiative in setting up schools or designate where they should be located, as was done when money was voted for grammar schools.

The significant innovation in elementary education was that public money formerly voted only to religious or philanthropic societies was now voted in recognition and encouragement of community action by the people themselves. Common school legislation in all three provinces was intended to provide grants only after the people locally had built a school or provided money for a school and its operation; and either the original legislation or a subsequent amendment required that the teacher should have discharged his duties for six months before the public money would be forthcoming. State recognition of such action was a radically new departure since the assumption had formerly been that educational initiative by the people was neither possible nor desirable.

The failure to recognize and encourage local initiative was the basis of Protestant criticism of the grants voted by the legislature in Lower Canada during the 1830's. There were men who offered to assist the government "by distributing moneys to School Masters or for School Houses upon warrant of inspector of accounts or other office" on a commission basis, and those who operated schools were ready to receive the money. But a committee of the legislature in 1831 warned its colleagues against "placing public money in the hands of societies or individuals practically liable to no sufficient responsibility, or regular or strict accountability, unless they at the same time have to apply a considerable portion of their own money along with that of the public." The phenomenal increase in the number of schools in Quebec between 1829 and 1836 was achieved not by local initiative aided by government but rather by government initiative in providing financial means for setting up local schools.

(3) Establishing a Representative Local Authority

Even today it is sometimes forgotten that people have little interest in enterprises over which they have no control and even less enthusiasm about paying out money to support them. When aristocratic views dominated in government, unusual perspicacity was required to see the necessity of local education authorities who represented the people. This essential step was not achieved at the same time in all provinces. It came late in Nova Scotia and New Brunswick, where abortive attempts were made to get local communities to provide free schools long before the power of electing trustees was granted — an incongruity sufficient in itself to defeat any free school legislation, even if the people had been prepared in other ways to accept such an advanced idea.

Early practice in the Maritimes, based on a distrust of the people, was to make the justices or the courts responsible in some measure for local administration of schools. In New Brunswick, in 1802, the justices of the general sessions were themselves designated as local trustees; in 1816, justices of the peace were entrusted with the appointment of two or more trustees in each of the towns or parishes. Not until 1858 were the three trustees elected. In Nova Scotia, the act of 1811 called for the nomination of six trustees by a meeting of the inhabitants who were freeholders or possessors of an income of forty shillings a year in real or personal property, but the court of sessions selected only three of the six for appointment. For a time under an act of 1826 the inhabitants nominated only three trustees, who were therefore virtually elected; but in 1832 this practice was changed, and the three trustees were designated by a board of two commissioners appointed by the governor. In 1845 the rate-payers were empowered to elect two of the three trustees, but the third was still to be appointed by the board of school commissioners. Only in 1850 were all three trustees elected by the rate-payers.

In Lower Canada because of the unique position and authority of the Roman Catholic Church among the French-Canadian people, the fabriques, designated as local authorities in 1824, may be regarded as acceptable if not representative boards. In the same province between 1829 and 1836 school acts called for the election of five trustees in each of the designated educational districts. After the rebellion, in 1841, provision was made again for local boards, elected but with little power. From 1846 it became the established practice to elect five school commissioners for the parish or locality and also to permit, on request, the election of three trustees by dissident residents, usually Protestants. In Upper Canada the standard North American procedure of electing three trustees was established immediately by the first common school legislation of 1816.

(4) Encouraging Community Responsibility

An essential step towards public control of education was the renunciation of dependence by a large proportion of the population. Since poorer families had been unable or unwilling to look after the education of their children, organized philanthropy, sponsored largely by the churches, had provided the poor with schools. Government grants to philanthropic organizations, like those first paid to educational societies in England in 1833, and like many of the early grants in the Canadian colonies, were paternalistic in that they financed a gift conferred on the poor and did not encourage the people themselves to take over the responsibility. This philanthropy and paternalism, however praiseworthy its efforts, had to be repudiated if the people were to act for themselves. Nothing retarded the development of public education more than the continued willingness of people to accept charity. When state grants for education were introduced, they were too often regarded as cash donations from the ruling class, a charity that was accepted with more eagerness but productive of less advantage than the free education provided by philanthropy. The final withdrawal by 1836 of the Society for the Propagation of the Gospel from educational operations in North America marked the almost complete disappearance of paternalistic charity, which had to cease before schools of the people could be fully established. Unfortunately it did not mark the end, among all people, of a preference for accepting aid instead of contributing to community effort.

STATE AID AND COMMUNITY INTEREST

The means of stimulating local initiative was the offering by the state of sufficient financial assistance to make a start possible without giving enough to subsidize lethargy. We have seen that Upper Canada took no risk on that score, especially after the reduction of the grant in 1820 — a measure for which the council and the Church of England were not solely responsible, for the bill passed the assembly on its second reading by a vote of 12 to 5. The reason for the legislation cited by the lieutenant-governor, that "a large amount paid to the district treasurers remained unemployed," seems hardly at first glance to warrant a cut in the amount payable to the individual teacher from £25 to £12 10s. A similar reduction from £25 to £15 was made the same year in Nova Scotia, and a reason may be found by examining the various amendments in the act to correct abuses in that province, where, according to Harvey, "a number of schools had been organized more with a view to securing government assistance than to further the aim of the act."[5] Economy in provincial grants was an unpalatable but necessary tonic for developing local authorities.

The Nova Scotia legislation of 1811 required that from £50 to £200 should be raised locally before the trustees could collect a government grant of one-half of the amount so raised. If the local funds were obtained in part by assessment, no charge was to be made for tuition in the schools; but if they were raised by subscription, rate-bills or fees were in order. The second option was the one chosen by local communities, so that an amendment was passed in 1819 to require that free places be provided for some children at least. The same amending legislation contained the revealing regulation that no trustee could exact a commission for his services and that clerks of the peace could

charge no more than one-third of their regular charge for issuing half-yearly certificates. After 1821 the grant was payable only after the trustees had given full particulars about enrolment and attendance and had also given assurance that one-half of the required local funds had actually been raised and used for the support of the school.

Precautions of this kind may reasonably be interpreted as evidence of local corruption, but the next action of the council shows that they may also have been motivated by prejudice. During the next two years the council refused to vote any money at all to the common schools because its members were unwilling to "concur in any bill which provides for the education of the children of the Rich and the Poor indiscriminately." The educative effect of the grant was hampered no less by the hostility and impatience of the government than by the continued lazy dependence and propensity to cheat the government shown by some local people.

THE EXPERIENCE OF NOVA SCOTIA

In 1824 the lieutenant-governor of Nova Scotia appointed commissioners to investigate educational conditions in the province, with the result that voluminous reports regarding the schools were accumulated. After examining some two thousand of these documents, Harvey published in 1934 a detailed analysis of what happened between 1811 and 1824. He shows, for example, that Annapolis township had received a grant for five schools in 1813 but for only three in 1821 and one in 1822. Evidence of this kind led him to the following conclusion:

There is no doubt that all of the counties and districts were stimulated to action in varying degrees when the Provincial Treasury was wide open; but it is not so clear that they all realized to an equal degree the aim of the Act, or thought of more than sharing a distribution of public funds. This rather doubtful virtue becomes apparent immediately after the Act required that a number of poor children be taught free, in return for the Provincial grant. It becomes even more apparent when a certificate was required to the effect that the money subscribed or assessed, in order to get the smaller provincial allowance, had actually been paid and devoted to its intended use. These tests found most of the townships wanting and leave a rather unfavorable impression. But certain facts emerge quite clearly. The government wanted to encourage the establishment of common schools and to that end gave assistance freely for nine years. They then tried to see if the various communities had got the idea and would in turn assist the poorer parents to receive some benefit for their children also. They found that very few were willing to comply with these conditions, preferring rather to do without any provincial aid. Suspecting further that £50 were not raised each year for the support of schools seeking provincial aid, they insisted on the more rigorous regulations of 1821; and, with few exceptions, they found their suspicions confirmed. It would seem, therefore, that, in the main, the Act of 1811 had not created a love of education *per se,* or a recognition of the fact that certain "essential parts of general education" are necessary to "persons of every rank and station in civilized society." Rather, the majority still were inclined either to do without schools or to provide more or less irregularly for their own children exclusively, and to leave the poorer classes or children of the more scattered settlements in ignorance.[6]

Grants were renewed in Nova Scotia by legislation of 1826. As in Upper Canada, by a provision of the Common School Act of 1816, the erection of a schoolhouse was made a necessary condition for the receipt of a grant. The legislation provided a special appropriation of £2500 for the education of the poor. It also made cautious provision for raising local funds by assessment when two-thirds of the rate-payers agreed. But conditions did not improve until an act of 1828 increased the total grant and attempted to apportion it more equitably, with consideration of local ability to pay. Whereas the returns for 1827 showed that only 44 schools had been established under the act of the previous year, 204 schools had been established or come under the operation of the new Act by the end of 1828.

DEVELOPMENTS ELSEWHERE

There was less experimentation in most other provinces, but the principle of giving moderate assistance to encourage local initiative was applied everywhere. In New Brunswick substantial grants totalling £3000 were introduced in 1816. In Prince Edward Island in 1825 the government began to pay one-sixth of the teachers' salaries — probably too little to be effective. On the other hand, in Lower Canada between 1829 and 1836, something in the neighborhood of £24,000 annually, or nearly one-fifth of the revenue of the province, was paid out with no permanent progress towards the development of local responsibility or the establishment of a regular system. In Upper Canada, where the people were comparatively well off, the grants to common schools were relatively small, even after the increase of 1833. It is probable that considerably larger grants might have been paid in Upper Canada without danger and with good effect towards the expansion of local responsibility and the improvement of education.

DISINTEREST AMONG THE WELL-TO-DO

The growth of community initiative was impeded no less by the excessive independence of some individuals than by the complete dependence of larger numbers. Some who possessed or earned enough money to consider themselves unique had no interest in schools for ordinary people. This disinterest extended even to the grammar schools, which fell into a sorry state of neglect in the third and fourth decades of the nineteenth century. We have seen that in Upper Canada they attracted only 311 pupils in 1838. In New Brunswick, in 1846, it was found that seven grammar schools drawing £100 each from the public funds had among them a total enrolment of only twenty pupils in Latin and seven in mathematics and were instructing only a few other pupils in elementary subjects. In Nova Scotia by the 1820's, the local grammar schools, in contrast with the institutions of reputation at Halifax, Windsor, and Pictou, were languishing and at the verge of expiration. People of extreme independence preferred private schools or the more pretentious establishments maintained by government. They showed no concern about local schools apart from an objection to contributing to their support. Little could be done about this attitude until a majority of the people were converted to the maintenance of schools by taxation — an achievement of a later period.

UNEVEN PROGRESS

Progress, of course, was very uneven among people and communities whose attitudes and values differed because of their previous experience and present resources. For example, in the early nineteenth century there was extreme educational destitution in settlements of fishermen in Prince Edward Island and Nova Scotia. It is said that in 1830 in an Acadian community of 330 families and 2500 people only three young men under instruction by the curé had any education and that the rest were wholly illiterate and ignorant. Under such circumstances it is no wonder that the people locally were unwilling to do their part to take advantage of the assistance offered by the government. To interest the Acadians in education and to induce them to take co-operative action in founding schools required the indefatigable leadership of individuals, notably of the Abbé Sigogne, to whose efforts during the first four decades of the nineteenth century later Acadians were largely indebted for the appreciation of education that prevailed among them.

PROGRESS NONE-THE-LESS

In typical communities, however, from Prince Edward Island to Upper Canada, where some of the people were ready to act, there was less need for local individual leadership than for assistance by judicious and regular government grants. By 1840 the operation of the grants had accustomed the people to take responsibility for the provision and maintenance of schools.

(5) *Establishing an Acceptable Central Authority*

Once the machinery of community responsibility was in working order, but only then, something in the nature of a central authority became desirable. It was needed in order to define better-than-average practice and thus to make laggard communities aware of their deficiencies. In a later period central authorities went much further than this to stimulate and direct progress and to develop some uniformity of content and standards throughout their respective provinces. But in the early period, before local initiative was fully ensured, strong central administration might have produced a stultifying bureaucracy. The problem at first was to provide not a powerful but an acceptable central authority and to move slowly in setting up controls. Progress towards a solution was made by the rejection of unacceptable partisan authorities and by the introduction of very moderate requirements as a condition for the receipt of grants.

We have seen how in Upper Canada a Central Board of Education with minority bias failed to gain acceptance during the ten-year period 1823-33. In Lower Canada, the Royal Institution, with greater initial prerogatives but less chance of gaining favor, expired in the early forties. In Upper Canada and in the Maritime Provinces, the movement towards the establishment of a central authority that would command respect was initiated by setting up intermediate boards to examine and license teachers. In Upper Canada, district boards, appointed by the lieutenant-governor, were given this duty in 1824. In Nova Scotia, a Board of School Commissioners, similarly appointed, was established in 1826 and strengthened in 1832; it had the same duty and other duties as well, including inspection of schools. In New Brunswick, by an act of 1837, the lieutenant-governor was empowered to appoint county boards of education to examine teachers and issue licences. These first moves towards the establishment of central authorities were motivated no less by anxiety about the infiltration of republican ideas through teachers from the United States than by desire to improve instruction. But they established precedents for more definite and comprehensive action.

Central authorities recognizable as such were set up at the end of the period. Prince Edward Island had a superintendent of education from 1837 to 1848 and re-established the office in 1853. In Lower and Upper Canada, and in Nova Scotia, provincial boards of education appeared in 1841, and superintendents were appointed soon after — in 1842 and 1850 respectively. In New Brunswick the first provincial board was created in 1847 and the first superintendent was appointed in 1852.

The State of Public Education, 1830-1840

An attempt will be made here to give a brief survey of conditions in the fourth decade of the nineteenth century. This will serve as a summary of progress in the six provinces up to that time and as a starting place for topical discussion of certain aspects of education in later chapters. Since statistics of the time are neither comparable nor accurate, a tabular presentation would be misleading, and quantitative achievement must be indicated in general terms.

UNRELIABILITY OF STATISTICS

As an illustration of the difficulty, let us look at the figures in reports of enrolment in the schools. In the first place, all such enrolment figures of the nineteenth century must be discounted heavily if comparisons are to be made with present conditions, since the average attendance was then seldom more than fifty per cent of the enrolment, whereas now it is in the neighborhood of ninety per cent. In the second place the school year in the early nineteenth century was no more than six months, if the teacher could be retained that long; and in places where another teacher was employed in the summer, the enrolment was added to the winter figures, although there may have been some overlapping.

With only these factors taken into consideration, it is apparent that early enrolment figures must be divided by three or four if they are to be interpreted as indicative of the number of children actually in school and of the days of instruction received, in terms of criteria used today. When school enrolment is stated in relation to total population, allowance must also be made for the higher proportion of young people at the earlier time; in 1842 the population of Canada West (Ontario) between the ages of five and sixteen was twenty-eight per cent of the total population, whereas a hundred years later in Ontario children from age five to sixteen inclusive represented only twenty per cent of the total population.

On the other hand the impression should not be gained from low enrolment and attendance figures that only a small proportion of the population ever went to school; the fact is that many children attended school, but most of them only for about one-third of the total number of months that children spend in the first six or eight grades today.

Lack of confidence is increased by discrepancies between enrolment figures in reports only a few years apart. In Upper Canada, for example, we have seen that the report of a Commission on Education indicated a total enrolment of 20,000 in common schools in 1838. Yet Ryerson, on the basis of very imperfect returns compiled by his predecessor as superintendent, estimated the number of pupils in common schools in 1842 at just under 66,000. Even allowing for a growth in population of more than twenty per cent and for a much larger grant under the rather ineffective legislation of 1841, one can hardly credit so great an improvement within so short a time. A marked change in the number of schools in operation and pupils enrolled was possible from year to year because a smaller or larger number of schools might be closed for lack of a teacher. But even this fact raises a question about the significance of enrolment figures when complete data for only occasional years is available. For all of these reasons some of the following brief statements of what was achieved in the various provinces are less generous than those which accept contemporary statistics and estimates at their face value.

NEWFOUNDLAND

The people of Newfoundland, whose number increased from about 70,000 to 85,000 in the decade 1830-40, were dependent mainly on philanthropic or religious school societies, of which the Newfoundland School Society, with some forty schools, was the most important. Private

schools and voluntary instruction by individuals helped to compensate in some measure for educational resources which were quite inadequate even by the standards of the time. When state grants were introduced in 1836, it was reported that there were seventy-nine schools with 4614 pupils on the roll, or about one in sixteen of the population. Conditions varied greatly in different parts of the island; in the St. John's district one in eight of the population was at school; in Trinity Bay, one in twenty; in the district of Fogo, one in fifty-seven. There was no system of public education similar in structure to the systems which were seeking to encourage local responsibility in the Maritime Provinces and in Upper Canada. It is likely that only a minority of the children received even the most meagre education.

PRINCE EDWARD ISLAND

In Prince Edward Island a report in the Journal of the Legislature for 1842 showed an educational advance even greater than the gain in population.

In 1833 the population was 32,292, the number of schools 74 and pupils 2176; and the proportion of pupils to population was 1 to 14.8. In 1841 the population was 47,034, the number of schools 121, of pupils 4356; the proportion was then 1 to 10. Progress could be attributed largely to the appointment in 1837 of a superintendent, John McNeill, for if we can believe another report the number of schools and pupils when McNeill was appointed was only 51 and 1553 respectively. Apparently there was a gain until 1844, when 134 schools enrolled 5272 pupils, or better than one pupil for every nine persons in the population. But in 1848, when the office of superintendent was dropped, the proportion of the population enrolled in schools was reported to be only 1 to 14. And statistics of this kind were characteristic of the period. The most favorable data are probably the least trust-worthy. The truth may have been reflected by a report of 1836, which showed an average attendance of only 860 pupils in 28 schools benefiting from government grants, which stated that there were 30 other schools not assisted by the govern-ment, and which estimated that altogether only a small percentage of the children were in school. Taking into consideration all these data and the fact that the first educational legislation and the first grant came as late as 1825, one is led to con-clude that during the decade 1830-40, on the average, only about one-half of the children received an average of twelve months' schooling and that the rest re-ceived very little, or none at all.

NOVA SCOTIA

The population of Nova Scotia during the decade grew from about 135,000 to 215,000. Reports on the number of teach-ers and pupils in the province show a consistent increase for some years pre-ceding 1835, when there were 530 teach-ers and 15,292 pupils. These figures may be regarded as a reasonably accurate basis for the inference that during that period two-thirds of the children attend-ed school for an average of from twelve to eighteen months. Statistics for the 1840's give a much more favorable impression, but the more careful returns after 1850, when William Dawson was appointed as superintendent, suggest that the higher enrolment figures were inflated. The cost of common school education in Nova Scotia in 1835 was about $5.00 a pupil, or in all about $77,000, of which more than $27,000 was paid by the government; hence the grants in relation to the popu-lation of the province were at least fifty per cent higher than in Upper Canada. This fact and the longer history of Nova Scotia also make more plausible its statis-tics of the 1830's, which show a consider-

ably higher standard of education in that province than in the others.

NEW BRUNSWICK

New Brunswick's population increased from about 90,000 to 155,000 during the decade. Reports on education between 1845 and 1852 suggest that about one in eleven of the total population was at school as contrasted with about one in nine for the same years in Nova Scotia. It seems likely, therefore, that the stand-ard of education in 1835 was proportion-ately lower than that suggested for Nova Scotia: perhaps only a little more than half of the children received an education averaging from twelve to eighteen months each.

UPPER CANADA

In Upper Canada the population of 215,000 in 1830 had doubled by 1840. But, as we have seen, the enrolment in com-mon schools in 1838 was only 20,000 — or one person in twenty of the total popu-lation at the time. This ratio is no better than that revealed by school returns about ten years before and much inferior to the ratio of one in eight claimed in the early 1840's. Yet even if it be assumed that the method of counting heads was relatively strict and that a generous interpretation may be given to the data for 1838, the conclusion must be that hardly more than one-half of the children in the 1830's at-tended school for periods averaging twelve months in length.

LOWER CANADA

In Lower Canada, where the popula-tion was about 500,000 in 1830 and 715,-000 in 1840, estimates of enrolment in all types of schools near the end of the decade are about twice as high as the numbers reported in common schools in Upper Canada. For example, Dunkin's report placed the number of pupils in 1835 at 38,387 for grant-aided country elementary schools, and at 12,000 to 15,000 for city schools of all types and country academies. But reports in the late 1820's give a very different impression: in Lower Canada in 1829 the number of schools is stated to be 78 and the number of scholars to be 3772; in Upper Canada in 1828 the number of schools is given as 291 and the number of scholars as 7731.

It seems unlikely that even with the assistance of the generous grants in the 1830's the French-Canadian population could have made before 1840 a recovery which placed them in a position educationally superior to that of the English-speaking people of Upper Canada. The cities and some of the more populous parishes were comparatively well served by the schools of religious orders, including the Ursulines, Sisters of the Congregation, and the Sulpicians, and also, of course, by monitorial schools. In the country the fabrique schools were supplanted or reinforced by the mushroom growth of grant-aided schools under elected school boards in the 1830's. But the quality of the teachers and of the instruction in rural schools was represented in the reports of Buller and Durham to be very wretched indeed. In the reports of a painstaking school visitor around 1840 the French-speaking population in several rural districts, including some of the more prosperous, was represented as apathetic towards education or as unable to pay for schools because of heavy prior demands of the church.

The educational position of the English-speaking population in Lower Canada, though it was not admirable, could hardly fail under other circumstances of the time to be superior to that of the French-speaking people, or of the people in Upper Canada. A reasonable overall estimate is given by Woodley in her study of education in Quebec — that "roughly one-third of the children of the province were receiving an education in 1836."[7]

Summary

It is probable that in the various provinces between 1830 and 1840, from one-third to two-thirds of the children received from twelve to twenty-four months of schooling. Except in monitorial and other town schools they were likely to receive this formal education in periods of no more than six months at a time and at irregular intervals. Among English-speaking people the diffusion and extent of education appears to have been relatively good in Nova Scotia, followed probably by New Brunswick and Lower Canada, by Upper Canada, by Prince Edward Island, and by Newfoundland, in that order. One should remember, also, that except in special circumstances there had been no development as yet of prescribed courses of studies or textbooks, of inspection or supervision, or of teacher training. Hence educational achievements, qualitatively, were as low as or lower than the achievements quantitatively.

As for higher education, universities and colleges had a relatively early start in Nova Scotia, where King's College was established in 1789, Dalhousie in 1818, and Acadia in 1838. In New Brunswick, a college created in 1800 obtained in 1827 a royal charter as King's College, which later became the University of New Brunswick. In Lower Canada, the medical faculty of the future McGill University opened in 1829. In Upper Canada, King's College had been granted a charter in 1827 but was not opened until 1843. Some other colleges and academies had begun to offer more advanced work.

By 1840, therefore, most of the bare framework of systems of public education had been erected in the eastern provinces. The structure was much more advanced when it served as a model for the western provinces towards the end of the century. Part Three of this book continues the history of various wings of the administrative building; meanwhile the next chapter on classroom practice will lay the foundation for subsequent discussion, in Part Four, of the development of philosophy and methods.

CHAPTER 9

A School of the People

**THE BUILDING · EQUIPMENT · BOOKS · PUPILS · THE TEACHER
CLASSROOM ORGANIZATION AND CURRICULUM · METHOD · TEXTBOOKS
A DAY IN SCHOOL · AN ADULT WORLD**

This is a description of a school that might have been found in 1830 anywhere among English-speaking people in Upper or Lower Canada or in the Maritime Provinces. There were, of course, differences between one school and another – even greater differences than now, for there were then no developed systems of public education to produce an outward uniformity. In some places the buildings were larger or smaller and the teachers better or worse. But the attempt here will be to describe a common school of the ordinary type, with characteristics frequently mentioned in reminiscences of teachers and contemporary reports, and to add only occasional references to less usual conditions and practices.

The Building

The school is a log structure about 18′ x 20′ in size. It is crudely made and finished. Into the chinks between the logs clay or moss has been pressed to keep the wind from whistling through in winter, but the interior is not lathed and plastered. Our school has a wooden floor, although some did not. It has two small windows in each side wall and a huge fireplace at the far end opposite the entrance door.

Equipment

The furniture is rough and scanty. In the centre of the single room are about eight benches, 5 feet long and 10 inches wide, made by cutting slabs from logs and boring holes at the corners for the supporting legs. There are no backs to these benches to support the bodies of the pupils; and the benches, though not the pupils, are all of the same height, so that the feet of the little ones dangle above the floor and the legs of the taller boys are stretched out as a hazard to those who make their way to the front to say their lesson. Under the windows at one side of the room a long slanting board has been fastened to the wall and strengthened by supporting brackets of wood; this serves as a writing desk for senior pupils, who may drag up one of the benches for a seat. A deep cut in the board directly opposite a window serves as a sun dial to indicate the time for a break at noon. The teacher has a stool or a chair and a high desk of the lectern type, cased in to provide storage space.

Other equipment is meagre. There is no blackboard. There are no maps, pictures, globes, or other visual aids. There is not even a bell. There is a water pail at the back of the room, with a mug or dipper, although the water has sometimes remained frozen in the pail at this remote distance from the fireplace while the youngsters near the front were roasting in the heat of a roaring blaze. The older pupils have slates and slate pencils; they have also, if they are lucky, copy-books, and quill pens, although the scarcity of paper makes it necessary to use, for practice, any scraps of wrapping or writing paper that can be found. The quill pens will require frequent mending by the teacher with his penknife, and the ink is a home brew of maple bark, to which lampblack and iron sulphate have been added. Anyone who asks for a ruler is told to make one. The teacher's desk contains aids to learning in the form of stimulants — certainly a supply of birch rods for application to the hides of the pupils, and sometimes a bottle of whiskey for the pedagogue himself.

Books

A scant and shabby collection of miscellaneous books completes the equipment of the school. Each pupil has what his parents have given him — the book or books appropriate to his age among textbooks purchased for the eldest child in the family. Different pupils may have different spelling books or arithmetics, and it is unlikely that the teacher has one of every kind. It is not worth the teacher's while to insist that all pupils have the same books, since that would be regarded by the parents as a new-fangled and extravagant idea and would make it even more certain that his tenure of the school would be short, as it probably will be in any event. The parents have the excuse that books are not easy to buy, except in larger towns, and expensive even there; they can hardly be expected to waste their money on the whims of every new teacher that comes along.

The most frequent controversies regarding books have to do with the use of American textbooks laudatory of institutions in the United States and derogatory of England and the English throne. In a later chapter this question will be discussed in its broader context of Canada-United States relations, as will also the associated issue of employing American teachers, who are mentioned only briefly in the present chapter.

Pupils

Those who attend the school are the sons and daughters of ordinary people — of farmers, workmen, small tradesmen, and all who make up the great majority. Except under unusual circumstances they do not include the children of office-holders in the government, commissioned officers of the army, doctors, clergymen of the Church of England, and others of established wealth or position. Since most

An artist's reconstruction, based on the author's suggestions, of our conjectural school of the people

of the population is rural, our typical school is located in the country and the pupils have to walk some distance to reach it.

Our pupils are from five to twelve years of age. In some districts where school is conducted in the summer months by a woman teacher, those who attend in winter are older boys of eight to twelve and some of the older girls whose help is not required on the farm. But in our district even the youngest come in winter if the distance is not too great. When we happen to have a good teacher, and especially after the school has been closed for some time, you may find among the scholars a few young men and women of twenty years of age or more. The enrolment at our school in 1830 is 25 and the number in anything like regular attendance is about 15. We hope that the school will remain in operation for a full six months. In Lower Canada the number of pupils is often twice as large and the school term only four months in winter and four months in summer. But our en-rolment and length of term are, on the whole, more common.

The Teacher

Our district has had difficulty in hiring a teacher. Those willing to teach in common schools are usually men unfitted by physical condition, temperament, or circumstances for regular employment in some more remunerative occupation. Those who admire the good old days may question this statement. Since the reputation of teachers as a class has seldom been enhanced by contemporary literature, they will not be inclined to accept, for example, the impression of a Nova Scotia teacher gained from Haliburton's *The Clockmaker*. But they will find reports and factual accounts of the early nineteenth century no less severe in their criticism of schoolmasters. Take for illustration the following statements of contemporaries in Upper Canada.

Gourley, in his Statistical Account of

Upper Canada, wrote that the common schools in 1817 were inundated with "worthless scum under the character of schoolmasters." An essay on education by J. M. Flindall in the Kingston Gazette stated in 1818 that "in many townships a teacher of twelve months' standing is a prodigy; one of as many weeks the most common," and mentioned "continual accounts given in the public papers of the most abominable impostors finding employment and encouragement as schoolmasters." A legislative assembly report for 1831, moved by Dr. Charles Duncombe, attributed conditions to inadequate grants:

. . . insufficiency of the common school fund to support competent respectable and well educated teachers has degraded common school teaching from a regular business to a mere matter of convenience to transient persons and common idlers who often stay for but one season and leave the schools vacant until they accommodate some other like person; whereby the minds of the youth of this province are left without due cultivation or what is still worse frequently with vulgar, low-bred, vicious and intemperate examples before them in the persons of their monitors.[1]

But if that report be regarded as special pleading, the same cannot be said of the evidence given by the Reverend Robert McGill before the Commission on Education already mentioned as reporting in 1839:

I know the qualifications of nearly all the common school teachers of this district and I do not hesitate to say that there is not more than one in the ten fully qualified to instruct the young in the humblest department.[2]

Some of the better teachers were immigrants who had not yet found themselves in the new country and who took teaching as a temporary job, to the bewilderment of the pupils who might hardly have learned to understand an English dialect before a Scotsman turned up next year. Some of the best were "slick Yankees," whose skill and assurance made them popular with children and parents in spite of disapproval from many higher authorities.

As the teacher of our school the trustees have employed another common type — an old soldier, not seriously incapacitated. Though lame and slightly stooped, he can get around readily enough and is handy with the tawse or the rod, or even with his fists if need be. He has taught in a rougher school than this, where he was compelled to break through a door barricaded by some older pupils and establish himself by licking the culprits one by one. Although there are occasional outbreaks in our school, he has the pupils in terror of his wrath and usually under control. In short he is an unhesitating disciplinarian and therefore has the reputation among the parents of being a very good teacher.

Our teacher has only a common school education himself, for people of his class did not attend secondary schools. He has had, of course, no training for teaching. Yet he is better equipped than some, since he has a knowledge of grammar and is prepared to teach it if required in addition to reading, spelling, writing, and arithmetic. He knows his pupils by name and has them classified as smart or lazy. He even knows their parents, since he boards with each family in succession for a week at a time. For his six months' hire he will get $60.00 from the government money and hopes that he will be able to collect a total of $40.00 more from the parents of most of the children attending the school.

All the incidental work about the school has to be done by the teacher or by the pupils under his direction. There is no caretaker to clean the windows or sweep up the floor. The parents of each pupil must supply a share of the fuel; if they do not, the teacher may send boys out to the woods with an axe. The trustees may occasionally visit the school to see how things are going, but they leave the teacher to his own resources.

Classroom Organization and Curriculum

This is an ungraded school in the strictest sense of the word. There are no classes, books, or grades to indicate level of achievement. For the most part pupils progress at their own rate. Most of the assignment and recitation is individual, although not individualized in the sense of being adapted to the capacity or interest of the pupil. For convenience the teacher may call up two or three or more pupils together; but there is little expository teaching of any kind and there is virtually no class activity of the type that became familiar later when the question and answer method was introduced. It would therefore be misleading to suggest that there is any class teaching or class organization within our 1830 school. Nevertheless the following scheme will give an idea of what is attempted, what books are used, and what is ordinarily accomplished by pupils who remain at school for varying lengths of time.

Conjectured Organization of a School of the People, 1830

FIRST YEAR: Learning the alphabet; learning to read and spell syllables and short words; reading short-word sentences. The books: *The English Spelling Book,* by William Mavor, D.D.; or one of the following: *The New Guide to the English Tongue,* by Thomas Dilworth; *The New England Primer; The American Spelling Book,* or its revision, *The Elementary Spelling Book,* by Noah Webster, LL.D.

SECOND YEAR: Oral spelling and reading continued; reading and memorizing New Testament verses. One of the above books and The Bible.

THIRD YEAR: Oral spelling separate from reading; reading the Bible and a more advanced reader; writing; arithmetic. Books of the second year and/or one of *The Scholars' Spelling Assistant,* by Thomas Carpenter; *Cobb's Spelling Book,* by Lyman Cobb, A.M.; and probably at least one of *Introduction to the English Reader,* by Lindley Murray, or *The English Reader,* by Lindley Murray; and probably *The Tutor's Assistant,* by Francis Walkingame; or, less likely, some other arithmetic textbook by Strachan, Dilworth, Gough, Gray, Daboll, Bonnycastle, or Colburn; plus a ciphering book.

FOURTH YEAR: Spelling, reading, writing, and arithmetic continued; possibly some grammar and geography; probably three of the books indicated for the third year — say Cobb's *Speller,* Murray's *English Reader,* and Walkingame's *Arithmetic;* and possibly one of *The Principles of English Grammar,* by William Lennie, *English Grammar,* by Lindley Murray, *English Grammar,* by Samuel Kirkham; possibly, also, either *A Practical System of Modern Geography,* by J. Olney, A.M., or *The Elements of Geography,* by Jedidiah Morse.

FIFTH YEAR: Spelling, reading, writing, and arithmetic continued; grammar and geography; possibly history; books as indicated for the fourth year; and possibly *The History of Rome,* and *Abridgement of the History of England,* by Oliver Goldsmith.

All of the above is based on six months' instruction each year.

Method

The method almost universally used was (1) with little or no preliminary explanation, to give the individual pupil an assignment; (2) with little or no questioning, to hear the individual pupil recite the material assigned for memorization. Ex-

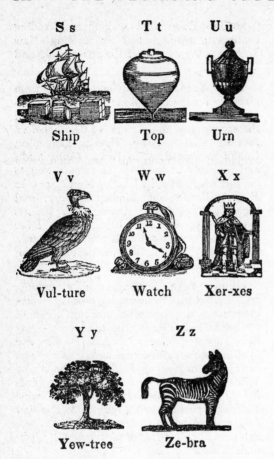

A page from Mavor's Spelling Book (Toronto, 1851)

kind; faithful to his friends, generous to his enemies, warm with compassion to the unfortunate; self-denying to little private interests and pleasures, but zealous for public interest and happiness; magnanimous, without being proud; humble, without being mean; just, without being harsh; simple in his manners, but manly in his feelings; on whose word we can entirely rely; whose countenance never deceives us; whose professions of kindness are the effusions of his heart: one, in fine, whom, independently of any views of advantage, we should choose for a superior, could trust in as a friend, and could love as a brother—this is the man, whom in our heart, above all others, we do, we must honour.   BLAIR.

SECTION XIII.

The influence of devotion on the happiness of life.

WHATEVER promotes and strengthens virtue, whatever calms and regulates the temper, is a source of happiness. Devotion produces these effects in a remarkable degree. It inspires composure of spirit, mildness, and benignity; weakens the painful, and cherishes the pleasing emotions; and, by these means, carries on the life of a pious man in a smooth and placid tenour.

Part of a page of Murray's English Reader *(1830)*

ercises given subsequently for practice were treated in the same way. If the method did not work, the pupil — not the teacher — was punished for laziness. The method aimed primarily at rote memorization of textbook content and secondarily at ability to apply memorized rules without deviation. It required above all docility and obedience in the pupil, and in the teacher an ability to make punishment an imminent reality. Such teaching relied slavishly on the textbook, and an examination of a few of the books in common use will show more clearly what the content was and how it was presented.

SPELLING

Mavor's *English Spelling Book* was a favorite text for beginners. It was distributed gratis to the schools about 1830 by the Central Board of Education in Upper Canada and was approved by a committee of the New Brunswick legislature in 1838 as decidedly the best of the spelling books examined. Following the plan of all such books, it starts with an illustrated alphabet and proceeds through syllables and words of increasing length to dissyllables and polysyllables, interspersing the word lists with reading lessons in sentence and paragraph form. By page 80 the words in columns have become strange and formidable; yet the reading lessons, though insufficient and not overly attractive, are at least simple and free from oppressive moralizing.

The little volume of one hundred and sixty-seven pages in all contains a mass of other content, included because the author was aware "that a Spelling Book frequently constitutes the whole library of a poor child." The latter part of the book gives measurement tables, prayers, moral exhortations and observations, worldly advice on getting good interest, a few pages of encyclopaedic facts, some stodgy poetry, a little grammar, composition, French and Latin, and catechisms on the duties of loyal churchmen and subjects. A little of everything could be taught from this book if the teacher were so minded and the pupil had no other text.

The more advanced spellers, like Cobb's *Spelling Book* and Carpenter's *Scholars' Spelling Assistant* had no pictures; the latter book had no reading lessons. These books were mainly or entirely composed of lists of words and differed only in some peculiar complexity of arrangement. What strikes the modern observer is the ingenuity of logic and the want of common-sense psychology displayed by all compilers. Carpenter, for example, made a boast of his elaborate sub-classification according to accent, in lists arranged at the same time alphabetically and according to the number of syllables. Neither he nor any other author was influenced in the slightest degree by the suitability of the words to the capabilities or experience of the child. Of such spelling-books Edgeworth had said:

The formidable columns rise in dread succession. Months and years are devoted to the undertaking; but after going through a whole spelling-book, perhaps a whole dictionary, until we come triumphantly to spell "zeugma," we have forgotten how to spell "abbot" and we must begin again with "abasement."[3]

In the 1840's the Superintendent of Education in Upper Canada condemned the spelling-books as an "ingenious device for relieving the teacher of labor and imposing it needlessly and perniciously upon the pupil." Some of the spelling-books attempted to improve the understanding of the pupil by laconic definitions of the meaning of words, wherein "nightly" was explained by "nocturnal" and "rice" was identified as "a foreign esculent grain."

READING

Murray's *English Reader*, if school reports can be credited, was the most widely used book of the time. Anyone who examines it today may be tempted to question the veracity of teachers who claimed to have succeeded in getting youngsters to read it, but since it went through untold editions one must accept the fact of its use and marvel at the youthful stamina of scholars who persisted and survived. Even in 1835 J. O. Taylor, author of an early American book on education, *The District School,* described it as "a book for a literary man, but entirely unfit for children." But that is a mild assertion, which avoids the risk of criticizing the crushing respectability of the pious volume.

According to Murray himself the *English Reader* contained "pieces in prose and verse selected from the best writers, designed to assist young persons to read with propriety and effect; to improve their language and sentiments, and to inculcate some of the most important principles of piety and virtue."

The pieces are classified and arranged as narrative, didactic, argumentative, descriptive, and so on; but one of these categories, "pathetic," might appropriately have embraced them all. Opening at random we find such titles as "The misery of pride," "The mortifications of vice greater than those of virtue," "On the immortality of the soul," "The close of life," and, under poetry, "The death of a good man a strong incentive to virtue," "A man perishing in the snow; from whence reflections are raised on the miseries of life," and "The pursuit of happiness often ill-directed." Almost without exception the selections are so ponderous in style and so uniformly oppressively moral in tone that even the most docile student of 1830 must have smoldered with rebellion. There is no attempt in the book at gradation of material: the first sentence reads, "Diligence, industry, and proper improvement of time, are material duties of the young."

Murray's *Introduction to the English Reader* is simpler in language but similar in tone. The first two sentences are: "To be good is to be happy," and "Vice, soon or late, brings misery."

ARITHMETIC

Walkingame's *Tutor's Assistant,* the most widely used arithmetic textbook at the time, is an almost perfect exemplar of the rule method. When a new topic is introduced, the author first gives a definition and a rule to be memorized, then sometimes further instructions, then usually a few examples worked out without explanation, and finally other examples or questions to which only the answer is given. For example, one of the basic operations is introduced as follows:

Multiplication

Teaches to repeat a given number as many times as there are units in another given number.

The number to be multiplied is called the Multiplicand; that by which we multiply is the Multiplier; and the number produced by multiplying is the Product.

Rule. When the multiplier is not more than 12, multiply the units' figure of the multiplicand, set down the units of the product, reserving the tens; multiply the next

figure, to the product of which carry the tens reserved; proceed thus till the whole is multiplied, and set down the last product in full.

Example:
713097
  x 4
———
2852388

Say 4 times 7 are 28, set down 8 and carry 2; 4 times 9 are 36 and 2 are 38, set down 8 and carry 3; 4 times 0 (naught) and 3 are 3, set down 3; 4 times 3 are 12, set down 2 and carry 1; 4 times 1 are 4 and 1 are 5, set down 5; 4 times 7 are 28, set down 28.

Between the rule and the example the multiplication table to 12 x 12 is given. After the example are fourteen questions, then an explanation of how to multiply by numbers between 12 and 20 and a few examples, and then the following:

When the multiplier consists of several figures, multiply by each of them separately, observing to put the first figure of every product under that figure you multiply by. Add the several products together, and their sum will be the total product.

This is rapid progress, made within the space of hardly more than a page.

Whether or not the pupil had an arithmetic text like Walkingame, he usually kept a ciphering book. In this he copied, under the appropriate headings, definitions and rules followed by examples previously worked out on a slate and corrected by the teacher. The method was to have rules copied and memorized and to have examples worked out, corrected, and copied. There was very little explanation at any stage, and no teaching by inductive methods. No occasion was given, if it could be avoided, for requiring the pupil to think, devise a solution of his own, or understand a procedure he was learning to follow. Obedience to the rule was the one desideratum. Of the pupils it might truthfully have been said, "Theirs not to reason why, theirs but to do or die." Understanding came, if at all, after the process had been mastered.

GRAMMAR

Murray's *English Grammar*, first published in 1795 and distributed in annual editions over the English-speaking world for more than fifty years, was the standard textbook of the early nineteenth century. It begins with the definition, then undisputed, that "English grammar is the art of speaking and writing the English language with propriety." It then enlightens the pupil by setting forth the major divisions of grammar — "Orthography," "Etymology," "Syntax," and "Prosody." Murray intended his text to be committed to memory, for which purpose he was "felicitous to select terms that are smooth and voluble." To "effect a compromise between presentation of whole and part," he used heavy and light type; the former gave definitions in technical language to be memorized by the pilgrim on his first journey through the book, the latter used other words to make the formal statements "more intelligible to the student." The scholar went through the book, "getting up" one page after another and simply repeating what he had memorized. He might then have to repeat the process, for only after "getting up the book" was he considered ready for parsing, the favorite exercise. The disheartening mass and nature of the material to be memorized gave Murray reason to hope that he had provided "an employment calculated to exclude those frivolous pursuits, and that love of ease and sensual pleasure, which enfeeble and corrupt the minds of many inconsiderate youth."

Parsing, to judge from examples given by Murray, was a fearsome exercise, far removed from the "art of speaking and writing." Martyn, in his study of Grammar in Elementary Schools, selects these two illustrations:[4]

Specimens of Etymological Parsing
"VIRTUE ENNOBLES US"

Virtue is a common substantive, of the neuter gender, the third person, the singular number, and in the nominative case. (Decline the noun.) *Ennobles* is a regular verb active, indicative mood, present tense, and the third person singular. (Repeat the present tense, the imperfect tense, and the perfect participle.) *Us* is a personal pronoun, of the first person plural, and in the objective case. (Decline it.)

Specimens of Syntactical Parsing
"VICE PRODUCES MISERY"

Vice is a common substantive, of the neuter gender, the third person, the singular number, and in the nominative case. *Produces* is a regular verb active, indicative mood, present tense, the third person singular, agreeing with its nominative *vice* according to Rule 1 which says: (here repeat the rule). *Misery* is a common substantive, of the neuter gender, the third person, the singular number, and the objective case, governed by the active verb *produces*, according to Rule XI which says, etc.

Barren exercises of this kind in English were obviously a carry-over from the teaching of Latin. But it is doubtful whether one teacher in a hundred in the common schools would have essayed such an arduous path. There is evidence that parsing in common schools was less thorough and more mechanical. In his *Pioneer Life in Zorra*, Mackay wrote (p. 247): "The pupil was taught to parse a word, not by studying its relation to other words, but simply by committing to memory a list of 'prepositions,' 'adverbs,' 'interjections,' et cetera. He knew that a certain word was a preposition, because he had committed to memory a list of prepositions, in which that word occurred; and so on with the other parts of speech."

It is only fair to say that the authors of the other two grammars mentioned, Lennie and Kirkham, were both opposed to purely memoriter methods. Kirkham states that he is "anxious to have the absurd practice, wherever it has been established, of causing learners to commit and recite definitions and rules without any simultaneous application of them to practical examples, immediately abolished." Lennie went so far as to suggest preliminary remarks and explanations by the teacher in assigning lessons. Both of these grammars contain exercises, including a good proportion of false syntax to be corrected. In its later editions at least, Lennie's grammar was much lighter in style than the older books, even to the point of mild attempts at humor in some of the examples.

GEOGRAPHY

Geography textbooks by Olney had a considerable circulation in Canada. A fifty-fourth edition of, *A Practical System of Modern Geography* published in 1847, was partly catechetical but largely descriptive in character and followed almost wholly an arrangement by political divisions of the world. The introductory catechetical section under Political Geography begins:

Q. What is a village?
A. A small collection of houses.
   Is this place a village?

Q. What is a city?
A. A large collection of houses, usually situated on a river, or near the sea.
   Is this place a city? How many cities can you mention?

This is indicative of the method to be used by teachers throughout the book.

Almost one third of the 300 pages are devoted to the United States, so that other countries receive relatively scanty attention. The first paragraph descriptive of the United States reads:

The United States are the most interesting and important division of the western continent. They are distinguished for the excellence of their government, the rapid increase of the population, and for the intelligence, industry, and enterprise of the inhabitants.

British America on the other hand is described as being "mostly inhabited by Indians, among whom the whites have established trading houses for the purpose of procuring furs and skins." This type of thing was naturally annoying to the people in the Canadian provinces, even if these provinces received individual attention later. To illustrate further, Nova Scotia is said to have "a cold, damp climate, and in most parts a thin and unproductive soil."

A Day in School

As suggested in the previous chapter, there was no uniformity with respect to the length of time a pupil might remain in school. There were no compulsory attendance laws, there was no certainty that a teacher could be found for a particular school in any one year, and there were other determining factors in the attitudes and circumstances of the parents. Practically all who went to school for any time learned to read. A majority of those who attended the common schools made at least a beginning with writing and arithmetic. Very few remained long enough to study geography and grammar. These statements are generally true of all provinces, but should be interpreted and modified in the light of what was said about provincial differences in the previous chapter. In our typical school there were eight pupils enrolled in what we have called the first year, nine in the second, seven in the third, one in the fourth, and no others.

Picture the school-house just described somewhere in a Canadian province in the year 1830. The teacher has swept up the floor and has the wood in the fireplace blazing. Sam, one of the older boys, has brought in a fresh supply of logs. The teacher hobbles to the door, opens it, and shouts: "All in! All in!" When the pupils have hung up their hats and coats on pegs along the back wall and taken seats in the centre of the room, the teacher calls them to order. He has several older pupils recite a verse of the New Testament which they have been told to memorize, and assigns another verse for the following day. The pupils then settle down to work — not in silence, for there is the buzz of many lips saying over their lessons for the day. The teacher then calls up Tom and Marjorie, two young beginners, to his desk at the front of the room.

THE READING LESSONS

"Fetch your books," he says. "Give them to me. Now, Marjorie, can you say the last six letters of the alphabet?"

Haltingly Marjorie succeeds.

"That's fine. But ye'd have larned them a lot faster if ye'd had a good book like Mavor with pretty pictures. That tarnation Webster your father gave you — fit only for republicans and sinners."

The teacher points to the letter *M*. "Now Tom what's that letter?" "*N*," says Tom.

"No! What's this nixt letter?"

"*N*."

"That's right. But they can't both be *N*. The first letter is *M*. What is it?"

"*M*."

"Now the two of you take your seats and really larn that alphabet. I want to start ye on the syllables tomarra."[5]

The teacher limps about the room and glowers at any who are not repeating their lessons. Three of the older pupils are at the writing-desk and the teacher is called on twice to go over and mend a pen. There is a minor disturbance when Tim on his way to the back of the room to get a drink trips over Sam's legs, but

the teacher is patient and contents himself with kicking Sam's shin while telling him to keep his big feet out of the way. Then he calls on Tim, who comes to the front of the room with his Mavor.

"Now Tim let's hear you read the first line of Lesson 5."

Tim reads: "a-b, ab; a-c, ac; a-d, ad; a-f, af; a-g, ag; a-l, al."

"That's fine. Maybe we could turn to Lesson 9 and look at some of the sentences. See if you can read them."

After some difficulty Tim manages to pronounce appealing titbits like these: "He is up," "We go in," "So do we," "It is so," and "Lo we go."

The next to come up is Will. He reads the last part of a story about boys who mistreated a dog: "It is a sad thing when boys beat poor dumb things: if the dog had not been good, he would have bit them; but he was good, and ought not to have been hurt."

"Well," said the teacher, "I guess you are ready to go on to the next lesson — words of two syllables. Let's hear you read the first word."

In Mavor the first six words appear as follows: *ab-ba, ab-bot, ab-ject, a-ble, ab-scess.* Poor Will has a hard time getting it into his head that "ab-ba" is one word; but he manages at last to stumble through the spelling: a-b, ab; b-a, ba and to pronounce the word *abba*, although he has no idea what it means, and probably the teacher hasn't either.

They get through the next two words but Will reads the fourth word: a, ay; b-l-e, blee and pronounces it "*ayblee.*"

"No," roars the teacher impatiently, "a-b-l-e, *aybul;* you ought to know that."

Will tries to defend himself: "Well, *a* is ay and *b-l-e* is blee, so why isn't it *ayblee*? How can you tell?"

"I'm telling you and you remember," shouts the teacher. "Read the next word."

"a-b, ab; s-c-e-s-s, skess; *abskess.*"

"That's right. Now larn those six for tomorrow."

SPELLING

And where does all this lead to?

We shall see, because the teacher is making an announcement: "We are now going to have the advanced class in spelling. The rest of ye young 'uns can listen, and keep in mind if ye work hard and get up yer lessons properly, ye'll be able to spell words like these some day. Now Matt, Saul, Martha, and Hanna, you come up. Toe the mark."

The four line up along a crack in the floor.

"First we'll take some words from page 101 of Mavor. That Yankee teacher down the road won't know these words and when we have the spelling match with his school we'll get the better of them. Spell *apostolically*."

The youngsters spell the words syllable by syllable. Anyone who misses goes to the foot of the class. A few other words on this page are *archiepiscopal, beatifically,* and *genealogical*.

"Now we'll take some words from Webster because that teacher down the line will be using it to get an unfair advantage of us. I told ye to get up the list at the top of page 124. Spell *cachexy . . . chalybeate . . . synecdoche . . . bronchotomy . . . ichthyology*. That's fine. Now we'll take a few from Carpenter. I told ye to get up page 98 — some of the words of five syllables. Spell *amphitheatre . . . anathematize . . .* Here's a good one: *assafoetida*. Good work, Matt. We'll win the spelling match on Thursday night for sure."

DISCIPLINE

Just at the point when the teacher is expressing his satisfaction at the progress of the brighter pupils, an uproar breaks out at the back of the room. It appears Zeke has poured a dipper full of water down Sam's back and that Sam immediately lets loose with the first blow of a wholehearted scrap. The teacher picks up a stout rod and manages to separate the two combatants, whom he hales to the front of the room.

Then, to the delight of some of the younger pupils but to the horror of one or two, he selects two more rods and gives one to each of the boys with the command, "All right, you two varmints. Lay on and cut jackets."

The two boys who were eager enough to get at each other a few moments before proceed with rather less enthusiasm to flog each other with the beech rods. But the teacher has a way of lending energy to their blows. If he sees that either is inclined to spare the other, he himself gives the more lenient one a stinging lash with the rod he holds in his own hand and all the while keeps urging the two to lay on harder. When this unhappy event is over, quiet reigns for a time.

ARITHMETIC

The teacher calls up Matt and Sol — the advanced class in arithmetic. They hand over their copies of Walkingame and the following dialogue ensues:

TEACHER: Well, Sol, how about the rule of three? Have you learned the rule?

SOL: Yes, sir, but I don't know what it means.

TEACHER: Well, give the definition. What's simple proportion?

SOL: 'Simple proportion teaches to find a fourth from three given numbers; two are always of the same name and one of the same name with the number sought.' Please, teacher, what kind of sum does that rule work?

TEACHER: Well, look at the example: If 9 yards of cloth cost £6 10s., what will 72 yards cost? Now, Matt, you give the definition.

MATT: 'Simple proportion teaches to find

a fourth from three given numbers; two are always of the same name and one of the same name with the number sought.'

TEACHER: Well, what are the three given numbers?

MATT (*after a pause*): 9 yards, £6, 10s, and 72 yards.

TEACHER: Right. Hold down your books. Now, Matt, you state the rule.

MATT (*in a sing-song; he has learned it by rote*): 'Place that sum for the second term which is of the same name with the number sought. Consider whether more or less be required by the question. If more, place the less of the two remaining terms for the first and the greater for the third. But if less be required, place the greater for the first and the less for the third. Multiply the second and third terms together and divide the product by the first. The quotient will be the answer.'

TEACHER: All right. Now say the first sentence again.

MATT: 'Place that number for the second term which is of the same name with the number sought.'

TEACHER: Well, what is the 'number sought'?

MATT: I don't know. I suppose that's what I've got to find out.

TEACHER: Now, don't be stupid. Read the example again.

MATT: 'If 9 yards of cloth cost £6 10s. what will 72 yards cost?'

TEACHER: Now what are you trying to find out?

MATT: How much 72 yards cost?

TEACHER: Well, what kind of name will the number be that tells that?

MATT: It will be pounds and shillings.

TEACHER: Then by the rule, the second term will be the pounds and shillings. Write that down. Now say the next sentence of the rule.

MATT: 'Consider whether more or less be required.'

TEACHER: Well, is more or less required in that example? Will 72 yards cost more or less than 9 yards?

MATT: It will cost more.

TEACHER: Then what does the rule say?

MATT: 'If more, place the less of the two

remaining terms for the first and the greater for the third.'

TEACHER: Well, what are the two remaining terms?

MATT: 9 yards and 72 yards.

TEACHER: And which is the less?

MATT: 9 yards.

TEACHER: Then put that for the first term, and the other for the third. What next does the rule say?

MATT: 'But if less be required . . . '

TEACHER: But you know less isn't required. Skip that, what does it say next?

MATT: 'Multiply the second and third terms together and divide by the first.'

TEACHER: Well, isn't that easy?

Matt scratches his head dubiously. Saul looks completely baffled. They stare at the problem as worked out: 9 : £6   10s :   72

$$72$$
$$9\overline{)468 .. 0 .. 0}$$
$$£52. \text{ Ans.}$$

They then go back to their seats to work at the exercise in Walkingame.

MORE DISCIPLINE

Later in the day the teacher has a chance to get back again at Zeke. Zeke, though an older boy, has never been able to get past page 24 in Walkingame — subtraction of money weights and measures. He comes unhappily to the front to recite the following rule:

Rule. Subtract as in integers, only when any of the lower denominations are greater than the upper, borrow as many of that as make one of the next superior, adding it to the upper, from which take the less; set down the difference, and carry 1 to the next higher denomination for what you borrowed.

When Zeke bogs down at "adding it to the upper," a bright young lad named Bill, prompts by hissing "from which take the less." But Zeke can go no further even when motivated by a stinging blow on his already sensitive back. He is warned to have the rule up by three o'clock or prepare for a worse licking than any he has received so far.

Then the teacher turns to Bill and asks him whether he thinks that ten minutes of the peg would quiet him down. The peg is a device whereby the hair of a restless boy can be pegged to the wall at a height to keep the boy standing on tiptoe for the period of the penalty. There are holes in the wall one above the other, about an inch apart, from four feet to slightly over six feet above the floor. Actually our teacher has never used this instrument of torture, but it remains in the schoolroom as a reminder of a teacher who did and as a constant threat to noise-makers in school.

An Adult World

Those who have a nostalgic admiration for the good old days may think that few schools were as bad as this. There were at least as many that were worse as there were schools that were better. There is a wealth of information about them in the first six volumes of Hodgin's[6] *Documentary History of Education* and in the first two volumes of his *Schools and Colleges of Ontario,* and corroborating evidence in contemporary accounts elsewhere and in local histories. To understand the reason for educational practices of the period, one has only to realize what reliance was placed on set forms — on crystallized articles of belief, on fixed codes of conduct, on the concept of a static society, on shibboleths about the propensities and treatment of the young, on rules of thumb for this and rules of thumb for that, on standard remedies, on made-up prescriptions of subject matter, and on traditional methods of teaching. To have a child read a sentence in praise of virtue must have a good effect; to have him memorize the sentence must make that effect more permanent. Who could think otherwise when to doubt was a ma-

jor offence and to test such assumptions a process almost unknown?

The adult formulae for the improvement of the young were applied without thought of the reaction of the child. His only virtue was receptivity and obedience. With the intention of facilitating the learning process, material was arranged in the logical order helpful to those who have knowledge to organize but often meaningless to the youthful learner. Hence formal content without significance had to be memorized, not understood. For this uncongenial task there could be only one motivation — the fear of punishment. It was not the difficulty of the work which made the rod necessary, but the complete absence of any other motivation.

Yet the pioneer school was not ineffective as judged by the values of the time. It helped to ensure routine obedience and a show of respect to elders and uncritical acceptance of concepts and notions approved by those in authority. The pioneer school discouraged the independence of thought and the ability to co-operate that might have been used by the people to their own advantage. Although content and method were backed by force and sometimes perhaps by conscious deception, the child was at least spared any hypocritical pretence that he was being taught to think. He was told what opinions to express and what rules to follow.

It is a truism, however, that the school usually lags a generation or two behind the new movements and more advanced thinking of the time. By 1830 reform was in the air and livelier minds were unhampered by the cloddish stuff still prevalent in elementary education and in ordinary lives. In succeeding chapters, we shall see how complacency regarding this old-time adult-centred education for children was upset by economic and political developments favorable to a new social and educational philosophy.

CHAPTER 10

The West

The regions now covered by the four western provinces had a relatively short history under European settlers before systems of public education were established. Since settlement was late, the early period of educational history is chronologically out of line with the corresponding period in older provinces. But it had the same essential characteristic — a beginning of educational work under paternalistic auspices.

At the beginning of the nineteenth century all British territories west of Upper Canada were controlled as a field of operations by the Hudson's Bay Company. Although this monopoly was challenged by the North West Company with headquarters in Montreal, the challenger was forced to come to terms and to unite in 1821 with the more powerful organization. The rule of the Hudson's Bay Company continued until 1869, when the territories were transferred to the newly formed Dominion of Canada. The company was interested in the fur trade, not in colonization, and the white population did not increase greatly until the last part of the nineteenth century.

Manitoba

The first area of the west to be settled was located in what became the province of Manitoba. In 1811 Lord Selkirk procured from the Hudson's Bay Company, in which he had acquired a controlling interest, a large tract of land on the banks of the Red River, extending southward into Minnesota and North Dakota. Impoverished Scotsmen and other settlers from Britain came by sea to York Factory on Hudson Bay, then south by river, lake, and land to this new home. Although harassed by the North West Company, by swarms of locusts, and by Red River floods, the inhabitants of the area were said to be sufficiently numerous by 1820 to send 500 Red River carts to the buffalo hunt. But the white and part-white population was hardly 4500 twenty years later, and only 12,000 in 1870, when the province of Manitoba was formed.

The early settlers in the Red River area included not only the Scots, but Irishmen, Orkneymen, Englishmen, and numerous French-Canadians. As time passed, the white men were joined by their offspring born of Indian mothers. The census statistics of 1871 show 1565 whites, 5757 French half-breeds, and 4083 English half-breeds, so that there were more French-speaking Roman Catholics than English-speaking Protestants in the total population. A few of the latter, as agents and employees of the Hudson's Bay Company, were outpost representatives of commercial society. But the rest became accustomed to a way of life not characterized by driving ambition and persistent industry, although severe hardships and heavy work were often unavoidable. Manners and morals were less closely supervised than in agricultural communities of the older colonies. These conditions, which persist among the *métis,* or half-breeds, even today, exerted a stronger influence in the early nineteenth century than the educational traditions of European civilization.

ROMAN CATHOLIC SCHOOLS

Among the Indians and French-speaking people the Roman Catholic Church strove from an early date to extend, maintain, and strengthen the Christian faith. In July, 1818, Father Provencher and two companions arrived in the colony; by the time snow fell they had a house contain-

ing a chapel, and in the latter they opened a school. The following year the missionaries had two schools, in which they taught reading, writing, and the catechism. In 1821 they introduced the teaching of Latin, and shortly afterward they began to give instruction in agriculture and weaving to the natives.

Father Provencher was anxious, also, to have special schools for girls. As early as 1819 he expressed a desire to have teaching sisters come to the area. Ten years later a first school for girls was opened by Angelique Nolin, the part-Indian daughter of an employee of the North West Company. This young woman, who had been sent east for her education, taught for a number of years. But the priest, then Bishop Provencher, continued until 1844 to pray: "Oh, that I might have some religious, religious, religious!" In June of that year his repeated efforts to obtain this help met with a first success when four Grey Nuns arrived from Montreal. A year later the sisters had eighty pupils in their school.

In 1845 further religious assistance came with the arrival of the first Oblate fathers. As part of their service to the colony they taught senior pupils at St. Boniface. Then Christian Brothers came out to take charge of elementary instruction in the same centre. In 1857, when the number in attendance had increased to fifty, the school, then known as the College of St. Boniface, moved into a newly erected building of its own.

By 1872 there were seventeen Roman Catholic schools. Up to that time they had been maintained almost entirely by the unselfish efforts of teachers devoted to the spiritual and temporal improvement of their fellow men. Some financial assistance was obtained from parents able to pay and some from the Hudson's Bay Company, which realized that an instructed population would improve business. In 1833, to cite an instance, the Council

Fort Garry, in the Red River Colony

of Rupert's Land voted £100 for a Roman Catholic school.

But the hard work and sacrifice was borne by the religious. The nuns at St. Boniface were up at half-past four; after hearing mass and having breakfast, some went out to visit families in need of help, others sewed or washed clothes, and still others taught in the school, which was attended by boys as well as girls. By any modern standard, educational facilities were meagre and the achievements more heroic than extensive and solid. Nevertheless the beginning, made under extreme difficulties, was truly impressive.

Not all of the remaining white population were English-speaking and Protestant. Most of the Scots spoke Gaelic, and Selkirk expressed the hope that they would find teachers of that tongue and not be in a hurry to learn the "language of the Yankees." Some were Roman Catholic. But since the majority of those who did not speak French were, or became, English-speaking, and were at least nominally adherents of a Protestant Church, all other educational efforts may be grouped as English-speaking Protestant.

PROTESTANT SCHOOLS

What may be regarded as the beginning of English education in the Red River area? Schoffield in his *History of Manitoba* says that the Hudson's Bay Company brought out three teachers in 1808 at salaries of £30 each; but if these men came to the west as teachers, they apparently found other work more pressing and exciting than teaching school. There is a record that school was conducted for the boys and girls on the ship that brought out the fourth party of Selkirk settlers in 1815 and that "it proved a source of entertainment for the adults as well as a benefit to the children."[1] Newfield says there is conclusive evidence that a school was opened on the banks of the Red River on January 16th of that same year. But in spite of Lord Selkirk's expressed anxiety to see schools established, the first persistent educational effort dates from the arrival in the colony in 1820 of the Reverend John West, who served for four years as chaplain of the Hudson's Bay Company. He was, of course, a priest of the Church of England.

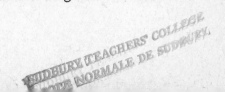

In his journal in 1821, West stated his purpose: "to erect in a central situation a substantial building, which should contain apartments for the schoolmaster, afford accommodation for the Indian children of the Settlers, enable us to establish a Sunday School for the half-caste population, and fully answer the purpose of a church for the present."[2] He used instead a log building, which was repaired to serve as a teacherage and a school. This was occupied by George Harcourt and his wife, who taught the sons and daughters of settlers and of the Indians. The curriculum stressed religious instruction and reading; it included other fundamentals for the white children, household arts for the girls, and agriculture for the Indian boys. West claimed in 1823 that the latter took delight "in hoeing and planting their separate gardens."

Several other schools were opened by Anglican clergymen during the next few decades at different places in the colony. Soon the usual pattern of differentiation by sex and social status was revealed. Continued efforts with Indian children were marked by the erection, in 1833, of an agricultural school with the characteristics of schools of industry in England, for the carding and spinning of wool were introduced later "to assist in clothing the children, and to teach them habits of industry and economy." At the elementary level there were Sunday schools as well as day schools; the former acquired a special importance when religious instruction in the latter became less denominational and definite.

Those at a higher social level could send their daughters to a school opened in 1828 for young ladies in the families of gentlemen in the service of the company. They might have their sons attend the school at St. John's which had been founded by West and which had become a boarding school in 1833. This school was subsequently combined with a similar institution in a neighboring parish to become St. John's College in 1866. A few people at the highest economic level had governesses for their daughters and sent their sons to school in Montreal and across the Atlantic for an Old Country education.

Many of the Scottish settlers were anxious to have the services of a Presbyterian minister and a school of their own. They established an elementary school of the ordinary type in 1849 and finally obtained a clergyman of their own faith two years later. This school, which soon began to offer secondary education also, became the basis of the College of Manitoba, which was established in 1870.

The description in Garrioch's *First Furrows* of St. Mary's parish school, built at Portage la Prairie in 1855, gives a graphic impression of earnest efforts to provide education under rigorous pioneer conditions:

It was a log building of the frame style. It was forty feet by twenty with walls nine feet under ceiling, was thatch roofed and the walls were daubed within and without with what was then called white mud, which, however, was many shades on the wrong side of white. No paint was laid out on this building except on the blackboard, which, of course was black, but there were white lines on one side to form staves for music. On the sunny side of the building were three twelve-light windows, the lower halves raisable, and underneath them and fastened to the wall, was a desk twenty-five feet in length. A large chimney built against the centre of the west wall was the only means of heating. The chimney end of the building was reserved for the girls, of whom in the school's best days, there were from twenty-five to thirty. The other and more frigid zone, was allotted to the boys, of whom there were about an equal number, and it goes without saying, that as their faces were instinctively turned toward the warmer place, there were depicted upon them expressions of envy as well as admiration, and also a look of disgust at one's chivalry having to stand such an icy trial.[3]

These Church of England parish schools used books published in England by the Society for the Promotion of Christian Knowledge, and were therefore similar to the S.P.G. schools in the older colonies. Once a week all pupils together were instructed in the Church catechism. When pupils had learned to read by use of a primer, they did much of their reading in the Bible — first in the four gospels, and when they were further advanced, in various books of the Old and New Testaments.

From this brief account of early education in the Red River area it will be clear that the church had a primary responsibility in providing schools, as had previously been the case in the older colonies. The Anglican Church Missionary Society sometimes contributed the whole of the £40 ordinarily paid to a teacher as salary. As a rule, however, the parents were expected to pay something — perhaps five dollars a year — towards the cost of a child's elementary education. As a subsidy to be divided among teachers, the Hudson's Bay Company set aside revenue from certain sources, such as fees for marriage licences. The Company did not make regular direct grants-in-aid to all schools, but did vote money — in one case £25 annually — to encourage the efforts of a teacher. In 1833, for example, the sum of £100 was voted to the Reverend D. T. Jones and his wife for the deep and lively interest they took in the improvement of the young folk committed to their care and for the unremitting attention they paid to their health and comfort.

By the 1860's the appurtenances of civilization had begun to change conditions in the west. A steamboat, not the first in operation but called the "Pioneer," was launched on the Red River in 1861, and by 1874 there were seven steamers. Mails and supplies, which had begun to trickle in from the south in the fifties, soon came regularly by that route rather than from England via Hudson Bay. In 1876 the first grain was shipped out by river steamer, and in 1878 a railway was constructed. A first newspaper, *The Nor'-Wester* had appeared in 1859, and by 1880 there were three dailies in Winnipeg alone. Entertainment of a mildly intellectual kind began to supplement social gatherings for dancing and other recreation, as may be illustrated by the formation at Portage la Prairie in 1868 of a "Young People's Mutual Improvement Society," which arranged programs of music, recitation, and lectures. When the territories of the Hudson's Bay Company were taken over by the Dominion and surveyors appeared from the east, the French-Canadian Indian *métis* and others who were fearful of losing their country and the old way of life were unable to hold back the inevitable.

In 1871, a year after the province of Manitoba was formed, an education act introduced a system of public education with central and local authorities similar to those which had been established in the east.

Saskatchewan and Alberta

In the vast expanse of the Northwest Territories between the Red River area and the Rocky Mountains, permanent settlements and the beginning of white men's education came considerably later. After being taken over from the Hudson's Bay Company, these territories were governed from 1871 to 1875 by a council of twelve men presided over by the lieutenant-governor of Manitoba; from 1876 until 1887 they had a resident lieutenant-governor of their own and a council, consisting at first of only five appointed members; from 1888 until 1905 they had a legislative assembly and an executive council which became responsible to the assembly in the 1890's. In 1905 the whole area except the region far to the north was divided to form two self-governing provinces, Saskatchewan and Alberta.

FATHER LACOMBE

In the first few decades of the nineteenth century there were numerous trading posts but very few permanent residents. One of the most important areas for the fur trade was in the vicinity of Edmonton, now the capital city of Alberta. Roman Catholic missionary efforts began there in 1836. Mission schools were established by priests at Lac Ste Anne in 1842, at Fort Edmonton in 1852, and at Lac La Biche in 1854. But the place of instruction was no more than "a circle around a campfire, a smoke-filled tent, at best a room in a fort."[4] Probably the first mission school with a permanent abode was the one opened in 1859 at Lac Ste Anne by three Grey Nuns, or Sisters of Charity, who had arrived the previous year. Sisters of the same order established four other teaching centres by 1874. Among the priests who performed notable service, Father Lacombe deserves special mention for his work among the Indians from the time of his arrival in 1852.

He was also responsible for the establishment at Edmonton in 1861 of the first ordinary school for children of Hudson's Bay Company employees. In the following year this school was conducted in a log chapel by an Oblate novice, Brother Scollen. Katherine Hughes in her biography of Father Lacombe, said that the twenty pupils were wild as hares and that "at the sound of the voyageurs' songs or cheers in autumn, they flew like arrows from their bows out to the bank (of the North Saskatchewan River) to welcome the brigade home."[5]

THE McDOUGALLS

The first Protestant missionary was sent out to the Edmonton district by the Wesleyan Methodist Church in England in 1840. On his travels he called the children together for instruction and at Lesser Slave Lake for a short period he kept a school in operation. One of two other Methodist ministers who arrived in 1855 was an Indian from a district of Upper Canada where Egerton Ryerson had worked as a young missionary. He procured a teacher and set up a school at Whitefish Lake, where there were soon eighty pupils on the roll. This school was kept in relatively steady operation, although the minister and the teacher had to follow their charges to the buffalo hunt to keep in contact with them. The best known of the Methodist missionaries, however, were George McDougall and his son John, who were appointed to work in the west in 1860 and who arrived in the Edmonton district two years later. It was said of the McDougalls that schooling was part of their religion.

By 1864 they had built a school in the Victoria settlement on the North Saskatchewan at a place later called Pakan, about 180 miles east of Edmonton. When the first teacher of the school was drowned in 1864, the missionaries obtained as his successor Benjamin McKenzie, who had received his education in the Red River area and had taught there in St. Mary's parish school. The mission school soon had a good attendance — about forty half-breeds, twenty Indians, and some whites. The teacher had the initiative and training to organize the first school choir in the Northwest.

Among other schools in the district was a night school which was opened in Edmonton in 1870 for employees of the company. Farther south the McDougalls established a school for the Stoney Indians at Morley, about 1872, and one at Fort Macleod for the Blackfoot Indians a few years later. These Indian mission schools were less successful, in the latter case because Fort Macleod became a centre of white settlement. In Calgary, what was probably the first school opened in 1883.

OTHER DENOMINATIONAL SCHOOLS IN SASKATCHEWAN

In the territory that is now the province of Saskatchewan, the Presbyterians established a school at Prince Albert in 1866. In this district the Roman Catholics, by 1871, are said to have had five schools, including a mission school at Isle à la Cross. At various places throughout the territories were other mission schools of different denominations; one school of the Church of England was located at Fort Simpson. The denominational schools were maintained with the help of any local support that could be procured. Assistance was also given by central bodies, as when the Methodist Church in 1875 made grants for educational work. The government of the Territories also voted grants-in-aid. Virtually all schools in the Northwest Territories before the 1880's were of the mission type and were church-sponsored. It was inevitable, therefore, that the Northwest Territories Act of 1875 should provide for the continuance of denominational schools, especially because there was no provision at the time for a publicly controlled system of education.

FURTHER PROGRESS

Although there was no real control by the state over education, acts were passed in 1874 regarding Indian children. It was made legal for any school or orphanage of a religious denomination to receive children to be brought up and educated to the age of sixteen. Provision was also made for the commitment to one of these schools or orphanages of any child under fourteen found wandering and destitute.

There was a beginning of local responsibility for education. In Edmonton there appears to have been a school in the lower town from 1874, but it was closed in 1882 because of financial difficulties and lack of pupils. In the upper town there was a schoolhouse, but there, too, difficulty was encountered in keeping it in operation. A committee of nine men came to the rescue in 1881 by assuming a liability of $150 each in order to guarantee the teacher's salary.

There were also the usual petitions from local communities to the government for aid. In 1877 St. Laurent asked for assistance in erecting a schoolhouse. Although the council gave careful consideration to the request, they could do nothing for lack of funds. In 1878 the governor included in his estimates an item of $2000, from which he intended to pay half the salaries of teachers in schools founded by voluntary agencies or local subscribers. In 1880 this type of government assistance was made available. After that date some localities were fairly well provided with schools. In 1881, St. Albert, near Edmonton, had a well-established school, attended by from 60 to 75 pupils, including 15 boarders. By 1884 three more schools were being organized in the vicinity. In that year an ordinance was passed by the council to provide for schools under state control.

By then, conditions had begun to change in the Northwest Territories. The Free Land Homestead Act of 1872 induced farmers to leave exhausted land in the east and migrate to the west. In 1880 two newspapers appeared — the *Edmonton Bulletin,* and the *Saskatchewan Herald* of Battleford, which was the early capital. The Canadian Pacific Railway had been extended across the prairies by 1883, and in that year five thousand settlers entered the Northwest. An event of educational significance was the creation, ten years before, of the Northwest Mounted Police, with headquarters soon after in Regina, which became the capital of the Territories in 1882. The Mounties, numbering only three hundred at first, succeeded remarkably not only in maintaining law and order over a vast domain but in creating a respect for the institutions of justice.

Though rough enough in many ways, the Canadian west did not encourage gun-toting and private enterprise in the exchange of shots.

British Columbia

The land between the Rocky Mountains and the sea, with the adjacent islands, now forms the province of British Columbia. The first British landing on the west coast was made in 1778 by Captain James Cook. In 1794 Spain and Great Britain agreed to abandon any exclusive claim to the coast, which for thirty years was open to traders of any country, with resulting scenes of violence. During the same period Alexander Mackenzie, Simon Fraser, and David Thompson, all partners in the North West Company, came into the territory from across the Rockies. The latter two, by the establishment of trading posts, gave Great Britain a sound basis for a claim to the area. In 1821 the Hudson's Bay Company, newly amalgamated with the North West Company, had a monopoly of trade. In 1849 the company was granted Vancouver Island on condition that a colony be settled there. Although the population was only a few hundred in its early years, the colony in 1850 acquired a governor and in 1856 an assembly. Shortly after, the discovery of gold in the Fraser River Valley caused an inrush of prospectors and others to the mainland. In 1858 the mainland of British Columbia was organized as a crown colony separate from Vancouver Island. The same year marked the end of the company's exclusive monopoly of trade and also of its control over Vancouver Island.

Inevitably, the governor had some difficulty in maintaining British rule in a region remote and separated by mountains from the rest of British North America and in relatively close communication with the states to the south. In 1865 economic depression caused the population to decline to about ten thousand people. The next year the two colonies were united for more economical administration. Burdened by debt, the united colony welcomed the promise of a railway linking it with eastern Canada, and for this and other reasons agreed to enter Confederation. In 1871 it became the province of British Columbia, with an elected assembly and responsible government.

HUDSON'S BAY COMPANY EFFORTS

On Vancouver Island in 1849 the Hudson's Bay Company took steps to provide schooling for the children of officers of the company. The Reverend Robert J. Staines was brought out from England to act as chaplain and to establish a school. Before he arrived at his destination, this Church of England clergyman must have thought of the new colony as a land of promise, for he had assurances of a generous stipend. The first shock was to find that Fort Victoria was a small, undeveloped settlement, so muddy that the inhabitants had to wade through the mire in sea boots and lay planks to enable the newcomers to reach the fort. It seems that the only educational work Staines was able to do was to have his wife conduct a school, although a letter of the governor dated 1851 mentions a company school under the clergyman's direction. By 1853 he had become so disgusted with conditions that he started back to England as the champion of the settlers to voice their grievances against the company. His ship foundered and he was drowned.

The following year the company obtained the services of the Reverend Edward Cridge, who was given to understand that a grant of £100 would be forthcoming to support a boarding school, and that the school would have further revenue from fees for the tuition and keep of some 30 or 40 pupils at £20 each. The suggestion was that a teacher and his wife come with Cridge from England to take charge of this school. In the event, all that was done immediately for the children of gentleman officers of the company was again to have the clergyman's wife open a school. But Cridge was keenly interested in education. In November 1856, less than two years after his arrival, he was appointed inspector of schools for the general population.

COLONIAL SCHOOLS

Probably the first school for the people was one opened by an Oblate priest, described by the governor as a very zealous teacher. In 1851, the Oblate left Victoria to live and work among the Indians. The first common, or "colonial," school was set up in Victoria in 1852 and the next two in Nanaimo and Craigflower in 1853. In the latter year a building was erected by the government for the Victoria school, and two years later a schoolhouse was built at Craigflower. The colonial schools were financed at least in part by grants from the government or the company.

The reports of Cridge in his capacity as inspector, and later as acting superintendent, gave definite information about the schools and his judgment regarding their achievements, deficiencies, and needs. In 1856 the only colonial schools in operation appear to have been those at Victoria and Craigflower. The former had on the roll seventeen boys, of whom nine were boarders, but only three boys and no girls "of the laboring class" for whom the school was primarily intended. The attendance of both the pupils and the master were decidedly irregular and their performance correspondingly indifferent. The supply of books and other necessities was sadly deficient. Three girls had been withdrawn and sent to a private

school, two boys had been removed to a newly-opened Roman Catholic school, and other pupils were known only to have ceased attending. The school at Craigflower had an enrolment of 11 boys and 10 girls; of the 21 pupils, 11 were "of the laboring class" and 3 were boarders; 12 were under ten years of age, and 9 were ten years of age or older. This school had a somewhat better attendance record and a more adequate supply of books and maps. Both schools taught elementary subjects, including a little grammar, geography, and history to pupils who remained at school for some time; one boy at Craigflower was receiving instruction in Euclid and Algebra.

By the fall of 1859, the enrolment at the new school in Victoria had increased to 77, of whom 13 were girls. In the winter this number fell to 44, since one had been expelled for immoral conduct, about six had been removed for various causes, and "about 26 had left on account of the state of the weather." The achievement of the pupils had improved greatly, although their attendance was still irregular. In 1861 there was a total enrolment in the three colonial schools of 111 — of whom 21 were girls and 51 pupils over ten years of age. At Victoria 20 pupils were being taught drawing, and 4 bookkeeping; at Craigflower there were 2 pupils in geometry and 1 in Latin; all other pupils were in elementary subjects. In all three schools the pupils were said to be making good progress. Increasingly generous salaries were being paid by the government to the teachers: instead of £40 or £60 as formerly, the amount paid to each master in 1860-61 was £150, and the amount shown in estimates of the superintendent for 1863 was £200. In addition to this government assistance, the schools collected fees from parents to the amount of about £1 per pupil per year.

An unsigned document in the handwriting of Cridge is quoted by MacLaurin[6] to show the number of schools of all types on Vancouver Island about 1864 or 1865. There were then five colonial schools. In Victoria, the Church of England had established a collegiate school for boys and a ladies' college, and the Roman Catholic Church had two similar institutions, although probably not of a socially selective character. The Church of England had also a school for girls in Nanaimo. There were at least four Sunday schools in Victoria — Anglican, Methodist, Congregationalist, and Presbyterian. In addition, there were on the island possibly five private schools conducted by women. The superintendent added that he believed there was also another school under the auspices of the Presbyterian Church.

COMMON SCHOOL ACT, 1865

Prosperity and a growing population led not only to an increase in the number of educational institutions but engendered the optimism necessary for a major educational advance. Cridge realized that satisfactory attendance of children from every economic class could be obtained only by abolishing school fees. The district of Esquimault, where the Craigflower school was located, had abolished fees for at least the one year 1863. Two years later the government passed a free school act and assumed the whole cost of education in common schools. This "Common School Act, 1865" established a general board of education to hold and manage all school property and made provision for a superintendent of education to act as the agent of the board. The central authority, appointed by the governor, had power to establish schools, to prescribe courses of study, textbooks, and rules for conducting schools, and to inspect schools. Even the appointment of teachers was the prerogative of the governor. Under such a highly centralized system of administration there was no

distinct need for local authorities, and the act provided merely that the governor might appoint a local board of three trustees in any school district if he considered it expedient so to do. The schools were to give no denominational teaching and were to be open to all.

According to a contemporary writer, Victoria in 1865 was abundantly supplied with schools — not only "colonial" schools for the poor but others offering every branch of a superior English education. There was a "Collegiate School" in which the classical curriculum of a Latin grammar school was supplemented by the more practical subjects of an academy, and there was also a "Ladies' College" — both under Church of England auspices. Altogether there were not less than six Protestant day schools.

Immediately on the passing of the Act of 1865, the government's expenditure on education rose from about $5000 to nearly $10,000. The numbers of schools and pupils increased, as they always did whenever and wherever education became free and non-sectarian in English-speaking Canada. For the year 1866 the General Board of Education estimated expenditures at more than $25,000. Unfortunately the money was not forthcoming: a depression had followed the gold rush boom, and the Free School Act broke down through inability of the government to meet its generous obligations.

Although the attainment of free schools, even temporarily, provided educational benefits remarkable in a colony founded only sixteen years before, it should be observed that the action was taken not by the people but by a government formerly associated with a powerful company. These two agencies, government and company, had previously taken most of the responsibility in providing education for children who were not reached by private schools or were not benefiting sufficiently from the limited efforts of the churches. All that the people had been asked to do, formerly, was to pay fees if they had children. With the exception of certain efforts made by the residents of the district of Esquimault, there was no direct co-operative action of citizens locally to take control and pay the cost of education. Hence the gain on Vancouver Island in 1865 may more accurately be regarded as an abolition of fees through the increased generosity of paternalism rather than as the attainment of free schools by democratic process.

On the mainland of British Columbia, when the population had suddenly increased, a first school was conducted in 1862-63 by the Reverend Robert Jamieson immediately after his arrival in New Westminster. Then, on the advice of this clergyman, a meeting of the citizens was called to take the steps necessary to establish a common school. An initial grant of £100 was obtained from the government on the understanding that the same amount would be raised locally and that the school would "be open to all persons and be maintained on non-sectarian principles." Subsequent grants were procured for annual support, for buildings, and for the purpose of reducing fees from 10 shillings to 6 shillings a month. There was an active school committee, locally appointed, which not only managed but expanded the services of the school. Before the two colonies were united in 1866, common schools had been established in three other places. All received government grants, which after 1864 were voted by the assembly, which met for the first time in that year. The only regular local support continued to be the fees paid by the parents of children attending school. As on Vancouver Island, the grants were increased until 1866 and then sharply reduced. But the four schools, and one other established in 1868, appear to have remained in operation on this basis until the passing of new legislation in 1869.

PUBLIC SCHOOLS ACT, 1869

On Vancouver Island, the period 1866-69 was one of extreme difficulty for the General Board of Education and for teachers in the schools. Both attempted to carry on without assurance of adequate financial support. The board and the superintendent fought to maintain the free school system in spite of mounting deficits. The governor and council took the position that it was the function of government to encourage the educational efforts of others and not to supplant them by a state school system, which they contended was impracticable in any case under conditions at the time. Actually, Governor Seymour, although a benighted reactionary in the eyes of those who were moved only by the need of providing education for all, showed keen insight into the confused issues and the implications of establishing schools under public control. He was prepared, for the time being, to have denominational schools look after the greater number of children, with some moderate assistance from government. But he saw that education under state control would have to be of an entirely different character. As reported in the Journals of the Legislative Council:

He believes that the community in which he resides is one where complete toleration in religious opinion exists. It is not therefore, under these circumstances, for the State and its Salaried Officers to interfere with the belief of any one. The Government has not undertaken to prove to the Jew that the Messiah has indeed arrived; to rob the Roman Catholic Church in her belief in the merciful intercession of the Blessed Virgin; to give special support to the Church of England; to mitigate the acidity of the Calvinistic doctrines of some Protestant believers, or to determine, authoritatively, the number of the Sacraments. Therefore, the Governor is of opinion that when the time comes for the establishment of a large Common School, religious teaching ought not to be allowed to intrude. It is vain to say that there are certain elementary matters in which all Christians, leaving out the Jews, must agree. It is merely calling upon a man picked up at random, allured by a trifling salary, to do what the whole religious wisdom, feeling, and affection of the world has not yet done. The paring down of all excrescences, which a man on a hundred and fifty pounds a year may think disfigure the several religions, and the reducing them to a common standard, becomes a sort of Methodism which may locally be named after the School master who performs it.[7]

Obviously religious difficulties were a complicating factor in the issue. But it was lack of money which forced the General Board to capitulate. Funds were raised by theatrical performances in Victoria to help pay arrears in the salaries of teachers, but when payment of money voted by the legislature for free schools was withheld, members of the board held a meeting in 1868 to consider the "propriety of resigning," and in March, 1869, the board met for the last time.

In the same month there was passed "An Ordinance to establish Public Schools throughout the Colony of British Columbia." This enactment made the governor-in-council the central authority over education and dispensed with the General Board and superintendent. It did provide, however, for elected local boards, and required local support for education. The decision as to whether the money be raised by taxation was left to an annual meeting of freeholders and resident householders, but a two-thirds vote was needed to make taxation lawful. The trustees did not have the power to appoint or discharge teachers. In the following year, Governor Seymour's successor gave assent to an amending ordinance providing again for the appointment of a committee and an official by the government — a committee to examine and certificate teachers and an Inspector General to examine the pupils and report to the governor-in-council.

In 1870 there were altogether fifteen government schools on the island and mainland, with a total attendance of about 370 children. The equipment of the fifteen schools was considered by the Inspector General to be "of the scantiest description." The efficiency of the teachers was judged to be "better than could have been expected" considering the small remuneration, although salaries were considerably higher than in Ontario. In the opinion of the inspector the system had two major defects. Even when local taxation was approved, the method was to impose a poll tax on all male residents over eighteen years of age rather than to levy against real estate a tax likely to be proportional to ability to pay. The other defect was the constitution of the local boards: in Victoria and New Westminster the municipal council was empowered to act in this capacity, and in both cities support for schools was hard to obtain — so hard in Victoria that the schools remained closed for two years, 1870-72.

British Columbia entered Confederation in 1871. This date will serve to mark the end of the early period in education. The total enrolment in all schools was close to one thousand and the average attendance perhaps half that number. The schools were usually better in many respects, than those of the east thirty years before. But as in the older colonies at the earlier date, local responsibility for education had yet to be permanently established.

PART THREE

The Development of Public School Systems

Although Canada has eleven independent systems of public education — one in each of nine provinces and two in Quebec — most of them have had a similar development and all have some characteristics in common. It is possible, therefore, to present the later history of Canadian education topically rather than province by province. Part Three follows this plan in dealing with the administrative side of our educational development and with aspects of education related thereto. Only in Chapter 14 are separate accounts given of developments in the individual provinces.

The geographical area under discussion hereafter is the whole of Canada, including chiefly the ten provinces. Some brief attention is given in Chapter 16 to the vast but less populous extra-provincial territories of the far north. The total area of land and fresh water of Canada is over 3,690,000 square miles.

The period under discussion in Part Three extends from the first appearance of schools under organized local control by the people — roughly from 1830 in the east and from 1890 in the west — to the present. Before 1867, of course, the various parts of the country were separate colonies with no political unity except through membership in the British Empire. By 1880 virtually the whole area had become part of Canada through Confederation or by annexation, with the exception of the island and adjacent territories of Newfoundland, which became the tenth province of Canada in 1949.

CHAPTER 11

A Growing Democracy
The Country

POPULATION · ECONOMIC DEVELOPMENT · GOVERNMENT · FROM APATHY
TO RESPONSIBILITY · SOCIAL AWARENESS · SELF-CONFIDENCE

The purpose of this chapter and the following two chapters
is to give an overall view of the expansion of Canada and of her
educational facilities to meet the needs of a growing country.

Population

Among the factors that influenced the
development of public education in Canada, the most obvious was the growth of
population. In rough approximations the
number of people doubled in twenty years
from 362,000 in 1801 to 750,000 in 1821;
again in twenty years to 1,650,000 in
1841; then in thirty years to 3,690,000 in
1871; then in forty years to 7,200,000 in
1911; and again in forty years to 14,000,-
000 in 1951. Two periods of rapid expansion, from 1830 to 1860 and from 1895 to
1915, made necessary a correspondingly
rapid expansion of school facilities from
1840 to 1870 in the east and from 1900 to
1925 in the west. There was a similar need
for more buildings and more teachers in
the years following World War II. But
the educational problem was more acute
in the earlier periods because the increase
in population resulted largely from immigration. It was not simply a matter of
enlarging existing plants to extend the
operation of a well-established organization, but of creating school systems to do
new educational work made all the more
urgent by the need for assimilating the
newcomers.

IMMIGRATION

Immigration has had considerable influence at all times on our educational

history. In the 1830's and 1840's great numbers of people risked the dangers of shipwreck and disease and suffered untold miseries in wretched transport ships to come to the new land. Even when they landed, their trials were far from being over. Some who reached Montreal lived for weeks in crowded squalor and, not knowing where they might settle or how to get there, drank themselves into an even deeper confusion. In 1832, when over 50,000 came, cholera broke out and spread from the port, as it did again in 1834. The threat of starvation after the potato famine in Ireland, drove tens of thousands to flee that unhappy country in 1846 and 1847. Most of the immigrants went to Upper Canada, where the problem of looking after the destitute was embarrassing. The numbers fell off shortly after. But for the most part immigration was encouraged without thought of consequence. New Brunswick sent lecturers to Britain and sold books there extolling the resources of the province. Although many of the more enterprising immigrants moved elsewhere when they learned what conditions were, the population of the small province tripled in thirty-three years after 1824. One result of excessive numbers and insufficient resources was that too many people took little interest in education.

But the problems created by early immigration were not merely quantitative. The attitudes and intellectual values of many newcomers were anything but conducive to educational advance. This handicap made all the more necessary the setting up of strong central authorities to counteract lethargy and to set minimum educational standards which localities were required to attain. The need for educational direction was greatest among the Irish, and especially among the Irish Roman Catholics, since their church had not the same educational privileges as the Protestants until 1831. Evidence of their condition is the large majority of Irish

among those Roman Catholics who were convicted of crimes in Canada towards the middle of the nineteenth century.

In 1871 and in 1931 the number of immigrants was about 28,000, but in all but a few of the intervening years it was considerably higher. Between 1882 and 1884 the annual count exceeded 100,000. The greatest numbers came between 1903 and 1915, the peak being 402,432 in 1913. The numbers fell off during the depression and World War II to less than 10,000 in a year, but rose again to 125,000 in 1948. The proportion of immigrants from European countries other than the United Kingdom increased at the turn of the century and added greatly to the problem of educational expansion in the west, since some were indifferent about education and others wanted only schools which taught the language and religion of the parents. In the first two decades of the twentieth century the number of children born of Canadian parents was only one-quarter of the number of newcomers from other countries, and one-third of the latter could not speak English when they came. One township of Saskatchewan had at one time 102 children of school age, not one of whom could speak the language of the country. Many districts were settled entirely by Norwegians, Swedes, Finns, Germans, Hungarians, Russians, Austrians, Poles, French, Galicians, Icelanders, Bohemians, Mennonites, or Doukhobors. It was necessary again, under these conditions, to have a vigorous central agency, and the western provinces appointed an official trustee to get schools built and opened and to see that taxes were collected and the teachers paid. The rapidity of the expansion may be illustrated by the increase in number of schools in operation in the Northwest Territories within a four-year period — from 492 in 1900 to 917 in 1904.

Even among later immigrants from England there were many who directly or in-

directly aggravated educational difficulties. Reports of commissions pointed out
that the newcomers in the late nineteenth
and early twentieth centuries included
people weak and infirm, children without
parents, and girls who found no better
means of livelihood than prostitution.
Social problems were most serious when
the new arrivals poured into already
crowded cities, and were intensified when
many who came had standards of living
and morality different from those of Canadians. Although the number of immigrants from the United States exceeded
the number from all other countries in
the 1880's and was also high during the
first part of the present century, a large
proportion of them were also recent arrivals from Europe.

CHANGE IN RURAL-URBAN DISTRIBUTION OF POPULATION

Another factor of importance was the
rural-urban distribution of the people. In
1851 nearly 90 per cent, and in 1871 more
than 80 per cent of the Canadian population were rural; by 1921 percentages of
urban and rural were about equal; and
in 1941 over 54 per cent were urban. In
Ontario 70 per cent of the population were
rural in 1881 and 70 per cent were urban
in 1951; the total rural population had
dropped slightly and the urban population
had increased sixfold. Before the end of
the nineteenth century the schools were
accused of depopulating rural areas by
encouraging a movement to the cities. The
Minister of Education in Ontario felt
obliged in 1897 to issue a pamphlet in
which he pointed out that the increase of
urban population in Ontario — from 19.4
per cent in 1871 to 33.2 per cent in 1891
— had resulted from causes apparently
unrelated to education — the low profits
to be made from farming, the reduction
by labor-saving machinery of the number

of farm-hands needed, the opening-up of
new country by the railways, and the expansion of industry.

Education was, however, in a long-
term sense largely responsible for urbanization because of practical applications
of knowledge; and conversely the extension of public education, especially at
the secondary level, was greatly facilitated by the growth of urban centres. But
the distinction between country and city
had less and less significance as transportation and communication improved; and
public education in the twentieth century
adopted measures to reduce rural disadvantages, although these continued to retard educational progress.

BIRTH-RATE FACTORS

Another population factor affecting the
provision of schools was the birth rate.
In 1851 the percentage of the male population under five years of age was 18.6,
in 1901 only 11.9. The change, of course,
was due partly to fewer deaths among
older people as well as to fewer births.

During the present century, and especially after World War I, the number
of births per thousand of population showed a marked decline — from 29.4 in 1921
to an average of 20.5 for the years 1936-
40. These national figures were higher
than they would otherwise have been because of the relatively high birth rate in
the province of Quebec — 37.6 in 1921 and
24.6 in 1936-40. The effect of this decline
was to reduce somewhat the amount of
accommodation required in elementary
schools. The effect was not apparent in
secondary schools, because school life
lengthened during the moderate economic
prosperity of the first three decades of
the century and during the recession of
the fourth decade from established high
standards of living conditions that were
apparently associated with the lower birth
rate.

During World War II and the period of post-war optimism the birth rate rose to 28.6 in 1947. After that year there was again an increasing need for elementary school accommodation, and from about 1956 there will be a growing need for high school expansion. But even in the kindergarten and at the primary level, the pressure of larger school population had only begun in 1953. In Ontario the number of children up to four years of age increased by nearly 73 per cent between 1941 and 1951, whereas the percentage increase in the five to nine age group was less than half as great and in the ten to fourteen age group practically zero.

Changes in birth rate produced apparent anomalies in educational statistics. For example, the proportion of elementary school enrolment in relation to the entire population was higher for some provinces in 1900 than in 1940, although the length of schooling had increased. Such data, of course, were affected also by immigration and the longevity of the population.

LIFE EXPECTANCY

The increase in life expectancy has begun to have considerable significance for education. A visitor to a cemetery in an old Canadian city, like Saint John, New Brunswick, is impressed by the large numbers who, up to the middle of the nineteenth century, died in infancy and childhood or before the age of thirty or forty. Even when allowance is made for the relatively small number of older people in a new country, it is clear that there could have been no secure confidence among the many in a protracted life on earth. In 1851 the percentage of the male population 60 years of age and older was only 4.5; in 1931 it was 8.4. As life expectancy rose, it became reasonable to provide a longer period of education for all. But as longevity continued to increase in the present century, it became neces-

sary to provide for the old as well as the young. Old age annuities were introduced in 1908, old age pensions for the indigent in 1929, and old age pensions for all in 1950. In the seventeen years between 1931 and 1947, life expectancy at birth increased from 60 to over 65 years for males, and from 62 to 69 years for females. Between those years public expenditures on education increased from $145,000,000 to $308,000,000, but on old age pensions from $7,000,000 to $44,000,000.

REGIONAL MOVEMENTS OF POPULATION

Inter-provincial movements of population also affected education. A comparison of the number of young people in the provinces between 10 and 14 years of age in 1931 and between 20 and 24 years of age in 1941 shows that Nova Scotia suffered a loss of 1600, whereas Ontario gained 5700. Of the seven other provinces only British Columbia showed a gain (of 9400) and Saskatchewan showed the heaviest loss (of nearly 25,000). Some provinces have thus paid for the education of many young people who migrated at an early age to take up work in another province. Such movements, regionally, are an economic and sometimes a cultural drain.

Economic Development

EDUCATION AND THE NATIONAL ECONOMY

This brings us to a consideration of the growing number of rival claimants for a share of the public and private purse. No doubt it is to be expected that when education is well established people should spend proportionately more on the material goods and other consumer benefits for which learning and science are basically though not immediately responsible. But reversals like the following give grounds for unease. During the first twenty years of the present century public expenditures on education increased in the ratio of ten to one (i.e. $11,000,000 to $113,000,000), while the value of manufactured products increased in the ratio of five to one ($215,000,000 to $1,124,000,000). During the next thirty years expenditures on public education increased in the ratio of only three to one ($113,000,000 to $347,000,000), while the value of manufactured products increased in the ratio of four and a half to one ($1,124,000,000 to $4,940,000,000). It is probable that the apparent increase in expenditure on education since the depression of the 1930's was more than offset by an increase of a third in population, by a continuing increase of more than a quarter in the birth rate, by a drop to nearly one-half in the value of the dollar, and by a rise in construction costs to proportionately even higher levels. It is certain that support for education has ceased to keep up with the much greater production of material goods and the much higher national income.

BASIC ECONOMIC CHANGES

There were other factors of significance to education in the economic development of Canada. In the period up to 1850 people were engaged almost entirely in primary occupations — in lumbering and trapping, in fishing along the Atlantic, and in agriculture in Upper Canada. There were saw mills and grist mills to process lumber and grain. There was some manufacturing of wood products — shipbuilding and the making of potash, staves for barrels, and a little rough furniture to supply domestic needs. There was a flourishing commerce in timber. But on the whole industrial development was exceedingly limited. The economy had little need for education, and provided no adequate surplus of time or money for its support.

Between 1850 and 1900 wood yielded to grain as the chief primary product for commerce and to iron as the essential material for industry. By the time of Confederation half the vessels sailing down the St. Lawrence were carrying cereals instead of lumber. In the last quarter of the century manufacturing was promising enough or strong enough to seek and obtain a protective tariff. Towns and cities in central Canada profited from trade flowing east and west and from the beginning of agricultural development in the prairies. In 1858 decimal currency was introduced, and in 1871 a Dominion currency was made uniform throughout Canada. But to avoid an exaggerated impression one should think of this half-century as a transition period. Although manufactured products included agricultural implements and steam engines as well as many consumer goods, and although the factory system was demonstrating fully its unpleasant nineteenth-century aspects, the change from a rural to an industrial society was only partly accomplished. In the first part of this period the economy provided the money to establish schools and in the second part tried to make them efficient in operation. The result was a horse-hair sofa type of education, outwardly durable and economical, undoubtedly solid, but cold and unyielding in its service to the young.

The first half of the present century brought a full development of agriculture in the west, a new importance to mining, new sources of hydro-electric power and oil, and an industrial expansion whose magnitude makes the industries of the past seem as nothing. A chief characteristic of the age is big business and big industry, highly organized and with vast resources. This development may be illustrated by railway amalgamation, like that of the Great Western Railway and the Grand Trunk Railway under the name of the latter in 1882, with the Northern Railway added in 1888. The change to bigness may be illustrated, also, by the relatively small (50 per cent) increase in the number of manufacturing plants as compared with the great (300 per cent) increase in the value of their products between 1920 and 1948. Educational administration has begun to follow the example of business in organization, but a long tradition of niggardliness, euphemistically disguised in terms of virtue, has left the school further and further behind in employing the new and greater resources of a rapidly changing society.

Benefits from these economic developments have not been distributed equally across the country. The Atlantic provinces have gained the least. In 1838 Durham said of the Maritime Provinces: "Their scanty population exhibits, in most portions of them, an aspect of poverty, backwardness, and stagnation." The decline after 1850 of shipbuilding from wood, of lumbering, and of fishing intensified this condition. Attempts were made before and after that date by governments and voluntary agencies to establish agriculture on a secure foundation, but agriculture, like forestry, was practised inefficiently and wastefully, and the narrow margin of profit inevitably disappeared. Coal mines in Cape Breton found a market in the United States in 1856 and soon after in central Canada. In 1876 the Intercolonial Railway provided communication and transportation between the Maritimes and the larger provinces, and overseas freight was handled by the eastern ports in the winter. But even with fruit-growing in Nova Scotia and the potato crops of Prince Edward Island, prosperity was limited. This condition is reflected in expenditures on education, and in demands for federal aid. A New Brunswick author in 1926 accused politicians of putting a low value on education and of being interested only in keeping down the cost, with consequent low standards of reading and culture. Although such allegations

are not quite fair, it is likely that adverse economic conditions did have an influence on other factors, including attitudes of men in public office, with unfortunate effects on educational progress.

UPS AND DOWNS

Throughout the century and a half under consideration there were alternating ups and downs of economic activity. The brighter interludes held out the lure of gain to business venture, and hard times may sometimes have goaded the lethargic worker, but the recurrent cycles left education without the necessary assurance of adequate support. Prosperity came with the war of 1812-15, as a delayed postwar boom in 1821-25, and in some measure from 1830 to 1835. An influx of English capital led to further economic expansion between 1841 and 1845. The Crimean War of 1851-56 was a period of mild prosperity, while the American Civil War occasioned a boom that lasted from 1861 to 1872. Again in 1879-81, and from 1896 to 1912, the Canadian economy experienced good times. World War I, the period from 1922 to 1929, and World War II were times of prosperity for an increasing number of the Canadian people. Depressions usually followed each war-time boom, or post-war boom. These occurred in 1816-21, and in 1826-29, though the latter was felt chiefly in New Brunswick. In 1837 a commercial crisis suspended the operation of banks. There was a severe depression from 1846 to 1850, and another, brought on by post-war deflation and a financial panic, in 1856-70. The economy was again hit hard from 1873 to 1878, and recurrently during the 1880's and the early 1890's. A threat of depression, averted by the outbreak of World War I, was felt in 1913-14, while after the war came a recession in 1920-21. The world-wide depression which began in 1929 with such dire consequences had shown little promise of coming to an end when World War II broke out ten years later.

The immediate effect of a severe depression on school administration may be illustrated by the drop in educational expenditures in British Columbia from a high of over $11,000,000 in 1928-29 to a little more than $8,000,000 in 1933-34, and by the increase in average daily attendance of pupils in the same province from 91,700 in 1928 to 104,978 in 1933. Even the brief recession after World War I, which was felt severely in the middle west, caused in Alberta a 30-per-cent increase in the number of pupils in Grade VIII between June 1921 and June 1922 and a cut in educational expenditures in 1923 which closed the normal school at Edmonton and reduced the number of school inspectors from 40 to 36. The effect of the depression of the 1930's and of World War II on provincial grants to schools may be seen from the accompanying table of educational expenditures:

EXPENDITURES OF NINE PROVINCIAL GOVERNMENTS
(Thousands of dollars)

	1921	1931	1941	1947
On all purposes............	$102,570	$190,754	$349,818	$480,406*
On grants to schools........	12,226	16,969	20,789	55,134*
— per cent............	12%	9%	6%	11%

* Eight provinces, Quebec omitted. Data from *Canada Year Book* (39) and *Biennial Survey of Education* (38)

But the lag in response of education in all its aspects to social change makes periods of inflationary prosperity like 1947-52 even more embarrassing financially than periods of recession. The less direct but more important effects of economic fluctuations on pupils and teachers will be discussed in later chapters.

STATUS OF LABOR

Another movement of educational importance associated with our economic development was the improvement in status and attitude of labor. Before Confederation, unions of workingmen had only local influence and very little power. The first trade union, the Typographical Society of York (Toronto), was established in 1832. But the need for such unions was not clearly apparent when cheap land and small-scale business offered a convenient alternative to wage employment. With the development of the factory system, however, legislation was passed in 1872 to counteract the one-sided power of capital by granting labor the legal right to organize and strike when necessary. In the same year there was a strike of the Toronto local of the Typographical Union. In 1877 a strike of the Grand Trunk Railway engine drivers disrupted business and the mails and brought the intervention of the militia. The first national organization of labor, the Trades and Labor Congress of Canada, was first established in Ontario in 1883 and spread to other provinces; it had 1000 locals in 1902, and 2000 before World War I.

Although membership in trade unions increased, the number in relation to total population remained low in comparison with other countries. In the latter part of the nineteenth century and for some time after, organized labor had to contend not only with long hours and low pay but with unhealthy and dangerous working conditions in factories, with the annual trial of seasonal unemployment, and with the bitter hardships escaped by management in depression years. "In industrial communities," says Lower, "employers have habitually met hard times by discharging employees and dumping the responsibility on the local community."[1]

The appalling conditions of unemployment and partial employment under this policy in the 1930's were a stern lesson, and when prosperity returned during and after World War II, labor asserted its power and improved the condition of the workingman immeasurably. Always favorably disposed to free schools of the people, organized labor was, by 1950, able to give strong and enlightened support to public education. Whereas in the nineteenth century a middle or white-collar class was the mainstay of education beyond the minimum, even the high school now rests on a broader foundation of popular approval. Members of trade unions almost without exception send their children to schools under public control, and parents have now the education, position, and influence to demand and obtain good educational facilities for their children.

COMMUNICATION

Ease of communication greatly facilitated the operation of schools. Improvements in travel and transportation by water were marked by the appearance of steamships — the first on the St. Lawrence in 1809 and many others on the Great Lakes in the 1820's and 1830's — and by the opening of canals, including the Lachine in 1825, the Welland in 1829, the Rideau in 1832, and the complete St. Lawrence route in 1848. Then came the railway and great haste to extend the steel at quick profits to the promoter and at any cost to the public.

The first trains drawn by steam locomotives ran in 1853 from Montreal to Portland, Maine, from Toronto to Bradford, and from Hamilton to the Niagara River, to London, and Windsor. These lines and others were rapidly extended — in 1855 from Toronto to Collingwood on the Georgian Bay, in 1856 from Montreal to Toronto and from Toronto to Hamilton, in 1858 from Halifax to Truro and from Port Hope to Lindsay. The lengthy Intercolonial Railway from the Maritimes to central Canada began operation in 1876, and the first Canadian Pacific through train reached the Pacific coast in 1886. By 1901 there were over 18,000 miles of railroad and by 1914, when a second transcontinental route was built to the west, another 12,000 miles of track had been added.

Roads for ordinary vehicles improved after the 1820's. Bridges were built, notably the Suspension Bridge in 1848 and the International Bridge in 1873 over the Niagara River. The St. Clair River tunnel was opened in 1891. The first power-propelled heavier-than-air flying machine was flown in Canada — in Nova Scotia — in 1909. Since then changes and improvements in transportation have been remarkable.

The extension of new school services and of secondary education has been assisted most directly by the motor car and the school bus. But throughout the whole period of 120 years greater ease of travel brought more adequate schooling within reach of more and more people.

The value of education as a public service was enhanced also by greater convenience and speed in the communication of ideas. High postage rates were reduced and the efficiency of the mails improved when the British government turned over the control of postal facilities to the North American colonies in 1849. Postage stamps were first used in 1851. Between then and 1867 the number of post-offices increased, in Nova Scotia, for example, from 143 to 640. A three-cent letter stamp was issued

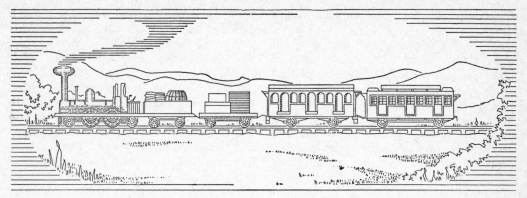

Canada's first train: it ran from LaPrairie, P.Q. to St. John's, P.Q., in 1836

in 1868, and penny postage was introduced in 1898. A telegraph went into commercial operation in 1847 between Toronto and Niagara, the first transatlantic cable was laid in 1866, and the telephone was first used commercially in 1877. The first experimental message to be sent across the Atlantic by wireless was received in Newfoundland in 1901. During the present century quick communication over almost any distance has become commonplace, and few are completely out of educational reach even if instruction has sometimes to be carried to the spot by a school railway car or sent by radio.

Government

Of greatest importance to the establishment and extension of public education was the development of Canadian democracy. The first great step was the attainment of responsible government.

RESPONSIBLE GOVERNMENT

In the early years of the nineteenth century all the older Canadian colonies had representative governments. But the prerogatives of the assembly were limited. The only effective power it had was a control over finances supplementary to the sources of revenue in the hands of the governor and council. Even the legislative function was shared with the legislative council. But what chiefly prevented the assembly from giving expression to the will of the people who elected it was its lack of control over those who held executive power. This was vested in a council appointed by the governor as the representative of the crown. The executive council was in no way responsible to the assembly or the people, and members of the council belonged almost invariably to a few influential families. They were superior in educational attainments and often in ability as contrasted with the mass of the people, and of course lived on a higher social and economic level. But they carried out the affairs of government in the interests of their own class. Even the governors, when willing to do so, were unable to resist their executive councils for long.

Two years after the rebellion of 1837 in Upper and Lower Canada, Lord Durham recommended that the governor should be instructed to appoint as an executive council men who could command a majority in the assembly. This same principle of responsible government was advocated by Joseph Howe in Nova Scotia. In practice it was to mean that the leader of the party having a majority in the assembly should recommend to the governor the men who should be appointed to form an executive council and that they should continue in office only with the support of the assembly.

Responsible government was attained in the older colonies of Canada in 1848 or immediately thereafter. In January of that year the assembly of Nova Scotia passed a vote of want of confidence in the administration, forced the resignation of the executive council, and secured for the leader of the assembly the right to name members of the executive — in other words to form a government. In the same year governments responsible to the people were set up in central Canada and in New Brunswick, and a few years later in Prince Edward Island. The newer provinces obtained responsible government at or before the time of their entrance into Confederation. The right to responsible government in all provinces does not rest on explicit statements in provincial or federal constitutions, but on firmly established custom.

SELF GOVERNMENT

Control by the people of the colonies over their own affairs at first applied only to matters within their borders. But after Confederation and especially during the present century there was a growing demand for self-government in relation to every aspect of a nation's business. With the passing of the Statute of Westminster in 1931, Canada obtained a complete and exclusive right to manage its own affairs as a fully autonomous country within the British Commonwealth of Nations.

Government by the people was not acquired without opposition. An article published in the *St. John Gazette and Daily Advertiser* on January 18, 1799, accused the assembly of trying to usurp power which would introduce "a pure democracy — a Government to avoid which his Majesty's loyal subjects in this province left their native country." A lieutenant-governor in Upper Canada spoke with disapproval of the "spirit of equality and want of subordination which too much prevails among the lower ranks of this province." In the colonies, as in England, the beneficiaries of society asked: "Why should we let down a ladder that the people may climb up and dispossess both us and our children?"[2] Robert Gourlay in Upper Canada was hounded for years and finally banished because he upheld justice and the rights of the people. The minority in power had no scruples about stirring up the ignorant and hot-headed to prevent the election of reformers to the assembly.

The battle to overcome such early opposition taught people the value of self-government more effectively than the school could do in later, less turbulent years. But the present provision of public education would have been impossible without the victory. The characteristic attitude of the old aristocratic governments towards education was illustrated by the council in New Brunswick, which as early as 1793 rejected a resolution of the assembly to give £10 to each parish for an elementary school and as late as 1839 defeated a bill passed by the assembly to amend the denominationally exclusive charter of King's College.

THE FRANCHISE

A responsible attitude of all people towards public education became possible only with the extension of the franchise. As a rule voters before Confederation had to qualify by ownership of real estate and later in the nineteenth century by receipt of a minimum income. Economic qualifications were set at a low uniform level for federal elections in 1885, and, not long after, virtually complete manhood suffrage was attained. During the early part of the twentieth century provincial franchise arrangements prevailed even for federal elections, and by this time votes for women had become a live issue. Before World War I women in all provinces had the right to vote for school trustees and in most provinces to run for election to that office. During the war they obtained the general franchise, first in the mid-western provinces and in Ontario. In 1917 they obtained the vote in federal elections, for which a virtually complete adult franchise was in operation thereafter. The restrictions against the Japanese and indigent residents of government institutions were removed in 1948. In provincial elections, a comprehensive adult suffrage also applied generally by 1917, although women in Quebec did not receive the provincial franchise until 1940. The potentialities of the women's vote for increasing public support to education have not been fully developed in any province.

MUNICIPAL GOVERNMENT

Essential to the creation and growth of public systems of education was the organization of municipal government by the people. In the early nineteenth century before local government was achieved, even such matters as the improvement of roads, the provision of street lights, and police protection in towns were held up by the indifference of remote officialdom in the colonial capital or across the Atlantic in London. What chance did the less tangible need for schools have of receiving attention from a central bureaucracy? The answer is suggested by a refusal of the legislative council of Upper Canada in 1837 to concur in legislation authorizing an assessment for education. Although it was stipulated that the levy could be made only at the discretion of the justices of the peace and at a rate no higher than three-quarters of a cent on the dollar, the council objected on grounds that the taxpayers of several districts had already been assessed to pay for the building of gaols and court houses and for the construction of macadamized roads.

Although the election of school trustees commonly preceded the election of municipal councils for general purposes, the efficacy of the former depended on the latter. Only after the setting up, first in Upper Canada in 1849, of the present system of self-government by villages, towns, townships, and counties, could tax-supported free public education become a real issue. The municipal franchise also was extended gradually, as may be illustrated by the granting of a vote on local matters to widows and spinsters in Ontario in 1884. The ordinary condition now is that all adult householders may vote to elect municipal governments, but that a much smaller percentage exercise that right than is the case in federal and provincial elections.

From Apathy To Responsibility

Practice in local self-government and local provision of schools was the chief means of overcoming popular apathy towards education. As one of the members of the New Brunswick legislature said in 1870, "If you want to interest the people in the education of the youth of the country, they must have some share in paying for that education and sustaining it." The indifference of people in that province had for decades been recognized as a chief obstacle to educational progress. Some of the least concerned had been temporary residents, like those who came to make a quick fortune in the shipping business in order to return home to a life of ease and enjoyment. Reports of New Brunswick school inspectors appointed in the 1840's attributed the inefficiency of the schools to the grudging support accorded them by people who used as a favorite excuse their disapproval of what was taught. The solution the inspectors suggested was that the interest of the people should be kindled by keeping education close to their lives and by setting up an institution to prepare young people as teachers; not by imparting a higher learning, but by instructing them in the homely art of keeping school.

The same indifference was encountered and deplored by school visitors and inspectors in other colonies; for example, in the school returns for Stanstead, Lower Canada, for 1830-31 the visitor found in one school "the Mistress and the Scholars more engaged than the Parents" and attributed the backwardness of another school to "the dullness of the parents," which he "endeavoured as much as possible to correct." By 1881 the importance of cultivating the interest and good opinion of the public was sufficiently recognized for an article to appear in the *Canada Educational Monthly* on "The Teacher Out of the School-room"; the author advised the young beginning teacher to be "more anxious to become popular with parents than with young people of his own age." Governments soon after found it advantageous to use special means of seeking public approval of educational policy. In 1919 an Ontario pamphlet, "Educational Problems and How They Have Been Met," dealt with the prices of textbooks, increased grants to rural areas, the teachers' pension fund, vocational training, and other matters. Voluntary effort formed a Saskatchewan Public Education League, secured the approval of the Minister of Education and the leader of the opposition, and organized in 1916 Saskatchewan's great "Campaign for Better Schools."

Persistent work to foster interest in education is now conducted by organizations like Home and School Associations, and there is at least a conviction that some regular attention must be given by the school systems to public relations. Newspapers and periodicals have generally been helpful. Typical of their service in the early nineteenth century was an editorial in the *Upper Canada Gazette* for August 31, 1815, urging the desirability of giving an elementary education to children between the ages of five and ten instead of putting them to work. Singled out for praise by a professional journal in 1879 was the *Lunenburg Progress*, which devoted a column each week to local matters of interest in connection with the schools. The problem today is to secure balanced publicity with constructive attention to activities other than games, auditorium performances, and escapades of pupils.

Social Awareness

An increasing awareness of social responsibilities was also essential to the expansion of public education. As we shall see in a subsequent chapter, many people as late as 1860 disclaimed any obligation to pay for even a minimum of education for other people's children. In 1948, through Family Allowances, all payers of income tax contributed through the government to the general support of all children for the first sixteen years of their lives. Recently many employers have adopted policies that make provision for the welfare and security of employees. There is no longer a callous disregard of the safety of workers and of the public. Government and big business have shown some anxiety to avoid disaster — whether of the type that killed fifty miners by a pit explosion in Stellarton, Nova Scotia, in 1880, or a general economic collapse like the one that occurred fifty years later.

Unfortunately the same feeling of greater security has not extended to international affairs. Although wars have focussed attention on health education and have given occasion in England for legislation to extend educational opportunity, their effects on Canadian education have been chiefly detrimental. Conflicts like the Crimean War, the American Civil War, and the Boer War had little effect on the public school systems in Canada, except to stimulate cadet training and physical education. But the two world wars of the present century usurped classroom time, interrupted school careers of older pupils, diverted public spending from education to the more urgent purposes of defence and destruction, and made calamitous inroads on teaching personnel. Regulations issued in Ontario in 1916 granted to pupils leaving school at Easter for farm service or enlistment an ordinary promotion, the Senior Public School Diploma, high school entrance, or pass matriculation. Those who enlisted while still attending high school were promised that, upon their return home and after completion of a special summer course, they would be allowed to enter a normal school or faculty of education. The regulations also permitted school boards to engage unqualified persons if the boards had failed to find teachers after advertising the positions and offering "adequate" salaries. Even in 1953 the fear of war and heavy defence expenditures deprived senior pupils and educational administrators of that serenity and confidence in the future which is most favorable to educational advance.

Self Confidence

Social as well as political independence was needed for the growth of education under popular control. In 1847 one Abraham Gesner wrote a handbook on *New Brunswick; with Notes for Emigrants* in which he said: "It is a common remark in this province and in Nova Scotia that it is vain to cultivate the higher branches of learning, so long as the Home Government bestows the principal offices and best pecuniary situations in the Colonies to persons from the Mother-country, who are sent out to fill them."[3] According to an editorial in the *New Brunswick Courier*

for May 31, 1856, the men sent out from England "received enormous salaries, and strutted on their little platform with all the airs of a genuine aristocracy, to the wonder and admiration of the poor Provincials who had to work for a living, and who could only look from a distance at the honors and dignities which were placed beyond their reach."

Even in 1880 the *Canada Educational Monthly* had reason to complain that Englishmen had recently been brought out to occupy the chairs of practical science, of chemistry, and of classics at the University of Toronto. The *Monthly* admitted that the presidency of the university had been tendered to Daniel Wilson, a professor of long standing in the institution, but "in a tardy and ungracious way that made the overture rather an insult than an honor."[4] It appears that the Minister of Education had scoured England "like a new Diogenes without a lantern" and failed to find an applicant who would take the position at the salary offered. To offset this one failure the government, according to the *Monthly*, could count not only the three professorial appointments already mentioned but imports to fill two other vacancies, one in the Ontario Agricultural College and one in the Toronto Lunatic Asylum. The tone of these remarks shows the resentment that was engendered, as did also the comments that English appointees were not acceptable to their colleagues or students, that Englishmen who were accustomed to divisions by social class had an arrogant air of superiority, and that in nearly all cases the results were most unhappy. Yet, as Lower says, universities in 1890 were still largely staffed by old-country men, who regarded themselves as exiles. Institutions that had courage to break the rule, like Mount Allison in New Brunswick, rendered a far-reaching service; but even in very recent years, and even in the west, top-level or wholesale appointments of the old colonial type have not entirely disappeared.

At the elementary and secondary school level, very few top administrative officers were brought over from across the Atlantic. The nature of the work required a familiarity obtainable only by previous experience in the country, and virtually all later appointees were residents of long standing. In the city of Quebec and its vicinity in 1830 teachers in Roman Catholic schools had been born and educated in the province, except for one French-speaking Roman Catholic who had been brought out from Bordeaux to teach in a Protestant school. But in the same district at that time all English-speaking Protestant teachers were products of schools in England, Ireland, and Scotland. The latter condition seventy years after the conquest was due partly to colonial attitudes and an exclusively overseas loyalty, but partly also to the difficulty of finding capable men for educational work in a country of economic opportunity. The difficulty would have been aggravated if the better positions in public education as well as in the universities had been regularly filled by men from England. It was necessary as a condition of full public support for education that young men and women of Canadian parentage should be able to enter the field of teaching as an open career and work with a good heart for the improvement of the schools at every level of responsibility.

The above are some of the forces in Canadian society that affected the growth and operation of the public school systems.

CHAPTER 12

A Growing Democracy Interest in Education

STAGES OF GROWTH · SCHOOL ENROLMENT · INCREASE IN SECONDARY SCHOOL
ENROLMENT · LENGTH OF SCHOOLING · ATTENDANCE · COMPULSORY SCHOOLING
PROVIDING SCHOOLS

Stages of Growth

This chapter gives a statistical account of the expansion of public school systems. But it will be helpful first to distinguish four stages of development. These successive stages are differentiated by changes in the administrative system and by the types of school provided.

STAGE ONE

The first stage extended to about 1840 in eastern Canada, to about 1870 in Manitoba and British Columbia, and to about 1885 in the territories that became Saskatchewan and Alberta. Its characteristics have already been described in previous chapters. This first stage ended with the beginning of our present system of public education.

In this stage of development schools for the people included church or parish schools, and charity schools, monitorial schools, Sunday schools, and infant schools operated by organized philanthropy. For the few there were Latin grammar schools and private schools. Secondary schools of a newer type, called academies, were established by the common enterprise of middle class people in a community, or less frequently by a religious denomination; they had a somewhat wider appeal either because they included more practical subjects in the curriculum or because they were not narrowly sectarian. Community schools of the people had appeared and had begun to supplant all other elementary types. As indicated in previous chapters, schools during this period were supported by subscriptions, government grants, and fees, but not by local taxation.

In any one province other schools of a special type might also be found. A report on schools in Prince Edward Island in 1846 listed the following: primary schools, teaching chiefly reading and spelling; French Acadian schools; two infant schools; a National school; female schools, teaching elementary subjects and giving practical instruction in household

179

economics; and district schools, teaching elementary subjects and sometimes Latin and mathematics also.

STAGE TWO

The second stage extended to about 1870 in eastern Canada and up to twenty or fifty years later in the west. It is marked by the establishment of strong central authorities, by the introduction of local taxation and free schools, and by the attainment of almost universal elementary education. For secondary education it was a period of transition from social exclusiveness to public support. It was a stage during which the people were educated by exhortation and experience to assume local responsibility for the provision of schools and during which facilities for elementary education were greatly expanded. Because of the great influx of newcomers into the middle west early in the twentieth century, this second stage was protracted or repeated in the Prairie Provinces until after World War I.

In this second stage of development, the dominant educational agency was the common school, the basic institution of provincial systems of education. It was financed at first by government grants and fees, and later by government grants and local taxation. It became a free school for all, operated by the people locally under the supervision of the provincial authority. In this period the unpopular grammar schools were taken over by the public authority, deprived of their social distinction, and made to serve as a second storey in the educational edifice. In this period, also, there evolved universities of a more public and less sectarian character. They formed a small and lofty third storey, which could now be reached by one who entered the common school if he had time and ability to climb the steep and narrowing stairs.

STAGE THREE

The third stage, from about 1870 to 1900, had the characteristics of organized efficiency. Provincial departments of education trained teachers, issued courses of study, authorized textbooks, sent out professionally qualified inspectors, and conducted an impressive number of examinations. School boards, if they could, built enduring plants for local branches of the education industry. Central and local authorities had already done, and still do, many of these things, but not with the solid confidence of Queen Victoria's later subjects. During this stage Ontario set a pattern for English-speaking Canada, which the west copied as promptly and faithfully as circumstances allowed.

In this third stage communities maintained, by local taxation and with the assistance of provincial grants, both elementary and secondary schools, which even then were known in most provinces as public schools and high schools. Elementary education was free and virtually universal, if not everywhere compulsory. Secondary education was cheap, even if not everywhere free. In less populous places secondary education was offered in a department attached to the elementary school, or even in the single classroom of the elementary school. In urban centres the high school had a building of its own. But in any event secondary education was separated from elementary education by a new academic barrier, with a gateway known as the entrance examination. It was differentiated also by its teaching of distinctly secondary subjects, including algebra, geometry, and foreign languages.

STAGE FOUR

The fourth stage, like the third, is a period characterized by developments that occurred more or less simultaneously across Canada. It extends from 1900 to the present. Provinces which, in the previous period, had not established a department of education under a minister, did so in the present century, although Quebec remained an exception. But there was nothing radically new in administrative organization, although increasing flexibility and tolerance gave it a touch of the more human quality which had come into the curriculum and the classroom. Two characteristics of this period distinguished it from the nineteenth century: (1) the extension of more than a minimum of education to all, by providing additional years at school for those whose academic ability was not exceptional and by offering a greater variety of educational fare; and (2) a greater willingness to be guided by what proved workable in practice even when the alternative procedure was more likely to hold or gain the respect of those with strong convictions.

During the present century an increasing number of urban centres, but not all, extended the public school downward by providing kindergartens, which had first been introduced in the previous period. Most cities after World War I, and more recently many rural areas, provided vocational schools or courses at the secondary level. The number and size of secondary schools increased greatly. Other notable extensions of educational services will be described in later chapters.

School Enrolment

The table on page 182 gives a comprehensive record of educational expansion in terms of enrolment figures for all provinces. The data in the table must not be regarded as exact or comparable within narrow limits, because methods used to arrive at the totals of pupils enrolled differed from province to province and from time to time. But the table does give a reasonably true impression of the growth that has taken place.

At the beginning of the second period, in 1841, we see school systems in imperfect operation in eastern Canada with an uncertain number of pupils, for no regular annual count was made as yet in all provinces. In Quebec education was still disrupted as a result of political troubles; in Ontario the schools were poor, to say the least; and nowhere was the organization well established and efficient. The enrolment figures are merely estimates.

From 1851 onward we see the effect of setting up strong provincial authorities to supervise the operation of the school systems. There were marked gains in enrolment beyond what might be expected as a result of increased population, and the totals were accurate to the extent that they were calculated by counting those who showed up at school sometime during the year.

From 1861 in Quebec and Ontario, from 1871 in Nova Scotia, and from 1881 in New Brunswick the result of local taxation and free schools is reflected in the totals. The gain in Prince Edward Island by 1861 had a similar cause, the assumption of a large proportion of school costs by the provincial government.

From 1871 we see the development of school systems in the western provinces, with rapid expansion shown from 1901.

In the third period, from 1871 or 1881 no great increase in enrolment took place in the older provinces, except Quebec, where the natural and total increase of population was high and the state of education poor at the start. Indeed, the whole period was a time of improvement in efficiency rather than of expansion.

If school enrolment and population figures are compared for different provinces at different times, apparent anomalies appear. Between 1871 and 1921 school enrolment in Nova Scotia increased at a slightly higher rate than in Ontario, although the increase of population was 81 per cent in Ontario as compared with 35 per cent in Nova Scotia. It appears that

APPROXIMATE ENROLMENT IN PUBLICLY CONTROLLED DAY SCHOOLS

	Nfld.	P.E.I.	N.S.	N.B.	Que.	Ont.	Man.	Sask.	Alta.	B.C.	Terri-tories	Canada
1841		4,500	20,000	14,000	60,000	65,000						160,000
1851		5,500	29,000	18,000	100,000	176,000						330,000
1861		12,000	33,000	28,000	181,000	344,000						600,000
1871		18,000	76,000	34,000	210,000	463,000	1,000			500		800,000
1881		21,500	79,000	65,500	228,000	496,000	5,000			2,500		900,000
1891		22,500	83,500	69,000	265,500	515,000	24,000			9,500	5,500	1,000,000
1901		21,000	98,500	66,500	315,000	492,500	52,000			23,500	24,000	1,100,000
1911		17,500	103,000	69,000	389,000	518,500	81,000	72,500	61,500	49,500		1,400,000
1921		17,500	109,500	73,500	518,500	637,500	129,000	185,000	138,000	86,000		1,900,000
1931	60,500	17,500	115,500	89,000	606,000	682,500	153,500	230,500	166,000	114,000		2,200,000
1941	66,500	18,000	117,000	92,000	644,000	643,500	131,500	201,500	163,500	119,500		2,200,000
1951	79,000	19,000	134,500	105,500	646,000	764,000	129,000	167,500	174,000	173,500	2,000	2,400,000

Based chiefly on data in publications of the
DOMINION BUREAU OF STATISTICS

the percentage of the population in school in Ontario in 1871 was amazingly high — nearly 28 per cent — and that it dropped to less than 22 per cent, whereas the Nova Scotia percentage gained conservatively from slightly less than the usual 20 per cent to slightly more. The conclusion to be drawn from this is not that Ontario suffered an educational decline, but that school enrolment in relation to total population may be misleading as a measure of educational progress, especially after universal education was attained. The ratio may be affected by such factors as interprovincial movements of adult population and comparative birth rate.

For this reason enrolment figures do not reflect the major educational development of the fourth period, the present century. It would appear that more than one in five of all Canadians were to be found in school in all census years between 1871 and 1901, and that the proportion has grown smaller, if anything, since that time. But one must keep in mind that the number of school-age children per hundred of population has declined — for males aged five to fourteen from 25.9 in 1851 to 22.3 in 1901, and to 19.8 in 1941. The fact is that, since the latter part of the nineteenth century, virtually everyone has attended school for an elementary education, and that in the later years of the present century the majority have received some secondary education as well. Since this development has had far-reaching consequences, it deserves amplification.

Increases in Secondary School Enrolment

In 1841 secondary schools were class institutions attended by a very few. Between then and 1871 these class institutions gave way to high schools, superim-

posed upon the elementary schools. By 1901 the high schools were attended by many preparing to be teachers, by a smaller number intending to enter university, and by some others. Then a spectacular expansion began.

In British Columbia there were less than 1000 pupils in high school in 1901-02, over 2000 in 1911-12, and about 18,000 in 1931-32. Whereas elementary school enrolment quadrupled during the thirty year period, secondary school enrolment went up in the ratio of over twenty to one.

What was happening may be illustrated by grade enrolment figures for Saskatchewan:[1]

SCHOOL ENROLMENT BY GRADES SASKATCHEWAN

	1910	1920	1930
GRADE I....	21,775	48,045	42,961
GRADE II...	8,815	20,839	26,337
GRADE III..	9,683	23,141	27,916
GRADE IV...	9,199	22,777	27,905
GRADE V...	5,377	16,791	24,015
GRADE VI...	3,152	12,453	20,746
GRADE VII..	2,199	8,355	13,925
GRADE VIII.	2,567	10,887	19,527
GRADE IX..}	1,840	4,421	9,865
GRADE X...}		2,736	7,025
GRADE XI..	547	2,327	5,294
GRADE XII..	238	652	2,265
TOTAL....	65,392	173,424	227,781

Data from the *Historical Statistical Survey of Education*, 1921, and the *Annual Survey* (38), 1921 and 1930.

Observe the relatively large increase in enrolment in grades above VII especially between 1920 and 1930.

In Ontario between 1900 and 1950 the population doubled, enrolment in elementary grades went up by one-third, and enrolment in secondary grades increased to six times the earlier figure. Secondary school enrolment was less than five per cent of total school enrolment in 1900, more than twenty-three per cent in 1950.

In New Brunswick in 1884 the provincial department of education was discouraged by the failure of its efforts to encourage attendance in high school grades. Only 258 pupils were engaged anywhere in the study of subjects of a distinctly secondary character, and of that number the high schools of Fredericton and Saint John accounted for all but 78. In 1895 less than one per cent of pupils in the province were enrolled in secondary grades, but in 1910 nearly three per cent, and in 1948 well over eight per cent were so enrolled.

The same phenomenal expansion of secondary education occurred across the whole of Canada from the beginning of the present century. It continued in later years, for the number of pupils doing work of secondary grade went up from 84,000 to 278,000 between 1921 and 1948, a period during which elementary school enrolment declined.

Some of the contributory causes of secondary school expansion were greater wealth, smaller families, less need for immediate wage earning, more need in business for educated employees, fewer jobs in depression years, new secondary school courses of utilitarian value, more consideration of pupils' interests and needs, and the cumulative effect of a growing appreciation of the value of education in successively better-educated generations. The educational implications of this expansion are discussed in chapter 22.

Length of Schooling

Obviously more young people have been attending school longer in recent years. Between 1911 and 1941 the average length of the school life of Canadian children increased from 8 to 10 years. At the later date it ranged from 9.15 years in Quebec to 10.73 years in British Columbia. It is difficult to estimate the average length of schooling in earlier periods. In Saskatchewan in 1896 the public elementary schools had five standards, but 88 per cent of the pupils did not proceed beyond the third standard, which the average pupil could complete in not more than six years. In 1881, Ontario children usually began school at seven years of age and took six or seven years to complete the work of the elementary school, but less than half as many pupils were in the highest elementary grade as were in the lowest. In British Columbia in 1876 Superintendent Jessup said that pupils took from four to five years to gain high school entrance standing. In many schools of Quebec in 1868 an inspector rarely found children over ten years of age. A study of the ages and grade distribution of Ontario pupils between 1850 and 1870 suggests that most pupils stayed at school from four to six years. Before the middle of the nineteenth century, comparison is complicated by the considerable number who attended hardly at all and by the short length of the school year.

As we have seen, schools around 1830 were open for terms of no more than six months, although some had also a summer session under a different teacher and for the most part with different pupils. The usual school career was about four of these short sessions; but if we include those who received no schooling or hardly any, the average can hardly have been more than two. Towards the middle of the century the winter term was extended into a school year, which in Ontario increased from less than eight months in 1844 to eleven months in 1871, although it was then reduced again to slightly more than ten months by the 1890's. Hence five years of schooling in the 1870's represented a much more substantial gain over four years in the 1840's than the number of years alone would indicate.

For the whole of Canada, therefore, the average length of total schooling received by children over the span of a century appears to have increased approximately as follows:

How children in rural areas went to school

AVERAGE NUMBERS OF MONTHS IN SCHOOL

1830	1850	1870	1890	1910	1930
10	20	50	60	80	100

The gain up to about 1860 was achieved mainly by getting more children into school; after 1860 the gains were made mainly by keeping the children in school for a longer time.

Attendance

There is still another factor to be considered in estimating the amount of education received. It is one thing to have a pupil's name on the roll, but quite another thing to keep him in regular attendance at school. Before the middle of the nineteenth century the irregular and spasmodic nature of school attendance was a chief worry of teachers and officials. The Royal Institution in Quebec found that attendance fluctuated with the seasons and was poorest in the spring when the roads were muddy and the farmer needed help at home. New Brunswick inspectors complained of the same conditions and particularly of the practice of sending one child and then another of the family to school for a few weeks at a time. It was evident that many parents thought the chores more important than book-learning. Schools were often intolerably cold and drafty in winter, the time when children had leisure to attend. But even in balmy British Columbia attendance was very irregular. In New Westminster in 1863 there were 35 on the roll but never more than 24 present at any time; for September two years later the average number present was only 12 of 30 on the roll. Even between 1870 and 1890 the average daily attendance for the whole province was only about 55 per cent of the enrolment. For all eastern provinces together the average was scarcely higher than 50 per cent at mid-century.

Interestingly enough, very much the same difficulties were encountered in the mid-western provinces early in the twentieth century. Children of the prairie pioneers found it very hard to get to school in winter, when they were least needed at home. Distances were great in the new districts, which were more spread out than the old settlements along the rivers. In Saskatchewan in 1911 an inspector drove up to a school and found that the teacher — a good one — had been the only one in attendance for five days. In school after school of some districts no more than 5 or 10 were present out of an enrolment of 15 to 25. Sometimes as many as a quarter of the pupils rode horses, for which stables were provided at school; quite often they carried their own drinking water, for among a group of 162 school districts, 24 had safe and reliable wells and 132 had no wells at all. Even in Manitoba at the beginning of the century nearly half the pupils attended for less than half the time, and some schools could muster an average of only 2, 3, 4, or 5 actually on hand.

By 1901 the average daily attendance for the whole of Canada had been raised to nearly 62 per cent. By 1911 it was just a little better than 64 per cent, but by 1948 it was nearly 88 per cent. Part of the gain resulted from the west's catching up with the east in the 1920's. Most of it was earned by enhancing the value of instruction. But some of it came from changes in the method of calculating school attendance.

In Ontario, for example, pupils who transferred from one school to another were until 1921 counted twice, a practice which added fictitiously to the provincial enrolment and reflected adversely on average attendance. In 1933 the old method of counting attendance for the calendar year was abandoned. Under the old method, pupils who graduated from school in June were marked absent in the fall, and the new pupils were marked present although they were not included in the enrolment until January. The enrolment thereafter was totalled for the last school day of May, so that pupils who dropped out before that time were not counted in the enrolment although their presence up to that point was credited in aggregate total attendance. Chiefly as a consequence of this change, curious figures for Ontario

appear in the records of the Dominion Bureau of Statistics:

	ENROLMENT	AVERAGE DAILY ATTENDANCE
1933	774,868	613,084
1934	698,020	614,357

The uninformed might conclude that tens of thousands of children had died of starvation during the depression and that the survivors had so improved in virtue as to cause a sudden improvement in average daily attendance from 79 per cent to 88 per cent in one year.

In Ontario again, the year 1934 marked the final disappearance of a practice of not counting absence for "certified" illness. In that year the report of the provincial school attendance officer explained that average daily attendance was then and thereafter to be the ratio of actual attendances to possible attendances of pupils. Calculations show that these statistical adjustments caused apparent gains up to an aggregate of fifteen per cent or more in regularity of attendance but that the inflationary effect did not persist because of other factors. For example, changes in calculating enrolment in 1942 and 1943 added 25,000 to the number of pupils and caused attendance to seem less satisfactory.

The import of all this is to emphasize the need for a wide latitude in attaching significance to any school statistics. Nevertheless there has been a marked improvement in regularity of attendance. If cognizance is taken of the child's bodily presence in school, it is probable that the average length of time Canadian children actually attended school was something like this:

AVERAGE NUMBER OF MONTHS IN SCHOOL

1830	1850	1870	1890	1910	1930	1950
5	10	30	35	55	80	90

Other facts regarding attendance are of some interest. In no province during recent years has average daily attendance fallen below 80 per cent, and only in Quebec, which had shown a superior record throughout the century, has it exceeded 90 per cent.

Epidemics caused great local variations in the past, and as late as 1918 influenza had a wide effect, as illustrated by the drop of the Ontario average in that year to 57 per cent as compared with 65 per cent in the years preceding and following. In 1946-47 the National Committee for School Health Research made the first nation-wide and thorough investigation of "Absenteeism in Canadian Schools." The report showed a relatively high percentage of absences from non-medical causes in rural schools as compared with urban schools, and a high percentage of absences caused by respiratory diseases.

Compulsory Schooling

Among the devices used to get children to school in pre-Confederation days was making the grant dependent on the attendance of a minimum number of pupils. Thus in New Brunswick in 1862 the government stipulated that the average daily attendance must be not less than ten in rural schools and not less than seventeen in certain designated centres of population. Schools that failed to meet the condition forfeited the grant. Although parents tried to comply by sending their six-year-olds to swell the enrolment, seventy-six schools were closed in the following year — many of them because grant support had been lost. The regulation was apparently dropped after 1864. Between 1877 and 1900, after free schools were in operation, an attempt was made to improve the attendance by offering prizes, but with little effect.

There was reluctance everywhere to pass and enforce legislation to compel parents to send their children to school. Some sincerely objected to compulsion on grounds of principle; others were anxious to avoid the taxation which such a measure implied. The Toronto *Globe* in 1848 argued editorially against compulsory attendance:

The cold and withering effects of such a system would soon develop themselves on the public character which nothing but a return to the sure land-marks set up by the Almighty would ever efface.[2]

Like many other opponents of compulsory education, this newspaper favored legislation to force parents and factory owners to limit hours of work for children in order that time might be left for education. But the only real alternative to compulsory attendance would have been far too costly and on other grounds impracticable in the nineteenth century. The alternative was the plan suggested by a minority of the Cross Commission in England in 1888 — to make education so convincingly attractive and valuable that no one would willingly forego the privilege.

Ontario took the first step in 1871, when the last remaining school districts were required by law to provide free schools by local taxation. In that year parents were obliged by threat of legal penalty to have children attend school for at least four months a year between the ages of seven and twelve. During the 1880's municipalities were required to compile registers of all school-age children and were empowered to appoint officers to enforce attendance. But the law remained only partially operative: 23 per cent of rural children within the compulsory school attendance age limits failed to attend for the minimum annual period, which had been raised to 100 days. Legislation in 1891 was more definite in stipulating penalties for parents or guardians who refused to comply and for employers who hired children who should have been at school, and more definite also in stating the conditions on which children might be exempted from attendance. The latter included sickness, distance from school if the child was under ten, the passing of the high school entrance examinations, and approval for other reasons by the school principal or a justice of the peace. The same legislation raised the requirements of attendance; throughout the school year children between the ages of eight and fourteen were required to go to school. There was still failure of parents to comply and of authorities to enforce, especially in rural areas. In the very year of the new legislation one school section levied a special rate on parents whose children did not attend regularly and claimed in that way to have improved attendance considerably. But many municipalities and townships did not appoint truant officers until required to do so by the School Attendance Act of 1919. Meanwhile in 1912 it had been made permissible for the locality to require the attendance of older children. The Adolescent School Attendance Act raised the age of compulsory attendance, in spite of opposition from employers, to sixteen years in urban areas in 1918 and throughout the province in 1921; but many parents in the country took advantage of loop-holes in the act to get their children out of school at fifteen or even fourteen years of age. In 1950 the Royal Commission on Education in Ontario pointed out that improvements in transportation had removed any valid reason for not requiring the attendance of younger children and recommended that the period of compulsory attendance be from six to sixteen years.

British Columbia made provision in 1873 for requiring the attendance of children between ages seven and fourteen for periods to be determined by the local trustees. Exemption might be obtained on such grounds as living more than three miles from school or having attained a certain educational standard. When it was found these provisions did not work, trustees were empowered in 1876 to enforce attendance, for six months in the year, of pupils between seven and twelve years of age. Compulsory attendance throughout the year was introduced for pupils aged seven to twelve in city school districts in 1901, for pupils aged seven to fourteen in all municipal districts in 1912, and for all pupils over seven and under fifteen everywhere in 1921. Two years later responsibility for enforcement was imposed on trustees.

Most other provinces introduced compulsory attendance before 1900. In Manitoba in 1876 the Act permitted central and local authorities to enforce attendance of pupils aged seven to twelve, and in 1888 a similar provision was made in the Northwest Territories. In Nova Scotia from 1883 a two-thirds vote in favor of compulsory attendance in any school section sanctioned its application to children aged seven to twelve, with the usual penalty of a fine and the usual exemptions of children living two miles from a public school or attending a private school; in 1888, 1895, and 1915 Halifax, and then other towns, were permitted to extend schooling by forbidding employment to upper limits of fourteen and finally sixteen years of age. New Brunswick finally introduced compulsory attendance in 1905. By the end of World War I eight provinces had compulsory attendance laws: in Prince Edward Island between 7 and 13 years of age for 20 or 30 weeks; in Nova Scotia from 7 to 12 at the option of the locality; in New Brunswick from 7 to 12 for at least 80 days; in Ontario from 8 to 14 for the full year; in Manitoba, Saskatchewan, and British Columbia from 7 to 14 for the full year; in Alberta from 7 to 15. Boards could forbid employment to age 10 in New Brunswick and in towns of Nova Scotia. Exemption when Grade VIII standing was attained could be secured in Saskatchewan and Alberta. In only two provinces was the exactment of compulsory attendance postponed until the second quarter of the present century.

In Quebec the issue of compulsory attendance was raised on several occasions. In 1912 the central authority for Protestant education tried unsuccessfully to have it introduced for their schools. Claims were advanced then and subsequently that it was unnecessary: that Quebec in 1911-12 had the highest average daily attendance in relation to pupils enrolled; that by 1931 the enrolment of children between seven and fourteen years of age was from 95 to 98 per cent of the total number; and that legislation forbidding the employment of children was sufficient. But in 1942 the Council of Public Instruction expressed itself in favor of compulsory attendance legislation, which was enacted forthwith. Children were obliged to attend from six to fourteen years of age in rural areas and from six to sixteen years of age in urban centres. In Newfoundland also legislation of 1942 provided for free education and compulsory attendance in elementary grades between the ages of seven and fourteen.

At the end of World War II, attendance was compulsory in all provinces up to 14, 15, or 16 years of age.

Providing Schools

The erection of a school building was not regarded at first as a major problem in providing education for a growing population in Canada. Whereas in England the first educational grants of 1833 were made for buildings, government assistance at that time on this continent usually took the form of a subsidy towards paying a teacher. The men of a rural community could easily put up a log schoolhouse. But aid towards the construction of buildings was granted in Quebec to education societies in large centres before 1829 and to trustees anywhere during the 1830's. By the time of Confederation it had become necessary there and elsewhere to see that adequate school accommodation was required. That the need was dire in some places is shown by this extract from the 1873 report on education in the Journal of the Legislative Assembly for Prince Edward Island:

The very low ebb to which the common schools of Charlottetown have fallen, ought to be the cause of alarm . . . . an army of about 800 children, of school age, within the limits of the city, or about one in three, never enter a Schoolroom at all. The twelve or thirteen poor Schoolrooms now in use, with difficulty accommodate the 630 children enrolled.

If there were not enough schools for children of the people, there was also a lack at first of good schools for the few — or at least for those who were most particular. In the Red River settlement around 1830-40, "many of the officers who were financially able sent their children away to be educated. Some were sent to the Old Country by Company's ships, while a great majority were educated at St. John's College. Some had governesses at the Forts . . ."[3]

Regulations in British Columbia will illustrate measures taken by provincial authorities to ensure adequate school accommodation. Schools were to be opened and a school district set up, in 1872 if there were fifteen or more children between the ages of five and sixteen, in 1893 if there were fifteen children between the ages of six and sixteen, and in 1897 if there were twenty children in the same age group. From 1872 schools might be opened with fewer children, but no district was to be established. The requirements of school accommodation were gradually extended. In 1891 cities were obliged to provide places for children between six and sixteen years of age desiring to attend, and in 1934 all school boards were obliged to provide accommodation for pupils up to eighteen years of age and might provide for older pupils.

The difficulty everywhere in Canada was to provide adequate school accommodation without encouraging the building of too many small schools, in deference to the narrow preferences of local democracy. The seriousness of this problem was well stated by Superintendent John Bennett of New Brunswick in 1865:

It has been more than once pointed out in these reports that a mere addition to the number of schools in the aggregate, irrespective of their locality, and the felt wants of the community, is no sign of advancing education; that in fact it may be, and often is, the very reverse; and I am not quite sure whether a few, perhaps only a very few, of the additional schools now reported, must not be regarded as a disadvantage than otherwise. The tendency of this increase in the larger towns is usually very great; and nothing but the restraining power of the Board can keep such places from being deluged with a useless multitude of petty rival schools and the Province from being saddled with many thousands of Dollars or worse than useless expense. Nor are the rural districts entirely free from the tendency in question. There, it has its origin in dissensions amongst the inhabitants who seek to escape from the pernicious effects of dissension by sub-dividing the districts, and establishing additional schools. These fledglings are necessarily poor affairs, and are all the more to be deprecated, that one of the first and worse effects of them is to reduce the schools from which they have swarmed, to the same low level with themselves.[4]

When distances were great and population scanty, some curious regulations were found necessary to control the operation of small schools. In the Northwest Territories in 1888 a school was required to remain open for the whole year if fifteen pupils resided within a radius of one and one-half miles, but only for half a year if only ten pupils lived within such an area. At the elementary level, the problem of the small school has persisted in rural areas. In six provinces for which such information was available in 1948, the most common number of pupils in average daily attendance in one-room rural schools was from 11 to 15, and there were almost as many such schools with 6 to 10 pupils as with 16 to 20. In city classrooms of the same provinces the number was more than twice as high.

At various times in various places expansion of school accommodation was necessarily rapid. In Ontario there were some 1750 school buildings in 1842, some 3000 in 1851, and about 4700 in 1871. In Alberta there were about 600 schools in operation in 1905, about 1750 in 1911, about 3000 in 1918, and about 4000 in 1939. In the whole of Canada the number of classrooms increased from 27,000 to 51,000 between 1901 and 1919, chiefly because of the opening of the west. In Saskatchewan there were 1400 elementary school districts in 1908 and 4800 twenty years later. For secondary education in Manitoba in 1896 most of the 1730 pupils simply remained in public school, for the only special provision was one small collegiate department. But in 1929 there were 126 intermediate schools, 44 high schools, 10 collegiate departments, and 11 collegiate institutes accommodating over 15,000 pupils.

More recently in Canada the shift of population to the cities, accelerated by industrial expansion and prosperity during and after World War II, and augmented in effect by the higher birth rate, has necessitated the construction of one school after another in growing suburban residential areas. The annual gross capital outlay of school boards in Ontario in 1943 and the five years following was, respectively, $927,000, $1,864,000, $3,395,000, $5,720,000, $11,129,000, and $16,279,000.

CHAPTER 13

A Growing Democracy
School Organization

THE GRADED ELEMENTARY SCHOOL: EARLY EXAMPLES AND DIFFICULTIES ·
THE APPROACH TO GRADED CLASSES: · GRADING ACCOMPLISHED
THE EVOLUTION OF THE SECONDARY SCHOOL: LATIN GRAMMAR SCHOOLS ·
ACADEMIES · BRINGING SECONDARY SCHOOLS UNDER DEMOCRATIC CONTROL
· IN THE OLDER PROVINCES · GRADE ORGANIZATION IN SECONDARY SCHOOLS
· JUNIOR HIGH SCHOOLS · VOCATIONAL SCHOOLS · UNIVERSITIES ·

SUMMARY OF CHAPTERS ELEVEN, TWELVE, AND THIRTEEN

This chapter is a continuation of chapters 11 and 12. The discussion turns to the organization and reorganization of grade levels and of sections in the educational ladder.

THE GRADE ELEMENTARY SCHOOL

In the early nineteenth-century school the pupil progressed at his own rate in learning the content required. But one should not be misled by any apparent advantage in this arrangement. The youngster might have benefited from individual instruction if there had been any instruction. He might also have been accelerated, or given an enriched program, or helped to catch up when retarded, if any teachers had had the insight, the time, and the ability to do any of these things. But the fact is, as we shall see later, teaching did more for the individual child when it became class teaching. The instruction of a class necessitated the distribution of pupils in grades, whether among several rooms or within a single

191

classroom. The "want of proper grading" was considered by many school visitors and inspectors at mid-century to be a major defect of the schools. The organization of the graded school was therefore an administrative development of importance.

Early Examples and Difficulties

Grading had been one of the improvements introduced by the monitorial schools. In a manuscript *Guide aux Instituteurs,* Guillaume Benziger in the early nineteenth century urged teachers of Lower Canada to organize their pupils in from four to eight classes and to have them instructed simultaneously by monitors. It is probable that the popularity of the monitorial method led to more attempts at grading in the ordinary schools of Lower Canada than elsewhere, but the decline and disappearance of the monitorial school left the problem to be solved in other ways.

The introduction in cities of another type of paternalistic school also set a pattern for grading of a kind. This institution was the infant school, which had been originated in Great Britain by Robert Owen, developed by Samuel Wilderspin, and caused to multiply by the Home and Colonial Infant School Society during the first half of the nineteenth century. Its purpose was to give instruction to children while they were very young, and its significance in connection with grading is that it established a primary department separate from the usual elementary school.

There were at least two infant schools in Quebec and one in Montreal. The Quebec Infant School Society opened its school in 1832 after writing to the society in London for books and a teacher and obtaining a government grant. It had 220 children on the roll in 1835. In the same year the British and Canadian Infant School Society of Quebec had a school

for 100 children. A Montreal Infant School Society had 106 children of all denominations enrolled in 1834. An infant school in Charlottetown, P.E.I., had an average attendance of 95 in 1846. In these cities and others where infant schools were in operation, at least some children had the experience of attending one school for preliminary work and another school for the continuance of their elementary education. Infant schools were vanishing by 1850, but they had set an example of separating younger and older children.

What was probably the nearest approach to grading in the early schools of the ordinary type is illustrated by the distribution of fifty pupils in the district common school of London, Upper Canada, in 1832. The report preserved in the Canadian archives shows that of the 36 boys and 14 girls in the school:

all 50 were in spelling, including 3 aged four, six, and seven who were in spelling only;

47 were in reading, and most of those under eleven were in reading and spelling only;

36 were in writing, and most of them were eleven or older;

28 were in arithmetic, and most of them were eleven or older;

9 were in geography, including two precocious youngsters of nine, although the rest were older;

2 were in grammar — both of them girls, whose ages were fourteen and fifteen.[1]

This grading by subjects reflected the curriculum sequence ordinarily followed in common schools.* Occasionally there were pupils who reached an even higher level where Latin was begun; there were two such pupils in London in 1834.

When the number of pupils increased in an ordinary common school and it be-

---

* See p. 141.

Central school, Hamilton, Ontario, 1853

came necessary to provide additional accommodation, the first thought that occurred to the parents even in towns was to build a second school nearer home. When the number increased to a point where distance ceased to be a consideration, those with strong views on the subject were often successful in getting one school or classroom for boys and another for girls. Division by level of achievement was also retarded in some places by the adoption of another alternative, the setting up of a different school for a Roman Catholic or a Protestant minority.

The Approach to Graded Classes

The first approach to the graded school in Upper Canada was the building of a senior school near the centre of a town in which one-room schools for junior pupils continued to operate in different wards or neighborhoods. This arrangement placed all the more advanced pupils in rooms of their own; but if the senior school had two rooms, it was still common practice in the 1850's to divide these advanced pupils by sex rather than by age or achievement. The next step was to have more than one division by grade level of pupils in a larger urban school. The Toronto Model School in the 1850's had six rooms — a junior, an intermediate, and a senior division for the boys and the same for the girls.

In the Maritime Provinces a more direct transition to graded classes was stimulated by the nearby example of Massachusetts. When a school in Saint John, N.B., became crowded in the 1850's, assistant teachers were engaged, and when additional accommodation could be found, classes were split up. In 1864 there were three graded schools in the province, a Roman Catholic school in Carleton County, the district school in Milltown, Charlotte County, and the so-called Commercial School in Saint John. The Milltown school had three departments, primary, intermediate, and high school. The Saint John school after 1852 had three graded departments accommodating 120 pupils in all and was praised by the inspectors as a model for others to follow.

By the 1850's graded readers had appeared. The most widely used of these in Canada was the Irish National series, in which there were five books, the first four of which carried the pupil to the point where the grammar schools took over when it became their function to give further education to graduates of the common schools. Some of the Irish National books, and most books of some later series, were published in two volumes, junior and senior. From this organization of school readers arose the practice of indicating a pupil's grade by the book he was using. He was said to be in the first book, the second book, and so on. By the 1880's, when the eight grade system had evolved, pupils were said to be in the junior first, the senior first, the junior second, and so on to the senior fourth. Those who remained at elementary school for more advanced work instead of going to high school were said to be in the fifth book, a term which has retained its meaning in Ontario up to the present day.

Grading Accomplished

By the 1870's the fully graded school had appeared in cities and larger towns, and the organization of the school program by "books" or grades was well established in smaller schools. For example, in

New Brunswick the Act of 1871 recognized three divisions of the school, elementary, advanced, and high; between 1871 and 1876 the introduction of uniform textbooks facilitated grading; by the latter year one-quarter of all schools had pupils classified in graded departments; and in 1878 the course of study was based on an eight-grade organization. The elementary school of eight grades became standard, but not in some provinces until considerably later, and not everywhere even then. In Saskatchewan the eight-grade public school was introduced in 1908. In British Columbia the elementary school program was reorganized on an eight-grade basis in 1923. The English-language schools of Quebec reached a seven-grade arrangement.

An addition to the number of grades in the elementary schools appeared with the introduction of the kindergarten in some Ontario cities in the late nineteenth century. In Toronto private kindergartens were advertised as early as 1877, and eight years later provincial legislation permitted the establishment of kindergartens as part of the school system of the province. By 1892 there were 160 kindergarten teachers in 66 Ontario schools, and by 1900 there were 250 in 120 schools. In 1948, kindergartens were permitted by legislation to be included in the publicly supported systems of education of the six provinces from Quebec westward, and were to be found in many of the larger centres. An innovation during World War II was the junior kindergarten: there were 18 junior kindergartens in Ottawa in 1948 and 10 in Toronto. Actually, the number of grades was increased by kindergartens of any type in only a few places across Canada. In some provinces, on the other hand, the number of elementary grades was reduced to six around 1930 by the introduction of junior high schools.*

* See p. 205.

THE EVOLUTION OF
THE SECONDARY SCHOOL

The evolution of the secondary school from an institution for the few to a community school for the people was a development of very great significance, if only because it left to the present generation a legacy of curricular problems more difficult than any that have been encountered in the elementary grades. These problems will be discussed in later chapters. We shall deal here with the function and organization of secondary schools and their place in the public school system.

Throughout the centuries the ruling and more favored classes in society were given a training which differentiated them from the great majority of ordinary people. In the mediaeval period chivalry gave the knight courtly manners and skill to fight in full armor. Subsequently the gentleman learned simply to use a sword; after the Renaissance he began to reinforce this less obvious claim to distinction by the acquisition of classical learning.

Latin Grammar Schools

As we have already seen, the universities and great secondary schools of England by the eighteenth century had become the resorts of bluebloods rather than the habitations of scholars. When Latin grammar schools were imported into Canada around 1800, they were intended for the education of young gentlemen, only a few of whom were preparing for further study. A major function of the grammar schools was to give future leaders of society an educational mark of distinction which would assist them to command respect.

We have seen in previous chapters that the Latin grammar schools were regarded by most people with suspicion and hostility. They were attacked in the legislature by the advocates of democratic reform and were criticized by observers like Lord Durham as not meriting the proportionately high grants they received. In the Maritime Provinces they languished at the point of expiration in the third and fourth decades of the nineteenth century. The fact was that local schools of the type had an insufficient clientele of the class to which they made appeal. Forced by circumstances to enrol girls and younger children of both sexes — among them some children of ordinary people — they were unable to maintain their distinctive characteristics.

Parents who were conscious of their superior social tradition preferred to send their sons to a few superior schools like Upper Canada College in Toronto, the Royal Grammar Schools in Montreal and Quebec, and the schools at Halifax and Windsor in Nova Scotia. The result was that the Latin grammar schools in smaller places had the support neither of the common people nor of the select few. Even people of a new prosperous middle class were lukewarm at best in their support, partly because they regarded the classical curriculum as old-fashioned and narrow, and in some cases because the schools were closely associated with the Church of England.

Academies

These more prosperous citizens in the towns were the first to establish community secondary schools to serve at least a limited section of the people. Corresponding groups had set up proprietary schools in England and academies in the United States, in both countries by organizing a number of subscribers to build, buy, or rent a school and get it into operation. The subscribers had some things in common: they either lived in the same town, or belonged to the same church, or were united in their opposition to the assumptions of special privileges in education by a single church. As a rule these new groups of commercial society wanted to provide a reasonably practical education for their sons and daughters.

IN LOWER CANADA

Academies, in this accepted sense of the term, were quite common in the English-speaking Protestant communities of Quebec. These academies were founded and supported by the contributions of subscribers. They admitted only pupils who had a good elementary education, so that those in attendance ranged from fourteen to twenty years of age, with a median age of close to sixteen years. In 1846 there were academies in Stanstead, Hatley, Shefford, Clarenceville, and Lennoxville. When government assistance was made regularly available in 1846, at least fifteen additional schools were established within a decade. But the "academies" were then in the first stage of transition into high schools. The change was complete when taxation replaced subscriptions as the means of local support.

Detailed information on one academy, the Stanstead Seminary, was given in reports of 1840. In December of that year there were two teachers, a man and a woman, and sixty-one pupils, of whom forty-nine were over the age of ten, thirty-nine were boys, and twelve were boarders. The school ran for four terms of twelve weeks each, and for five and one-half days a week. Boys and girls were taught in separate departments, but from the beginning of the second term they were both to be in one department

under the preceptor, or male teacher, "it being deemed adviseable through the winter season to have but one school." Under the two teachers twenty-five subjects in all were offered.* The school had suffered over £50 damage from use as a barracks for troops during the rebellion, but had received reimbursement. It had also received for the year £100 as a government grant and £41 in fees from the pupils, and therefore in terms of financial administration it had become indistinguishable from a grammar school. The preceptor was given £62 10s as salary for half a year and the preceptress £36 5s for services up to November 2nd. Pupils could get board for from 7s 6d to 10 shillings a week. Three boys and five girls in a smaller class the previous spring were preparing to be teachers.

IN UPPER CANADA

In Upper Canada the first academy was established by the people of Ernestown in 1812 as a practical measure of protest against the setting up of a grammar school at Kingston. The school was located at Bath, known as the Ernestown Academy, and taught by Barnabas Bidwell. Another local academy was the Grantham Academy established by subscriptions in St. Catharines in 1829. Ten years later it was refused government aid on the ground that the grammar schools had first claim on the limited fund. Since the school was in debt and unable to pay adequate salaries, its agent asked that it be made a grammar school, but also gave assurance that he could sell additional shares in the academy if financial assistance was assured. The original four-room building is still in use in the centre of a structure which expanded on either side after the academy became a high school, and which in 1952 was modernized and extended still further to house an elementary school.

* See p. 441.

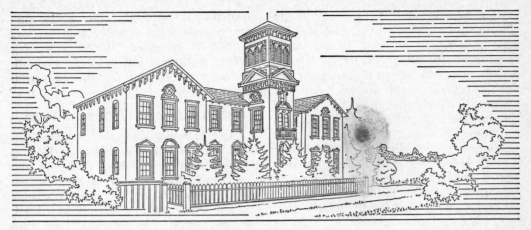

Grantham Academy

Academies of the denominational type were Upper Canada Academy, founded by the Methodists in 1836 at Cobourg, and the predecessor of Pickering College, founded by the Quakers near Picton in 1841.

Altogether about eleven academies were opened in Upper Canada before 1850; after that date they either became grammar schools and eventually high schools under public control, or developed into a university, as in the case of Upper Canada Academy, or continued as what would now be called private schools, as in the case of Pickering College, or disappeared.

IN THE MARITIME PROVINCES

Since the groups who were responsible for the founding of academies in Canada were in many cases able to obtain government grants, such schools were not always easily distinguishable from other types. As Harvey pointed out, interested people established regional or denominational schools of an academy type in Nova Scotia, partly to be sure of getting a share of the government grants for their own districts. Academies in the Maritime Provinces were thought of as public institutions superior to the grammar schools.

Legislation of 1841 and 1845 in Nova Scotia indicated that academies were expected to provide a whole range of secondary subjects, whereas the grammar schools were expected to offer instruction in the classics and in the ordinary subjects of the common schools. Forrester, a distinguished educationist of the province, wrote in 1867 that an academy "when conducted in accordance with its position in the school series, occupies . . . a kind of intermediate place between the grammar school and the college" and that the "grammar school, sometimes called the high school, differs from the common school by the addition of higher departments of grammar, mathematics and classics."

This concept of the academy as a superior institution caused the term to be applied to such establishments as Fredericton Collegiate School, although this was actually a preparatory school attached to King's College and supported by college funds, an Anglican institution opened and closed each day with the reading of Church of England prayers, and considered to be aristocratic. Yet this school was like an academy in that it required the beginning students to have an elementary education, the actual stipulation in this case being that the entrants be able to read a chapter of the Bible. Like many academies, also, it finally came under the jurisdiction of the provincial school system: in 1861 it was brought under the supervision of the chief superintendent of education and in 1873 it became the high school for the city of Fredericton.

A school of New Brunswick which had a much more humble beginning also exhibited certain characteristics of an academy. In 1854 Father Lafrance founded at Memramcook a "seminary" which was really just a parish school. In 1855 it acquired a second teacher, Miss O'Regan, to give instruction to girls. The school later closed for a while, then reopened, and became in 1864 the bilingual College of St. Joseph, which in 1928 became the University of St. Joseph. Lynam says that this college was truly "one of the people, built for the improvement of their intellectual and moral health."

Academies, denominational or otherwise, had financial difficulties. After its establishment in 1818 Pictou Academy was financed in the first instance by substantial contributions of subscribers. But for its continued support it was necessary to organize "Ladies' Penny a Week," "Gentlemen's Dollar a Year," and other funds and collecting agencies throughout Nova Scotia and the adjoining provinces. Even so, voluntary contributions proved inadequate, and for a few years the trustees were successful in obtaining grants from the legislature. Regular support from the government was secured in 1832 and eventually Pictou Academy became a high school, though one of traditionally high reputation, in the provincial system.

A later school founded by the Presbyterians was the academy of Chatham, New Brunswick, which opened in 1861. The following year it had a full staff of teachers and 160 pupils enrolled in French, Latin, Greek, algebra, geometry, and more

elementary subjects. In spite of its success, educationally, it was forced to close in 1865. It reopened later as a teacher training institution but its work was subsequently taken over by the provincial normal school.

HISTORICAL ROLE OF THE ACADEMY

These examples show that academies in Canada played a role similar to that of academies in the United States in the evolution of the secondary school. By admitting pupils from the common schools and by restricting to the secondary level, the instruction they offered, they provided a working model of the now familiar educational ladder. They were commonly co-educational and offered a broader program than that required for university entrance. In these ways they set a pattern for the later high schools. One of their chief functions was the preparation of teachers for the common schools. To the extent that they were established by a group of people locally, they represent a transition to the community high school supported by general taxation. Nevertheless academies were less numerous and influential, especially in Upper Canada, than they were in the United States. In Upper Canada the transition to the high school was made by the democratization of the Latin grammar schools in the manner about to be described.

Bringing Secondary Schools under Democratic Control

IN UPPER CANADA

One of the objections to the grammar schools in Upper Canada was that their small number kept them geographically out of reach of people who could not afford to send their sons away to board in another town. In 1839 an act to provide

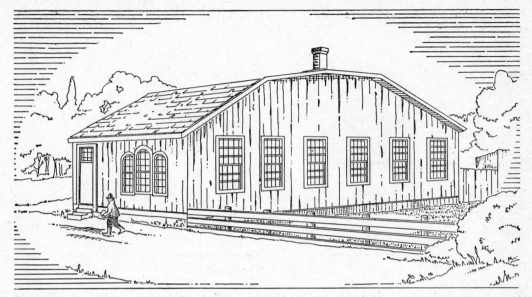

District of Toronto Grammar School, 1864-70

for the advancement of education set aside a definite endowment for the grammar schools and made grants available for the building and operation of additional schools on condition that the new school was at least six miles distant from any existing school and was able to enrol sixty pupils.

Another cause of complaint was that the grammar schools were managed by trustees appointed by the lieutenant-governor and were thus not in any sense controlled by representatives of the people. In 1853-55 the grammar schools were brought under democratic local control: they were to be managed by six trustees appointed by their county council, and permission was given to municipal councils, either of the counties or of the towns, to raise money by taxation for their support. The grammar schools were also made subject to the regulations of the Council of Public Instruction, which prescribed the course of study and textbooks and also appointed a grammar school inspector. The same legislation went much further in providing for additional schools:

grants of £100 each were to be given to the so-called senior grammar schools in each area, and proportionate grants were paid to additional schools, according to the population of the locality. Provision was also made for union schools combining the functions of elementary schools and grammar schools under the management of joint boards, a provision that led to the establishment of so many small inefficient schools that it had to be restricted in 1865 and revoked in 1874.

Prior to the legislation of 1853 Egerton Ryerson, the chief superintendent of education, had expressed his disapproval of the grammar schools because they duplicated the services of the common school by teaching elementary education to pupils of parents who thought the grammar school "more respectable than the common school," with the result that the grammar school fund operated "to a great extent as a contribution to the rich." When the grammar schools came under the Council of Public Instruction, the regulations stipulated that pupils be admitted only after an oral examination by the principal

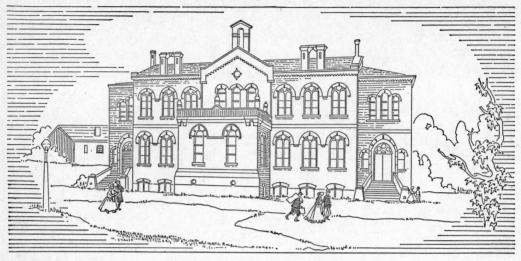

Toronto High School, 1871

on common school subjects. Thereafter it was the function of the grammar schools to provide a second stage of education for pupils who had graduated from the common schools.

Even under the new administrative arrangements, municipal councils were reluctant to assume responsibility for the financial support of grammar schools; town and city councils because they did not appoint the trustees, and county councils on the ground that the urban centres derived most benefits from the grammar schools and should therefore pay for their operation. In 1865 the foundation for these excuses was removed by having three of the six trustees appointed by the village or town in which the grammar school was located, and by making a city the equivalent of a county for grammar school purposes, so that a city appointed all six of the trustees. An amount equal to at least one-half of the grant had to be raised locally, although not necessarily by taxation. All grammar schools were put on an equal footing by distribution of the grant according to the average attendance in the grammar school program. The final step was to secure adequate support by local taxation. This step was taken in 1871, when legislation required that at least one-half the amount of the grant be raised by taxation — generally from the county — and that further amounts required by the high school board also be raised by taxation — generally from the municipality in which the school was situated. The same act changed the name of the grammar schools to high schools, which were legally co-educational and which charged only moderate fees. After 1873 entrance to high school was obtained by a written entrance examination.

The aristocratic grammar schools of Upper Canada were thus metamorphosed into democratic high schools in a period of slightly over thirty years. In 1839 a limited number of socially exclusive grammar schools under the management of the lientenant-governor's appointees gave elementary and secondary education to a very few children. By 1871 the same institutions had increased in number and had become high schools, publicly controlled and financed and designed to provide education at the secondary level to pupils who had completed the elementary grades.

In the Older Provinces

Similar changes in the administration of secondary education took place elsewhere. In Nova Scotia in 1865 the government for the first time took complete control of secondary education, and the secondary schools became, as Bingay said, "part and parcel of the general public school system." There, and in New Brunswick, secondary education by that time was offered in schools of two types — superior schools, which were really elementary schools in which the teacher or teachers taught secondary subjects as well, and county grammar schools or academies, which were essentially high schools, although they commonly had pupils in elementary grades.

In New Brunswick, superior schools and special grants for their support were introduced in 1858, and the grammar schools were brought under the control of the provincial board of education in 1861. Apart from a very few city high schools, facilities for secondary education in the Maritime Provinces became so closely associated with the public elementary schools that the change to democratic support and control was less noticeable than in Upper Canada. It was more closely linked with the establishment of free schools, an important movement which will be discussed in a later chapter.

Partly because of the close connection with the elementary schools, high schools in Nova Scotia became free at an early date. In 1892, at the first meeting of the Dominion Education Association, A. H. MacKay, superintendent of education in Nova Scotia, could point to this achievement in his own province when he spoke to educational administrators from other parts of Canada on the advantages of free high schools. It is interesting that he felt it necessary to reassure his hearers that there was no danger that free high schools would become "too crowded with those not adapted for high school work" — partly because the cost of board was a deterrent to such further education but chiefly because the hard life of the student would prevent everyone from taking advantage of such an opportunity. In this forecast he was mistaken.

In the 1840's the two Royal Grammar Schools at Quebec and Montreal were succeeded by secondary schools closer to the high school type. An academy established in Montreal about 1844-45 received in 1846 the grant formerly payable to the master of the Royal Grammar School on condition that it educate twenty pupils free and report twice a year to the government. In 1843 a school at Quebec had been able to make a similar arrangement, and both schools received these special grants up to the twentieth century. Their evolution to high schools supported by local taxation is also linked with a broader question to be discussed later — the financial privileges and powers of urban boards in Quebec. But an address delivered at the opening of a new high school building in Montreal in 1878 shows the continuance of traditional characteristics. The speaker explained carefully that there were really two distinct schools — each with its own entrance from a different street — one for boys and one for girls. In that year there were 444 pupils in the high school, or Royal Grammar School, but 203 of these were in a preparatory department. The high school for girls had 226 pupils, so that the grand total was 670. If the whole institution could be thought of as a unit, the size of this enrolment was impressively large for the time.

Inevitably different in certain respects because of the small size of the province, was the development of secondary education in Prince Edward Island. A central academy which had opened in Charlottetown in 1836 became in 1860 Prince of Wales College. This institution, which was

Prince of Wales College, Charlottetown

designed to give a "first class mathematic-al, classical and philosophical education," was placed under the management of a board of governors of thirteen appointed by the lieutenant-governor-in-council. In 1879 Prince of Wales College and the normal school were united, an action which reflected the teacher-preparation function of secondary schools and the small size of the province. In 1863 legis-lative provision was made for smaller grammar schools in Georgetown, Summer-side, and Charlottetown; but Prince of Wales College remained the only distinct-ly secondary institution, and elsewhere elementary and secondary education were closely linked as in the other Maritime Provinces. To enable students from other parts of the province to attend Prince of Wales College six scholarships offering £20 plus free tuition were provided, two to each county.

In Newfoundland, the influence of the churches forestalled the development of public high schools. According to Shaw,

the first attempt of the legislature to provide for secondary education was the provision in the Education Act of 1843 for a non-denominational academy in St. John's. This was opened in 1845, but suc-cumbed five years later to religious op-position. Bishop Feild of the Church of England, who was strongly opposed to this non-denominational school, established in 1844 a Church of England academy to "mitigate the evil of a public academy on liberal principles" — that is, of a school with religious teaching excluded. In the early 1850's the government yielded to pressure from the churches, gave up the hope of establishing one superior insti-tution of secondary education, and voted grants to the denominations for three academies. At the same time, to provide some more advanced education in larger settlements outside St. John's, money was ear-marked in the grants for "commercial schools." In 1890 an addition was made to the education grant to assist boards of education in establishing superior schools, or high schools. To qualify for the grant a superior school had to have not less than twenty pupils of Grade V standing or higher and not less than two certificated teachers. Since the boards of education were not elected and obtained no support for education from local taxation, none of the schools had the essential characteristics of high schools elsewhere.

The development of secondary education for the French-speaking Roman Catholic people of Quebec was entirely different. The traditional secondary school was the *collège classique*, or classical college, offering to entrants who had had elementary education, a course of about eight years leading to the baccalaureate, or a shorter course of much less prestige including some commercial subjects. The classical colleges were financed by fees, by contributions of former pupils, especially clergy, and by income from property or from agriculture. They were controlled by regents, including professors, who were almost all members of the clergy. After 1846 an increasing number of new classical colleges were founded by groups of more prosperous parishes, to the total of at least eleven additional institutions by 1875. Apart from this numerical expansion there was no similarity to the development of publicly controlled high schools elsewhere. As we shall see later, these classical colleges are not even part of the system of schools under the provincial department of education.

To summarize for English-speaking Canada: the typical North American high school evolved in all provinces except Newfoundland, either by transition through academies or by bringing Latin grammar schools under democratic control. In the Maritime Provinces, small schools made a close connection with elementary schools inevitable, but in all of the more populous centres and areas the high school became a separate unit in the public school system.

Grade Organization in Secondary Schools

When the Latin grammar schools taught both elementary and secondary subjects, they sometimes used the sequence-of-subjects organization similar to that of the common schools. The grammar school of Peterborough, Upper Canada, in 1834 had 30 boys. All 30 were in spelling, 29 in writing, 25 in reading, 23 in arithmetic, 21 in grammar, 18 in geography, 15 in history, 10 in mathematics, 6 in algebra, and 6 in classics. Some of the better schools offered a course of six divisions. The grammar school of the Midland District at Kingston had six graded classes and two departments, classics and mathematics. Upper Canada College, which offered some work of college grade, had seven forms above the preparatory school in 1831. School years in the early grammar schools were full years of close to eleven months.

After the middle of the nineteenth century when secondary schools were superimposed on the elementary schools, the usual length of the course for university entrance was a nominal three years. But it might be covered in less time. Good students in the late nineteenth century could, and did, complete the work of a form in half a year, and work for the other half-year, so that the actual time spent in high school might be less than that which the number of forms would suggest. Acceleration was facilitated by the traditional practice of admitting pupils at more than one point during the year. Records of Upper Canada College for 1830-32 show admissions in January, March, and August. When introduced in 1873 in Ontario, the examination for entrance to high schools could be written either in June or in January.

Lambert Norman, who became a teacher and, from 1913 until 1939, an inspector of public schools in Ontario, passed his entrance examination in December 1881 when he was twelve years old after five and one-half years in public school. In 1882-83 he spent only the winter in a Fifth Book class. From January to June in each of the years 1884, 1885, 1886, 1887 he attended high school; by June, 1885, after only one and one-half years of attendance at the secondary level he had obtained Second Class, Grade A professional standing — almost equivalent to pass matriculation; in June, 1887 he matriculated with honors in moderns on the examinations of the University of Toronto after a total of only two and one-half years' attendance in secondary grades.

It is more accurate, therefore, to say that the high school course for graduation at the junior or pass matriculation level required only about two years' attendance until around 1890, and three years thereafter. Where work of the first year college level was offered for honor or senior matriculation, the student might remain for an extra year. In 1887 New Brunswick issued a course of study for secondary school standards IX, X, and XI. In Ontario, the regulations for 1878 indicated simply a lower school and an upper school and left such details as the order of subjects to the individual high school, whereas the regulations of 1891 required the organization of four forms in all, or three to pass matriculation. These and certain other adjustments resulted in what the minister of education for Ontario modestly described in 1898 as "the most perfect system of secondary schools in any English-speaking country."

The western provinces could not introduce the same organization immediately. In Saskatchewan, in the 1890's, the three high school standards were VI, VII, and VIII — following five elementary standards. In British Columbia there were two divisions in the high school before 1889, three until 1899, and four after 1900; but the last two of the four covered the work

of first and second year university Arts. In 1907 the junior division was split up into two grades, and in 1921-22 the top three divisions were replaced by junior and senior matriculation requirements. In 1923 an eight-grade elementary school was followed by a three-year high school, with an optional additional year for senior matriculation.

Three or four years beyond Grade VIII became the standard length of the high school course in most provinces. In the English-language high schools of Quebec, after 1897, pass matriculation was reached by four secondary grades beyond a seven-year elementary school. But in Ontario the high school course was lengthened to four or five or even six years beyond Grade VIII and standardized at four or five years in 1919. British Columbia introduced the four- or five-year course in 1929. This means that two provinces, Ontario and British Columbia, have high schools with Grades XIII. Nova Scotia made plans in 1950 to extend the high school course by a year and to have Grade XI replaced by Grade XII, without any definite policy regarding an "honor" matriculation Grade XIII.

The curious discrepancies in the levels of high school graduation and university entrance in Canada may be attributed to at least three conditions: the independence of provincial education authorities looking only to the universities of their own area; differences in admission requirements to pass and honors courses; and the smaller amount of money for education in some provinces than in neighboring states across the border where the twelve-grade system became the standard. There is probably not a full year of difference in terms either of time taken or work covered between systems with twelve or thirteen grades and those with eleven or twelve. But there is a further complication in a growing tendency to have students spend two years in the honor matriculation grade.

For a substantial number of young people seeking university entrance, the Ontario high school continues to require fourteen years of schooling.

One may summarize roughly as follows the increase in length of a complete elementary and secondary school course leading to university entrance:

PREPARATORY PERIOD FOR
UNIVERSITY ENTRANCE

YEAR	1840	1860	1880	1900	1920	1950
TIME SPENT, years	8	9	10	11	11–13	11–14

If the period of higher education were added, the increase in maximum length of schooling might possibly be less. In King's College, New Brunswick, in the middle of the nineteenth century, students spent four years in residence to secure the B.A. Those preparing for the legal profession spent another three years in a law office. Those preparing for medicine might secure an M.B. in one year after the B.A., but needed three additional years to acquire an M.D. To produce a full-fledged theologian took fourteen years — four for the B.A., three for the M.A., and seven for the B.D. If the whole time was spent in attendance, the requirements in the last case were extensive, to say the least. An article in the *Canada Educational Monthly* in 1881 gave a credible account of preparation for a learned profession at that time — six or seven years in elementary work, four years at high school, four years at university, and three or four years in professional courses thereafter.

Junior High Schools

The point and the method of the pupil's transition from elementary to secondary school have changed more than once during the past hundred and fifty years. In the early nineteenth century when the two schools were for different social classes, the only means of transfer from the elementary school for children of ordinary people was to gain a free place in the secondary school by superior ability or special influence. Such transfers were seldom made.

Around the middle of the nineteenth century, when secondary education became secondary in the modern sense, union schools were established as the only practical means of providing secondary education in smaller centres of population; in these the pupil who had had five or six years of elementary education and who wished to continue in school might be advanced into secondary work when the teacher or principal teacher considered him ready. If the transfer was from one school to another, as from a common school to a grammar school, the principal of the latter examined the pupil, often by an oral test, to see whether he met standards outlined in broad terms by a provincial authority. Around the 1870's written entrance examinations to high school were introduced to ensure that pupils had the grounding and ability to do satisfactory work in the subjects of the academic high school. This examination had the effect of sharpening again the distinction between elementary and secondary education, although the basis of cleavage was to be intellectual achievement rather than social level. When the length of elementary schooling increased, during the last third of the nineteenth century, from about six years to eight years, the point of transition to secondary work was correspondingly advanced. The result was that in English-speaking North America children entered secondary schools or began work of the secondary character at a later age than in other countries.

When in the early twentieth century a larger and larger proportion of the pupils from elementary schools began to attend high school, the unsuitability of this point of transfer became apparent. On psychological grounds alone there were convincing reasons for preferring a break at age twelve to a break at age fourteen. Again, the curriculum of the eighth grade elementary school had been devised to give a complete education to pupils who would go no further; but when a considerable proportion were going on to high school, it became more reasonable to make a break at a point where the elementary tools of learning had been acquired and not in the middle of the stage at which a broader program was being introduced. Nevertheless, in the Canadian provinces, desirable reorganization was postponed for decades, adopted sparingly, or not introduced at all. Apart from mere conservatism and reluctance to follow what could be represented as an American example, there were reasons for tardiness in adopting a different point of transfer. In Eastern Canada, where secondary education, except in a few towns, was given in small combined or union schools, the break could be made in any event only in terms of curriculum. In Ontario, where a junior high school or intermediate school might otherwise have been introduced, the alternatives of curtailing or extending the privilege of Roman Catholic separate schools caused the storm clouds to gather and convinced politicians and administrators that maintenance of existing arrangements was basic to the preservation of religious and educational peace.

In Winnipeg, Manitoba, the first junior high school was opened in 1919. It was composed of Grades VII, VIII, and IX and was designed to prepare young people for occupations in business, industry, and the home. The city enlarged on the provincial course of study to offer elementary science in a suitable laboratory and also typewriting and stenography. Probably because of the practical program, the school became very popular. In 1924 the six-three-three plan was adopted

for the entire city. In 1928 one other Manitoba city, Brandon, opened a junior high school.

In Alberta, also, the first junior high school was established in 1919, the Westmount School in Edmonton. Since it was set up chiefly for convenience in accommodating pupils, the only noticeable innovation was the introduction of French in Grades VII and VIII. The real change in Alberta came in 1936, when Grades VII, VIII, and IX became the intermediate school.

In 1933 J. F. K. English, in connection with his study of the combined junior-senior high school in British Columbia, discovered by correspondence with deputy ministers and chief education officers in other provinces that the status of the junior high school across Canada was as follows. In Prince Edward Island there were no junior high schools. In New Brunswick there was little or no agitation to reorganize the schools on the six-six (or, presumably, on the six-three-three) plan. In Nova Scotia, although the law provided for reorganization and grants-in-aid, no local board had qualified for the grant by setting up a junior high school in a separate school building. In the Protestant system of Quebec there was no movement in the direction of establishing junior high schools or the six-year high school. In Ontario nothing had been done by the provincial department of education towards establishing junior high schools, although there was a strong demand for schools of the type and regulations regarding "intermediate schools" were being prepared. In Manitoba the school systems of Winnipeg and Brandon were organized on the six-three-three plan and the curriculum for the province was similarly organized, with Grades VII, VIII, and IX designated the intermediate school. In Saskatchewan, although considerable thought had been given to reorganization, nothing had yet been done. In Alberta the junior high school reorganization had been introduced locally but had not yet been extended.

In British Columbia as early as 1906 the superintendent of schools in Victoria tried experimentally to provide a more appropriate education for adolescent pupils by setting up special classes in Grades VII and VIII in Victoria. He gave this explanation:

The only new subjects pupils entering the high school at the age of fourteen or fifteen encounter are algebra, geometry and Latin. It is well known that, except in the public systems of America, these subjects, if taught at all, are invariably introduced to children very much younger than fourteen. Then there is the fact that in the United States reputable authorities on secondary education have for years been urging that a shorter elementary course be required of prospective high school pupils than pupils must have whose schooling will end with the elementary course . . .[2]

When the superintendent died in 1908, his plan was dropped.

Vancouver in 1922 and New Westminster in 1924 set up schools of a vocational or "opportunity" type for adolescent pupils unlikely to complete an academic high school course. The municipal inspector of Vancouver said that his purpose was:

to give at least two years academic and practical work to boys and girls who have completed the Public School course, but who are not in a position to take one of the ordinary and regular school courses.[3]

But real impetus towards the establishing of junior high schools came with the publication in 1925 of the *Survey of the School System of British Columbia* by Putman and Weir. It was recommended in this report (p. 110):

That the public school system of British Columbia provide elementary schools for children from six to twelve years of age, middle schools for pupils from twelve to fifteen years of age, and high schools for pupils who remain in school after reaching fifteen years.

That the middle schools be organized where possible distinct from either elementary or high schools, but combined with one or the other of these where the number of pupils makes such an organization necessary.

The following year a junior high school was opened in Penticton. By 1930, the province had eleven junior high schools with an enrolment of 5186 pupils. Five of these were of the segregated, or separate-building, type; six were in combined junior-senior high schools. Three of the former and two of the latter were in Vancouver.

For the reasons previously stated no similar progress in setting up junior high schools was made in eastern Canada, although a few cities and municipalities of Ontario established some type of intermediate school organization after 1930.

Vocational Schools

In a way the term "vocational" suggests a distinction which does not exist, since academic secondary education was a prerequisite in the early nineteenth century for professions and gentlemanly occupations and in the late nineteenth century for elementary school teaching as well.

Practical courses and schools were established first at a higher level. At McGill University a course in applied science was offered in 1855. But jealousy or niggardliness or simply the perennial want of funds limited expansion there or elsewhere. In 1870 Principal J. W. Dawson of McGill made a plea for university extension, in which he lamented the limited extent to which the university had been able to promote the practical applications of science and art. He said that the school of engineering, though successful in attracting students, had been suspended because of the university's lack of money and the public's lack of interest. Although the most eminent chemist in the country occupied the chair of practical chemistry, the course failed to attract either artisans or manufacturers. A regular faculty of applied science and engineering was set up in McGill in 1878, at about the same time as the School of Practical Science opened in Toronto, where the university had offered evening classes in technology since 1871.

But as occupational opportunities increased, more people with practical training were needed, and by 1881 it had become clear to many that new types of schools or courses should be provided at the secondary level. Keen competition in trade was developing between nations and little had been done as yet in Canada to improve industrial efficiency. An editorial in the *Canada Educational Monthly* in 1881 pointed out that although other countries had already made a beginning with technical education, no province in Canada had even given serious consideration to its introduction, that there was some teaching of science, but not of the applications of science, and no training of the hands as well as the head.

An article later in the year on "The Need of the Useful in Education" suggested that the needed technical schools might be established in connection with larger academic high schools, or possibly by changing the nature of mechanics' institutes. The author expressed himself strongly on the need:

If the people of Canada can afford to support one of the most useless establishments on the face of the earth, in the shape of a Military College, surely we in Ontario should do something for the advancement and proper education of those upon whom we have to depend for the development of the country.[4]

In 1882 the Council of Arts and Manufactures of the province of Quebec arranged for lectures on technical education by Professor Walter Smith, who had been educated in South Kensington, England, and had become the principal of the Boston Conservatory School of Fine Arts. The speaker pointed out that the introduction of technical education was an economic question, that the wealthiest nations at the time, France and England, were the two that had done the most for education and science.

By 1896 in Ontario there was legislation which empowered the trustees of any high school or any board of education to establish a technical school or to change any existing high school into a technical school. Regulations suggested in broad terms a program of arts and sciences related to the industries of the province. Municipal corporations might also establish technical schools for adults. Grants were offered, but they could not be higher than for the regular high schools. Toronto in 1901 added day classes to the evening technical classes organized ten years before, and in 1904 established a technical school. Up to the time of World War I, however, there were vocational schools in only a few cities. In Quebec in 1910 the provincial government opened schools of higher commercial studies, and in 1911 technical schools in Quebec and Montreal. In Winnipeg, Manitoba, a technical school was established in 1911.

After 1913 agricultural instruction, and after 1919 other vocational training, were encouraged by grants from the federal government.* From then on the expansion was more rapid. In Ontario there were 16 day vocational schools with 9000 pupils in 1922-23 and more than three times as many ten years later. There was a check during the depression, and a decline during the war from 35,000 pupils in 52 schools in 1939-40 to 31,000 pupils in 38 schools in 1947-48. In Quebec by 1950

* See p. 344.

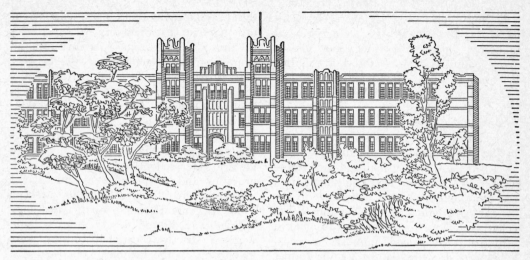

Provincial Institute of Technology and Art, Calgary, Alberta

there were technical schools in five cities offering four-year courses, and trade schools in thirty-two centres offering the first three years of the same program as well as two-year courses in various crafts or trades.

In British Columbia in 1913 interest in vocational education was marked by the appearance of the title "Supervisor of Industrial and Technical Education." Next year there were appointments of an organizer of technical education and of a director of elementary agricultural education. Boards of trustees were empowered to establish day or evening classes and grants from the Council of Public Instruction were made available. The first technical instruction was offered in night schools, but in 1916-17 the first day class was organized in King Edward High School, Vancouver.

Provinces in which industrial development was not marked also enacted vocational school legislation. In New Brunswick, acts were passed in 1918, 1923, and 1927 to match and procure the federal grants. In 1919 a vocational board was set up and a director of vocational education appointed. A vocational school

was established in every year but one between 1919 and 1924, and three were set up in 1925. These were schools with one or more, and often with three or four, of five departments, — agricultural, commercial, industrial, home-making, and prevocational. After 1925 there was practically no further expansion until the regional high school development at the end of World War II. In Saskatchewan the Vocational Education Act of 1919 offered school boards from fifty to seventy-five per cent of the cost of equipment and fifty per cent of the teachers' salaries if they set up three-year vocational programs of a commercial, home economics, or industrial type. In the 1920's such courses were offered in four large high schools. In 1929 Regina began to build a technical school, and by 1934 there were also technical schools in Moose Jaw and Saskatoon. Alberta appointed a director of technical education in 1914. In that year Edmonton had a technical school, Calgary had a prevocational school, and Camrose was experimenting with practical courses. The provincial Institute of Technology and Art in Calgary was organized in 1916 and its building was completed six years later.

During World War II and after, facilities for technical education were expanded to accommodate War Emergency classes and rehabilitation programs. For example in Charlottetown, P.E.I., where virtually the only vocational school was the commercial department set up in Prince of Wales College in 1925, a building was erected nearby to house industrial shops. In the far different surroundings of Red Deer, Alberta, an agricultural and technical school also acquired equipment from war-time and post-war activities of the federal government. Even Newfoundland, not then a province of Canada, had a sufficiently awakened interest in vocational education in 1940 to ask the former director of vocational education in New Brunswick, Fletcher Peacock, to visit the island and make recommendations. Although the war prevented any possible program of school expansion, an Office of Vocational Education and Civil Re-establishment was set up in 1942.

When vocational education was introduced in eastern Canada at the beginning of this century, it was kept apart from academic education. The Ontario regulations of 1896 required that the building of the vocational school be separate although admission was to be obtained through the same examination. This isolation of the practical to maintain the superiority of purely intellectual subjects resulted from a strong attachment to the existing form of secondary education. Differentiated schools persisted in some cities of Nova Scotia, Quebec, Ontario, and Saskatchewan. In Nova Scotia and Quebec technical schools were administered by a distinct branch of the central authority. In Ontario later schools established in smaller cities and towns after World War I were not separate. In Saskatchewan from 1936 a general course with vocational options was offered in academic schools, whereas strictly vocational courses were given only in the technical schools.

In spite of the separation of academic and vocational at first, the trend was towards the composite or multilateral school. The tendency was dictated in part by administrative convenience where the population was small, but was fostered also by a conviction that intellectual and manual workers should intermingle at school. The superintendent of schools in Winnipeg gave an instance of that belief in 1925 when he pointed out that his city was not in favor of separate commercial schools and that the commercial course was offered in all high schools.

UNIVERSITIES

In most of the older provinces the sequence of events in university history was (a) the founding of a Church of England institution, (b) the setting up of colleges by dissenting groups, and (c) a reduction in the denominational characteristics of the original foundation and of some of the other colleges. The small institutions so established had some advantages; but, as Bourinot said in 1880, it is a question "if the perpetuation of a system which multiplies colleges with university powers in each province, will tend to produce the soundest scholarship in the end."[5] The problem was most serious in the Maritime Provinces. In Nova Scotia, for example, where the Anglican King's College had opened in 1790, Dalhousie was founded in 1818, Acadia in 1838, St. Mary's, Halifax, in 1841, St. Francis Xavier in 1853,

McGill College, Montreal, about 1875

and the Collège de Sainte Anne in 1890, so that in 1896 six institutions with a total staff of eighty-two had a total student body of 533 and conferred 124 degrees. Efforts had been made to consolidate Dalhousie and King's in 1823, 1835, and 1885. In 1876 a University of Halifax had been formed and supported by grants for five years in the hope that it might become the one university, of which other institutions would be colleges. The idea was dropped in 1881. Some forty years later generous Carnegie grants were offered to induce other universities to move to Halifax and unite with Dalhousie, but only King's accepted.

The history of King's College, Fredericton, shows how Anglican foundations were changed. In 1827 King's secured a royal charter which required all members of the staff to subscribe to the Thirty-nine Articles of the Church of England. Although it had a good endowment, it graduated only thirty-eight students in sixteen years. After repeated attempts of the assembly to have the charter amended, the council assented in 1846 to the abolition

of the religious test, except in the faculty of theology, the continuance of which was the one special privilege remaining to the Church of England. In 1854 the government appointed a royal commission on education to investigate the university problem and included in its membership the superintendents of education in two other provinces, William Dawson of Nova Scotia and Egerton Ryerson, the champion of Methodism in Upper Canada. As a result of the commission's recommendations the college was merged in the University of New Brunswick in 1859 and so became secular. The history of King's College, Upper Canada, was an almost exact parallel. The charter obtained by Strachan in 1827 had to be modified at the insistence of the assembly before the college was built in 1843. By then it was Anglican only to the extent that it supported a chair of Church of England theology. In 1849 this last prerogative of the church was abolished and King's College became the secular University of Toronto. Bishop Strachan then secured a charter and funds for a new Church of

England institution, Trinity College, which opened in 1852.

In Quebec the first university was Mc-Gill, which opened with a faculty of medicine in 1829 and a faculty of arts in 1843. Partly because Strachan and others had not succeeded in making McGill an exclusively Church of England institution, Bishop's College, Lennoxville, was incorporated in 1843, opened in 1845, and elevated to a chartered university in 1853. Laval university opened in 1852.

In 1880 Bourinot said that there were twenty-one colleges and universities with 2200 students. All but one of the institutions not yet mentioned were in Ontario: Victoria, founded in 1841; Queen's, 1841; Knox, 1844; Regiopolis, 1846; St. Joseph's (Ottawa) 1846; and St. Michael's, 1852. In New Brunswick, the University of Mount Allison College had begun in Sackville in 1843 as a Wesleyan Academy for boys, to which Mount Allison Ladies College was added. It was authorized to grant degrees in 1858.

In western Canada one provincial university was established in each of the four provinces: the University of Manitoba in 1877, of Saskatchewan in 1907, of Alberta in 1908, and of British Columbia in 1915. Meanwhile in the east other developments had occurred. Victoria and St. Michael's in 1887 and Trinity in 1903 entered into federation with the University of Toronto. Queen's circularized her graduates and supporters on the question and found them opposed. The University of Western Ontario was founded in 1878, and McMaster University in 1887. The University of Montreal, which had been a branch of Laval, became a university in its own right in 1920. Memorial University College in St. John's, Newfoundland, was established as a junior university college in 1925 and became a degree-granting institution in 1949. In Prince Edward Island St. Dunstan's College opened in 1855. In addition to the universities mentioned by name in this brief summary, Canada has many other institutions of higher education, French-speaking and English-speaking, including several which have independent degree-granting powers.

Undergraduate enrolment in Canadian universities was about 22,000 in 1919-20 and about 69,000 in 1950. There was a peak enrolment of 79,000 undergraduates in 1947-48, when nearly 30,000 war veterans were in attendance. The increase of post-graduate students was more striking, from less than 400 to more than 5000 during the thirty-year period. Recent undergraduate expansion occurred in faculties of arts and even more in faculties of applied science and engineering, but not in faculties of dentistry and medicine.

Summary of Chapters Eleven, Twelve, and Thirteen

Population changes, immigration, economic and political developments, and the slow process of building public interest in education were factors of major importance in the growth of our school systems. The first stage in the construction of public education was a transition from paternalism accomplished around 1840 in eastern Canada and considerably later in the west. The second stage of about thirty years was marked by the establishment of strong central authorities, the introduction of local taxation, and the attainment of free universal elementary education. The third stage extending to 1900 in eastern Canada gave time to improve the efficiency of administration. The fourth stage, or the half-century just completed, extended more liberal educational benefits to all.

School enrolment through the years reflects these accomplishments, as do increases in the length of schooling and improvements in regularity of attendance. Legislation from 1871, and especially from World War I, made school attendance compulsory for the benefit of children of the minority who had not been educated to an appreciation of educational advantages for the young. The people of local communities learned by practice to meet minimum requirements of school accommodation, although problems were created by insistence on a school for each small neighborhood and also by sudden increases in school population.

In the latter half of the nineteenth century the graded elementary school evolved and secondary schools became the second section of an educational ladder. Secondary education then increased in length and became more like an extension of the common school. The junior high school reorganization evolved in some western provinces during the first two or three decades of the present century. Vocational schools, in spite of local interest, were not established in any number until after World War I. Although traditional views on education would have preferred to keep practical training distinct and separate from academic education, the tendency in most places was to set up composite high schools.

Most universities of eastern Canada were established in the second third of the nineteenth century. In the Maritime Provinces an early start was made with denominational institutions, which became and remained numerous in relation to population. In western Canada the necessarily late establishment of universities made it the rule that one institution should serve most people of the province, although there are also numerous denominational colleges.

CHAPTER 14

The Provinces

NEWFOUNDLAND · PRINCE EDWARD ISLAND · NOVA SCOTIA · NEW BRUNSWICK · QUEBEC · ONTARIO · MANITOBA · SASKATCHEWAN ALBERTA · BRITISH COLUMBIA

In all provinces of Canada except Newfoundland the development of provincial systems of education followed a fairly regular pattern. When the people locally had assumed some organized responsibility for education through elected trustees, provincial governments set up strong central authorities which sooner or later had power to make regulations, prescribe courses of study, and authorize textbooks. In nearly all provinces at some time since Confederation the offices of minister and deputy minister of education have been created to head the department of education. The major achievements of the nineteenth century were organized inspection of schools and a beginning of teacher training under the central authority, and free schools paid for by local taxation under the local authorities. In all provinces there has been an expansion of secondary education and of new educational services during the present century.

These and other important aspects of education will be discussed in later chapters. To avoid repetition they will be mentioned only occasionally in these brief accounts of developments in the individual provinces, the chief purpose of which is to point out characteristics that are differentiating rather than common.

Newfoundland

The educational system of Newfoundland, unlike that of any other province, provides for schools under the separate control of five denominations, four of which are represented by superintendents on the council of education, which virtually decides the policy of the central authority. There are local boards of education of from five to seven members in some 300 school districts throughout the island. New members are either selected by the existing board to replace retiring members, or are chosen by the people at a public meeting at which the general affairs of the community are being discussed. In either case the recommendations for appointment are forwarded to the proper denominational superintendent and the new appointments are legally confirmed by the governor-in-council. Direct election by the people is becoming more general and the government of the province is giving encouragement to the trend. Nevertheless the government pays nine-tenths of the cost of education, for which there is no support from local taxation. In many places, moreover, the local clergyman, appointed ex-officio, is predominantly the most influential and active member of the board. Thus local responsibility of the people for education has not yet been fully developed.

Why has this been so? It will be recalled that schools in Newfoundland during the early nineteenth century had been operated mainly by religious and philanthropic societies — that is, by the so-called voluntary system. In 1836 the assembly's select committee on education submitted a report approving of these arrangements:

Your committee consider that the voluntary system works advantageously and therefore they would recommend that assistance be given by the Legislature by immediate grants of money, to be placed at the disposal of the several Societies.[1]

But the first education act, passed in that year, divided the country into nine educational districts, each to be under the direction of a board of twelve persons, none of whom was to belong to the clergy. Immediately the clergy voiced a protest, secured in 1838 an amendment which admitted them to membership on the boards, and soon dominated the other members. Then the denominational influence gained in strength. By an act of 1843 the country was divided into eighteen Roman Catholic and eighteen Protestant

districts. The original grant of £2100 was increased to £5000 and apportioned among the denominational boards. But there was continued bitterness and strife. For example, the superior position of the Church of England among the Protestant groups was challenged by the Methodists, who had increased in number and strength. Finally in 1874 the state capitulated to the demands of the religious leaders and subdivided the Protestant grants among the larger denominations. In 1876 Roman Catholic, Church of England, and Methodist superintendents of education were appointed.

In all of this, Newfoundland followed the English model and was apparently indifferent or opposed to developments elsewhere in North America. In 1869 and again in 1895 negotiations for the union of Canada and Newfoundland ended in failure. The chief administrative similarity between the Newfoundland system and other Canadian systems is in the head of the department of education. In 1893 a member of the executive council, the colonial secretary, was given particular responsibility for education. A department of education was established in 1920. After Newfoundland joined Confederation in 1949, the portfolio of minister of education was created and the chief civil servant of the department became deputy minister of education. As Newfoundland has had responsible government since 1855, except for the lapse during the depression and World War II, there is some popular control over education at the provincial level.

One may wonder how a new school can be built without elected local boards and local taxation. Shaw, a former head of the education department, gives this answer: At a board or district meeting the project is decided on and the local board is charged with the responsibility of carrying it out. The board and the department of education after consultation agree upon a plan and estimate the cost. If a community is unable to bear the entire expense, as is usually the case, the board applies to the department for a grant of up to about fifty per cent of the total estimated cost. If the department is satisfied that there is need of a school the grant is usually forthcoming. The contribution of the local community is usually in the form of lumber and free labor.

In Newfoundland at the time of World War II there were thirteen hundred different and distinct settlements scattered mainly along a coast-line of six thousand miles, or, including Labrador, of seven thousand miles. In many districts these settlements are isolated from one another, without communicating roads, and can be reached by sea only. Many of the supervisors and helping teachers have to do all their travelling by boat. The one who works in the northern peninsula of the island and in Labrador frequently uses dog teams in winter.

The population of Newfoundland grew from about 74,000 in 1836 and 96,000 in 1845 to about 221,000 by 1901 and 361,000 by 1951. Roughly half of the people live in the Avalon peninsula at the southeast. In 1949 the school enrolment of 75,000 pupils included 26,000 in Roman Catholic schools, 21,000 in Anglican schools, 18,000 in United Church schools, 4600 in Salvation Army schools, and 230 in three schools of the Seventh Day Adventists; of the rest, some 4750 were in "amalgamated" schools for combined Protestant denominations.

Prince Edward Island

Canada's smallest province has an area of only 2184 square miles. Its population of 98,000 in 1951 was not 5000 higher than in 1871, although it rose to a peak of 109,000 in 1891 and fell to a low of 88,000 in the 1930's. Once covered with fine trees, it has been for more than a century an agricultural community. It is a province which prefers to run its own affairs.

Apart from limited resources and expenditures, the most noticeable characteristic of the educational system in Prince Edward Island has been the large proportion of the educational costs borne by the provincial government. The markedly paternalistic role of the government in education was pointed out in an editorial in the *Educational Review* for December, 1898. The government of the island then devoted about two-thirds of its revenue to the financing of schools, about one-half of which had no other support than the government money. The editor saw the consequence of this policy.

In not placing the responsibility of school maintenance on those who should bear at least a portion of it, there is a lack of public spirit, and little or no interest in many communities in educational matters.

There had always been difficulty in finding adequate local support. The first grants in 1825 were intended to pay only one-sixth of the cost of teachers' salaries, but some localities did little more than give the teacher board and provide a wretched shack to serve as a school. Grants under the Free Education Act of 1852 paid almost the whole cost of salaries. During the present century up to about 1941, grants in Prince Edward Island paid two or three times the percentage of the cost of education which governments assumed in other provinces. Since then the difference has been much less. In 1948 the government grants in Prince Edward Island paid fifty-four per cent of the total cost as compared with a thirty-eight per cent average in seven other provinces.

In other respects the development of the provincial system of education followed more or less closely the usual Canadian pattern. A chief education officer was appointed at an early date — from

1837 to 1847, then permanently from 1853. But the central board of education, first set up in 1829 and reorganized frequently, had insufficient power. Only in 1877, twenty-five years after the passing of the Free Education Act, was a strong central authority established. This consisted of the superintendent of education, the principal of Prince of Wales College, and the executive council. It had power to make regulations, prescribe courses of study, and authorize textbooks. The legislation of 1877 also aimed at getting local education authorities to take their work seriously, by providing for fines to be imposed on trustees who refused to act or neglected their duties. Finally in 1945 an education department was placed under a minister and deputy minister of education.

Nova Scotia

Of the four small and comparatively poor Atlantic provinces, Nova Scotia is the most populous and the most prosperous. The population for a century showed a slow but steady gain from 277,000 in 1851 to 460,000 in 1901 and to 643,000 in 1951, although by North American standards such a rate of advance comes close to standing still. In expansion, therefore, as in most other respects, the province has been conservative. In its government, Nova Scotia did away with the legislative council only in 1928. In the department of education the first minister took office in 1949 and the first deputy minister in 1950.

Conservatism is shown in strong attachment to traditional forms and names and in geographical and sectarian loyalties. Pictou Academy is still so called, although it has been supported by local taxation since 1885. The Normal College at Truro, opened in 1855, was still in operation at the same place under the same name in 1950; and arguments about its location in newspapers and periodicals nearly a century apart professed the same

distrust of Halifax and the same fear that life in that seaport city would corrupt teachers-in-training from rural areas. As we have seen, the small denominational universities of Nova Scotia maintained their independence against strong inducements to unite. Even among the Roman Catholics there are separate degree-granting institutions for those who speak French and for women and also two rival English-speaking universities, St. Francis Xavier and St. Mary's. Much of Nova Scotia is solid rock, and all educational institutions appear to have been built on this enduring foundation.

But this did not mean a lack of progress and new ideas. Various agencies of special education were established in Nova Scotia, some of them to serve the whole of the maritime area, including the Halifax Institute for the Deaf and Dumb, 1851, the Halifax Asylum for the Blind, 1867, the College of Agriculture, 1899, and the Technical College, 1907. Nova Scotia had one of the first lively summer schools for teachers, a Summer School of Science, from 1887. Though traditional in many respects, the province had a reputation for interest in science. The distinguished geologist, J. W. Dawson, was born in Nova Scotia, was educated at Pictou Academy, and between 1850 and 1856 was the first superintendent of education for the province. Like other able Nova Scotians later, he then moved farther west to become head of a large university.

The hostility of the province to any sudden change — no matter how good in purpose and effect — may be illustrated by the fate of the Tupper administration which enacted free school legislation in 1864 and compulsory local taxation one year later. In recompense for this greatest single service of a government to education, the Nova Scotians in the next election defeated every candidate but one of the Conservative party. After World

Nova Scotia Technical College

War II, when the major educational movement was the establishment of composite high schools in rural areas, a Liberal government avoided risk of a similar fate by paying all the capital cost and most of the maintenance cost that would fall on the rural municipality, an arrangement more conducive to local importunity than to community responsibility in educational finance. At present, as in the past, Nova Scotia has capable educators and administrators who know what should be done and how to do it, but they are under unusually strong pressure to subordinate the general advantage for fear of offence to jealous minorities.

New Brunswick

The third of the small Maritime Provinces was to have been "the most gentlemanlike on earth." But returning Acadians and immigrant Irish and English depressed social standards, and Scot and Yankee speculators in the lumber business upset serene gentility. Boom years in the lumber trade and crop failures in 1836 and 1845 militated against steady agricultural development. There were forces for enlightenment and culture: subscription libraries in Fredericton and Saint John, the latter, before mid-century, one of the most complete in the Canadian provinces; the Fredericton Athenaeum Society, a literary and scientific organization to which leading educators and other intellectuals belonged; the Young Men's Debating Society, organized in Chatham in 1837; other debating societies, quiz clubs, and dancing academies; mechanics' institutes, the first in Saint John and others after 1840; and a New Brunswick Society for the Encouragement of Agriculture, Home Manufactures, and Commerce, which sent out lecturers on tours after 1849. But the lumber economy created an indifference to public education. The rich merchants preferred to send their children to private schools. The younger adventurers with money and the intermittently employed lived loose, spendthrift, intemperate, and rowdy lives. These opposing forces made the position of education equivocal.

In spite of a century's progress, public education in New Brunswick still gives no one-sided, clear-cut, impression. To a visitor from the west, most of the province seems a pleasant, old-fashioned place, whose poorly-paid teachers appear to do better work than the public has a right to expect. But in one area of educational improvement on which attention has been centred since 1940, the establishment of rural, composite high schools, New Brunswick has been a leader. By 1949 eighteen of these schools had been built and arrangements were being made for twenty-one others, a remarkable achievement in a small province.

New Brunswick's system of education has marked similarities to that of Nova Scotia. Neither province has separate schools, although both have within the public school system schools that are frankly Roman Catholic. Both have French-speaking minorities, whose "Acadian" schools are also treated as public schools. Recent administrative reorganization of rural areas since 1940 in both provinces introduced a large unit, roughly the county, for educational finance although not for all administrative purposes. New Brunswick's first minister of education took office in 1936, thirteen years before Nova Scotia's.

Like Ontario, New Brunswick began to offer teacher training in 1847, and like Ontario passed legislation in 1871 to make free schools obligatory after twenty years' experience with an optional law. But in New Brunswick, provision for the election of local trustees in 1852 had come thirty-six years later than in Ontario, the appointment of a provincial superintendent in 1852 had come ten years later, and the taking over of the grammar schools into the school system in 1861 had come eight years later. The smaller province entered the twentieth century with no compulsory attendance law and with other educational handicaps.

The population during the past 100 years has shown about the same small steady gain as Nova Scotia. It was about 194,000 in 1851, 286,000 in 1871, 331,000 in 1901, and 516,000 in 1951.

Quebec

For the province of Quebec a longer account of the provincial development is required for three reasons: there are virtually two systems of public education; the organization of schools for the French-speaking children is unique and cannot conveniently be covered in chapters devoted to particular aspects of the English-speaking systems; and nearly thirty per cent of all Canadians live in Quebec.

TWO EDUCATIONAL SYSTEMS

The reason for thinking of two systems of education in Quebec is that there are two virtually independent committees within the central authority — one Roman Catholic, the other Protestant. As in four other provinces there are also separate and independent local boards of trustees. In Quebec the Roman Catholic committee is the central authority for local commissioners or trustees of Roman Catholic schools, which therefore have curricula, textbooks, regulations, teacher training institutions, and nearly all appurtenances and services separate from those of the Protestant system. The enrolment in the Roman Catholic system was about six times that of the Protestant system in 1881 and nearly seven times that of the Protestant system by 1936. For educational purposes in Quebec, the term "Protestant" includes all who are not Roman Catholic.

The evolution of this dual system began in 1841 when preponderantly Roman Catholic Lower Canada was united politically with preponderantly Protestant Upper Canada. Educational legislation of that year provided for Roman Catholic and Protestant schools under separate local control. When a more workable act for Quebec, or Canada East, was passed in 1846, the separate school principle was retained: that is, when a school had been established by the religious majority, a separate school might be set up under certain conditions by the religious minority. The majority elected five local school commissioners for a three-year term to run their school or schools. The minority also elected a board, usually of three trustees, for the same purpose. This act also introduced local taxation for schools. It made the parish the local unit of the Roman Catholic system.

The Act of 1841 had also made provision for a central authority. In 1842 a provincial superintendent of education was appointed. The first incumbent, J. B. Meilleur, enhanced the prestige of his office and strengthened the central authority by having it set up boards to examine teachers (1849) and appoint inspectors of schools (1852). Meilleur was succeeded as superintendent in 1854 by J. O. Chauveau, a distinguished speaker and author and a member of parliament. Two years after his appointment the central authority took definite shape as a Council of Public Instruction. When appointments were made a little later, this council consisted of fourteen members, ten Roman Catholic and four Protestant. In the meantime, in 1857, three normal schools, two Roman Catholic and one Protestant, had been opened, and about the same time a *Journal of Public Education* began publication in two languages.

When Confederation was about to be realized, the Protestant minority in Quebec expressed fears that their educational interests might be submerged under a permanent arrangement. One of their handicaps was their ineffective, though numerically fair, representation on the Council of Public Instruction. Immediately after Confederation, in 1869, two committees were formed, one Roman Catholic, having fourteen members, and the other Protestant, having seven members. In

1875 these two committees were given complete independence of action, so that the Protestant committee ceased to be affected by the larger Roman Catholic committee, even though nominally the two committees together formed a council over which the superintendent presided. This made it possible, without giving cause for objection, to include in the membership of the Roman Catholic committee all bishops of that church.

Meanwhile, in 1867, Chauveau had become minister of public instruction. He was succeeded in 1873 by Gédéon Ouimet, who was replaced in 1874 by de Boucherville. The latter in 1875 abolished the office of minister, restored the office of superintendent, and appointed Ouimet as superintendent. Thereafter education was represented in the assembly and the cabinet only through the provincial secretary. Obviously, one reason for the less direct political connection is the Roman Catholic belief that the church, rather than a government elected by the people, is the fitting body to have strong influence in the central authority. As a corollary, the Protestant central authority, without the dominating influence of any one church, is also further removed from support and control by the voting public than departments of education in other provinces.

These, then, are the Roman Catholic and Protestant systems of public education in Quebec. Over both there is a superintendent and a council made up of the two committees. In practice the secretaries of the two committees each have a position equivalent to that of deputy minister of education in another province. This statement, however, has to be qualified.

The Roman Catholic committee, or department of education, is the central authority only for elementary schools and related institutions. In other provinces we have seen that secondary schools, around

1860, were brought under control of the central authority previously established for elementary schools. In the French Roman Catholic system this was not done. Post-primary work came to be offered in complementary and superior schools under the provincial department of education. But the traditional secondary schools for French-speaking pupils, the classical colleges, have remained apart.

We have seen how the *collèges classiques* were founded and how they increased in number after 1840. They were taught by regular or secular clergy, who received only nominal salaries, so that fees were kept low. An event of supreme importance to the secondary school system was the granting in 1852 of a royal charter to Laval University, Quebec, since this institution became not only the goal of the student but a co-ordinating influence in secondary studies. In 1867 the Pope authorized the foundation of another university, the University of Montreal, which was recognized as an independent seat of learning in 1889 and given a charter in 1920. With one or the other of these two universities, most of the classical colleges and other secondary and higher institutions became affiliated. Classical colleges for girls were founded also, but no co-educational schools at the secondary level.

In the Protestant system, of course, secondary schools are part of the public system of education under the Protestant committee.

But separate again from both the primary and the secondary divisions of the Roman Catholic system, and from the Protestant system, are undenominational technical schools, under the direct supervision of the provincial secretary. There are also many other schools in far greater variety than is to be found elsewhere in Canada, including schools to teach many different occupations and trades, schools of fine arts, and schools for homemakers. Some of these are under departments of government other than education.

DUAL AUTHORITY IN OPERATION

To return to the history of education under the two committees, the system has operated since 1875 with little disturbance from the legislative assembly of the province. There was talk more than once about restoring the ministry of education. In 1897 the members of the legislature actually voted forty-four to nineteen in support of a government measure to abolish the office of superintendent and re-establish the portfolio of minister. The government named a minister, and he held office for thirty-six hours until the upper house vetoed the bill. There were also at least three vain efforts to introduce compulsory attendance, the last under Bouchard in 1918. Legislation for this purpose was, as we have seen, passed in 1942, but only after the Council of Public Instruction had indicated its approval.

But the central authority was not inactive. One of the first pension schemes for teachers was introduced in 1856. A depository, or *dépôt de livres*, was set up in 1876 to handle books, maps, and school apparatus, but it was abolished in 1879 on grounds that it had the effect of restricting the choice of books. The *Journal of Public Instruction* was suspended in 1880, but replaced by a French-language periodical on elementary education and subsequently, from 1898, by both *l'Enseignement Primaire* and the *Educational Record*. A law in 1897 set up a central committee of examiners concerned with the issuing of licences to teachers. A law of 1899 required the use of uniform textbooks, but was apparently not enforced. Three recent acts have been concerned with disputes between school boards and teachers (1944), with the provision of free textbooks (1944), and with a new source of revenue for school corporations unable to meet their obligations (1946).

The increasing number of schools and pupils gave tangible evidence of progress. According to Magnan, there were approximately 1800 schools and 69,000 pupils in 1849, 2800 schools and 120,000 pupils in 1854, 4350 schools and 230,000 pupils in 1875. In 1950 there were about 10,000 schools and other educational institutions, about 720,000 pupils, and about 33,000 teachers in the province. Since only about half of the Roman Catholic teachers in Quebec are lay men and women, educational statistics are not comparable with those of other provinces and are of less significance to Quebec itself than such an event as the arrival from France in 1837 of Brothers of the Christian Schools. Within the next hundred years, more than fifteen new religious congregations had been founded in Quebec and a still larger number had come from France. By the 1930's the teaching orders numbered ten communities of men and twenty-six of women.

Marks of educational progress in the present century included the following. There was a striking increase in the number of normal schools for girls and a growth of other teacher training institutions, especially since the scholasticates of religious were recognized in 1931 as normal schools. In 1951 there were 51 Roman Catholic normal schools for one sex or the other, and 44 scholasticates — 15 for brothers and 29 for sisters. For advanced study in education *l'Institut pédagogique St. Georges* was established in 1929 by the Christian Brothers, and a similar institution was founded in 1923 by the Sisters of the Congregation of Notre Dame, both at Montreal. The number of inspectors of schools was increased early in the century and three inspectors general were appointed. Even without compulsory attendance, school enrolment by the 1930's was reported to have reached from ninety-five to ninety-eight per cent of the total number of children between the ages of seven and fourteen. The government had increased ordinary grants, paid additional grants on buildings, and introduced new subsidies to universities and classical colleges. Many important new institutions were built, including the polytechnical institutes at Montreal, Quebec, Three Rivers, and Hull, two schools of fine arts at Quebec and Montreal, and the School of Higher Commercial Studies at Montreal.

The Protestant committee in 1875 set about drawing up regulations and courses of study. But they found the condition of the rural schools so bad, and the funds at their disposal so limited, that they became discouraged about doing much for them and concentrated their attention on the improvement of superior schools. Since 1847 there had been a Superior Education Fund for the support of institutions other than elementary schools. In 1878 the following news item appeared in the *Canadian School Journal*:

The Protestant Committee are making great efforts to organize that portion of the educational system which they control. Hitherto educational institutions, especially those which are supposed to be devoted to superior education, have gone on in a haphazard kind of way — partly under the control of religious bodies, partly aided by the State, without uniformity of text books, and without any sufficient test of the qualifications of masters and teachers. Secondary education has languished. Of late, however, matters have begun to change. The appointment of Professor Weir, of Morrin College, and F. C. Emberson, M.A., to inspect those institutions which obtain grants from the Superior Education Fund will induce a more rigid classification, and give the Protestant Committee something more than mere names as a basis for the apportionment of the annual grants.[2]

From this and other comments on conditions in Quebec, readers of educational journals elsewhere gained the impression that in the 1870's the improvement of Protestant education had just begun. The position of the chief officer of the Protestant system was strengthened in 1886 when the English secretary of the department became also the secretary of the Protestant committee. The holder of the former office from 1882 had been the Reverend E. I. Rexford, a trained and experienced teacher, who in the dual capacity did effective work of the Horace Mann type for the improvement of the Protestant schools.

As a minority group the Protestants in Quebec were somewhat hampered, especially outside the few cities where their numbers were substantial. Even for Montreal a law requiring the Protestant board to make schools free was passed only in 1904, more than fifty years later than the establishment of free public elementary schools in Toronto. In 1912 other school boards were authorized by law to make schools free, forty-one years after Ontario boards were required to abolish fees. But the same act authorized the boards to provide free textbooks, and in that it was not behind the times.

The handicap of the Protestant minority could not be attributed to discriminatory treatment in educational finance, since revenues not collected from real estate of individual taxpayers were divided in proportion to enrolment. But the inexpensive services of religious teachers, and other factors, caused Roman Catholic schools to set an example of demanding rather little from local taxation. This made it more difficult to accustom Protestant residents to increasing taxes for schools. But the Protestant system in Quebec has long since overcome any disadvantage which resulted from the late second start in 1875. Its schools are similar to those of the English-speaking provinces, and will receive further attention in later chapters.

AN EXAMPLE OF HARMONY

The educational system of Quebec is described by Bolger as an expression of the harmony between two races with different cultural traditions. The educational values of French-speaking Quebec have remained fundamentally the same as they were in the seventeenth and eighteenth centuries. Secondary and higher education in the classical tradition have retained their position of prestige in spite of the newer institutions in which science and applied science are taught for employment in the modern world. Moreover, the Roman Catholic Church, the French language, and the French-Canadian way of life have all retained their hold. They inspire a type of patriotism which it is difficult for the English-speaking Canadian to understand. He looks on the whole expanse of Canada as his country. His French-speaking compatriot thinks of *la Province de Québec* as his homeland, just as the old imperialist thought of England as the heart of the empire. Yet the two peoples with their different attitudes live together; their children attend the very different schools of two distinct systems and still learn to get along with one another.[3] The example of the province of Quebec is Canada's best contribution towards a tolerant and unified world.

The gain in population over the past hundred years was considerably greater in Quebec than in the Maritime Provinces — from 890,000 in 1851, to 1,192,000 in 1871, to 1,649,000 in 1901, to 4,056,000 in 1951.

Ontario

By 1851 Canada West, formerly Upper Canada and later Ontario, had the largest total population, and much the largest English-speaking population, of any Canadian province. One hundred years later, when the number of inhabitants had increased from less than a million to well over four and one-half million, the comparison still held. In the development of its educational system Ontario was often enabled by its size to do first and more thoroughly what newer or smaller provinces could attempt only partially and sometimes belatedly. Up till the end of World War I, the western provinces frankly copied Ontario practice, although the east was less happy to be found doing later what Ontario had already done. All of this makes it exceedingly difficult to do justice to the large central province without giving the impression that the rest of Canada is merely an outer fringe. The following account gives only brief synopses of achievement during periods already defined.

The period of expansion between 1841 and 1871 was a time of improvements in communication, of rapid growth by immigration, and of newly achieved democracy, provincial and municipal. The superintendent of education, Egerton Ryerson, secured through legislation in 1846 and 1850 the strong central authority necessary to give direction. The Council of Public Instruction drew up schedules of what must be taught, of the qualifications teachers must have, and of the textbooks they must use. The people locally, and the school trustees they elected, were given the opportunity from 1850 to raise money by taxation and to improve their schools. Moreover they were given constant encouragement to take advantage of the opportunity.

The result was that by 1871 nearly all elementary schools were tax-supported and free, that school enrolment had increased twice as fast as population, that three and one-half months had been added to the school year, that most teachers had academic qualifications possessed by few twenty years before, and that all teachers had certificates based on definite accomplishments, though only about fifteen per cent were trained. School buildings were greatly improved, and during the early 1850's they rapidly acquired blackboards, maps, and seats with desks. There were even "frills"; 1150 of some 4450 schools had acquired school libraries, with collections averaging 200 books.

Next came the period of consolidation and efficiency, from 1870 to 1900. As we have seen, the act of 1871 set up a popular system of free public schools and high schools, with compulsory attendance at the former and compulsory taxation to support the latter. One function of the high schools was to educate teachers; and uniform, province-wide examinations were set up for teachers' certificates. The course of study was now outlined with precision to show exactly what should be covered and the time to be taken. Two years later a written high school entrance examination was introduced, and two years from then an intermediate high school examination was established to determine the efficiency of the school and the grant it should receive. Many other written examinations were conducted for various purposes. School inspectors, after 1871, were men who had been certificated teachers, well qualified to appraise the faults and merits of their former colleagues. After 1877 all elementary school teachers were trained, cheaply and quickly, it is true, but at least to the satisfaction of the regulations.

We have seen how the grammar schools of Ontario became high schools in 1871. From 1872 they had to have two teachers at least; and from 1874 they had to be distinct high schools with boards of their own, not just elementary schools with a higher department attached. In 1871 very few of the 107 schools of secondary grade employed more than one master. In 1878 there was an average of three masters to each of the 103 schools and not a single instance in which one master was attempting the impossible task of teaching all subjects of the curriculum. The result, according to Inspector McLellan, who had sound reason for his statement, was "better classification, better discipline, better teaching, greater industry on the part of the pupils, and, on the whole, a state of efficiency incomparably in advance of that of former days."[4] New optional subjects appeared in the high school program and the number of pupils increased. Large, well-equipped high schools might qualify as collegiate institutes.

By 1890 Ontario had a truly solid system of education. In cities massive buildings of brick, three or four stories high, with smoke in winter proudly pouring from their central heating systems, symbolized the strength and efficiency of the educational organization. At the top, since 1875, there had been a minister of education. At the bottom, after 1883, was the Toronto youngster entering a kindergarten in September. What did it mean to go to an Ontario school in the census year 1891?

It meant that you, as a pupil, were one of almost half a million on the register of the schools, although the average attendance was only half that number. There were more than 5700 public schools, mostly brick or frame, nearly all freehold, and nearly all with maps and other simple equipment. These schools were taught by more than 8000 teachers, two-thirds of them women, and half of them with only a year or two of high school education. Most of the schools were open for a full year of 208 days.

Seven out of eight pupils who had managed to get through the first reader in 1891 were destined to reach the fourth reader (nominally, Grades VII and VIII). During all of their public school career they studied reading, writing, and arithmetic, and, during nearly all of it, drawing. During two-thirds of their elementary school career they studied geography, grammar, and composition. For about half that length of time the time-table included Canadian history, temperance and hygiene, drill and

calisthenics, English history, and music, although not every pupil received instruction in all these subjects.

Let us look for a moment at the 85,000 youngsters in the fourth reader of the public school. Presumably 35,000 or 40,000 of them were in the senior fourth or highest elementary grade. Of that number about 22,000 wrote the high school entrance examination, and about 12,000 passed.

Those who went on to high school attended either one of the 31 collegiate institutes having an average of over 300 pupils on the roll, or one of the 89 high schools having an average of over 100. Altogether in 1891 there were 19,000 enrolled in these schools and an average attendance of over 11,000. No less than 15,000 of these pupils were in Form I, 3600 in Form II, only 772 in Form III, and only 85 in Form IV. Obviously a fair number stayed for more than a year in the first form, but only a minority went any higher. About 500 matriculated, mostly at the junior or Form III level. More than four times that number received commercial certificates. About a quarter of the students leaving high school went into teaching.

At high school all students studied English — grammar, composition, and literature — and history, geography, arithmetic, and algebra. Two-thirds studied geometry, drawing, and book-keeping. More than one-third studied French, less than one-third Latin, about one-quarter physics, and about one-sixth chemistry. Very few, by this time, were studying Greek; in fact there were about twice as many studying German.

Ontario people of position were very proud of their school system in the last quarter of the nineteenth century. It was a model of formal efficiency, the envy of other provinces at the time. Even in 1950 there were some older citizens who looked back with nostalgia to the solid program of those Victorian schools. But a few people even in 1890 regarded the whole system as a pretentious machine incapable of true education.

1900 TO THE PRESENT

The final period, from 1900 to the present, was characterized in Ontario as elsewhere by decreasing confidence in the forms of the past and more concern for the needs of the individual pupil here and now. We have seen that the years of compulsory schooling were extended and that some attendance at high school became almost universal. There was a striking development of vocational education. In the period between the two great wars, the number of pupils in vocational schools and courses increased from a negligible proportion to thirty per cent of the total secondary school enrolment. New school services included free textbooks, medical and dental inspection, and transportation to school.

Gradually, throughout the period, measures have been taken to make the system less rigid and more elastic. More and more pupils were excused from the high school entrance examination until in 1950 it was abolished. Recommendation by teachers was accepted from 1932 as an alternative to passing Grade XI and XII departmental examinations, which were abandoned altogether a few years later. Since 1950 experimental efforts have been under way to overcome retardation resulting from a lock-step system of grading, to encourage adaptation of the school program to local needs, and to have teachers take over responsibility for curriculum planning. All of these movements will be discussed in later chapters.

Manitoba

When Manitoba became a province in 1871, it had a population of 25,000, of whom less than one in thirty were known to be attending school. By 1901 the population had increased to 255,000, of whom one in five was enrolled in the schools. The population continued to grow, to 700,000 by 1931 and to 777,000 by 1951. But as elsewhere, the proportion of the population in school declined in the present century, although school life lengthened and average attendance improved from about fifty-three per cent in 1900 to about eighty-four per cent in 1950. Except for the more rapid expansion around the turn of the century, the development of education was similar to that of Ontario.

Educational legislation in 1871 established the Manitoba school system. The central authority was a board of education appointed by the lieutenant-governor-in-council. The local authorities were boards of three elected trustees, who in 1873 were required to support the school by local taxation. But at first there were virtually two systems of education modelled after those of Quebec. The provincial board as a whole selected textbooks for secular subjects, but Roman Catholic and Protestant panels looked after other matters: the control, management, and discipline of schools; the regulations for examining, grading, and licensing teachers; and the prescription of books relating to religion and morals. The grant was divided equally at first between the two panels, then in 1873 according to aggregate attendance in the respective schools, and in 1875 according to population between ages five and sixteen. At the local level, the religious minority had the privilege of establishing a separate school, and after 1875 more than one such school. After 1873 it was definitely established that no taxpayer was obliged to support more than one type of school. Of major interest in the history of education in Manitoba is the development which changed these arrangements.

The population of the province in 1871 consisted of various elements. There were the métis, who were hostile to the new-comers and anxious to preserve their semi-civilized ways. A few were English métis, the sons of officials of the Hudson's Bay Company. But more were French métis, inclined to the wild free life of the Indian, strong in their feeling of French-Canadian nationalism and in their unwillingness to take responsibility for education away from the church. Nearest to the métis in this respect were the older Scot settlers, who were also content to have the church provide and control the schools. Officials of the Hudson's Bay Company, probably for other reasons, approved of this attitude. Opposed to such an educational policy, and opposed as well to any arrangements likely to strengthen the Roman Catholic Church or to gratify the company, were English-speaking settlers from Upper Canada. Both they and settlers from the United States were in favor of democratic government and the management of affairs, including education, by the people themselves. The English-speaking people, as Simms says, felt "no compelling urge" to preserve their religion, or the religion of others, by means of the schools.[5]

The latter point of view gained in strength and prevailed. The majority of an overwhelming number of new settlers believed in a single public school under popular control, or were converted to that belief by western conditions. In 1875 the membership of the provincial board of education was changed to twelve Protestants and nine Roman Catholics. In 1890, as we shall see later, a new school act did away not only with the divided central authority, but with tax-supported separate schools. The Roman Catholics failed in their efforts, first to have the new school act declared *ultra vires* and next to get the Dominion government to disallow the act. They did obtain a decision from the Privy Council that as a religious minority they might appeal to the Dominion government for remedial legisla-

tion. The Conservative government in Ottawa ordered the government of Manitoba to pass supplementary legislation, but the government of Manitoba refused. The Conservative party decided to introduce remedial legislation but was defeated at the polls in 1896.

If the denominational system had been upheld in Manitoba, a major difficulty during the twentieth century period of expansion might have been much more complicated. Great numbers of settlers came from Germany, Scandinavia, the Ukraine, and other countries of Europe. They settled in clusters and some tried to set up schools to teach their own language and religion or to have no schools at all. Among them were Mennonites, who lived in strict theocratic communities, and Doukhobors, who had a communistic system of land holding and a religion of extreme simplicity. The claim of groups like these to special educational privileges or exemptions might have been irresistible under a divided central authority, and the difficulty of securing Canadian schools would have been greatly aggravated.

Secondary education in Manitoba was hampered by the problems inevitable in a large area with small population. In 1888 special grants were offered to intermediate departments in elementary schools, and by 1913 there were forty-five such departments each under one teacher. As for full-fledged high schools, in 1882 there was a collegiate department only in Winnipeg. By 1913 there were seven centres in the province outside Winnipeg with collegiate departments of four or more teachers, six centres with collegiate departments of three or more teachers, and thirteen centres with high schools. Altogether in 1913, some 186 teachers and 4100 pupils were engaged in high school work.

Expenditures on education in Manitoba dropped from $14,000,000 in 1930-31 to $9,400,000 in 1935-36. By 1948, when they were only slightly over $19,000,000 they had not been restored to the same extent as in the two other Prairie Provinces to the west. A comparatively small proportion of the province had been reorganized in those larger units of administration that result in extensions of educational services.

Saskatchewan

In a previous chapter the history of the beginning of education in the Northwest Territories was carried to about the year 1883. There were then about 60,000 people in the territories and only nineteen schools which qualified for the government grant of one-half the teacher's salary. The next year an ordinance created the skeleton organization of a school system. It dealt with the foundation of school districts, the duties of trustees, assessments for schools, and even with inspection and the certification of teachers. Thereafter an increasing population put flesh on the bare bones:

Year	Population	Schools	Teachers	Pupils
1886	75,000	76	84	2,550
1900	200,000	492	592	20,350

The first report of the secretary of the board of education for the territories, published in 1886, showed only two teachers in Regina and only one at Saskatoon, centres that are now the chief cities of Saskatchewan. In Saskatoon, school was open for only the first two or three months of the school year, in the fall. Schools and teachers were classified as Roman Catholic or Protestant. The first certificates were issued in 1886 on the basis of separate examinations set by a Protestant and a Roman Catholic clergyman. In 1888 fourteen school visitors, or part-time inspectors, were appointed, and at least four of them were clergy. But although the number of Roman Catholic and Protestant schools was about equal in 1883, the new population was so predominantly Protestant that even by 1886 schools of that category outnumbered Roman Catholic schools in the ratio of five to one, and the difference continued to increase.

In 1892 the central authority took the form of a Council of Public Instruction, which shortly after appointed a superintendent of education. In 1901 the council was replaced by a department of education headed by a commissioner of education, who was a member of the executive council. This arrangement was in force when the provinces of Saskatchewan and Alberta were formed in 1905.

The history of education in Saskatchewan was characterized by rapidity of development. The numerical growth in twenty years was remarkable:

Year	Schools	Teachers	Pupils	Grants
1905	700	1000	25,000	$ 157,500
1925	4400	7700	217,000	$ 2,595,000

Expansion at this pace meant that in a peak year, 1912, new school districts were formed at the rate of more than one a day.

In 1905 the department of education consisted of only the commissioner, the deputy commissioner, three or four others in the office, and five school inspectors in the field. The commissioner was replaced by a minister in 1909. By 1919 the inside staff numbered 78, and the outside staff 77. New officials in charge of new branches appeared every two or three years. In 1915 new appointments included two directors of school agriculture, a director of household science, and four supervisors of school districts in foreign language communities. In 1917 there were two new officials, a chief inspector of schools and a director of school hygiene. In 1919 there were appointments of an assistant registrar, a director of education among new Canadians, an inspector in charge of school district organization, a director of rural education associations and school fairs, and an assistant in extension work in school hygiene. That made a total of fourteen new positions, half of them of top importance, in six years. The nature of the appointments indicate some of the educational problems of a vast agricultural area rapidly settled by people from many countries.

One of the problems was to obtain a sufficient number of teachers. In 1906 two-thirds of those granted licences had received their training in other provinces. But the normal school that had opened in Regina in 1901 was supplemented by a second one in Saskatoon in 1912, and by 1916 only one-quarter of the new teachers had to be imported. When teachers' salaries went to a new high in 1921, normal school enrolment increased from 900 in that year to over 1600 in 1922. By 1925 the deputy minister was able to announce that the province could train a sufficient number of its own young people as teachers to staff the schools. In that year the number so trained and certificated was 2280. Next year the normal schools were unable to accommodate the number of applicants, and standards were raised by the elimination of third class certificates. Subsequently, in 1938, after years of economic depression, the old second class qualifications were abolished, and all who entered normal school were required to have full Grade XII standing.

As in other provinces, educational services in Saskatchewan expanded not only with the growing population but with the broader concepts of the function of the school. After the passing of the first Secondary Education Act in 1907, high school enrolment grew rapidly. After the passing of the Technical Education Act of 1919, increasing attention was given to the practical side of secondary education. Growing concern for the health of school children could be demonstrated in 1925 by visits of nurses to over 1300 schools and by their inspection of over 14,000 children. Many other such services might be enumerated. But Saskatchewan had the misfortune to be distinguished even more for its demonstration of the disastrous effects on social welfare of the depression of the 1930's.

Expenditures on education in 1929 had reached almost seventeen million dollars. By 1931 they had fallen to twelve and three-quarter millions, and by 1935 to only a little over eight and one-half millions. The effect on teachers and the teaching profession was calamitous. The salaries of women teachers holding first class certificates in rural areas fell from $1142 in 1930 to $864 in 1931 and $442 in 1934. But even salaries at this level could not always be collected. In many districts teachers were given only the government grant of a dollar a day and usually, but not always, their board. Arrears in teachers' salaries amounted to over $600,000 in 1933 and to over $850,000 in 1935. Attendance at normal schools dropped from an ordinary total of about 1500 to about 1250 in 1931 and about 625 in 1933.

The almost complete dependence of Saskatchewan on agriculture caused the effect of the depression, intensified by years of drought, to be even more severe and prolonged than in other provinces. The population, which had increased from 91,000 in 1901 to 922,000 by 1931, declined thereafter to 896,000 by 1941, and to 832,-000 by 1951.

In 1944 the first socialist government in Canada came to power in Saskatchewan, and during World War II and after, the province shared in the revival of economic prosperity. The expenditure on education, which had been restored to only $10,000,-000 in 1941, rose to $15,000,000 in 1946 and to $30,000,000 in 1951. In 1949 Saskatchewan ranked third among the provinces in expenditures per capita and in expenditures per pupil in average daily attendance. By that time most of the province had been reorganized into larger areas of school administration, as was the case also in the two provinces to the west, where the expenditures were higher.

To summarize briefly, public education in Saskatchewan since 1905 has had twenty-five years of expansion, ten years of retrogression, and ten years of recovery, with more extreme ups and downs than most other provinces.

Alberta

Five movements or events have been prominent in the history of education of Alberta. The first was the rapid increase of population and the correspondingly rapid expansion of school facilities in the first decades of the present century. Since this development has already been discussed with reference to Saskatchewan, it will be sufficient here simply to mention that there were 746 school sections in Alberta in 1906 and 3027 school sections in 1912. The second movement was the campaign to assimilate the large new foreign born population. The third was the introduction in 1936 of a radically new program in the elementary schools. The fourth was the administrative reorganization, about the same time, of the whole province into large school districts. The fifth was the transfer in 1945 of all responsibility for teacher education to the provincial university. In these last three developments Alberta was not only the pioneer but the most thorough-going of all Canadian provinces, and the contributions of Alberta in these fields will receive attention in later chapters. Chief emphasis in this brief history of education in the province will be given to the second of the developments mentioned, the assimilation of the foreign born.

In the early 1880's there were only 5000 whites in the area now covered by Alberta. The first considerable influx of new population came between 1887 and 1890, when 10,000 Mormons settled in the southern part of the territory. Then came the great waves of immigration already noted. Fortunately a fair number of the newcomers were Americans, or Europeans who had lived for a few years in the United States before coming to Canada, so that the problems of language and customs were not as grave as they might otherwise have been. Fortunately, too, some of the European immigrants were easily assimilated, as were the Icelanders who settled west of Red Deer.

Members of a national group who posed a serious problem were the Ukrainians, consisting of Ruthenians and Galicians. At least one-half of these people were illiterate, and all had customs, attitudes, and ideas of political organization entirely different from those of English-speaking North America. They settled in clusters, among which one of the largest was a Ruthenian "colony" of some 15,000 persons east and north-east of Edmonton. Some attempt was made by church groups to establish schools among the settlers, but the government decided that the regular machinery must be set up locally to enable the people gradually to take responsibility for the operation of their own schools. Extreme difficulties were encountered. In one place not one of the three Ukrainian trustees could read or write English, and one of the three could not read or write Ukrainian. Ruthenian priests were often opposed to the establishment of English schools and helped to foster among their people distrust of public education, passive resistance to the establishment of schools, and sometimes active hostility.

Soon after the formation of the province the department of education appointed a supervisor of foreign schools for Alberta. Robert Fletcher, who assumed this office, found a strong desire among the Ruthenians for teachers who could speak their language. To obtain bilingual teachers, Manitoba and Saskatchewan had set up English schools for the foreign born, and Alberta between 1912 and 1918 also gave prospective Ukrainian teachers instruction in English in a pre-normal Ruthenian training school at Vegreville. Although the plan achieved good results, many of these young teachers proved to be troublesome. Some acquired a mere smattering of English and taught their pupils nothing of value from a Canadian point of view. Some who came from Manitoba and Saskatchewan proved to be agents of an organization anxious to defeat the purposes of the schools. The supervisor of foreign schools secured laws that made it impossible for these reactionary agitators to collect their salaries by legal process and enabled him to impose fines for teaching without proper qualifications.

Other groups caused trouble. A branch of the German-Lutheran church set up private schools, the teachers of which were theological students from colleges of the sect in the United States. Most of the instruction they gave was related to religion and the German language. The department's method of dealing with these schools was to refuse a certificate that they were doing efficient work and thus to leave the parents of children who attended them liable to penalty under the Truancy Act. By 1914 many of these Lutheran schools had closed and their children had returned to the public schools. Others who presented difficulties were the Huterian Brethren, or Hutterites, who came to Canada in 1917 from the United States when the government there attempted to conscript their young men for World

War I. In Alberta there was less trouble than elsewhere in getting the Hutterites to establish schools. They agreed to operate public schools with certificated teachers on five days a week during regular school hours, but the buildings for the rest of the time served as Hutterite churches, in which the children were taught the religion and history of the group, and a composite language formed from its several dialects. There were settlers of a great many other nationalities and denominations, only a few of which gave trouble by insisting on the teaching of their own language and religion.

There were other difficulties of a more general kind which aggravated the problem of Canadianization. The inspector at Red Deer in 1909 listed the following as major needs in public education: the operation of schools for a full ten-month year and not merely for short terms; qualified teachers who would remain in the profession instead of permit holders and transients; a more practical course of study and a more practical program of teacher training; better roads and improved transportation; more money; and more energetic and zealous attention of citizens and educators to the rural schools.

The policy of the government was highly successful in overcoming educational difficulties with ethnic groups. By 1911 the supervisor of foreign schools was able to report a marked improvement in the ability of local communities to look after their own affairs, including the establishment and operation of schools. By 1949 the expenditures on public education of local school boards were higher in Alberta than in any other province in proportion to population and second highest per pupil in average daily attendance. In Alberta today there are many towns and districts in which the inhabitants are largely or almost wholly of one national origin; but in spite of the retention of some characteristic customs, the people and the schools are unquestionably Canadian.

For fear that this account of only one aspect of the development of education in Alberta may leave a one-sided impression, it is worth pointing out that the organization of public education in the province follows the common Canadian pattern in nearly all particulars. In fact the provincial department of education in Alberta might be cited as typical of Canada. It has been headed since the first years of the province by a minister of education. The chief of the civil servants is the deputy minister, and under him are the officials most usually found in other provincial departments. As in other western provinces there is one provincial university, although there are also several colleges, not all of which are affiliated. Alberta deviates, as was suggested at the beginning of this section, only in the extent to which reorganization and innovations have been carried out since 1935. Its population of 940,000 in 1951 was the fourth highest among the Canadian provinces.

British Columbia

The province of British Columbia extends west from Alberta to the Pacific Ocean, north from the state of Washington to the Yukon, and covers about 366,-000 square miles. Its population increased from 36,000 in 1871 to 179,000 in 1901, then more rapidly to 525,000 in 1921 and to 1,165,000 in 1951. In that year the school enrolment exceeded 173,000 and the average attendance 154,000. Expenditures on education in 1949 were the highest in the Canadian provinces per pupil in average daily attendance, and the second highest per head of population.

A reasonable question to be answered in a brief historical account of education in British Columbia is how such high standing was achieved. One answer, of course, is that the province became wealthy. In per capita income it was the third highest in Canada for the period 1919-1937, and the second highest as measured by the net value of production per person in 1948. It profited by gold rushes to the Fraser Valley in 1858 and to the Klondike forty years later and by the discovery of silver in the 1880's, from the development of fisheries dating from the first export of canned salmon in the 1870's, and from lumbering and more recently from the manufacturing of materials and products from wood. But educational improvements were effected chiefly by a belated reform of educational finance, beginning in the late nineteenth century, and by major reorganizations within the schools after 1925.

The free school controversy in British Columbia* failed to develop local responsibility, so that until 1888 the province paid the whole cost of education. In that year, however, the four cities on the coast were required to refund one-third of the provincial grant for teachers' salaries by a tax on rateable property. Three years later the ratio was raised to one-half, and in 1893 the cities were given the responsibility of erecting and repairing schools and simultaneously the power to fix salaries of teachers. By 1901 city school districts had full financial responsibility for the operation of schools with assistance from provincial grants. After 1905, rural municipalities and rural school districts began to assume a share of school costs. As a result the following changes took place in the distribution of educational expenditure:

School Year	Government Expenditure	Local Expenditure
1888 — 1889	$126,000	$ 11,000
1899 — 1900	$307,000	$ 82,000
1900 — 1901	$350,000	$182,000
1907 — 1908	$545,000	$675,000

* See p. 284.

Some credit for this revolution must go, no doubt, to the central authority, including superintendents S. D. Pope (1884-1899) and Alexander Robinson (1899-1919). But the grant system was not particularly ingenious. After 1901, grants to cities were based on average attendance but after 1905, grants generally were determined by the number of teachers, with supplements favorable to smaller centres and rural areas. One chief factor in the success of the development appears to have been the introduction of the desired change in cities first. In contrast, the cities of Quebec and Montreal were deliberately handicapped from 1846 to 1868-69, and generally the tendency in other provinces was to adjust the pace of educational advance to rural areas. Another factor was direct provincial taxation for education by means of a poll tax. This method of raising money had been tried locally and half-heartedly before Confederation with indifferent results, but in 1876 every male resident over eighteen years of age was required to pay an annual tax of three dollars to support public schools. Such a universal tax was possible only because the act of 1872 had made the schools strictly non-sectarian. Although moral training was to be emphasized, no religious dogmas or creeds were to be taught. Hence in 1876 no new religious issue was raised by the introduction of direct taxation. Roman Catholic opposition to one system of publicly supported schools for all was expressed again in stronger terms, but the act was passed.

Later improvements in the organization and work of the schools of British Columbia are discussed elsewhere, especially with reference to junior high schools and the curriculum.

Though typical of provincial universities in western Canada, the University of British Columbia was the last to come into actual existence. As early as 1872 the superintendent of schools advocated land endowment for a university. But legislation eighteen years later to establish such an institution proved abortive because a quorum of the senate could not be assembled. As a temporary expedient in 1894 an amendment to the Public Schools Act made it lawful for high schools to affiliate with one of several Canadian universities. In 1899 and 1902 respectively, high schools in Vancouver and Victoria became associated with McGill University and offered first year and subsequently second year arts. In 1906 a familiar title reappeared with the incorporation of a Royal Institution for the Advancement of Learning of British Columbia, under which the McGill University College of British Columbia was established at Vancouver in 1906, and the college at Victoria acquired similar status in 1907. Within a short time the former was offering three years, and the latter two years of arts and science and both were offering two years of applied science. In 1908 a new University of British Columbia Act was passed, in 1915 the university opened in Vancouver, and in 1920 the college at Victoria was affiliated with the University of British Columbia. These bare facts reveal none of the denominational and institutional rivalry which enlivened the proceedings.

British Columbia in 1947 ranked first among the provinces of Canada by a considerable margin in the percentage of teachers who were university graduates, in the percentage of men teachers, and in the median number of years of experience of its teachers.

CHAPTER 15

Central Authorities

Each of the British colonies which later became part of Canada had taken some state action to assist education before they had entered into any permanent union. Education was therefore a provincial prerogative before Confederation and continued to be so thereafter. The autonomy of the federating provinces in this respect was ensured by constitutional guarantee chiefly as a safeguard of religious privileges in education but partly to maintain vested political interests in a field which had already become an important function of government.

Evolution

Early central authorities tended to be aristocratic and unpopular. One of this type was the central board of education in Upper Canada, whose appointed members under the chairmanship of John Strachan attempted to control the schools there between 1823 and 1833. William Lyon Mackenzie in the *Colonial Advocate* gave what he called "some particulars of the history of this concern." The motto of the chairman, he said, was "Give me a good salary and I'll be your minister." He objected to the expenditure of £1050 on Church of England catechisms and on Strachan's favorite primers and denounced with equal vehemence "Strachan College" and the "University of Strachan."[1] Although a violent critic, Mackenzie probably reflected the antipathy of many people towards this type of central authority.

In Lower Canada the first central authority over education was the Royal Institution for the Advancement of Learning, provided for by legislation of 1801 and set

234

up in 1818. It consisted of a board of eighteen appointed members, whose essential function was the distribution of government money to assist in maintaining schools. But the Royal Institution was doomed to failure from the start. It was fashioned in accordance with the views brought over from England in 1793 by Dr. Mountain, who became Anglican Bishop of Quebec in that year. That fourteen of the eighteen members were Protestant was enough to ensure its non-acceptance by the great majority of the population. That the Anglican bishop was chairman, and the secretary a teacher preparing for holy orders in the Church of England, was sufficient to inspire distrust not only among Roman Catholics but among dissenting Protestants as well. But even in a secular way it went counter to North American feeling in school administration. To obtain a grant from the Royal Institution the people of a local community were required to give up ownership of their school and turn over the deed to the central authority.

Where influence in favor of denominational control of schools was strong, there was inevitably opposition to the setting up of a purely secular state authority over education. In Lower Canada after the passing of the act of 1829, a committee of the legislature was to all intents and purposes the central authority. This body could not possibly be charged with pro-English or Protestant bias, but it was not wholly satisfactory to the church. As Dunkin wrote in 1839, "A newer jealousy between the political leaders of the French-Canadian population and their clergy was now beginning to spring up."[2] When a new central authority was established after the Act of Union, it evolved, as we saw, into a divided body, one section of which was heavily weighted with members of the hierarchy of the Roman Catholic Church. In Upper Canada in 1853, the presbyter of the Diocese of Toronto ex-

pressed in a pamphlet the opposition of many of the Anglican clergy to education under public control. In Newfoundland the creation of any real state authority over education was delayed until the end of the nineteenth century, and even then the influence of the major denominations restricted the power of the state.

Provincial authorities, set up over public education about the middle of the nineteenth century, had control as a rule only over elementary education. Aristocratic influences still held sway over secondary education. For example, in New Brunswick, where the lieutenant-governor and the executive council had been constituted a board of education in 1847, and where a provincial superintendent of education was appointed in 1852, a member of the legislature pointed out during a debate in the house in the latter year that a disproportionate amount of about £2300 had been spent separately on twenty-three pupils in King's College. A royal commission appointed in 1854 would have had the university and all the schools of the province united under the control of the provincial superintendent. In 1861 the board of education and chief superintendent in New Brunswick did take over control of the grammar schools, although even then the schools in Fredericton and Saint John remained apart. Secondary schools sooner or later came under the control of the provincial central authorities, except in the Roman Catholic system of Quebec. The universities, of course, remained apart from the public school systems.

FOUR STEPS IN DEVELOPMENT

The usual steps by which central authorities came into being were *first* the establishment of some regular system of grants, *second* the setting up of boards intermediate between the locality and the government to examine and license teachers, *third* the establishment of a provincial board with wider powers, and *fourth* the employment of a provincial superintendent and subsequently of additional expert personnel. The order of the last two steps was sometimes reversed. In Upper Canada, for example, grants to the common schools were introduced in 1816, district boards to certificate teachers in 1824, a superintendent of education in 1842, and a provincial board in 1846. The beginning of school grants was discussed in a previous chapter, but something more should be said here about the other three steps.

Intermediate boards for the licensing of teachers sometimes continued to function, as in Ontario, long after the central board was established, although eventually the central authority took over the work. In New Brunswick the courts of the general sessions were intermediate county authorities from 1816 to 1858, and a central board of education was set up in 1847. In Prince Edward Island, however, the central authority developed from a single board established to license teachers in 1830. In 1852 this became a board of education of seven members appointed by the governor-in-council not only to examine and license teachers but to re-engage those who were satisfactory and generally to exercise control over all the common schools. The board was enlarged in 1861 and given charge of the normal school and again enlarged in 1868 and given power to alter and re-arrange school districts and to open not more than eleven grammar schools. In 1877 the board of education was reorganized to consist of the members of the executive council, the superintendent of education, and the principal of Prince of Wales College. It was then a full-fledged central authority.

The third and fourth steps, and the relationship between the provincial board and the superintendent, may be illustrated by the example of Nova Scotia. In that province a general board of five members appointed by the governor-in-council was set up in 1841 in order "that greater uniformity in the system to be pursued by the respective boards of school commissioners may be promoted and the enactments of the act rendered more effective." In 1850 a superintendent of education was appointed. He was instructed to report annually on the condition of the schools, and on means of improving buildings and equipment, to encourage teachers' institutes, to help destitute districts acquire teachers, and "to establish as far as may be done, without undue interference with the functions of commissioners and teachers, an efficient and uniform system." Here as elsewhere the intention was that the central authority should do what was necessary to secure at least minimum standards without usurping local initiative.

A FIFTH STEP

Nevertheless there was a distrust of control by appointed provincial boards, and a subsequent fifth step was in the direction of bringing the central administration under direct check by the people's representatives. In Nova Scotia in 1864 the central authority became a council of public instruction consisting of members of the executive council, and the following year the superintendent was given responsibility as their agent for general supervision of the schools. Across the continent in British Columbia the same change occurred some years later: an act of 1872 had set up a board of education consisting of six members appointed by the governor-in-council and exercising very full powers; in 1879 the board was abolished and most of the duties were transferred to the superintendent; in 1891 members of the executive council were constituted a council of public instruction. When the two-denominational type of central authority was abandoned in Manitoba in 1890, a member of the executive council acted as head of the department of education until 1907, when a minister of education first took office. Similarly in the Northwest Territories an appointed board of the two-denominational type, set up in 1884, was replaced in 1892 by a council of public instruction whose voting members were members of the executive council. This was abolished in 1901, but in that year the government took the final step of having one member of the executive council — in this case a commissioner of education — given special responsibility for the schools.

In Ontario this last step was taken in 1876, when legislation transferred the powers of the former council of public instruction and chief superintendent of education to an "education department" consisting of members of the executive council and, in particular, a minister of education. In discussing the change some twenty years later, the second incumbent of the ministerial office, the Honorable G. W. Ross, admitted some disadvantages in this more direct political control. But he emphasized the value of having a spokesman for education in the house and in the cabinet, and even more the value of having the head of the education department sensitive to the will of the people.

"There is no constitutional reason" he said, "why public opinion should not be brought to bear as directly upon educational questions as upon any other which affect the welfare of the community and the pockets of the taxpayers."[3]

As we have seen, the province of Quebec had had a minister of education from 1867 to 1874, but abolished the office in the same year that the two committees of the central education authority gained complete independence of action, so that the church was free to play an unhampered role in the direction of Roman Catholic education. Few who speak for education in that province would express themselves in favor of re-establishing a minister of education and making educational policy through him subject to the control of the electorate.

In the three Prairie Provinces, ministers of education first took office about 1907, and in British Columbia in 1920. All provinces, with the exception of Quebec, had departments of education headed by a minister and deputy minister of education by 1951. In terms of constituted authority and democratic control, the department of education in any of the nine English-speaking provinces is essentially the cabinet, or executive council. In British Columbia and New Brunswick members of the executive council and the chief education officer are explicitly designated the council of public instruction and the board of education, respectively. In Manitoba and Prince Edward Island there are appointed advisory boards. But as operating bodies the provincial departments of education are thought of, and are in effect, the civil servant officials of whom the deputy minister is chief. In making appointments, effecting major reorganizations, or introducing controversial changes the minister of education is the active head. But in the ordinary executive functions and even in some matters of policy the deputy minister and his assistants exercise control. This arrangement of affairs as carried out in most provinces is familiar to the majority of Canadians. But in Newfoundland there are complications.

Newfoundland created a department of education under a minister by an act of 1920. But this legislation failed to withstand the power of denominational influences and the effect of an economic depression. By an act of 1927 a bureau of education with the prime minister as president was substituted for the department of education. This bureau included, in addition to the president, the deputy president or secretary for education, the three denominational superintendents of education, three assistant superintendents of education, the educational secretary of the Salvation Army, and other members nominated by each of the three larger denominations, making a total of twelve persons in all. By amendment passed in 1935 the department of education was re-established under the direction of the commissioner for home affairs and education. There was to be a committee of education consisting of the commissioner and six members, two from each of the three major denominations. In 1939 a further revision of the Education Act provided for a department of education under a commissioner with a secretary for education and three executive officers. There was also a council of education consisting of the commissioner, two chief officials of the department, and one representative for each of four major denominations, Church of England, Roman Catholic, United Church, and Salvation Army. After Confederation in 1949, Newfoundland re-introduced the offices of minister and deputy minister of education, but the denominational superintendents and the council remained.

APPRAISAL OF THE NEED

When strong central authorities were set up from the Atlantic to Ontario around 1850, and in the west around 1890, they were very much needed, in spite of the charges of "Prussian despotism" from advocates of denominational, local, or individual freedom. In explaining this need, Theodore Rand, who had been superintendent of education in both Nova Scotia and New Brunswick, referred to an observation of John Stuart Mill that those who need to be made wiser usually desire it least. Rand said it was the obligation of government to offer to the people a better education than the majority would spontaneously elect. To do this the central authority did not take responsibility for the schools into its own hands. Egerton Ryerson, who was frequently accused of being an autocrat, declared just as frequently that the provision of education was essentially the responsibility of the people in their local communities. The chief function of the central authority was to offer grants to stimulate local initiative and thus to establish minimum provincial standards. The powers given to the central authorities by law were really definitions of the arrangements under which provincial grants would be paid.

Functions

Logically one of the first steps taken by governments when they began giving grants was to obtain reports on schools so assisted. Great numbers of school returns in the Canadian archives attest to assiduous efforts along this line. In Lower Canada under the Act of 1829, school reports prepared by teachers for trustees gave the following information: the teacher's name, the average number of children in attendance throughout the year, the fee charged, the number of poor children taught gratuitously, the books used, under whose superintendence the school was operated, when the school was established, by what authority (e.g., under the school act of what year) the school had been established, how the school was supported, and remarks on any particular system of teaching that was used. A typical return of one of the elementary schools at Pointe aux Trembles in 1829 showed that Benjamin Spillsbury, the teacher, had forty-two pupils of whom twenty-three were taught gratis, the rest paying seven pence ha'penny a month and contributing their share of twenty cords of firewood, that the teacher used the "Canadien (sic) Spelling Book" and taught English and French, and that the school had been established under the Act of 1829. Before 1840, reports of larger schools were made on printed forms requiring similar and additional information, including the subjects taught, the dates of the school year, the number preparing to be teachers, and an account of the receipts and expenditures of the school. Other reports giving a judgment on the work of the teacher were sent in by school visitors, who were appointed from an early date and who, as they became paid inspectors, took over the full work of reporting. Chief inspectors or superintendents (appointed in Prince Edward Island 1837, Nova Scotia 1850, New Brunswick 1852, Lower Canada and Upper Canada 1842) received the local reports and soon began to compile complete school returns.

When the central authorities were fully established, their powers were regularly as follows: making regulations, *e.g.* regarding the length of the school day and year; authorizing textbooks; drawing up courses of study; defining qualifications for teachers, and, sooner or later, issuing certificates and conducting examinations for certificates; training teachers; and inspecting schools. In Ontario the central authority acquired most of these powers by 1846 and all by 1850, although those regarding courses of study, teachers' certificates, and inspection became more sharply defined after 1870. After that date control of written examinations became another powerful instrument of the central authority.

There were variations, of course, in different provinces. In Prince Edward Island most of these powers were defined in an act of 1877, when the first superintendent was appointed. In New Brunswick in 1858 the central board exercised control over the inspection of schools, but did not prescribe textbooks or make ordinary regulations regarding the organization or government of schools until 1870. In British Columbia in 1872 the central board

of education not only prescribed but also purchased and distributed textbooks, not only examined and certificated teachers but also fixed their salaries and for that one year appointed them. But in spite of these and other deviations mentioned below, all provincial authorities by the present century controlled these listed *interna* of education and left to the local authorities the management of *externa,* such as the provision of school facilities and the employment of teachers.

Throughout the years the central authorities issued a multiplying number of regulations supplementary to successive education acts, on conditions affecting grants, on the time that schools should be open, on textbooks, and on scores of other matters. Intended to facilitate the work of administration, the rigid rules were often a source of embarrassment in particular cases.

Here is one illustration, from the early days, of the administrator's problems. John Salmons, a teacher of Upper Canada in 1837, sent the lieutenant-governor a straightforward, well-written letter in an attempt to collect his share of the government money. The central board had rejected his claim because he had not taught in the same school up to the first of July. He wrote: "I taught the full time that I agreed to teach, *viz.* for 6 months, faithfully and honestly."[4] He pointed out that local boards were compelled to hire teachers when they could. The petition was referred to Strachan, who made a note to the effect that the central board could not depart from its rules because the fixed amount of the school grant was divided twice a year among those who produced a certificate from the trustees of a school to show that they had taught for the previous six months. What could an administrator do for a deserving teacher who had taught for three months before and three months after a semi-annual day of reckoning? Nothing.

Grants

LAND GRANTS

The earliest grants for education were in the form of land. In Prince Edward Island in 1767 thirty acres in each township were set aside for the support of a schoolmaster. In New Brunswick the royal instructions of 1784 stipulated that 200 acres in each township should be set aside to encourage the settlement of a schoolmaster and 500 acres for the maintenance of any schoolmaster in charge of a school. In Lower Canada land grants were promised by the governor in 1801, but nothing was done. In 1797 in Upper Canada 500,-000 acres were designated as an endowment for grammar schools and a university at the request of Governor Simcoe. Naturally endowments for such purposes were preferred by the early governments. In New Brunswick in 1788 the government of the new colony set aside 6000 acres adjacent to Fredericton for the endowment of a college. In Prince Edward Island in 1804 the government under Fanning made a grant of ground for an institution named Kent College, which was to educate young men in "the learned languages, the liberal arts and sciences, and all the branches of useful and polite literature." The grant also set aside land for residences for the president and professors and for a botanical garden or nurseries, although for these lands a small yearly rent was to be paid.

Actually these early land grants did very little for education. One reason was the low value of land: 81,000 acres of crown land sold in Upper Canada in 1800 for £411, 16s., or at the price of about two and a half cents an acre. In Upper Canada the original school lands were carelessly selected, remote, and almost unsalable, although in 1828 half of them were exchanged for more valuable land as an endowment for the university. Later

legislation — for example, that of 1834 in Prince Edward Island — authorized the sale of such lands. Such action provided some revenue for the provincial government and it was possible to argue that education profited. When 250,000 acres were re-allocated to the grammar schools of Upper Canada in 1839, it was stipulated that the land should be sold for not less than ten shillings per acre. In 1849 a million acres were granted for the support of common schools in the two Canadas. This endowment also was sold and the proceeds were invested in provincial debentures, an ironical form of book-keeping which ostensibly provided money for the schools but really did nothing but reduce current taxation by the liquidation of capital. Some institutions, including even a few public schools in addition to several private schools and colleges, managed to retain land until the rental or sale price was high. Individuals and families must have profited more than the schools in this way, since 15,000,000 acres of crown land in Upper Canada are said to have been given up with nothing substantial to show for them, largely because of favoritism displayed by the Family Compact.

In later years land was set aside for education in the west. In Manitoba after 1870 two sections (1280 acres) in each township of 36 square miles were designated school lands, which were to be administered by the Dominion government. The province was to get the interest on money derived from sales, but apparently education received very little benefit. In Vancouver Island, as early as 1853, some 2200 acres were set aside as a church and school reserve in Victoria. In 1870 the inspector general of schools in British Columbia pointed out the desirability of school reserves of the kind that had been set aside in the United States. In 1879 a land amendment act designated sections 16 and 27 of townships thereafter surveyed as land for the support of education, and in 1882 it was enacted that no public reserve was to be alienated without the consent of the school trustees in the district.

MONEY GRANTS — A LEVERAGE

Grants of money were introduced during the period of transition to schools under public control. At first they were paid in a paternalistic way by governments in response to requests which found official favor. Petitions by the hundred poured into the offices of the governors — for aid in acquiring a lot and putting up a building, for assistance towards paying a teacher and maintaining a school, for infant schools, for national schools, for common schools, for secondary schools, for schools of every type. When regular machinery was set up for the distribution of grants, the petitions became claims, and communities were assured of some support if they met the simple conditions. But, as we saw, money was voted for limited periods and the amounts fluctuated. Only towards mid-century, when the central authorities had been organized in definite form and permanent school funds had been established, did the municipalities have a guarantee of reasonably constant assistance.

During the nineteenth century grants were designed by the central authorities chiefly to enforce the adoption of practices considered essential and to encourage localities to improve or extend their educational services in other approved ways. Thus grants were almost always dependent on the employment of a certificated teacher and were commonly graduated according to the qualifications of the teacher. The amount of the grants in Prince Edward Island was determined wholly on this basis in the third quarter of the nineteenth century, in the Northwest Territories largely on this basis between

1885 and 1901, and in Ontario partly on this basis between 1908 and 1930.

Grants often depended also on teachers' salaries: in the Northwest Territories after 1888 the grants paid 75 per cent of the salary of a first class teacher, 70 per cent of a second class, and 65 per cent of a third class; in British Columbia between 1931 and 1933, grants paid from 25 to 52 per cent of salaries of urban teachers and from 52 to 90 per cent of salaries of rural teachers. Earlier grants were also calculated according to total population, school population, or the number of pupils on the roll, but this basis was changed to average attendance (Ontario 1859, New Brunswick 1876, Northwest Territories 1888). Ontario and New Brunswick after the dates just mentioned and the Northwest Territories after 1901 based grants also on the length of the school year. Grants were used to enforce the use of authorized textbooks, as in Ontario from 1846. They were also used to induce trustees and teachers to set up school libraries (in Ontario after 1859, in the Northwest Territories after 1903). They were sometimes dependent on the teacher's achievement, which about 1880 was measured in New Brunswick by inspection and in Ontario by examinations. During the early decades of the present century grants were used to ensure the introduction of new subjects like manual training, household science, arts, agriculture, and new services like free textbooks and medical and dental inspection.

EQUALIZATION OF MONEY GRANTS

Gradually this "leverage" use of the grants gave way to a new purpose, the equalization of educational opportunity. Nova Scotia before 1832 had put aside the small sum of £70 a year to be divided among poor sections, and in that year decreed that part of this amount be used to establish schools for neglected Negroes. In 1865 in the same province it was found that grants which varied in amount according to the licence of the teacher left poorer sections unable to make up the difference by local taxation, and legislation was therefore passed to require a county tax to give special aid to these poorer sections. In New Brunswick after 1876 an inspector might recommend that a district be designated "poor" and that it receive supplementary grants. Newfoundland introduced in the early 1890's a "sparsely populated localities grant," which helped to reduce the number of illiterate persons over five years of age from 47.6 per cent of the population in 1891 to 30.5 per cent in 1911.

Grants predominantly for this purpose came into general use only in the present century. In Quebec the growing rural population and the many poor municipalities forced the Roman Catholic committee to go far in the direction of special grants to poorer districts. The principle of making the grant depend inversely on the amount of assessable land was introduced in the Northwest Territories in 1901. Although bonuses were still given then for length of school year, teachers' qualifications, and regularity of attendance, these were dropped in Alberta in 1913, when special grants were introduced for new schools during the first four difficult years of operation. There after 1926 an equalization grant on a graduated scale assisted schools with assessments below $75,000, and because of this many rural schools were able to keep open during the depression of the 1930's. In Ontario, grants to rural areas were made partly dependent on the amount of assessment in 1907. The principle was applied to all municipalities in the 1930's, and the leverage use of the grant was weakened by using as another chief factor all ordinary expenditures of the local school board. After 1945 Ontario grants paid a proportion of approved expenditures varying from thirty per cent in large cities to ninety-five per cent in

the poorest rural areas. In Saskatchewan, which had special grants for new school and small districts from before World War I, an amendment to the School Act just before World War II gave a scaled increase in grants to districts assessed below $100,000 per teacher. In 1943 this equalization supplement was doubled. In that same year New Brunswick passed a rural schools assistance act, which set aside $1,000,000 to assist rural municipalities in capital expenditures on elementary and high schools.

These illustrations of particular measures adopted by individual provinces reflect the general trend across Canada: from grants administered with partiality to grants based solely on population (1800-1850); from a leverage use of the grants (1850-1930) to an increasing emphasis on equalization during the present century and especially since World War II.

Changing policy in educational finance reflected the general evolution of society. At first a few regarded themselves as rightful beneficiaries and custodians of what the economy could afford; they allocated a small surplus for purposes they thought fit. Then political democracy and laissez-faire liberalism tended to stimulate enterprise. Finally came a new appraisal of human rights and an acceptance of the idea that the amount of assistance given in any particular case should be governed only by the need. In educational policy most provincial governments accepted this development because poorer areas were rural constituencies, where each single vote is of greater weight than in the more affluent urban centres.

Length of the School Year

Paternalistic schools of the early nineteenth century were kept in operation throughout the year, but schools of the people had winter or summer terms of six months. One of the major concerns of central authorities at mid-century was to lengthen the common school year to ten months or more. The longer school year introduced the question of vacation periods, regarding which there was little disposition to be generous. In Lower Canada three masters of Royal Institution schools in Bedford county protested

that a certain amount of time ought to be set apart for Vacations . . . that a vacation of three weeks each quarter year is not too long for the benefit of the Scholars, and that with such vacations they will learn more in the year, than they will when kept constantly on the drill.[5]

The Royal Institution issued supplementary regulations fixing the summer vacation at no more than a month, the Christmas vacation at no more than a fortnight, the school week at not less than five days, and the school day at not less than five hours. By an act of 1832 schools were required to be open at least 190 days in the year from nine to twelve and from one to four o'clock.

In Prince Edward Island a special committee of the legislative assembly appointed in 1839 recommended three weeks of vacation — ten days in May and eleven in October — with other holidays limited to Christmas Day, Good Friday, and alternate Saturdays. In the same province in 1852 it was decided that there should be three vacations during the year — one week in June, the second week in October, and December 24th to January 6th — with every other Saturday a holiday. Again in 1861, except in Charlottetown and Georgetown, the periods of vacation were defined as from May 15th to June 1st with two weeks in October and alternate Saturdays free. In British Columbia in 1872 the schools were given a five-day week and vacations of two weeks at Christmas and four weeks in summer; the long

vacation was extended slightly in 1879, when it was set for a fixed period, from the last Saturday in June to the first Sunday in August. As late as 1884 in New Brunswick the summer vacation was set at four weeks and the remaining holidays throughout the year at ten days in all.

In Ontario in 1880 a private member's bill was introduced to shorten the summer vacation to three weeks. Thereupon a deputation of the board of directors of the Ontario Teachers' Association

. . . waited upon the Minister of Education by appointment on Saturday, 21st February, to lay their views before him against the proposed shortening of the summer vacation, and some other matters. Though the time was of his own choosing, the deputation, after dancing attendance in the halls of the Education Department for an hour or more, and trying to see good in everything from the cobwebs on the ceiling to the pictures that adorned the walls, were compelled to give up the hope of an interview and reluctantly withdrew.[6]

Contrary to the wishes of the teachers the government passed legislation giving rural trustees discretionary power to shorten the summer holidays from six weeks to four. The same kind of thing was going on in Quebec, where the superintendent reported in 1878 that there was a proposal to abolish eight holidays and to reduce the summer vacation from six weeks to four because, it was said, there were 167 days in the year when the schools were not open.

Such niggardly attitudes were overcome around the turn of the century by three factors — prosperity, consideration for the child, and the establishment of summer schools for the professional improvement of teachers. From then on, it became established practice for schools to be closed in July and August, for a week or so at Christmas and Easter, on statutory holidays, and on all Saturdays.

The School Day

If distance from school and chores at home had not been considerations, early nineteenth-century schools like those of ancient Rome might have been opened from dawn till dusk. In Newfoundland in 1809 an advertisement in the *Gazette* of a private school stated that in order to accelerate the progress of the pupils preparing for an examination in August, the hours of attendance commencing the first of May would be from 6 a.m. to 8 a.m. in the early morning, from 9 a.m. to 12 noon, and from 2 p.m. to 5 p.m. In the grammar school of Saint John, New Brunswick, in 1812 the hours of attendance were set at 6 a.m. to 5 p.m. in May, June, July, and August, with two breaks of two hours each; only of necessity in the darker months was the day proportionately shorter. In the same school in the 1830's the period of instruction was fixed at from six to six and one-half hours daily. The condition of the roads and the brightness of daylight had to be considered everywhere. In British Columbia in 1872 the hours were 9 a.m. to 12 noon and 1 p.m. to 3.30 p.m. from April to September, and from 9.30 a.m. to 12 noon and 1 p.m. to 3 p.m. from October to March. There was then a fifteen-minute recess in the morning and after 1879 a ten-minute recess in the afternoon. Regulations in Ontario in 1878 stated that the school day should not be longer than six hours, exclusive of breaks for lunch and recess, and, in characteristic Ontario fashion, permitted shorter hours at the option of the trustees. In Kingston, Ontario, in 1879 the board at the request of the teachers increased the lunch hour to an hour and a half but eased their consciences by cancelling the afternoon recess until forced by the protests of the teachers to restore it. In many places in the early nineteenth century half-holidays on Wednesday and Saturday were the rule. Kingston made the adjustment to a single full-day holiday in 1859.

It is rather surprising to find that as early as 1879 there was criticism of the length of a school day not much longer than we have at present. In Hamilton, Ontario, the question was raised whether the health of the pupil and his educational progress were best served by five or six hours' incarceration in school. Homework also came in for criticism. In Montreal "after-dinner schooling" was denounced by some who contributed to a discussion in the press. In an editorial the *Canada Educational Monthly* cited with approval a statement that "two hours in the morning and one in the afternoon is about as long as a bright, voluntary attention can be secured from young children."[7] The editorial urged teachers to use their influence to have two hours lopped off the school day for young children and at least one hour for older pupils and to break the remaining period for intellectual study with physical activities and exercise.

Supervision

The inspection or supervision of schools was always to some extent a function of the central education authority in Canada. Reports of early school visitors were sent to the central authority. From about the middle of the nineteenth century many part-time or full-time inspectors were appointed and paid by a local district. But the trend was towards the assumption of a dominant role in supervision by the provincial departments, which set out the qualifications for inspectors and eventually became their direct employers. This trend followed practice in England, where after 1839 Her Majesty's inspectors were the employees and agents of the central authority. In Canada now superintendents and inspectors responsible only to local boards are to be found only in larger cities, although there are signs that more responsibility for the supervision of teaching will be assumed by principals and other employees of the locality, as is the practice in the United States. The deputy minister of education in New Brunswick in 1953 entitled his master's thesis *The Administrative and Supervisory Functions of a School Principal Who is also a Superintendent of Town Schools*. An attempt in Toronto in the 1890's to have four senior principals inspect other schools failed when the "walking principals" earned a reputation for officious behavior by listing weak teachers and checking the work of other principals. A feeling has persisted in Canada that there is more freedom under remote authorities.

THE SCHOOL VISITORS

Those who inspected the schools in the early nineteenth century were usually men designated as school visitors and asked to give voluntary service. At the middle of the nineteenth century they were part-time paid officials. By about the time of Confederation they were regularly employed officials, and before the end of the nineteenth century they were professionally qualified agents of the central authority.

School visitors in the early period included the trustees themselves, clergymen, justices of the peace, and men in other capacities. In Upper Canada after 1816 and in New Brunswick after 1833 they were the local trustees, although they seldom bothered to carry out supervisory duties. Clergymen were invited to visit the schools under the Royal Institution in Lower Canada and were designated as inspectors in a correspondingly early period in the Northwest Territories in 1887. In Lower Canada nineteen school visitors appointed under an act of 1831 were all members of the legislative assembly. In Nova Scotia in 1826 supervision of schools was put in the hands of boards of commissioners appointed by

the lieutenant-governor as intermediate authorities between the local trustees and the government. School visitors in Upper Canada, first mentioned in 1846, were supplementary to the officials designated to perform the regular work of inspection.

The varying quality and nature of early supervision may be illustrated by examples in Lower Canada. Dunkin mentioned a certificate given to a teacher at Old Lorette dated September 17th, 1838. Of the five persons who signed it, two did so by marks, a third apparently spelled his own name incorrectly, and a fourth used handwriting remarkable for its "defective character." Dunkin said that this was not an extraordinary example. Buller was told that under the supervision of members of the legislature the masters were political appointees, ill qualified at best. As for the officials, a teacher giving evidence in 1836 said: "Il y a eu des sindics qui ne sont pas fait scrupules de prendre l'argent des maîtres pour payer les frais de leurs élections."[8]

Yet a large number of the reports suggest conscientious work by capable people. Here is an example dated April 20th, 1837:

We the undersigned school visitors of the County of Megantic certify that we have visited the Elementary School No. 1 in the Township of Inverness kept by M. W. Hargrave on the twentieth day of April in the present year and having examined the Journal and Minute Book of the said school the regulations thereof and the Certificate of qualifications of the Teacher and having examined the Teacher out of the presence of the Scholars and also the Scholars themselves we verily believe . . . [that the school and the teacher are satisfactory] . . . And we recommend that said School continue to be the Superior School in this Township and receive the sum of ten pounds in addition to the usual allowance . . .[9]

The more thorough reports of school visitors covering the schools of a whole county were like school surveys giving population, the location of schools, the history of their operation, their condition at the time, and so on. Under the date 1840 the first report of the school visitor for the County of Chambly comprised twenty-eight large handwritten pages, and that of the County of Two Mountains forty-seven pages. Some of the early school visitors had the virtue of being kindly and good natured at least. J. L. Gourlay in his *History of the Ottawa Valley* gave this account of one inspector:

He made the tour on horseback, the roads admitting of no other mode of travel except on foot, which was much more common. He would dismount at the schoolhouse, and with the bridle rein on his arm, place a hand on each side of the door frame, the horse looking in as if to examine the furnishings, to the great enjoyment of the young folks, who seldom saw a horse in that early time. The gentleman would ask a little boy how to spell a word of one syllable to which the little man would address himself with energy, but with his eyes fixed on the horse. After a short standing examination he would dismiss them with a benignant smile, and very gracious words of which he had an abundant treasury at easy, ready command.[10]

In Upper Canada in 1850, in New Brunswick in 1852, and in the Northwest Territories in 1888, paid inspectors were appointed on a part-time basis. The earlier practice was to pay a small amount per visit to a school, 7s 6d in New Brunswick, and £1 in Ontario. In the west the inspectors received twenty dollars per year per school, plus expenses. No piecework or pay-by-production arrangement ever worked satisfactorily in education. Perhaps because some of the fourteen or fifteen part-time county inspectors in New Brunswick managed to make over £50 a year by hasty visits, Superintendent d'Avray recommended in 1856 that the number of inspectors be reduced. Two years later only four inspectors were appointed

at salaries of £250 each. Nova Scotia abandoned payment by number of visits in 1865. In the Northwest Territories three full-time inspectors on regular salary were appointed in 1891. In Quebec in 1850 a law divided the province into twenty-three school districts each under the direction of an inspector, and inspectors were appointed two years later. Manitoba appointed a regular staff of five inspectors in 1888. In British Columbia after various expedients a paid inspector was appointed temporarily in 1879, and the Council of Public Instruction was regularly empowered to appoint one or more inspectors in 1891.

THE UNQUALIFIED INSPECTOR

There was considerable vacillation before permanent arrangements were made. In Prince Edward Island a school visitor for the whole province was appointed at the early date of 1837 at the penny-wise salary of £63, 13s, 11½d. This modest expense for a chief official was saved when provision was made in 1847 for the appointment of a school visitor in each of the three counties. Five years later an inspector of schools was appointed, but he was dismissed in 1856. After trying a two-inspector arrangement in 1863, the province returned to three county inspectors in 1868. In Newfoundland the first school inspector was appointed in 1843. He was a member of the assembly and a Roman Catholic. In his letter of appointment the colonial secretary said: "His Excellency wishes you to confine yourself to inspection of Roman Catholic Schools except that, where Protestant Boards may desire, you should visit schools in their districts."[11] The next year a Protestant clergyman was appointed as inspector for one year with corresponding instructions. There were no further inspectors until 1858, when regular arrangements were made.

The work of inspectors without professional qualifications was very uneven. The great number of extracts from their reports printed by the superintendent of education in Canada West between 1850 and 1870 sometimes reveal discernment and usually show an honest effort to further the campaign of the chief superintendent to improve the work of the classroom. Similarly in Prince Edward Island, the reports in the *Journal of the Assembly* are evidence that many of the inspectors at mid-century had a clear understanding of the educative process and commendable insight into what was desirable. Those employed full-time by the government, it is true, disclosed in successive reports an anxiety to prove that the schools were improving under their supervision. But if they gradually abandoned stringent criticism of practices in the schools, they achieved somewhat the same purpose by explaining repeatedly the better way which they had urged the teachers to adopt.

Supervision by non-professionals, however, was sometimes vain and ridiculous, and up until the 1870's in the province of Quebec it appears usually to have been a farce. There were stories of an inspector who used to allot prizes by letting the pupils stick pins into the Bible held edgewise and giving the prize to the first lucky competitor whose pin point ran against a letter "a." Another inspector is said to have given a teacher three weeks' notice of his visit and to have sent in advance the questions he intended to ask the class. The Montreal *Gazette* in 1877 printed the following account by the principal of a leading academy of the first inspection of his school:

A gentleman once suddenly entered my school whom, by dryness of appearance, primness of attire, and air of immense but polite superiority, I recognized as my Inspector. He approached my desk, making three bows on the road. He uttered a swift sentence in French. I blushed to the roots of my hair and incontinently replied "Wee." He then turned his back on the boys; opened his little bag, took out a little comb, combed his whiskers and moustache, and finally put on a black hat or cap of indescribable shape and uttered another short sentence or long word in French, waved his hand and took a chair. I examined the boys in geography. After a while he waved his hand again and I took history. He then rose, said little, waved his hand much, put some expensive books by second-rate authors in my hands, packed up his cap, put on the unofficial hat and withdrew with more elaborate bowing than ever.[12]

PROFESSIONAL QUALIFICATIONS REQUIRED

As a safeguard against supervision of this kind and for other positive advantages, central authorities from about 1870 began to require professional qualifications for appointment as a school inspector. The Roman Catholic board in 1877 required that a candidate for the position of inspector produce a diploma of qualifications from one of the normal schools of the province, or at least a certificate from one of the boards of examiners for teachers, and that he also have a testimonial from the schools in which he had taught during the last preceding five years. The candidate was required as well to be between twenty-five and sixty years of age and be able to furnish a baptismal certificate and a certificate of good conduct. He was examined in various subjects, including the construction of a school building.

The reorganized Protestant central authority in Quebec appointed its first inspector in 1875 to visit superior schools, called model schools and academies. A narrative account of the inspection of a school two years later showed a conscientious attempt to grade every pupil, to demonstrate a new teaching technique, and to interest parents in the school. In

British Columbia by the Act of 1872 the superintendent of education had to be a certificated and experienced teacher. After 1876 New Brunswick inspectors had to be professionally qualified. In Manitoba from that year inspectors in cities and towns were required to hold a first class teaching certificate or to be graduates of a university. Ontario in 1871 required that a candidate for the post of county inspector hold the highest grade of elementary school certificate and submit to examination. The advantages of the innovation were explained by an official in the Ontario Department of Education in 1878:

By the new system the schools in each inspectorate were placed under the supervision and to some extent control of an officer thoroughly equipped by high literary attainments and long professional experience to help teachers improve their methods and discipline. This gave everyone greater confidence — the teachers, trustees, the government, and the people.[13]

Although it was undoubtedly true, as the above statement claimed, that marked improvement was achieved after 1870, we must guard against the impression that crudity and arrogance disappeared everywhere immediately. As late as 1911 there was a letter in the *Globe* on inspection in rural schools by "one who has been through the mill":

The inspector . . . would visit the school in a state of intoxication or when just recovering from a drunken spree . . . He would question the children in a bullying fashion and frighten them into dumbness. One time . . . he came in and lay down beside the stove for an hour: then he got up and was going away without his hat, and a scholar had to take it to him. He had done his duty to the school for that term.[14]

Inspection of that sort must have been close to the vanishing point by the turn of the century, but it had not been forgotten entirely. Progress in education, even in the personal characteristics of personnel, has been slow and continuing but not spectacular.

Once introduced, academic and professional qualifications of inspectors were continually raised. In Ontario in 1879, the candidate was required to hold a first class provincial certificate, Grade A, which involved training in model school and normal school and academic standing equivalent to a year or two at university. In 1908 an applicant for a position as inspector had to hold a permanent first class certificate and a degree in arts with at least second class honors, have had at least seven years' teaching experience, and have passed an examination on a special course for inspectors. In 1913 it was stipulated that his university degree must have been obtained in part by at least two years' attendance at university. In 1920 the department found it necessary to lower academic requirements to a pass B.A. in order to obtain candidates. When the depression made it possible to stiffen requirements, the advance was made in terms of professional qualifications involving graduate courses in education.

The supervisory work of inspectors has always been hampered by the burden of administrative duties. Administrative work in the early period was heavily weighted with reporting and in recent decades with the reorganization of local education authorities. These duties have persisted, even into a period when the expanding responsibilities of the school have obliged inspectors to pay increasing attention to physical facilities and additional services. About the only duty from which inspectors were in time relieved was that of examining teachers for initial certificates, a responsibility they had in some older provinces before Confederation and in the Northwest Territories until about the end of the nineteenth century. In supervision the early inspectors were expected to be no more than the name implied, estimators of the adequacy of the teacher. School visitors in Lower Canada in 1831 recommended suspension of the government allowance for 126 out of 1305 teachers. Brown has shown how this older concept changed gradually to the modern view which holds that the purpose of supervision is the improvement of instruction and the encouragement of teachers, rather than their evaluation.

An extreme example of the inquisitorial type of teacher supervision was provided by New Brunswick from the late 1870's until 1884. There were eight full-time inspectors who were required to grade teachers as a basis for determining the amount of the grant, an echo of the notorious payment-by-results system introduced in England in 1861 and retained there with modifications until about the end of the nineteenth century. Superintendent Rand of New Brunswick soon found himself alone in supporting the plan. But the old concept persisted. As late as 1925 the Alberta Teachers' Alliance said that inspection was still regarded as the means of discovering weakness in a teacher, although in their province they had just been granted the concession that the inspector should hand a copy of his report to the teacher as well as to the school board and to the department of education. This practice had been introduced in 1919 in British Columbia, where it was modified after ten years' experience to require that only the final report of the inspector be submitted to teachers and trustees. After World War I, Saskatchewan was divided into smaller inspectoral areas with the declared purpose of enabling inspectors to give supervision as well as inspection. One means of providing the type of supervision desired was to appoint under the inspector "helping teachers," sometimes called supervisors, as was done in Newfoundland under legislative authorization in 1920, and in other provinces also

during the present century. But most important was the change of attitude associated with the new social and educational philosophy.*

Since high school inspectors were not only appointed by the department of education, but usually had offices and homes where the central authority was located, they were more likely than local inspectors to exhibit an official point of view at variance with that of the teacher. Ontario first appointed such inspectors in 1855. The early appointees were clergymen, and one a personage of note. Twenty-five years later the professionally qualified inspectors seemed to take very seriously their own importance and the importance of their work of teacher evaluation. But as to the influence for good of such supervision, an educational journal of the time said that an exalted opinion of inspection was held only by departmental officials and not shared by others. There was need for better relations between inspectors and teachers: ". . . Confidence should be encouraged, and frankness responded to and respected. . . . In the classroom repellent looks and frigidity of manner should be alien to the place."[15]

INSPECTORAL LOAD

The load imposed on inspectors varied from time to time, and between one place and another. In Saskatchewan in 1905, before the days of the motor car, one of the five inspectors travelled 2865 miles by road in addition to 1072 miles by rail. There the number of inspectors increased to ten in 1908 and to forty-one in 1918. In Alberta, where a similar growth had occurred, a large number of inspectors were suddenly dismissed in 1923. According to McNaughton, Inspector Duval of New Brunswick had to supervise 270 schools in 1869, whereas, at the same time,

* See Chapters 21 and 22.

the Ontario law required that no inspector be responsible for more than 120 schools. In most provinces the number of inspectors was increased in relation to the number of schools up to the year 1930 and reduced thereafter. In Quebec in 1910 the number of Roman Catholic inspectoral districts was increased to thirty-nine and two visits a year to a school were required. In Prince Edward Island, where there were ten inspectors by 1920, there were only seven in 1939. In 1943, Miller's study of the supervisory load across the country showed considerable differences among the provinces and generally too little time for essential duties. Improvement came by such actions as that of New Brunswick in 1943, when inspectors were renamed county superintendents and given qualified secretaries, professional assistants, and expense accounts to enable them to visit schools more often. The change to the name superintendent had occurred previously in the west — in Saskatchewan in 1939. The three types of assistance were common but not general in 1950.

Textbooks

One of the vexing problems which hampered Canadian education at the beginning was the scarcity of suitable textbooks. During the French regime and for half a century thereafter French-speaking Canadians were dependent for textbooks on France, with which country trade was always difficult and sometimes virtually impossible. At the beginning of the nineteenth century booksellers and private individuals often paid the *Quebec Gazette* two shillings and sixpence for a six-line advertisement to offer books for sale. A French arithmetic was offered in 1809 for the same amount, a substantial sum in those days. Then came books from England. The prolific Lindley Murray wrote a *Lecture française,* which was used in the schools of the Royal Institution. We saw that in ordinary schools for English-speaking Canadians books by Murray, Mavor, Walkingame, and other British authors were much favored by the authorities and commonly used.

EARLY EFFORTS TO PUBLISH IN CANADA

Many individuals sought patronage or assistance in efforts to publish books in Canada. In 1827 a printer named Mac-Farlane at Kingston in Upper Canada announced his intention of printing a spelling book and again in 1832 his proposal to publish a Canadian edition of Murray's *English Grammar,* with some simplification of terminology, to take the place of the half dozen editions which he said were complicating the work of teachers. In 1830 Alexander Davidson of Port Hope sent the lieutenant-governor a dedication page of an "Upper Canada Speller" to secure his approval; in 1836 he was still writing to the lieutenant-governor in an effort to get the education authorities to examine the manuscript, since the publishing committee of the Methodist Conference had agreed to print it if it received official sanction. In the Toronto *Globe* of August 14th, 1844, Mr. R. Brewer advertised that he was publishing, from the latest English editions, Lennie's grammar, Walkingame's arithmetic, and Brown's primer and that he also had available a Canadian edition of Mavor. Between 1831 and 1835 the government of Lower Canada received three petitions for aid to publish textbooks: from the widow of Jacques Labrie, who had a manuscript of a history of Canada, and from a layman and a clergyman with English names who had written respectively a geography and a history of Lower Canada.

Probably the earliest book for educational use published in Canada was a catechism printed in Quebec in 1765. John Strachan wrote and published an arithmetic in 1809. J. F. Perrault wrote and published a spelling book, *L'ortho-*

graphe, which was used in the schools of the Royal Institution; he also wrote in 1822 a *Cours d'Education Elémentaire à l'usage de l'école gratuite établie dans la cité de Québec* on the mutual or monitorial system of instruction; and he sent to the governor in 1830 a copy of his *Manuel pratique,* or Book of Practical Exercises. By 1880 there was no longer need to import any but the less usual textbooks, although in paper and print the Canadian products were inferior. Two of the many Canadian authors were J. B. Calkin of Nova Scotia and J. H. Sangster of Ontario.

LOCAL CHOICE OF TEXTBOOKS

In the early part of the nineteenth century the choice of textbooks was left to the locality, nominally to the trustees. But if any choice was actually made beyond mere acceptance of what parents had already bought, the few teachers who remained in one place for any length of time could have their own way. Where a good many of the teachers as well as the parents had come from the United States, as in the Eastern Townships of Quebec, there were obstinate objections to relinquishing this local right to choose familiar American texts. Audet says that even the Royal Institution did not insist on approved books: "on accordait une très grande liberté dans le choix de livres de classe."[16] The superintendent of education for Quebec, Dr. Meilleur, said in his report for 1850 that most of the schools for English-speaking children were using the National school books, which were of British origin, except in the Eastern Townships, where the people still persisted in using American books.

In Upper Canada about 1830 the central board did consider "the propriety of recommending to the district boards the use of the same books in all the schools," although they realized the difficulty of enforcing the measure and thought it would be of no effect unless books could be printed in Canada for less money than the cost of alternative importations. In 1825 Strachan, as chairman of the board, asked for the purchase of 1100 copies of the *Charity School Speller* by that staunch churchwoman of England, Mrs. Trimmer. He also requested 488 copies of a treatise on Bell's system and 2200 copies each of certain religious books like the *Chief Truths of the Christian Religion.* But although the board purchased and distributed books in 1825 and 1826, they stopped doing so for the next three years. In the *Colonial Advocate* in 1830 one of Strachan's critics suggested other books which the board might purchase with the £150 a year the government had put at its disposal.

It was not easy to get agreement when people took pride in obstinate adherence to a particular religious or political bias. The author of a *Universal Spelling Book* used in Prince Edward Island claimed that he had "furnished material to counteract the machinations of Popish emissaries." A committee of the legislature in New Brunswick reporting on books for schools took objection to *The Distinguished Men of Modern Times* because, as they said, "the religious and political tendency of some of the characters appears to us not entirely unexceptionable" and disapproved even more of another book of history, admittedly comprehensive, graphic, and attractive, because some portions of it were "calculated to cherish a democratic and disaffected spirit."[17]

TOWARDS AUTHORIZATION AND UNIFORMITY

Nevertheless the need for authorized, uniform textbooks came to be recognized. In Prince Edward Island in 1841 the school visitor, John McNeill, said that there was "no greater obstacle to the advancement of education than the deficiency of suitable books," and that "not only the deficiency, but the heterogeneous mixture of books . . . sets all classification at defiance and presents a serious obstacle to the successful introduction of any improved mode of education." Egerton Ryerson in Ontario obtained the authorization in 1846 of the Irish National Series of school books as "the most unobjectionable and at the same time the best that could be introduced." In spite of difficulties he soon had the same books used by all pupils in all publicly supported schools throughout the province.

But elsewhere the change came more slowly. In reports of the board of education of Prince Edward Island for 1876 and later years there were still statements like this: "The great variety of textbooks in use in the schools is an unmitigated evil. Teachers are everywhere loud and incessant in their complaints thereof." In New Brunswick an act of 1847 authorized the board of education to spend £1000 for the purchase of books from the education office in Dublin. Thereafter the Irish National books came into frequent use in that province, but no decisive action was taken immediately to make their adoption imperative. There were various sanctions of individual books in addition to the approved list issued in 1847. Even in the 1860's rural schools of the province did not insist that all pupils have the same books for any one subject. There was progress towards uniformity, but not complete uniformity until after 1870. In Quebec the council of education introduced authorized textbooks in 1860 and decided in 1865 to permit no others; but legislation definitely requiring uniformity was passed only in 1897, and even then it seems not to have been enforced.

Because of the early adoption of uniform textbooks in populous Ontario, there was a tendency for other provinces to use the books that Ontario had authorized. Permission had been obtained to have the Irish National Series printed in Canada; and from the time of Confederation, when other books were authorized, nearly all of the more commonly used textbooks were printed in Toronto or Montreal. Because of their assurance of a wide sale they were relatively cheap. Manitoba in the late nineteenth century was using at least thirteen of the Ontario textbooks, including the public school readers, arithmetic, geography, and grammar, and the high school textbooks in geography, history of England and Canada, arithmetic, algebra, physical science, and book-keeping, all with such prosaic names as "Public School Arithmetic" or "High School Algebra." The Northwest Territories used twelve of the Ontario books, British Columbia six, Quebec six, New Brunswick three, and Nova Scotia apparently only one. In the last four provinces, however, the most commonly used books, like public school readers, arithmetics, and geographies, and high school algebras and histories were not those of Ontario, so that in the Maritimes any duplication may have been less intentional than unavoidable. New Brunswick and Nova Scotia showed independence even of each other: of the two dozen or so books that each province had on its authorized list in 1888, only about eight books or series were the same.

GOVERNMENT DEPOSITORIES

Ryerson went a step further than requiring the use of authorized textbooks by setting up an "educational depository," which purchased and sold to the schools at low prices textbooks, books for school libraries, maps, and other teaching aids. This institution was the cause of prolonged and recurrent controversy. In 1858 the Book Sellers Association published a pamphlet objecting to the interference with individual enterprise and to the government's making schools "the organ of its own doctrine."[18] Although the first objection was not disinterested, there were grounds for the second, since Ryerson in his purchase of books undoubtedly discriminated in accordance with his personal principles and views. Nevertheless the depository made available many excellent materials which might never have appeared on the market, and its low prices enabled school boards to buy more than they would otherwise have done.

After an investigation of the operation of the depository, the minister of education in 1877 ordered it to give up the handling of books and four years later closed it entirely. Although no admirer of the government, the editor of the *Canada Educational Monthly* approved of these actions as a long overdue reform which had been recommended by the Council of Public Instruction as its last official act before the ministry was established. According to the *Monthly* the depository had accumulated a stock of "literary rubbish." In the province of Quebec there was a "dépôt de livres, cartes, et globes" between 1876 and 1879. It also was abolished on grounds that it restricted freedom in the choice of books.

In the twentieth century agencies, generally called textbook bureaus, similar to the old depository were set up in all of the provinces except Ontario and Quebec. In Alberta in 1926 a school libraries branch was reorganized as a school book branch. As in the other provinces, it took control of the wholesale distribution of public and high school textbooks and distributed them prepaid to school boards and retail book-sellers usually at a discount of 15 per cent from the bureau's list price. The dealer had to agree to sell the books at no more than the list price but had the privilege of returning books.

THE EDUCATIONAL OFFICIAL AND THE PUBLISHER

Since authorization of textbooks ensured a wide sale and protection from competition, it was almost inevitable that de-partments of education should sometimes be charged with favoritism. Acrimonious controversy occurred most often in Ontario. In 1866 a firm which published many authorized textbooks put out a pamphlet of letters accusing the editor of the Toronto *Globe*, George Brown, of carrying on ceaseless warfare against the education department partly in the interests of his brother-in-law, who represented another company in the textbook trade. In 1877-78 there were charges of collusion between members of a committee of the department of education and a publishing firm, which was thereby enabled to put out textbooks remarkably useful in preparing for departmental examinations. Mr. Justice Patterson, who was appointed as a commissioner to investigate these charges, reported that they had been successfully rebutted. The same enterprising firm published a *Canadian School Journal*, which announced in April 1878 that it was recommended by the minister of education in Ontario, by the Council of Public Instruction in Quebec, and by the chief superintendent of education in New Brunswick. To this impressive list it added shortly after the chief superintendent of education in British Columbia. The journal was offered to teachers at moderate cost and carried advertisements in which the books of the publisher received some prominence.

Individual officials of the department of education were accused of unethical association with publishing firms in order to acquire profit from textbooks. A rival of the *Canadian School Journal*, the *Canada Educational Monthly*, may not have been disinterested but was certainly outspoken in its criticism of the senior high school inspector. An editorial spoke of "the gross impropriety of Dr. McLellan's pecuniary interest in these books while holding his official position." The books in question were among the "three or four a year" said by a school inspector in a letter to the *Hamilton Spectator* to have been produced by members of the central committee of examiners in their avocational role as a "Torontonian Board of School Book Compilers." They were sold as keys to success in the all-important examinations, were sometimes quickly produced by adapting American texts, and, although not authorized, were "industriously circulated" and authoritatively recommended.

While the teachers are practically coerced by the influence of an inspector who is also supreme, or believed to be so, at the Department, to force illegal text-books into use in the Schools, the teacher's moral sense and self-respect are injured. While base piracies of foreign school manuals are thrust on the public, with a cynical contempt for law, and a perseverance worthy of professional book agents, the whole tone of the Education Department is fatally lowered.[19]

It was also charged that local inspectors were invited in a "scandalous circular" from a publishing firm to earn a fifty per cent commission selling a "School Examiner" to teachers in their inspectorates. There was probably enough truth in these allegations of 1880-81 to convince the department of education that commercial alliances should be carefully shunned by an inspector and "his hands, above all things, kept clean from publishing house subsidies."

The controversy became less acute, but continued to recur in minor form as late as World War II, with the result that rather stringent regulations were issued regarding the writing of school textbooks by departmental officials.

PRICES

Complaints regarding the price of school books were another cause of trouble for the government of Ontario. During the administration of the first minister of education thirty-four books were added to the authorized list, and thirty-six were removed. Two series of readers were authorized in 1883 and then withdrawn in 1884 in favor of a new series when a new minister of education took office. In 1887 a newly formed trustees' association met for the first time in Toronto to protest against the cost to the people of introducing new textbooks. The minutes of the first meeting described the "blundering" of the department of education as "an outrage on the poorer classes." It was stated that the eighty-nine books authorized for high schools cost a total of $65.75. "It is to be hoped," said an officer of the association, "that the parents are not compelled to purchase, nor the pupils to read, the whole of these books during their race through the four forms." Ten years later the Liberal party still found it necessary to discuss this question in a political pamphlet entitled "Ontario's School System." The pamphlet pointed out that the average cost of textbooks to the pupils attending public schools was less than twenty cents a book, much less than in comparable American states. A commission appointed to investigate the prices of school books and related questions corroborated this claim in its report. It found that in the public schools of New York the cost of books to pupils was $9.96 as compared with $4.95 for books covering the same subjects in Ontario. But the responsibility of provincial government for the choice of textbooks, and the pressure from voters that they should be cheap, made it inevitable that Canadian textbooks should be less attractive in appearance than many of their American counterparts.

FREE TEXTBOOKS

From an early date limited efforts were made to supply free textbooks to schools. New Brunswick voted a sum of money in 1847 for the purpose. The annual grant of £150 was still provided in Upper Canada in 1839; a letter protesting the delay in its distribution that year indicated that teachers in "remote townships" were unable to get books without it. In the nineteenth century, school books were supplied to children of indigent parents — a charitable duty imposed on local trustees in the Northwest Territories by the ordinance of 1885. But the regular distribution of free textbooks to pupils is a service characteristic of the present century. Toronto introduced it in 1892, and Hamilton and Brantford before 1904, when an Ontario law offered grants to rural schools introducing the practice. In 1908 Saskatchewan and Alberta began to distribute free readers. By 1917 all western provinces supplied some books, and British Columbia supplied all books for elementary schools. In the west those books that were free were provided by the departments of education. At first books were lent to pupils, so that in Toronto in 1904 the cost of textbooks per pupil enrolled was only nine cents a year. In British Columbia from about the time of World War I until the depression, textbooks were given to the pupil outright. In 1950 most books were lent to pupils, either by the province or by the districts, in elementary grades in five provinces and in many districts of Manitoba, Ontario, and Quebec. In Prince Edward Island and Newfoundland, the province subsidized sales and sold books at prices much reduced from the publishers' list prices. In British Columbia, the province bought all high school books and rented them to the students.

School libraries, which had become common in Ontario by the time of Confederation, were encouraged by central authorities in other provinces. By an act of 1858 the government in New Brunswick offered to pay one half of local expenditures on books for school libraries, so that 946 volumes were purchased the first year and libraries were set up in about nine schools a year for a decade or so

thereafter. In the Northwest Territories a clause was included in the school grants ordinances in 1903 to require every school district to use for the purchase of library books one half of the supplementary grant which was paid to a school when the school was declared by the inspectors to have attained a minimum standard of efficiency. In Alberta a little later the books were selected from a catalogue issued by the department of education, and in 1913 the School Act was changed to allow the department to supply books instead of a special grant. The books were priced low and included a large selection of five-cent classics. By 1916 in Alberta almost ninety per cent of the 2300 schools had libraries.

Leaders in Educational Expansion

In some of the older provinces of Canada between 1840 and 1870 there was a period of accelerated improvement in education corresponding to the common school revival in the United States. It was made possible by economic developments and was given power by the related expression of democratic principles in government and society. The chief education officers first appointed by the provinces had the opportunity to give the movement direction and increasing impetus. Some, like Dawson, Forrester, and Rand of Nova Scotia, and Ryerson of Upper Canada, showed the energy and resourcefulness of Horace Mann, and achieved comparable success. In Quebec the improvement of education was delayed by religious difficulties, in New Brunswick and Prince Edward Island by economic limitations, and in Newfoundland by both. In Manitoba and British Columbia a similar opportunity was presented after 1870. In the former province, however, a central authority, split on denominational lines, could not act with single-

J. W. Dawson

ness of purpose. In British Columbia the first superintendent, Jessop, made very creditable progress considering the small population and the brevity of his term of office. In the two middle western provinces the corresponding period was one of creation, rather than of revival. It came at the end of the nineteenth century when Goggin was superintendent.

MARITIME LEADERS

John McNeill, appointed school visitor in Prince Edward Island in 1839, had keen insight and farsighted vision. In his first report he said that a teacher must have not only knowledge but "aptitude for imparting knowledge" and for "infusing energy into others," and that unless teachers were to be imported a normal school must be built. Right at the start he put his finger on what proved to be a continuing weakness in administration on the island when he urged that each school be allotted a permanent grant and that the inhabitants be obliged to give it the

further support necessary. Four years later he not only came out strongly for financing schools by taxation but anticipated by almost a century the equalization principle in educational finance by urging a general rate for the island, or a rate for each county, thrown into a common fund to "provide the means of education for poor equally with rich settlements."

John William Dawson was born in Pictou, Nova Scotia, in 1820, continued his education at the University of Edinburgh, and became a naturalist and geologist of note. In 1855 he became principal and professor of natural history in McGill College and University, and from 1857 to 1870 he was also principal of the McGill Normal School. In the 1870's he was a member of the Protestant committee of the Council of Public Instruction of the Province of Quebec and also of the Protestant board of school commissioners in the city of Montreal. Between 1850 and 1855 he was the first superintendent of education in Nova Scotia. In an autobiography he wrote of his work:

In summer I travelled from county to county, convening meetings of the commissioners of schools and of persons interested in education; examining schools and collecting statistics concerning them; lecturing on education, and explaining the means of introducing agriculture into the schools; occasionally convening teachers' institutes in central places; introducing uniform textbooks and new apparatus; devising plans for better schoolhouses . . .[20]

The limited powers attached to the superintendency and the wretched condition of the schools made it necessary for him to serve rather as an educational missionary than in a merely official capacity.

Dawson's two immediate successors deserve mention. Alexander Forrester, who acted as superintendent between 1856 and 1864, was also principal of the normal school. He was a Scotsman and a minister of the Free Church, who first came to Nova Scotia at the age of forty-three and later accepted a charge at Halifax. As superintendent he improved the standard of education and emphasized spiritual and ethical values. More specifically, he was chiefly responsible for the free school legislation of 1864, in support of which he obtained signatures on a petition from five thousand respectable citizens. Forrester also wrote *The Teacher's Text Book*, an impressive and praiseworthy work. He was highly respected by teachers of the province.

Theodore Harding Rand, who succeeded Forrester, was born in Cornwallis, Nova Scotia, and educated in Horton Collegiate Academy and Acadia College. For a period in his younger days he was a liberal and a free thinker, but was converted to strong religious conviction and an intense self-respect which enabled him to take precedence over others in a characteristically engaging manner. In 1860 he became an instructor in English and classics under Forrester at the normal college. In 1864, when he was hardly thirty, he supplanted his superior as superintendent of education for the province. During the next five and a half years the attendance at school doubled, the salaries of teachers increased, and the quality of instruction was evidently raised. The improvements were due largely to the free school legislation secured by his predecessor but also to the passing in 1865 during Rand's superintendency of further legislation to make taxation compulsory. In 1871, after being dismissed from Nova Scotia, Rand displaced the superintendent in New Brunswick, where the passing of similar free school legislation had just set the stage for him to repeat his former achievements. After introducing payment by results in that province and maintaining his faith in its operation in the face of growing skepticism, he left for Ontario, where he was a founder of McMaster University.

Theodore Harding Rand

After the creation of a central board of education in 1847, New Brunswick had a quasi-superintendent in the person of the secretary. When the office of superintendent was established in 1852, the first appointee was a clergyman, who resigned after a year. He was succeeded by J. Marshall d'Avray, who had come to Canada in 1847, when his influence with the British government secured him appointment as master of the first training school for teachers in New Brunswick. D'Avray was an educated gentleman of charming manner, ready wit, and brilliant mind. His thinking about education was independent, realistic, and in advance of his time, but was sometimes expressed in language which recognized social distinctions offensive to the new democracy. D'Avray might have achieved much under different circumstances. But as a professor at King's College serving only part-time as superintendent, he could do little more than lend dignity to the office and write excellent reports.

J. B. Meilleur

Egerton Ryerson

MEILLEUR IN LOWER CANADA

Jean Baptiste Meilleur was a native of St. Laurent on the Island of Montreal. Continuing his studies in New England, he became a scholar in medicine, philosophy, and science and wrote treatises on a variety of subjects. Before his appointment to the superintendency he was a professor in the Collège de l'Assomption, of which he was a founder, and also a member of the assembly. He became superintendent in 1842 at the age of forty-five and occupied that position for thirteen years. His scholarship and position of prestige in society gave him a primary interest in secondary education and he was instrumental in the founding of several institutions of note. But in his eighteen official reports and thirty circulars to teachers he showed a deep understanding of education generally. In planning the reorganization of education in Quebec, Meilleur showed a wisdom which facilitated the work of his successors.

EGERTON RYERSON

Egerton Ryerson (1803-1882) for length of service and magnitude of achievements must be given first place among the early superintendents. He was a native of Upper Canada, son of a Loyalist father and a mother who is thought to have been the first white woman born in Canada after the British conquest. Ryerson was educated in a district grammar school, worked on the farm, taught school, entered the Methodist ministry, and became a chief opponent of John Strachan and of special privileges for the Church of England. In 1829 he became editor of the *Christian Guardian,* in 1835 obtained a charter for Upper Canada Academy, and in 1841 was made first principal of Victoria College, which had evolved from the academy. From 1844 to 1876 he was superintendent of education for the province.

Against all obstacles, discouragements, and the bitter attacks of his many critics, Ryerson worked with unflagging energy to build the educational structure of Ontario. Through his annual reports and monthly *Journal of Education* and by public meetings, conferences, and correspondence, he maintained a steady pressure of constructive propaganda. Five times, in 1847, 1853, 1860, 1866, and 1869-70, he travelled around the province conducting county conventions, where he hoped "to meet the District School Superintendent and as many of the Clergy, District Councillors, School Trustees, Teachers, and Friends of Elementary Education as may attend."[21] By the more direct means of teacher training, inspection, control over textbooks and courses of study, regulations, and new legislation when necessary, he raised the poorest schools to a minimum standard of adequacy and encouraged the more able, within somewhat regimented limits, to do considerably more.

IN THE WEST

When Manitoba became a province in 1871, the two-denomination board was made up of eight clergymen and four laymen. Joseph Royal and Molyneaux St. John acted as superintendents and secretaries. The latter was succeeded by an Anglican clergyman, Cyprian Pinkham, a native of Newfoundland, who had been educated at the Church of England Academy in St. John's and in England. Pinkham went to the west in 1868 at the age of twenty-four, became a member and then superintendent of the Protestant board in 1871, and showed both vigor and consideration of the views of others in securing the establishment of elementary schools.

David James Goggin was a native of Ontario, where he became a teacher and a principal. In 1884 he went to Winnipeg to become principal of the Manitoba Normal School. He secured his bachelor's degree from the University of Manitoba in 1887. From 1893 to 1902 he was su-

perintendent of education in the North-west Territories, where he discharged his multifarious duties with ability and credit. He was a president of the Manitoba Teachers' Association and of the Dominion Education Association, and an effective speaker at teachers' conventions and at evening meetings for the public. Possibly because of repeated carping about his salary he resigned and went into the publishing business.

John Jessop, superintendent of education in British Columbia from 1872 to 1878, was born in England in 1829. At the age of seventeen he arrived in Halifax in a vessel shorn of most of her rigging and in a sinking condition. He went to Ontario in 1847, attended the Toronto Normal School in 1855, and taught school. In 1859 he joined a party of eight who set off on foot from Fort Garry. He reached the Pacific coast early next year, the only survivor. In Victoria after an attempt at newspaper publishing, he opened a private school. Then as a master in one of the state-supported schools, he held out to the bitter end when Governor Seymour refused to pay salaries in 1866-68. Jessop tried without success to secure a seat in the assembly, but helped draw up the school legislation of 1871, which created the office to which he was appointed. During his six years as superintendent the average attendance in the schools increased from 575 to 1375 and the number of pupils in regular attendance from 55 per cent to 63 per cent of the total enrolment. Jessop had ideas. One which he put into practice provoked much controversy — the building of a co-educational boarding school under public control, a venture which ended in failure.

Educational Politics

It has been assumed in Canada, with good reason on the whole, that chief ed-

John Jessop

ucation officers were appointed for their merits and were secure in their positions thereafter. But there were instances of favoritism and arbitrary dismissal in the nineteenth century.

ARBITRARY DISMISSALS

Apparently it was dangerous to attempt too much. Jessop as superintendent worked with vigor and imagination for the improvement of education. During his six-year term in office provincial expenditures on education increased from $25,000 to $43,000, or from 5.9 to 9.7 per cent of the total expenditures of the province. In one year they went up to a high of over $68,000. But a new administration in 1878 made changes in the Education Act contrary to his wishes. It also reduced his salary from $2000 to $750. When Jessop by this action was forced to resign within the year, the whole board of education resigned with him.

In Prince Edward Island there was a noteworthy example of dismissal for

honesty of utterance, not for dishonesty of behavior. John M. Stark was brought over from Scotland as an expert on new methods of teaching and on teacher training. As inspector of schools in the province he successfully advocated a normal school. At the opening of this institution in Charlottetown in 1856 Stark was frank enough to say:

I would, however, warn my friends here, and the people of this colony, against supposing that three months' training at a Normal Institution can make perfect teachers. They must not suppose that this institution is a patent machine which receives ignorant and inexperienced young persons and at the end of three months turns them out judicious and well-informed teachers.

These remarks caused a furore and Stark was forced to resign.

Marshall d'Avray lost his position as superintendent of education in New Brunswick in 1858, the year after he had conducted a survey which showed that conditions in the schools were very bad. It is probable, however, that this was no more than a supporting cause. He was only one of the civil service victims dismissed by a "smasher government." Henry Fisher, the brother of the leader of the government, was appointed as d'Avray's successor.

Another educator whom we have already mentioned failed to secure the preferment which he and others in the profession took for granted would come to him. Alexander Forrester, according to Calkin, who knew him, and Laidlaw, who recently studied the case, had every reason to assume that he would continue as superintendent of education and give all his time to the work when the government passed the free school legislation for which he had been largely responsible. He recommended that Rand, who worked under him, should succeed him as principal of the normal college. He appears to have had no inkling of what was going on until he discovered from a newspaper item, as Calkin has it, or from a letter on a routine matter, as Laidlaw says, that his subordinate had stepped over his head. The government — "to please some of their supporters," says Calkin — made Rand superintendent and left Forrester with only the inferior post of principal of the normal college. Forrester was deeply hurt but said that he would be able to work under Rand, for whom he expressed admiration.

Retribution came to the aggressive administrator, but only temporarily. After six years as superintendent, Rand was dismissed. As a former advocate of Confederation he was out of favor when a new government came into power. Exasperated by difficulties in obtaining co-operation, he committed an administrative blunder by writing a compromising letter of sympathy to an inspector who had been replaced by the government for political reasons. He continued in office, but, chiefly because of diminishing support from the cabinet, became entangled in local religious issues. One of these served as a ground for his discharge. Next year, in 1871, he was appointed superintendent of education in New Brunswick. This appointment was made at the expense of another abrupt dismissal.

John Bennett, as one of the inspectors of schools, and after 1859 as superintendent of education in New Brunswick, had shown a keen understanding of education in many printed reports. In September, 1871, he returned to Fredericton in obedience to a telegram from the provincial secretary and found waiting for him a letter from the attorney-general. The letter stated that Bennett's resignation, if tendered, would be accepted. Bennett in a simple dignified letter submitted his resignation and enclosed a copy of the attorney-general's letter to indicate that the action was not taken of his own volition.

Perhaps because of the continuing strength of traditional factions, uneasiness about dismissals and appointments was more in evidence in the Maritime Provinces than elsewhere. A subsequent superintendent of education, Crocket, was dismissed in the late nineteenth century by the government of New Brunswick. Some said it was for having taken sides, one way or the other, on the Roman Catholic school question. Others gave as the reason that his sons in their newspapers had not supported Premier Blair. After 1877 in Nova Scotia, however, superintendents enjoyed such a long tenure of office that there were only three incumbents in a period of seventy years.

PROFESSIONAL CRITICISM

Departments of education in the nineteenth century were not held in such respect that criticism from professional sources could not appear in print. The *Canadian School Journal* in 1877 reported charges of irregularities in the Nova Scotia department involving the provincial superintendent, the Reverend A. S. Hunt, a Baptist minister. Mr. Hunt was exonerated, but when he died the same year, his successor was given a much more adequate salary, $2400 instead of $1600 a year. In Ontario in 1880 the senior high school inspector, James McLellan, was described in another professional journal as "a rough, self-asserting person, with much practical talent for money-making, great love of power, and a keen sense of his own interests."[22] When he published a *Handbook of Algebra for Teachers* the reviewer wrote that "its industrious, but unabashed author came to his task ill-equipped, in a literary point of view," that he used "bad English" and "inaccurate grammar," that he showed a "total lack of judgment in its preparation," that he made "mistakes literally by the dozens," and that by publishing it he "contributed to an illegal and contraband trade." A lengthy article the same year expounded the thesis that the Reverend George Paxton Young ran the educational machinery of the Ontario department with the minister and deputy minister as chief agents in the bureaucracy: "Now centralization and martinetism reign rampant, but very little good, after all, has resulted from them." Advice regarding appointments was freely offered. When J. M. Buchan, an inspector of high schools, resigned in 1881 to become headmaster of Upper Canada College, the *Canada Educational Monthly* recommended that his place should be filled by John Seath, who was in fact appointed and who soon became the most influential member of the department. This same journal was quick to turn the spotlight of publicity on any practice judged to be illiberal or shortsighted and on any possibly dangerous use of power, for example the high cost of administering low grants to secondary schools and the use of influence by inspectors to secure the appointment of teachers.

Prominent educators and departmental officials sometimes expressed opinions in print with a candor that twentieth-century governments would be unlikely to tolerate. In Prince Edward Island in 1859, R. B. Irving, the acting school visitor, could write for publication in the *Journal of the Legislative Assembly* his views on the salary attached to this position:

. . . unless the amount of the emoluments fairly correspond to the amount and importance of the duties to be performed, and are such as to enable the Visiter to disregard, and act independently of substantial favors at the hands of those with whose interests he has to deal in the capacity of a judge . . . he will . . . be unduly warped in his judgment. . . . The annual salary of the School Visiter, — £200 —, is a very insufficient remuneration for his services.

In a signed article published in the *Educational Weekly* in 1885, John Millar, a high school principal who five years later was made deputy minister in the province, criticized Ontario, and by direct implication its government, for not increasing high school grants, "though enjoying the advantages of a large surplus and distributing its tens of thousands among the various municipalities." By statistics on enrolment and provincial expenditures he showed that the province was giving "hardly a dollar more than when Ryerson was superintendent" — "an increase hardly sufficient to meet the requirements of additional collegiate institutes"[23] among the many new secondary schools.

But a change was on the way. One who compares the annual reports of chief education officers around 1850 with those of the present century sees a striking difference. In the old reports strong words are used to make faults plain. On the glossy pages of later years complaisant generalities portray nobler accomplishments in a soft light which leaves the shabby background misty and obscure. An early sample of the Polyanna-in-a-frock-coat jargon appeared in the Report of the Minister of Education for Ontario for 1878: "There are many considerations, which enable me to state to you that the wave of progress flows onward to the maturity of perfection, gradually deepening and widening." Contrast Ryerson's derogatory statement in his report for 1872: ". . . the internal condition of the Schools generally has not improved for years." As for civil servants in the departments, when democracy came to be regarded not as a campaign, as in the 1840's, but as an achievement, it became a principle of democratic administration that public utterances of experts should be obsequious. There were fewer sparks and fewer fires.

COMMISSIONS

A device occasionally used by provincial education authorities when faced with difficult problems was the appointment of a special committee or commission. Special committees of provincial legislatures were common in the 1830's. Prince Edward Island had rather frequent recourse to this expedient. In 1852 the Free School Act followed the report of a special committee to inquire into the desirability of making education free. In 1876 there was a report from a parliamentary committee appointed to make a thorough investigation of the educational system and its administration. Equally broad in terms of reference was the commission of three appointed in 1908 to study the "whole matter of education" in the province. Although it submitted, after two years' work, recommendations based on an exhaustive analysis of school consolidation and on an intelligent consideration of teacher training, nothing at all was done. A teachers' strike in 1929 led again to the appointment of a royal commission, whose report two years later resulted in the passing of a school teachers' superannuation act and the appointment of a minister of education and public health, although other major recommendations were ignored. In other provinces, also, commissions and surveys were fairly common in the present century. Manitoba in 1924 appointed a commission to consider the educational needs and facilities in more recently settled portions of the province, and in 1945 a "Special Select Committee of the Legislative Assembly" to look into education generally. In 1938 the Protestant system of Quebec set up a survey committee under an educator brought over from Scotland. In Saskatchewan a comprehensive survey of education and related social problems was made by H. W. Foght, who reported in 1918.

Results achieved by commissions, and particularly by those with broad terms of reference, have seldom been noteworthy. After nearly five years' work a Royal Commission on education in Ontario published in 1950 a most comprehensive and

Hon. Adam Crooks, Ontario's first Minister of Education, 1876

creditable report; but a majority of the members had the temerity to offer an ingenious solution to a seemingly insoluble separate school problem, and the government understandably helped to restore peace by inaction. In Nova Scotia during the same year a much less pretentious commission on teacher education sought to achieve a needed advance without disregarding or over-emphasizing denominational and sectional interests, but its report led to no immediate action. In British Columbia, however, a survey of schools by J. H. Putman and G. M. Weir, with the assistance of Peter Sandiford, had considerable influence. It provided the most thorough examination of any school system in Canada up to the time of publication of its five hundred page report in 1925. It recommended, *inter alia,* a more equitable distribution of taxation and more help to rural schools, recognition of domestic science and manual training as regular subjects, a more flexible high school curriculum, and a three-year junior high school. Action followed on the last two of these recommendations rather quickly. Again, during World War II, a British Columbia commission composed of one capable man, M. A. Cameron, recommended drastic administrative reforms which were immediately implemented.

Summary

Central authorities over education arbitrarily appointed in the early part of the nineteenth century commanded little respect. But by mid-century permanent authorities over elementary education evolved as successors to committees formerly set up to license teachers, and provincial superintendents were appointed. Subsequently in English-speaking provinces these authorities assumed control over secondary education also and came to be headed by a minister of education. Aid to education often took the form of land grants at first but was given later as regular grants of money — in the nineteenth century to stimulate local effort and in the twentieth century to equalize educational opportunity. Necessarily powerful in 1850, the central authorities continued to expand their functions, which included the regulation of the length of the school day and year, inspection of schools, and the authorization of textbooks. The central authorities and their chief education officers must be given a considerable share of the credit for the steady improvement of education for a century, although in the choice and treatment of personnel, as in other matters, less disinterested motives were sometimes in evidence. Questions regarding the extent to which control over education should still be centralized are raised in the following chapter.

CHAPTER 16

Local Authorities

The establishment of representative local authorities provided the administrative machinery by which the people could
take full responsibility for maintaining schools. This chapter
deals historically with the organization and functions of local
boards, with the size of the community they served, with local
finance of education and free schools, with the relationship of
local boards to other administrative bodies and to the public,
and with certain schools that were of special interest to local
authorities.

Election of Trustees

As long as education was provided for
the people by a controlling minority,
aristocratic or ecclesiastical, the election
of local school authorities would obviously have been an anomaly. In Newfoundland, where the denominational system
prevailed, local boards from 1836 were
appointed by the government and had to
include the "senior or superior clergyman
of each of the several religious denominations, being actually resident in the district."[1] But the people took over some control of elementary education and began
to elect trustees in other provinces: Prince
Edward Island, 1847; Nova Scotia, 1850;
New Brunswick, 1858; Quebec, 1829; Ontario, 1816; Manitoba, 1871; Northwest
Territories, 1884; British Columbia, 1869.

Where the people, after previous experience in providing schools for themselves, sought and secured legal recognition of the practice, local administration

under elected trustees worked fairly well from the start. But in Quebec most people were unprepared for the innovation of 1829. They had had some experience in local school administration through the *fabriques* after 1824, but in close association with the church. The act of 1829 gave virtually no share in the management of the schools to the clergy, and the *habitants* were too ignorant and inexperienced to carry on independently. Buller found that school returns were falsified by local authorities anxious only to obtain the grant; the names of children not at school were included in the roll and "parents were known to lend themselves to this good-humored arrangement." The education committee became alarmed at the amount of money misspent and expressed the hope that the people of the province would "trust to themselves" to provide education and not rely wholly on the legislative grants. The situation was not improved by making supervision a responsibility of elected members of the assembly, who sometimes set examples of graft in expense accounts, in acceptance of bribes for not recommending the dismissal of teachers, and in misappropriation of prize money entrusted to them for distribution to schools. Another difficulty was that the legislation did not require assent, much less a request, from householders, but simply stated that school boards should be set up. There was no provision at first for permanency of the school corporation or for its right to own real property. According to Dunkin, the assembly in its ambition to be the one great power in the province would not endure, much less create, any rivals and preferred the school boards to be dependent and inferior in status. Dunkin's analysis of the act was shrewd:

The principle, then, so long contested, of allowing a direct local administration of schools to be aided by the Government, is at last fully conceded, and this concession,

had it been hedged round by enactments calculated to carry it fairly into effect and prevent the thousand abuses to which it is liable, would indeed have been a great point gained.[2]

Political democracy, introduced suddenly and with no restraining influence, was unlikely to be honest and efficient there or elsewhere.

After the rebellion, when Quebec became Canada East, new issues in local school administration were raised. The Act of 1841 copied an earlier New England practice of entrusting responsibility for schools to a general instead of an *ad hoc* municipal authority, an arrangement wholly at variance with Canadian custom, though introduced as a twentieth-century development in England. In Quebec the municipal council was made responsible for levying and collecting taxes, for sending reports on schools to the government, and for receiving government grants. There were school commissioners, also, but they were "merely exalted errand boys of the municipal council."[3] Any appearance of democracy in this plan was deceptive. Although the councillors were elected, property restrictions and other qualifications reduced the number of those eligible to such an extent that successful candidates were virtually government appointees. In 1846 the scheme was abandoned, and the complete management of schools was entrusted to elected commissioners. It is of interest that in British Columbia in 1869-70 the local authority over education was vested in the municipal councils of Victoria and New Westminster and that the schools in this instance also were not given adequate support.

The essential problem of all education was clearly illustrated in the development of local boards: the incompetence of trustees made it risky to entrust them with responsibility; limitation of opportunity for the trustees to take responsibility kept them from becoming competent. In Up-

A meeting of school trustees. (Drawing based on a painting by Robert Harris now in the National Gallery of Canada)

per Canada there were many complaints against trustees. In 1823 the board of education for the Home district, an appointed intermediate authority, told the lieutenant-governor that the elected members of local boards could not be trusted to choose teachers, and the next year the power to examine and certificate was transferred from the trustees to the district boards. But in this case the trustees, retained other powers and improved in ability. In the Maritimes, where control by local representatives of the people was withheld for another thirty years, Calkin said: "It was seldom that the Trustees stood in any responsible capacity between the teacher and the people. The contract was made directly between the Teacher . . . and the parents."[4] In Prince Edward Island at the time of Confederation there was little local interest in the schools, but ten years later, when responsibilities were extended, trustees, "feeling the importance of the work committed to them . . . manfully set to work," and parents appreciated "as they never did before the benefits of a good education for their children."

The franchise in the election of trustees was usually extended at first to freeholders, householders, or resident ratepayers. Then, in British Columbia for example, wives of eligible voters could vote for rural trustees in 1885 and run for office from 1896. In 1932 all who had paid the special school tax could vote to elect trustees, but could not vote on money matters. There was more caution regarding cities. Although city women could stand for election as trustees at an earlier date (1889), city trustees were appointed in 1891-92. Although after that they were again elected in British Columbia, they continued as a rule to be appointed in Quebec and in the Maritime Provinces. In the province of Quebec no provision was made in 1846 for the election of school boards in the cities of Montreal and Quebec, and the Act of 1868 stated that there should be boards of six members, three to be appointed by the government and three by the city council. In Charlottetown and Summerside, Prince Edward Island, boards similarly constituted in 1877 became more democratic only to the extent that in

Petition of a school trustee, Lower Canada, 1829, objecting to clerical interference. (Public Archives of Canada)

Charlottetown a larger number of members was in later years appointed by the municipality instead of by the government. In Fredericton and Saint John, New Brunswick, four and five of the nine and eleven members, respectively, including the chairman, were still appointed by the provincial government in 1950. A probable reason for not permitting the direct election of any or all members of city boards was that the many who paid little or no direct taxation on urban real estate might elect those who promised generous spending on schools. Similar considerations sometimes caused election privileges to be revoked in urban or rural areas which had fallen into financial difficulties. In British Columbia, legislation of 1919 authorized the appointment of an official trustee with all the powers of elected trustees to conduct the affairs of a school district. During the depression,

in 1934, 170 rural districts were under official trustees.

There was reluctance also to have trustees of secondary schools elected to office, partly for the reason already stated with respect to urban centres. Another reason was that secondary education was of less general interest than elementary. The academic type was esteemed chiefly by the few who used it professionally, and the vocational type was expensive and seemingly of benefit only to particular workers and employers. In Ontario, secondary school boards were appointed by the lieutenant-governor after 1807 and by municipalities after 1853. The local administration of sizable secondary schools remained separate from that of elementary schools, except that after 1903 an increasing number of urban municipalities were permitted to elect boards of education as local authorities over all schools.

Saskatchewan legislation of 1907 copied the Ontario system of a separate high school administration. Trustees were elected, of course, in nine provinces, for rural schools offering secondary education of sorts. Ontario had made this concession to rural areas when combined and partly elected boards were permitted to operate union schools between 1853 and 1874, and continuation classes and schools after 1896. In the Maritime Provinces trustees of small rural schools with pupils at a secondary level, or in an attached high school department, were also elected. But full-scale secondary schools in most centres of many provinces remained under appointed boards. Hence the Royal Commission on Education in Ontario, having only the advantage of the schools in mind, found it necessary to recommend in 1950 that all members of all school boards be elected by the people. The commission also expressed a preference for regional boards concerned with both elementary and secondary education.

Size of Rural Administrative Areas

Under the conditions of the early nineteenth century, the only practicable unit for local administration in rural areas was the small district or section, supporting usually a one-room school. In Roman Catholic Quebec, legislation in 1824 and in 1846 recognized the parish as the appropriate unit. Elsewhere the tendency for a long period was to reduce the size of the local administrative unit. New Brunswick began with the parish as the local area, had it subdivided by parish trustees into districts in 1833, provided for both parish trustees and district commissioners to be elected from 1858 to 1871, and thereafter made the small district the one local unit. In the Northwest Territories the ordinance of 1884 permitted the formation of a school district of not more than thirty-six square miles, if

there were four heads of families and at least ten children between the ages of five and sixteen; shortly after, requirements were made more strict by requiring that there be four resident ratepayers and twelve children within the smaller area of twenty-five square miles. In Saskatchewan in 1910 the area was reduced again to twenty square miles, with the result that there were over 5000 school sections there by 1936.

The desirability of larger areas for local administration in Ontario was recognized in proposed school legislation in 1831, and in enactments of 1850, 1871, 1896, and 1921, all designed to give districts the option of forming township school areas. An editorial in the *Canadian School Journal* in 1878 supported township boards chiefly because of the inequality of the burden of school taxation — "an evil that, when its magnitude comes to be fully realized, one can only wonder how the section system has remained in existence so long."[5] The writer gave as other reasons in favor of the reform that trustees under the existing system were illiterate men and that better board members might be found for a larger area, especially if they were paid. But any such change was jealously resisted by district trustees. Mandatory legislation introduced in 1925 was withdrawn because of their opposition. Similarly in the Northwest Territories in 1903 the deputy commissioner of education wrote in his report: "There is no doubt but that the small rural district with its inferior school house, poor equipment and irregular attendance is a distinct educational loss."[6] But when legislation was proposed in Alberta twenty-five years later, there was trouble. The bill was printed six months before presentation in the legislature to permit discussion by farmers' locals. The minister of education supported it in public addresses but failed to obtain support from the agricultural population. The *Edmonton Bulletin,* on the other hand, gained reader approval by attacking the proposal as an attempt to centralize power. The bill was given a six months' hoist and, after a debate in the legislature in 1930, it was withdrawn.

Convinced that bold and drastic action was the only solution, a new government in Alberta amended the School Act in 1936 to provide for the establishment of large school divisions at the order of the minister of education. By the end of the following year there were five divisions comprising 744 local districts. Rapid progress in succeeding years reorganized the whole province before 1950 into fifty-seven divisions, each ordinarily covering 1000 to 1500 square miles and employing sixty to eighty teachers. The former 2500 school districts remained in existence to the extent that they continued to elect trustees, but their responsibilities were limited to looking after only a few local matters and keeping the divisional board informed about local conditions.

Two other western provinces used strong measures to bring about reorganization. Saskatchewan in 1944 passed an act under which the minister could take the initiative in setting up larger school units without a local vote unless such a vote was requested by a petition of twenty per cent of the ratepayers. By 1950 four-fifths of the province had been reorganized. In British Columbia, thirty-nine rural school districts in the Peace River section were abolished between 1934 and 1936 and the area was reorganized into four districts, temporarily under one official trustee. Other experiments with larger school areas demonstrated that greatly improved educational services could be provided at less cost by reorganization. Then, after the Cameron report* came a complete reform. In 1946 nearly all of the 650 school districts of the province were abolished and replaced by 77 larger

* See p. 264.

districts. But in the other western province, Manitoba, apart from the setting up of a municipal school district in 1919, and one other large school area in 1947, there was no administrative reorganization.

In Ontario reform was moderated in deference to local democracy and the weighted voting power of the rural electorate. In 1932, township councils were empowered to organize even part of a township, if not the whole, into a "township school area." From 1938 an organized campaign of persuasion was conducted, chiefly by the elementary school inspectors. By this diversion of much supervisory effort, more than sixty per cent of the province was induced to adopt the plan by 1950. Although the reorganized administrative areas were far smaller than those established in the west, they brought similar advantages to some degree and left their administration close enough to the people to permit the complete dissolution of former sections without loss.

In the Protestant system of Quebec a law of 1943 also required local approval to effect reorganization by the establishment of central boards. By 1950 there were nine central boards, whose members were appointed by delegates from local boards and whose chief responsibilities were to engage and supervise teachers and to keep watch over the spending of the local boards. In the Roman Catholic system, for obvious reasons, no attempt was made to reorganize the parish system, although recently the multiplication of local boards has been discouraged and union of boards encouraged.

Nova Scotia in 1942 and New Brunswick in 1943 set up intermediate units for financial administration in a county or equivalent area. Though the legislation was permissive, reorganization throughout both provinces was completed before 1950, largely because the local boards retained important prerogatives. In Prince Edward Island seven small school districts were united to form a larger administrative area in 1949.

The following table gives a summary of the reorganization accomplished during the recent period of concentrated attention to the rural administrative problem:

Approximate Number of School Boards Operating in Rural Areas

Province	Before Recent Reorganization (1935-45)	After Reorganization 1949-50		
		In districts not yet reorganized	Over larger areas	As continuing local boards under larger area boards
B. C.	650	20	74	....
Alta.	2,500	....	57	2,450
Sask.	4,000	800	48	3,200
Man.	1,700	1,650	1	43
Ont.	5,750	2,282	536	....
P. Q.				
—Catholic.	1,635	....	....	....
—Protestant.	350	200	9	90
N. B.	1,350	....	15	1,325
N. S.	1,800	....	24	1,750
P. E. I.	500	472	1	7
Nfld.	300	....	....	....

Consolidated Schools

Early in the twentieth century, local authorities were encouraged to improve rural education by co-operating to establish consolidated schools. An original impetus was given to the movement by donations of Sir William Macdonald, who in 1902 offered to pay all excess costs of any experimental establishment for three years. In spite of obvious educational benefits, however, local communities showed little disposition to shoulder the expense and carry on at the end of the initial period. In Middleton, Nova Scotia, for example:

An excellent school building was erected and equipped; superior teachers engaged; and the attendance improved greatly. But during the three years' experiment the local assessment was not increased, and when the special grant was withdrawn four of the eight sections originally consolidated reverted to their little red school houses.[7]

Throughout the province 53 sections had formed 22 consolidations by 1905, 60 had formed 26 by 1908, and then the movement ground to a stop. The commission of 1908 made a thorough study and recommended the setting up of consolidated schools throughout the province of Prince Edward Island. However, in 1912 the Macdonald Consolidated School at Hillsboro, the first of its kind in Canada, closed for financial reasons after nine years of operation. All those who believed that better education was worth the extra cost were greatly disappointed.

Local authorities were empowered by provincial legislation to unite for the purpose of establishing a consolidated or central school. In New Brunswick authority was given to any three or more contiguous districts in 1903 and a special grant of $1000 was offered. That year one consolidation of six districts was formed at Kingston, but by 1944 there were only eight consolidations, although only one of those set up in the thirty-year period had been abandoned. Districts in the Northwest Territories were given permission and inducements to consolidate as early as 1901, but no enthusiasm was engendered. In Manitoba an enactment of 1905 authorizing arrangements for consolidation and transportation of pupils led to small consolidations, usually of only two districts. There were two schools by 1906, 46 by 1913, and 108 by 1925. Saskatchewan legislation of 1912-13 provided for the organization of larger districts up to fifty or more square miles, for unions of districts, and for conveyance of pupils; and legislation of 1917 permitted the organization of a district for the purpose of conveying pupils to a school in another district. In that province the number of consolidations was 9 in 1914, 19 in 1917, 39 in 1921; but although good gravel roads were constructed a few years later, the consolidation movement slowed down. In Alberta an enactment of 1913 assured localities that they would receive no less in provincial grants after consolidation than would have been forthcoming otherwise. A first consolidated school was erected at Warner at a cost of $30,000. In 1918, when four such schools had been built and about forty minor consolidations organized, a supervisor of consolidated schools was appointed. Distances were a great handicap in the west. A grant of a fixed sum per day towards costs of transportation was offered in Alberta in 1913 and a grant for the operation of vehicles in 1919. British Columbia in 1905 offered a fifty-per-cent grant to help provide conveyance to graded schools established by two or more contiguous districts and between 1917 and 1922 broadened the conditions for conveyance grants.

At the beginning of the twentieth century in Quebec, one-quarter of all the Protestant schools were attended by ten pupils or less. Movements to the city from the scanty Protestant rural populations intensified the problem, so that consolidation seemed the only solution. Assurance was given to the people that existing small schools would not be removed for

three years after a consolidated school was established. Special grants were offered in 1914-15, transportation grants in 1923-24, and grants for new buildings in 1925. Most of the consolidations were successful, and forty-nine consolidated school districts were in operation in 1943. In Ontario, legislation of 1919 ensured districts against loss of provincial grants if consolidated schools were established. A pamphlet explaining the inadequacies of rural schools and the advantages of consolidation was published in 1920, and another of the question and answer type in 1922. But although 10 consolidated schools had been established by 1920, there were in 1938 only 28 and in 1950 only 20, all of which had been set up before 1927.

Except in special circumstances, therefore, consolidated elementary schools did not win support from rural parents in spite of better teaching, superior facilities, and a program commonly enriched by manual training, domestic science, school gardening, and expert instruction in music and art. Mothers objected to transportation of young children to a distance from their homes, fathers to the higher cost of the superior education, and trustees to their loss of importance when the neighborhood school was closed. If roads and motor vehicles had been of 1930 quality in 1905, the enthusiasts might have succeeded. But after the depression, efforts to encourage consolidation were redirected towards the improvement of secondary schools.

This purpose had not been overlooked earlier. British Columbia in 1905 authorized unions of districts to support high schools, then withdrew the permission in 1906 in favor of rural municipal school districts, but in 1921 empowered the central authority to unite districts for the original purpose. Quebec consolidated schools frequently included secondary grades. But the object of later efforts was to establish regional composite high schools. Ontario boards by 1948 were spending more than $1,500,000 on the conveyance of pupils to secondary schools as compared with a little over $800,000 on transportation to elementary schools. In six years between 1944 and 1950 the number of pupils transported increased from 600 to over 25,000, about forty new high schools were built, and high school districts were organized in over seventy-five per cent of the southern portion of the province. Consolidation of this type involved administrative reorganization at the request of county councils and with the approval of local municipalities concerned. Its chief purpose, however, was to replace small, inadequate "continuation" schools by high schools with accommodation, equipment, and staff to offer a modern secondary school program. Ontario established as a criterion that a minimum of 300 pupils in Grades IX to XIII was needed for the efficient operation of a regional high school. Unfortunately, concessions to the usual pressure from rural constituencies from about 1950 caused a breakdown of this standard. Reference was made in chapter 14 to corresponding efforts in other provinces.

City School Systems

Until 1847 cities had no administrative organization for the whole municipality but simply embraced a number of school sections with independent boards. In that year, however, boards were set up over all public elementary schools in the cities of Canada West. At first the boards were appointed by the municipal councils, but chiefly because of difficulties in securing local financial support for the schools in Toronto, election of members by wards was introduced three years later. Appointed secondary school boards remained separate until the end of the nineteenth century — in Toronto from 1807 to 1903. In 1892 Kingston began to appoint a member of the public school board to the collegiate board for liaison, and after receiving a favorable report from a committee to study the desirability of closer association, the two boards joined forces in 1897. From 1903 to 1909 successive acts gave authority to large cities and other urban municipalities to set up elected municipal boards of education over schools of all types. Toronto established such a board in 1904 and Kingston in 1931, although some cities retained their two boards. On the whole, a single elected board became typical in provinces from Ontario westward, and a single appointed board in the Maritime Provinces.

It became common practice in the present century to have cities help carry the cost of services in rural areas, whether in providing telephones under private enterprise or schools under government auspices. But there was discrimination against certain cities long ago. Montreal and Quebec from 1846 received in grants only one-quarter and two-thirds respectively of the sums to which they would have been entitled in the ordinary way. In these cities, moreover, no provision was made for local support of the schools. In 1868-69 the grants to the two cities were made equitable and the city corporations were required to raise three times the amount of the grant by the separate assessment of Roman Catholic and Protestant ratepayers. Thereafter the Protestant commissioners had adequate funds to offer the advantages of a good education to the city children and by their example to stimulate educational progress elsewhere.

A few of the improvements introduced by some city school systems between 1875 and 1925 were, in chronological order: well equipped buildings made more cheerful by pictures and flowers; trained teachers in every classroom; kindergartens; improved methods of teaching reading; teaching of art, music, nature study, manual training, and household science; su-

James L. Hughes

pervised playgrounds; and classes for physically and mentally handicapped children. Cities had the services of superintendents on the spot. Toronto had a combined superintendent and secretary from 1844 to 1857, a clergyman superintendent from 1857 to 1874, and from then a professional inspector of its own, although the first superintendent over both elementary and secondary education was not appointed until 1932. The Montreal Protestant board had a secretary-treasurer after 1846 and a superintendent after 1871. After the number of schools and pupils had doubled in a decade, Moncton in 1897, appointed as part-time superintendent a lawyer who had formerly been a teacher. Larger British Columbia cities after 1901 might employ superintendents if the central authority approved.

Outstanding among city school superintendents was James L. Hughes, who was well known throughout Canada and in many of the United States. Fearless, energetic, and self-assertive, he took the position of inspector of public schools in Toronto in 1874 at the age of twenty-nine. With well-directed blasts he swept the dust and cobwebs from the city system, showed up its deficiencies, and drove in reforms. In five years there were few untrained teachers remaining in Toronto classrooms. In ten years, attendance and punctuality had greatly improved. Before retiring in 1914 he had introduced all the improvements mentioned in the previous paragraph and many more. His patriotism, love of fun, and generosity caused most people to forgive his amazing insensitivity to the feelings of others. The Toronto Board of Education's *Centennial Story* which was published in 1950 reveals his arrogance and rudeness as well as his exceptional ability. He was described as a dominating individual, an ardent patriot, and a man with high ideals and with "faith in God and in himself."[8] He was an Orangeman, a Mason, an athlete, and unquestionably an administrative success. Men who had the characteristics necessary to acquire and hold city superintendencies were largely responsible for making the city systems what they were by World War I.

Large city school systems became differentiated, to a degree, from the provincial systems of which they were a part. Montreal in 1916 began to use textbooks different from those used elsewhere in the Protestant schools of Quebec and shortly after had inspectors and many distinctive regulations of its own. The Roman Catholic system in Montreal began also to assert some independence. Manitoba in 1876 gave incorporated cities and towns authority to appoint their own inspectors, and Winnipeg in the twentieth century introduced many other services which made it seem different educationally from the rest of Manitoba. Some city school systems became very large, and were in a position to become larger by amalgamation. In 1925 the Montreal Protestant Central School Board was formed to cover five cities and six other towns and municipalities on the Island of Montreal. In 1953 Greater Toronto became the municipality of metropolitan Toronto with a metropolitan school board consisting of representatives of the Toronto board and of the suburban boards. This administrative area was as large in school enrolment and as elaborate in its ramifications as the combined systems of two or three of the smaller provinces.

School Premises

TENANCY

Schools before the time of Confederation were commonly held in any makeshift premises available. As late as 1862 one school in three in New Brunswick, and one in six in Canada West was conducted in a rented building or room. Houses, stables, stores, warehouses, saloons, and blacksmith shops — or a portion of such premises if they were still in other use — served for school accommodation. Anything was good enough: in Owen Sound, Upper Canada, a log shelter originally used by prospectors; in Collingwood a kitchen; at Lakefield a board shanty. In the Eastern Townships of Quebec the Misses Sally Pierce and Betsy Daniels taught for two summers in the attic of Ephraim Magoon's distillery at Danville. The improvement of education was retarded by the failure of trustees to acquire school premises under the ownership of the public. In New Brunswick the people sometimes saved expense by letting the teacher provide accommodation, although anything he could afford was "miserably ill-adapted to the efficient or economic working of a public school system of education."[9] Sometimes the teacher was expected only to provide equip-

ment: in British Columbia in 1856 a master requested that "the furniture & fixtures . . . might be bought at a valuation for his successor." Even in Toronto some school premises were still rented as late as the 1920's.

DESCRIPTION OF EARLY SCHOOL HOUSES

Rented or freehold, most school premises at mid-century were wretched buildings, often in bad repair, commonly without conveniences or equipment, and always uncomfortable in any weather. D'Avray of New Brunswick said in 1850:

Look at the miserable huts which in many parts of the country are made to answer the purpose of a school, many of them in such a state that every wind of heaven has free entrance; so small, so inconvenient that they would make indifferent pig styes, and yet in them the unfortunate teacher must perform his laborious and imperfect duties, he must teach reading and spelling without books, geography without maps, and oftentimes writing and cyphering without paper or slates.[10]

As for sanitary facilities, 380 of 700 New Brunswick schools in 1852 admitted that there was no provision whatever, 205 claimed to have some provision, and 115 simply did not report. Superintendent Porter advocated the circulation of Henry Barnard's treatise on "School Architecture," which Ryerson used to advantage in Canada West. But conditions changed slowly. "In fact," said Superintendent Bennett thirteen years later, "anything filthier and more unsuitable as places of education than some of the school rooms which I visited in the city of Saint John and the Parish of Portland, it would be difficult to imagine and impossible to describe."[11]

In Nova Scotia in 1864 Rand found only 100 satisfactory schoolhouses, no building at all in 200 school sections; among the other 700 schools reporting he found hundreds which were private prop-

An early stone schoolhouse around 1840

erty and other hundreds which could "scarcely be designated schoolhouses, many being without floors, without glass windows, without plastering, without desks, without seats except rough slabs, without apparatus."[12] In Prince Edward Island the inspectors frequently pointed out how education was handicapped by the wretched buildings and meagre equipment. They said that the poor, shabby schoolhouse too often reflected the apathy of the people, even of those who took some pride in their homes.

Log buildings persisted. Ontario in 1875 still had more than 1000 log schoolhouses as compared with about 1350 in 1844. In British Columbia three of the twelve publicly owned schoolhouses in 1872 were log structures. In New Brunswick, however, almost half of the 107 log buildings in 1852 had been abandoned by 1865, perhaps because they were too utterly crude to be worth preserving. Construction in the 1860's was mostly frame, but in Ontario masonry was becoming common, for there were 500 schoolhouses of stone and 1200 of brick in 1875, as com-

pared with only 80 and 50 respectively thirty years before.

Early schools were often very small. The tiniest, reported by the Royal Institution in Quebec, was sixteen feet by seventeen feet. About four hundred or five hundred square feet was a common size. Not much thought was given to school grounds: in one case a lot thirty feet by forty feet was chosen for a schoolhouse measuring twenty feet by twenty-five feet; but several of the Institution's schools had half an acre, and some had four acres. In the Western District of Upper Canada, one of the better schools of 1829 measured thirty feet by fifty feet, was twelve feet high to a plastered ceiling, and had a flue for a stove instead of the usual fireplace. During the 1850's and 1860's schools in Canada West were rapidly equipped with maps, globes, desks, and blackboards. The "great lack of blackboards" in British Columbia in 1872 shocked the superintendent, who had formerly been a teacher in Ontario.

In exceptional cases private individuals erected superior schoolhouses at their own expense. An example was a school built near Fredericton in 1864 and described by an inspector in these words:

The internal arrangement is very superior. The furniture was imported from the States and is of the most costly kind. There are twenty desks to accommodate forty pupils and for small children sixteen separate seats with pockets, besides five settees for the classes while reciting. The teacher's desk is at the back of the room on a slight elevation, and immediately behind it, and running the whole length of the wall, is a nicely prepared blackboard. On the walls are hung eight maps, four of which were furnished by Mr. Gibson. There are five windows on each side of the building, and so arranged as to lift or let down as convenience may require. All of these are furnished with green window shutters. The school room is ceiled up to the windows, and painted an oak colour, and the walls are papered with expensive material, in panel work; the whole presenting a beautiful experience. The Library, a neat little room between the two entrance halls, fitted up in the same style as the school room, contains three hundred volumes for the use of the school. In addition to all this $40 have been expended to light the building in case it should be necessary to use it in the evening.[13]

NINETEENTH-CENTURY IMPROVEMENT

Improvements between 1840 and 1900 may be illustrated by the schools of Toronto. At first the city had rented premises designated only by number in a dozen houses or other buildings. In three years, however, after the free school victory in the early 1850's, the city erected six identical two-storey school buildings — "handsome, spacious and commodious, suitably fitted up and supplied with all needful appliances," including two hot air furnaces. After a battle with ratepayers who preferred to have classrooms overcrowded or to tack on additions at best, there was another burst of new school construction in the 1870's. Three "wonder-schools" were equipped with individual desks,

cloakrooms, ventilation, and running water. Actually, by that time, washroom equipment and made-in-Canada desks and classroom supplies were widely advertised. Though the schools appeared to be mighty forts, the classrooms were brightened considerably by pictures on the walls and by growing plants on the window sills. But still a source of trouble and of unscheduled holidays were the heating systems. In a principal's diary from 1877 to 1887 were recurrent items: "temperature could not be raised above 38°"; "tinsmith is busy putting up stoves . . . the furnaces having been rejected"; "furnaces are now in operation . . . this morning rooms were too cold . . . the stoves were directed to be lit at 10.15 a.m."; "pipes connected with the steam heating . . . were burst by frost."[14]

Elsewhere in the 1870's there were "new and elegant schoolhouses of improved architecture and enlarged size" — seven in Queen's County, Prince Edward Island, within the year of the Act of 1877. Here is a contemporary description of a high school under construction in Halifax in 1878:

The building is eighty-four feet in length, seventy-four in width. The style of architecture is altogether befitting an educational edifice. The material is pressed brick, with basement of rustic granite. The dulness (*sic*) of the brick is relieved by granite trimmings and ornamental work in white and black brick. The structure is two stories in height, with mansard roof; so that practically there are three floors available for school purposes. Besides, the basement is only a basement in name, being as light and airy as the upper stories. Here the City Board of School Commissioners will have their Board Room, and their Secretary his office. A very comfortable gymnasium will be fitted up in another part of the basement. The first floor proper comprises four class rooms, Principal's private office, etc. On the second are four other class rooms, private room for teachers' use, and an elegant chemical laboratory. The third

A superior rural school near Fenelon Falls, Ontario, 1873

contains the large hall, or assembly room, and two good-sized class rooms. Here is provided ample accommodation for at least two hundred pupils; we may safely say for two hundred and fifty. Though the building has been designed specifically as a high school for boys, it is possible that the Commissioners may consider the propriety of admitting girls, should the attendance of the rougher sex not exhaust the seating capacity.[15]

Typical of the school buildings in which citizens at the end of the century took pride was the Aberdeen High School at Moncton, completed in 1898. The secretary of the school board described it in detail in his report. It measured one hundred and twenty-nine feet by ninety feet, was three stories high, and had an elaborate basement. It had seventeen classrooms, averaging in size about thirty-five feet square. It had an assembly hall capable of seating six hundred people, a library, two rooms for the teachers, and in the basement a science laboratory well-equipped for teaching chemistry to forty-eight pupils. On the ground floor "connected with the Principal's room by roll-

ing doors is the natural history room, which is shelved and protected by glass for the reception of natural history specimens. In this room is the large sink and tables upon rollers, capable of being moved into the main room, thus enabling the Principal to demonstrate small experiments before the school without going to the laboratory in the basement."[16] The halls of the building, considered a striking feature, were "exceedingly wide, admitting eight abreast marching through the hall" and the three stairways were "of ample and easy ascent" for four marching at ease and comfort. Various precautions were taken against fire, and the nine hundred occupants could in case of emergency be dismissed from the building in one minute. The school boasted the very latest furniture, uniform in every classroom, including ball-bearing desks, noiseless in action. The building was lighted by electricity, had a system of electric alarm bells in each room, and was heated and ventilated by nine furnaces with fans to force the air through the building. The interior trim of white wood and native

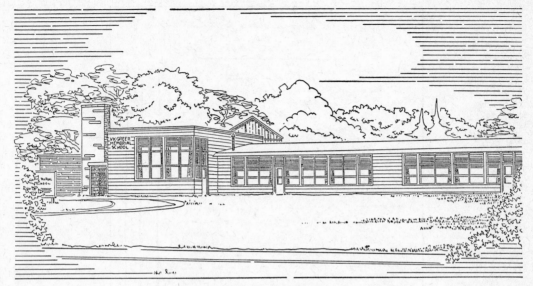

A superior rural school near Utterson, Ontario, 1950

spruce was finished to give a bright and pleasing effect. The school was supplied with maps, a lantern and slides, and apparatus for chemistry and physics. As was usual in "high schools" of the Maritime Provinces, most of the pupils were in elementary grades. Though built of brick and stone, the school was destroyed by fire in 1915.

A MODERN SCHOOL

A generation later in 1934-35 Moncton erected another high school which was considered a model at that time. It is much less compact: the main building extends two hundred and thirty feet across the front and a wing runs two hundred and eight feet back; there are two stories instead of three above the basement, which has a high ceiling and windows above grade to make it useful for instructional purposes. Two science laboratories, for chemistry and physics, are located there. In the main block are twenty-five classrooms of a size to accommodate thirty-five pupils, each lighted by a bank of five high windows and six hanging lights in

two circuits. There are many other rooms including suites of offices for the school board and for members of the high school staff, a library with boys' and girls' study rooms opening from it, rest rooms for the teachers, and a "doctor's room." The building is fire-resistant, built of steel and masonry with concrete floors covered with asbestos tile. Ceilings are covered with squares of wood-fibre boards to absorb some of the sound. The wing containing the auditorium and gymnasium can be shut off from the main building and used independently. The auditorium has a seating capacity of thirteen hundred and forty and a large elevated stage which can be thrown open by folding doors to the spacious gymnasium floor at the same level. Around the sides of the gymnasium is a balcony for spectators and under the floor are rest rooms, showers, and toilets.

It is not possible to summarize briefly the changes in school construction during the present century. The trend to lower buildings has been particularly noteworthy. Around 1907-08, newspaper editorials condemned the dangerous econ-

An itemized bill showing the cost of materials and labor for construction of a school at Cape St. Ignace, 1829 (Public Archives of Canada)

omy of structures three or four storeys high. They were described as fire-traps, which should be "immediately and peremptorily prohibited." After World War II new suburban and larger rural schools were commonly built on the ground level only, without basements or second storeys.

Costs

The cost of school construction was very low in the first few decades of the nineteenth century. In Lower Canada labor for the erection of a fieldstone house thirty-two feet by thirty-five feet was estimated at $80, and labor and materials for a wooden house eighteen feet by twenty-four feet at $100. Grants for the purchase or construction of schoolhouses averaged £40 sterling. The above illustration of a record of expenditures on a school building shows that this amount was adequate. Monitorial schools were more expensive: the school of the Midland District School Society cost £300. The rent allowance for the Royal Grammar School in Quebec, 1814-18, was probably exorbitant — £120 a year. Upkeep of school buildings was amazingly cheap. A record has been preserved of the maintenance costs in 1839-40 of the British and Canadian school at Quebec:

Maintenance Costs

	£	s.	d.
Insurance and Prizes	3	6	3
Stationery and Books	15		
Two Years' Ground Rent		4	8
Repairs	13	3	0
Cleaning School	3	12	0
Scrubing *(sic)* School		5	0
Ink Powders		2	0
Pencils		1	6
Broom		2.	0
Cleaning Privy.		10	0
Notices		2	6
Cartage			10
Advertising		6	8
Sweeping Chimneys.		10	0
TOTAL.	37	6	5

Scarcely $150 for two years' maintenance, excluding fuel and salaries, of a school to accommodate about 250 pupils!

At mid-century the finish and equipment of buildings was somewhat better and the cost was higher. In British Columbia £500 was appropriated for a school in Victoria in 1853, and a tender for $1930 was approved by the governor for a school to accommodate eighty pupils in New Westminster in 1865. The six schools erected in Toronto in the 1850's cost a total of about $80,000 and provided accommodation for 3000 pupils. The Moncton High School of 1898, with its seventeen classrooms and other facilities, cost $40,000, and a replacement with twenty rooms, auditorium, and shooting gallery ran in 1915 to slightly over $100,000. Costs increased sharply in the 1920's, fell again almost to the pre-war level in the 1930's, and then all but tripled by 1950. Comparisons in the twentieth century are impossible because of the wide range of possible facilities and equipment.

The Fight for Free Schools

From about the middle of the nineteenth century until shortly after Confederation, the champions of a new era fought the greatest campaign in our educational history. Their one goal was to secure free schools supported by the people through local taxation. Three preliminary achievements had set the stage: the establishment of determined central authorities, of regular grants, and of elected local trustees. A little had been done to accustom the people to local responsibility. But those who distrusted public education kept open two easy escapes, the rate-bill and charity education for the poor.

RATE-BILLS AND CHARITY EDUCATION

The rate-bill was a fee levied only on parents of children attending a common school. The amount was usually twenty-five to seventy-five cents a month, although there were wide variations. If the parents were unable to board the teacher for a week, they were charged in some districts from ten to thirty cents more. If they did not supply a share of the fuel, as most parents did, they paid for its cost. Children in excess of three from one family might be admitted free. In British Columbia before Confederation fees were as high as two dollars a month. In Quebec in 1830 the amount a teacher could charge was supposed to vary according to the means of the parents and in 1832 was limited as a condition of his receiving a grant. Parents without money, who seemed to be numerous everywhere, might be permitted to pay in kind, such as "good merchandisable wheat," which the unfortunate teacher found it hard to sell. In New Brunswick, cattle, musquash, skins, rum, making shoes, and hauling hay were among the goods and services offered and accepted in lieu of cash.

The effects of the rate-bill were vicious: it reduced attendance, especially if the teacher was permitted to charge more when the number of pupils fell off; and it caused the school to close if the teacher's income fell. In New Brunswick it re-

sulted in parents' paying a fee for one pupil and having their children take turns
at going to school. In the words of d'Avray:

John Brown has subscribed a certain sum
and is entitled to send his son Richard Brown
to the school during a period of six months.
Richard attends for a week or ten days, and
is then kept at home to work for a month or
six weeks — during that time William or
Tom, or Sam goes in his stead, or none of
the Browns go, and then the whole family
is sent so as to make up the full time. Eight
or ten Browns stand on the School returns
as having attended the school during the
year although it is plain that their attendance
has been extremely irregular, little profitable
to themselves and very annoying to the
teacher.[17]

Everywhere the rate-bill gave improvident
parents an excuse for not sending them
to school, or sending them for too short
a time.

Another obstacle difficult to overcome,
in this case because of laudable or seemingly laudable motives, was the provision
of education as a charity. Occasionally
ragged schools were provided for the
poor. In a New Brunswick city as late as
1860 a number of ladies engaged in charitable visiting were shocked at the large
number of children without adequate
clothing. They organized a school, each
taking a day to look after it, until one of
them took over the whole work. Seventy-
six pupils were enrolled in the first year,
and in six years a second teacher was
needed. At this school children were given
both instruction and clothing, which was
either donated or purchased with money
raised by subscriptions, concerts, and
bazaars. Similar work was done by the
Midland District School Society, formed
originally to conduct a monitorial school
and revived in 1837. From that date in
Kingston, Ontario, the society operated
two schools and provided free education,
books, and sometimes clothing to the poor.
In the winter of 1842 it clothed 234 children of sixty-seven families to enable the
children to attend school. These schools
in Kingston were also attended by pupils
who paid fees, including some children
whose parents were fairly well-to-do. One
school continued until about 1883, when
the society was disbanded. A common
method of raising money for charity education was indicated in an advertisement
in the *Quebec Gazette* in May 1815, which
invited benefactors to subscribe twenty
shillings and so acquire the right to send
one free scholar to school.

In common schools in some places the
teacher, either by agreement or of his own
free will, accepted some pupils free of
charge. In Lower Canada, where the
practice was most common, the Royal Institution advised the school commissioners of Hull and vicinity in 1824 to divide
the £60 grant among their three schools
according to the number of poor scholars
taught free by their respective teachers,
and to collect fees from the substantial
farmers who were well able to pay. In
returns of country elementary schools receiving a grant in that province in 1835,
only 24,000 of 38,000 pupils were shown
as paying scholars. But usually the charity
pupils were in a minority and were conscious of their position. The effect was
noted by the trustees of Charlotte County,
New Brunswick, in 1842: "The poorer
classes frequently, from a feeling of false
pride, and the notion that they may become in a manner Parish paupers by sending their children on the Provincial allowance, leave them to grow up in ignorance; the few of such class who attend
have been sought out by the Trustees."

TAX LEVIES IN INTERMEDIATE AREAS

Although the issue of support for schools
by taxation was fought out in local communities, central authorities sometimes required that their grants be matched by
sums raised in an intermediate area such

as a county. Various acts for Canada West from 1843 required these supplements, which from 1850 had to be raised by county councils by means of property assessment to an amount not less than the legislative grant. Taxation of this type was of value in helping to equalize opportunities for schooling over such an area. It was introduced sooner or later in some form everywhere — in New Brunswick in 1871 as a thirty-cent levy on every inhabitant to provide a county fund that was apportioned among the districts; in Manitoba in 1885 as a general school tax over large municipal areas; and so on.

But in relation simply to the struggle for tax-supported free schools, these intermediate levies were significant only in showing that the issue was not as simple and clear-cut as it might otherwise seem. There was little objection to taxation for education from those who were not aware of paying the tax, and awareness varied inversely as the area over which the tax was collected. Government grants were cheerfully demanded. Where free schools were introduced at the expense of the government — as in Prince Edward Island in 1852 or in British Columbia around 1865 — there were no shrieks of pain. But an early law requiring local taxation to support free schools, passed in New Brunswick in 1816, before the people had any training in responsibility, raised such an outcry that it had immediately to be repealed.

MOVEMENT FOR LOCAL TAXATION AND FREE SCHOOLS

The arguments of the more enlightened had won sufficient support by 1840 to inspire many public declarations in favor of tax-supported schools. In Prince Edward Island that year a special committee of the legislature went as far as to recommend the "assessment of persons not subscribing to any school within three miles of their residence and having a child or children betwixt the ages of six and eighteen." Next year the school visitor, John MacNeill, came out strongly for assessment to enable the poor man to send all his children to school. In Nova Scotia the lieutenant-governor in his speech from the throne had spoken in favor of the "principle of general assessment" for the support of schools. In 1842, the following year, G. R. Young published his *On Colonial Literature, Science and Education,* which demonstrated the need for this reform.

The year before, Judge Charles Mondelet of Quebec had written a series of letters asking not only for the restoration of aid from the legislature but also the introduction of local taxation for schools, although he insisted that parents should still be required to pay a small fee. His recommendations and those of Meilleur were embodied in the legislation of 1841, which made the mistake of requiring local taxation by municipal authorities appointed by the crown, not elected by the people. Justifiable objections were exploited by the opposition in the legislature to compel the government in 1845 to reinstate voluntary contributions as an option to taxation, without making clear whether the municipal councils or the school commissioners should have the unpopular duty of imposing taxes, so that a great number of schools closed because the teachers received no salaries.

Within a decade the weight of argument was heavy on the side of reform. In New Brunswick, for example, the Mechanics' Institute in Saint John had in 1849 a number of lectures in favor of free schools. The *New Brunswick Courier* conducted a campaign in 1851, and by 1860 all newspapers in the province but one were advocating tax support and free education. A specific example of the advantages to be attained by local taxation was offered in 1850 by the examiners of the training school in Saint John. In the parish of Hampton less than one-quarter of the population supported the schools by subscriptions of at least nineteen shillings each. The amount so raised, added to the government grant, provided insufficient salaries for teachers, no more than £22. 8s at most, and part of that was paid in board. A number of parents were unable to subscribe and their children were left without any education. The report of the examiners showed that an additional hundred pounds for the parish would staff the schools with competent teachers at an average salary of thirty pounds and provide an education for all children. The money could be raised by taxation at an average cost of 14s 6d to every taxpayer, and at much less than average cost to poorer families. Three benefits would result: all parents would be supporters of the school; all would take advantage of the opportunity to send their children; and better teachers would be secured.

School trustees in the city of Toronto in 1847 used another argument in their effort to get funds from the municipal council:

A perfectly free education in the Common Schools of this City would prove to be productive in a short time of the most beneficial results in withdrawing from idleness and dissipation a large number of children who now loiter about the streets or frequent the haunts of vice, creating the most painful emotions in every well regulated mind.[18]

A committee of the school board in 1851 presented an impressive report which showed that not one-half of the population from five to sixteen years of age was at school. In arguing for free schools, the report pointed out that contributory causes of the lamentable conditions were insufficient school accommodation, poverty, parental indifference, and sectarianism; it was very emphatic about the necessity of "excluding everything of a sectarian character from the instruction given."

OPPOSITION TO FREE SCHOOLS

The type of opposition which the committee had in mind was provided in Upper Canada by the Reverend John Roaf. In one of his letters to the editor of *The Globe* he categorized the free school system as "communism in education" which undermined property and society and pauperized the people. He denied the right of "mechanics and labourers . . . to educate their children at the expense of their more wealthy neighbours . . . Though it is our duty," he said, "to give this blessing to the poor, it does not follow that the poor should forcibly take from us. . . . The French people and the Mormons ought to serve as warnings of the abyss to which this plausible socialism is enticing us."[19]

Most of the arguments against free schools were clearly inspired by personal interest. Proprietors of private schools were among the obstinate opponents. Because of hostility to Ryerson, the editor of the Toronto *Globe* tried to build up an honest case against local taxation, but abandoned the attempt and went over to the other side. Most of the objectors were moved primarily by a fear of being taxed. In 1853 in Quebec the superintendent observed that the people were strongly opposed to the free school law: "the system of direct contribution which it imposes being previously unknown to them, and everywhere odious." Political agitators or "extinguishers" described even the optional assessment law of 1845 as "arbitrary, tyrannical, unjust, oppressive, absurd, and impractical." They tried to prevent the adoption of local taxation by playing on the selfish immediate interest of the people.*

Not all of the opposition to free schools, however, was utterly benighted. A message of Governor Seymour to the legisla-

* Woodley (214), pp 84-87.

ture of British Columbia on February 27, 1867, had a little wisdom behind its prejudice:

He thinks that any man who respects himself would not desire to have his children instructed without some pecuniary sacrifice on his part. The state may aid the parent, but ought not to relieve him of his own natural responsibility else it may happen that the promising mechanics may be marred, and the country overburdened with half-educated professional politicians or needy hangers-on of the Government.[20]

The governor wanted to have secular schools charge a low fee and to give some assistance also to denominational schools to enable them to compete with the secular schools operated by the government and the people. The issue was confused in his province because most of the advocates of free schools expected the government to pay the whole cost, whereas some who were classified as opponents of free schools were actually in favor of local taxation. It was claimed by government supporters that free schools in Victoria alone would require all the money the government had available and that free schools had to be opposed if any help at all was to be given to other centres.

OPTIONAL AND COMPULSORY LEGISLATION

At mid-century the first decisions in favor of free schools were secured in the older provinces less by argument than by force of circumstances. Economic improvement, democratic government, large numbers of immigrants, and more liberal thought made the first step possible and necessary. In Ontario and New Brunswick, in 1850 and 1852 respectively, this first step was the passing of an optional law which invited the locality to decide whether to introduce general taxation or continue the rate bill. In Quebec and Nova Scotia legislation of 1846 and 1864-65, respectively, made local taxation obligatory almost immediately. But whether optional or compulsory, the first free school acts had to be preceded and followed by much propaganda to make them effective.

ONTARIO

In Ontario the vigorous campaign of Ryerson was so successful that 4000 of 4400 school sections by 1870 had adopted local assessment for free schools, so that compulsory legislation of the following year did little more than ratify an achievement.

NEW BRUNSWICK

In New Brunswick, however, mistakes were made. Although right in an assumption that direct taxation for free schools could only be adopted by degrees, the legislature erred in exempting the property of non-residents. This obvious injustice made resident ratepayers who had no children at school even more unwilling to pay. Worse still, New Brunswick had no native-born, indefatigable superintendent with a sense of mission to draft the original legislation and drive it into operation. The inducement of a twenty-five per cent higher grant from the government to the teacher when free schools were established, though copied later in Nova Scotia, was not in itself sufficient. The result was that by 1871 only a few districts and not a single county municipality or parish had adopted the assessment principle. When compulsory legislation was passed in 1872 it was revolutionary and many years had to be spent in getting it into smooth operation before attendance laws could be enacted and other advances made.

QUEBEC

In Quebec there was a see-saw contest. The government had introduced unpopular taxation in 1841, had then given way and paid grants in 1843 to recalcitrant municipalities, had made a further concession by restoring optional voluntary subscription in 1845, and had re-introduced taxation in 1846. Again in 1849 there was a concession in principle which enabled the people of a local community to escape taxation by voluntary contribution of an amount equal to the government grant. Although this law remained on the statute books for fifty years, taxation was introduced everywhere before 1860. Much of the credit was deserved by Superintendent Meilleur, who drafted the legislation of 1846, which not only required local taxation but placed school affairs in the hands of elected commissioners. But the rapid acceptance of local taxation in Roman Catholic parishes was due chiefly to the zeal of the clergy, who were as ready later to support confessional schools of their own people as they had been ready earlier to resist the establishment of institutions of which the church did not approve.

Nevertheless there was resistance to be overcome. The *habitants* regarded the law of 1846 as a device to take money from them by taxation. Children were withdrawn from school, unqualified commissioners were elected to circumvent the law, leading citizens who supported it were threatened with retaliation, and schools were burned. The Archbishop of Quebec imposed on one parish an interdict which was lifted only when the provisions of the act had been carried out. Under the influence of the clergy, and with thoughts of the security of French-speaking Canada in mind, the people ceased to resist the law. By 1855 the opposition to taxes had died out among the French-speaking Canadians, although the Irish Catholics continued to resist for five or six years more on grounds that they had come to this country to escape taxation in Ireland.

NOVA SCOTIA

In Nova Scotia, after Forrester's preliminary work in rounding up support and helping to draft the bill, the Conservative government under Dr. Charles Tupper in 1864 passed an act which gave school sections the choice of rate-bills or assessment and offered a twenty-five per cent bonus in the grant to those which chose the latter alternative. The leader of the Liberal party voted with the government, but many back-benchers of both parties voted against the measure. Throughout much of the province the operation of the act was resisted by refusal to call meetings and vote funds. In one of the western counties only twelve of about one hundred school sections submitted to organization under the law. Tupper was denounced in the press as an "angel of discord and confusion . . . wrecking and destroying the sacred cause of education . . . rending and dividing districts . . . setting neighbor against neighbor . . . kindling the fires of intense hatred and strife."[21] His response, on the advice of Rand, was to pass next year a much stronger act which required assessment in all counties for ordinary expenses and assessment in school sections for capital expenditures. As a result of these two acts and the vigorous work of the superintendent, the number of pupils attending school in the winter increased from about 35,000 in 1865 to 45,000 in 1866 and to 60,000 in 1867. The government then suffered an honorable extinction at the polls, and the superintendent shortly after was discharged, but the free school system was secure.

PRINCE EDWARD ISLAND

In Prince Edward Island in 1852 the lieutenant-governor called attention to the "lamentable want of education and the great apathy which seems to have prevailed." He urged the legislators to make it their business that "the inestimable blessings of education be extended to every corner of this colony." A committee of the legislature was appointed. The committee reported that the number of children in the schools had failed to keep up with the increase in population, saw no solution but to have the salaries of schoolmasters paid wholly by the government, and recommended legislation "to establish schools on the free system throughout the Island." Accordingly legislation was passed abolishing school fees, establishing local taxation for school purposes, and providing grants to give teachers a salary of forty-five pounds or fifty pounds. The results were immediate and spectacular. Whereas in 1852 there had been only 133 schools and not one child in fourteen at school, in 1855 there were 270 schools and one child in five in attendance. But local taxation was not enforced until 1877, when the trustees were empowered to collect from the resident householders either a poll-tax not exceeding one dollar per head or a property tax, or both. There were the usual objections that it was unfair to make householders without children contribute to the salary of the teacher, "an idler in their midst." Yet enforcement of the act increased the number of teachers from 344 to 450 between 1876 and 1879, reduced the number of vacant schools from 68 to 21, and caused new and more commodious schools to be built.

MANITOBA AND THE NORTHWEST

In Manitoba optional local taxation was introduced in 1871 and compulsory taxation two years later. In the Northwest Territories the battle for free schools began with the passing of the ordinance of 1884. There the obstacles were the indifference of settlers towards education, the usual objection to taxation, and the opposition of certain interests to bringing schools under public control. Nevertheless the increased grants led to numerous applications for aid. One of these asked for the setting up in Edmonton of a Protestant school district with power to tax. Opposition to taxation came chiefly from officials of the Hudson's Bay Company, which had favored church schools in the past and which still had very great influence. One of the chief proponents of free schools was the editor of the *Edmonton Bulletin*, who emphasized the need of an *ad hoc* body with power to tax not only residents but absentee land-holders, including chiefly the company and its officials. The vote on the question was taken between December 20 and December 27, 1884. The issue was hotly contested and order had to be kept by a sergeant of the police and two special constables. By nine in the morning the teams were out to bring in voters, first a sleighload of anti's, then a sleighload of pro's. When the anti's claimed voting rights for company employees as tenants of rooms in the company building, the pro's brought over to the polls occupants of rooms in the Edmonton hotel. There was plenty of liquor in evidence in spite of a prohibitory law. When the polls closed at four o'clock, the vote was 54 for and 43 against. The Edmonton school was established as the first in Alberta, although the seventh in the Northwest Territories, under the ordinance of 1884. Opposition to taxation continued for a year or two but then subsided. Between 1885 and 1892 the securing of responsible government was a concurrent issue in the Northwest Territories. During 1892, when democratic government was established and the population increasing, about half as many schools were built as in all the years before.

BRITISH COLUMBIA

In British Columbia, schools nominally free were maintained by the government on Vancouver Island in 1865. But in 1867 the governor refused to continue paying the whole cost of operation and ordered the free schools to close at the end of the year. Nevertheless the board and the teachers attempted to carry on. The board divided its remaining funds among the teachers, who received in this way from twenty dollars to ninety-four dollars each as their salaries for the year, plus a share of $434 raised by a benefit performance in the theatre. In 1869 when the Victoria board had given up the struggle and many schools elsewhere were closed, an ordinance gave local boards authority to call a meeting of residents to decide whether local support should be provided by fees and subscriptions only or by taxation. The latter took the form of a two-dollar poll tax on male residents, so that well-to-do absentee property holders escaped. In Victoria in 1870 little effort was made to collect the tax. When the teachers received only the government money they resigned, and one school at least was closed for two years. In Nanaimo in 1870 only 26 of 142 children between five and fifteen were in attendance. In the whole province only $3000 was raised locally for education. After Confederation, the whole cost of education from 1872 was again assumed by the provincial government. Hence the early struggle for free schools in British Columbia was simply an attempt to escape both school fees and local taxation. Local responsibility was achieved later, as we have seen.

OBJECTIONS CONTINUED

Even after the triumph of free schools there were people who tried to nullify the victory and to impede further progress for public education. An educational journal in 1879 classified these people as follows:

1. Those who look upon Public Schools as "pauper schools" very good for the "vulgar herd."

2. Those who believe that it is "dangerous to the State, and productive of communistic views, to give the children of the poor too much education."

3. Those who say, "I done fusrate wi' no eddication, wy shouldn't the childer?"

4. Those who say, "Joggerfy don't help no boy to drive a yoke o' oxen."

5. Those who are rich, niggardly, and have no children to go to school.[22]

INCREASED COST OF EDUCATION

One of the consequences of free school legislation was a great increase in expenditures on education. In Nova Scotia the cost per pupil remained at less than five dollars until 1864 and then leaped to over $12.50 in 1870. During the same six years the number of pupils more than doubled. Not surprisingly, there were public objections to increased costs.

A handbook on Toronto claimed that between 1844 and 1857, when the population rose from 18,500 to 45,000, the cost of city schools increased from £1377 for 1194 pupils under 12 teachers to £6054 for 1863 pupils under 36 teachers. Since the proportionately lower enrolment could not be attributed wholly to immigrant adult population and to the 1857 depression, the board wisely spent $350 on a special school census a few years later, with the result that attendance jumped to three or four times the former number. But compulsory attendance was needed to give children the full benefit of the free school system.

FREE HIGH SCHOOLS

A long period elapsed in most parts of Canada before free high schools followed free elementary schools. Grammar school fees in the early nineteenth century were usually about thirty dollars for the full calendar year. The charges per quarter at Kingston, Upper Canada, in 1830 were £1 for junior elementary subjects, £1.10 for advanced elementary or English subjects, £2 for Latin, and £2.10 for Greek, plus a levy of two shillings on all pupils for school repairs. Board and tuition was £30 at Brockville in 1837 for pupils "in the usual branches" and £50 for theological students. The latter always paid high fees: at Quebec and Montreal in 1829, ordinary grammar school charges ranged from £8 to £12 a year; but at Chambly, where ordinary students paid £15 to £20 for instruction, or £40 to £50 with board, divinity students in residence paid £75. This was a reflection of the advantageous economic and social position of the Church of England clergy. In Roman Catholic colleges or seminaries, however, charges were low: at Quebec, £1 for tuition and £17.10 for tuition and board; at Montreal, £1.15 and £21. Also inexpensive were such institutions as Mount Allison: in 1851 fees covering all expenses for forty-three weeks were £25 to £30.

The fees charged in high schools after Confederation were moderate. In Ontario the trustees could make the schools entirely free to resident pupils and could not charge pupils from other parts of the county more than one dollar a month. The average fee for the province in 1895 was less than five dollars. There was some reaction against free high schools in the late nineteenth century. In British Columbia during hard times in 1878, a motion was put forward in the house to "disestablish" the high school of Victoria. It did not pass, but there was strong support for high school fees, which trustees throughout the province were empowered to collect in 1888. The year before that date a meeting of Ontario trustees in Toronto passed a resolution introduced by the Reverend E. Cockburn of Uxbridge that a minimum fee of fifty cents a month be charged, on the ground that high schools were within the reach of only a minority of the citizens. In Nova Scotia, however, where high schools had been closely associated with the elementary schools since 1864, fees were abolished by the 1890's.

An Ontario pupil might escape high school fees by taking a year or two of secondary work in the "fifth book" of an elementary school. In Toronto before 1911, fees in collegiate institutes ranged from six dollars in the first form to twenty-seven dollars in the fourth form. They were then reduced, and in 1921 abolished there and everywhere in the province. The first Secondary Education Act of Saskatchewan in 1907 authorized fees of up to one dollar a month for resident pupils but no fees for out-of-town pupils, and in 1920 the high schools became free to all. Except in Quebec and Newfoundland, free public secondary schools became general about that time.

Expenditures of Local and Central Authorities

Although school trustees served without remuneration, they were subjected to criticism from the first. Their traditional fault was bargain hunting for cheap educational services, and until World War II they were usually under pressure from central authorities to spend more money. But local taxpayers blamed them for extravagance as educational services expanded. For example, at the opening of the new high schools in Montreal in 1878, the chairman of the Protestant board found it necessary to defend the high school system against the attacks of those who considered such institutions a useless and expensive luxury. In his address he said that many of the commercial population in the province of Quebec, and even some of the wealthiest merchants, considered the merest smattering of writing and arithmetic sufficient educational equipment for their sons.

Criticism of trustees was strong in language, if weak in logic, when inflation and sudden increase in school population sent costs soaring. It appeared often in anonymous letters to newspapers. A typical letter signed "Taxpayer" appeared in the *Moncton Times* in January, 1921. It appears that the number of pupils in the schools of the city had increased between 1915 and 1920 from 1766 to 3152, the number of teachers from 48 to 75, and the salaries of teachers from around $450 to around $900. The irate taxpayer claimed that there was no need for this increased expenditure. J. F. Edgett, a member of the board, answered the letter. The former salaries had been disgracefully low, and inflation due to the war had made them utterly inadequate. If educational expenditures had remained at the former level, the cost of additional buildings for the larger school population would have had to come out of teachers' salaries, which would have been reduced to $5.32 per month.[23]

LOCAL TAXATION AUTHORITY

A foundation stone in local finance of Canadian public education is the independent financial responsibility of *ad hoc* authorities. The effect of permitting municipal councils to decide the amount of expenditure was demonstrated when Toronto in 1848-49 refused to support schools from general funds raised by taxation. Immediately after, the Act of 1850 in Canada West stated plainly that it was the duty of the board of trustees to prepare an estimate of the amount needed and the duty of the municipal council "to provide such sum, or sums, in such manner as shall be desired by said Board of School Trustees." When the Toronto city council in 1860 reduced the school board's estimates from $30,000 to $24,000, the board took the question to the Court of Queen's Bench and won their case. They gained another court decision in a similar dispute regarding salary increases in 1901. But demands for control by municipal councils of school board expenditures recurred there and elsewhere from time to

time, and again recently because of the effect on educational costs of a higher birth rate. Only in Quebec have school commissioners, since 1846, had power of their own to tax for school purposes instead of the right to have municipal councils raise money for schools by taxation.

In 1879 legislation in Ontario enabled the municipal council by a two-thirds vote to refuse to raise money requested by the school board for capital expenditures and, if requested by the school board to do so, to submit the question to the electors who were supporters of the public schools. The government gave as the reason for this measure the need for a check on extravagance. An immediate effect was the refusal of the Toronto city council to pay $7000 for an addition to the collegiate institute, not on grounds that the accommodation was unnecessary but on grounds that taxes had to be reduced. The following year the council refused a very reasonable amount for new buildings and capitulated only after the minister of education had threatened to cut off the provincial grant. Actually, however, the Ontario legislation proved less restrictive than corresponding restraints on capital expenditures in most other provinces, where school debentures could be issued only after approval by a vote of the ratepayers.

SUBSIDIES TO INDIFFERENCE

A basic problem in educational finance was to obtain an advantageous adjustment of local and provincial responsibility. To get schools into operation in the early nineteenth century, the central authorities had to pay a large part of the major current expense — the teacher's salary. But the improvement of education was greater in the long run where the proportion of government expenditure was reduced. Although the miserly grants in Upper Canada in the 1820's and 1830's provided less educational sustenance than was offered in the Maritime Provinces, when the time for advance came later the people were better prepared to pay. Around 1840 provincial grants were about twice as high in proportion to population in Nova Scotia as in Upper Canada, but around 1860 total expenditures per capita on education were about fifty per cent higher in the larger province.

There was plenty of testimony regarding the deleterious effect of grants proportionately high enough to permit local communities to escape financial responsibility. The 1831 report of the Committee of the Legislature on Education in Lower Canada mentioned "evidence that in several instances too much dependance (*sic*) has been placed in Legislative Aids, and in some cases to a degree which seems to have had the effect of relaxing the exertions which were formerly made."[24] In New Brunswick in 1844 a committee of the legislature reported that although the province had provided ample funds for education as compared with the United States, Nova Scotia, and the Canadas, the money was not producing as effective a system of elementary education as was to be found in these other areas. In the 1850's many speeches in the legislature showed an awareness of the problem. D'Avray in 1856 pointed out in his annual report that popular indifference might increase rather than diminish as a result of the liberal aid granted by the legislature and the "facilities afforded the people" of evading any local contribution. After the optional free school law had failed for eighteen years to get the people to take hold, the attorney-general of the province said in the legislature: "The present system is founded on centralization, which has its merits, but it does not provoke any interest in education or local responsibility." He laid the blame for the reluctance of the people to act, on the shoulders of provincial forefathers who had set up institutions providing for very little self-government.

Grants unrelated to local effort were offered in early years because paternalism preferred to give the people anything rather than power. But they were maintained or restored later by democratic governments which relied on the votes of backward areas. In New Brunswick when the grants were raised from £180 per parish in 1837 to £260 per parish in 1840, the maximum grant per school was kept at the original £20, so that there was no incentive for a locality to spend more on better schools but simply a wider distribution of gratuities. These, as Superintendent Bennett said in 1866, had "saddled the country with a heavy burden" of wretched little unnecessary schools. In 1836 a committee of the legislature piously declared its belief in the need for better qualified teachers, but ruled out a suggestion that teachers be examined and licensed by county boards, on the ground that it would increase the difficulty of people in remote settlements in securing schoolmasters and "thereby prevent the benefit of Education being extended to many poor inhabitants of the province." Later it became only too clear that such policies provided not educational benefits for children but subsidies to adult indifference.

PROVINCIAL-LOCAL RATIOS

Obviously the ratio of provincial and local expenditure was affected by other factors, notably by the average income of the people. In poor provinces, as in poorer areas of a province, the proportion of provincial to local expenditure tended to be high. But there was almost certainly some reciprocal effect, and it is not fantastic to assume that government policies conducive to higher local expenditures on schools improved the economic habits and industry of the people and created conditions which retained and attracted ambitious citizens who were prepared to work for further educational and material advance.

In two provinces, British Columbia and Prince Edward Island, the central authorities assumed a major share of the financial burden from the time of Confederation – in the former the whole cost, and in the latter from 70 to 80 per cent of the cost. But British Columbia, as we have seen, changed her policy, and had the municipalities pay an increasing proportion of school costs, 35 per cent by 1900, 60 per cent by 1910, and 72 per cent by 1939. In the relatively poor province of Prince Edward Island, however, the localities continued to meet only about 30 or 40 per cent of school costs up to World War II. Only after 1944, when the proportion of provincial expenditures in other provinces began to increase sharply, while it fell off in Prince Edward Island, did the financial responsibilities of municipalities in the island province become comparable with those of municipalities elsewhere. The expenditure on public elementary education per pupil in average daily attendance in 1949 was $244 in British Columbia and $83 in Prince Edward Island – by far the highest and the lowest respectively among the provinces of Canada, except Newfoundland. In that province, where there is no local taxation, denominational boards raised by various means only about one-sixth of the cost of schools, and the total expenditure per pupil was $77.

Provincial and local expenditures on education over a period of more than a century in one of the older provinces, as shown in the table at the top of the next column, illustrate the long-term trend in Canada. The years have been chosen to show periods during which educational expenditure doubled. The sudden jump in 1866 resulted from the introduction of tax-supported schools the year before. The two other sharp increases came with inflation

Expenditures on Education in Nova Scotia

YEAR	PROVINCIAL	LOCAL	TOTAL
1836......	$ 28,000	$ 60,000	$ 88,000
1861......	47,000	130,000	177,000
1866......	137,000	232,000	369,000
1891......	214,000	511,000	725,000
1916......	415,000	1,205,000	1,620,000
1921......	577,000	2,866,000	3,443,000
1946......	3,425,000	4,261,000	7,686,000
1950......	7,583,000	6,034,000	13,617,000

during and after the two world wars. Observe, however, that after World War I the increased burden fell chiefly on the municipalities, which in 1921 were paying more than eighty per cent of the cost of education, whereas after World War II provincial expenditure increased until in 1950 it represented well over half of the total outlay.

CHANGING RATIOS

A radical change in the distribution of local school costs accompanied the formation of larger areas of rural school administration in recent years.

Changes in Percentage of Local School Costs Borne by Provinces

	1936	1941	1950
Nfld...............	—	—	75.76
P.E.I.............	59.2	59.3	52.74
N.S...............	15.4	17.9	45.05
N.B...............	14.6	17.5	28.83
P.Q...............	4.9	10.6	21.11
Ont...............	9.6	19.9	40.08
Man...............	12.4	15.2	27.82
Sask...............	16.1	15.7	30.20
Alta...............	13.7	23.3	33.37
B.C...............	22.7	30.0	41.32
Average...........	11.2	16.7	35.09

This transfer of cost burden was a source of satisfaction to educators who had advocated such a move to secure greater equality of opportunity for young people in rural and poorer areas. Cameron in his study of *Property Taxation and School*

Finance in Canada concluded that "the percentage of the total cost to be paid by the provincial government might exceed fifty without danger to local autonomy."[25] But the average was greatly exceeded in grants of ninety per cent or more to low-assessment areas. Hence the finance of rural education by 1950 reflected economic trends away from community enterprise and financial responsibility and towards the welfare state. The new paternalism cast urban big business and industry in the role of benefactor and the people of rural areas as the dependent poor. If nineteenth century experience is any guide, there was danger in 1950 of retrogression. As in Quebec in the 1830's, the high grants after World War II placed some central authorities in a position where their efforts were directed towards curbing local extravagance in spending the money of others, and not towards encouraging local effort for the improvement of education. Under the new arrangements, moreover, much of the increased revenue needed for schools during the period of inflation was obtained by concealed taxation on liquor rather than by declared assessments on real estate, and collected in cities for expenditure in rural areas. The educative effect might have been doubly corrosive to local responsibility. Fortunately, from this point of view, a school population greatly expanded by the jump in the birth rate was likely to keep local taxpayers aware of their obligation to the schools, at least in suburban areas.

EXPENDITURES ON SCHOOLS

Until about 1890 provincial expenditures on education made up a rather large proportion of total provincial expenditures, commonly about twenty per cent. During the twentieth century the average for all provinces was usually around twelve and one-half per cent, though considerably less during the depression and still less

during World War II. Municipal taxation for education in Ontario amounted to thirty-three per cent or less of all municipal taxation between 1927 and 1937, rose to nearly forty per cent by 1944, fell back when higher provincial grants were introduced, and rose again to almost thirty-eight per cent in 1951. Both provincial and municipal expenditures on education were then on the point of rising to a considerably higher proportion of all expenditures. Total public expenditures on education in Canada tripled in each of the first two decades of the twentieth century, increased relatively little for the next two decades, and more than tripled before the 1941-51 decade was over. It was about $11,000,000 in 1901 and was close to $400,000,000 in 1949.

CENTRAL OR LOCAL RESPONSIBILITY – A CHANGING CONCEPT

In the early nineteenth century an assumption still prevailed that ordinary people could not be trusted to provide education themselves. In commenting on the decline of education among French-speaking Canadians after the conquest, when the church was no longer in a position to conduct schools, the Abbé Groulx made this generalization:

L'expérience, hélas, l'a trop démontré: dans l'ordre intellectuel comme dans l'ordre moral, les peuples, laissés à eux-mêmes, ont plutôt tendance à s'abandonner. C'est le propre de tous les maux, sans en excepter l'ignorance, d'aller s'aggravant, pour peu qu'on cesse de les combattre.[26]

It is true, no doubt, that any education of people away from their inclination must be carried on unceasingly by someone with authority and funds. But another idea began more than a century ago to work in the minds of many in North America. If given only enough help to get things started and sufficient opportunity to run school affairs in their own way at their own expense, the people could and would dispense with charity from above and themselves provide education for their children. This was the concept on which the provincial systems were built. At the middle of the twentieth century its continuance was not quite certain.

Maintaining Local Interest

LOCAL RESPONSIBILITY FOR THE CURRICULUM

The extent of local financial responsibility cannot be separated from the expansion or contraction of powers of local school authorities and of community interest in education. We have seen that the tendency until recently was to centralize control of the interna of education, including teacher training and certification, supervision, and curriculum. Movements in the opposite direction have been the reduction of departmental examinations, greater flexibility in courses of study and choice of textbooks, and latitude for additional activities and services in cities and larger administrative areas.

In school curricula local trustees and teachers had a relatively free hand before 1850, but little discretion thereafter. In Kingston, in 1829, trustees expressed a willingness to accept a uniform grammar school program only "so far as local circumstances render it feasible." Between 1882 and 1884, when demands for more practical subjects were gaining strength, trustees in the same city asked the principal of the high school to prepare a program that would emphasize subjects useful to pupils who planned to enter business. They engaged teachers for drawing and shorthand and were considering other innovations, such as telegraphy and mechanical drawing, when the city solicitor gave his opinion that it would be illegal

to offer subjects not prescribed by the central authority. The trustees planned to issue a pamphlet designating the school as a "Technical and Commercial College," but dropped this unorthodox title at the request of the minister. Local authorities had made little headway when Foght in 1918 wrote in his *Survey of Education in Saskatchewan*:

It is doubtful whether this centralised control in matters of detail and local professional policy is in every respect wise. There is danger that too little flexibility of study courses and too little opportunity for local initiative will result where a central authority prescribes the details of work for teacher and pupils whom it is impossible to know in an intimate way. This phase of departmental control may, therefore, be considered as subject to modification to accommodate itself to local needs.[27]

By the 1940's however, the prescribed courses of study gave considerable latitude to the local school, and officials of the central authority in Ontario encouraged regional high schools to modify their programs to meet community needs. Alberta experimented with an elaborately organized scheme of consultation with lay and local groups on curricular revision. Ontario in 1950 invited local communities to organize committees to draft curricula of their own. Saskatchewan since then has had remarkable success in securing two-way communication regarding curriculum problems between the provincial department and the people locally. In short, there was by 1950 a trend towards new responsibilities for school boards and their electors and employees.

TRUSTEES ASSOCIATIONS

Trustees in the late nineteenth century gave other indications of attaching higher importance to their work. In 1887 the Provincial Association of Public and High School Trustees of Ontario was formed to strengthen the influence of trustees in dealing with the central authority and to "consider all matters having a practical bearing on Education and the School System." Although the agenda of the first meeting dealt almost exclusively with financial matters, the president's address criticized the excessive pressure of the uniform course of study and of the examination system for high schools. Provincial associations of trustees were formed in British Columbia in 1905, in Manitoba and Alberta in 1907, and in Saskatchewan in 1915. A Canadian Trustees' Association was established in 1923, but it proved difficult to hold the national organization together until it was reorganized in 1943. Ten years later there were associations of five provinces in the Canadian School Trustees Association and a sixth was being organized in Nova Scotia. By 1943 a considerable number of school trustees had begun to attend educational conventions.

INTEREST OF PARENTS

As local administrative areas became larger by growth of population or reorganization, it became increasingly important to foster a direct interest of parents in the school. A century ago the residents of most communities knew by sight and name the trustees they elected and also the teacher whom the trustees engaged. Public oral examinations and interschool spelling matches brought parents occasionally into the schools. A sign of change to a less personal era was the introduction of ballot voting for school trustees in cities around 1880. Probably most teachers in the nineteenth century welcomed the increasing isolation of the urban classroom. Two educational journals in 1868, one in Quebec and one in Nova Scotia, quoted a barrister who condemned vehemently the parent who interfered with the discipline of the school. But a new note was sounded in 1880 at the Waterloo Teachers' Association, where

a teacher pointed out the need of getting to know parents and to encourage their support in the work of education. "If our usefulness in the community is thus made to extend beyond the routine of school work," he said, "we will be looked upon with greater respect."[28] Before the century was over, according to Penrose, there were instances of parents forming groups to make school life more attractive to their children. One group was organized in Baddeck, Nova Scotia, to study the feasibility of introducing "such necessary educational features as Manual Training, Household Science, Physical Training, and School Libraries."[29] Another in Toronto the following year organized an art league in the belief that they could awaken children's interest in the school if they brightened the walls with good pictures. Before World War I there were several parents' associations in Ontario, and at least one for a short time in Calgary. Without any central organization to give direction, they sometimes interfered with school authorities and ran into difficulties.

HOME AND SCHOOL ASSOCIATIONS

Then came the formation of parent-teacher, or home and school, associations and the setting up of city and provincial organizations. Probably the first of the local parent-teacher groups was set up in Craigflower, B.C., in 1915. The following year Mrs. A. C. Courtice took the initiative in forming a home and school council to co-ordinate the work of the nine Toronto associations, and three years later she became the organizing secretary of the newly formed Ontario Federation of Home and School. Provincial federations were organized in British Columbia (1922), in Alberta (1929), in Nova Scotia (1936), in New Brunswick and Saskatchewan (1938), in Quebec (1940), and in Manitoba (1943). Membership increased about fifty per cent during World

War II and in 1945 reached a total of some 60,000 in some 1300 local associations. The eight provincial federations were united in the Canadian Federation of Home and School, which had been formed in 1927. Penrose found in 1945 that in the opinion of educators in key positions the home and school movement had been successful in improving parents' understanding of their own children, in giving an appreciation of the work done by the school, and in developing co-operation and good relations between parents and teachers.

Private Schools

Before the setting up of local education authorities, schools established by private initiative frequently performed a public service. Thereafter they catered usually to limited groups — often to those who wanted their children to be educated in an exclusive environment, preferably remote from home. In Kingston, Ontario, as late as 1847 there were 25 private schools with 621 pupils and only 10 common schools with 798 pupils. At the time of Confederation, Protestant schools in Montreal under the direct control of the board had only 15 teachers and 750 pupils, while private Protestant schools had 88 teachers and over 3000 pupils. But by 1878, if not before, educational opinion within the public school system was no more than tolerant of private schools. In that year an editorial in an educational journal quoted a statement that had appeared in a Canadian newspaper to the effect that "private schools are a necessity and should be encouraged, and parents who can afford it should leave the public schools to the children of the poorer classes."[30] The professional journal not unnaturally expressed regret at the tone of this statement and pointed out that the public schools were the schools of the nation, not

of a certain class. It did not object to permitting well-to-do parents to send their children to private schools but strongly condemned the notion that they ought to do so.

PRIVATE SCHOOLS AND THE PUBLIC

By that time also there were strong protests against support from public funds to any institution charging high fees and regarded as exclusive and private. Upper Canada College, founded in 1829 as a superior grammar school, had aroused popular disapproval from the first. It had been favored by the government with an original endowment of land, with advantageous adjustments in its endowment, and with substantial grants of money. After the secondary schools had been brought under the control of the central authority, there was bound to be trouble about exceptionally generous treatment of any one institution. Attacks at the time of Confederation resulted in little more than the appointment of a parliamentary committee and the publication of a pamphlet in defence of the college by its principal. Around 1880 the indignation of teachers in ordinary schools and of the public was expressed with renewed vigor. It was claimed that about one and one-half million dollars had been spent on the college during its fifty years of existence. Comparisons were made between the annual grants of about $23,000 to the college and $2000 to the Toronto Collegiate Institute. An attack in the *Brantford Expositor* admitted that Upper Canada College had once been the principal feeder of the university but had since "degenerated into a high-toned boarding school, exhibiting nothing remarkable in its teaching or management." The *Canada Educational Monthly's* version was that it had in the main "degenerated into a nursery for the propagation of youthful priggism." In 1881 a special report of the minister of education defended the college as a provincial high school, claimed that its annual income from endowment exclusive of land and building was only $15,000, and pointed out that $10,000 was received in fees. The minister was anxious to obtain a special appropriation of $30,000 to enlarge its boarding facilities. But a petition of high school teachers and trustees requested that the money used for the college be "restored" to the public secondary schools. At the end of the century Upper Canada College became wholly dissociated from the government and strictly a private school.

Another curious attempt was made between 1900 and 1902 to provide special privileges for a few, partly at public expense. The so-called experiment, supported by Goldwyn Smith in a pamphlet reprinting his article in the *Canadian Magazine*, purported to combine the public and voluntary school ideas. In January, 1900, the Avenue Road Voluntary Public School opened with twelve pupils and enrolled over thirty by 1902. The scheme was to have parents pay a voluntary fee to supplement the money expended through the public school board. They planned in this way to obtain specially qualified teachers and to offer an enriched curriculum, including such subjects as elementary Latin, drawing, music, and religious instruction. To impartial school administrators the import of such an arrangement must have been apparent.

If minority groups had been permitted to supplement the standard educational diet in detached little public schools of their own, they would inevitably have become pressure groups to reduce the basic program paid for by taxes. The principle which safeguards public education from degeneration into a shabby charity is that those who want better schools for their own children must help to provide them for all children in the administrative area. Unfortunately those who had no objection to providing special education for their sons and daughters at their own expense were usually advocates of strict economy and bare essentials in public education for the many.

The ratio of private and public school enrolment in the twentieth century was fairly constant in Canada. In nine provinces together, one pupil attended a private elementary or secondary school for every twenty-three pupils who attended publicly controlled day schools in 1921, and one pupil for twenty-two in 1948. Two-thirds of the private school enrolment was in the province of Quebec, where the ratio to enrolment in the publicly controlled system was roughly as one to ten. In the rest of Canada the ratio was one in thirty in 1921, and one in forty in 1948. It was considerably lower in Saskatchewan and Alberta.

THE PRIVATE BUSINESS COLLEGE

Although there were always private schools whose proprietors offered to prepare young people for positions in the commercial world, the private business college as we know it dates in Canada from 1860. In that year the British American Business College was opened in Toronto to give the student specific training for employment as a clerk, bookkeeper, or stenographer. The school with the longest history is probably the Ontario Business College, established at Belleville in 1868. Shaw Schools, Limited, traces its origin to the founding of the Central Business College of Toronto, in 1892. In Vancouver, the Pitman Business College was established in 1898 by Miss E. A. C. Richards.

The period of rapid expansion for private business colleges was from 1880 to 1920. During the 1920's the public school systems expanded their offerings of commercial education and made a serious effort to meet the need. The result was reduced enrolment in the business colleges.

A further drop came during the depression, when there was little chance to obtain tuition fees and little incentive on the part of students to pay them. Between 1935 and 1938 attendance increased, then fell off, then increased during World War II. The marked swings are illustrated in the following table:

YEAR	BUSINESS COLLEGE ENROLMENT
1921	30,000
1922	23,000
1933	17,000
1947	41,000

There were several reasons for the appeal of private business colleges. Until the 1920's they provided, in many places, the only efficient instruction in commercial subjects. Then and later they were convenient in not requiring any set level of educational attainment for admission. Since the instruction was largely individual, a student might enter at any time. Since the program was strictly vocational, effort was concentrated and directly motivated, so that much could be achieved in a short period. Courses usually extended over six to ten months, the shorter period being sufficient for stenography or bookkeeping alone and the longer period for complete secretarial training. Fees ranging from fifteen to twenty dollars a month, at the dollar values before the inflation which began during World War II, were obviously a good investment when jobs were likely to be available.

COMMERCIAL EDUCATION IN PUBLIC HIGH SCHOOLS

The chief reason, however, that private business colleges were both necessary and successful was the prejudice against practical education at the secondary level. In Canada this prejudice was the more effective because the curriculum was controlled by central education authorities, which were more susceptible to university influence than local school boards. Many of the latter would have been willing to accede to a popular demand for vocational courses if they had had the power. In exceptional cases academic secondary schools did offer students the alternative of a commercial course. In the province of Quebec an institution called Masson College, founded in 1847 to give classical education, offered at the time of Confederation a "comprehensive commercial course" of five years, in which the third year, and the third year only, was devoted to such subjects as bookkeeping, commercial arithmetic, commercial correspondence, and other commercial subjects, including stenography. The high school in Montreal introduced a commercial department in 1870, abolished it in 1877 to strengthen the position of Latin, and reintroduced a commercial option in 1891. In 1889-90 eleven of fifteen classical colleges in Quebec had commercial courses. From 1885 Ontario offered a vocational option in high schools and a commercial diploma, and British Columbia a commercial course as one of three optional high school programs. But in practice, most schools simply taught a few commercial subjects, notably bookkeeping, and offered nothing equivalent to the vocational preparation available in the business colleges.

Events in Winnipeg will illustrate the introduction early in the twentieth century of comprehensive commercial courses in city schools. The Collegiate School Board of Winnipeg set up a two-year commercial course as an option in the last two years of high school in 1899. The enrolment at first was somewhat disappointing — only 39 in the spring, and 59 in the fall. Commissioners of the department of education expressed the opinion that possibly the academic environment did not develop the "business idea" and suggested that it might be well to adopt the arrangement and methods followed in private business colleges, in order to give the commercial department a stronger hold on students who were disposed to elect that option. But by 1906 the commissioners of the department were well pleased with the progress of the commercial department in the Winnipeg Collegiate Institute. Whereas it had begun with "a couple of score of boys and girls who found the regular courses of study rather irksome," it had in the later year 122 bright boys and girls with a definite purpose in mind. The commissioners recommended the establishment of similar departments in Brandon and Portage la Prairie.

In 1906 British Columbia introduced a two-year commercial course leading to a commercial diploma, lengthened it to three years in 1914, and in 1930 offered a four-year course leading to a senior business diploma and high school graduation.

Real impetus to commercial education in publicly controlled schools came with federal grants to vocational education in 1919. In Ontario, the Vocational Education Act of 1921 made specific provision for commercial schools and vocational departments in vocational schools. The ease of obtaining money for vocational education and the great demand for such education caused a building boom between 1920 and 1930 in nearly all commercial centres of the province. Most of the schools were composite to some extent — academic-commercial-technical, academic-commercial, or technical-commercial. But Toronto, Ottawa, and Hamilton had large commercial high schools.

Development in the Maritime Provinces was somewhat retarded. In New Brunswick a commercial course which included instruction in typewriting and other subjects was introduced in 1921-22. The following year the Vocational Education Act was passed, in 1926 the Saint John Vocational School was opened, and during the next few years commercial departments were established in four or five other high schools. The full courses in New Brunswick and Ontario were usually three and four years respectively, but some schools in both provinces introduced a one-year course for those who had completed high school.

Summary

The characteristic local authority became an elected school board although there was reluctance to have city trustees and secondary school trustees elected directly by the people. The size of rural administrative areas tended, if anything, to grow smaller until about 1935, but reorganization since then has established larger units throughout almost the whole of English-speaking Canada. The consolidated school movement made only limited progress in the early part of the twentieth century, but numerous regional high schools for rural pupils have been built during the last decade. City school systems showed the way in introducing many educational improvements, including better school buildings. But the most significant advance was the assumption of local responsibility for the support of education during the third quarter of the nineteenth century, when taxation on all property was substituted for rate-bills on parents who were not always able and willing to pay. Until recently in most provinces the relatively large share of school costs that fell to the local communities kept the people aware of their role as school supporters. The trend towards assumption of a larger proportion of educational costs by the provinces has given added importance to other ways of maintaining local interest, including the home and school movement, which has greatly expanded since World War I.

Private schools in Canada became relatively unimportant after 1850, although private business colleges answered the demand for practical education before the publicly supported schools.

Over the past 150 years more people locally have assumed more responsibility for public education, in spite of recently increased help from provincial governments. Through payment of taxes, election of school boards, and direct interest in the work of schools, they have provided more education and more varied education to meet the needs of a larger proportion of Canadian children.

CHAPTER 17

The Church
and Public Education

CONTINUATION AND DECLINE OF CHURCH RESPONSIBILITY · THE SEPARATE
SCHOOL ISSUE · NEWFOUNDLAND · QUEBEC · AN OPPORTUNITY LOST?
CHURCH AND INDIVIDUAL RIGHTS · HOW SEPARATE SCHOOLS WERE FORMED
HOW SEPARATE SCHOOLS WERE PERPETUATED · SPECIAL PROBLEMS · MANITOBA
SASKATCHEWAN AND ALBERTA · THE MARITIME PROVINCES · BRITISH
COLUMBIA · RELIGIOUS INSTRUCTION AND RELIGIOUS EXERCISES · SUMMARY

In nearly every aspect of education the Canadian position is between that of England and that of the United States. Denominational schools and religious instruction within the public school system are found virtually everywhere in England, in some parts of Canada, and virtually nowhere in the United States. Much of this chapter deals with the history of "separate" schools, or tax-supported denominational schools, in Canada. The chapter also includes a brief history of religious education and related issues.

Continuation and Decline of Church Responsibility

Acceptance of a close relationship between religion and education was part of the educational tradition inherited from the old world. If any education was to be provided for ordinary people, the church, or some philanthropic organization associated with the church, was assumed to be the only proper agency. A type of school which continued to reflect this traditional attitude in some places was the Sunday school. Religious denominations co-operated in obtaining support for such schools. In Kingston, the Union Sun-

RULES

FOR THE

SUNDAY SCHOOLS.

1. **T**HE hours of School are, from 9 o'clock in the morning till public worship begins ; and from 3 o'clock till 4 in the afternoon. At the opening and closing of the School, it is expected that all the children should be then present.

2. Any Scholar who shall be absent from School three successive Sundays, without a sufficient reason being given, shall be dismissed ; but with liberty of appealing to the Committee.

3. If any Scholars do not come clean, washed, and combed, or be guilty of lying, swearing, pilfering, talking in an indecent manner or otherwise misbehaving ; and if, after repeated reproof, the Scholar shall not be reformed, he or she shall be excluded the School.

4. No book shall be taken away from the School on any pretence, without the permission of the teacher.

Part of an early nineteenth-century notice regarding Sunday Schools (Public Archives of Canada)

day School Society was under a general committee comprised of all ministers of religion in the town and fifteen laymen "of whom six shall be of the Church of England, three of the Roman Catholic Church, three of the Presbyterian, and three from the Wesleyan Methodists." [1] The duties of the committee included the purchase of books, catechisms, and supplies and a quarterly examination of scholars, who received instruction in schools of their respective churches, in which an annual sermon was to be preached "for the benefit of the General subscription." In New Brunswick, where Sunday schools were very common, all denominations were said in 1847 to have united cheerfully for their support and to have kept them well supplied with books and teachers. Sunday schools for secular instruction had been succeeded by mid-century in most of Canada by church Sunday schools for religious education only, but there were curious survivals of the older type. In 1886 the inspector of schools in Yarmouth and Shelburne Counties, Nova Scotia, found that Sunday schools aggravated his difficulties in raising the low standard of education in his inspectorate:

Lately I had the opportunity to introduce the subject to a "leading" citizen and told him the opponents of the school were depriving the young people of an education. He promptly contradicted me, asserting that they had a good "Sunday School" where all were taught to read the "word" and added triumphantly, "That is enough for any man."

Other denominational schools, supported as a charity, were to exist for some time. The Newfoundland School Society began operations in Canada in 1838 and was said to have had about 70 schools there in 1844. A Church of England school society had 16 schools in Quebec in 1849. Because of the retarded development of community schools of the people in parts of New Brunswick, a few Madras schools in that province survived until almost the end of the century. These schools had flourished in the 1820's and 1830's. With support not only from the government of New Brunswick but from ardent church people in England and in the colony, they had been able to provide education at very little cost to parents. They modified their rules regarding church attendance to attract the children of dissenters, who could then take advantage of the moderate fees with a clear conscience. But when schools of the people began to be established and some more active interest in education was stirring, the Madras schools ceased to command respect. Lynam says that a commission of 1845-46 reported their efficiency as doubtful, and that the chief superintendent in 1862 mentioned only four Madras schools and rated only one as good. Yet there were eleven Madras schools still in existence when the free school legislation in 1871 made their extinction only a matter of time. The Madras School Society relinquished its charter in 1900. In spite of these few survivals, however, schools of paternalistic origin had been numerically overwhelmed by public schools more than fifty years before.

The educational work of the church and clergy received commendation from many quarters. King Louis XIV of France praised Laval for his "continued care to hold the people in their duty towards God and towards me by the good education you give or cause to be given to the young".[2] More than a century later and far to the west, the Hudson's Bay Company recognized "the great benefit being experienced from the benevolent and indefatiguable exertions of the Catholic mission at Red River."[3] Regarding early educational efforts of religious philanthropy in Newfoundland, the first archdeacon attested that "many are the children who have learnt to read and pray, who, but for the teachers of these schools, would have known nothing."[4] Grammar school trustees appointed by lieutenant-governors welcomed the services of clergy as masters. In 1825 when there was difficulty in finding a suitable teacher at Kingston, even

for an inducement optimistically estimated at £350, the trustees asked that the incumbent be also given an appointment as clergyman, "for which he would receive competent remuneration." Only for the clergy of the Church of England was appreciation expressed so handsomely in monetary terms!

Time was when the church of the aristocracy had enjoyed a unique position. Lands were reserved for the support of its clergy. Only they could perform a marriage ceremony, and only the bishop could license teachers of children. These exclusive privileges were gradually relinquished. John Strachan at one time calculated the number of Anglicans by subtracting the number of known adherents of other denominations from the total population.* But even he saw reason to suggest to the lieutenant-governor in 1830 that it might be "expedient to insert the names of Roman Catholic and Presbyterian clergymen" in revising the list of grammar school trustees.[5] Such conciliation of respectable error did not extend to Methodists, who were gaining a disturbing number of converts by going out among the people even in remote areas. The Church of England had too few capable and energetic clergy and too many with airs of social superiority which made people feel more at home elsewhere. An observer in 1851 wrote that the church had less hold on the people than Presbyterians, Baptists, and Roman Catholics for the very reason that its clergy were "independent of the people in pecuniary matters" and had therefore not "cultivated them as the other sects have."[6] If that was true, Anglican influence declined for the same reason that religious schools provided for the people gave place to schools which the people themselves maintained. By mid-century the Church of England

* Lower (131), pp 236-37

had lost all but a remnant of its former educational prerogatives.

Before then, in the 1830's, even the Church of Rome was in temporary danger of losing control. When French-speaking parliamentarians in Quebec became increasingly assertive, many of their people seemed as ready to follow new secular leaders as to follow religious leaders. An intelligentsia of sorts was threatening to break the rule of the curés. But the rebellion of 1837 discredited the new movement and strengthened the church. By mid-century the clergy, specifically mentioned in the School Act as eligible for election as trustees, exerted a strong influence on local boards, and immediately after Confederation the hierarchy was fully represented in the central authority.

Protestant revolt against Anglican domination extended to a distrust of any ecclesiastical influence in the management of school affairs. In Nova Scotia in 1821 an amendment to the school act stipulated that one trustee had to be a licensed minister of the gospel or a justice of the peace. In Upper Canada in 1832, grammar school trustee Leslie of Perth tendered his resignation in deference to "the wish of the Lieutenant-Governor to appoint as members of the Board of Education some clergymen of this District."[7] The people and their representatives began to express other views. In New Brunswick it was enacted that after June, 1830, no clergyman in charge of a congregation of any Christian faith could be appointed as master or usher in any grammar school. In the same province during debate on the Act of 1847 a member named Porter warned against having clergymen for inspectors, on the ground that they were always jealous of one another and interfered with one another's suggestions. In Prince Edward Island a Dr. de St. Croix advised the legislative assembly to have local boards consist of seven members, three of whom should be *ex officio* the rector of the parish, the officiating Roman Catholic priest, and the minister of the Presbyterian congregation; but in 1840 a special committee of the legislative assembly advised that no clergyman should be a trustee of a school unless he sent his child or children to that school. In 1861 in the Eastern Townships of Quebec at the fifth convention of the Teachers' Association of St. Francis a resolution was passed "that no priest, curé or officiating clergyman shall have power to prescribe what books shall be used in the schools, and that part of the law conferring such powers be repealed."[8] The Act of 1876 in British Columbia included a clause to the effect that no clergyman should be eligible as superintendent, deputy superintendent, teacher, or trustee. In 1892 in the Northwest Territories a man prominent in political life and actively interested in education moved a section of a bill "to bar any clergyman from taking any position whatever in the school system."[9]

The chief reason for such actions and the attitudes they reflect was the perpetual difficulty caused in educational administration by denominational zeal and bigotry. Another reason was the indifference or hostility shown by many clergy to public education. Montreal's first Protestant board of three clergymen and three laymen seldom met because of the difficulty of obtaining a quorum. When they received $558 from the city in 1847 for the operation of schools, they invested the money because "they had no use to which to apply it." But whatever their cause, these developments illustrate a decreasing respect for ecclesiastical authority in school affairs. At the end of the nineteenth century, in the election of 1896, it was possible for Laurier to win 49 of the 65 Quebec seats in spite of denunciation by Roman Catholic clergy, who admonished their parishioners to vote for candidates opposed to his policy on the Manitoba school issue.

The Separate School Issue

As an educational issue, the separate school problem is logically insoluble. The Roman Catholic concept of the purpose of education and of the function of the school is not the concept which produced the public school system. Arguments for or against separate schools are based on entirely different assumptions. Members of the Royal Commission on Education in Ontario could not agree after five years even on the history of separate schools in the province and had to write two versions of the past. To have devised a dialectic acceptable even for discussion of present difficulties would have been a major achievement. To have arrived at recommendations acceptable to both points of view would have been a miracle. Yet the majority and minority reports of the commission were admirably thorough, and the plan proposed by the majority so truly ingenious that its merit had to be ignored by the government if they were to escape embarrassment.

Roman Catholic education accepts authority in a way that is not only inadmissible but apparently incomprehensible to Canadians of another mind. Those who rely on their own judgment are unlikely to appreciate an institution which defines truth and requires observance with a precision that leaves little scope for individual discretion. The Roman Catholic Church holds that it is the primary and essential function of a school to teach revealed truth of a definite and indisputable character in order to ensure the eternal salvation of the child. To a large number of people such a statement is no more than a sequence of words — a sentence intended to convey a thought, but with no more practical sense in it than in such teachings of Jesus as may seem not meant to be taken literally. But if the statement is taken as true, it follows that the Roman Catholic Church must insist on control of what is taught to Roman Catholic children. Since it is difficult for those already taxed for one school to pay for another, the church must fight tenaciously for existing separate school rights and aggressively for their extension.

Public school education in North America, on the other hand, was constructed by the people to meet a community need. The ground was cleared for the public school by repudiation of paternalistic authority. The foundation was laid by the people's assumption of responsibility to provide education. The structure was completed by the ability of people to exclude differences of religious faith and of economic status from community school affairs — whether in classroom instruction or in providing financial support. The only school that could operate on such a principle was the common school. Its primary purpose was to educate the children for life in the community that founded it. The teacher was expected to stress good morals and broad religious content helpful to adherents of various faiths, but never to expound divisive doctrine.

The separate or denominational school was not an invention of 1841, but a survival from the eighteenth century and earlier. Government grants were not always given first to public schools and then diverted to sectarian schools. They were given at first to sectarian schools in countries where old-world views continued — in England for thirty-seven years before schools under local boards appeared belatedly in 1870, and in Quebec spasmodically before and after public schools appeared temporarily in 1829. When central education authorities were set up in England in 1839 and in Canada shortly after, grants to denominational schools, where there were such grants, were channelled through these central education authorities. But all such assistance was paternalistic, for the common people had no thought that they were spending what they themselves had contributed. The anomaly in the continuance of public financial support to denominational schools stems from general taxation for educational purposes and from democratic concepts of government and taxation. The anomaly became immediately apparent with reference to local finance when free schools were established, and gradually more apparent with reference to provincial grants as popular awareness of provincial taxation grew more acute.

Since the beginning of this country a growing number of people have become more and more convinced that it is right for people to control their own affairs. By 1850 this principle was established, and thereafter applied increasingly in government. At the time of Confederation not many would have consciously acquiesced in taxation for purposes over which they had no control. It is as certain as any conjecture can be that a large majority of non-Catholic Canadians would, if they could, refuse financial support from public funds to schools controlled by any religious denomination. They would also refuse to exempt from taxation any group that claimed exemption on the ground that the group was paying for equivalent services of a special type. The reason for this attitude is an anti-authoritarian conviction which is anathema to the Roman Catholic Church and perhaps incomprehensible to many Roman Catholics.

Democracy is a form of civil government acceptable to the Roman Catholic Church, and a form of civil government preferred by Roman Catholics in Canada. But to a large proportion of the non-Catholic population democracy is also *the* right way of life. Whether they think about it clearly or at all, and whether they have reconciled it with the sometimes fuzzy doctrines of Protestantism, the non-Catholic Canadian ordinarily acts on the assumption that it is right for the

people to decide for themselves on any question, religious or political. This concept of democracy — that self-determination is unquestionably right, and that democratic government is the only acceptable form of government — is condemned as error in Roman Catholic teaching.

Hence the issue of public versus separate schools is more than an educational problem. It is a clash between control of the people by traditional old-world authorities and a way of life still being worked out by the people of North America. The issue cannot be resolved by arguments about schools. Within the limited field of educational administration, it is probably most advantageous to advocate nothing and to resist pressure that anything be done — to try to maintain classical serenity, though not beauty, by an existing arrangement to which nothing can be added and from which nothing can be taken away. Social and political evolution will bring about educational changes in this respect as in others. For the sake of the young, who are surely innocent, both sides might avoid making the school a battleground for fighting out basic disagreements, if fight they must. An understanding of how the present Canadian arrangements came about should be conducive to educational peace. The exaggerated tensions of the past have a humorous aspect which engenders good-natured tolerance now.

Newfoundland

In Newfoundland the little that had been done educationally before 1836 had been done almost entirely as a religious charity. The beginning of a state-supported denominational system, in the opinion of Rowe, was marked by a grant that year to the Irish Benevolent Society. At the same time the assembly made an effort to provide schools under the control of local boards of laymen. The churches, as we saw, scotched this attempt. Clergy were admitted to control of local boards in 1838, grants and school districts were divided between Roman Catholics and Protestants in 1843, and the whole school system was subdivided among denominations in 1874. Bishop Feild of the Church of England was the most powerful proponent of Church schools. With somewhat unwelcome support from the Roman Catholic Church on principle and from Protestant non-conformists as jealous rivals, he won a victory, not for the Anglican faith, but for denominationalism. For example, when the government opened an undenominational academy in St. John's in 1845, students were deterred from attending by thunder from the Anglican and Roman Catholic Churches. Though it had a good staff of three, it had never more than twenty scholars and closed its doors in 1850. Eight years later, according to Hickman, there were four separate academies with salaries fixed by legislation rating the denominations as follows: Roman Catholic, £600; Church of England, £400; Wesleyan Methodist, £200; and general Protestant, £150. Thus secondary education, like elementary, came under denominational control.

It is not possible to identify cause and effect in the interaction of forces which has left the government, the economy, the churches, the schools, and the people in their present relationship and condition. By Canadian standards, the money provided for schools in Newfoundland is insufficient in amount and inefficiently spent, the educational achievements correspondingly low, and the denominational influence inordinately strong. That educators in the province are dissatisfied with conditions is clearly indicated by Hickman, who gave this graphic illustration in 1941:

But schools are built and Government money *should* be spent to provide the best possible education for the children. The denominational system does not do this. The writer knows very well a town of about 2000 inhabitants. There are five schools with an average attendance of about fifty. This means that there is one teacher in each, and that teacher usually has to do the work of all Grades from I to XI. This is practically impossible, and since we have an external examination system, the younger pupils are generally neglected, the evil of which is cumulative. If this town had one school instead of five, a well equipped building could be maintained, and the work of all the grades could be divided among the five teachers according to the aptitude of each teacher for a particular phase of the work. This would make for efficiency, and the pupils would get a much better education.[10]

But Newfoundland as a province has a right to its own educational values, which presumably are those that interested people prefer. The people generally in local communities have not undertaken to develop a controlling interest in schools of their own provided at their own expense. The denominational school system was given a constitutional guarantee by a statute of Canada in 1949.

Quebec

In the province of Quebec a unique situation made public schools and denominational schools synonymous. This was possible only because of the religious homogeneity of the French-speaking Canadians. Among them, and among them only in Canada, it was possible for the people to unite in support of a denominational school. Since the church immediately sought supervisory power when schools under elected local boards were established in 1829, the schools were never as completely schools of the people as in Protestant communities. Contented to have limits set to the area of their intellectual responsibility, and protected from the influence of liberal thought, the ordinary people of French Canada did not take

Plan of a school at St. François du Lac (Public Archives of Canada)

complete control of education. The anti-clerical influence of the *Institut Canadien* and the *Rouge* party had too little time and scope to arouse any widespread enthusiasm for non-sectarian schools. Strengthened by the discrediting of any such forces associated with the rebellion, the Roman Catholic bishops protested against the power given to the superintendent and the exclusion of ecclesiastical authority in the Act of 1841. In that year the Jesuits returned as a teaching order. As we have seen, the influence of the church in educational administration was greatly strengthened by subsequent developments. The Roman Catholic system of Quebec became a public denominational school system similar in structure to the undenominational systems elsewhere; but the central authority of the state, the local authority of the people, and the teaching staff are permeated and controlled by ecclesiastical personnel and religious influence.

In Quebec the separate schools of the dissentient minority are classified as Protestant. Since the conglomeration of reli-gious groups so defined embraces all non-Catholics, including Jews since 1903, it would appear at first glance that their schools must be wholly undenominational. But the Church of England, emerging with commendable grace from its fortified position as the church of a ruling aristocracy, was not unreasonably anxious to retain the denominational school privileges granted by its government to the church of the majority. Private schools with an Anglican atmosphere therefore continued. Moreover, even the public schools of assorted Protestants retained a consciousness of religious differentiation and a tinge of the characteristics of the denominational school, including greater prominence to religious instruction and payment of fees by parents able to afford them. On the other hand, the comparatively small number of Protestants in most places made a common public school all the more necessary, and the schools are essentially of this type.

When Lower and Upper Canada were united in 1841 as Canada East and Canada West, the government of the two prov-

A school at St. François

inces was subjected to pressure not so much to get schools established as to secure or prevent denominational control of schools. There were forty petitions to the legislature asking that the Bible in its entirety be used as a textbook in common schools. Other petitions, including one from Roman Catholic bishops, asked that the Roman Catholic Church and other denominations be consulted before legislation was passed. Deadlocked because of the strength of Catholicism in Canada East and of Protestantism in Canada West, the assembly turned over the drafting of an education bill to a committee, two-thirds of whose members, according to Hodgins, were representatives of Canada East. The act that was passed gave the right to any number of adherents of a religious faith, different from that of the majority, to set up a separate school if they dissented from the "regulations, arrangements, and proceedings made by the Common School Commissioners." The principle thus established was applied subsequently in separate legislation for the two provinces. In Canada East after

1846 a Protestant minority, or a Roman Catholic minority in the few places where Protestants were more numerous, could withdraw from support of the majority school, elect trustees, and operate a school of their own. They shared in the government grant, were exempted from taxes for the majority school, and were empowered to determine and collect taxes for the support of their own school.

The Protestant minority in Quebec was granted equality and independence much more rapidly and fully than the Roman Catholic minority in Canada West. For example, school municipalities of the majority and the minority could be set up or altered independently of each other, and no stipulated number of heads of families was needed to establish a dissentient school. In contrast, legislation in Canada West imposed irritating restrictions obviously designed to obstruct and limit the expansion of separate schools. The minority in Quebec acquired a distinct central authority, which was virtually independent after 1875, and secretaries of this Protestant committee attested that

French-Catholic superintendents gave the committee a free hand and supported its decisions. They also acknowledged the generous support of the Roman Catholic committee on such occasions as the passing of an amendment in 1869 to permit independent taxation of the two categories of school supporters in Montreal and Quebec; the Roman Catholics suffered financially by this change, whereas Protestant revenues from taxation increased — in Montreal from $8000 in 1868 to $23,000 in 1871 and to $59,000 in 1875. Again, since 1869 corporation taxes in Quebec have been divided between the two systems in proportion to school enrolment. In other provinces Roman Catholic minorities maintained ·that they were at a great disadvantage for the want of such an arrangement.

There is, however, another side to the argument. In Quebec the majority were supporters of the denominational school principle, so that the independence of both central and local authorities was no more a concession than a desire. Legislation of 1841 to provide for an undenominational normal school met a cold reception from the Roman Catholic Church. When the Protestants were given a normal school of their own in 1856, the privilege could hardly be regarded as a concession to the public school idea. It could be argued also that in a division of corporation taxes by school population, more was taken from relatively well-to-do Protestants and more was given to relatively numerous Roman Catholics. Such an argument would have no validity if applied to an entirely public school system, but it does carry weight if the premises of denominationalism are accepted. The director of Protestant education in Quebec (1953) characterized as an "unhappy incident" a request of the Protestants in the late nineteenth century for an amendment which would have had all members and shareholders of corporations declared Protestants or Roman Catholics for taxation purposes. Also to be considered, though not to be overemphasized, is a slight reduction of minority privileges in 1899: an amendment took away from the two committees the right of nominating school inspectors, although candidates for appointment still had to have qualifications determined by the committees. On the whole, however, the English conquerors of Quebec are right in thinking that they have been fairly treated by the majority of Her Majesty's loyal subjects of that province.

An Opportunity Lost?

In spite of the principles and logic of Catholicism, the English-speaking Canadian inevitably asks whether it might not have been possible for all Canadian children to attend the same public schools. A previous chapter offered evidence of such mixed education in the early nineteenth century. There were many other instances. An advertisement in the *Upper Canada Gazette* in 1817 indicated that a commercial academy and boarding school in Quebec was taught jointly by Protestant and Roman Catholic teachers. The National School Society of Montreal in 1835 had on the roll 295 pupils of various denominations — 148 Church of England, 48 Church of Rome, 55 Kirk of Scotland, and 44 Protestant dissenters. A return of the British Canadian School of Quebec in 1841 showed the highest attendance on any day as 227 and the lowest as 55, and added that the smallness of the latter number could be "accounted for by the circumstances of none of the Roman Catholic Boys attending School during any of their holidays."[11] In 1840 a capable and conscientious school visitor named Robert Armour reported that in the parish of Dorchester a private school for boys and girls was taught by a Protestant who gave the Irish Catholics the church catechism.

Armour recommended the establishment of a "superior seminary" at Dorchester and was confident that it would be supported by "the numerous better-class British population and a few Canadians of the towns" if it were "conducted on a liberal scale without privilege to any Religious community."[12] In 1848 a school conducted at Sorel by the Church of England School Society was crowded by the attendance of Roman Catholics as well as Protestants; in the evening it was attended by from fifteen to twenty French-speaking Canadians. One faraway example must suffice to show that the same conditions existed generally: the St. John's School in the Red River area was attended by sons and daughters of well-to-do French-speaking families living farther up the river.

What had the church to say about the education of Roman Catholic children at mixed schools? In the archiepiscopal archives at Quebec is a document dated August 5, 1820, in which Rome advised the bishops that the Methodists, especially in Ireland, were seeking to "infest" Catholic children with "false Bibles" and to open biblical schools for them. The bishops were therefore urged to advise parents not to send their children to such institutions, and to open schools themselves, particularly for poor children in rural areas.[13] The conclusion to be drawn from this communication must surely be that the Roman Catholic Church objected to Protestant religious teaching in schools attended by its children, and that the occurrence of such teaching was a cogent reason for the establishment of Roman Catholic schools. The same reasoning was followed in canons of the Roman Catholic Council of Baltimore, which Bishop Charbonnel in 1852 quoted in a letter to Egerton Ryerson. With reference to attendance of Roman Catholic youth at public schools, pastors were admonished to "take especial pains lest such youth use the Protestant version of the Scriptures,

or recite the hymns or prayers of Sectaries." "It must be carefully provided," the canon continued, "that no books or exercises of this kind be introduced in the Public Schools, to the danger of faith and piety." In his letter to Ryerson the bishop wrote that "if the Catechism were sufficiently taught in the family or by the Pastor, so rare in this large Diocese; and if the Mixed Schools were exclusively for secular instruction, and without danger to our Catholics, in regard to Masters, Books and companions, the Catholic Hierarchy might tolerate it."[14]

One answer to our question, therefore, is that public schools might have been acceptable to all if they had been secular. But in Canada the old-world tradition was too strong to permit the sharp break with the past that was made in the United States. An amazing aspect of the separate school controversy in Canada West was the complete assurance with which Protestant non-conformists maintained that the religious exercises and the reading of the Bible were entirely undenominational. Had it not been for this zealous lack of perception, successful legislation might have been drafted early in the 1840's to establish two-denominational schools in Canada East and neutral common schools in Canada West. There would then have been no separate schools in Ontario or the middle west, and no mention in the British North America Act of educational rights of religious minorities, except in Quebec.

Not that clergy and staunch churchmen would have been happy about the public school. When the union came about in 1841, John Strachan, Anglican Bishop of Toronto, petitioned the legislature for public support of denominational schools. Twelve years later Adam Townley, presbyter of the diocese of Toronto, published letters demanding separate schools for members of the Church of England. A sample from one of his diatribes against

Ryerson shows the strength of feeling engendered by religious views at the time:

We can assure the Reverend concocter of our most insidiously irreligious Common School Acts, that Churchmen have consciences *almost* as tender concerning distinctive religious truth, as those of the followers of the papacy; and that, consequently, we would sooner entrust our children to the care of even the idolatrous worshipper of the blessed Virgin than to the cold neglect of a Protestant sectary who would keep them from the arms of their Saviour, by denying them the blessed Sacrament of baptism.[15]

But the Anglicans soon became supporters of the public schools and won the commendation of Ryerson when they "stood forward as a phalanx against the seductions presented to them" in separate school amendments proposed by the Roman Catholics in 1855.

The attitude of Roman Catholics at first appeared to be quite tolerant. According to a report of a council of the Society for Promoting Christian Knowledge in Quebec, the Roman Catholic bishop had been perfectly satisfied with the instruction in the Church of England National School. In Quebec in 1841 Judge Charles Mondelet advocated the setting up in each locality of a French school and an English school, both non-sectarian in the sense that religious instruction should be restricted to beliefs common to Roman Catholics and Protestants. According to Ryerson, Bishop Power in Canada East between 1841 and 1847 lamented separate schools as a misfortune and wanted them only in so far as they were necessary as a "protection from insult" to Roman Catholic children in cases where they could not attend a public school without being subjected to opprobrium. But later, when separate Roman Catholic schools had for a long time played the role of inferior rivals of a public school of Protestant aspect, there was bitterness. In 1879 the headmaster of a separate school in Belleville, Ontario, wrote, with particular reference to undenominational teacher training:

The boasted state school, in all its intellectual glory, is but the cradle of infidelity, the noxious nursery of a Godless race.[16]

There was no dearth of strong statements of the clergy, of which the following reported utterance of the Roman Catholic archbishop in Kingston, Ontario, in 1887 is among the more sweeping:

Our public schools are destroyers of modesty, an abomination and a disgrace . . . I have heard boasts of the school system of the country, but I tell you such an ignorant system the world never saw before.[17]

It is unnecessary to show that the Roman Catholic clergy in more recent years have not only spoken but worked unceasingly for the extension of denominational education.

These developments confirm the impression that a chance for completely public education in eight provinces was missed in the 1840's. It is true that the earlier attendance of Roman Catholic children at mixed schools may have been due partly to the extreme difficulty of setting up schools of their own. But the Roman Catholic people, of their own volition, would hardly have discontinued such arrangements. Had their clergy not been aroused by active Protestantism in the schools, the mixed school of 1830 might have become the public school of 1850.

Church and Individual Rights

Actually, as the majority of the Royal Commission on Education in Ontario pointed out, "no right or privilege in our school system was granted at any time, or preserved, inferentially or otherwise, to the Roman Catholic Church or any other church as a religious body, organization, or denomination."[18] The privilege of setting up a denominational school and securing public support was offered to people in local communities. In Canada West, at least, the law indicated that the decision rested with the individual whether he would join with others of the minority religious persuasion in asking for a separate school. After various amendments, the wording in the last pre-Confederation Act of 1863 stated that the decision was to be made at a meeting of "persons desiring to establish a Separate School." The same act provided that any Roman Catholic might withdraw his support of a separate school — a safeguard of individual discretion inspired by public school preference and contrasting with the repeal of the same privilege in Quebec in 1908 to ensure continuance of relatively costly support to the minority. Hodgins, who was Ryerson's secretary and right-hand man, also emphasized that it was one of the important issues "to recognize and uphold the individual right of parents — without compulsion or interference — to choose for themselves the school to which they would send their children."[19] Ryerson believed that there was a "general disinclination of Roman Catholics in Upper Canada to isolate themselves from their fellow-citizens in school matters" and could claim that the number of separate schools, never more than 50, had declined to 20 in 1851, when there were about 3000 common schools in the province. Apparently some new cause or influence was at work thereafter, for there were 100 Roman Catholic separate schools in 1857 and a steadily increasing number thereafter. At the time of Confederation less than five per cent of elementary school pupils were enrolled in separate schools, and at the end of World War II nearly twenty per cent.

In Canada West ten years of relative peace after 1841 were followed by twelve years of religious warfare. In those twelve years the Roman Catholic Church won ad-

ditional privileges for the separate schools: the right to have more than one such school in cities and towns in 1851; exemption from common school rates while the taxpayer's children were at school in 1853, and at all times in 1855; trustee boards with power to tax in 1855; abolition in 1863 of the requirement that separate school supporters so declare themselves year by year; and other concessions, including a reduction from twelve in 1850 to five in 1863 of the minimum number of heads of families who could take the initiative in establishing a separate school. Every step of the way the issues were fought against stubborn resistance. Although Ryerson and the Protestants saved the public school system, their begrudged and partial concessions exasperated the Roman Catholic clergy, who renewed the assault when Ryerson complacently believed that lasting peace had been signed. Accusations provoked counter-accusations. Reciprocity in prejudice and deception made questionable statements and practices all too frequent.

An extract from a letter of the Honorable John A. Macdonald to Ryerson in 1855 illustrates the political handling of the issue:

Our Separate School Bill, which is, as you know, quite harmless, passed with the approbation of our Friend, Bishop de Charbonnel, who, before leaving here, formally thanked the Administration for doing justice to his Church.

He has, however, got a new light since his return to Toronto, and now says that the Bill won't do. I need not point out to your suggestive mind, that, in any article written by you on the subject, it is politic to press two points on the attention of the public.

First. That the Bill will not injuriously affect the Common School System. (This for the people at large.)

Second. That the Separate School Bill of 1855 is a substantial boon to the Roman Catholics. (This is to keep them in good humor.)

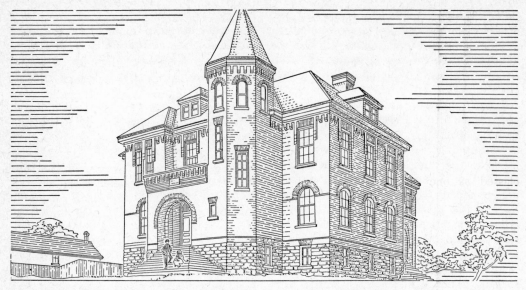

Roman Catholic separate school at Mattawa, Ontario, about 1895

You see that, if the Bishop makes the Roman Catholics believe that the Separate School Bill is of no use to them, there will be a renewal of the unwholesome agitation, which I thought was allayed.[20]

The gains made for separate schools were nevertheless substantial. Eight years later, against the opposition of Ryerson, the government of Sanfield Macdonald passed legislation making further concessions and establishing the pattern which Confederation made permanent. This act of 1863 had been drafted earlier by R. W. Scott, a prominent Roman Catholic member of the legislature. It was supported by John A. Macdonald and his friends, who accused the government of changing sides. Although members from Canada West voted 31 to 21 against the bill, 55 votes from Canada East passed the law for the neighboring province by a whacking majority of 45.

In spite of everything, however, one basic right was preserved for the people of Ontario regardless of their religious persuasion — the right of the individual to decide whether he would support or continue to support a separate instead of a public school. This right of the individual was wholly or partially lost in other separate school provinces. In Saskatchewan after disputes, legislative amendments, and judicial decisions on the issue between 1911 and 1917, it evolved that the religion of the taxpayer left him no choice in supporting either the public or separate school, and that once declared to be a separate school supporter he had no right to withdraw. Although the issue did not go to the courts in Alberta, the law there was the same and presumably would have been sustained to the same effect if challenged.

How Separate Schools Were Formed

The law in Ontario, therefore, from 1841 to the present imposed no obligation on anyone to establish or support a separate school. A number of schools taught chiefly or entirely by Protestant or by Roman Catholic teachers could remain under the control of a single board, and still did in some places in 1950. How, then, did it come about that local communities took advantage of the easy divorce? Lapp, in his study, *The Schools of Kingston,* gives an illuminating account of events in that city.

From 1841 there had been in Kingston a school of the Sisters of the Congregation of Notre Dame. When the first elected school board for the city took office in 1850, this Roman Catholic school was classed as one of the common schools under the board. Similarly a school opened by the Christian Brothers in 1852 came immediately under the board's supervision. In 1853 there were 718 pupils in the schools, including 275 children in the two schools mentioned, including, also, Roman Catholic as well as Protestant children in another school taught by a Roman Catholic teacher named O'Donnell. Both Protestants and Roman Catholics were members of the board.

No trouble occurred until the summer of 1853. Then a short flare-up was started by a rumor that the public examination of the Christian Brothers school would be held in the Roman Catholic cathedral and that admission would be by ticket only, to keep the general public from attending. Feeling subsided when arrangements were made to hold the examination elsewhere and tickets were found to be readily available. But another fuse was lighted when a visit of inspection was paid to Mr. O'Donnell's school by several trustees, including a priest of the Roman Catholic Church and a priest of the Church of England. It was alleged that when the latter began to address the pupils, the former interrupted and challenged his right to speak to the children of that school.

An acrimonious controversy ensued. Thirteen letters on the subject appeared in the *Kingston News* between July 19th and August 12th. "These letters," says Lapp, "did not show how the argument at O'Donnell's school really started, nor

who was chiefly to blame; in fact they showed little except the intolerant and unchristian attitude adopted by all parties concerned. The point in dispute was soon obscured by attacks on doctrine and principles."[21]

The next year the chairman of the board was the Reverend Mr. Smith, a professor of Queen's University. The chairman and six other Protestant members voted against paying the salaries of teachers in the two schools conducted by religious orders, but the vote was a tie. Ryerson, when appealed to by Smith, pointed out that persons belonging to religious orders were not thereby disqualified as teachers of common schools. Then, in the fall of 1854, one of the Roman Catholic trustees died and a Protestant clergyman was elected as his successor. Thus reinforced, the other two Protestant ministers, who had moved and seconded the amendment regarding salaries, were able to carry a motion that the two schools be struck off the list. Immediately the Roman Catholics petitioned for a separate school.

The disruption in this case must be attributed chiefly to bigotry and prejudice. No doubt the election as board members of several clergymen with strong professional bias made the clash inevitable.* In spite of the potential cleft in the school system, division of local communities might not have come so frequently or so soon if only laymen had been concerned with school administration. When a split had been made, controversy did not necessarily cease. In 1853 in Toronto, where Roman Catholics had separate school privileges in all wards, the *Globe* accused both Roman Catholics and high church Anglicans of conspiracy to defeat the ablest member of the common school board by having votes cast by women, by separate school supporters, and by men who had voted before.

* See p. 304.

How Separate Schools
Were Perpetuated

To achieve Confederation in 1867, it was necessary to guarantee provincial autonomy in education. This alone might have satisfied the Roman Catholic majority in Quebec. The danger of a constitutional guarantee of the rights of religious minorities to separate schools was pointed out in the Confederation debates by John Sanfield Macdonald. A Roman Catholic, he opposed any restriction on provincial rights, as did Laurier in the Manitoba school question thirty years later. These were Macdonald's words:

I say, sir, that by making a constitutional restriction in respect to the schools of the minority, we are sowing the seeds from which in the end will rise a serious conflict, unless the Constitution be amended. The minority will be quite safe on a question relating to their faith and their education in a colony under the sway of the British Crown; but if you expressly withdraw that question from the control of the majority, the rights of the minority will not be safe in either section of the Province, if you distrust the action of the majority. It is our duty, sir, to see that a question which affects us so dearly as the education of our children . . . shall not be withdrawn from the management of the local Legislature. . . . You may rely upon it, other religious bodies will be sure to protest against any particular creed having special rights, or an exclusive monopoly of certain privileges, whatever they may be.[22]

Nevertheless Section 93 of the British North America Act as ratified in 1867 did impose restrictions on provincial democracy in these terms:

In and for each Province the Legislature may exclusively make laws in relation to Education, subject and according to the following provisions:
    (1) Nothing in any such law shall prejudicially affect any Right or Privilege with respect to Denominational Schools which any class of persons have by law in the Province at the Union.

Against this rock of the first proviso, arguments regarding separate schools have broken, and approved plans for school reorganization have been shattered. It is doubtful whether any other law or pact in later Canadian history has evoked controversy, bitterness, litigation, and frustration in comparable measure. Who were primarily responsible?

Woodley argued that major concern in the Confederation debates was shown for the rights of the Roman Catholic minority in Canada West. It is true, as she says, that there was pressure for privileges enjoyed by the Protestant minority in Canada East. On the other hand, Weir rejected the "widespread but erroneous belief to the effect that the Roman Catholics of Upper and Lower Canada were primarily responsible for the introduction of the element of separatism into certain of our school systems."[23] He regarded the Protestants of Quebec as the group responsible. They considered their rights to dissentient schools were inadequately safeguarded by law and sought legislation to strengthen their position. Evidence of their concern has been preserved in a pamphlet expressing the views of Sir William Dawson, Principal of McGill University.* Subsection 2 of Section 93 in the British North America Act was designed to give Protestant dissentient schools in Quebec the security and privileges enjoyed by Roman Catholic separate schools in Ontario. The third subsection permitted an appeal to the governor-general-in-council, an authority likely to be sympathetic towards English-speaking Protestants. Immediately after Confederation the Roman Catholic majority in Quebec fulfilled a pledge to pass legislation granting further concessions to the Protestant minority, whereas

* See bibliography, 65.

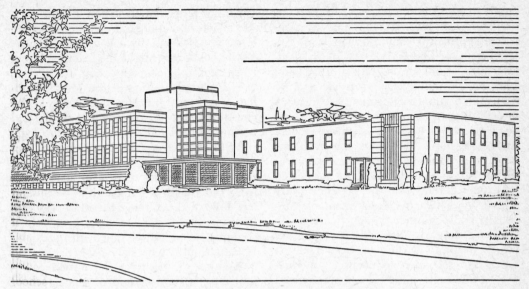

Ecole Notre-Dame de l'Assomption, Arvida, Québec, 1951

Ryerson and others in Ontario were indignant at pre-Confederation demands of the Ontario minority. Clearly the Protestants of Quebec were both advocates and immediate beneficiaries of the separate or dissentient school clauses in the constitution.

After Confederation there was little controversy or difficulty in Quebec, as might be expected in a province favorably disposed to denominational schools. In Ontario, however, hope for a unified system survived. In 1881, when the *Toronto Telegram* published interviews with various people on the perennial question, the editor of the *Canada Educational Monthly* expressed views held by many educators:

In the past history of the Province, the concession of Separate Schools was a necessity, and, at the time, an act of wisdom. Now-a-days, when bigotry, it is to be hoped, is buried, and our Public Schools are thoroughly secularized, a return to a common system, with all the advantages which a common system has to offer, would seem to be wisdom.[24]

The next year, however, the separate schools were first given inspectors of their own. Periodically, suppressed antagonisms broke out, as in 1922 during an aggravated dispute about corporation taxes, which caused the Roman Catholic Archbishop of Toronto to write a pamphlet in refutation of the social unity argument for public education and in support of religious education. On the whole, the separate schools held their own, although they suffered financially with the increase in services and costs of public education, as did denominational schools in England.

Special Problems

Destined to be a persistent problem in Ontario was determination of the upper limit of separate school rights within the graded school structure. Secondary education has always been more sharply demarcated from elementary education in Ontario than in other English-speaking provinces, although even in Upper Canada some common schools occasionally had pupils in Latin before the Act of 1841, as in London in 1834. At the time of Confederation many common schools and a few separate schools had pupils in post-elementary subjects. Between 1896 and 1908, when public school trustees were empowered to offer secondary education in continuation classes and schools, where no high school existed, separate school trustees acquired the same power. But a privy council ruling in 1928 made it clear that separate school privileges permitted only an alternative form of elementary school, for which the department of education could determine curriculum. In Ontario, therefore, the religious minority has no right to exemption from taxation for public secondary education. In Quebec, Protestant minority rights extend through the academic secondary school grades.

But the two-denomination system of Quebec raised another issue not encountered where public schools exist, the educational rights of Jews. Obviously there was no appropriate place for those who belonged to neither the Roman Catholic nor the Protestant category. Provision was made in 1869 for a neutral panel to receive taxes from sources not so classified. These sources included individual Jewish taxpayers, who in the following year were enabled to request that they be taxed for support of either school system. Under this arrangement the money received by the Protestant school authorities proved to be insufficient to cover the cost of educating Jewish children in Protestant schools. The problem in the city of Montreal was serious enough by 1888 to occasion one of the rare meetings of the entire Council of Public Instruction. The Protestant committee asked that Jews be regarded for educational purposes as Protestants; but a deadlock ensued. Not until 1903 did an act of the legislature provide that Jews should pay local taxes as Protestants, count as

Protestants in the allocation of the provincial grants, and send their children to Protestant schools. By a conscience clause, Jewish children might be excused from Protestant religious education.

This partial solution of the Jewish problem was not entirely satisfactory. The constitutionality of the act was challenged because it violated to an extent the legal right of the larger minority group to conduct schools of a Christian Protestant character. The act was also inadequate from the Jewish point of view because it left Jews without the right of representation on the Protestant board of school commissioners. After much dispute and litigation, an act of 1930 gave the Jewish population of Montreal the option of establishing a third system of schools under Jewish school commissioners, or of entering into an agreement with either of the existing boards. Choosing the second alternative, they made an agreement with the Protestant board in Montreal for a fifteen-year period on much the same basis as that provided for by the Act of 1903. The Roman Catholic board, however, was to share with the Protestant board the excess cost over revenue entailed in the education of children of Jewish taxpayers.

Woodley points out that in the cosmopolitan city of Montreal it is by no means impossible that other minorities, neither Protestant nor Roman Catholic, may claim identification. Since it is unlikely that either the Jews or any new minority group will want to establish a separate system of schools, it is conceivable that in the Montreal area the structure of denominational schools may someday be successfully challenged.

Manitoba

On joining Confederation, Manitoba in 1871 set up a dual system similar to that of Quebec. The two sections of the central authority had independent control of school management, discipline, curriculum and examinations, of the grading and the licensing of teachers, and of textbooks for moral and religious training. There were then 639 pupils in Roman Catholic schools and 876 in Protestant schools. But the Protestant system outgrew the Roman Catholic and by 1887 had more than four times as many pupils in attendance. By then, the great increase in rural population necessitated the establishment of many new school sections and made people keenly aware of the relatively high cost and economic inefficiency of duplicate school facilities. As early as 1876 the Protestant section of the board tried to obtain the abolition of the dual central authority, but action was postponed by an increase in the number of Protestant members. Then in 1890 legislation was passed to set up a single system of free, non-sectarian, public schools. This action led to a spectacular nation-wide battle on the Manitoba School Question.

The point at issue was whether the Manitoba legislature had power to abolish separate school privileges. The Manitoba Act of 1870 had reiterated the guarantees of the B.N.A. Act and had inserted two words in the first provision to cover denominational school rights possessed not only by law but by "practice" at the time of union. A test was made in the courts by a case arising from a Winnipeg by-law under the Act of 1890, according to which all property-owners were to be taxed for the support of public schools. The validity of the act was upheld by two courts in Manitoba, denied by the supreme court of Canada, and confirmed by the privy council in 1892. The pre-Confederation right to conduct denominational schools at private expense had not been abolished by the Act of 1890, which had revoked the privileges of provincial and local support and control granted by legislation in 1871 and 1873. The Roman Catholics, therefore, under the second

provision of the Manitoba Act, sought and secured by a privy council decision in 1895 an appeal to the governor-general-in-council. Their rights had been prejudicially affected, as Weir says, "in fact although not in law." In response to the appeal, the Conservative government at Ottawa tried to get the Manitoba government to restore separate school privileges and, having been unsuccessful, promised to pass remedial legislation compelling such action. The passing of such legislation was blocked by the Liberals until an election intervened in 1896. Laurier took a stand for provincial autonomy in education and for no coercion. Under his leadership the Liberals were elected to power.

Next year, in 1897, minor concessions were granted to the Roman Catholics by amendments legalizing religious education from 3.30 to 4.00 p.m. and the employment, by request, of a Roman Catholic teacher when there were 25 or 40 pupils of that faith attending respectively a rural or urban school. Of 91 separate schools, 25 were disbanded and 27 accepted metamorphosis into public schools. In Winnipeg and Brandon, however, former separate schools continued in operation as parochial schools without support from public funds. Subsequently there were contortions to secure denominational privileges within the school system: a 1912 amendment made "school" mean "classroom," so that the employment of a full complement of Roman Catholic teachers could be legally ensured in a graded school attended exclusively or predominantly by Roman Catholic children; then in the following year the Winnipeg board was asked to take over two parochial schools and retain their teachers. The board refused, and a new provincial government in 1916 repealed the amendment. The sequence of events in the four years 1912-16 was accompanied by a commotion of pledges by French-speaking Roman Catholics, resolutions of the Orange Grand Lodge, bitterly fought elections, and storm clouds everywhere.

Newspaper items on the basic issue of 1890 are quoted by Simms to illustrate the opposing points of view. The *Manitoba Free Press* on the tenth of February, 1880, stated the public school creed:

The ground we take is that it is not the duty of the state to teach religion but the duty of the Church. We stand upon the broad ground, that public money should in no case be devoted to the propagation of the dogmas of any particular class or denomination.

A letter signed "Irish Canadian" in the *North West Review* appealed in September, 1889, for sympathetic consideration of the Roman Catholic archbishop's position:

We see him, afflicted in spirit, because of the demon of intolerance which is abroad. It must indeed be painful to His Grace to reflect that popinjays, who rode but yesterday into the country, can embitter the closing years of his life by suggesting legislation which would deprive his people of rights they hold most sacred.

Early in 1890, a discussion in the *Manitoba Free Press* supported this argument for the *status quo*:

Will the abolition of separate schools result in the improvement of these schools? If the Roman Catholics will accept such legislation and conform to the school the State offers them, then an affirmative answer may fairly be given to this question.

They will continue to maintain their distinctive schools at their own cost, but with much less efficiency and with a rankling sense of injury, bearing fruit in protests, agitations and class animosities. Can any patriotic citizen contemplate such a prospect with satisfaction?[25]

Saskatchewan and Alberta

As for Saskatchewan and Alberta, the North West Territories Act of 1875 established and limited provincial autonomy over education in the following terms:

When, and so soon as any system of taxation shall be adopted in any district or portion of the North West Territories, the Lieutenant-Governor by and with the consent of the Council or Assembly, as the case may be, shall pass all necessary ordinances in respect to education; but it shall therein be always provided, that a majority of the ratepayers of any district or portion of the North West Territories, or any lesser portion or sub-division thereof, by whatever name the same may be known, may establish such schools therein as they may think fit, and make the necessary assessment and collection of taxes therefor; and further that the minority of the ratepayers therein whether Protestant or Roman Catholic, may establish separate schools therein, and that, in such latter case, the ratepayers establishing such Protestant or Roman Catholic separate schools shall be liable only to the assessments of such rates as they may impose upon themselves in respect thereof . . .[26]

The first issue to be settled later was whether the Quebec or Ontario pattern should be followed. At first, a preponderance of Roman Catholics secured the adoption of the Quebec pattern when the ordinance of 1884 set up a dual central authority. Thereafter, however, increasingly strong opposition to denominationalism secured the adoption of several amendments and new ordinances, which between 1891 and 1901 took away the privilege of licensing teachers and appointing inspectors, introduced unified teacher training, textbooks, and examinations, provided for denominational schools only where public schools had been established first, and established a single central authority with an advisory council as the only vestige of the two former denominational sections. After 1889, when the Territorial Assembly petitioned the Dominion government for removal of the restrictive clauses from the N.W.T. Act, it was clear that an increasing majority of the people resented the system of education which had been fastened on their country when it was new and sparsely populated. In that year there were only 969 pupils and 36 teachers in 31 Roman Catholic schools out of 4574 pupils and 183 teachers in the 163 schools of the territories.

As the population increased, the discrepancy became greater and the commitments of the past more irritating. In a twenty-year period after 1884 only 16 of 1360 newly organized districts were for separate schools, of which two were Protestant. From the abolition in 1892 of Roman Catholic control of school districts independent of public school districts, only four separate schools had been established, although the 1901 census had shown twenty per cent of the population as Roman Catholic. At the beginning of the twentieth century the Territorial Assembly passed a resolution requesting provincial autonomy. Action was delayed by the Laurier administration, allegedly because of Roman Catholic clerical influence at Ottawa. In 1905 Laurier introduced an autonomy bill which might have restored the conditions of 1875. In March, Sifton resigned from the cabinet as unable to believe "that it would not be better that the Legislature of the North West Territories should be free" and as unwilling that there be any "taint of what I call ecclesiasticism in schools . . . unless the people of the North West choose to have it . . ."[27] Laurier's bill was also fiercely attacked by Haultain, the leader of the government in the territories. Laurier compromised by passing an amendment bill which in effect made Section 93 of the B.N.A. Act apply to Saskatchewan and Alberta in such a way as to perpetuate separate schools as organized under the ordinance of 1901. Throughout these proceedings there were expressions of strong feeling not only in the west but throughout Canada. From one point of view traditional rights of the church were threatened; from the other, new world democracy was fettered and the universality of the public school endangered.

In the controversy that re-appeared in Saskatchewan, one of the issues was the allotment of school taxes paid by corporations. Amendments passed by Alberta in 1910 and Saskatchewan in 1913 stipulated that a company might specify that money paid in taxes be distributed to public and separate schools according to the proportion of its non-Catholic and Roman Catholic shareholders, and that otherwise revenue from taxes so paid would be divided according to the proportion of the taxes paid by persons who were public and separate school supporters. In Saskatchewan this issue was a subject of acrimonious dispute and litigation from 1913 to 1915. In Quebec after 1869 the taxes paid by corporations were allotted to Protestant and Roman Catholic schools in proportion to the number of pupils enrolled, or, in Montreal and Quebec city, to the school population. In Ontario after 1886 corporations were permitted to require that the whole or any part of their property be assessed for the support of separate schools. This was in accordance with the principle applying in Ontario alone that any individual, and presumably any taxpayer, might contribute to either type of school entirely at his own discretion. If the proportion of a corporation's taxes that might go to separate schools were limited by the proportion of Roman Catholic shareholders, this principle would be violated, since such action is logically based on the contrary assumption that the taxpayer's religion should determine the destination of his taxes. In 1936 Ontario legislation designed to apply the latter hypothesis fully was actually passed. It required a division of corporation taxes on the basis of shareholders' religious profession; the law proved unworkable, and was repealed in the following year. Even Weir, who in 1934 had written that amendments of the Alberta-Saskatchewan type "would probably remove the prejudice to which separate school supporters in Ontario consider themselves subjected," had emphasized also that the western provinces were different from Ontario on the critical issue of the taxpayer's right to decide. Perhaps because equity in any enforced division of such taxes would inevitably be specious and ironical, the Royal Commission on Education in Ontario recommended that they be turned over entirely to the undivided secondary schools.

One paradox of several connected with public and separate school systems of Canada is that the federal government, usually punctilious in avoiding interference with the educational systems of the provinces, should be in a position to throw its weight on one side only. Sheane mentions a written agreement of 1873 between Canada and certain Mennonite delegates from southern Russia:

The fullest privilege of exercising their religious principles is by law afforded the Mennonites, without any kind of molestation or restriction whatever, and the same privilege extends to the education of their children in the schools.[28]

Such a commitment did not protect established rights of religious minorities but compromised the educational autonomy of the provinces in favor of denominational schools. The document is dated two years before the passing of the North West Territories Act, which subsequently restricted the operation of public education in Alberta and Saskatchewan, where ethnical and religious minorities caused great difficulty. In the event, the people of the Canadian west were compelled to choose between breaking agreements which had been made by others in their name and, alternatively, failing to provide adequately for the education of their children. Not only Roman Catholics but numerous Protestant sects attempted, perhaps with prior assurances of their right, to educate their own children. But as Goresky says, the multiple divisions among the people made "agreement upon a state system almost a necessity" and forced provincial governments to curtail denominational school rights which impeded the establishment of schools for the majority.

The Maritime Provinces

"In Nova Scotia there has never been the bitter antagonism between Catholics and Protestants which has unfortunately prevailed in some other provinces of Canada," said the Honorable Mr. Justice F. A. Anglin in 1910 in an address before the Catholic Educational Association in the United States. No arrangement regarding denominational schools can please everyone, and in 1930 the Grand Orange Lodge of Manitoba vehemently attacked the Nova Scotia system in a pamphlet which purported to show "how the excellent non-sectarian school law is violated in the interest of the Roman Catholic Church." But one is inclined to agree with Mr. Anglin and to accept the explanation of the Honorable Mr. Fielding, a Protestant, who for many years was Premier of Nova Scotia:

We have no separate schools by law in Nova Scotia, but I say that we could not have brought about that happy condition if we had not been disposed to meet our Roman Catholic brethren in a generous spirit...[29]

More than sixty years before, on February 19, 1846, the Honorable Joseph Howe had sounded the keynote for such a policy:

We may make education a battle ground, where the laurels we reap may be wet with the tears of our country . . . But without mutual forbearance, and a spirit of compromise, we can do little good, and make no satisfactory and permanent settlement of these questions.[30]

Conceivably the strong traditional loyalties in the Maritime Provinces fostered a respect for denominationalism. Possibly a longer history in closer contact with Great Britain built a firm base for the continuance of attitudes favorable to the denominational school. But geographical propinquity to New England, where Horace Mann won his notable victory for the non-sectarian common school, and the similar views of people who had come to the Maritime Provinces from the United States in previous years were no less influential. Both sides were willing to compromise. The working arrangement arrived at in Nova Scotia and New Brunswick was the same, but developments in the latter province were more eventful, even if relations between Protestants and Roman Catholics were not always as happy.

Long before Confederation there were many Roman Catholic schools. At least one in New Brunswick, established by the Reverend James Dunphy in 1835, was a free school for the education of poor children of any denomination. Shortly after it opened, the school received a government grant and had an enrolment in its two divisions of about 200 boys and nearly as many girls. Other Roman Catholic schools were of various types. Most of them were elementary, some were secondary, and in one at Bathurst both English and French were used as the languages of instruction. Many of the earlier schools were co-educational. Secondary schools for girls were established after 1854 by the Religious of the Sacred Heart and by the Sisters of Charity, and in 1864 by the Congregation of Notre Dame in Newcastle. About that time the Christian Brothers came to Saint John and established schools for boys.

Around 1852 when the optional free school law of New Brunswick was passed, there were many petitions to the legislature: against state aid to denominational schools, for a separate school law, in favor of Bible reading in all schools, and in favor of denominational instruction. A compromise clause in the Act of 1858 permitted Roman Catholic children to use the Douay version when the Bible was read in school. This provision was retained when the Act of 1871 required that all elementary schools in the provincial system be free, tax-supported, and non-sectarian. Regarding that bill, which passed the council by a narrow margin, Lieutenant-Governor Wilmot said:

Most sincerely do I hope that under its operation we may soon see, in every part of the Province, children of all denominations of Christians gathered into the same schools . . . sitting on the same forms . . . forming youthful friendships to be continued in after years when the real life-work is entered upon, and when all denominations are inevitably gathered into the World's Great School . . .[31]

But the *Morning Freeman,* a Roman Catholic paper, mockingly called the lieutenant-governor "Pope" Wilmot and referred to his council as "Methodist Cardinals." The paper also made reference to "Red Republicans of Paris, now in revolt against God and Society." As usual the Roman Catholic argument was that the schools would be "either Protestant or Godless and Infidel" and that in either case they would not be acceptable to the Roman Catholic population. They claimed that the requirement in the Act that schools be non-sectarian was a violation of rights established by the Act of 1858, in which the teacher was enjoined to "exert his best endeavors to impress on the minds of the children committed to his care the principles of Christianity. . . ." But the supreme court of New Brunswick found no support for this contention and the privy council in 1874 dismissed an appeal with costs.

Then came an interesting development. The minutes of the executive council show that five members of the assembly, on behalf of the Roman Catholics, submitted four propositions:

That the pupils residing in all populous places where there may be a sufficient number of children to form two or more schools, should be permitted to attend schools outside of the districts in which they may reside.

That regulations be made to provide for the granting of licenses to persons holding certificates from the superior of any religious order, or where such persons hold no such certificates that provision be made for the examination of such persons at their place of residence or school rooms.

That in schools taught by the Christian Brothers and Sisters of Charity, or which may be attended by Roman Catholic children, the teachers shall not be compelled to use any books which may contain any thing objectionable to them in a religious point of view. . . .

That provision shall be made that the trustees shall allow religious instruction to be given in the schoolrooms under their control after regular secular school hours, said hours to be shortened to the extent allowed for religious instruction.

There is a document in Fredericton, presumably authentic, giving the replies that the executive council recommended that the lieutenant-governor should make to these propositions: that the trustees might permit children to attend any of the schools within a district; that a candidate holding a certificate from the superior of any of the Roman Catholic teaching orders might be examined for a teachers' licence without attendance at training school; that the greatest care had been and would be taken to keep the school books free from objectionable matter and that the board of education would be asked to consider the insertion of notes in a history textbook on certain portions of the text to which exception had been taken; and that where the trustees agreed, school buildings might be used for reli-

gious instruction after the end of the school day. This gentlemen's agreement is said to have restored a fair degree of harmony.

In both Nova Scotia and New Brunswick the following procedure was devised to set up publicly supported schools of a character acceptable to the Roman Catholic Church. The public school trustees might rent schoolrooms or the entire building of denominational schools, appoint as teachers those recommended by the owners of the rooms, and operate the school in accordance with the law. In some towns pupils were withdrawn from public schools to form convent schools as a preliminary to the above process, which was then carried out with the help of favorably disposed members of the public school board. In Halifax the school board appointed as teachers in certain schools applicants nominated by Roman Catholic members of the board. Presumably any other denomination or group of people might obtain the same privileges by appropriate action.

Developments in Moncton will serve as a particular illustration of the procedure. Before 1886 all Roman Catholic children of St. Barnard's parish, whether English-speaking or French-speaking, attended the same schools as other children. Then the parish priests gathered all Roman Catholic children together and got Sisters of Charity to teach them. Shortly after, when a convent had been built, the two-language groups were taught in separate rooms. Then the parish was divided — the English-speaking congregation retained the name St. Barnard's and the French-speaking congregation formed the parish of Notre Dame de l'Assomption. In 1923 the latter parish completed the building of Sacred Heart Academy and rented it to the city. The pupils in the sixteen classrooms were taught by nuns. This completed the transition from public schools, attended by all, to denominational schools in which pupils were segregated not only by religion but by language.

Those who suspect that arrangements of this kind were not always conducive to harmony will find confirmation in McNaughton's account of the Bathurst school case. In the New Brunswick town and village of that name boys attended public schools, although there was a parochial school for Roman Catholic girls. But in 1890 the Roman Catholics of the district engaged Sisters of Charity as licensed teachers of boys as well as girls, and the school board took over several convent classrooms for operation as publicly supported schools. The enrolment at the former public schools was reduced to a number which made efficient grading impossible. In 1892, on grounds of economy, the board engaged a primary teacher with an inferior licence valid only in Acadian, or French-speaking Roman Catholic, districts, with the result that Protestants withdrew their children until the teacher resigned. In 1893, in spite of an agreement of all ratepayers that the principal of the grammar school should be a Protestant, the position was given to a Roman Catholic without a grammar school licence, a son of one of the trustees and a former inspector who had been removed from office for gross neglect of duty. Protestant ratepayers opened a private school, and two Protestant clergymen were moved by subsequent incidents to telegraph the premier that Bathurst was on the verge of a riot.

High feeling was aroused throughout the province. In the press and on the public platform defamatory remarks and accusations were exchanged. The Honorable John J. Fraser, judge of the supreme court, was appointed to investigate the charges. Although he criticized the appointment of the teachers mentioned and the crowding of convent classrooms, he upheld the actions of the board on most counts and found no support in the evidence for a contention that the clergy had interfered with the operation of the schools. He found that the Roman Catholic catechism had been taught in some schools at noon, but not in wilful violation of the law; and although Roman Catholic prayers had been used, there was no regulation against their use and certainly no ground for belief that Protestant pupils had been compelled to kneel or to cross themselves. Peace was not restored immediately.

In 1953 such issues were still recurrent. In Edmundston, Protestants objected when the school board allegedly refused to build them a school of their own and offered instead more economical premises for Protestant classrooms on the third floor of a convent school building. On the whole, however, arrangements in the Maritimes for denominational schools appear to have caused relatively little friction.

British Columbia

Only in the far western province did no vestige remain, after Confederation, of denominational schools supported by public funds. A major cause of this exceptional development is to be found in the close association between religious education and the denominational school — an association which some have always regarded as obvious, but which others have been unwilling to face.

In the early days religious instruction was emphasized no less in British Columbia than elsewhere. In 1851 Governor Douglas in recommending the establishment of elementary schools indicated that their purpose would be "to give a proper moral and religious training to the children of settlers." Five years later reports of the clergyman superintendent made it clear that Biblical instruction was customary if not always efficient. Of his visit to one school he wrote:

The examination in Scripture was inadvertently omitted till too late on the day of the public examination, but I had examined the school previously in this subject, in which I did not find that the children had made the same improvement as in some others.[32]

But the government had become so impatient of religious controversy by 1863 that it gave a first grant to a school on the mainland "upon the clear understanding . . . that the School which the grant is to aid be open to all persons and be maintained on non-sectarian principles."[33] During the next two years religious education was debated everywhere with some vigor, and resolutions were passed at a public meeting in New Westminster in favor of education on a religious but non-sectarian basis. Governor Seymour saw the incongruity of definite religious teaching and publicly supported schools.*

An act of 1865 made the implications of non-sectarian principles clear:

All Schools established under the Provisions of this Act shall be conducted strictly upon Non-Sectarian Principles. Books inculcating the highest Morality shall be selected for the Use of such Schools, and all Books of a Religious Character, teaching Denominational Dogmas shall be strictly excluded therefrom.[34]

The clergy were permitted to visit schools and impart religious instruction. In 1865 this was given in a separate room to children of each denomination, but in 1869 only after school hours. By 1870 the inspector-general reported that there were no longer religious difficulties; and the Act of 1872 confirmed the position that schools should teach the highest morality and no religious dogma. Subsequently, in 1876, when clergymen were debarred from holding positions in the school system, religious exercises were limited to the use of the Lord's Prayer and the Ten Commandments and were left to the option

* See p. 233.

of the trustees. For two years after 1879, the central authority forbade even these religious exercises, but thereafter permitted them again on condition that the trustees approved. By these measures, however objectionable to some, the schools were kept wholly public in character.

Religious Instruction and Religious Exercises

In the early period of our educational history, great stress was placed on the teaching of religion by leaders in church and state. Protestant leadership went almost as far as the Roman Catholic Church in making such instruction a primary function of the school. The Royal Instructions of 1784 to the governor of New Brunswick included this statement:

It is our further will and pleasure that you recommend to the Assembly to enter upon proper methods for the erecting and maintenance of Schools in order to the training up of youth to reading and to a necessary knowledge of the principles of religion.[35]

The same directive was given to the governor of Upper Canada and Lower Canada in 1791. But those of superior station who advocated religious teaching had almost always a political purpose in mind. They spoke in the same breath of maintaining loyalty to existing institutions and forestalling democratic aspirations among the populace.* There was not the same insistence on religious education by the people themselves. Hence public utterances on the subject in the early nineteenth century give an exaggerated impression of what was actually done in the classroom.

The central board of education in Upper Canada urged that school be opened and closed with prayer, that the New

* See p. 404.

Testament be read aloud, and that the forenoon of each Saturday be devoted to religious instruction. But Ryerson declared that "in not one school out of ten, if one out of twenty, were there daily prayers and Scripture Reading, or Religious Instruction of any kind . . ."[36] Moreover, the quality of the teachers and the teaching made it unlikely that pupils had any real understanding or appreciation of the Bible or of religious exercises in some of the schools where approved practice was observed. On the other hand, school reading books were compiled by authors who were zealous in giving religious direction, so that the verbal content of the curriculum was heavily weighted with that intent. It was also the common practice of teachers to have pupils memorize New Testament verses.

When public education systems were set up, central authorities as a rule abstained from prescription of religious activities. The characteristically cautious attitude was illustrated by Ryerson's statement regarding legislation of 1846 in Upper Canada:

The government does not assume the function of religious instructor; it confines itself to the more appropriate sphere of securing the facilities of Religious Instruction by those whose proper office it is to provide and communicate it. The extent and manner, in which this shall be introduced and maintained in each School, is left to the Trustees of each School.[37]

The same formula was followed in most provinces. Religious exercises, and religious instruction after hours if permitted at all, were left to the discretion of trustees in the local community.

Prince Edward Island was exceptionally cautious. The report of a special committee of the legislative assembly stated in 1840 that:

in regard to religious catechisms, it appears to many of the committee, that the insisting on the teacher giving lessons therein, is intruding on him a duty more incumbent on the parent.

In 1857 and again in 1858 the government refused to act on petitions that the Bible be read and Biblical instruction given in all schools; but in 1860 the government did authorize the reading of the Bible without comment at the opening of school to those who voluntarily attended for the purpose. From 1868 the school visitor in Queen's County made a check of the number of pupils "reading Scriptures" as compared with the number reading class books. As a result of his efforts the proportion of the former rose from thirty per cent to forty-five per cent in 1871, but fell back immediately afterward in 1873 to the former level.

The Act of 1877 and subsequent legislation also provided for Scripture reading without comment as an opening exercise, but emphasized that the schools must be non-sectarian. Trustees might have the Ten Commandments and other passages from the Bible memorized and recited, and have Scripture reading at the close of school.

The type of provision for Roman Catholic schools in the Maritime Provinces caused Nova Scotia and New Brunswick to be almost equally careful about prescription of Protestant religious teaching and exercises. In Nova Scotia at the end of the nineteenth century the superintendent stated that it was assumed that religious exercises were conducted, and that they were held before or after school hours if any objection was made. The nearest approach to religious instruction was the injunction that the teacher should "inculcate by precept and example respect for religion and Christian morality." In New Brunswick, opening and closing exercises with the use of either the Protestant or the Roman Catholic version of the Bible were permitted at the discretion of the trustees. The conditions in all three of the Maritime Provinces were unchanged in 1950, although Protestant church groups had tried during World War II to have religious instruction introduced in Nova Scotia and New Brunswick.

In the middle west, also, the decision was left to the trustees. In Manitoba, the Act of 1890 permitted them to have religious exercises conducted at the close of the school day. Subsequently, local clergymen or teachers as their representatives were also permitted at the option of the community to offer religious instruction during the last half-hour. In the Northwest Territories the ordinance of 1884 permitted religious instruction between 3 p.m. and 4 p.m., but a revision of 1896 allotted only the last half-hour of the day to such religious instruction as the trustees might allow, on condition that children of objectors might withdraw. This type of local option was confirmed on the formation of Alberta and Saskatchewan in 1905. Until 1918 in Alberta demands for religious education came from various pressure groups in the new country. During World War I, moreover, the Ministerial Association of Edmonton prepared a syllabus for religious education and tried by a public campaign to influence members of the school board to support its introduction. But the board refused to permit religious instruction in the public schools of the city.

During World War II, however, clergy and zealous laymen of the Protestant churches had greater success. In Saskatchewan and Alberta they redoubled their efforts to persuade local boards to use the optional half-hour for religious instruction. In Edmonton and Calgary and some other urban centres the boards agreed. In Manitoba in 1943, revised regulations increased the number of approved prayers, chosen from both Roman Catholic and Protestant books, and authorized for the first time the use of prescribed hymns in the optional religious exercises. Even in British Columbia, where recitation of the Lord's Prayer had been the only religious exercise permitted, a reversal of policy in 1944 made Bible reading without comment and use of the Lord's Prayer obligatory. High school credit was also given for Bible study taken extra-murally. In Nova Scotia in 1940 an interdenominational church committee obtained authorization of a syllabus of graded scripture reading lessons and of a form of devotional exercises, although their use was optional. Religious instruction was permitted, but only after school hours. In Canada as a whole, the coincidence of war and of gains for religious activity in public schools is striking, especially in contrast with failures at other times. In British Columbia in 1927 an effort was made to introduce Scripture reading and religious exercises, as was done eventually in 1944; in the peace-time year a motion to achieve the purpose by legislative amendment aroused so much opposition in the house that it had to be withdrawn.

By far the most basic change during World War II occurred in Ontario. There, for almost a century, the public school system had been conducted on the principle enunciated by Ryerson that it was not the function of the central authority to prescribe religious instruction. Religious exercises until 1884 were left by law to the discretion of the trustees, and in practice largely to the decision of the teacher, but were recommended by the central authority and were in general use. Religious instruction, also with the approval of the trustees, might be given by visiting clergymen — from 1857 until 1924 after four o'clock, and from 1924 to 1944 before or after school hours. Instruction by the teacher, as illustrated by a "general lesson" recommended in 1847, was ethical in character, though supported by references to Scripture. Such instruction was also optional, except from 1871 to 1875, when Christian Morals was included in the prescribed program for senior classes. Conditions and events connected with this innovation were of special interest.

Under the local option arrangements, formal lessons on Christian ethics by teachers, and after-school lessons on Christian dogma by clergymen, were seldom offered in the 1860's. Even in Toronto, a trustee favorably disposed to religious instruction lamented in 1866 that no clergymen, with the exception of a few Anglican ministers, had ever arranged to give such instruction, although he claimed that all pupils in one school had petitioned to be allowed to remain for classes taught by an Anglican minister. Hamilton set an unusual example in 1862 by having religious instruction offered by clergy of different denominations to the thousand or more pupils of the Central Union Grammar and Common School from three to four o'clock on Fridays, under a regulation that permitted school hours to be shortened once a week for that purpose. But there had been strong criticism even of recommended religious exercises in the popular press, which questioned the right of the central authority to establish any connection between church and state. During the period of prosperity before Confederation and for a decade thereafter most people were content to leave religious instruction to the Sunday schools. Such quiescence was provocative to Ryerson, who, in spite of the contentions of his opponents, and in spite of his honest caution in legal enactments, had an intense determination that the schools should be an active force for Christianity.

He wrote a textbook entitled *First Lessons in Christian Morals,* which a special committee of Protestant ministers in 1871 examined and recommended for sanction by the Council of Public Instruction. At first it was commended in reviews appearing in church publications, but it was then subjected to blasting criticism by *The Globe* and other newspapers. A protest against its authorization was signed by seventy-three clergymen, among whom Baptists were most prominent. An editorial in *The Ontario Teacher* said that the hostile criticism proved that:

> Even with the most ripened experience and the most extensive knowledge, it is difficult to avoid collision with those denominational preferences which, at the present day, so largely prevail.[38]

An alternative textbook was permitted, and in 1874 after a three years' trial Christian Morals as a prescribed subject was dropped from the curriculum.

After 1876 the appointment of a minister of education in Ontario opened to the churches and to others an avenue for political influence, and lack of secure confidence in worldly prosperity during the next twenty years made the time favorable for directing more attention to religion in schools. Adam Crooks as minister, in response to requests of the Anglicans and Presbyterians, interpreted the law in 1878 to mean that school boards might "require their Teachers to use the Bible or portions thereof as part of the ordinary exercises of the school, giving, however, such explanations only as are needed for a proper understanding of what is read." The next minister, George W. Ross, in whose own home Bible reading was regularly observed, proved amenable to recommendations from the clergy and a committee of the Ontario Educational Association. In 1884 revised regulations, making it obligatory for teachers to read the Bible without comment and to conduct religious exercises, were submitted to the house for approval and, according to the minister, were adopted without a dissenting voice. The next year an expurgated version of the Scriptures was authorized for use in schools. According to Matthews, it omitted verses "which might be considered objectionable reading for young minds"; but according to certain contemporary critics, it also omitted passages offensive to Roman Catholics. This "Ross Bible" was a cause of heated controversy until the full Bible was authorized as an alternative in 1887. In that year, because of other agitation, the teachers of the province thought it necessary to pass a resolution to categorize as "unreasonable" a request that they be obliged to give religious instruction in schools. Up to 1905 various church conferences and the Ontario Educational Association reiterated demands for such compulsory religious teaching. Having held out until then, the central authority was relieved of any strong pressure for many years.

Soon after the beginning of World War II, however, certain clergymen began to give religious instruction during the traditional school day. The regulations required schools to open at nine in the morning and close not later than four in the afternoon, but permitted the local board with the approval of the minister to make other arrangements. The procedure for the introduction of religious instruction was to persuade school boards to take advantage of the permissive regulation — that is, to have the school hours altered — in order to offer religious education between nine and nine-thirty, when children were at school, but legally before school opened. By 1941 the minister of education had approved forty applications of the kind, and at the end of the year clergymen were teaching at least one lesson a week in 628 schools. Devious arrangements were made with a minimum of publicity to provide for religious instruction at other times — at 11.30 a.m. and at 1.30 and 3.30 p.m. Then an interchurch committee and a committee of the executive of the Ontario Educational Association pressed strongly to secure a regular place for religious education on the school program and to have instruction given by either teachers or clergymen. In 1943 the Conservative party came to power, and the speech from the throne in February, 1944, announced that religious education would be offered in public and secondary schools. During the following school year textbooks were issued for a prescribed program of religious instruction in the first six grades. Regulations required not only opening exercises, including Bible reading, but religious instruction for two half-hour periods a week at the beginning or end of morning or afternoon sessions, either by teachers or, if local boards so decided, by clergymen or lay people selected by clergymen. As in all other requirements concerning religion in Ontario and other provinces in the nineteenth or twentieth centuries, parents of pupils could claim exemption. So, in this case, could the teacher or the school board. But the offering of religious instruction became the regular procedure, and the onus was placed on the objector to declare himself an exception.

Whether revolutionary or reactionary, this innovation was contrary to precedent in a North American public school system. In the denominational systems of Newfoundland and Quebec the churches and the central authority had long required and prescribed religious teaching. But in the other provinces of Canada and in all states of the United States, demands that the central authority exert such power had been rejected as contrary to public school principle. The minister of education in Ontario at the time, the Honorable George A. Drew, was moved by strong attachment to Great Britain to graft on the Ontario school system the religious instruction required by legislation of 1944 in England for a system of schools different in its origin and development. Although the plan was carried out in the elementary schools of Ontario, the proposal to introduce Protestant religious education in high schools was quietly dropped, presumably because permanent officials in the department of education advised the minister of its implications.

Millar, a deputy minister of education in Ontario at the end of the nineteenth century, made a clear statement on the issue in his book, *School Management.* He had been a proponent of Bible reading without comment and believed that the school should support the Christian religion as the foundation of morality. But as for the actual teaching of religion, he held it to be the responsibility of the parent to establish the particular religious sanctions that would serve as a basis for moral training in school. "The end of the school," he wrote, "is not to teach religion, but to train children to become good citizens."[39] To those who claimed that school instruction in religion was necessary for this purpose, he replied:

The efficiency of the national schools is crowning evidence of the soundness of the principles upon which they have been established. . . . Our High Schools are supported by all religious bodies, and scarcely a whisper is heard in favor of establishing secondary schools under sectarian control.[40]

Hughes, the notable superintendent of schools in Toronto, gave the Dominion Education Association in 1892 a more practical reason for not relying on formal instruction. "Religious education," he said, "does not consist in memorizing a creed but in living one." Daniel Wilson, President of the University of Toronto, told a story of a boy who was asked by his Sunday school teacher, "What is persecution for righteousness' sake?" The answer was somewhat revealing: "Being drove to school, and being drove to Church." Wilson thought it possible to give undenominational instruction on the parables and the miracles, but he was convinced that the truly important factor in ethical teaching was the example of the teacher.[41]

In Quebec, Arthur Buller in 1838 was hopeful that there were surely some points on which all Christians could agree. His plan was to have certain extracts from the Bible taught in school, and supplemented, if desired, by denominational teaching before or after school. He put his views before the Roman Catholic Bishop of Quebec and before some of the principal members of the English and Scottish churches. The answers were anything but encouraging. But even though the Church of England clergy were almost unanimously hostile, and the Presbyterians divided, he was confident that he could win the sympathy of a "vast majority of the different bodies of dissenters."[42] When the two-denominational system developed later, it became possible to require Protestant religious education.

The first course of study for Protestant schools in Quebec was prescribed by the central authority in 1883, and Scripture was included as a subject of study from an early date. Before the end of the nineteenth century the regulations provided that the first half-hour of each day should be devoted to Biblical instruction, with no sectarian teaching. Regulations in the twentieth century required that the first twenty minutes of the day should be used for devotional exercises, including the reading of the Bible, and for instruction in morals and Scripture History. By 1950 an elaborate outline of Biblical lessons was used with the aims of imparting a knowledge of the Bible, of stimulating interest in the Bible as a masterpiece of literature, and of providing an opportunity to emphasize the moral and religious foundations of western civilization.

Roman Catholic Quebec is reputed to have a more complete and thorough program of religious education than is to be found in publicly supported schools of any other province or of any other country. Religion is not only taught as a subject; it permeates other subjects and the whole life of the school. Teaching is reinforced also by regular religious observances. The school program has had these characteristics since the educational prerogatives of the church were restored.

In Newfoundland a short-lived effort to limit religious education and denominationalism was made in 1838. An amendment to the Act in that year provided that all ministers of religion should have power to visit schools "provided, nevertheless, that no minister shall be permitted to impart any religious instruction in the school, or in any way interfere in the proceedings or management thereof." This act, says Hickman, forbade the use of any books except those chosen by the board or boards of education and forbade the use of "any book or books of a character having the tendency to teach or inculcate the Doctrines or peculiar tenets of any particular or exclusive Church or Religious Society whatsoever."[43] As we have seen, the advocates of denominational schools nevertheless won out. It became established practice to have religious instruction by denominational teachers for from two to five half-hour periods a week.

An indication of the content of religious education in the nineteenth century was given briefly in the prescribed programs of the Roman Catholic and Protestant sections of the central authority in Manitoba about 1880. The Roman Catholic program for the fourth division of the school included: (1) religious instruction, i.e. the catechism, the commandments, and the unseen part of the catechism; (2) becomingness, or manners and morals, including habits of order, politeness at table, and manners of greeting; (3) music, with emphasis on plain chant and religious music; (4) history, including the Old Testament from the death of Solomon and the New Testament, with related religious instruction. The Protestant program required that exercises at the opening and closing of school include: (1) the reading of a portion of the Scrip-

ture; (2) prayer by the teacher, as outlined; (3) recitation by the teacher and the children of the Lord's Prayer; (4) benediction. Obviously there was as much difference then as now in the time allotted by the two religious systems to religion and related instruction.

The purpose of religious education, like the purpose of the denominational school, was linked in the past to a concept of society opposed to movements which led to schools of the people and government by the people. In 1835 the bishop of the Protestant Episcopal Church in the diocese of Vermont preached two sermons in the cathedral church of Quebec on "The Importance of Providing Religious Education for the Poor." He explained the limitation of his subject by remarking that the rich may be destitute of piety and yet be friends of government, but not the poor. He warned:

The age in which we live, my brethren, is full of fearful warnings. The spirit of insubordination — of revolution — of the overturn of all most sacred and dear — seems to be abroad throughout the earth; and the instruments of that spirit, everywhere, are the lower orders of the people. Excited by the oratory of demagogues, filled with impracticable notions of liberty and equality, taught to band together for the correction of alleged abuses . . . the laboring classes of every community exhibit a growing hostility to law and order . . . which can only be effectually prevented by the early inculcation of religious principle.[44]

Considerably later there was still emphasis on the special value of religious education for the poor. In the pamphlet "Denominational or Free Christian Schools in Manitoba" (1877), Archbishop Taché wrote:

The culture of the intellect without that of the heart, develops the spirit of vanity in children of the poorest classes. Associated in school, with children in better circumstances, the child of the poor bears, in that respect, a pression which has the most deplorable consequences. Such a child often becomes insolent towards his parents, on a mere question of dress. . . .How many mothers have shed the bitterest tears, how many fathers have over-worked themselves and injured their health to have peace with their unfortunate sons, who had received instruction without being educated?[45]

The purpose of religious education as stated in the teacher's manual issued in Ontario in 1944 emphasized Protestant idealism and life in democratic society. The teacher was to help the child understand and accept as his own the ethical principles of Christianity. Specific religious instruction would be sterile, said the manual, unless conducive to this end. Although it would not be safe to generalize from a comparison of this and the two earlier statements quoted, it does seem probable that the content and stress in religious education and the possible effects could differ as greatly as the social environment.

Summary

In spite of the decline of church responsibility for education, denominational schools continued to receive support from public funds in Canada after taxation for schools was introduced. In this issue, old-world traditions and the solidarity of the French-speaking Roman Catholic population outweighed the influence of the North American environment. But Protestantism became identified with the common school under community control and wholly unsympathetic to the educational philosophy which led the Roman Catholic Church to insist on confessional schools for its adherents. The sharp cleavage between the numerous Roman Catholics and Protestants of central Canada led to separate school legislation which acquired permanency at the time of Confederation and spread to the middle west. In the Maritime Provinces tacit local agreements permitted the equivalent of separate schools and public schools under one local authority. Manitoba renounced and British Columbia avoided denominational cleavage. Among nine provinces of Canada only Quebec set up and retained a divided central authority, although the pattern was followed in the middle west for a time towards the end of the nineteenth century. Newfoundland, which was influenced more by early nineteenth century England than by the rest of North America, set up a state-supported denominational system with no local taxation for community schools. These developments were accompanied almost everywhere and for much of the time by acrimonious disputes which penalized the schools for differences among adults on religious and social issues by no means restricted to education.

Religious exercises and religious instruction, though prominent in paternalistic schools, were less evident in practice than in theory in early schools of the people. Recurrent efforts were made by the Protestant clergy and more zealous laymen to secure more specific religious teaching in public schools. Roman Catholic education was at all times permeated by religion. The universal nature of the public school and changes in the political structure and social attitudes have raised problems regarding the place and nature of religious education in schools and regarding the import of the teaching.

CHAPTER 18

National and International Factors in Education

EDUCATION IN THE TERRITORIES · EDUCATION OF INDIANS · LANGUAGE
ISSUES · NATIONAL DEFENCE · FEDERAL AID · OTHER FEDERAL ACTIVITIES
· CONFLICTING VIEWS AND INTERESTS · EDUCATIONAL RELATIONS WITH
THE UNITED STATES · EDUCATIONAL RELATIONS WITH OTHER COUNTRIES
· NATIONAL AWARENESS

The British North America Act gave the provincial governments complete authority over education within their own provinces, with the one important reservation explained in the previous chapter. Hence the federal government assumed at Confederation one educational prerogative, assertion of denominational school rights, which it came near to exercising in 1896 and did exercise in 1905 to control public education in the middle west. It also engaged, increasingly in recent years, in other activities of an educational nature, acceptance or disapproval of which was based more often on group or provincial interest than on strict interpretation of the "constitution." This chapter deals briefly with the role of the federal government in education and with other educational activities of a national or international character.

Education in the Territories

One responsibility retained by the federal government was the provision of education in extra-provincial territories. Although territorial governments assumed jurisdiction over schools and other institutions, grants to such schools were still paid from federal funds. For example, half the salaries of teachers in ten Protestant and nine Roman Catholic schools in the Northwest Territories in 1883 were paid out of the sum voted by the parliament of Canada for the expenses of government in the territories, as were grants under the ordinance of 1884. After the formation of Saskatchewan and Alberta in 1905, the regions north of the provincial boundaries were still vast, but sparsely settled. Even in 1951 the two divisions, the Northwest Territories and the Yukon Territory, had a total population of only 25,000. Many of the schools, provided for Indians and Eskimos by religious denominations and the federal government, were of a type to be described below. Other schools, for whites and the native population, were maintained by the territorial governments with federal assistance. Only one, a school completed at Yellowknife in 1947, had the characteristics of a community school of the people — administration by a local board and support from local taxation. Since its grant assistance came from the federal government, it was unique in 1950 as the one national public school.

Education of Indians

The education of Indians living on reserves within the provinces and anywhere in the territories has also been a responsibility of the federal government since Confederation. In the early part of the nineteenth century, governments gave some financial assistance to Indian education. Prince Edward Island in 1831 voted £50 to provide primary books in an Indian dialect. Nova Scotia in 1842 empowered a Commissioner of Indian Affairs to contract with the trustees of any school for the board and tuition of Indian children at the government's expense. In Lower Canada by a similar arrangement the "Indian Department" paid the cost of educating Indian pupils in ordinary schools. In the county of Chambly a teacher named Forrest, described as a catechist of the Church of England, had six such pupils in 1840 in addition to a score of fee-paying white pupils. Indian boys were enrolled also at a farm school attached to

the Seminary of St. Sulpice at Oka. In Upper Canada Indian schools were made eligible for grants in 1824, but there is record of only two grants being paid.

EDUCATION BY CHURCH AND CHARITY

For the most part Indian education in the early days was financed by organized philanthropy and by the churches. The New England Society carried on work not only in New Brunswick, but after 1827 in Upper Canada, where it succeeded to the management of a school on the Grand River, near Brantford. At this site in 1785 a church had been erected for the Indians, probably the first Protestant church building in the province. On the Bay of Quinte, the year before, the Society for the Propagation of the Gospel established what was probably the first Protestant school in the province, a school for the Iroquois who had come in from the United States. Methodists of Upper Canada were particularly active in the education of the Indians. One school attended by forty children was located on the Credit River, where Ryerson went as a missionary in 1827. A well-known Methodist residential school was founded at Mount Elgin in 1849.

In Lower Canada, Roman Catholic missionaries were attached to nearly every Indian settlement or wandering tribe. Some of the work of churches and of philanthropic organizations in Lower Canada has already been mentioned. Illustrative of casual efforts was an appeal to the governor in 1822 by a resident of Three Rivers named Wagner. He said that he had obtained £200 for Indian education from a wealthy benevolent association in London, England, and asked for "rations or half rations," or some money, for the support of Indian youth coming for instruction to the school he proposed to set up in the county of Durham.

The failure of efforts in the Maritimes was illustrated by the record of an Indian lad of thirteen, who as "a solitary exception" to his people's indifference to the white men's education had attended different schools as his family migrated from place to place; he acquired excellent ability in the three R's and taught other children in his tribe, but four years later, in 1846, he refused a grant of £15 offered by the government to enable him to pursue his studies and continued his customary pursuits of trapping and hunting. At the time of Confederation the Indian office recognized only fifty schools for Indians, all in Ontario and Quebec, and all day schools except the establishment at Mount Elgin. There were also at the time several Indian schools of a strictly missionary character. Very extensive work, including the operation of three schools, was conducted by the churches in the Red River area.

The work of converting Indian children to Christianity and educating them for peaceful life within a limited area was a charity that had intrinsic appeal. There was need also to counteract the influence of white men with less worthy motives. In 1839 the Reverend Richard Flood reported in a letter to Sir George Arthur that:

> The Indians have been and are to this day, when Christian Instruction is not imparted, the dupes and victims of the designing speculator, who would purchase their valuable furs and in return pay them with the scota-wawoo (fire-water).[1]

He considered the condition of the Indians in Upper Canada to be desperate. His advice was to select some for education as teachers, but if possible to "keep them out of public seminaries, where they might contract vicious habits from their intercourse with white children, who may not be under the influence of true religion."

CURRICULUM IN CHURCH EDUCATION

The content of Indian education included not only instruction in the Chris-

tian religion and the three R's but in simple practical skills. The school on the Grand River, which had boys and girls in residence, included mechanical arts and industrial science in the curriculum. At Mount Elgin agriculture and crafts were taught to boys and household affairs to girls. A Methodist school founded in 1826-27 on Grope Island in the Bay of Quinte had a fifty-acre farm and seven cows; it taught housekeeping, spinning, knitting, needlework, and dairy management to girls and farming to boys, in addition to the usual subjects. Fundamental education of this type was attempted in the better schools everywhere. James Evans, superintendent of Methodist missions in the west in 1836, reduced the Cree language to eight consonants and four vowels which could be represented by nine characters in four positions. He produced birch-bark books and cast type from lead taken from tea chests. John Sinclair, a Methodist missionary in the west in 1854, requested "some kind of musical instrument that would amuse the children, or start out our tunes (such as accordeon and tune fork)."[2] Miss Adams, another Methodist missionary in the Red River Area, had Indian girls help her stitch and bind three thousand copies of the Gospels and four Epistles printed in the Cree language in a crude press. She taught school during the day, trained mothers and daughters in household duties during the evening, and visited the sick and needy when special need arose.

UNDER FEDERAL JURISDICTION

After Confederation the education of Indians was placed under the newly created office of the secretary of state in 1868, under the newly created department of the interior in 1873, under a separate department of Indian affairs from 1880 until 1936, then under the department of mines and resources, and since 1949 under the department of citizenship and immigration.

Legislation and regulations of 1894-95 set up the first important code for Indian education. The code required the attendance at school of all Indian children between the ages of seven and sixteen and made parents or others who prevented their attendance liable to penalties. Indian agents and justices of the peace might issue warrants authorizing search for a child and his removal to an industrial or boarding school. The governor-in-council was authorized to establish these schools and to declare any existing school to be such an institution.

One of these, the Rupert's Land Industrial School, was described in the *Canadian Church Magazine* in 1893 as an academic and industrial boarding school for sixty-four Indian boys and girls drawn from seven Church of England missions. The school program covered five grades, each considerably lower in standard than a corresponding grade in public schools. For each pupil the government gave the church $100 a year, which had to be supplemented by at least $50 to cover the cost of the pupil's tuition and maintenance.

In 1920 the governor-in-council was given authority to establish day schools. In 1930 the superintendent general of Indian affairs was empowered to extend the age of compulsory attendance to eighteen years of age in particular cases. In 1946-48 a special joint committee of the Senate and the House of Commons brought to light deficiencies in the Indian school system, and the government voted greatly increased sums of money to extend and improve facilities. In 1951 personnel in the education division of the Indian affairs branch included a superintendent of education, a survey officer, two supervisors, and regional inspectors in four provinces. The Indian population was about 75,000 at Confederation and about 136,000 in 1951. In that year all but four

per cent were listed as members of Christian denominations and more than half as Roman Catholics.

PRESENT CONDITIONS AND TRENDS

The total number of schools for Indians increased from 287 in 1900 to 345 in 1916, remained close to that number until the end of World War II, and then increased rapidly to 597 in 1951. The enrolment increased from 10,000 in 1904 to 18,000 in 1936, fell to 16,500 in 1944, and increased to nearly 25,000 in 1951. Less than three per cent of these pupils lived in the territories; most of them were in the provinces from Quebec westward. In 1936 there were 79 residential schools conducted by the various denominations with government assistance of $150 to $250 a pupil per year. Of these schools 44 were Roman Catholic, 20 Church of England, 13 United Church, and 2 Presbyterian. The enrolment in residential schools since then has remained at about 9000, so that the expansion has occurred in government day schools. In 1951 there were in addition some 1200 Indian pupils in provincial and private schools, including a few in institutions at the post-secondary level. Since the enrolment in higher grades in Indian schools was still relatively low and the facilities for secondary education meagre, a few hundred better pupils were encouraged and assisted to continue their education in provincial schools.

These and other facts suggest a trend in the direction indicated by a recommendation of the parliamentary committee in its report of 1948: "that wherever and whenever possible, Indian children should be educated in association with other children." The number of Indian pupils in provincial schools was increasing. Schools in reservations used the program of studies of the province in which they were located, partly to facilitate transfer. The Royal Commission on Education in Ontario recommended in 1950 that the province assume responsibility for the education of Indians in order that they might not be left with educational resources inferior to those of the public school system. It seems unlikely that Ontario or any other province will provide boarding schools, the benefits from which are not lasting if the pupils return later to the life of the Indian band. The industrial schools at the end of the nineteenth century were less successful than was hoped because the Indian boys and girls who graduated with training as carpenters, blacksmiths, tailors, printers, or skilled workers in other fields proved unable to maintain their places as tradesmen or tradeswomen in the white man's world.

There has been little opportunity as yet for the Indians to provide schools of their own. More than a century ago, in 1848, some Indian bands of Upper Canada assumed a degree of responsibility by agreeing to devote to education one-quarter of certain funds received as compensation from the government. In 1880 the chief or chiefs of any band in council were given a little responsibility, but only with respect to the religious denomination of the teacher to be appointed. This power was confirmed in 1927 and supplemented by power to make rules and regulations regarding the construction and repair of buildings and the attendance of children within prescribed limits. Although only a measure of local authority was thus made possible, the central authority in the Indian affairs branch has recently acquired the characteristics of provincial departments of education. As a result, the entire system of Indian education could in the future more easily be converted to the public school pattern. Apart from the difficulties which the Indians themselves would have to overcome in assuming responsibility, there would be reluctance to permit the disappearance of denominational schools under church control.

After 1939 the Eskimos were classified with the Indians for educational purposes. In recent years increasing control over education in the north has been exerted by what is now the federal department of northern affairs and national resources. This department in 1954 was not only conducting or supervising schools for Eskimos under its own jurisdiction, but was inspecting northern schools of the Indian affairs branch and operating schools for the government of the Northwest Territories. At the end of that year there were eight schools for Eskimos, of which five were day schools maintained directly by the department. There were plans for the department to take over the operation of classes in church boarding schools — from Grade VI at Aklavik and throughout the grades at Chesterfield Inlet. The department employs in its northern administration and lands branch a superintendent of education and two inspectors of schools, prescribes the curriculum which must be taught as a condition of receiving a grant, and is establishing a unified system of education for all children — whites, Indians, half-breed, and Eskimos. But the widely scattered and nomadic Eskimo population, of slightly less than 10,000 in 1951, are most difficult to reach. In 1954 only about 20 per cent of the Eskimo children were receiving any formal education, even including those attending mission classes for an hour or two a day.

Language Issues

The development of nationalism and the increasing importance attached to communication within the country because of commercial expansion and democratic government led to an insistence after Confederation on the use of the English language in schools of provinces other than Quebec. But in the early part of the nineteenth century divisions among the people were compatible with concepts of society and government, and the retention of a language other than English in a community and its school caused no grave concern. In Canada West, Ryerson insisted that French was not a foreign language and was also quite willing to accept a knowledge of German grammar instead of English grammar in granting certificates to teachers for communities in which German was spoken and in the schools of which German was recognized as the language of instruction. It was not until 1885 that all schools in Ontario were required to teach and use the English language.

Early law and custom, therefore, sanctioned the operation of French or other language schools. In Prince Edward Island the school acts provided in 1847 a grant of £10, and in 1852 a grant of £35, to Acadian teachers certified by the clergyman as able to teach French. These amounts in both cases were less than the grants to other teachers, but legislation in 1863 gave Acadian teachers full standing and equal support. In Nova Scotia an act of 1841 authorized payment of the grants to schools using French, German, or Gaelic as the language of instruction. The Free School Act of 1864 was indirectly a blow to these schools because of their denominational characteristics.

As for New Brunswick, Lynam says that expelled Acadians and refugees from Quebec who settled in isolated areas were poverty-stricken, lacking in vitality and ambition, ignorant, and dominated by the church. In the few parochial schools before 1850 most of the teachers lacked knowledge to face the simplest test and probably for that reason few shared in the grants. The government then showed some interest by authorizing for use, in French-language schools, books used in Quebec — le Guide de l'Instituteur in 1852, and le Syllabaire de Québec and le Devoir du Chrétien in 1858 — and by providing £100 in 1853 for books in French. The Free School Act of 1871 imposed no requirements regarding the language of instruction. But even in 1885 the difficulty of obtaining capable Acadian teachers was so great that the marks made by Acadian candidates at the normal school on an extra examination paper in French counted as a bonus to help them achieve a passing grade.

In Manitoba after 1871 and in the Northwest Territories after 1878 French was recognized as an official language, and some of the schools were as completely French as others were English. Clause two of article seven in the Manitoba School Act specifically mentioned English books for English schools and French books for French schools. People from Edmonton visiting St. Albert School in 1885 heard the public examinations conducted both in English and in French.

Then came the requirement that English be taught in all schools. This meant that schools using other languages should either be eliminated from the public school system or that they should become bilingual. In the latter case, the problem was the rapidity of transition to English-language instruction as pupils moved upwards through the grades. Discussion of pedagogical advantage and of tact or abruptness in regulations did not conceal the basic conflict. Out-and-out champions of the universal public school advocated the introduction of English language instruction at an increasingly early stage, in the hope of eliminating the need for bilingual schools as soon as possible. Other language groups, with strong denominational backing, were primarily concerned about the preservation of the native language in family and religious life.

In the Northwest Territories in 1892, publicly supported schools were required to use English as the language of instruction, with the proviso only that local boards might permit a primary course to be taught in French. In Saskatchewan in

1930 this concession was withdrawn, and boards were permitted only to have French taught as a subject for one hour a day. Since the direct method was undoubtedly used, the distinction made less difference in practice than was intended, and the following year about one pupil in thirty was receiving instruction in French in the elementary schools.

In Manitoba the French language lost its status in 1890. In 1897, as compensation to denominational interests after the abolition of separate schools, it was enacted that in schools where ten pupils spoke a native language other than English their instruction should be conducted partly in that language, a requirement politely described by Weir as a "mongrel provision in the school law," which was fortunately repealed in 1916. In 1915 there had been 421 bilingual schools, in which about one-sixth of the pupils in the province were enrolled.

In the 1870's and 1880's New Brunswick authorized English-French textbooks, some of which were adopted by Maine in 1879 and others by Ontario in 1889; they were intended, as the name implies, for use in bilingual schools. Prince Edward Island in 1868 offered a supplementary grant to teachers certified by central authority as capable of teaching French — clearly for bilingual ability. The island province in 1892, New Brunswick in 1901, and Nova Scotia in 1908 appointed special inspectors for their Acadian schools.

The quality of instruction in bilingual schools was notoriously poor. The Roman Catholic Bishop Fallon declared in Ontario in 1911 that bilingualism "encourages incompetency, gives a prize to hypocrisy, and breeds ignorance."[3] The next year on the basis of a report by F. W. Merchant, the province issued "Instructions 17," which in crisp, mandatory style cut down French-language privileges to instruction in the primary grade and made it clear that the business of the school was to see that the pupil learned English as quickly as possible. Special inspectors were appointed. After a stormy fifteen years, the attempt to enforce stringent regulations was abandoned in favor of co-operative arrangements to help schools do the best work possible in view of their particular problems. The new plan of 1927 was based on a second report by Merchant, then chief director of education, in association with two others. A University of Ottawa Normal School was set up to train teachers for the bilingual schools, thereafter designated "schools in which French is a subject of instruction with the approval of the Minister of Education." Its enrolment soon exceeded ten per cent of the total normal school enrolment of the province. The department of education also appointed two special officers, a director of English instruction and a director of French instruction, to work for the improvement of these schools in the teaching of the respective languages.

Partly for the sake of brevity, hardly a mention has been made here of the bigotry, controversy, and uproar associated with the bilingual issue. It will be enough to say that the conflict was similar to the separate school conflict, to which it was related. But a detached observer could hardly fail to see the humor in the scheming and diplomacy, as in the undercover working of Ontario's dual supervisory system of 1927. The Royal Commission on Education in 1950 stated, without comment, curious facts regarding a change in the incumbents of the office of director of French instruction in 1937 and added recommendations clearly designed to reverse a tendency since then of French language schools to acquire the autonomy of an independent dominion within the departmental empire. The counter office of director of English instruction was not regularly filled in later years. Clearly those devoted to maintaining and extending the use of the French language outside Quebec had resorted to more subtle means when court decisions went against them. To cite one Ontario case, a decision of the privy council in 1916 made it clear that no separate school privileges were guaranteed by the B.N.A. Act with respect to language of instruction, regarding which the provinces were competent to make decisions as they saw fit. The French language in English-speaking provinces has special claims only because courtesy and common sense demand some deference to the large number of Canadians who speak it as their native tongue. A bulletin published by the U.S. Bureau of Education in 1919 stated, with perhaps too little reservation, that in Canada "relations between French and English have always been so amiable, and legal compromises have been so skillful, as to forestall all friction."[4]

A brief account has been given of twentieth century difficulties with language groups in Alberta. The same problems were faced elsewhere in the west. Mennonites in large numbers came to Manitoba in the last quarter of the nineteenth century. Among these people the elders exercised a controlling power and opposed the learning of English, general education, and intellectual advance. In their villages they preferred to have schools under their own supervision teach the German language for Bible reading. The Galicians, or Ruthenians, gave even more trouble by keeping their children at home to work on the farms. Saskatchewan appointed a supervisor of Ruthenian schools in 1908, began training Ruthenian teachers in 1909, had four supervisors of school districts in foreign language areas in 1915, and established the office of director of education among new Canadians in 1919. Doukhobors, who came just before 1900 and set up communistic villages, were also extremely difficult to educate and assimilate. The essential difficulty in the case of most language groups

was the same: the leaders and institutions of the group, to retain their authority, were obliged to resist educational activities which would give their people wider understanding and lead them to become members of Canadian society at large. Since German or a dialect of German was spoken by many groups, World War I caused the closing of a large number of their schools. Women's organizations during the war brought pressure on governments to accelerate the assimilation of new Canadians. In 1930 a decision of the privy council put an end to appeals by the Mennonites against the Manitoba legislation of 1916, which required that instruction in public schools be given in English.

National Defence

Much of the federal government's educational effort has been related to national defence. To educate officers for the army the government established in Kingston in 1876 an institution which two years later became the Royal Military College. Since the military establishment could not absorb an unlimited number of officers, arrangements were made to have graduates admitted to professional faculties of the universities to complete their training for civilian employment. A Royal Naval College of Canada was established in Halifax, N.S., in 1911, moved to Esquimault in 1918, and closed in 1922. It reopened at Royal Roads, B.C., in 1942, and offered an alternative to the first two years of the four-year program at R.M.C. Chiefly since World War II the armed services have provided directly or indirectly for the training of men in many technical skills. Education of service personnel in broader fields such as current affairs was also provided by education divisions in the services during World War II and by the bureau of current affairs after 1951.

Extensive educational work of this broader type was carried on with federal government support by the Canadian Legion Educational Services. Less than six weeks after the beginning of World War II the Canadian Legion applied for and was granted a charter for its educational organization. The work was carried on chiefly by correspondence courses at the secondary level and during military service, although the great variety of offerings included elementary, advanced, and non-academic courses, pre-enlistment courses, and some tuition. Between January 1, 1941, and March 31, 1947, nearly 216,000 individuals registered for 268,000 C.L.E.S. correspondence courses. For the 91 different courses offered 3,800,000 textbooklets were printed and nearly 2,000,000 had been issued before the end of 1946. Expenditures on the work of C.L.E.S. up to the end of 1945, when its operations were drawing to a close, totalled nearly six and a quarter million dollars, of which about 90 per cent had been paid by the federal government.

When the number of unemployed single men reached an estimated 70,000 in 1932, the federal government established relief camps under the department of national defence. In the next three years 113,000 passed through these camps, where they were given work and sometimes education at a total cost of more than three and one-half million dollars. In 1937 the Dominion Provincial Youth Training plan was initiated to train young people between sixteen and twenty-five years of age for employment. The training could be strictly occupational or, as in British Columbia, for the improvement of health and morale. Grants were made available through the federal department of labor, which made agreements with provincial departments, chiefly those of education and labor, which were prepared to pay half the cost of training projects. Although all provinces did not

co-operate fully, the federal grant was increased in 1939 from one million to one and one-half million dollars. Soon after, of course, employment opportunity improved, but the administrative arrangements established for the Youth Training plan were used for the War Emergency Training Program, with which the former was merged in 1940.

The depression years had left the country unprepared for machine warfare by depleting the number of skilled workers and the quantity of productive equipment. To make good the former deficiency it was necessary to give short courses of training to men and women available for employment in industry and to enlisted men needed for mechanical trades in the services. Under the War Emergency Training Program, municipalities made available the shops and equipment in technical schools, the provinces paid certain administrative costs and one-half the cost of all machinery and equipment purchased, and the federal government paid all other expenses. In 1941-42 classes were attended by nearly 74,000 persons, of whom about half were preparing for employment in industry. In 1942 more comprehensive arrangements were made, through the Vocational Training Co-ordination Act, for the co-operation of the federal department of labor and the provincial governments in various training projects.

At the end of the war the major project became the rehabilitation of veterans. Between April, 1944, and October, 1948, some 85,000 veterans attended courses under Canadian Vocational Training at rehabilitation centres. Of these, about 55,000 enrolled in one of some sixty different courses of the skilled trade type and the remaining 30,000 studied ordinary secondary school subjects in preparation for entrance to university or other academic work. By March 31, 1949, the expenditures of the federal government on the vocational training program for veterans had reached more than $25,000,000. Apart from this program, the government by the same date had spent about $115,000,000 to provide university education for some 35,000 veterans. This expenditure covered fees and supplementary amounts paid to universities, and living allowances paid to students.

For obvious reasons cadet or military training of school pupils came to be supported by the federal government. Its beginning on any considerable scale dated from the American Civil War and the Fenian raids. The change in attitudes may be illustrated by the actions of the public school board in Kingston, Ontario. In 1865 members of the board censured a teacher for appearing in school in a military uniform, but three years later they applied to the Adjutant-General of Militia for permission to establish cadet corps in the schools. Military drill had become part of the gymnastic instruction in the normal school at Toronto in 1864, and in 1865 legislation in Canada West provided grants of $50 for military drill in schools setting up cadet corps. In 1879 the militia department at Ottawa authorized the formation in high schools and some other educational institutions of companies for military drill, and offered to supply equipment and instructors. At least a few secondary schools in Ontario and Quebec established companies. Ontario in 1898 again voted a $50 grant for a corps of twenty-five cadets.

But the rapid expansion of cadet training in all provinces came ten years later. Lord Strathcona in 1909-10 donated $500,000 as a trust fund to provide $20,000 a year for physical and military training. To secure maximum results the money was used chiefly to encourage teachers to take such training. In 1908 in Nova Scotia, where Strathcona money was then available, physical training certificates were required for the higher grades of

teachers' licences and the training was provided by the department of militia and defence, which by 1913 had given instruction to 3000 teachers of the province. Department of militia and defence grants provided one dollar per cadet in 1910 and one dollar per uniform in 1912. In Ontario the High Schools Act and the Public Schools Act were revised in 1909 to provide for military instruction in regular classes, and in 1911 a circular was issued on courses, equipment, and other details. The number of corps in the province increased from 72 in 1910 to 578 in 1915 under the impetus of World War I. By the latter year even Saskatchewan had 39 corps, with 38 instructors, 139 officers, and 2142 cadets.

In the period between the wars, there was growing opposition to cadet corps. Grants from the federal government were reduced in 1922. Aylesworth says that in Alberta in the 1920's the strong desire to get away from war caused abolition of cadets and sometimes of marching pupils in and out of school; but this did not occur in all localities, for an Alberta teacher of the period says he trained cadets and underwent inspections all through the twenties. In the 1930's the Manitoba department of education decided to discourage the continuance of cadet corps. The school board in Toronto in 1933 voted fourteen to two for doing away with cadet corps in the schools of the city. But during World War II cadets associated with all three services were established.

Federal Aid

Keen competition for world markets by the beginning of the twentieth century caused English-speaking countries to subsidize vocational training to improve the efficiency of production. The Canadian government, by the Agricultural Aid Act of 1912 and the Agricultural Instruction

Act of 1913, made available to the provinces sums of money increasing annually and amounting in all to $11,400,000 by 1924. Much of the money was used directly or indirectly for agricultural education. In 1919 the Technical Education Act provided $10,000,000 over a period of ten years for any form of vocational or technical education "to increase the earning capacity, efficiency, and productive power" of employees in industry and mechanical trades. Grants under this Act could not exceed provincial expenditures on vocational education, and in 1929 an extension of time was provided since only Ontario had used its full allotment. The Vocational Education Act of 1931 promised $750,000 a year for fifteen years, but its operation was postponed by the depression.

The Vocational Training Co-ordination Act of 1942 was designed primarily for defence training but led to the co-operation of provincial departments of education and the department of labor at Ottawa in a variety of vocational education activities. Under this and subsequent legislation, $30,000,000 was made available to the provinces for vocational secondary schools, including $10,000,000 for capital expenditures between 1945 and 1952 and $2,000,000 a year for maintenance and operating costs.

In 1944 the federal government passed the Family Allowances Act, under which monthly allowances of $5 to $8 according to age were paid on behalf of every child up to sixteen years of age. Since parents or other adults responsible for the child forfeited the allowance if provincial school regulations were not observed, one immediate effect of the Act was to improve school attendance in many places. Although its effect on the birth rate cannot be measured, it was clear by 1953 that to maintain additional schools for the increased number of pupils would soon cost the taxpayer more than the $173,000,000 spent in 1946 for family allowances. Event-

ually the educational implications of this Act may be greater than any other action of the federal government.

In recent years federal government money has been made available for purposes affecting education in several forms, including Dominion-Provincial scholarships and research grants, especially in the field of mental health. In 1951, in accordance with the recommendations of the Massey Commission, the federal government provided $7,100,000 for distribution through the provinces as grants to universities.

Increasingly during the present century as equalization became the dominant consideration in school finance, there has been a demand from the poorer provinces for federal aid to elementary and secondary education. The demand was supported on a national scale by the Canadian Teachers' Federation, which was responsible for the publication in 1945 of *Wealth, Children, and Education in Canada,* a brochure presenting statistical evidence on the need for larger provincial grants and for equalization grants from the federal government to the provinces. After World War II, advocacy of federal aid became a chief activity of the C.T.F. and subsequently of the Canadian School Trustees' Association. The Canadian Education Association, however, mindful of provincial autonomy in education and of the wealthier as well as the poorer provinces, restricted itself in the *Report of the Survey Committee* in 1943 and in its continuing policy, to pointing out the discrepancies existing among the provinces — for example, an interprovincial range in 1936 from $35 to $80 in the cost of education per child, and in 1941 from $422 to $1321 in the median salaries of teachers. Presumably a federal grant policy acceptable to all provinces and to the C.E.A. would increase the revenues of the provincial governments from the coffers of Ottawa, whereas the C.T.F. and the

C.S.T.A., being unconcerned about governmental rivalries and anxious only to increase the money available to the schools, would prefer grants earmarked for education. In 1953 there was no likelihood that the federal government would risk criticism by unnecessary generosity.

At the end of World War II, strong pressure was put on the federal government by the C.E.A., on behalf of and in association with provincial and local education authorities, to obtain war surplus equipment for the schools, including machine and hand tools, typewriters, and motion picture projectors. A parliamentary committee on war expenditures and economics seemed favorably disposed towards the request and there was assurance at one point that the equipment would be made available to education authorities through the C.E.A. on very favorable terms. Unfortunately for education, the ready support of the proposal by opposition party members in the committee, and the concomitant lack of strong backing from departments of education in provinces with Liberal governments, weakened the case for the schools. The President of War Assets Corporation, who consistently maintained that all equipment and materials of value should be sold to dealers, was able to prevent any significant breach in this policy. Education gained token concessions, a quantity of cheap materials, and some costly, unsaleable leftovers of little use to anyone. Valuable equipment was obtained through the war emergency program and, in exceptional cases, under other arrangements, but not by the schools generally through the ordinary distribution of war surpluses.

Other Federal Activities

After World War I the dominion bureau of statistics set up an education division, which began in 1921 to issue regular and occasional publications that collated statistical data on education in the various provinces. One well-known and useful series came to be called the *Biennial Survey of Education in Canada*. In later years the professional educator in charge of the education division of the bureau was useful to the federal government as an expert consultant in a field which is almost exclusively the prerogative of the provinces.

From the beginning of World War II certain divisions of other departments of government carried on an increasing amount of work of an educative character. In the department of national health and welfare the nutrition division published display materials and booklets that were used in schools, and a National Physical Fitness Program, initiated by legislation in 1943, provided money and services utilized by departments of education in most provinces. The citizenship branch in the department of the secretary of state was concerned with the education of various ethnic groups for Canadian life and citizenship. The department of agriculture through experimental farms, publications, and films contributed to the more direct work of education.

Other agencies associated less directly with the federal government have engaged in recent years in educational undertakings. The Canadian Broadcasting Corporation, established in 1936, began shortly afterward to co-operate with provincial departments of education in producing programs for schools. In addition to provincial series it offered national school broadcasts, planned since 1944 by a national advisory committee on which provincial departments of education were well represented. Although the National Film Board also produced many films excellent for school use, it was less successful in establishing working arrangements with some provincial education authorities. But in Saskatchewan, Nova Scotia, and other provinces, close co-operation made possible the joint employment of personnel in visual education and was particularly effective in bringing educational films to adult groups in rural areas. Another organization, much smaller but wholly educational in purpose, the Canadian Citizenship Council, was formed early in World War II and was given limited and rather precarious support by the federal government. Its chief work was the production of books deemed valuable in education for citizenship.

Conflicting Views and Interests

The brief account above of financial assistance to education from the Canadian government and agencies associated with it is sufficient to show that the provinces have not maintained a complete independence in educational affairs. From the eve of Confederation there were advocates of more extensive participation by the federal government in public education. Extreme views were expressed in *Kosmos* in 1885 by one who saw "two distinct and hostile peoples" in Canada, classified them as "the English-speaking and progressive race and the French-speaking or stand-still class," urged legislators to "give up cringeing to and fawning upon sect and party," and came out for a "truly national system of education."[5] Unfortunately statements of this kind raised suspicion regarding the motives of the moderates, who urged only the formation of voluntary national associations to give some degree of unity.

Speaking in 1864 on educational questions raised by Confederation, William Dawson, Principal of McGill University, recommended supervision of higher education by the federal government to ensure university degrees "of national quality." At a meeting in 1867 of the Provincial Association of Protestant Teachers of Lower Canada, in which Dawson was

very influential, a committee was appointed to "mature a plan for a connection with the different Associations of the Dominion of Canada." Twelve years later, when all provinces except Prince Edward Island had an educational or a teachers' association or both, James L. Hughes addressed the Ontario Educational Association on the need for a national organization. Nearly a decade later, in July 1888, a convention of the teachers of the Maritime Provinces in Saint John, New Brunswick, marked a limited achievement in that direction. Then in July, 1891, when the National Education Association of the United States met in Toronto, Canadian teachers held a meeting to form a similar association for Canada. They appointed a provisional council representative of education in all provinces and Newfoundland. The resulting Dominion Educational Association held its first session from July 5 to July 8, 1892, in Montreal.

CANADIAN EDUCATION ASSOCIATION

This was the origin of the organization now known as the Canadian Education Association. From the first it was essentially a voluntary association of the provincial departments of education, four of which originally contributed to its support. Although its membership included many teachers, the officers and directors were regularly administrative officials of the provincial departments and of city school boards, and people engaged in teacher training and supervision. The association met usually once in three years until 1917, somewhat more frequently until 1942, and annually except in one year thereafter. Its influence was limited by lack of personnel and resources to carry on work between conventions. But activities of the association increased with the publication of a *Report of the Survey Committee* on educational needs in 1943, and with the employment of paid staff from a small beginning in the same year.

Hon. G. W. Ross, first president, Dominion Educational Association

A few years later it had become a consistently active institution representative of educational authorities and closely associated with other voluntary organizations concerned with elementary and secondary education. Since its chief function was to serve as a clearing house for educational information, it engaged in research and the publication of surveys. Three major projects have been a five-year study of school health beginning in 1944, a similar five-year program in practical education beginning in 1947, and a program for the improvement of rural supervision and administration which began in 1952. The C.E.A. also undertook to act on behalf of education authorities and other educational associations, at their request, in matters affecting all provinces or the country at large. Its increasing activity raised the question whether a voluntary inter-provincial association might make unnecessary the establishment by the federal government of a central office or bureau, as had been done in the United States and in Australia, countries with a number of independent education authorities similar to those of the Canadian provinces.

Since the Dominion Educational Association was not equipped at the beginning to perform any such function, one of its prominent members, J. M. Harper, began to press actively for a central bureau at the third convention of the association in 1898. Harper was an inspector of high schools in the Protestant system of Quebec. His address at the Halifax convention was hedged with a profusion of literary allusions and lofty sentiments but in essence asked the association to request the federal government to set up an information and statistics service for the benefit of public education in Canada.

In spite of fine language and caution, the import of the proposal was clear enough to the Roman Catholic superintendent of education in Quebec, who was at hand to answer a further speech by Harper at the next convention of the association in Ottawa three years later. Harper reported that a deputation from the D.E.A. had waited on the prime minister to ask what steps were likely to be taken by his government to organize a bureau. Sir Wilfred, he said, had listened attentively and promised to look into the whole matter carefully. At the conclusion of Harper's address, Superintendent Boucher de La Bruère made any further investigation unnecessary by the first sentence of his reply. Quebec regretted that such a proposal had been made. At the end of a reasoned argument the superintendent said that it would plainly be wrong and imprudent for the D.E.A. to pursue the matter further. Apparently the directors of the association had by then reached the same conclusion. An address on "National Education" at the next convention dealt with moral and spiritual values and not with administrative innovations.

At the seventh convention of the D.E.A. in Victoria in 1909 the possibility of a Canadian government statistical service for education was discussed again. The beginning of this service was marked by a conference on educational statistics attended by representatives of the federal and provincial governments in October, 1920.

NATIONAL COUNCIL ON EDUCATION

A notable attempt to secure a national bureau was next made in 1922 during the *floruit* of a rather remarkable organization, the National Council on Education. The creator of this body was Fred J. Ney, who as an official of the Manitoba department of education had inaugurated, in 1910, with strong departmental support, excursions of teachers to England — the beginning of an extensive teacher exchange program. In 1919, after some two years of preparatory work, Ney convened at Winnipeg under the patronage of the governor-general a most impressive conference of influential people and some 1800 representatives of institutions and groups with high tasks in mind for the schools to perform. The National Council on Education was formed and its chief author became general secretary. The council consisted of five representatives from each of the nine provinces and five from the Dominion at large. It was a lay rather than a professional organization and decidedly high-caste rather than cross-section in make-up. At the time of the Council's formation the Canadian Education Association, so re-named in 1918, was in the doldrums, with the result that prominent members of the latter gave support to the new body. The Council sought annual donations of $20,000 from the provinces, matched by an equal amount from the federal government. Its publications announced such aims as the realization of a Canadian ideal in education and the establishment of a clearing house of education information, including two

specific objectives, a national university and a national bureau of education. In connection with the latter, a meeting of the deputy ministers and superintendents of education of the various provinces was held in Toronto at the invitation of the government of Ontario on October 30, 1922, just before the annual conference of the Dominion Education Association in the same city.

R. H. Grant, minister of education in Ontario, and chairman of the conference, spoke in favor of a national bureau. He was supported by President Falconer of the University of Toronto, and by Canon Cody, who was later to hold the posts then occupied by the previous speakers, and by Robert Fletcher of Manitoba. Canon Cody asked: "Why should not this power, this wonderful power of education, be rightly directed in securing national unity and in developing national ideals?" The ministers of education from Nova Scotia and Saskatchewan were skeptical, although willing to give the proposal consideration. The Alberta minister wanted more information, and the British Columbia minister was guarded in his remarks. But the answers to Canon Cody's question became clear to all when the Honorable L. A. David, Provincial Secretary of Quebec, addressed the gathering. The conference passed a very cautious motion asking the provinces to consider the proposal and to communicate with Ney if they were in favor. This allowed the scheme to expire without indecent haste. Then, on the motion of Mr. David, the conference passed a robust resolution declaring the unwillingness of the provinces to tolerate any interference of the federal authorities in educational affairs.

The National Council on Education conducted another big-gun affair in Toronto in 1923, a national conference on education and citizenship. Thereafter for many years it gave useful service in the circumscribed field of teacher exchange,

C.T.F. House, the office of the Canadian Teachers' Federation, Ottawa

but had dropped almost out of sight by World War II. Even in 1922 one of its strong supporters, Vincent Massey, had found it necessary to explain that the Council was not fully understood. To its critics it was an attempt to superimpose aristocratic leadership in order to exert a controlling influence for esoteric purposes over the schools of the people and the democratically constituted school authorities. To the extent that this was true its rejection was important evidence that public education in Canada had achieved a mature independence.

Since 1922 public requests for a federal bureau have been made periodically by voluntary organizations, but not by the Canadian Education Association or by representatives of many provincial authorities. Even as a member of the C.E.A., the province of Quebec has sometimes felt obliged to leave its continued co-operation in doubt at the risk of weakening the inter-provincical association which, by the success of its work, is best able to make a national office unnecessary. Meanwhile the increasing educational opera-

tions of the federal government are creating without intention a climate and a personnel for action from that quarter.

OTHER NATIONAL ORGANIZATIONS

Other voluntary associations of a national character appeared after World War I. The National Conference of Canadian Universities was formed in 1911 and met annually thereafter. The Canadian Teachers' Federation, made up of all provincial associations except that of the Roman Catholic teachers of Quebec, was inaugurated in Calgary in 1920. The Canadian School Trustees' Association was formed in 1923, the Canadian Federation of Home and School in 1928, and the Canadian Association for Adult Education in 1936.

Educational Relations with the United States

In education, as in other departments of life, English-speaking Canadians have been subjected to strong influences from two other countries, Great Britain and the

United States. In the early part of the nineteenth century the pull of these two forces was in opposite directions. The ruling aristocracy and those associated with them were whole-heartedly British, as were the important colleges and secondary schools supported by the state and most of the elementary schools provided paternalistically for the people. A large number of the ordinary settlers, on the other hand, were North Americans if not pro-American in outlook, and their attitude was usually reflected in community schools of the people and in academies maintained by the subscriptions of those who had prospered by economic enterprise. Since loyalty to Britain and support of aristocracy were officially respectable, and American ideas and democratic tendencies correspondingly reprehensible, evidence of the latter is found chiefly in deploratory statements. As R. P. Baker put it, "a proper hatred of the United States and an equally proper love of England became social decencies to be expressed in traditional terms."[6]

PREJUDICE AND LOYALTY

John Strachan set a continuing fashion by ascribing a uniform iniquity to American schools:

Now in the United States a custom prevails unknown to or unpractised in any other nation; in all other countries morals and religion are made the basis of public instruction, and the first books put into the hands of children teach them the domestic, the social, and religious virtues; but in the United States politics pervade the whole system of education; the school books, from the very first elements, are stuffed with praises of their own institutions and breathe hatred to everything English.[7]

In the year of that declaration, 1830, Strachan was accused in the *Colonial Advocate* of sycophancy and the use of anti-Americanism and politics to further his own ambitions. But everywhere those who held high positions in the church and education took a similar stand. In Fredericton the Reverend Dr. Somerville, headmaster of the Church of England Academy, who had a reputation as an Anglophile and an upholder of traditions, became in 1829 Professor of Divinity at King's College. That institution was regarded by its vice-president, the Reverend Dr. Edwin Jacob, and by the whole college council, as a bulwark against the levelling influence of the United States.

A fear frequently expressed was that even the sons of respectable parents might be corrupted if they crossed the border to complete their education. Strachan added to his previous remarks:

To such a country our youth may go, strongly attached to their native land . . . but by hearing its institutions continually depreciated, and those of the United States praised . . . some may become fascinated with that liberty which has degenerated into licentiousness, and imbibe, perhaps unconsciously, sentiments unfriendly to things of which Englishmen are proud.[8]

Others were sure that very few who went to schools in the United States returned to Canada "without some taint of Democracy." But in spite of their professed anxiety, many of the well-to-do did send their sons to school or college in the neighboring republic.

Even more disturbing, because they mingled with ordinary people, were the Americans who came into Canada to make a living. Of all who exerted a baneful influence, according to a Toronto citizen of 1839, the worst were the "Yankee pretenders" to the science of medicine — worse even than the United States ministers and teachers who had "overrun the Provinces" for many years. "It is really melancholy to traverse the Province," said Dr. Thomas Rolph in 1833. "You find a herd of children instructed by some anti-British adventurer, instilling into the young and tender mind sentiments hostile to the Parent State."[9] In correspondence between the lieutenant-governor of Upper Canada, the colonial secretary and the Lord Bishop of Montreal in 1838, grave concern was expressed regarding "American School-masters who have most diligently instructed their pupils in revering republican principles and ridiculing all monarchical institutions." Arthur believed that untold damage had been done by "the madness of allowing the Americans to be the instructors of the Youth of the Country" and held it impossible for Upper Canada to be "retained by Great Britain, if the evil be not got rid of root and Branch and that too *at once*".[10] On the other hand the citizen of the United States who in 1799 wrote *A Tour through Upper and Lower Canada* attributed the "destitution of learning" in the provinces to the exclusion of American teachers and American clergy. The law of 1816 in Upper Canada set as the one qualification of a teacher that he be a British subject, but this law was not always observed.

The same conditions prevailed in other provinces. In Nova Scotia, Haliburton urged the requirement of a teacher's licence that would exclude Americans. In academies of the English-speaking people in Quebec, teachers and principals at mid-century were commonly American-born. In New Brunswick in 1838 the lieutenant-governor advocated in a message to the House of Assembly the importation from England of methods of instruction, teachers, and textbooks, that might develop a "sounder principle of loyalty and attachment to the parent state" than were likely to be instilled by publications "emanating from a foreign press."[11]

TEXTBOOKS

American textbooks were a cause of worry in all provinces. Audet says that the Royal Institution asked for and apparently was given a special grant in 1825 to purchase English textbooks for free distribution in schools near the border, where books of American origin and political bias were commonly used. Ryerson, like Strachan, considered American textbooks unique in expressing "hostility to the institutions and even governments of other countries — especially to those of Great Britain." A printer trying to get a subsidy to publish Canadian books in 1828 claimed that nine-tenths of the textbooks used in the schools of Upper Canada were from the United States. Ryerson placed the proportion at one-half in 1846. Efforts were made by central and intermediate authorities to buy books from England. In 1818 in Upper Canada, the Midland District Committee admitted that the use of Webster's speller was injurious and reported that they had ordered the use of books by Murray and other English authors; in the same year the Western District reported the arrival of textbooks ordered from England. The Bishop of Montreal said that American textbooks colored the history and institutions of their republic in a manner very dangerous to the principles and loyalty of the rising generations in Canada. "Next to the religious wants of the Province," he said, "this evil is that which in my humble judgment most loudly calls for remedy."[12]

What made the problem all the more difficult for the leaders and beneficiaries of the British-Canadian status quo was that many of the "slick Yankees" were preferred because of their superior pedagogical skill, if not for their notions of social equality. A petitioner to the lieutenant-governor in Upper Canada in 1834 claimed that, after teaching for a year in Markham and bringing the school up to a flourishing condition, he found his scholars enticed away by the Yankee teacher of a school set up in the immediate vicinity by the "disaffected Faction who are laboring indefatigably for the subversion of British supremacy."[13] Although he had the support of loyal members of the existing board, he said there was every reason to fear that the trustees next elected would expel him from the school and complete his ruin. In another district in 1839:

A British subject, well qualified, was appointed to the Charge of a common school, in a well settled neighborhood; but as no lodging could be procured for him, he went away: the next applicant, however, being an American, every one eagerly offered him all necessary accommodation.[14]

One example of a skilful and painstaking American teacher was a man named Haskin who came from Rochester, New York, and taught in Simcoe, Upper Canada, in the 1840's. He won public support by conducting quarterly public examinations and having pupils sing and take part in recitations, dialogues, and debates. American textbooks, also, whether superior or not, were better suited to the needs and mood of the country than imports from England.

In the third quarter of the nineteenth century all of these problems were greatly reduced. Canadian schools and colleges improved. Adaptations of English books and an increasing number of textbooks of Canadian authorship were printed in Canada. Capable teachers of Canadian birth became more plentiful with the introduction of teacher training and the admission of women into the profession. As fears subsided, progress was achieved by frankly copying American practices, particularly in administration, and adapting them to Canadian conditions. The school systems of the older provinces were constructed on patterns set by New York and the New England States. Woodley points out, for example, that the introduction in Quebec between 1841 and 1856 of a Council of Public Instruction and a superintendent of education, of the district council as an in-

termediate board, of *ad hoc* local authorities, and of local equivalents to government grants was based on practices introduced in the northeastern United States ten to thirty years before. Superintendent Dawson of Nova Scotia in 1852 devoted nearly a third of his 96-page report to an account of his visit to the United States and to descriptions of institutions in Massachusetts and New York. Superintendent Ryerson of Canada West did not hesitate to quote Mann and Barnard as authorities in the earlier years of his campaign to improve education, or in the 1870's to cite higher expenditures on schools in the United States as an argument for more money in Ontario.

EXCHANGE

Throughout the latter half of the nineteenth century, as Canadian independence in education grew stronger, there was even less hesitancy in using material of American origin. Official publications of central authorities after 1850, and an increasing number of professional journals after Confederation, republished articles from American magazines. The *Canadian School Journal* in the 1870's made free use of exchanges with the United States in quoting extracts from their pages and pointed out editorially how leadership south of the border might be copied to advantage in Canada, as in the introduction of psychology as a subject for teachers in training. The journal also carried a large number of advertisements of American professional journals, which presumably received some subscriptions from Canadian teachers. In the last quarter of the nineteenth century, when the basic textbooks in the common subjects were almost all Canadian, American textbooks for other subjects and supplementary purposes were used without question by Canadians, either in the original or in an adapted form.

There was comparatively little exchange in the opposite direction. The Oswego Pestalozzian movement in the United States derived its original impetus from a visit to Toronto in 1859 of Superintendent Sheldon who was filled with enthusiasm by a display of apparatus for teaching a formal type of object lesson, apparatus which the Toronto Normal School had imported from England. According to Copp, a United States authority on physical education in the 1890's stated that Canadians had "settled upon a plan of practical work sooner than the Americans did."[15] Ryerson recommended gymnastics in his report of 1846, had a gymnasium included in the normal school building in 1852, and thereafter published in the *Journal of Education* a syllabus of gymnastic exercises. These events were cited in the United States to show that Canadians sometimes did things while the Americans merely talked.

American educators sometimes came to Canada, and Canadians took part in conventions in the United States. Plans were made for an international normal educational conference in the Thousand Islands in August, 1879. Superintendent Hughes of Toronto was scheduled to speak on "The Kindergarten in Relation to the Public School" and Principal McCabe of the Toronto Normal School on "The Aesthetic Influence of the School Room," while many Americans were to speak on methods and a few on the philosophical and psychological aspects of education. Hughes was fairly well known in the United States, and teachers often came from American cities to visit Toronto schools. At an international congress of educators held in New Orleans in February, 1885, J. G. Hodgins was made honorary secretary and was asked to give an account of the Ontario system, which did not suffer in the description at a distance. The deputy minister, in preparation, had had twenty-three papers prepared by Ontario officials on various aspects of the system, including such imaginary projections as "technical education."

Early in the present century in the west, a few American authors like Longfellow found their way into English courses, and Swinton's *Outline of World History*, an American publication, was used as a textbook. After World War I, when friendship with the United States was even stronger, more American authors were represented in junior literature courses, and a composition textbook by Rhodes was used in Grade XII although its illustrative material and its methods were obviously designed for use in the United States. But in 1924 a revised American textbook on world history caused dissatisfaction because of its treatment of World War I, and changes were demanded in the text for use in Canadian schools. Similar trouble arose during World War II in Ontario, where the leader of the Conservative party, later prime minister and minister of education, objected to the treatment of British policy in China and elsewhere, and eventually caused the American book to be replaced by a world history of Canadian authorship. The prevalence of national bias in school histories of many countries prompted a survey to be made between the world wars of the content of history textbooks used in Canadian schools, and an undated report was published by the Women's International League for Peace and Freedom. In 1947, in an effort to reduce grounds for ill-feeling and to encourage a more constructive treatment, *A Study of National History Textbooks Used in the Schools of Canada and the United States* was published by the Canada-United States Committee on Education.

This committee was set up in June, 1944, on the initiative of the American Council on Education. Its Canadian members were appointees of the Canadian

Education Association, the Canadian Teachers' Federation, and the National Conference of Canadian Universities. The committee carried out or co-operated in a variety of activities to strengthen through education the foundations of knowledge and understanding basic to good relations between the two countries. Testing programs and studies of newspaper content showed that many Americans had little knowledge of Canada and that many Canadians had retained prejudices about the United States. But another published report of the committee on *Current Practices in Canadian American Interchanges of Educational Personnel* indicated a frequency of communication across the border possibly greater than similar exchanges between the provinces. The report showed that in 1948 arrangements of many kinds were in operation in many different places for short visits, extended stays, conferences, and even a joint parliament of American and Canadian students. In 1947 the first formal arrangements were made for teacher exchange between the United States and Canada.

"BIN" OR "BEEN"

Various minor prejudices persisted, including objections to American usage in speech and writing. A teacher in Lower Canada urged that a revised edition of Webster's Spelling Book should be printed in Montreal to bring the orthography and syllabication in line with English books like Murray's. Half a century later, in 1881, the editor of the *Canada Educational Monthly* devoted a column to an attack on Hughes for his pronunciation of "been" to rhyme with "sin". He wrote:

Now it is bad enough to import professors for our educational institutions from England, but let us stop short of importing the American language with all its dialects and "fonetics" and thus save the Queen's English from dishonour while we remain subjects of the Crown.[16]

METHODS

American educational methods were another favorite target. When much was heard in 1880 about the Quincy plan, the same editor referred to the "great deal of irrational talk among our neighbors." But a few years later Colonel Parker of Quincy was invited to speak at a convention of the Ontario Educational Association, where he did not hesitate to comment unfavorably on practices of an undemocratic nature in England. Hughes and Parker were friends, and the chief exponents in their respective countries of the educational doctrines of Froebel. It was apparent then, and even more apparent by 1950, that Canadian views on American education were based not on consideration of facts but on the personal, political, and social leanings of those who expressed them. There was also, unfortunately, a tendency among some Canadians to take cover behind ludicrous claims to superior educational standards, which obviously differ greatly among provinces, states, and institutions but not demonstrably in the aggregate between one country and another.

EXODUS

A recurring worry to Canadians was the exodus to the United States of people educated in Canada at public expense. Between the census years 1901 and 1931 the total loss of Canadian population to the neighboring country was 102 per cent of the natural increase or 70 per cent of the accretion by immigration into Canada. A pamphleteer in British Columbia in 1925 complained of the educational cost of this movement: "We are training men and women at great expense to the community in professions and as experts, fifty per cent of whom go to the United States for employment."[17] Between 1939 and 1949 the increase of Canadian students in American universities was twice as great as the increase of Canadian students in the universities of Canada. But most of the Canadian veterans who attended educational institutions in the United States after World War II expressed a preference for subsequent employment in Canada. By 1950 there were indications that Canada would be well able to retain its school and university graduates in the future.

Educational Relations with Other Countries

In its few educational contacts with other countries, Canada, as represented chiefly by Ontario in the nineteenth century, appears to have bolstered its morale by overestimating educational achievements. A foreign visitor who had been greatly impressed by the Ontario school exhibit at the centennial exhibition in Paris was shocked to find when he inspected fifty schools of the province in 1880 that conditions in practice were entirely different. He wrote a letter to the educational press:

In forty-four no globe is there: in thirty-nine no map of Canada itself exhibits: in alone two are there charts like the charts of Paris and Philadelphia, of the body and of plants, and they the teachers say they find no time to employ. For object-lessons, in all the schools did I discover not one. Philosophical apparatus, most of the teachers do explain they never have heard with . . .[18]

He asked whether it was British fair play to put on a show of superiority when actually the schools of many European countries were better furnished and taught than those of Ontario. He was particularly shocked to find that the majority of the teachers were "only young members of the population in third-class certificates."

But from the time of World War II educational relations with other countries ceased to be a novelty or an opportunity

for boasting. To the annual budget of UNESCO the Canadian government contributed its 3.7 per cent share — $323,500 in 1948. As a member nation, Canada sent representatives yearly to the General Conference of UNESCO. Some difficulty was encountered in selecting educational representatives equally acceptable to the provincial governments as educational authorities and to the federal government as the UNESCO member financially responsible. This was handled in 1946, but not subsequently, by the agreement of the federal government to accept the nominees of the C.E.A. and C.T.F. as representatives of public elementary and secondary education. But understanding and appreciation of UNESCO in Canada, and the contribution of Canada to world education, were very much handicapped by the reluctance of the federal government to set up a national commission. This reluctance was understandable in view of the coolness towards UNESCO of Roman Catholic Quebec and Social Credit Alberta and the lack of enthusiasm in some other provinces. Since public elementary and secondary education is more sensitive than higher education, adult education, or the arts, to possible encroachments on provincial autonomy, voluntary agreement of public education authorities has appeared from the first to be a prerequisite to any federal government move towards setting up a national body in which education is represented. Nevertheless Canadians have participated in seminars and other projects both as guests and as temporary employees of UNESCO. Many Canadian teachers and a few administrators have undertaken other educational assignments abroad since World War II, as in Ethiopia, Lebanon, Burma, Indochina, and the Philippines.

After World War II a considerable number of educators from other countries began coming to Canada. In 1949-50 the Canadian Council for Reconstruction through UNESCO, a voluntary organization, brought to Canada for periods of six months or more people from fifteen or twenty countries that had suffered severely in World War II, including one or two educators from each country. After 1951 the Colombo plan brought in a few educationists each year. At the Ontario College of Education from 1949 to 1953 there were from six to fifteen certificated teachers from as many countries among the small group of Canadian students taking regular session courses for post-graduate education degrees.

National Awareness

These various developments suggest a much greater awareness of Canada as a nation, but a continuing reluctance to do anything definitely national in the field of education. To some this is weakness. To others it is the strength of Canada's character that any unnecessary agreement or conformity is avoided. Consider one aspect of the problem, the teaching of Canadian history in Canada. In 1878 the Protestant secretary in Quebec, Henry H. Miles, wrote school histories of Canada, one of a primary nature, and one more advanced. An Ontario reviewer considered the books suitable for Quebec but less suitable for the rest of Canada because they gave considerable space and emphasis to the French regime. Later there were repeated efforts to procure a single textbook in Canadian history for the schools of all provinces. In 1892 the Dominion Educational Association took up the idea, and in 1893 the provincial governments contributed $2000 to conduct a prize competition to encourage the writing of such a text. The prize-winning manuscript, one of fifteen submitted, was published in 1897, but the scheme was neither widely nor permanently successful. During World War II there was again a strong demand from certain individuals and organizations for one authorized Canadian history textbook. If agreement could have been reached on such a book, very large concessions from the various provinces would have been required regarding not only factual content but also desirable pedagogical practice, and above all with respect to the social philosophy implicit if not explicit in the text. What was done? The Canadian Education Association appointed a committee for the study of Canadian history textbooks and published in 1945 the committee's report, which demonstrated how a more balanced and comprehensive treatment of Canadian history might be achieved in school courses and in textbooks and teaching materials. If nationalism in education had gone further, it would have ceased to be Canadian.

Yet many Canadians see no reason for excluding the federal government from control of public education. Their point of view was expressed by no less distinguished a father of Confederation than Sir John A. Macdonald, who in 1872 wrote in a letter to Egerton Ryerson: ". . . the subject of Education has been withdrawn, unwisely as I always thought, from the control and supervision of the General Government."*

* The Hodgins Papers, March 25, 1872 (67 and 205)

CHAPTER 19

The Expanding Scope
of Public Education

ADULT EDUCATION · REMOTE AREAS · HEALTH · EDUCATION OF NEGROES
SPECIAL EDUCATION · SUMMARY

The whole of our educational history might be related to this theme. Through the years an increasing number of pupils have engaged in more varied activities for longer periods of time. The school has been asked to assume many additional responsibilities discussed in preceding and following chapters. The present chapter illustrates the movement by reference to a few extensions and broader concepts of education — pre-school and adult education, the education of pupils in remote areas, attention to health in school, education of Negroes, and special education for the handicapped and more gifted. The following chapter on the education of girls and women continues the theme.

Adult Education

Adult education of an informal or spasmodic kind was carried on from pioneer days. The title pages of early textbooks on colonial geography indicated that they were intended for use not only in schools but by families, travellers, and immigrants. Examples were J. W. Dawsons's *Hand Book in the Geography and Natural History of the Province of Nova Scotia* and the Reverend George Sutherland's *Manual of the Geography and Natural and Civil History of Prince Edward Island*, published in Pictou and Charlottetown respectively in 1852 and 1851. Courses of public lectures were offered by grammar school masters. John Strachan in 1807 offered evening lectures in natural philosophy at Cornwall, Upper Canada, and thirty years later a select committee of the legislature recommended that inducements be given all grammar school masters to follow this early example. The masters of Pictou Academy, Nova Scotia, at mid-century took turns year by year in giving lecture series, typically from 8 p.m. to 9 p.m. Mondays, Wednesdays, and Fridays at rates of ten shillings a course for gentlemen and fifteen shillings for a lady and gentleman. The subjects were usually scientific and the recorded attendance for one year was thirty-four.

There was even a suggestion, during the War of 1812, of adult education similar to that provided by Canadian Legion Educational Services in World War II. A letter in the *Kingston Gazette*, December 1, 1812, probably from John Whitelaw, master of the grammar school in the Midland District, advocated fitting up one of the rooms of the school for the instruction in ordinary school subjects of young militia men garrisoned in the town. The writer pointed out that such instruction would provide them with a welcome relief from their regular work, prevent them from contracting habits of idleness and dissipation, and prepare them for a better life in the future.

MECHANICS' INSTITUTES

To reach men of lower social status and education, mechanics' institutes were organized in England in the 1820's. One of the first in Canada was set up in Halifax in 1831 with Joseph Howe as an energetic supporter. Institutes were founded during the decade in several towns of Ontario, in Charlottetown in 1838, and under a provincial charter in Saint John, New Brunswick, in 1839. The Saint John Mechanics' Institute had a library, a reading room, and a museum. It was supported by a provincial grant, by contributions, and by the fees of members, who numbered 560 within a year of its foundation. The need for mechanics' institutes and the purpose they were intended to serve were explained in the Journal of the House of Assembly of New Brunswick in 1841:

In a country where collegiate learning can by no means become general and where practical instruction in Natural Philosophy and Physical Science cannot be widely extended by the ordinary operations of colleges, any system whereby useful information is given to all classes, must be of the highest importance to the welfare and prosperity of the country. Besides an acquaintance with Philosophy and Literature . . . the Mechanic and Artist requires a perfect acquaintance with those sciences by which alone their industry is rendered most useful. . . . By combining instruction with a certain kind of amusement, they [mechanics' institutes] afford the best relief to all working classes after their daily labour has been completed. . . . The exercise of the mental facilities . . . enables men to discharge with zeal and fidelity all their social and moral duties and fits the mind for the practice of the important precepts of Christianity.[1]

But paternalism stifled the vitality of the institutes from the start. A clergyman addressing the Saint John institute in 1843 said that he was not one of those who looked "with extreme jealousy, not to say alarm, upon all direct efforts to instruct and advance the working class," but although he felt that all men were entitled to acquire such knowledge as the institutes conveyed, he nevertheless felt it necessary to emphasize that he was "no leveller in relation to the different sections of society." Members of the institutes were expected to take the advice of their superiors, who tolerated no free discussion of social, economic, and political problems, but provided lecturers of authority and approved outlook. Subjects for lecture topics were prescribed and books were selected for libraries without consulting the wishes of the members. In Ontario, mechanics' institutes were under the control of the Board of Arts and Manufactures until 1868 and under the direction of a Mechanics' Institute Association until

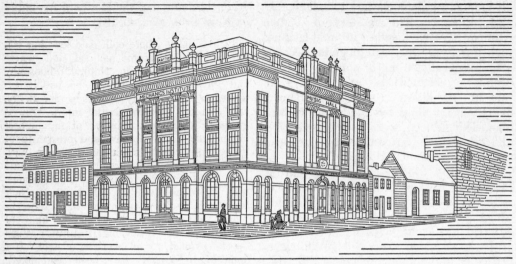

The Mechanics' Institute, Toronto, 1861

1879. By that year the number had increased to seventy-four and the total provincial grant for their assistance was almost $23,000. Soon after, they came under the control of the minister of education, who called a conference on adult education in 1891. At that conference Principal Grant of Queen's pronounced a fitting epitaph: "If you want to go to a place where you are certain not to find mechanics, go to the Mechanics' Institute." An act of 1895 in Ontario empowered the former directors of institutes to transfer their reading rooms and book collections to municipal councils as public libraries. The institutes disappeared elsewhere about the same time.

NIGHT SCHOOLS AND OTHER AGENCIES

Privately operated night schools have already been mentioned as early agencies of adult education. City school boards opened public night schools. Kingston, Ontario, started one for boys in 1861 and one for girls in 1879. Toronto's first venture about 1860 collapsed when attendance fell off until the cost rose to six dollars per pupil per night. The second venture in

1880 was immediately successful. Enrolment increased to about 1400 in 1891, when a more stringent day school attendance act caused attendance at the night school to decline. In Manitoba night classes for the improvement of general education and for teaching English to new settlers were started in 1907. In Alberta before World War I, Calgary had upwards of a thousand evening students in technical subjects and in the English language. In British Columbia grants were offered for academic night classes in 1910 and for vocational night classes after World War I. Since then in all Canada evening instruction has tended to be at an adult level for hobby interests or for academic or vocational advancement, although courses in English for newcomers to Canada were again numerous in 1950.

University extension began with courses for women at Toronto and McGill Universities about 1870. From 1890 Queen's University offered an extension course leading to a degree. A pioneer in extension work as a vigorous activity was the University of Alberta, which in 1912 appointed as director of the department a member of its first graduating class. Best known in the second quarter of the present century was the co-operative movement linked with the extension work of St. Francis-Xavier University at Antigonish in Nova Scotia. Also very active in the later period were the departments at universities mentioned and also at Macdonald College, McGill, and at the University of British Columbia. Extension lectures of the University of Toronto, regularized by the senate in 1894, attracted an enrolment of 15,000 by 1926 and 30,000 by 1936.

Among other early agencies of adult education were organizations of many types. In Quebec *la Société St.-Jean-Baptiste* was formed in 1834 to maintain French-Canadian identity and culture, and in Montreal *l'Institut Canadien* was set up in 1844 to develop intellectual and aesthetic interests. In Ontario the first women's institute appeared in 1897 at Stoney Creek. A Presbyterian minister began educational work among woodsmen of the Algoma District in Ontario in 1899, secured a helper in 1903, and so organized Frontier College, which carried education to lumber, mining, and other camps in various parts of Canada. The Workers' Educational Association began operations in Canada at the end of World War I. Since then adult education agencies and activities have multiplied in bewildering number and variety. Two radio forums deserve mention if only because of their national scope, National Farm Radio Forum and Citizens' Forum, initiated in 1941 and 1943 respectively. To reduce unnecessary duplication of effort by the many agencies and to help to pool resources the Canadian Association for Adult Education organized a Joint Planning Commission in 1946.

ACTION BY DEPARTMENTS OF EDUCATION

Newfoundland provides an example of provincial developments in recent years.

After the organization of the Newfoundland Adult Education Association in 1929, notable results were achieved. Prior to that date evening classes in scientific, practical, and other subjects had been available in St. John's, but little was being done in other parts of the island where adult education was most needed. Experts were brought in from other countries and a teacher was sent to the United States for special training. One of the most interesting types of work introduced was that of the opportunity school. Only a small proportion of the teacher's time — from four to six hours a week — was given to classroom instruction in the evenings; most of it was spent in daytime visits to homes, where the teacher acted as leader of a group. Adult education work of various types was extended throughout the whole island. In 1936 the association became a branch of the department of education. In 1938-39 there were thirty-eight centres of adult education instructing more than 2700 men and women, whose average attendance at classes was better than 80 per cent, and instructors or leaders made upwards of 5200 visits to homes.

In other provinces also recent administrative changes brought adult education into closer contact with the public school systems. In Nova Scotia in 1945, in Ontario in 1947, and in some other provinces divisions of adult education were established within provincial departments of education. Although this arrangement was a logical necessity if adult education agencies were to be given regular support from public funds, it sometimes proved embarrassing both to governments and to adult educators. Saskatchewan, under a democratic socialist government, in 1944 appointed to its newly formed Adult Education Branch a director who was dismissed a year or so later for publications and utterances judged to be pro-communist. In Ontario the department assumed responsibility for an adult education

Draping Class in Ryerson Institute of Technology

division reluctantly because education of the type was known to flourish under voluntary initiative without checks which a government agency is compelled to impose.

Remote Areas

In a large country, distance from school has always been a handicap. Even in 1941 the percentage of young people aged 15 to 19 at school was 50 per cent higher in urban Canada than in rural Canada, and for the group between 20 and 24 years of age the difference between urban and rural school attendance was twice as great. We have already seen how local authorities sought to improve educational opportunities in rural areas by consolidating schools and by providing transportation. An alternative that gained little acceptance within public school systems was the boarding school or day school with attached dormitory. In New Brunswick, Sunbury County Grammar School

in the 1860's set up boarding accommodation for forty pupils. In British Columbia from 1874 to 1876 the public school at Cache Creek had dormitories for girls and for boys and an attendance of up to forty-four under the supervision of a teacher and his wife; but partly because of financial difficulties and partly because such an arrangement was a scandal to Victorian morality, it closed and became a day school shortly after. The boarding school was alleged to have fallen into a deplorable state of ill-repute in spite of the fact that the girls and boys were isolated and forbidden to engage in conversation even at meals. Since the venture had the personal blessing of the provincial superintendent, its failure had some significance. Seventy years later in some school divisions of Alberta successful dormitories were operated where suitable buildings were erected. Pupils were brought in on Sunday evenings and returned to their homes on Friday evenings and provided with board and lodging at a cost to the parents of only $4.00 a week. But although the social development and training in responsibility were apparent to some, Roman Catholic school officials among others did not approve. In British Columbia, for a like reason perhaps, the one section of the Cameron Report not implemented by the government was a recommendation that school dormitories be provided in certain areas.

Correspondence school branches covering elementary grades were established by provincial departments of education in the decade following World War I. Dates of establishment show how the innovation spread from west to east: British Columbia, 1919; Alberta, 1924; Saskatchewan, 1925; Ontario, 1926; Manitoba, 1927; Nova Scotia, 1930. Ten years later the courses were extended through junior high school grades and shortly thereafter to the completion of high school work in the western provinces. New Brunswick in

1939 opened a correspondence high school with a triple purpose. It served young people in rural areas who had completed Grade VIII but who were unable for any reason to attend a secondary school, it provided further education for older people, and it enabled teachers with lower qualifications to improve their academic standing. In 1943 nearly 200 New Brunswick teachers enrolled for correspondence courses. In Newfoundland the small correspondence school with one teacher in charge expanded sufficiently to require a second teacher in 1940. From the early 1930's onward, school radio broadcasts were used more and more to increase the effectiveness of instruction by correspondence, and in some places the elementary school teacher was enlisted to give assistance to correspondence students. Another method of carrying the school to the child was the railway car classroom. Ontario from 1926 used this means of reaching children in scattered and shifting settlements along the three transcontinental lines in the northern part of the province. Newfoundland also used railway cars. In Nova Scotia shopmobiles were introduced to give shopwork experience to pupils in rural schools.

Health

The expanding scope of public education was marked by a growing concern for the health of the pupil. The first great wave of interest came around 1880. New Brunswick teachers in their institutes between 1875 and 1878 discussed cleanliness in school, methods of handling contagious diseases, and other questions related to health. "Thoughtful and practical educators," said the editor of the *Canada School Journal* in 1878, "are more and more directing their attention to the subject of school hygiene."[2] Reports of ministers of education in the 1880's and 1890's devoted many pages to sanitary conditions, to fenced playgrounds, and to the new conviction that a healthful environment, exercise, and instruction in hygiene could prevent disease. Popular journals carried articles on the health of school children. One in the *Maritime Monthly* in 1873 discussed the relation of academic progress to health, asked how much of school learning was really necessary, and condemned in the strongest terms "the injustice done, the misery inflicted, the health destroyed, the cruelty manifested . . . by parents and preceptors" against "dyspeptic children, beaten because they could not remember a lesson consisting of words carrying no meaning."[3] *Kosmos* in 1886 expressed approval of the concern shown by education authorities to secure healthful conditions in school and classroom.

Although provincial superintendents during the 1850's and 1860's had succeeded in eliminating some of the dirtiest and shabbiest buildings, most schools were still ill-ventilated, dingy, and uncomfortable. Centre Street School in Toronto in 1865 had an average of over ninety pupils in each of its rooms and such an offensive smell from the playground that windows had to be kept closed in hot weather. When in Quebec City in 1874 as many as eighty children were crowded into a classroom, an effort was made to improve the condition of the air in schools by running a square duct in the corner of the building up through the roof. *The Journal of Education for Lower Canada* carried an article two years later on calculations necessary to ensure adequate ventilation. Small windows, incorrectly located and often dirty, gave only half the useful light needed to spare the eyes. This condition also led to the publication of numerous articles by teachers and doctors on better illumination and care of pupils' eyesight. Among the provinces that issued new regulations regarding school premises was Manitoba, which in 1879 required

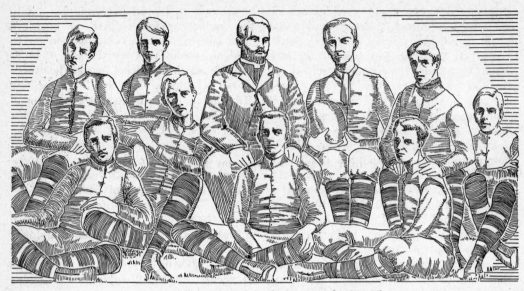

Football team, High School of Montreal, 1896-97

adequate ventilation in buildings, fenced school grounds no smaller than a prescribed minimum in size, and separate play areas for boys and girls in town schools.

PHYSICAL EDUCATION

Although trained teachers in Upper Canada had been given some acquaintance with physical education, little was done in the schools. Then came an increasing demand for physical training, as illustrated by an article in the *Journal of the Board of Arts and Manufactures for Upper Canada* in 1865 and two articles in the *Journal of Education for Lower Canada* in 1873 and 1874, all pointing out dangers in the neglect of physical culture in schools or benefits to be secured by its introduction. The model school of the New Brunswick Normal School in 1877 appointed an instructress in physical training who had sets of cards on which were printed exercises for use with pupils standing between rows of desks; the normal school students bought the cards because they feared the instructress as a disciplinarian, although they did not use them when

they obtained positions in schools of their own. In Ontario after 1879, when examination pressure in high schools was extreme, there was tremendous interest in getting pupils to take physical exercise. One article in the *Canada School Journal* that year described "Goodyear's Pocket Gymnasium" — a strong rubber tube with wooden handles inserted at the ends. Other articles by a New Brunswick teacher admitted that no serious consideration had been given to the physical development of school children until the previous few years, and that it would take time to convince the public that a teacher should be employed for any other purpose than teaching the famous three R's, and for the burdening of children's memories with dry bones of fact concerning Siberia and Patagonia, and equally dry rules of English grammar. She emphasized, however, the need for good posture in school, for permitting pupils a change of position, for avoiding drafts and cold feet, for warm clothing, and for health instruction. At the Ontario Educational Association in the same year a clergyman gave a talk on the use of calisthenics and gymnasium apparatus and emphasized the value of physical education as a means of inducing morality. In 1879 a high school inspector reported that the collegiate institute at Galt had a good gymnasium in constant and effective use and that Chatham, already distinguished for girls' calisthenics, had also procured funds for a gymnasium.

By then, in Ontario, gymnastics, drill, and calisthenics could be provided at the option of trustees. In 1881 a teacher from Galt spoke to the Ontario Educational Association on the value of systematic outdoor exercise, of gymnastics and drill, of having pupils move about in the classroom, and of getting pupils to sit and stand with proper posture. The minister of education in his report emphasized the importance of physical training. In 1885 there were gymnasiums in five collegiate institutes of the province. In the copious discussion of the next few years there were arguments between proponents of informal and formal gymnastics, pleas for supervision of recess, and claims that physical training in cities would probably be a panacea for urban vice. The Ontario regulations of 1909 gave collegiate institutes still without gymnasiums two years to make good the deficiency on penalty of forfeiting collegiate status.

In the decade following World War I there was another spurt of interest in physical education, which before World War II became established as one of the trio of compulsory subjects in Canadian schools. The related teaching of health will be discussed in a later chapter.

PHYSICAL RECREATION

After about 1880, also, there was a new interest in recreation and in the mental health of pupils. The first sports day in the Toronto Collegiate Institute was held in 1877. In a paper read before a teachers' association in 1880 the principal of the high school in Dundas, Ontario, urged

teachers to encourage outdoor games and take part in these games with the pupils. He said that chores and work done at home were no substitutes for activities that "not only divert and stir the courses of his blood, but cheer his spirits, and make him forget his studies for the time." One of the benefits to be secured, in the opinion of the author, was that children would like rather than detest school. His reason for the teacher's taking part in the games was to check the acquisition of habits of using bad language, for fear of which many parents kept their children from free association with other boys and girls and in some cases sent their sons and daughters to private schools. But in most of Canada it was not until the end of the century that schools engaged physical training instructors and made efforts to interest pupils in sports and extra-curricular activities. An inspector in the province of Quebec in 1901 was delighted to find at least one school in Montreal with a skating rink attached. Said he: "The boys and girls who take an active interest in toboggan slides and ice ponds have less time to devote to sensational and to silly sentimental reading."[4]

Once people began to realize that children had lives to live as well as brains to cram, surprisingly generous concessions were advocated. A contributor to a professional journal in 1877 urged frequent recess periods and advised that pupils should not be debarred for more than three-quarters of an hour at a time from enjoying a few minutes in the fresh air. In a paper on "Gymnastics of the Brain," read before the Canadian Medical Association at Ottawa in 1880, Dr. J. A. Grant emphasized the need for exercise of body and mind and strongly assailed methods which forced young people to stuff their heads with facts under a pressure that depressed their spirits. The superintendent of the Toronto Lunatic Asylum in his annual report for 1879 stated that the Ontario public school system was a "pregnant source of the mental and physical deterioration which, in a secondary way, affects the adult population as well as the youth of our land, from the senseless mental overstrain to which school children are subjected."[5] The same theme appeared in various publications: the *Journal of Education in Lower Canada* in 1875 explained causes of mental disturbances and offered appropriate advice to teachers; *Knox College Monthly* in 1883 had a doctor discuss the mental strain and physical harm caused by excessive study. Actually, in terms of school day and recess periods, children were not much more restricted than they now are; but in terms of pressure and stultifying drudgery unrelieved by lively activity, the lot of later Victorian children was indeed hard.

MEDICAL SERVICES

Almost a generation later came the beginning of medical services for school children. Illustrative of necessary preliminary steps was the establishment in Ontario of a provincial board of health and the extension of powers of local boards of health in 1882. Indicative of the obstacles to be overcome were views on immunization expressed in Toronto in 1900: the mayor said that vaccination in schools was "a dirty, filthy practice"; the school board declared that "it had been established that vaccination was powerless to prevent smallpox" and requested that it should not be made compulsory for children whose parents and guardians had conscientious objections. In 1905 at the Ontario Educational Association, attention was given to records made in the 1890's of the height and weight of Toronto school children, and to vision, condition of teeth, communicable diseases, and even to nutrition. In 1908 legislation, Ontario permitted public or separate school boards to provide medical and dental inspection of pupils. British Columbia in 1911 put

into operation a school medical inspection act, which called for a yearly examination by a qualified practitioner of all school children, teachers, and janitors. Several large cities in Canada had previously established medical inspection, for example, Vancouver in 1902. There a school medical officer had been appointed part-time in 1907 and full-time in 1910, when the first school nurse was also appointed.

World War I focussed attention on health, and health services were extended after the war. Ontario offered grants for medical and dental inspection in 1918 and permitted boards to provide surgical treatment of minor defects in 1920. British Columbia in 1920 empowered municipal school districts to employ nurses and dental surgeons and offered grants in assistance, in 1927 required such districts to appoint health inspectors, and in 1932 enabled school trustees anywhere to engage nurses. Manitoba was the first province to develop a public health nursing service in rural areas. Saskatchewan after 1918 empowered any trustee board or group of boards to provide medical and dental inspection and to employ a school nurse; in 1925, nurses of the province visited over 1200 schools and inspected some 14,500 children. Alberta had four public health nurses in 1918 and twenty-one in 1920. Health units established in Quebec in 1922 and strengthened in 1925 conducted educational campaigns and gave preschool care. Medical inspection was introduced in smaller cities — for example, in Moncton, New Brunswick, in 1918.

By 1941 all provinces had legislation permitting local authorities to provide medical and dental inspection, and New Brunswick, like British Columbia, required it. Generally speaking, full medical and dental inspection by doctors and dentists was to be found only in cities. In many rural areas there was no inspection except that of the teacher; in others there was inspection by a school nurse. Although no complete data were available, there was evidence that about one-third of the pupils in schools had defects other than dental and that about one-third of the defects were discovered and corrected. Treatment of such defects was seldom provided at public expense. Similarly, the proportion with dental defects appeared to be about two-thirds of all pupils and up to ninety-five per cent of the pupils in communities where no school dental services were required. About one-third of the Canadian cities had better than superficial school dental services, generally including both inspection and treatment. As a rule, immunization services were provided at the discretion of local authorities, who could make acceptance of the services virtually compulsory. In a selected group of sixteen cities, about eighty per cent to ninety per cent of the children received diphtheria toxoid and from forty per cent to one hundred per cent were vaccinated. Elsewhere the percentages were presumably much lower and more erratic. There had been a tendency to place school health services under provincial and local boards of health, as in the Prairie Provinces, and as in Ontario after 1925.

These conditions gave no ground for complacency. Vexing questions concerned the extent of responsibility that could be assumed by governments without overburdening taxpayers and without destroying parental responsibility and interest. In many places health services were provided as a charity to the poor. When a free dental clinic was first opened in Moncton, the school board provided supplies and the dentists of the city gave treatment without remuneration to the children of indigent parents; in 1926 a service club, the Gyro, sponsored the clinic and paid for the work. In a few places, the free school philosophy was extended to health services. Around 1930 a majority of Toronto citizens, regardless of economic status, had no compunction about sending their children for treatment to school dentists whose services were paid for by local taxation.

VARIATIONS IN CONDITIONS

In a country as large as Canada differences in conditions over a long period of years are likely to be no greater than differences between one area and another at a given time. As a corrective to any false impression that the passage of time necessarily implies progress, take Lysecki's description of a typical school in Manitoba as late as 1935. At Pikwitonei, two hundred and thirteen miles from The Pas on the Hudson's Bay Railway, was a settlement consisting of five stores and a post office, two section-houses, one bunkhouse, about sixteen dwelling houses, and the usual railway buildings. The school was built in 1916, although the district was not organized until 1931. Until 1930 the pupils sat on long benches, five on each bench. There were thirteen white and three half-breed children in 1934. The teacher obtained all her academic schooling in The Pas — up to Grade XII. She and the pupils did the caretaking of the school. She said: "During the long winter months, the first thing in the morning you must light your fire in the box-stove, as quickly as possible, then chop up the ice in your water pail and thaw out your wash cloth. The idea is to exercise as much as possible to keep from freezing." Dances were held usually once a week. At New Year's, 1934, a basket social was held and $120 was realized. With this money maple flooring and shingles were bought for the school.

During and after World War II the revived interest in school health led to widespread and varied activities. One problem, revealed more clearly by the first report of the National Committee for School Health Research in 1947, was the great variation in health conditions between rural and urban schools and between one province and another. Inadequate caretaking facilities, infrequently tested drinking water, outdoor toilets, and lack of artificial lighting were conditions common in one-room rural schools and rare in larger urban schools, but generally much worse in poorer provinces. Reports of this committee and of the National Committee for Mental Hygiene also revealed disturbing facts about the mental health of teachers and, by inference, of pupils. Although during a century vast improvements had been made in sanitary conditions, opportunities for recreation, and almost every aspect of education related to health, the complexity of life in 1953, new possibilities, new vision, and new problems left much more to be done.

Education of Negroes

Advertisements in early issues of the *Quebec Gazette* offered rewards for the return of runaway Negro slaves. But in 1793 in Upper Canada legislation prohibited the importation of slaves and provided for the liberation at age twenty-five of the children of slaves already in the country. In 1833, by an act of the British parliament, slavery was abolished in the colonies. Canada therefore became a refuge for a considerable number of Negroes, of whom there were said to be 30,000 in 1852. Upwards of 2000 lived in the neighborhood of Chatham in Kent County, Upper Canada, where John Brown held his convention in 1858. Nova Scotia also acquired and still retains a fair number of Negro settlers. A contemporary writer on conditions in Upper Canada at the middle of the nineteenth century described the Negroes as "performing the most burdensome and lowest descriptions of labor" and living in "the least valuable corners of the towns at a scale of civilization greatly inferior to the mass of the population."[6] A century later the comparatively few Negroes in Canada were more restricted in economic and social opportunities than those in parts of the northern United States where their numbers were large.

As might be expected, early nineteenth century differentiation applied to the education of Negro children. In New Brunswick in the 1820's two schools for Negroes were opened, one in Saint John and one in Fredericton. In 1841 Negroes petitioned for provincial assistance and received the usual grants as long as the so-called African schools met the required conditions. In Nova Scotia, as we have seen, a share in the small supplementary grant was offered in 1832 to schools for neglected Negroes; in 1845 up to one quarter of the provincial grant might be used by any district for the education of Indians and Negroes.

In Upper Canada, prejudice often deprived Negro children of a chance to attend school. As often occurs, those who bolstered their claims to superiority by showing contempt for possible inferiors belonged to a class similarly despised, "the lower order of whites," as the police commissioners of Hamilton described them. The Negroes of that town petitioned the government in 1838 for aid in setting up a school of their own, and in 1843 petitioned as taxpayers for admission of their children to the common schools, from which they were debarred. The Negro ratepayers of Amherstburg, Canada West, in a petition of 1846 quoted their white detractors as saying that "sooner than they will send them to school with niggers they will cut their children's heads off and throw them into the road side ditch."[7] The whites there had told them that the town school was private. Then, when the Negroes elected trustees, the whites said that theirs was the public school. When the Negro children then sought admission, the teacher, acting under orders, refused them entrance. Up to this date, Ryerson supported the right of the Negroes to attend public schools. But in the next two years he admitted that prejudice was stronger than law and "with extreme pain and regret" proposed a revision in the school law to provide separate schools for Negro children, who might otherwise have had no chance to receive an education.

The legislation referred to, was passed in 1850 and made it a duty of the municipal council to establish separate schools for "colored people" on the application of twelve or more heads of families. Interpreted in accordance with the Ontario principle of individual choice* this should have meant that action could be taken only on the request of the Negroes themselves. But as interpreted by Ryerson under pressure from Chatham and other places, it meant that the municipality at the demand of prejudiced white men could establish a separate school for Negro children and exclude them from the schools for whites. For a few years the separate school privileges of Roman Catholics rested on this same clause, a fact which adds to the confusion in the whole anomalous issue of divided public schools. Certainly the police commissioners of Hamilton had been right in advising the superintendent against any concession to prejudice by permitting the segregation of Negro children, for bigotry can make a mockery of the public school if ever its foundation of universality is undermined by recognition of a division among the people. Admittedly the issue was mainly of theoretical importance, since the maximum number of separate schools for Negro children at any time was only three. A Wilberforce Educational Institute was established in Dresden in 1840, to provide more advanced education for Negroes.

Unless compelled by the prejudice of others to segregate, the Negroes had no desire for separate schools. Their attitude was reflected in 1834 by an educated Negro lad who preferred "being employed as an assistant at the Central School rather than to open a school of his own for colored children." There was obviously no racial discrimination in this denominational central school — the Church of England school at Toronto — and probably less in other Anglican and Roman Catholic denominational schools than in some later truncated "public" schools in which no community of faith, sectarian or universal, made physical characteristics unimportant. Not until 1890 did the school board of Chatham, Ontario, reverse its policy of segregating Negro children. In that year separate schools for Negroes disappeared, and the Wilberforce Institute, which had acquired a new building at Chatham in 1887, soon lost its pupils to the public high schools.

In 1939 Tanser found that 188 Negro children in seven schools of Kent County had a median score fourteen points lower than 544 white pupils of the same schools on four of the white man's intelligence tests. If, as is likely, environmental factors past and contemporary were largely responsible, democratic education by school and society had even then some "levelling" work to do.

Special Education

As population and wealth increased and sensitivity to misfortune was heightened, provision was made for the education of those who could not profit from ordinary instruction. Prior to 1850 very little was done. Later in the nineteenth century institutions were built for some who were severely afflicted in obvious ways. In the present century special education was provided in some centres for those whose partial handicaps had escaped detection and provoked only punitive measures before.

* See p. 314.

THE HANDICAPPED

Typical of early efforts was a petition asking the government of Upper Canada in 1836 to vote a sum to provide for the education of two deaf and dumb children, and a report in the same year of a special committee of the legislature recommending the establishment of schools for the deaf and dumb. Eighteen years later an expenditure of $40,000 was authorized, but nothing was done. In 1858 a Society for the Instruction of the Deaf and Dumb and of the Blind was organized in Toronto. Supported by $2.00 fees of members and by $40.00 subscriptions which carried the right to nominate candidates for free instruction, it maintained a school which in 1868 was educating about twenty of the 300 deaf mutes in the province. Children in Toronto could be sent as fee-paying day pupils for $20.00 a year and boarders from outside the city for $140.00. In the fall of 1870 the Ontario Institution for the Deaf and Dumb was opened in Belleville. This institution had an enrolment of about 100 in 1871 and 280 at the end of the decade. Its methods attracted attention in Quebec and elsewhere. Meanwhile this Ontario development had been preceded by the foundation in 1857 of the Halifax Institution for the Deaf and Dumb. The Halifax School for the Blind was opened in 1871. These Halifax institutions served not only Nova Scotia but also the two adjacent Maritime Provinces, although New Brunswick established its own institution for the deaf and dumb at Fredericton in 1872. The Ontario Institute for the Education of the Blind was established at Brantford in 1871.

From these and similar beginnings elsewhere, this type of work was extended in the twentieth century to include, in ordinary schools, sight-saving classes and classes for the hard-of-hearing. Parallel developments were the placing of the older special institutions under the provincial departments of education and the provision, within departments, of a division or of supervision of some kind for special education. After about 1910, and in the largest cities first, there began to appear open-air and forest classes for tubercular and sickly children, schools and classes for crippled children, speech correction classes, visiting teachers for stay-at-homes, and a great many other special services, of which only a few can be dealt with below.

Special classes for the mentally handicapped were recommended in Toronto by Hughes in 1894. The first class of this type in the city did not, however, come into operation until 1913. Next year the Ontario Auxiliary Classes Act was passed and an inspector of auxiliary classes appointed. Immediately after World War I a summer course was offered for teachers of special classes, and by 1926 there were forty-four auxiliary classes for pupils of extremely limited intellectual ability. Subsequently much more was done in some places for the mentally handicapped, including the provision of special classes for dull normals at different levels. A survey by Russell and Tyler in 1941-42 indicated, however, that there were only about 525 classes in Canada for children of the 50 to 75 I.Q., or auxiliary class, level — still an extremely inadequate provision. Of these, 323 were located in Toronto, 66 in Montreal, 48 in Winnipeg, 29 in Vancouver, and the rest in other cities of all provinces except Prince Edward Island. Nevertheless rapid progress had been made within the preceding decade and the special class teachers were becoming a highly skilled professional group. The survey revealed only four special classes for gifted children, two in Montreal and two in Saskatoon, with a total enrolment of less than a hundred. But since experiments with such classes in London, Ontario, and elsewhere revealed social disadvantages that possibly outweighed intellectual benefits, this was not a serious deficiency in public school systems still geared in higher academic grades to the ability of the intellectually superior student. Nevertheless, several cities at present are planning to establish special classes for the gifted in elementary grades.

ATTITUDES TOWARDS CHILDREN

The treatment of children generally, and of orphan, neglected, and delinquent children in particular, changed with the schools during the past century and a half. The callousness of pious and impious adults of earlier generations is almost incredible. Children were exploited as cheap labor on the home farm, and as employees of others. Only as late as 1873 did Nova Scotia — the first province to take action — prohibit the employment of boys under ten years of age in or about the mines and limit the working hours of boys under thirteen to ten hours a day or sixty hours a week. In 1877 British Columbia forbade the employment below ground of boys under twelve. In 1882 a commission reported that the employment of children in mills and factories was extensive and increasing, that some of the child workers were as young as eight or ten years of age, that some were ignorant even of their own ages, that they worked the full day from as early as 6.30 a.m. and sometimes with compulsory overtime, and that they and older employees, in Montreal at least, might be chastised at their employer's discretion with the express permission of the recorder of the city, who justified the practice as conforming to law, both civil and divine. Ontario in 1884 passed a factory act prohibiting the employment of boys under twelve and girls under fourteen and restricting hours of work to sixty a week for boys of twelve to fourteen, girls of fourteen to sixteen, and women. Quebec passed a similar act in 1885. Ontario in 1888 restricted working hours of boys under fourteen and girls under sixteen to seventy-two a week in mercantile establishments, and in 1897 made the employment of children under ten illegal in retail stores.

Orphans, children deserted by their fathers, and children whose parents were in jail or dependent on public charity could be bound as apprentices by local authorities. This meant that boys were compelled to work for the master up to the age of twenty-one, and girls to the age of eighteen, under terms which even in later legislation of 1877 gave little protection to the apprentice and chief consideration to the master. Institutions for orphans first appeared in Ontario after mid-century and the number in receipt of government aid increased from five in 1868 to ten in 1871. In a typical institution of 1860 boys of seven to fourteen years were let out for hire at about a penny an hour. Large numbers of unwanted and deserted infants were kept alive, if hardy enough to survive, in numerous privately operated baby farms, which were not subject to regulation in Ontario until 1887. Infant homes established in Halifax, Montreal, and Toronto about 1875 began to rescue such infants and to save the lives of many. Forty per cent of children born in Canadian cities died during their first year, according to mortality returns in the *Canada Lancet* in 1878. Surplus children exported from Britain to Canada sometimes found employment during the harvest, only to be left destitute in the streets of a town in winter. In the Toronto jail in 1869 there were five boys who had been sent out in 1868 by an institution in London, England, and who for "want of any friendly shelter or advice" had resorted to crime. After 1870 such children were given a much better chance because they were escorted to the new world by a Miss McPherson to be placed in the service of "warm-hearted Canadian farmers," who were required to allow them to attend school for a specified number of months each year.

Many children who lived with parents were no better off, even around 1887, when it was estimated that between six and seven hundred boys and about one hundred girls — many of them mere infants — were sent out into the streets of Toronto by drunken and avaricious parents to get money by selling newspapers, pencils, and other articles if they could, or by begging and pilfering. A small brother and sister found begging on a cold November day were afraid to go home because they had been threatened with a whipping if they failed to collect at least twenty-five cents. Kelso, a contemporary historian of the Children's Aid movement, wrote of "indescribably shocking conditions among the little girls who thronged newspaper alleys and sold papers in the neighborhood of saloons, theatres and downtown thoroughfares until late in the night."[8]

Five years of intensive activity by Kelso and others were marked by such events as the establishment of the Toronto Humane Society in 1887, of the Toronto Fresh Air Fund in 1888, and of a children's playground in Jesse Ketchum Park in 1889. In 1891 the first Children's Aid Society in Canada was organized in Toronto to provide a shelter for children and to secure protection for children under the law. Two years later it became for the first time an indictable offence in Ontario to abuse or neglect children. The hardships of the young did not immediately disappear, but state action marked the awakening of a social conscience based on a growing adult capacity for sympathy and understanding. Ontario in 1893 appointed a superintendent of neglected and dependent children, and rapidly expanding Saskatchewan did the same in 1909. The achievement of more humane attitudes and

the improvement in conditions for children during the present century are too great to be related briefly and too obvious by contrast with the past to be denied.

CORRECTIVE INSTITUTIONS

Nevertheless there was criticism in 1953 of failure to discipline erring children by punishment. In 1813 when schoolmasters and parents were severe, the law was more so. That year in Montreal three men and a boy less than fourteen years of age were hanged for stealing — the boy for "grand larceny of a cow." For petty offences children were sentenced to confinement in the same jails and penitentiaries as adults, where they associated with "murderers, coiners, horse stealers, and scoundrels of the deepest dye."

Humanitarians were successful in securing the establishment of separate reform institutions for children in Penetanguishene, Ontario, in 1859 and in Halifax in 1864. The Ontario institution was housed in a barracks disused after the war of 1812 and was considered by a contemporary educationist to be well managed, perhaps because its one hundred inmates in 1861 were strictly confined to ensure their suffering an adequate punishment. The provincial inspector of asylums, prisons, and public charities reported in 1877 and 1878 that the appearance of the institution and the disciplinary arrangements were still those of a prison and that the juvenile offenders, until a short time before dressed as convicts, were still called by that name. The only schooling they received until 1875 was an hour's instruction before breakfast.

The inspector's efforts to improve conditions were backed by educators, who wanted industrial schools not as punitive but as protective and remedial institutions for destitute children and for children whose parents were incompetent to bring them up, whether the children had run

Drake House, Ontario Training School for Boys, Cobourg, Ont.

foul of the law or not. Legislation in Ontario providing grant aid for industrial schools in 1882 was followed five years later by the establishment of Victoria Industrial School near Toronto. A commission of investigation in 1890 found that this massive structure was simply a more commodious prison where boys were locked up every evening behind iron bars in a triple tier of cells. Nevertheless the principal of the school in 1892 claimed that many so-called incorrigible boys had been saved from a life of crime. For girls, the first reformatory in Ontario was built in 1878. But even in the 1880's some boys and girls were sent to the common jails, and until 1888 there were no separate courts or trials for juvenile offenders.

The contrast between 1900 and 1950 was clearly marked by comparison of these earlier institutions with later training schools. The Bowmanville Training School for Boys, successor to the Victoria Industrial School, offered not only regular classroom instruction and vocational training but also a generous program of extra-curricular activities. The routine and the discipline were such as to encourage responsibility and pride in the school community. On graduation boys went home or to carefully selected foster homes, as well prepared as possible psychologically and otherwise, to take jobs or to continue their education, and the school continued to take an interest in their careers. By nineteenth-century standards, the school failed to administer deserved punishment, but its success in rehabilitation was commendable. The same change could be seen in greater or less degree in the program of other training schools of similar type elsewhere in Canada.

Summary

Adult education has had a long history, since the need of formal provision is most obvious when schooling is meagre. Experience has shown that in democratic society adult education can succeed only when the participants have a share in its direction and active part in the educative process, except when instruction is sought for a definite purpose. Recently adult education has received financial and other assistance from provincial departments of education. Among devices to carry the advantages of education to remote areas, dormitories were seldom used in the public school systems, whereas correspondence courses and radio broadcasting increased in popularity. Towards the end of the nineteenth century the public school began to assume increasing responsibility for the health of pupils and to co-operate with health authorities. From the ignorance, bigotry, and indifference of 1900 a great advance has been made, but much remains to be done. A distinction of the mid-nineteenth century which disappeared was the separate education of Negroes. On the other hand, special provision for handicapped children was made in the nineteenth century only in the case of obvious and extreme defects, whereas after World War I various types of special education have been introduced to help the less fortunate. The contrast between conditions towards the end of the nineteenth century and at the middle of the twentieth century is amazingly sharp if comparison is made of the treatment of children whose parents were poor or neglectful — whether orphans and strays, or young workers and employees, or offenders against the law. Not only the scope but the humanity of public education has expanded.

CHAPTER 20

Girls and Women

The basic issue affecting educational development in Canada has been the retention or reduction of traditional distinctions. Human beings get satisfaction from a classification which places a restricted number of people, ideas, or things they cherish in a superior category. In the past there was little hesitancy about claiming divine sanction for any classification or distinction which could be exploited to advantage. Those who came first to this country were accustomed to assert or accept clear-cut distinctions between the governing and the governed, gentlemen and common men, the educated and the ignorant, rich and poor, and the good and the bad. But much land for a few people was a great leveller. Distinctions in kind tended to become differences in degree, and in some fields the validity of any differentiation was questioned.

The history of education in English-speaking Canada is largely a record of a struggle to achieve parity for everyone and for the aspirations of everyone against the resistance of those who sought to maintain the superiority of forms advantageous to the group with which they identified themselves. The theme is revealed with sharp clarity in the century-long transition from older ideas on the status and education of women. In 1850 differences between the sexes were emphasized, and in education every effort was made to keep the two apart. Around 1880 the differentiation was challenged. By 1950 retention or recurrence of such thinking and practice was considered reactionary.

Segregation in the Early Nineteenth Century

We have seen that authorities in the old days, including the Roman Catholic and Anglican churches in particular, tried to establish separate elementary schools for girls even against insuperable geographic handicaps in rural areas. In populous centres they were able to prolong the losing battle in graded schools of the people until after 1850. In Quebec City and the surrounding district Roman Catholic schools about 1830, except convent schools, were entirely for boys; the six Protestant schools were attended by both boys and girls, although girls were much less numerous. Grant legislation for the whole province in 1832 provided an additional allowance of £20 for the support of a separate girls' school in each Roman Catholic parish. In Upper Canada the master of the Church of England Central School at York asked in 1826 for a woman as an assistant because he did not want to have girls and boys taught together. In Preston, Upper Canada, in 1847, special schools for girls were prudently located in a part of the village remote from the school for boys. In the small province of Prince Edward Island in 1847 there were nine "female schools" in receipt of aid from the public funds. In British Columbia, probably because of English influence, special efforts were made to segregate the sexes. New Westminster kept open a separate school for girls in 1866 with an average attendance of twelve but had to abandon it the following year when the number fell to six and the teacher resigned. Even after Confederation, the central authority in British Columbia was given power in 1872 to set up separate schools for girls where it deemed such action expedient.

But the above instances are exceptions, for co-education was common in schools of the people in rural areas from an early date, and in virtually all schools of Protestant communities by the time of Confederation. In the early part of the nineteenth century girls received less education than boys. Where possible they were given special instruction in needlework and morality. But in spite of prevailing views it was not possible to keep the young daughters of the majority from association with the sons.

A Victorian Education for Women

Middle- and upper-class families of means and respectability protected their daughters from any such possible contamination. In towns and cities there were numerous private schools and convent schools for girls only. Young ladies from a distance attended as boarders, and others as boarders or day pupils. In Newfoundland, the Roman Catholic bishop in 1842 introduced the Congregation of the Sisters of Mercy, one of whose objects was to provide a higher order of education for the daughters of well-to-do citizens. In the Red River area in 1851, a Church of England school for girls was built and came under the direction of a Mrs. Mills and her two daughters, who gave young ladies very thorough instruction in all the social usages of the day in addition to solid intellectual fare. In Victoria, British Columbia, in 1864 there were two ladies' colleges, one Church of England and one Roman Catholic, each with an attendance of forty or fifty. In the older provinces of Canada there were numbers of institutions like these. In Canada East there were also academies for girls, including schools at Cowansville, Melbourne, and Waterloo in 1850. In Canada West there were dozens of private schools and academies describing themselves in various interesting ways, among them the Cobourg Ladies' Seminary, which in 1845 became

Burlington Ladies' Academy, and a school in Brampton which in 1863 became the Eclectic Female Institute.

The curriculum in pre-Confederation schools for young ladies was designed to ensure their escape from the hardships of the less fortunate by emphasizing female dependence. Women of the lower and lower middle class worked and endured more than men and for a smaller recompense. Opportunities for independent employment were limited and wages were pitifully low. Wives bore and reared many children and toiled laboriously about the house. Approval of their sharing in other work of the farm was expressed at mid-century even by an enlightened Nova Scotia editor who hoped that labor-saving machinery might be found to reduce household drudgery. This large majority of women received little attention or consideration and had no aesthetic or intellectual recreation. Though without the pleasure of participation, many women had to endure the effects of the amiable and less amiable vices in which men sought escape. Others must have found virtuous husbands no less forbidding. Small wonder that women of position or determination welcomed a type of education which would enable their daughters to escape the lot of ordinary women. Schools for young ladies carried their charges to the brink of matrimony with the attractions of unquestionable virtue, of an ingenuous manner complemented by adroit manners, and of purely social and ornamental accomplishments, with the further insurance against hard work of a seemingly delicate constitution. Everything about the young lady distinguished her from the common female as a precious exception from whom it would be sacrilege to expect any practical service.

Hence Miss Matilda Davis in the Red River area at mid-century was extremely particular about the propriety of her girls' behavior. She placed particular stress on their deportment as they walked two by two to St. Andrew's Church twice on Sunday and as all thirty sat at the long dining table under her watchful eye. Mrs. Mills in her school at St. Cross in the same district made discipline in diet a rule: she included bread and butter with meat in her plain menus only once a day. Schools in far-off New Brunswick differed only in the greater variety of useless skills they offered to impart. Sussex Vale Academy and Boarding School in 1819 taught "drawing, painting on paper or silk, all kinds of plain and ornamental needlework, embroidery with silk or gold, embroidery of flowers, figures, or pictures, filago work, etc."[1] Mrs. Huret's school in Saint John in 1840 offered music, painting, French, Italian, dancing, and deportment. But by far the greatest variety of accomplishments could be acquired at the school opened in 1843 in the same city by the Misses MacIntosh. The good ladies not only taught grammar, reading, ancient and modern history, composition, rhetoric, philosophy, natural and moral, botany, geography, astronomy, algebra, arithmetic, bookkeeping, French, and Latin for the cultivation of the mind; they also offered as contributions to gracious living: drawing (six styles — artificial, rice, water, oil, oriental tinting, and pencilling in two modes), transferring, writing (round and square), pianoforte, guitar, and accordion, needlework (plain, ornamental, colored, and netting), fancy knitting, velvet and crepe embroidery, point work (Italian, German, and French), fancy work, fly cages; letter racks; match boxes; water rices and aluminum work, wax fruit and flowers, bead, twist, and braid work, dancing (Victoria and Lowe's quadrilles, lancers, cotillions, and other fashionable dances). What more could a gentleman ask for in his bride? Advertisements of early schools in Upper Canada and elsewhere list only a few other "polite branches of female education," including mantel ornaments, Dresden work, miniature paint-ing, seraphim, and guitar.

Revolt from the Victorian Point of View

Published male opinion on the question showed no great admiration for "accom-plishments" and no anxiety to put the female mind to competitive trial. At the Mechanics' Institute of Saint John, New Brunswick, W. T. Wishart delivered an address on "The Female Sex," which was printed in *The Provincial,* a Nova Scotia monthly, in 1852 and distributed also in pamphlet form. The author was respect-able enough to subscribe in part to or-thodox views on the capabilities and defi-ciencies of female nature. Women were not likely to add to our knowledge of physical and moral science: "The severe searching mind that gives eminence to the lawyer is foreign to their usual constitu-tion." Their abilities, moreover, were "not calculated for those impetuous and concentrated efforts that are deemed re-quisite for the career of the politician and orator." But Wishart insisted that the minds of women could be and should be improved by intellectual pursuits and that their time should not be wasted on cro-chet, embroidery, and needless domestic drudgery. The editor of *The Provincial* had more characteristically masculine views. He was not among those who thought that the position of women re-quired either elevation or redress. "To our idea she has at the present day every legitimate exercise of her intellectual and social faculties . . . She occupies the posi-tion which her Creator intended her to fill, that of 'help meet to man,' the only 'right' she should ask for or require." He was afraid that the elevation of the female mind might interfere with essential family tasks and expressed a preference for "less of thinking and more of domestic com-fort."[2]

Most gentlewomen were prepared to support make-believe regarding themselves for the sake of their own security. *The Mayflower,* a monthly for women publish-ed in Halifax by Miss Herbert in the 1850's, carried articles and stories entitled "Virtue Alone is Beautiful," "A Sweet Pic-ture," "Love," and "The Oppressed Seam-stress." An essay on "Female Influence" conceded the divine right of male super-iority and claimed only a complementary function for women:

Woman in all her relations is bound to "honor and obey" those on whom she depends for protection and support, nor does the truly feminine mind desire to exceed this limita-tion of heaven. But where the dictates of authority may never control, the voice of reason and affection may ever convince and persuade . . .[3]

But in an article on the "Training of Daughters," the author dealt not only with "cultivating a taste of what is re-fined and beautiful," but urged mothers to set a good example of cheerfulness in the performance of household duties in order that their daughters might not be averse to making themselves useful. Such advice not only appealed to sensible peo-ple of both sexes but showed educational insight as keen as any in the twentieth century. A year later, at the time of Wish-art's address, the editor of *The Mayflower* was bold enough to quote with guarded approval an essay published in England which discounted the notion that women were intellectually inferior to men, lament-ed that ladies were "taught less to think than to shine," and advocated the same type of education for both sexes.

About this time, in 1848, a school of the more solid type opened in Toronto. The editor of the *Agriculturalist and Cana-dian Journal,* who may have had personal reasons for his favorable opinions, de-scribed its program as an "appropriate and thorough education of those destined to become the mothers of the next generation, and not the mere gilded butterflies that buzz and flutter in the saloons of fashion."[4] Instead of merely fitting young ladies to "sing, and dance, and yawn through a worthless existence," this school and another like it in Hamilton (probably Burlington Ladies' Academy) taught "useful and solid branches" like rhetoric, moral philosophy, general history and astronomy. In 1869 at the Royal Canadian Institute, Daniel Wilson, later President of the University of Toronto, urged Canadians not to strive, as many Americans were doing, "to clothe women in all that is costly" but to realize that women of the new world, like the male aristocracy of classical times, constituted the class who had leisure for intellectual pursuits. In 1873 the *Journal of Education* in Lower Canada, quoting from *Hearth and Home,* exhorted mothers not to be coaxed to send their daughters to "this or that delightful seminary" but to turn a deaf ear to the demands of Mrs. Grundy and give them the best education that the princely resources of a wealthy age could afford.

This mid-century revolt against female accomplishments had acquired steamroller power by 1880. Said Principal Grant of Queen's University in his inaugural lecture at the ninth session of the Montreal Ladies' Educational Association in 1879:

When I think of the varieties of dress, head-gear, and ornamentation that have been thought fashionable among us in this century, and of all that is involved in the disproportionate degree of time, thought, and money bestowed on these things, of the poor and false ideals set before our girls in good society, of the dreary, aimless, brainless round of exhausting frivolity to which they are doomed, I cease to wonder that there are so many unhappy marriages, and that the race should be so slow in learning the alphabet of Christianity.[5]

A woman who wrote militant anonymous letters to the press that year protested against standard prescriptions in the education of young ladies. She said that it could surely not be necessary to teach every girl music and singing whether she had a taste for it or not, and that "much pain would be spared musical persons if young girls were not set to play 'Rippling Rills' and 'Cascades' very indifferently in every drawing-room, or encouraged to disturb air-currents by appeals to rivers to bear them far away." She protested also against the teaching of drawing to every girl regardless of her aptitude or desire. And why, she asked, should all girls be given a smattering of German and Italian when they were likely to see neither Germany nor Italy and would be no better fitted to make themselves understood by the natives of those countries if they should happen to travel?[6]

More vigorous training was advocated at this later date. Miss de St. Remy of Kingston, Ontario, won the confidence of readers in an article on "The Training of Girls" by conceding the "feebler frame" and "higher-strung nerves" of women. But how, she asked, could a girl be made like the polished corner stone of the temple — strong to support, quiet to endure, a strength and a help and a constant pleasure to all with whom she associated, and not a burden? By hard work and exercise. By making daughters useful, as laboring class families did.

I will never acknowledge that to get up in the morning, dress prettily, and dawdle through the forenoon with the help of some self-imposed task of needlework, and spend the afternoon in an aimless walk, will make any woman contented.[7]

But in the last quarter of the nineteenth century mothers who had escaped from poverty and toil preferred to educate their daughters for idleness in the bonds of matrimony.

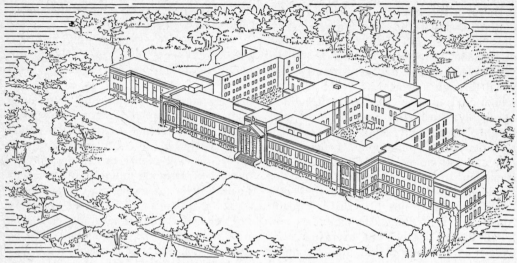

A private girls' school. L'institut pédagogique des Soeurs de la Congrégation de Notre-Dame de Montréal

The private schools which carried on the old tradition had lost some older clients to the public schools but acquired new pupils from the commercial class. Calendars and notices of recognized institutions towards the end of the nineteenth century emphasized high academic standards but did not conceal the earlier purposes. Ontario Ladies College at Whitby, founded in 1874, claimed to give a thorough knowledge of the elementary branches as a foundation and to carry the building upward "until the cap-stone is put on in the higher branches of Science and Philosophy."[8] At Dunham Ladies College, a Church of England institution in the province of Quebec, the course of study was said to be "comprehensive, aiming to develop the reflective faculties, imparting a solid culture combined with a Religious, Mental, and physical training." Perhaps the lower case initial in the third adjective indicated a significant difference! But there were "extras" at Dunham — instrumental music, vocal music, theory and harmony, drawing, painting, and the German language. Mount Allison Ladies' College in New Brunswick still advertised

in 1887 "painting on china, plush, wood, brass, terraline, etc. . . . among the novelties which illustrate the progressive character of the instruction imparted in the department of Fine Arts."[9] For moral development, chief reliance was still placed on protective isolation. "Instead of the impure air and temptation incident to a public thoroughfare," said the Whitby prospectus in 1884, "we have here a quiet and happy retreat," No calls or visits were permitted there on the Sabbath. The minimum program of intellectual and moral training with board in these institutions cost about $150 to $175 a year in the 1880's, and a "good variety" of social accomplishments about fifty per cent more. *Rose Belford's Canadian Monthly* in 1875 had given the private schools their cue in appealing to the fastidious piety of the carriage trade:

Most of all, therefore, we want in our ladies' colleges — and it is a *sine qua non* — a pure, high-toned atmosphere free from worldly frivolity and vanity. . . . We want an atmosphere in which our Canadian girls may grow up as pure and fresh and dewy as English violets . . .[10]

Co-education in Secondary Schools

The development of co-education was linked with the elementary and secondary schools of the people. Never a real issue in the former, it would probably have followed without question in the latter if it had remained an affair in which only the people were concerned. When the Midland District School Society through the columns of the *Kingston Gazette* in 1815 appealed to people for ten dollar subscriptions, it was to provide a school for both sexes. But educational and religious leaders were opposed to co-education, particularly at the secondary and higher age levels. Their efforts against natural, geographical, and economic forces slowed up the co-educational movement sufficiently to give it time to acquire an interesting history. At the more advanced educational level co-education became a real issue only after the establishment of non-denominational or secular universities. It had then to contend only with academic tradition and male insecurity when tenets regarding intellectual differences in the sexes were in danger of being subjected to test.

Before 1850 co-education was forced on the grammar schools to the extent that young girls of social standing attended to obtain elementary education. But senior pupils at the secondary level were almost always boys. Small academies and some larger academies were co-educational, as might be expected in view of their transitional nature.* Objectors to co-education in the Eastern Townships proposed that for five years Stanstead Academy should receive only young women and that Charleston Academy be restricted to young men, but were voted down. Upper Canada Academy, as typical of the denominational type, was co-educational with extreme precautions:

* See p. 195.

The front of the edifice is appropriated as a place of exercise for the females — the rear, and play-ground, for the males. And more effectually to preclude all intercommunication between the sexes, their corresponding, conversing, or, in any way associating together, save in the case of brothers and sisters, (and that by permission of the Principal or Preceptress) is expressly interdicted.[11]

Possibly the nearest thing to modern co-education was illustrated by a notice published in Saint John, New Brunswick, in 1805 of "a Drawing School for the instruction of young ladies and gentlemen in the accomplished and pleasing art of Landscape and Flower Painting." But even a dancing school, in Kingston, Upper Canada, advertised in the *Chronicle* on New Year's Eve, 1819, that instruction was offered to ladies from 2 p.m. until 5 p.m. and to gentlemen from 6 p.m. until 9 p.m. If the gentlemen had partners they were presumably not ladies! This staggered-hour system was an old device: James Tanswell in Quebec in 1786 taught gentlemen from 7 a.m. to 10 a.m. and from 3 p.m. to 6 p.m., and ladies from 10 a.m. to 2 p.m.

By the time of Confederation there were breaches in the opposition to co-education in publicly supported secondary schools. In Upper Canada Egerton Ryerson and George Paxton Young, Methodist and Presbyterian clergymen respectively, were no less distrustful of co-education than the Anglican Bishop Strachan. But they compromised in 1867 with grammar school trustees who admitted girls by allowing them to count a girl as one-half a boy for purposes of the grant, and they helped prepare legislation which made high schools largely co-educational four years later. Some places held out. In Kingston, where a committee of the common school board in 1852 had described as a great evil "the promiscuous attendance of the sexes at the same school," the collegiate

Co-education — a secondary-school orchestra

institute board in 1876 still refused to admit girls. Seven citizens then offered to pay the cost of fitting out a classroom for girls and the additional cost in teachers' salaries. In 1877 the board admitted girls to instruction in the separate room and in 1879 assumed the cost of their education. Twenty years later the number of girls in attendance exceeded the number of boys. In Toronto the collegiate institute building erected about 1880 had separate rooms for girls, as did the high school in Montreal.

Even at the time of Confederation, however, some educators had the courage to assert that co-education was not merely tolerable under close supervision but in itself desirable. The respected Dr. Forrester of Nova Scotia insisted that the mutual advantage to both sexes of association in school was demonstrable evidence of "the power and glory" of an important educational principle, the "sympathy of numbers."* The *Journal of Education* in the same province quoted with approval radical arguments that "men and women

* See p. 415.

possess the same order of faculties" and that there was "no fear of clandestine affairs in self-governing institutions." In 1879, John Millar, later deputy minister of education in Ontario, matched the common argument that association of the sexes was conducive to immorality by an assertion that co-education gave both sexes a stronger incentive to study. Against opposition, chiefly clerical, this point of view gradually reduced the restrictions on co-education in high schools — but not everywhere, and probably never to an extent that would permit the freedom allowed elsewhere in the community.

Co-education in Universities

At higher educational levels the conflict between male jealousy and pressure of circumstances was even more interesting. To get respectable teachers at a low price, education authorities were compelled to lower the barriers against the employment of women. In New Brunswick, where smaller grants to female teachers and a quota law limited their numbers in 1833, a shortage of teachers in 1841 led to the distribution of a circular inviting young women of twenty-five to forty years of age to apply for positions. By 1850 one-third of the registered teachers in the province were women. The issue of co-education arose when a girl in her early twenties, Martha Hamm Lewis, applied for admission to the New Brunswick training school for teachers. When her application was refused, not once but many times, she appealed to the lieutenant-governor and obtained an order-in-council directing her admission, although the council warned her that it took no responsibility for any ill results. The principal of the school, greatly perturbed, erected a barricade of special rules against the audacious female. McNaughton says:

She had to enter the classroom ten minutes before the other students and was required to wear a veil. She was asked to sit alone at the back of the room, retire five minutes before the lecture ended, and leave the premises without speaking to the male students.[12]

Alas for the quick passing of those days of high morality when bulls and men teachers alike were designated males! By 1860 women in the normal schools of all provinces were so common that Dawson in Montreal used their number as an argument against the extension of co-education to McGill University. He tolerated the presence of women in the McGill Normal School only because they constituted a large proportion of the student body and because teachers-in-training could be subjected to "strict rules of discipline impossible in the case of college students." Even so, the anxieties of the principal and his colleagues had "necessitated a large infusion of trained and educated women" in the staff of the normal school. It is safe to conclude that the staff acquisitions were not selected with a view to making conditions of work more

pleasant or permitted to set an example which would encourage "female infusion" in other faculties.

Co-education in universities was therefore delayed for some time. By 1870 Dawson had become a cautious advocate, desirous of having university examinations made open to women and even of having the university provide lectures for women on literary and scientific subjects. He said:

I do not propose either that the young women should attend the ordinary college classes, or that, except in special cases, the ordinary professors should lecture to them. I would have special classrooms, and in many instances at least, special lecturers appointed by the university.[13]

President Daniel Wilson of the University of Toronto was somewhat less liberal. Although he helped to organize the Toronto Ladies Educational Association in 1869 and gave regular courses of lectures to large classes of women at a safe distance from the university, he made a sharp distinction between higher education for women, which he had come to support, and co-education, against which he remained adamant. In this attitude he had the support of Goldwyn Smith who wrote in an article in the *Princeton Review*:

Supposing, however, that the final education of men and women is to be the same, it is a separate question whether they can receive it in the same universities. . . . We have to ask ourselves whether the young women of the wealthier class generally can be safely mingled in a university with the young men of the same class.[14]

But women were not to be denied full intellectual status and freedom of association in democratic society on the specious argument of protection from moral inferiors. The sequence of events at the University of Toronto was as follows. In 1877 the senate of the university established local examinations of women on the subjects of matriculation examinations

Calisthenics for girls, 1858

for men. In 1878 girls and women with matriculation standing applied for admission to the university and were refused. In 1879 a girl from Hamilton Collegiate Institute won a moderns scholarship but could not use it. In 1880 it was decreed that girls should be given the money attached to scholarships, could be enrolled on class lists at the university, but could not attend classes. In 1882, to the horror of men who relied on the argument of female inferiority, two other girls won scholarships, not in the congenial field of modern languages, but in the stern discipline of mathematics. In 1884 a motion in the legislature to admit women to the university, though opposed by Wilson and the university council, nevertheless passed. In February 1885 this legislation became effective, and eleven women students entered the university. Some months later there were 68 women in the first year, 19 in the second year, 4 in the third year, and 5 in the fourth year, the more advanced students having previously obtained standing extra-murally.

The Amazon victory was won elsewhere in Canada at about the same time — somewhat earlier at Acadia and Mount Allison, in 1882 at Dalhousie, in 1884 at McGill, and a few years later at the University of New Brunswick.

Wilson argued to the last that the presence of women would upset order and discipline. Like President Eliot of Harvard, he believed that co-education was at best a measure of expediency and necessity and that young men and women of college age would undoubtedly be educated separately when the country progressed in "wealth and refinement." But Principal Grant of Queen's University had broader ideas. Truly convinced that women should have "as thorough mental training as men," if only to make them fit companions for their husbands, he was prepared to admit them to the university in spite of the objections of those who cried out in alarm. Speaking before the Montreal Ladies' Educational Association in 1879 he said:

Surely by this time we have got far ahead of the gross idea that woman's virtue depends not on herself, her modesty, self-respect, and principle, but on thick veils, padlocks and duennas.[15]

Colleges for women helped to consolidate the victory, although at first they were a concession to isolationist views. When St. Hilda's College was added to Trinity University in 1889, separate lectures for women were provided at first. Medical colleges for women were established at Queen's and Toronto in 1883. Follow-up gains at the University of Toronto were marked by the establishment of the University Women's Residence Association in 1893, of the association's Queen's Hall in 1905, of Annesley Hall in 1903, and of two special schools, Margaret Eaton in 1907 and Lillian Massey in 1912. In the later 1920's the number of women enrolled in universities was well over half the number of men. Between 1920 and 1950 the number of women enrolled in graduate work increased eleven times. A woman advocate of colleges for women in 1908, Maud C. Edgar, argued that women's rights had been won, that co-education for all was not necessary, and that there was a tendency for women, unless they had colleges of their own, to avoid courses in which men predominated and to concentrate too much on fields like foreign languages.

Women in the Professions and the Vocations

The element of truth in that statement was linked to the final stage of emancipation, the admission of women to education and employment in practical affairs. Even Principal Grant refused to promise women support in their efforts to obtain admission to all professions. Others in 1880, like the Reverend Canon Norman of Bishop's University, still protected their complacency by the expression of definitely restrictive views:

Also, women I conceive, as a class are somewhat disqualified for certain callings in life, not from lack of ability, but rather because the requisite preliminary training, the love of study, and the duties of the calling, would be apt to crush out of them what is tender, delicate, and womanly. I do not intend the slightest depreciation of the mental capacity of the gentler sex when I say this.[16]

Any man could have some sympathy for the feeling of the good canon, who must have had contact with some of the formidable female types occasionally produced by more solid programs of education for women after 1850. The author of *Upper Canada Sketches* decried a "prevalent tendency among young women not to entertain matrimonial ideas" and the preference of an increasing number to take employment as nurses, telegraph operators, "typewriters," ticket sellers and stenographers — all to the detriment of women's "proper sphere as queen of the home." There must indeed have been many girls of independent spirit in accord with one of their number who wrote in 1879:

Why should I be obliged to give up to Society, to whom, as yet, I owe nothing, the most active and vigorous part of my life? Is the aim of my education only to be accomplished by a constant round of garden-parties, balls, and receptions, — if so, why have I been taught anything else, but to read, write, dance, enter a room gracefully, and chirp a feeble song to a wandering and uncertain accompaniment? These acquirements would have been enough to have given me a footing in what is called Society. No! I cannot submit to that kind of thing; I must have a purpose, a life-work, a determined end in what I undertake.[17]

Since that time the breakdown of barriers against the employment of women proceeded slowly as a rule, but with acceleration during the great wars of the twentieth century. By the end of World War II guidance material on careers for women mentioned particularly the occupations of food specialist, journalist, lawyer, librarian, occupational therapist, physiotherapist, optometrist, pharmacist, physician, and social worker, in addition to other obvious callings. In 1953 nearly all types of employment were at least open to women, though not always on equal terms with men, and at least some girls were enrolled in nearly all educational institutions and courses. Educators in sympathy with this new economy tried to prepare the young by easier association of the sexes at school. Yet the conflict of views continued, especially because a large though diminishing proportion of women preferred economic security and dependence to the hard responsibilities of freedom. Contrary to the fears of some men, the new tendencies were not detrimental to home-making. In 1893 a published plea for education in the practical work of the housewife was a novelty, whereas sixty years later such courses were commonplace and home conditions incomparably superior for that and other reasons. Among non-Catholics a high mark of emancipation was demonstrated by the educated young women who engaged in essential work during World War II, married, helped support a veteran husband during the completion of his education, and then raised a family. Co-education designed to prepare for this type of service was available in most of Canada in 1953 but was not appreciated by all.

Summary

The old world maintained a distinction between the sexes in relation to education and intellectual pursuits, but only at higher social levels. Differentiated female education prepared young ladies for dependent leisure. The new world outlook of the common people regarded boys and girls in school simply as pupils. Co-education prevailed in elementary schools of the people from the first and in high schools also as they became schools of the people in the latter part of the nineteenth century. By that time only private schools for the well-to-do and Roman Catholic schools kept the sexes apart. The secondary schools for young ladies adopted a heavy program of academic subjects no different from that of secondary schools for boys, except that some vestiges of the former curriculum of ladylike accomplishments remained. Women secured admission to universities after Confederation by pressing for one concession after another in quick succession. Chiefly since World War I they also secured an entry to nearly every type of work. No serious educational obstacle remains as a barrier against women who seek respect as equals, although many of both sexes no doubt still prefer that the sexes should receive differentiated treatment in their education and their later work.

PART FOUR

Educational Thought and Practice

In the fourth part of this volume attention is focussed on educational thought and practice. Again it will be instructive to consider developments in society at large, but with emphasis this time on less material aspects, on new ways of living and thinking. Then we shall turn in succession to changes in educational thought, in the elementary school program, in the secondary school program, in educational method, in discipline and ethical training, and in examinations and standards. The last two chapters will deal historically with the major determinant of quality and efficiency in education, the teacher.

CHAPTER 21

Changing Attitudes

TRADITION AND ENVIRONMENT · OUTLOOK ON LIFE · BREAKDOWN OF
HEREDITARY DISTINCTION · RELEASE FROM MATERIAL STRINGENCY · THE
WIDENING OUTLOOK · AMUSEMENTS · CRIME AND PUNISHMENT ·
MORALITY · RELIGIOUS TOLERANCE · INTELLIGENCE AND THE SCIENTIFIC
ATTITUDE · ARISTOCRACY AND DEMOCRACY · SUMMARY

Democratic society is not homogeneous. In no part of English-speaking Canada have all people shown in their thinking
or by their behavior equally strong attachment to the same
values. Nowhere have they changed at the same rate in their
attitudes. Even if there had been some uniformity or consistency
among residents of long standing, newcomers in most parts of
the country were sufficiently numerous to disrupt unity or alter
the pace of advance. The majority in one province held views
which did not gain the ascendancy in another province until
thirty years later. Most rural communities clung to notions and
ways which had ceased to be dominant in most urban communities sixty years before. There were always a few individuals,
including educators, who seemed to be a century ahead of the
times and others who seemed to be a century behind the times
— and even the times may be interpreted differently by different observers.

On the whole, however, attitudes of people in 1840 har-
monized with their confidence that society, institutions, creeds,
commandments, right, wrong, and everything else had a definite, fixed, and almost material form. A remedy was a remedy
no matter what its origin, its reaction under particular circumstances with a particular individual, or the record of its
failures. Indeed, to question or test any formula, belief, loyalty,
or duty was to incur the wrath of the individual or social group
who cherished the form or pattern. It was right and God's command that the son should respect his father even if the latter
was a drink-befuddled and vicious tyrant who was corrupting
other members of the family. The form, or literal interpretation
of the commandment — rather than its spirit or effective operation — was the primary consideration. Similarly, formal classi-
fications were accepted as objectively valid. Actual distinctions
in kind were taken to exist if it were to someone's advantage to
separate people or things into inferior and superior categories

on any convenient basis. Parentage made a gentleman or commoner, sex a stronger or a weaker mind. Books, sentiments, skin color, occupations, and the like were divided by earmarks into at least two classes — good and bad, acceptable or unacceptable. Most people in the old world lived a dog's life of strong attachment to familiar forms and distrust of the stranger's ideas. In these and other respects the new world of today is not wholly unlike the old world of yesterday, but it is different enough to make a large number of people today aware of the change.

The difference, it must be emphasized, is in the attitudes and behavior of people generally, not in originality of brilliant minds. If the activity of writers and leaders in reform were the criterion, the middle decades of the nineteenth century might be judged more lively in some respects than the present. But public education is by definition concerned with the whole populace, to whom the above statements apply.

After the middle of the nineteenth century a growing number of people revealed more and more clearly attitudes based on a different concept of the world. Their respect for particular forms declined as their trust in principle and their confidence in other people increased. Thinking replaced acceptance of established patterns in the production and distribution of commodities. Organization was found to pay dividends, and competition became less often a contest between unsupported individuals. Liberalism, founded on economic optimism, grew more and more willing to give everyone a chance — a chance to show enterprise and to share in the benefits. Distinctions became less clearly marked between those who had a say and those who must do as they were told, even in the superior-inferior relationships of old and young. Intelligence, no respecter of established forms, entered new fields, although the powers it unleashed were seized in 1950 as in 1850 by two-fisted, unregenerate believers in old-world values. On the whole, however, in the new world of 1950 more people were sensitive to the aspirations of others than ever before. They were less willing that the individual child or man, through inability to resist threats of deprivation and punishment, should forego the opportunity to live his own life in his own way. More people were moved by aesthetic, intellectual, and ethical considerations and less bound by formulae for keeping themselves secure and others in their place.

Broadly, in spite of exceptions, regressions, and regional variations, life changed and education changed during the nineteenth and twentieth centuries in the direction of open-mindedness. Manifestations of the change may be observed in aspects of social living which have important implications for the school.

Tradition and Environment

Two strong traditional influences tended to maintain the old-world point of view. In French-speaking Canada the values of seventeenth- and eighteenth-century France survived with little modification by later European thought of a liberal character. There developed a remarkably homogeneous French-Canadian civilization in which language, religion, and culture were closely linked in preserving a traditional way of life both before and after the British conquest and into the twentieth century. Even in 1953 the older attitudes remained, although industrialization, urbanization, and association with Americans and other Canadians had become a serious challenge. Among English-speaking Canadians of British descent a tradition originally paternalistic and subsequently conservative continued, although in diluted and weakened form, as a check on environmental forces. The attitudes of Canadians, strongly influenced by one or the other of these traditions, tended to accord with a formal view of the world — for example, in attaching high intrinsic importance to traditional school subjects without reference to circumstances or to the response of the learner.

The environmental influence of North America was related to energy rather than mass or form. As a dynamic force it attached little value to permanence and high value to progress. That people should do things was of more importance than that any form of life should be kept unchanged. The attitudes of Canadians, strongly influenced by the environment, became less attached to old-world forms and more in sympathy with the world of action and with the views of people generally.

Outlook on Life

Because of the limited use of scientific knowledge, life in the old world was short and precarious. Helpless under the constant threat of uncontrollable disaster, the bold were reckless and callous, the timid strict and restrictive in their narrow piety. As an immigrant the newcomer had risked shipwreck and plague. As a settler he was prodigal in fathering many children and bowed to fate when the Grim Reaper was equally greedy in carrying them or their mother away. Catastrophe struck frequently and without warning. In hardly more than a decade and as late as 1876-86 major fires destroyed 500 houses in St. Hyacinthe; almost all of Saint John; Acadia College, Nova Scotia; the parliament buildings of New Brunswick and Quebec; and most of Vancouver. Within these same years a devastating cyclone swept New Brunswick, and a steamship collapsed near London, Ontario, with a loss of 200 lives. The early record of the railways was punctuated with more serious disasters than the corresponding, later record of the commercial airlines: 47 killed in a collision west of London in 1854; 60 killed when a train went through a canal bridge near Hamilton in 1857; 86 killed when an immigrant train fell into the Richelieu River in 1864. In spite of two appalling wars in the twentieth century, more people travelled farther and faster and lived longer and more diverse lives with comparative safety and greater confidence.

Reflecting the tragedy of life, earlier school readers were gloomy in content and strong in their emphasis on man's dependence on God and on the one sure future beyond the grave. They changed as conditions of life changed. With the improvement of transportation in the 1850's, they became more practical; with the increase in production after Confederation, they became more human; and with economic progress and medical advance after 1900, they became quite cheerful. We shall see later how aims, curricula, methods, and discipline responded to the growing confidence of man in men and of adults in children. As adults ceased to cling for security to the time-honored forms and patterns of a tragic world, children had less reason to fear the rod and less compulsion to memorize the meaningless verbiage which had previously been accepted without question as the true form of education.

Breakdown of Hereditary Distinction

Gentlemen by birth tried hard to maintain their superior positions. In New Brunswick before 1850 the high-born were described as supercilious, the newly rich as self-important, the middle ranks as stiff and ceremonious, and all below the top stratum as eager for admission into the more select society they condemned as unjustly exclusive. People were sensitive about position: Christopher Widner of Toronto in 1837 tendered his resignation as a member of the Council of King's College when the name of a new appointee appeared above his name on a list. The author of *Three Years' Residence in Canada* in 1840 found many sons of the gentry unwilling to engage in agriculture or commerce, as pursuits beneath their station. Not until 1851 was the law of primogeniture abolished in Canada. But the new world had no place for those with neither money nor practical ability. An Oxford graduate who, as a cabin passenger, had helped in kicking and cuffing a steward's assistant on the steamship to Canada, was reduced to waiting on tables in a cheap restaurant operated by the former menial in Victoria, British Columbia, about 1870. There, too, a lady "of the most superior attainments" was compelled, when her husband took to drink, to keep herself alive as a tavern entertainer and prostitute.

Lower class immigrants from the British Isles were immediately able to sense the growing American spirit of equality, discarded the cloak of servility, and by open insolence revealed their hatred of those who treated them as inferiors. Newspapers appealed to a larger circle of readers by what seemed to some a licentious abuse of gentlemen in high positions. Symbolic of the disappearance of respect for caste was what Lower calls the "democratic promiscuity" of Canadian railway cars, in which formality was reduced still further by the off-hand familiarity of the conductors. The sleeping cars and parlor cars of a later day were for a mobile commercial aristocracy for which neither birth nor education was a necessary qualification.

Marshall d'Avray, Superintendent of Education in New Brunswick, expressed in his report of 1856 educational views that were realistic in the earlier two-class society:

Unless we grant that shadow and substance are identical — that quackery and science are synonymous — that a mere smattering of knowledge is equivalent to knowledge itself, and that as much can be learned in three or four years by the one class, as in the ten or twelve which the other can afford to devote to School and College, as well might it be asserted that they are entitled to lands and houses — to rich furniture and gay equipages — and at once overthrowing all the distinctions at present existing in the world, maintain that the poor have a right to the property of the rich.

The persistence of this attitude, and the fear of mass enlightenment even in the age of commercial aristocracy, were illustrated by a paper read before a section of the Royal Society of Canada by C. Baillairgé in 1894:

The education of the masses should not go too far beyond mere reading, writing, and arithmetic and the object lessons here proposed. . . . Let us beware of too much education. There is a danger of overdoing the thing and thus causing or inciting our should-be agriculturists to be dissatisfied with their parents' mode of livelyhood, flocking towards cities and towns or populated centres, there to become second and third class professionals of every hue, with little or nothing to do; with mischief and discontent and anarchical tendencies following in the wake.[1]

And that on the eve of the great increase of secondary school enrolment which was to make a high school education in 1940 as common an accomplishment as an elementary school education in the society of clearly marked social classes a century before!

Release from Material Stringency

A curious quirk of the human mind has made it conventional to categorize as materialistic those societies which produce an abundance of material goods and have time to spare for other pursuits, and to credit with spiritual and idealistic attributes those who from dawn to dusk must toil without machine power to get the bare necessities of life. But observers of early nineteenth-century life — whether in the fishing villages by the Atlantic, or on the backwoods farms of Upper Canada, or among the laborers in towns — found that preoccupation with working for a living left neither leisure nor aspiration for higher pursuits than drinking and crude physical pleasures. On the prairies in the first decades of the twentieth century it was demonstrated again that necessary concentration on making enough to live, left people indifferent to schools and cultural institutions and opposed to any expense for benefits not in material form. In his inaugural address at Victoria College in 1842 on the advantages of a liberal education Egerton Ryerson quoted Roger Bacon: "Seek first the goods of the mind, and the rest shall be supplied, or no way prejudiced by their absence." Although not many were able then to follow the advice, there were signs a generation later

of the new world that was coming. An article reprinted by educational journals of Upper Canada and Nova Scotia declared: "In future, the richest nation, and consequently the most powerful, will be that which shall apply the most knowledge to labor. . . ." and, with no less truth: "While education is indispensable to the increase of wealth, it is no less needed to teach its proper use."[2]

A few incidents may be selected to mark the development of an organized economy. Between 1817 and 1837 several banks were founded — the banks of Montreal, of Quebec, of New Brunswick, of Upper Canada, and, at Montreal, of British North America. The Massey firm began making farm machinery in the 1840's. New freedom for trade was marked in the same decade by the removal of restrictions against commerce with nations other than Britain and from 1854 to 1866 by reciprocity with the United States. Timothy Eaton's store in Toronto had four employees in 1868 and forty-eight in 1878. The report of a royal commission in 1889 indicated that trades unions were beginning to develop a spirit of independence and self-reliance in workingmen. The opening of the west in the twentieth century led to wide-scale organization of business. Financial concentration came after World War I and industrial expansion after World War II. In 1954 it was possible for most people to make an adequate living and have time and energy to spare for other pursuits. In 1841, in Canada West, life was as generous to the few as it was niggardly to the many: the chief magistrate received $8,000 a year, thirty or forty times as much as a laborer. A century later few such discrepancies existed in North America among people in ordinary pursuits, although there were fantastic exceptions. In Canada under the old-world conditions of 1841 domestic servants could be hired easily for $4 to $6 a month with board; in 1951 they were hard to find at $90 to $100.

Even the lowly female had escaped servitude and been granted the right to live.

The Widening Outlook

At the time of Confederation, Montreal and Toronto had sidewalks, some paved roads, horse cars, gaslighted streets, and a few houses similarly illuminated and equipped with such comforts as baths. But colonial attitudes, timidity, and narrowness of mind, according to Lower, kept Canada far behind the United States in material improvements and in vigor of life. The two countries were brought closer together, however, when the first locomotive crossed the suspension bridge over the Niagara River in 1855. Even so drastic a measure as annexation was advocated not only by some people during the troubles of 1812 and 1837, but by a thousand merchants and politicians of Montreal in 1848, and by many voters who elected Fielding in Nova Scotia on the secession issue in 1886. A wider outlook within the country was heralded also by the first sitting of the supreme court of Canada in 1876, by the "National Policy" of Macdonald in 1879, by the first meetings of the Royal Canadian Academy of Arts in 1880 and of the Royal Society of Canada in 1882, by the appointment of the first Canadian high commissioner in London in 1880, and by the annexation to Canada in the same year of all British possessions in the northern part of America except Newfoundland and its dependencies.

Access to information and exchange of ideas broadened the thinking of Canadians. The first newspapers appeared in Halifax in 1752, in Quebec in 1764; the first daily in Montreal in 1833. Just before Confederation there were not quite 300 newspapers, including a score of dailies; before the end of the century there were three or four times as many. At the later date they were judged by American critics to be high in quality.

They gave a broad coverage of the news and intelligent discussion of many issues of significance.

In the 1820's there were libraries in Halifax, Quebec, Kingston, and York, and one in Montreal with 8,000 volumes. But these libraries were for the few: at Kingston in 1819 the price of shares was five guineas and the fees were thirty shillings a year. Prejudice hampered the growth of libraries. As the author of a volume on New Brunswick put it in 1845, the selection of books "was a matter of some difficulty, the grave and serious declaiming against light reading and regarding the novel as the climax of human weakness."[3] Many people in the province restricted their reading to the *Bible, Pilgrim's Progress,* and the even more popular *Saint's Rest.* The author of a series of letters in the *Kingston Gazette* in 1815 wanted people to have books on religion, morality, and the manners and laws of the country and had no compunction about asking for legislation to exclude others, including those from the United States that were not conducive to respect for England and British institutions. The Booksellers' Association of Upper Canada in 1858, on the other hand, objected to the distribution of a restricted selection of books through government channels and urged free scope for "the natural action of literature on the popular intelligence and taste."[4] An article on "The Intellectual Progress of Canada" in the *Canadian Monthly* in 1875 pointed out that the dollar value of books imported into Canada had doubled between 1868 and 1874, from $479,000 to $959,000 — surely an effect in part of free elementary education.

At the turn of the century the schools began to turn out large numbers with a desire to read, and libraries, assisted by governments, sought to encourage rather than to control reading. In Ontario, libraries circulated some 7,200,000 books in 1920 and nearly twice as many in 1938; and a slight decline thereafter was accompanied by a greatly increased sale of books and magazines. There were laggards and retarding influences, of course. A survey made in Caledon, Ontario, in 1918 showed that only 21 out of 190 rural homes listed reading as a form of recreation. In a section of Manitoba in 1914, although nearly all families subscribed to newspapers and more than three-fifths to one magazine, booklovers were few. In the growing cities of the present century, a large proportion of the population were of rural origin and retained to an extent the attitudes, values, and habits of their earlier environment. Not a few continued to believe that urban society could be saved from perdition only through the restraining forms of an older generation. But the outlook of people broadened nevertheless.

Recent development of other means of communication made it difficult for the schools to restrict attention to narrow traditional content. In Ontario between 1895 and 1912 — the period, incidentally, when self-expression in school composition became the vogue — the number of letters per capita sent through the mails increased from 27 to almost 95. In the same province, telephones multiplied from a beginning in the 1870's and a small number before World War I to 825,000 before the end of World War II. In all of Canada the number of radio receiving sets, as indicated by licences, was less than 10,000 in 1923 and over 2,000,000 in 1940. Motion pictures and television became even more powerful instruments of enlightenment, though capable of limiting thought by propaganda and by the cynical insincerity of portrayals designed to satisfy both the censors and the general public. Travel could do little to broaden the outlook of even a few when, for example, in 1819 the steamship *Frontenac* made three trips a month between York, Niagara, and Kingston from April to November, whereas the facilities of trains, aeroplanes, buses, and motor cars were available to nearly all of the population 130 years afterward.

Later we shall see how education responded to the broadening outlook of people. William Lyon Mackenzie perceived the dilemma faced by those who sought to educate and control. The colonial aristocratic governments tried to find teachers who would train the people "to habits of servility and toleration of arbitrary power," but in so doing they could not always avoid giving also "the keys of useful knowledge," which enabled people "to form a just and correct estimate of their own situation."[5] Consider what had happened by 1879. A woman teacher in Fredericton argued against insisting that pupils memorize what they did not understand or what did not necessarily follow. "If every teacher would consider this matter," she said, "there would be fewer people following the opinions of others, and more who would think for themselves. . . ."[6] In the same year in Ontario the headmaster of Whitby High School expressed regret that daily newspapers were not studied as reading material in schools. He ventured the opinion that "in the hands of the judicious teacher, they could be made the instruments of incalculable benefit in quickening the intelligence of pupils."[7] In the late nineteenth century the emancipation of the teacher had begun: in 1892, a school principal of Kingston, Ontario, did not refrain from delivering an unorthodox address on "The Workman's Sunday"; three years later a woman teacher dressed in bloomers rode a bicycle on the streets of another Ontario city and survived the censure.

In 1893 a Manitoba lawyer gave food for thought to Protestants who were ready to indoctrinate children in a variety of "isms" if only Catholicism was excluded:

Perhaps you, reader, have been urging that certain things apart from mere secular education should, or should not, be taught in the schools because, as you say, those things are right, or are wrong although other people do not agree in your opinion of them . . . perhaps you are an Imperial Federationist, and want to instil Imperial ideas . . . perhaps you believe in militarism and the inculcation of a warlike spirit . . . or perhaps you believe that education is a vicious thing, unaccompanied by religion . . . you insist upon religious instruction in all the schools . . . perchance Sabbatarianism is your particular hobby . . . or is the abolition of alcoholism your particular ambition? . . . I would have all these, and every other ism, of such like, you can think of, in the schools; but upon this condition, that the parents of all the children should be willing to have them there.[8]

Later in the same decade, in 1897, the minister of education in Ontario discussed in a pamphlet the comparative restrictions on the academic freedom of universities imposed by state control and by private endowment. With reference to the latter, he cited the case of Professor Beemis, who was removed from the faculty of the University of Chicago because his remarks about trade combines and monopolies displeased Mr. Rockefeller, who had given the university nearly $12,000,000. He mentioned also the remark of President Harper: "It's all very well to sympathize with the working man, but we get our money from those on the other side." The outlook of Canadian educators had broadened sufficiently at least to recognize the problem of insisting that approved patterns and forms be taught and accepted as truth.

Amusements

Prince Edward Island, with a population of 23,000 in 1825, imported 54,000 gallons of rum, not to mention wines and other liquors — a sufficient reminder that the only thought of many there and elsewhere was bodily escape from toil and from an environment with few aesthetic or intellectual diversions. Everywhere in Canada, as Bourinot said:

Men who lived for years without the means of frequent communication with their fellow men, without opportunities for social intercourse . . . might well have little ambition except to satisfy the grosser wants of their nature.[9]

Cock-fighting, horse-racing, wrestling, and fisticuffs were common forms of physical activity, which was the only type of recreation appreciated by a very large number. It is noteworthy that individual competition was characteristic of sport in the first half of the nineteenth century. Team games then increased in popularity, gentlemanly British cricket gave place after Confederation to vigorous, slashing lacrosse, which was superseded increasingly by strategic baseball. Sensational spectacles probably drew a higher proportion of the potential audience than today. In 1859 Blondin walked a tight-rope over the Niagara River; in the 1870's hangings still drew, and were permitted to draw, large crowds. The most popular form of commercial entertainment around mid-century was the circus-menagerie of wild animals, troops of horses, tumblers, jugglers, and rope dancers, which came from the United States to pitch tents in a field near some tavern in the cities, towns, and larger villages of the Canadian colonies.

Theatrical performances were offered by professional companies and often by military garrisons. In Upper Canada the Kingston Amateur Theatre in 1816 advertised a *Comedy of Education*, with the caution that no children were to be admitted. Advertisements in the *Kingston Chronicle* in 1819 offered such plays as *She Stoops to Conquer, Hamlet,* and a farce entitled *Venice Preserved* to the relatively few who could pay 7s 6d or 5s a seat, with a weekly change of bill. The same prices applied in Toronto twenty-eight years later when *Love under a Lamppost* appeared at the Lyceum Theatre. But drama for everybody was not available until the movies supplanted vaude-

A public hanging around 1848

ville and burlesque after World War I. During the depression of the 1930's hundreds, perhaps thousands, of dramatic clubs were formed. On the whole, in spite of gags and routines demanding short attention-span, and other more obvious exceptions, modern entertainment, in contrast with that of the past, makes available to more people immeasurably more aesthetic and intellectual enjoyment.

If music, dancing, and various types of social activity were considered, the same tendencies would be apparent. The early nineteenth century was not without its sleigh rides, square dances, surprise parties, and Sunday evening sparking. The later nineteenth century had its band concerts, quartettes, glee clubs, parades, excursions, and regattas, its waltz, polka, and two-step. Those who see deterioration across the years may find lunacy in the post-war crazes of the 1920's — mah-jongg, the player piano added to the phonograph, motor cars tripled in number during the decade, pole sitting, marathon dancing, the Charleston, and the Black Bottom. In 1952 there were laments that conversa-

tion was a lost art, but in 1802 John Strachan found little opportunity for intellectual stimulation: "My time passes in tedious uniformity and having no society, I grow dull and study but little."[10] On the whole, as the twentieth century advanced, there was more widespread appreciation of even the more difficult in music and dance and greater frankness in speech — more ability and more confidence and not so much formal restraint. There was a report in Saint John, in 1847, that ladies went "riding down hill upon hand-sleds with the gentlemen." It was indignantly refuted with an assertion that the ladies of the province had as "high a sense of decorum as those of the most refined societies in England."[11] In 1947 there would have been no report and no comment on such activities.

Crime and Punishment

For the control of crime in the early nineteenth century, complete reliance appears to have been placed on a code drawn up for the protection of property without thought of the human reaction, and on severe forms of punishment similarly conceived. The curious institution of imprisonment for debt led to the formation in Halifax in 1811 of a philanthropic society which tried to supply bare essentials to the miserable offenders incarcerated for this cause and "without the means of procuring subsistence." In 1858 the royal assent was given to an act abolishing imprisonment for debt.

Another remarkable law in early Nova Scotia imposed a fine of ten shillings on the head of a family and of five shillings on every child over twelve and every servant for non-attendance at church for a space of three months without proper cause. It was enacted for Halifax that the church wardens and constables should at the times of divine service walk through the town "to observe and suppress all offenders."

In the following illustrations from Calkin of severity in the operation of law, we may see not only the callous attitude of the times but the unquestioning acceptance of physical forms in punishment as in all aspects of life:

For clipping, filing or debasing a coin the offender was placed in the pillory with one of his ears nailed to the beam, and he was afterwards publicly whipped through the streets of the town. For forgery the penalty was a fine of £20; and in default of payment the criminal was put in the pillory and both ears nailed to the posts. For publishing a libel or scandalous report he was placed in the stocks for three hours or whipped at the discretion of the court. In 1825, a man in Halifax found guilty of forgery was sentenced to a year's imprisonment, one hour in the pillory, and to have one of his ears cut off.[12]

As late as 1852 a young man in Hamilton, Canada West, was sentenced to death for abstracting a money letter from a mail bag.

In spite of the crudity and brutality of the penal system, crimes were frequent in the early part of the nineteenth century in English-speaking provinces. Canada West in the period 1856-59 sent nearly four times as many convicts to the penitentiary as Canada East, where the population was largely rural, settled, and under the close surveillance of the Roman Catholic clergy. Only in that province among the French-speaking Canadians was the validity of forms and patterns reinforced by unquestioned faith and authority and by the utter devotion of religious leaders. Elsewhere old-world values were at war with the new, and the new had to gain considerably more strength to win support for criminal-centred remedial education than for the child-centred school. Improvement of conditions of confinement and abandonment of faith in corporal punishment came only a little more slowly for the prisoner in jail than for the child in school. But the recognition of motivation and the possibility of securing socially desirable behavior by the development of individual interests were much harder to accept in the treatment of the criminal. As Clark puts it, with reference to the twentieth century:

The necessity of paying greater attention to the character of the criminal and less attention to the nature of the crime, and of devising improved methods of treating criminal offenders, was only slowly realized by Canadian judicial authorities.[13]

One of the promising developments was the introduction in penitentiaries, in 1947, of a vocational training program to which admission was obtained by the voluntary application of prisoners.

Those who read the dark record of crime for the past 150 years will find little support for laments that the world is getting worse. There was juvenile delinquency in Toronto during World War II, but probably more per capita in 1866 when 126 children under sixteen years of age were in the city jail, or a generation after when the lives of many unfortunate children were a scandal to increasingly sensitive people. Crime fluctuated as gold rushes, war, or economic changes created special conditions. Convictions for indictable offences increased from about one per thousand before 1900 to about double that ratio in 1921 and to nearly five per thousand in 1939, but then decreased somewhat to about three per thousand after World War II. Obviously such figures reflect the frequency of apprehension and conviction no less than the prevalence of crime. With the growth of cities in the present century, new problems were created when organization was applied in crime as in legitimate enterprises. But in spite of difficulties and conflicting attitudes regarding control, law-abiding citizens in communities of all types could proceed with their affairs by day or night in greater safety than in the past.

Morality

The old world did not recognize the use of alcohol by men as a form of immorality until Protestant non-conformists, largely Methodists, organized the temperance movement. The people's assembly in New Brunswick passed a prohibition act in 1855, but the governor saved the established order of society by dissolving the house the next year. A prohibition law was in operation in the Northwest Territories in the 1880's for the protection of the Indians, but it became unenforceable as the white population increased. A Royal Commission in 1895 reported its conclusion that prohibitory laws did not lessen the sale of alcoholic beverages. Later, during and after World War I, such laws were enacted but subsequently repealed, in part because of objections and new forms of lawlessness. Nevertheless the temperance forces performed a valuable service in reducing the abuse of liquor to small proportions and in improving the lot of women and children. They had a long

struggle. The Toronto Temperance Society was organized in 1830. Twenty years later the city had 152 taverns, 206 beershops, and cheap liquor for sale at twenty-five cents a gallon. For a long time afterward the bar-rooms, to put it moderately, were exemplars of life at a low level. The change to present conditions may have been effected in considerable degree by the fanatical zeal of reformers, by abstinence pledges, and by specific laws. But other factors were the development of moral discrimination and responsibility and greater freedom for social recreation of various kinds, including association with members of the other sex. Significant both as cause and effect was the extension to middle class women of freedom to drink without loss of respectability.

There was a similar but slower departure from a formal code in relations between the sexes. As suggested in an earlier chapter, the code was designed to ensure the chastity of respectable women and the permanence of marriage. From what evidence came to light, it would appear that obedience to the rules was restricted to the letter only and secured among lower and middle class people generally by keeping sexual relations close to the animal level, at a cost of embittering guilt to the more sensitive. Presumably in this area of behavior, as in the use of liquor, there was less trouble and unhappiness in French-speaking Canada, where the church took cognizance of human limitations. But unleashed ambitions, aspirations to freedom, and revolt against suppression in English-speaking Canada must logically have reacted, in conflict with a restrictive social code, to produce the stern cruelty of the thwarted or the cynicism of brute indulgence. Children bore the brunt of the former. Sufficient evidence of the latter may be found in the records of prostitution and of the seduction of women who were made easy victims by poverty and lack of social status.

In Halifax after 1755 the number of venereal patients in the military hospital was a problem. In 1818 an indignant citizen wrote that "the facilities of licentious intercourse" were "as great as the most vicious and hardened of either sex could desire."[14] In central Canada the Roman Catholic chaplain of the penitentiary reported in 1853 that immigrant women, arrested for petty theft to which they were driven by destitution, were seduced by lawyers and agents who visited them in jail with promises of help. In 1859 over 3500 women were sent to jail in Toronto, almost all of them prostitutes. One of the commissioners appointed to investigate conditions in the city in 1891 mentioned a tour of visits to thirty-five known houses of ill fame; but the commission concluded that there were hardly half as many prostitutes as in pre-Confederation days when the city was only one-quarter the size. By this time in the west there was slave traffic in Indian girls for prostitution; in mining towns there were flagrant red light districts and adjacent to prairie towns there were Indian prostitute camps.

The disruption of marriages was by no means unknown. In the *Upper Canada Gazette* for January 9, 1817, Charles Grant gave warning: "Whereas my wife, Christiana, has left my bed and board . . . I forbid any person harboring her or giving her credit on my account." In the *Kingston Gazette* for April 23, 1819, George Coil announced over his mark that Henry Coil ran away with the wife of Charles Witherey after beating his mother and stealing papers belonging to George — but the complainant lived in Pittsburgh, where Canadians might expect such things to happen. Upper class society was marked even in the old days by dashing young men and gaiety by night. But among the increasing majority of middle class people it is probable that considerably greater laxity in relations between the sexes has existed from the time of World War I.

An increasing divorce rate also attested a lessened respect for the rigid patterns of the past. To the extent that women have been emancipated to independent status, prostitution and legal exploitation in marriage and employment have obviously been reduced, as have the chances of maintaining stability by compulsion. Yet the older attitudes and forces are strong. The conflict of attitudes regarding relations between the sexes imposes problems for the young and new problems for secondary education.

Religious Tolerance

During most of the nineteenth century nearly all people went to church if they could and professed certain fundamental beliefs of the Christian religion. In pioneer backwoods there was a tendency to forget religious animosities and religious observances, but growth of population and the building of denominational churches brought a revival of both. Hence great importance was attached to literal interpretation, and particular literal interpretations, of formal articles of faith. Efforts were directed towards deterring, through fear of divine wrath, any departure from approved formulae of creed and conduct, but, to judge by results, little was done to inspire love of a loving God or a generous attitude towards human beings. The Church of England was distinguished for sanity and a willingness to confer respectability without excessive demands on the individual. The Presbyterians were noted for intellectual endurance and were given most of the credit for the characteristic Canadian Sunday of hushed activity and darkened windows. Methodism convened emotionally charged gatherings in a country where social opportunities were few, and it also kindled the fire which gave power to movements for social reform. The Roman Catholic Church served Protestants as a hostile fortress which gave vigor and direction to their attack; among the faithful it maintained the consistency of doctrine and practice which enabled most of them to accept the dependence of man and religious teaching as truth not subject to interpretation by the individual.

As the established state church of the homeland where government was centred, the Church of England emphasized the political function of religion. The government's representative in Nova Scotia in 1768 sent back this advice:

The Settlers are generally of various Persuasions, some of whom are replete with Republican Principles, and unless government place proper Clergymen among them before they are able to support teachers of their own, it will be difficult to Inculcate proper sentiments of Subordination to Government.[15]

Hence attendance at any other church was forbidden to members of the faculty or student body at King's College, Nova Scotia, in 1789. It was alleged that the Royal Institution in Lower Canada threatened to cut off the grant to Three Rivers because Methodist preachers had been allowed to use the schoolhouse. In 1827 the home government disallowed an Upper Canada bill for keeping registers of baptisms, marriages, and burials with the explanation that "His Majesty in Council cannot recognize the character of Ministers of Dissenting Congregations for exercising any civil or ecclesiastical rights."[16] These exclusive privileges were lost around 1830, as we have seen. The continuance of old attitudes was illustrated by letters of David Burn in the *Hamilton Gazette* in the 1840's on the endowment of the university in Upper Canada; his argument was that "the management of the lands so munificently set apart for its promotion should be at once and forever removed from all popular control." Anglican preference for acquiescence over shared responsibility continued for many decades to inhibit democratic tendencies in educational practice.

The Roman Catholic Church secured the repeal of discriminatory measures but continued to bear the brunt of attack. In New Brunswick no Roman Catholic could vote until 1810. In 1875 in Toronto a Roman Catholic procession was twice mobbed. In 1892 the *Knox College Monthly* carried an article on Presbyterian mission schools in Quebec and mission work among French Canadians. But the church had dealt effectively even with challenges originating among its own people in the stronghold province. In 1844 *l'Institut Canadien* was founded in Montreal to cultivate a taste for science, art, and literature. It marked the beginning of a movement for freedom of mind which appealed to young intellectuals of French-speaking Canada. The movement was spread by the establishment of institutes in other places and became liberal to the extent of admitting Protestant members, placing Protestant and skeptical works on the library shelves, and fostering reason and tolerance. Bishop Bourget of Montreal and the clergy generally declared their opposition, and by 1858 only the Montreal institute remained. In 1869, when the approval of Rome had been obtained, the church refused the sacrament to members of the institute. In the same year, a member who was a devout Roman Catholic died suddenly without the last rites, and the burial of his body in consecrated ground was forbidden. The institute successfully carried an appeal to the Privy Council and, though the hearse was stoned away from the cemetery, succeeded in burying the body and placed concrete and scrap iron over it to prevent removal. The bishop then deconsecrated the patch of ground in which the body was buried. Graphic illustrations of this kind helped to convince many Canadians in the twentieth century that the Roman Catholic Church was in earnest.

Greater tolerance in the twentieth century was engendered by the realization that neither of the opposing concepts of truth and education can be wiped out. Greater faith in the power of God, whether conceived in terms of immutable form, or of dynamic force, or of interaction of both, has enabled more Canadians to live constructively amidst differences. This change of attitude has helped to make education a more positive factor in human relations.

In predominantly English-speaking and non-Catholic communities, there was occasional evidence of audacious revolt early in the nineteenth century. The *Royal Gazette* of Fredericton published in 1830 without editorial approval a letter which objected to expenditure of the people's money on schools "where the children are taught the antiquated, obsolete, superstitious (sic) nonsense about fearing God and honoring the King, and submitting to governments, pastors, and masters, and ordering oneself lowly and reverently to one's betters."[17] But unorthodoxy was severely censured even at the end of the century. In 1893 newspapers devoted much space to a trial for heresy conducted by the Montreal Presbytery. In February at the invitation of the students' committee at Queen's University a lecture was delivered by Professor Campbell, who, as a result, was accused of impugning and discrediting the scriptures as the supreme and infallible source of religious truth and of representing God not as one who smites and punishes. The key accusation appears to have been the latter. In September the speaker was found guilty by the presbytery.

Failure of the churches to adapt themselves to changing social conditions in the twentieth century weakened their influence. In the west the older churches, and particularly the Church of England, had an eastern orientation which made it difficult for them to understand the lives and problems of prairie settlers. In the growing eastern cities there was a tendency to remain aloof from people and organizations not approved by nineteenth-century standards. To quote Clark: "Respectability was a condition of membership in the church, and respectability was maintained by ignoring undesirable elements in the population."[18] A counteracting force was the Salvation Army, which had worked in Canada since 1883. Since the churches often took sides with employers against employees, it was not surprising that a Presbyterian assembly in British Columbia reported in 1914 that "the attitude of a large number of wage-earners and members of labour unions towards the church has not become more friendly."[19] Much of the strength of the Protestant churches in cities rested on the membership of people from rural areas and smaller towns, who were not predisposed to an understanding of conditions in urban society and to dealing with social problems by the organization necessary for effective action in large centres of population. A counteracting source of strength was the formation in 1925 of the United Church of Canada, whose members forsook preoccupation with differences of theological belief and observance. Few members of Protestant churches were inclined in 1950 to control education by prescription and restriction of formal content. Most of them sought only freedom and strength for the schools.

Intelligence and the Scientific Attitude

We may accept Bourinot's judgment that civil authorities under the French regime were not anxious for popular enlightenment and that the people were not distinguished for intellectual activity at the time of the British conquest. Even in later years, freedom of inquiry and decision on fundamental issues was countenanced only with reference to ultimate acceptance of truth already defined. Hence the Roman Catholic Bishop of Quebec was reported to have said in 1789 that "in the stile of modern writers, a person unprejudiced in his opinions is one who opposes every principle of Religion."[20] The continuing attitude of the church, and of educators associated with the church, was reflected in the examination questions on philosophy set for baccalaureate candidates at Laval University in 1877. As given in translation by the *Canada School Journal* they were:

(1) Difference between faith and knowledge (*la science*). (2) How do we know the truths which surpass the reach of reason? Proofs. (3) How refute this objection: The indefinite progress of the sciences authorises us to believe that reason can attain to every truth? (4) How reply to the following objection: The form cannot exist out of its subject: The soul is the form of the body: therefore the soul will not survive the body? (5) Is man born for society? Proof. (6) Does the right of property arise from human laws or from natural law? Proof.[21]

Evidently the examiners expected the reproduction of approved answers to these questions. Most present-day students would consider such an examination requirement as tantamount to a preclusion of independent thought.

In English-speaking Canada there was little reliance on intelligence in the early nineteenth century. The Presbyterian minister, Proudfoot, found the people "very ignorant and full of prejudice against doctors" — perhaps with good reason, considering the limitations of medical science in 1834. After Confederation, when the influence of Darwin, Huxley, Spencer, and others had penetrated Canada from England, educational leaders in high positions sought to check the swing to reason and empiricism. In his convocation address in 1879 Principal Grant of Queen's spoke of what he considered the very

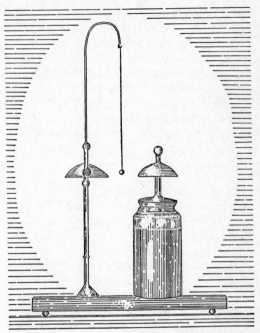

Electrical apparatus used for demonstration in 1857

critical spirit of the age. He quoted Goethe's remark that if the Romans were great enough to invent stories of heroism we should be great enough to believe them. Since then the same view was expressed often when there appeared to be danger of losing a cherished form which could not be sustained by rational means. But Grant spoke at a time when science laboratories were just beginning to appear in secondary schools. In New Brunswick at a teachers' institute in 1875 Theodore Rand introduced Professor Thomas Harrison, who spoke on the "Experimental Method of Investigation" — the method of agreement, the method of difference, the method of concomitant variations, the double method of agreement, and the method of residues. This must have seemed as abstruse and fantastic to the assembled teachers as an exposition of group dynamics seventy-five years later. Since 1875 reliance on observation and strict reasoning gained strength in school and out. By 1953 the achievements in physical empirical science had left far behind the earthbound concepts of nature and magic unchallenged by the populace at large a century before. In their attitudes people had come close to breaking the barrier which blocked a comparable application of intelligence to human affairs.

Aristocracy and Democracy

In the early nineteenth century, attitudes of people were dominated by concepts of right which were advantageous to leaders or beneficiaries in society and its institutions. As all men were dependent on God, so were the majority of men dependent on their superiors. The latter were represented as wise and capable. They rightly enjoyed a monopoly of power and of goods to keep or bestow. It was the duty of ordinary men to be grateful to their superiors for any charity, consideration, or recompense they received. It was also their duty not to seek power but to be humble and obedient — not to think about justice but to believe the teaching of their betters. Religion was commonly interpreted, or distorted, to support the privileges of the few and the duties of the many. The latter were forced to acquiesce under threat of dire punishment on earth and in the hereafter.

One consequence was obsequiousness among those on the fringe of the privileged class and among some in the lower classes. It was an age of petitions — in language regularly deferential, sometimes ponderous with adulation, often with pious overtones. Nepotism and patronage were assumed to be in order. Grant my son a king's scholar's free place in the royal grammar school; recommend my appointment as an agent for school lands; give me the more lucrative position my merits and years of service deserve; designate your humble servant the bookseller to Upper Canada College; make my son, George Cartwright Strachan, registrar of King's College because in spite of his excellent talents he has a horror of public speaking; consider that I was born in the same neighborhood as Your Excellency and read the manuscript of my spelling book; grace my school with your presence, dear lady, that I may secure donations from others: these are abbreviated samples of pleas which abound in the archives. One of the first purposes of school legislation as democracy became operative in Upper Canada was to reduce or eliminate patronage in the distribution of school grants.

It is logical to assume that another consequence must have been cynicism. The system condoned actions that would today be regarded as too flagrantly corrupt for any but a totalitarian state. In 1767 thirty acres in each of the sixty-seven townships of Prince Edward Island were reserved for the use of a schoolmaster, but in July of the same year the whole of the sixty-seven townships were disposed of by ballot in a single day to certain officers and members of parliament, who thus became a landed aristocracy to whom all inhabitants of the island paid tribute. Hannay suggested the educative effect of similar actions in New Brunswick. Though schoolmasters and ministers might teach that society needed and rewarded able and conscientious men, the citizen of the colony soon learned the embittering lesson that appointments to the government service were made on no such basis, but were merely handed out to friends and relatives who would safeguard the prerogatives of the privileged group. If there was teaching or preaching about the sacredness of truth or the right to appeal against injustice, there was the contrary object lesson of an enactment under which a heavy fine and imprisonment might be imposed on anyone who obtained more than twenty signatures to a petition or

Old Time Election, around 1880

complaint concerning matters established by law. Those who as children had been taught their duty to their superiors found out as young men that political power was used unscrupulously for the benefit of the few who held the power. When an election was first held in New Brunswick in 1785, a partisan official in Saint John struck off enough votes for opposition candidates to ensure the election of the governor's men. A protest was treated with contempt.

Snobbery and jealousy were characteristic of people with any pretentions and permeated the more important institutions of secondary education. Within a year of the opening of Upper Canada College, the masters of the classical department complained in a curt note to the lieutenant-governor that the principal looked on them as assistants or ushers, and not as colleagues, as they had understood their status would warrant. Next year the French and drawing masters had the temerity to ask that they, like the first three classical masters, should have seats of their own in the public hall at meetings and examinations. The latter request was un-British,

since in the public schools of that country at the time such frills were supplementary and subordinate to the regular school business, and not even the boys were required to treat a French master with respect.

These older attitudes were reduced to some extent by the cooperation necessary to establish political democracy and get it into operation around 1850. Subsequently when political parties were strongly motivated to achieve some purpose for the general good, the attitudes approved by democracy were strengthened by the experience. In the twentieth century the change on the surface was sufficiently great that candidates for office regularly professed a confidence in the ability of the people to think and decide and a conviction that government should serve the interests of all. They repudiated favoritism and declared their attachment to honesty, equity, and other democratic virtues. School teaching of social studies also assumed that governments were inspired by these ideals and devoted to the purposes of democracy.

Nevertheless the old attitudes persisted and were inevitably fostered as political parties consolidated for their own pre-servation. Parties evolved when reformers united to break the power of the oligarchy and when the latter rallied their forces in defence. In both groups there were ex-tremists and moderates. The Clear Grits became Liberals, and the moderates of both groups, with extreme Tories under cover, became the Liberal Conservatives. During the last quarter of the nineteenth century the old corruption was strongly in evidence. Lower remarks that the ger-rymander preceding the election of 1887 was hailed by Macdonald's followers as a strategic accomplishment of which any leader might be proud. After World War I a United Farmers Organization and a National Progressive Party introduced a new force in political life, but only for a short time. Three new parties appeared during the depression of the 1930's — the Co-operative Commonwealth Federation, Social Credit, and Union Nationale — and each of the three was in power in one province in 1955. Although the five prom-inent parties at that time made politics less simple and stable than before, the multiple division gave some evidence of popular interest in public affairs.

The potential of the school in education for democracy was recognized as early as 1808 by the staunch Tory, John Strachan.

He expressed the fear that as the result of an election the house would "be com-posed of ignorant clowns, for the spirit of levelling seemed to pervade the province." But he went on to say: "By and bye my pupils will be getting forward, some of them perhaps into the House, and then I shall have more in my power."[22] The usual type of statement in the later part of the nineteenth century ran like this:

Democracy is gaining ground, it is often repeated, by the friends of freedom with joy, by its foes with alarm. . . . Give the ballot to an ignorant nation, and anarchy will re-sult today, despotism tomorrow.[23]

During the present century talk about edu-cation for democracy became wearisome in extent. After World War II, however, it was occasionally given a new twist by demands for realistic teaching which would admit the persistence of selfish motives, lobbying by pressure groups, and under-cover deals. If it is true that old- and new-world attitudes both con-tinue to exist, disclosure of truth in school would prevent cynicism later. One is re-minded, however, of a remark of Father Lacombe in the Northwest Territories one hundred years ago that missionaries did not dare to discuss the ethics of the fur trade.

Summary

In the social developments discussed above there appears to be a pattern of two concepts of the world — one receding from dominance and the other gaining in strength. The outlook of the Canadian people broadened as their fear gave place to optimism. As they secured release from exhausting toil, their leisure interests became less crude and more varied. The treat-ment of crime became more enlightened and less severe. Concepts of morality became more discriminating as behavior ceased to be predominantly bestial or sternly forbidding. In religion tolerance increased, as did emphasis on the divine attributes of love and equity rather than on jealous wrath and partiality. The free use of intelligence and of the scientific method, though still in their infancy, gained acceptance by their achievements. The dominance of a few gave place to the growing responsibility of the many.

To the extent that the attitudes of Canadians changed in accordance with the above developments, the social environment became increasingly favorable to acceptance of the new educational thought discussed in the next chapter.

In order not to give a one-sided representation of the change, it is necessary to emphasize again that most Canadians in 1955 still held some strong old-world attitudes. Many were concerned because the diminishing respect for formal subject matter and for claims of superiority had left education without definite direction and standards of excellence. The levelling process had caused the mediocre values of the common man to spread like weeds and to endanger the cultivated gardens of the elect. In literature and art, in manners and morals, in religious faith, in entertainment, and in education, the old criteria of the good and the beautiful had been lost in the formless maelstrom of pragmatic activity and interaction. Educators of the twentieth century were more or less uneasy about these developments. Like other Canadians they differed from their predecessors and among themselves only in the degree of their confidence that more widespread ability was worth some loss in the prestige of traditional patterns. Old-world views and conditions had by no means disappeared.

CHAPTER 22

New Educational Thought

STATIC FORM: TO 1840 · POWER: 1840-1870 · FERMENT AND EFFICIENCY: 1870-1900 · MOTIVATION: 1900-1920 · INTERACTION: 1920-1950 · FROM DISTINCTIVE FORMS TO UNIVERSAL POWER: 1800-1950

In this chapter an attempt is made to allocate changes in educational thought to five successive periods. Since the new ideas came mostly from other countries, brief expositions are given of the thinking of European and American educators whose influence was felt in Canada during the respective periods. Then in each case attention is paid to the views of Canadian educators or to changes in classroom practice which reflected the ideas from abroad or showed similar originality.

Although this chronological arrangement is convenient for historical presentation, it must be remembered that no educational ideas were entirely novel or confined to any period of time. When we speak of a change in educational thought, we really mean that views formerly held by few began to spread more widely or to receive official recognition. Similarly, new educational practice was attained by recruiting and educating teachers who were not impervious to ideas emerging from the obscurity of disapproval in which exceptional teachers had applied them before. There were "new education" thinkers and teachers in all periods, but they could not make many converts while aristocratic attitudes prevailed. The apparent innovations in the successive periods, therefore, were in fact only a more general acceptance of "new" ideas under more favorable circumstances.

Static Form: to 1840

A few sentences will recall the concepts of education described in earlier chapters. The privileged few thought it proper to provide the ignorant many with carefully restricted knowledge of religion and of the duties of the poor, with practical skills sufficient only for reading the Scripture and for work of the humblest character. The most liberal philanthropy offered no more than this, plus writing and arithmetic, with grammar and geography for advanced pupils in exceptional cases. The basic educational aim of aristocracy was reinforcement of social stability, chiefly by the teaching of religion and morality. As schools of the people were introduced, and the people had a say, they showed an interest mainly in the three R's for practical purposes in everyday life. At the same time gentlemen provided a distinctive type of classical education for their own sons and sometimes education in lady-like accomplishments for their daughters. Self-made men in some places arranged to set up schools to teach their children more practical secondary subjects. Every orthodox person agreed, however, (1) that the substance of education was formal content; (2) that the process of education was getting this content into the mind; (3) that this could be done with least violence to the form by having the pupil memorize the words of a textbook; and (4) that the backward had to be punished and the bright rewarded to make them learn.

Altogether opposed to these congealed notions of education were the ideas of a Swiss ne'er-do-well, Jean Jacques Rousseau (1712-78). He was the first of four European educators whose thinking was to direct the course of an educational revolution in modern times. Rousseau had no use for the artificial life of aristocratic society or for the bookish and formal type of education everywhere in vogue. His aim was not to mold the boy into the form approved by convention but to help him grow into a free man able to face all vicissitudes of life. In his educational novel, *Emile,* he gave an account of the upbringing of a boy in rural surroundings remote from the corrupting influence of civilization. Emile's tutor took care that the early experiences of his pupil left him healthy and without fear. In outdoor ramblings he arranged situations where curiosity and practical necessity gave a motive for learning. But the tutor was in no hurry to begin the process of formal education. Emile learned to read only when he was ready of his own volition to do so. He was neither permitted to command nor required to obey, and was disciplined only by the natural consequences of his own actions. Not until he was fifteen years of age was he brought into close contact with society and with religion and literature. Strong and independent, he thus acquired sympathetic virtues and social abilities without loss to his integrity as an individual.

Educational ideas of this kind had little chance of serious acceptance in Britain at the end of the eighteenth century, and less chance of transmission to Canada. But Rousseau had a very great influence on the thinking of other educators, if only because he recognized children as children and did not regard them merely as small, imperfect adults to be trained and put to some use as soon as possible. Rousseau's scheme of education called for special attention to each of four periods: infancy to the age of five, childhood from five to twelve, boyhood from twelve to fifteen, and later adolescence from fifteen to twenty. He was radical and revolutionary in his respect for the individual child and man and in his renunciation of authorities which sanctioned the domination of one individual by another. His challenge of the existing political forms of society made him a progenitor of political revolution and of modern democracy. His views on education were similarly incompatible with contemporary concepts of society. Unfortunately Rousseau's mistakes and weaknesses were serious enough to be used against him by the opponents of human freedom. As a champion of nature against existing civilization, he painted a fantastic picture of the noble savage. As an exploiter of women, he preferred that they be given a conventional education to keep them subordinate to men. As a parent he refused to accept the responsibilities he urged on others. But millions of children and adults owe him much for kindling an intellectual fire which changed human existence into human life.

Among those influenced by Rousseau was an Irishman, Richard Lovell Edgeworth (1744-1817). Four times married, and blessed with eighteen children, he had considerable opportunity for educational experiments. A son brought up in accordance with the principles of Rousseau proved at the age of nine to be strong, healthy, agile, brave, generous, and good-natured, but "scarcely to be controlled." To guard against such intractability, some restraint was required in the process of education without a return to the opposite extreme. Both Edgeworth and his daughter Maria were noteworthy advocates of pleasurable learning, of learning through activity, of remedial rather than merely punitive discipline, and of reading material with appeal for the child. Edgeworth's book, *Practical Education*, put a higher value on ability to invent, think, generalize, apply, and work effectively than on memorized knowledge of traditional content. The book was widely read by educated and interested parents in England and had some little influence in Canada.

An account has already been given of the monitorial system, which helped a little in making the school environment favorable to learning. Some modifying

influence resulted also from the work of Robert Owen (1771-1858). Owen's ideas were too radical to gain immediate acceptance. He believed that the educative environment was all-important in determining whether people were to be slovenly, shiftless, and miserable, or respectable, prosperous, and happy. In his view the transformation could be accomplished fully only by the reorganization of society along socialist lines. But in the meantime, as part owner and manager of a textile mill at New Lanark, Scotland, he set up a new type of school for the children of workers in the community. The infant department for youngsters from one to six years of age was bright and cheerful and was supervised by a man and a woman chosen because of their love of children. There were pictures, games, singing, dancing, conversation, story hours, playground activities, and study of nature and objects. Owen and his teachers sought to banish the harshness of the ordinary school and to establish love and kindness as governing principles in human relations. The upper school also had a freshness and spontaneity notably lacking in other institutions.

Samuel Wilderspin (1792-1866) made his chief contribution by getting more infant schools established. But he was also an advocate of pleasant surroundings, rule by love, the use of objective methods, didactic verse to make learning more fun, practising rather than preaching, of group instruction in the schoolroom "gallery," and of moral training in a playground made attractive by swings and flowers. In the Wilderspin schools, as in Owen's, there was a mistress as well as a master to give a more gentle quality to the school environment.

The influence of Owen and Wilderspin was felt in Canada only in the form of infant schools, which did not fully reflect the spirit and ideas of the founders.

The ideas of European educators may have filtered through to Canada and had

Owen's Infant School, 1799

some effect in various ways. An article in the *Agricultural and Canadian Journal* in 1848 gave the advice, "Never deceive a child," which may have been an echo of Rousseau's dictum that "a single admitted falsehood will destroy forever the fruits of education" — a claim too disturbing for acceptance by many even in the twentieth century. The same journal in the same year reviewed a textbook, *Poetical Geography and Rhyming Rules for Spelling*, published in Toronto and perhaps inspired by Wilderspin. The editor of the journal, however, credited the author with having hit on something new in stating boundaries and positions of countries in verse — evidence that Wilderspin's practice was not familiar at least to him.

Power: 1840 - 1870

"Knowledge is Power" appeared on the masthead of *The Educationalist*, a periodical of Canada West which survived for a few months in 1860-61. This was the creed of an early nineteenth-century movement in England, where the Society for the Diffusion of Useful Knowledge was established in 1827. The purpose of the movement was to give the ordinary man and his children an opportunity to gain some factual knowledge of the world in which they lived through cheap publications, mechanics' institutes, and the schools. That this would mean power and eventually the end of subservience to a privileged class was apparent to some of the latter. Although attempts were made to suppress some of the new publications, the movement spread too rapidly and too far to be checked by direct opposition. Then the dissemination of useful knowledge was given approval, and control was exerted only by trimming and coloring information on political and social conditions to support the views of those who were comfortable under the existing order.

A typical compendium of useful knowledge, printed in Edinburgh in 1845 and sold in Canada, was *The Rudiments of Knowledge,* or *Third Book of Reading*, in Chambers' Educational Course. In eighty pages the little book covered most of creation, including *inter alia* water, ocean, ships, and rivers, colors, professions and trades, and the faculties and emotions of the mind. The best known textbooks of information, however, were the school readers of the Irish National Series, which were authorized exclusively in Canada West for twenty years after 1846 and were much used elsewhere. The readers were described by Ryerson in these words:

Beginning with the forms and various sounds of the letters, and one syllable dialogues and little narratives so congenial to the taste of the infant mind, they proceed through the simple elements of the essential branches of useful knowledge, until in the fourth and fifth books, the most important subjects of Physical Geography and Geology, of Jewish History and Political Economy, of General History and Chronology, of Vegetable and Animal Physiology, of Natural Philosophy, including elementary Mechanics, Astronomy, Hydrostatics, Pneumatics, Optics, Electricity, and Chemistry, are treated in a manner both attractive and scientific, and adapted to the intercourse and pursuits of life — the whole being interspersed with miscellaneous and poetic selections calculated to please the imagination, to gratify and improve the taste, and to elevate and strengthen the moral feelings.[1]

But education as power derived its real strength from another source, and not from content, but from method. "To have knowledge without practical power, to have insight and yet to be incapable of applying it in everyday life! What more dreadful fate. . . ." These are the words of Heinrich Pestalozzi (1746-1827), who followed Rousseau in the sequence of great European educators. Impressed by the ideas of his notorious compatriot, Pestalozzi followed Rousseau's plan in the education of his son and found it necessary, as others did, to introduce a greater measure of control. Unlike Rousseau, Pestalozzi was a classroom teacher. Largely for that reason his direct and immediate in-

fluence on education was incomparably greater, for he was compelled to work out practical methods instead of giving loose reign to theory. Pestalozzi's ideas were carried to other European countries by those who visited his famous school at Yverdun and by translation of his books, including the story of *Leonard and Gertrude* and the explanation of *How Gertrude Teaches Her Children*. The first country to introduce Pestalozzianism on a considerable scale was Prussia, which in the first half of the nineteenth century established a system of schools which were the model of the world until reactionary forces destroyed their spirit and vitality.

Pestalozzi had a deep sympathy for the poor and unfortunate and devoted himself to the improvement of their lives. Education for him was an instrument for this purpose. Intensely religious, he expressed his love of a loving God by a life of active benevolence. Pestalozzianism meant universal elementary education for social betterment by the development of individual abilities. It replaced memorization and rote recitation of a textbook by oral instruction of a whole class together. For harsh punishment it substituted a strict but kindly control of love; for verbal platitudes about righteousness it substituted the practice of unselfishness and consideration of others. The fundamental principle of Pestalozzian method was that learning must begin with observation and sense-perception of the object and that words and arithmetical symbols should be introduced only in relation to content thus made familiar and significant to the learner. A second essential was that the pupil should learn by activity.

The first superintendents of education appointed around 1850 were exponents of Pestalozzianism. Egerton Ryerson in 1846 wrote a lengthy report on education as a preventive of pauperism, on the development of all the faculties, on conversation in teaching, on intellectual teaching to

Pestalozzi

secure understanding of what was read, on practical bookkeeping, on grammar as a rational exercise, on the use of maps and blackboard in teaching geography, and on other Pestalozzian practices mentioned below. He condemned the previous neglect of elementary education, word-mongery and superficial teaching, and the frequent use of the rod. Ryerson made class teaching possible by the authorization of uniform textbooks, he had some teachers instructed in the new methods by establishing a normal school in 1847, and he encouraged the spread of the ideas through teachers institutes and through articles in the *Journal of Education*. Twenty-five years later the Pestalozzian spirit had brought life and kindness into the classrooms, although tyranny and stupidity had not disappeared. In 1871 Ryerson began a second drive to secure more attention to sense perception and the teaching of the spoken word before the written word.

At a time when most people saw reality only in form, it was inevitable that the formal pattern of Pestalozzi's methods should be adopted without the vitality of the idea. To get his pupils to observe and know what words meant, Pestalozzi seized on immediate opportunities. A pupil in his school at Burgdorf told how the teacher pointed with eager interest and had his enthusiastic pupils repeat after him: "I see a hole in the wall! . . . I see a l-o-n-g hole in the wall . . . Through the long hole in the wall I see the lath. . . ." Though the method was crude, pupils were given practice in observing the things and qualities to which words were applied. To give form to this Pestalozzian idea, Elizabeth Mayo of England wrote a volume of *Lessons on Objects* and made available a collection of articles for teaching object lessons. Allspice, for example, was to be observed by pupils, who were then to learn and repeat by heart its qualities — "aromatic, pungent, spherical, opaque, tropical, inflammable, friable, sapid, and conservative." The apparatus for this travesty of a plan to reduce word-mongery was imported for use in the Toronto normal and model schools, where object lessons were observed by teachers-in-training. Some twenty years later, in 1871, object lessons were given a regular place in the prescribed course of studies for all schools.

Alexander Forrester of Nova Scotia in 1867 gave the following illustration to show teachers in eastern Canada how object lessons should be taught:

You all know what this is. A piece of coal. Who can tell me some of its properties or qualities? It is pure black. Anything else? It is glistening bright. Can you see through it? No. Then it is not transparent, and if so, it must be . . . opaque. John, bring a hammer, I apply it and it breaks into a thousand pieces. You call this property . . . brittle. I am going to throw one of these pieces into the fire, watch what becomes of it? It burns with a bright flame, and gradually becomes . . . red hot, and then . . . a cinder, or ashes. This shows it to be . . . You don't know the term . . . combustible . . . like wood, or peat, or turf. It is then one . . . of the inflammables. Do you know any other quality this coal possesses? Yes — some kinds of coal have a great deal of gas. This is extracted and lights . . . cities and dwelling-houses. Will you now repeat the qualities of coal? It is black and glistening — brittle —opaque — combustible and gaseous.[2]

In the hands of a skilful teacher, and in an environment less restraining than the ordinary classroom, object lessons could provide effective learning experience. But the conditions were not often met.

Other manifestations, during this period, of Pestalozzi's ideas, including his insistence on "simple to complex," will be discussed in later chapters. His influence was revealed occasionally from the beginning and constantly towards the end of the nineteenth century in several textbooks and essays. In the *Upper Canada Gazette* in 1802 an essay on education referred, as Pestalozzi did, to the mother as the first and most important teacher of the child. A Pestalozzian *Geography and History of Lower Canada* by Zadock Thompson, the principal of Charleston Academy, was published in 1835: it had the pupil begin his study at home by direct observation and directed him next to draw a map of his own township to show all the important places and things that he knew. More than forty years later this idea was still new to most teachers, who were told in the Ontario regulations that "the school house and its surroundings, with which pupils are familiar, should be taken as the first subjects of lessons." They were also warned in these regulations of 1878 that object lessons were "intended to develop the faculties rather than to store the mind with information" and that the pupil should be told nothing that he could discover for himself. In Nova Scotia in

FIRST BOOK OF GEOGRAPHY.

—

LESSON FIRST.

DEFINITIONS.

Do you know what township you live in? Do you know what a *township* is? I will tell. It is a piece of land, usually, about ten miles square, but sometimes larger, and sometimes smaller. Here is a picture of a township.

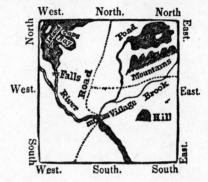

Page from Zadock Thompson's *Geography and History of Lower Canada, 1835*

1888, J. B. Calkin, principal of the normal school, published his *Notes on Education,* a teachers' handbook with strong Pestalozzian emphasis. He insisted that the common elementary school should not aim at training of a specific nature but at the development of abilities that were the foundation of success in all departments of life. The child's mind had latent possibilities to be developed by exercise. In Quebec in 1875 an article in the *Journal of Education* summarized the influence of Pestalozzi on elementary education. In 1892, S. P. Robins, Principal of the McGill Normal School, expounded to members of the Dominion Education Association the Pestalozzian doctrine that "clear and comprehensive conceptions of form and of form relation can and should be called up early in the minds of children."[3]

There was another educator who exerted a powerful influence on Canadian educational thought during the mid-century period. David Stow (1793-1864) learned by experience that telling was not teaching and that, without understanding, rote knowledge and the mechanical ability to read were hollow shams. As principal of the Glasgow Normal School in 1836 he wrote a book entitled *The Training System* which went through eleven editions within twenty-five years. Probably because of our British connection the effect of Stow's thinking was marked in Canada, although apparently negligible in the United States if we may judge by the absence of references to Stow in histories of American education. Stow not only accepted and developed the basic ideas of Pestalozzi but showed himself to be an advanced thinker and practitioner in other ways. He condemned not only corporal punishment but the giving of prizes or other extraneous rewards. He stated clearly that education must be education of the whole child. He forecast the teaching of social studies in his somewhat optimistic claim that the "uniting of geography with history is now getting very general." He was a strong advocate of co-education.

The essence of Stow's system was that children must be "trained" to understand and to do under the guidance of a mature and skilled instructor. In Bible training the teacher led the pupils by questions to "picture out" the meaning of what they read. In moral training the teacher used incidents observed on the playground to involve the pupils in discussion which touched them closely. In agriculture and bookkeeping, learning was to be accomplished by actual practice, for "all education is self-education, the key to which is doing." Much stress was put on oral class teaching, not only for

its inspirational value, but because the participation of pupils in class activity made what Stow called "the sympathy of numbers" effective in a desirable way. Otherwise the powerful influence of the group on the individual would be exerted only away from school. Clearly Stow was an educator, not merely an expert on the dispensing of facts.

Stow's influence on education in Canada began no later than 1838, when a committee of the assembly in Nova Scotia studied the educational systems of Prussia, Massachusetts, and Scotland. During the following decade a number of emissaries from the Glasgow Normal School came to the province. A Mr. and Mrs. Munro, who opened an academy in Boulardarie in 1839, frankly followed the principles of Stow and earned high commendation later from Superintendent Dawson. Ryerson visited the Glasgow Normal School before writing his report of 1846. Prince Edward Island in 1852-53 obtained from that institution its inspector of schools and advocate of teacher training, John M. Stark. The author of *The Nova Scotia Arithmetic*, published in 1864, stated that the subject could be taught effectively only by the Training System, which required the pupils to do the exercises themselves. There was evidence on the other hand that Stow's ideas were not fully acceptable to the old guard, in the large number of prizes distributed — during Ryerson's time in Ontario, during the last quarter of the nineteenth century in New Brunswick, and during the present century in Quebec, where the government donated 625,000 prize books between 1916 and 1931. Prize-giving was obnoxious to Stow, not because of the alleged characteristics of the Scots, but because incentives in extraneous form were more harmful to the many than necessary for the few.

The outstanding exponent of Stow in Canada was Alexander Forrester, whose opus, *The Teacher's Textbook,* appeared in

Alexander Forrester

1867. In acknowledging his obligation, Forrester described Stow as "the great pioneer of all modern improvements in the inner life of education." For the education of the child, he said, there was need not of instruction merely, not of example merely, but of training — of individual training and of training through group influence in the co-educational and preferably graded classroom. Because of the high esteem in which Forrester was held by teachers in eastern Canada, and because of his influence as principal of the normal school and superintendent in Nova Scotia, we may assume that many of the best teachers tried to follow the practices illustrated in his book. The following passage shows how every opportunity was used to introduce references to religion and how the ellipsis was employed to get the pupils to answer as a class:

TEACHER: What do I hold in my hand? A leaf of . . .
PUPILS: A rose.
TEACHER: What do you think of the rose?
PUPILS: It is a very beautiful flower.

TEACHER: It is the queen . . .
PUPILS: Of flowers.
TEACHER: Who is compared to a rose for beauty and fragrance?
PUPILS: The Lord Jesus Christ.
TEACHER: He is called . . .
PUPILS: The rose of Sharon.[4]

Forrester's teachers were trained to conduct lessons which pictured-out passages or incidents in the Bible. For example the following is a short extract from a lengthy lesson on Noah and the ark:

TEACHER: Would you like to know how Noah was preserved?
PUPILS: Yes, very much.
TEACHER: Well, when God revealed his purpose of destroying the world by a deluge, he entered into covenant with Noah, that is, he made an agreement with him by which he appointed him as the second head of the human family, gave instructions for the building of a house or ark, a large floating fabric, as big as forty men-of-war, a hundred and fifty feet long, twenty-five broad and fifteen deep. Noah believed God . . .
PUPILS: And did as he was commanded.
TEACHER: There were no clouds apparently loaded with rain . . .
PUPILS: But Noah believed God, and acted just as if he had seen it. Did Noah begin at once to build?
TEACHER: Yes, little children, at once, and continued the whole time that God had given space to the wicked to repent, that was . . .
PUPILS: 120 years.
TEACHER: At length the time arrived and God could wait no longer. He gave Noah seven days to get ready, to put all the necessary food and all the creatures . . .
PUPILS: Safely into the ark.
TEACHER: This was an extraordinary week with Noah. He did not lose a moment . . . in getting all stored away. And what do you think were the wicked doing and saying? . . .
PUPILS: They were eating and drinking, buying and selling, marrying and giving in marriage as usual.
TEACHER: And passing their jokes, and taking a loud laugh at the old dreamer. At last the seventh, or Sabbath day came, and

God shut in Noah. And now the fountains of the great deep gushed forth, the windows of heaven were opened. It was no ordinary rain, it came . . .

PUPILS: In torrents.[5]

The modern reader may think it remarkable that the children were able to give the desired answers or that they were able to extract from the story the lessons that Forrester expected — that God will fulfil His threats upon the wicked, that men ought to take God at His word and believe what He says, and that men should show their faith by doing whatever God bids them. Even so, these examples show a great advance over early nineteenth-century concepts of education.

Ferment and Efficiency: 1870 - 1900

By the last third of the nineteenth century the number of writers on education had become large enough to be confusing. In the early decades, in addition to books already mentioned, there were works by American writers, including the *Theory and Practice of Teaching* by David P. Paige, *The School* and *The Schoolmaster* by Potter and Emerson, to both of which Forrester acknowledged indebtedness, and *The District School* by J. O. Taylor, *Methods of Instruction* by J. P. Wickersham, and others which were purchased by many Canadians. Some of these writers, including Paige, showed flashes of understanding which placed them far in advance of most of their contemporaries. In the late nineteenth century several books published in Britain were lauded by education authorities, although they had more literary excellence than practical value to teachers in Canada. Two books that dealt with broader problems of education were *Lectures on Teaching* by J. G. Fitch and the *Theory and Practice of Teaching* by Edward Thring. There was also a late-Victorian tendency to upholster some educational journals with stuffy remarks on education by notable Britishers unconnected with the schools, including politicians and professors in England and imported presidents of universities in Canada. But two issues of clear-cut significance emerged from the fog.

One of these, related to a new extreme in veneration of written examinations, will be discussed in a later chapter. Respect for form reached a new high degree when ability to reproduce textbook content and teachers' notes was taken as the sole measure of education. This hard-shelled realism was soon cracked and weakened by persistent revolt, but never broken, and it continued to encrust secondary and higher education in the twentieth century.

The second issue was fought between science, as challenger, and the humanities, which from 1870 onward were put on the defensive. The arguments of Thomas Huxley and Herbert Spencer for science and of Matthew Arnold for the humanities were made familiar to Canadians by educational journals. At the meeting of the Educational Institute of New Brunswick in 1878, Principal Crocket of the normal school said:

With respect to curriculums for secondary or superior instruction, the battle has waxed hot between the two great classes — the partizans of the old classical studies and the partizans of what are known as the real or useful studies.

Most of the articles in educational journals championed science and the scientific method, as did one based on Spencer's essay of 1871. The Canadian author claimed that civilization could never have arisen but for science, which was the "Cinderella of knowledges, doing all the work, ministering to her gaudier sisters, and long since kept unrecognized in the background."[6] Bain, whose book on *Education as a Science* was highly regarded and prescribed as reading for higher certificates in Ontario, was definitely on the side of science both as method and as "the most perfect embodiment of truth." Bain considered the teaching of languages as justifiable only insofar as they were useful to receive or convey information, and would have placed grammar on the same level as algebra as a more technical and advanced study in its field of communication.

Against this position and in favor of literature, foreign languages, and history were most of the more conservative and religious people of position and influence. The real conflict was between science as method and the acceptance of particular forms and values in the study of the humanities. Champions of the classics who managed to ignore the report of the Schools Inquiry Commission published in England in 1866 were unhappy to read in Fitch, fourteen years later, that the testimony accumulated by that commission was "conclusive as to the prevalence in the grammar schools of a belief in the supreme efficacy of Latin and Greek as a means of mental training, but also as to the worthlessness of much of the result."[7] Many strong proponents of English literature and of history had also something definite in mind — the values and beliefs of a society that recognized the superiority of certain values, and that maintained the noble and the good by upholding a language and a set of concepts not susceptible to scientific analysis and disproof.

Then about 1890 North America discovered Herbart, an aggressive advocate of the humanities who out-mechanized teachers of practical subjects, an exponent of character education who had a method pedagogically more convincing than that of the scientists. Johann Friedrich Herbart (1776-1841), a German scholar, expanded Pestalozzi's thesis on the importance of sense-perception into a logically organized system of pedagogy. His *Outlines of Educational Doctrine* began by stating that virtue was the purpose of education, and proceeded to show exactly how the purpose could be achieved by the development of many-sided interests that would ensure right decisions at times of critical choice. These interests could be developed and made effective by the teaching of ordinary school subjects, provided (1) that a foundation of sense impression was laid down, and (2) that through the instruction, connections were established between clusters of significant knowledge. Then, whatever the problem or temptation, the right idea would rise to consciousness with an overwhelming array of allies.

Obviously the study of human relations through literature and history was of primary importance in providing ideas which would dominate the field when virtue was at stake. Obviously, also, the teacher must be a master of technique to be sure that pupils grasped, or "apperceived," the new knowledge presented to them and that they acquired genuine interest, which is a reaching out for more. Their interests, or knowledge, must not be scattered or disjointed. A supply of facts and miscellaneous information was of no avail. The educated person could survey his well-rounded knowledge as a connected whole.

This and much more came from Herbart and his successors, Ziller and Rein, who attracted the attention of the English-speaking world late in the nineteenth century. As a result, education after about 1890 became a science. We shall see in later chapters: that new training institutions for secondary school teachers and subsequently university faculties or departments of education were established; that ability to use the five formal steps of the Herbartian lesson became the professional asset of the teacher; that high school courses of study were whipped into shape, by means of examination requirements, to ensure many-sidedness with unity; that teachers began to study psychology and to appreciate the importance of securing interest; and that more history and more literature were taught with a new emphasis on understanding. These and other related developments at the end of the nineteenth century can be attributed in considerable degree to the influence of Herbart. A few specific examples will help to illustrate the expression or operation of Herbartian ideas in Canada.

William Lyon Mackenzie may have been acquainted with the work of the German educator in 1830, for in that year he published a pamphlet, *Catechism of Education*, which stated that character was produced by a sequence of ideas starting from a sensation. George Paxton Young, scholarly grammar school inspector of Canada West in the 1860's, was deeply concerned even then that pupils were not taught to understand and appreciate literature. The *Canada School Journal* published in 1878 an article that argued that it would be advisable to have pupils read "certain works entire," an innovation which came only when the full weight of the Herbartian influence was felt ten or twenty years later. Between January and June, 1885, the *Educational Weekly* published editorials and articles discussing various Herbartian ideas. They dealt with the need of treating education as a science, of gaining insight into "those psychological and physical laws upon which true education is based," and of establishing a "professorship of pedagogic" to round off the system. They forecast the study in school of complete books and suggested that no readers with extracts should be required beyond the third reader, or Grade VI. They reviewed a translation from the German of Diesterweg on methods of teaching history. Perhaps the emphasis on education as a science was derived from Bain, and one writer credited the

advocacy of whole works of literature for school study to Matthew Arnold. But the ideas were Herbartian also.

In Nova Scotia in 1892, as also in Ontario, the high school course of study for teachers' certificates, university entrance, and in effect for all purposes was unified in accordance with the Herbartian principles which were the basis of recommendations made in the United States the previous year by the National Education Association's Committee of Ten on secondary school studies. Guided by the same principles, British Columbia in 1892 made English a required instead of an optional subject in high schools, and the Northwest Territories in 1903 increased considerably the amount of English and general history in the curriculum. In Manitoba in 1897 the report of the Committee of Ten was prescribed for study by teachers seeking a First Class certificate, and the report of the Committee of Fifteen on correlation of elementary school subjects for candidates for Second Class certificates. From coast to coast the impact of the Herbartian doctrine was felt.

But there were other types of thinking in evidence towards the end of the nineteenth century. Always included when platitudes were mouthed were declarations regarding subjects which trained the mind. The assumptions of formal discipline and transfer of training were not questioned by leading citizens although they were not supported by reputable systems of pedagogical thought such as those of Herbart and Hegel. To give them an authoritative parentage, some writers attributed them to John Locke a century or two after he was able to reply. But although lack of evidence or authority did not weaken expressions of conviction by important laymen and administrators, experienced educators were more cautious. Calkin, principal of the normal school in Nova Scotia, admitted that "every study impresses its own specific character on its discipline" but refused to concede any clear-cut distinction between the so-called useful subjects like science and the so-called disciplinary subjects like the classics. "A study," he said, "may be best as useful knowledge or as discipline according to the way it is pursued." Statements of other educators on training the mind followed the Pestalozzian idea of developing power without attributing general value to particular subjects. According to Inch, who became superintendent in New Brunswick, exercise was the source of power:

For the Teacher the exercise of the child's body and soul is the only condition of their development. That is a truth which should be written in phosphorus upon the dark background of every unsuccessful Teacher's record. It is an idea which should permeate the Teacher's being until he acts from it unconsciously. It is by exercise alone that the muscles are strengthened; by exercise the brain in all its lobes is improved; by exercise moral stamina is secured.[8]

Neither Locke nor Pestalozzi would have objected to that. The argument is aimed chiefly against the older concept of the receptive learner.

Similarly there were exhortations to teach pupils "to think." This advice came from people who obviously meant that pupils should accept approved opinions and follow approved patterns of reasoning. But there were also educators who had given some thought to what was involved in clear thinking. A contributor to an educational journal in 1880 concluded that intellectual readiness was in evidence when "points of similarity and difference in any question are almost instinctively recognized and the judgment so invariably used that rapid decision follows on the heels of correct thought, which in turn is founded on indisputable facts."[9] Anticipating Gestalt psychology and the unit method, he advised teachers to see that the pupil understood the general outline of a subject and the relation in which each

part already observed stood to every other in the formation of the whole.

To counteract such dangerous thinking, the nineteenth century had the educational philosophy of idealism. It, too, was intellectual, but the approved, conservative type of idealism gave eternal and ubiquitous validity to ideas in crystallized form. Apart from W. T. Harris in the United States, there have been few declared and conscious exponents in North America of Hegelian idealism, but there were and apparently still are large numbers who have essentially the same views on education without knowing the why and wherefore.

The Hegelians attached high importance to society and its institutions and, in education, frankly made the curriculum a first consideration, not the pupil. The child coming to school for the first time was to be regarded as a little animal. The task of education was to transform him into a civilized man by having him study and master subjects representative of the highest achievements of mankind. There was to be no catering to his natural and undeveloped tastes. It was right that school should be unpleasant and formidable to him at first, that he should be forced under strict discipline to apply himself, and that he should accept the judgment and direction of his superiors. After years of hard study under close direction of teachers who knew what was right and fine and who enforced their authority, the pupil at last would feel at home in this new world. The individual would have become at one with the species. He might then be trusted to think and act for himself.

There is evidence that some teachers were aware of Hegelian theory. Manitoba in 1897 prescribed *Philosophy of Education* by Rosenkranz to be read in preparation for First Class certificate examinations. In his *School Management*, John Millar, Deputy Minister of Education in

Ontario, showed his respect for Rosenkranz and for W. T. Harris, whose *Psychological Foundations of Education* was also read by better qualified teachers. Rosenkranz and Harris were the chief exponents of Hegelian educational theory. A Canadian textbook strongly Hegelian in tone was published in 1893 — *Studies in Poetry, Wordsworth*, by M. F. Libby, a prominent Toronto teacher in a collegiate institute. Libby had no patience with the "ugly and petty" opinions of bumptious youth or with teachers who asked Grade IX pupils whether they liked a poem. Throughout high school, pupils were to be told what poetry was excellent and why it was excellent in the judgment of educated people who were qualified to speak. Poems were to be analyzed minutely, stanza by stanza, line by line, phrase by phrase, word by word to disclose the technique of their artistry. After four or five years of such intensive study, but only then, a pupil might be asked what he thought of a poem. He might then be expected to give — not a grunt, or an inarticulate "It's all right, I guess" — but an answer!

People who had been detached from the crowd by their own education found it hard not to approve of such ideas, regardless of their incompatibility with democracy. In the 1890's, work was work in school, and play was play out of school. Subjects were what the schools taught and what pupils had to learn. The words of the teacher were truth and law in his own classroom. But during the decade, confidence in these seemingly solid forms was shaken. At teachers' institutes up to 1890 the chief concern had been with subject matter and methods of instruction. From that time, attention was directed increasingly to such questions as the relationship of the school to society, to industry, and to the community. In particular there was a growth of interest in educational psychology. By the end of the century people were ready to appreciate the very different idealism of another German educator.

Motivation: 1900 - 1920

Friedrich Wilhelm August Froebel (1782-1852) was moved by his own unhappy childhood to devise a new type of education which was to bring joy and self-confidence to millions of children who followed him. Froebel's life was a search for harmony in the world, especially between the contradictory claims of the adult and the spontaneity of the child. He found his answer in a divine *Unity*. But for Froebel this *Reality* of the universe was not a person, or structure of truth, detached from nature and man. This Unity was dynamic — "all-pervading, energetic, living, self-conscious, and hence eternal." Moreover, this Unity, or God, lived and reigned in all nature and in all men — not among them as an agent, but in them as their true being. The theologian may recognize this as the same heresy for which Bruno was burned at the stake two centuries before. It had basic and revolutionary significance not only for religion but for education.

Since the true nature of the child was God-like and good, it followed that the essential method of education must be free self-activity of the pupil. Only by his own activity could the child develop as God moved him and in accordance with the divine plan. It was the purpose of education to enable the individual consciously to reveal God in his life. This purpose was to be achieved partly by nature study, through which the pupil learned to understand the operation of divine law in the world about him. The purpose was to be achieved also by expressive and creative activity, through which the pupil grew in power to make God manifest in his life. The purpose was thwarted, and the child physically or psychologically deformed, when the adult parent or teacher, himself corrupt, interfered with the child's development on some pious misconception or pretence. By attributing evil motives to the child, the corrupt adult destroyed the child's faith in the good within himself and thus made the child evil by a selfish falsehood or malicious lie. But in the good school or home, adults and children alike were disciplined by the divine law of freedom; the demands of education were "simultaneously double-sided — giving and taking, uniting and dividing, prescribing and following, active and passive, positive yet giving scope, firm and yielding." No form of man's life or of society was to be considered as distinct or perfect; rather one should view his own life and that of all others as part of a continuous whole in infinitely progressive development.

Even at the end of the nineteenth century such concepts were unintelligible to most, although the dynamic import was disturbing to those whose security depended on the permanence of form. Clergymen of the Church of England objected to the use in teacher education of Froebel's most important book, *The Education of Man.* During discussion in the synod of Toronto, as reported in the *Mail and Empire* in 1900, one stated that the "book was irreligious," another that "liberalism was spoiling Christianity." But a committee advised against denunciation:

Your Committee has examined with care Froebel's book on "Education of Man" which is being used by the Normal School Kindergarten. They paid particular attention to those passages which were indicated as containing objectionable teaching. They do not feel that they have a right to condemn a work written from a scientific and general religious point of view . . . however much they might prefer one with more distinctively Christian teaching . . . which takes for its ground the nature of man simply regarded as a creature of God.[10]

Fortunately the chief manifestation of Froebelian doctrine applied to the education of very young children, to whose inner urges the adult is least disposed to attribute evil, and of whose uncontrolled activities he is most indulgent. In 1837, at Blankenburg, Froebel concentrated his attention on classes for children of preschool age and in 1840 named his institution the kindergarten. The children engaged in play — the purest form of self-activity — including games and songs and play with the "gifts." The latter, consisting of simple playthings like a ball and a cube, were intended not only to provide a healthy or constructive outlet for energy but to teach the child first lessons on the laws and principles of the universe. Thus the sphere was the perfect whole which, in the form of a ball, absorbed the energy of the child and returned it by bounce or roll. Kindergarten experts up to the beginning of World War I continued to attach such mystical significance to the gifts, but subsequently retained the objects without claims as to their meaning for the child. Similarly various Froebelian methods and practices at a higher level were introduced or retained without the philosophy of dynamic idealism on which they were originally based.

Since James L. Hughes was the outstanding Canadian exponent of Froebel, it is not surprising that Toronto could claim to be the second city in the world to make the kindergarten a part of its regular school system. As early as 1878 the two morning newspapers of the city carried arguments in favor of the adoption of Froebelian principles either in kindergartens or in existing classes. A knowledge of these principles would effect a "revolution in the methods of disciplining and teaching," said the *Mail.* Even teachers of advanced pupils should study them, said the *Globe,* for the application of these "very natural principles" does not stop with the years of infancy.[11] After

A modern kindergarten, around 1950

an interchange of visits with kindergarten experts in St. Louis, Missouri, a Toronto teacher who had been sent there for training took charge of the first public school kindergarten in Canada in 1883. The number of kindergartens multiplied year by year and spread to other cities. Before 1900 there were 120 kindergartens in Ontario taught by 250 teachers and attended by over 11,000 pupils under six years of age. In the Maritime Provinces the *Educational Review* in 1887 carried an enthusiastic article by a Halifax author:

A few visits to a good kindergarten will soon settle the question as to whether his [Froebel's] principles work well in practice. All is life and stir, but no confusion. There is no restraint, for although the *reign of law,* in the teacher's thought, is skilfully applied, the children, too immature for abstraction, enjoy its benefits *unconsciously.* Innocent gayety enlivens the scene.[12]

The following year the kindergarten was on the agenda of the inter-provincial convention of teachers in the Maritime Provinces. At the convention of the Dominion Education Association in 1894,

there was a kindergarten section in which papers were given by the Inspector of Kindergartens for Ontario and by a teacher of Halifax, Nova Scotia. The kindergarten had been accepted.

A second concrete illustration of the Froebelian influence was the establishment of manual training and domestic science classes at the beginning of the present century. Manual activity and the education of the whole child for the whole of life were part of the Froebelian scheme. But early manual training was Pestalozzian, since it aimed at developing successive skills, like the ability to handle the saw, the plane, and the chisel. It became Froebelian as it discarded this approach in favor of allowing the boy to make some article as soon as possible. Similarly household science conducted in laboratory fashion became Froebelian as it evolved into home-making in a model apartment. These changes began soon after 1900 but were not everywhere far advanced even forty years later.

Other tangible evidence was the appearance, shortly after 1900, of nature study in the elementary schools as the successor, after an interval, of discreet and formal lessons on objects. Subsequently, about 1930, the scope of nature study was widened to admit general science — still in accordance with the Froebelian principle, in which the unity of the comprehensive whole must always be sought. We shall see in later chapters how this principle was given expression in such integrated activities as social studies and the enterprise. Again in the first few years of the present century Froebelian creative art began to replace Pestalozzian drawing of straight and curved lines. Later we shall see that similar changes occurred in other subjects of study.

Prominent Canadian educators from the time of Confederation onward, and classroom teachers in increasing numbers later, were moved to some degree by the views of Froebel. Forrester used the acorn metaphor to depict education as growth. Calkin in 1878 wrote that the child should be "placed in the position of the investigator who is exploring his own subject."[13] A little book by an inspector of schools, F. C. Emberson, published in Montreal in the same year, contained chapters on "How to Make the Children Like School" and on "Cheerfulness and Health of the Teacher and Pupils." Articles in educational journals stressed the importance of play and kindergartens from 1885 and of nature study, manual training, and household science from 1900. Hughes, author of *Froebel's Educational Laws* in 1897, urged in another of his books that the transition from the home to the school should be less sudden and that the work of the school should afford pleasure to the pupil. Some principals and instructors of model and normal schools by 1890 advised teachers-in-training to give the child's first year at school some of the qualities of the kindergarten, to look for "connectedness" in the nature of the child, and without extinguishing the vital spark

to direct the self-activity of the child into proper channels. Programs of national conventions of the Dominion Education Association announced discussion of "Child Study," "Emotions as a Factor in Education," and "The Overcrowded Curriculum." At a convention of the teachers of South Saskatchewan in 1904 one teacher explained in her paper that the school was a workhouse, in which a certain amount of noise was necessary, and that the best school is the least governed. Other papers at the convention dealt with nature study, drawing, and ways of making primary work more interesting. The next year J. M. Harper published an article on the "Law of Repression," in which he urged teachers to keep check on their own egotism lest their own personalities be dominant in the classroom and the children be suppressed. The school should provide for exercise of the child's potentialities, not for display of the teacher's power. To be justifiable and beneficial, repression must come from within one's being and not from without.

This and further evidence to be presented in later chapters points to a revolution in educational thought at the beginning of the twentieth century. Three major factors which influenced substantial numbers of people to swing over to the new-world point of view were Froebelian idealism, the upswing in prosperity and optimism which broadened the scope of liberalism, and the weakening of old bonds by irrefutable demonstrations of the scientific method. More people became willing to give others a chance to lead a fuller life. Among the minority of teachers who stayed in the profession, more were ready to argue for the release of the young from educational straightjackets even if their professional assets in organized knowledge and coercive authority suffered in consequence.

After about 1905 provincial departments of education in programs of study and other publications put the stamp of approval on education *for,* and not merely *of,* the child. In that year the *Canada Educational Monthly* quietly expired with swan song issues containing articles which might have retained interest fifteen years before: "The Ideal Teacher" by a distinguished young clergyman; "Hints on Memory Training" by one who assumed that education was the development of the mental faculties; "English Schools as Seen by a Canadian Teacher" of Victoria, B.C., who reported that "the average English assistant teaches what he has been told to teach, when he is told to teach it, and in the exact manner in which he has been taught to teach it — and he does it well." That was not the kind of thing to hold readers at the beginning of a new century.

In 1906 Principal Perrett of the Saskatchewan Normal School explained the new point of view by reference to teacher education:

> While we give plans and suggestions for teaching various subjects we are spending more time in helping our students to teach the child, realizing that the child is of greater and more importance than the subject. We are not only attempting to teach children various subjects but to teach these subjects that these children will be more suited to live the life of this country.[14]

In 1912 the superintendent of schools in Edmonton summarized changes in educational thinking and practice in a generation: the transformation of reading from a formal mastery of symbols to expression of the author's meaning, of arithmetic from trickery with number symbols to ability in common human transactions, and of drawing from formal imitation of things to expression of ideas, experiences, and observations. In old subjects and new the pupil no longer merely absorbed a body of information but learned to do things and to express himself in words and materials.

What had happened to education? More people had realized that others felt and behaved as they did, whether children or adults. Although fear of punishment or hope of extraneous reward would drive a person to work hard until the end was gained or avoided, neither a child nor a man would work with a will or take a real interest in anyone or anything except of his own volition under conditions that he recognized as fair. If there was to be virtue or knowledge for its own sake, and if education was to be more than indoctrination and practical training, then the Golden Rule had to be practised in the schoolroom, and not by pupils alone. Pallas Athene in the inducement that she offered to Paris had given a clue. The important gift was the power within. "Do unto others" must be interpreted as "Give unto others the same opportunity to decide and to act accordingly as you in practice claim for yourself." This greater willingness to allow others to direct their own affairs made it possible to provide for intrinsic motivation in general education. Recognition of the importance of motivation is the hallmark of twentieth-century thought and practice. But the motivation must operate as an inner driving force, as in Froebelian self-activity. For convenience the word "motivation" is used in this sense without explanation in the pages that follow.

Interaction: 1920 - 1950

Though given an original or renewed impetus by ideas from abroad, the new education in North America had also an indigenous development. Towards the end of the nineteenth century rapidly changing conditions in American society altered the function of the schools. Thereafter educational thought was modified by practice, as practice was modified by thought, and both by continuing social change, which education sought to influence as it in turn was influenced by new developments in society. In this ever-changing world of interacting forces no fixed point of reference was possible, unless in some academic stronghold out of communication with the lives of ordinary men. From the operation of dynamic idealism in this educational environment, p r a g m a t i s m evolved as a philosophy for the schools.

In 1884 Francis W. Parker, the leading American exponent of Froebel, spoke to the Ontario Teachers' Association on the conflict of two ideals — of limitation and of freedom. Courtesy did not restrain him from declaring bluntly that England among other European countries tried to keep its lower classes in ignorance and subjection by dogmatic teaching of textbook material. Where limitation was the ideal, quantity was the method, and dependence the result. Quantities of selected facts and work were prescribed, crammed under strict discipline into the pupils, and measured by examinations. Said Parker:

I remember visiting a school in which the children sat very still. They looked before them and stared at the walls. Their eyes had the expression of inmates of an insane asylum. When asked a question, a current of electricity seemed to set their mouths in motion, and the words came out. What were these children trained for? For the docile subjects of others; to be ruled over by political bosses.[15]

In place of this submissive learning Parker advocated education for freedom: "When the child learns to choose for himself, that moment he is free." He admitted that there might be a little confusion at first while the children were learning self-control, but urged his hearers not to extinguish the divine spark of curiosity which moved the child to seek and discover truth for himself. Parker's exposition of Froebelian ideas was clearly related to education for political democracy.

John Dewey (1859-1952), who was also strongly influenced by idealism in his earlier years, became the outstanding exponent of education in democratic society. It is impossible to do justice to the profound contribution he made to American education. He saw how the process of education was nullified by the unbridged gap between the authority of the teacher and the curriculum on the one hand and the interest and point of view of the pupil on the other. He showed how the two could be brought together by thinking of education as a continuous reconstruction of experience, as the drive of motivated activity brought the child into vital contact with his world in situations directed by the teacher to ensure constructive learning. Objectives had to be immediate and continuing rather than remote, and subject matter could not be predetermined in order and arrangement. Unfortunately some who were able to think only in terms of alternative forms of education — teacher-dominating or child-undirected — rushed from one extreme to the other. Only skilful teachers with democratic convictions were able to employ radically progressive techniques. But nearly all teachers during the present century profited sufficiently from Dewey's insight to improve the schools to a marked degree.

Some Canadian teachers became aware of Dewey's ideas from the beginning of the twentieth century. The *Educational Review* of New Brunswick in April 1899 published an article on Dewey's laboratory school at the University of Chicago. In the first calendar of the faculty of education of the University of Toronto, established in 1907, two of the four books listed under the teacher-training course in principles of education were *School and Society* and *Ethical Principles Underlying Education*, both by Dewey. In the Ontario Teachers' Manual on *History of Education*, published in 1915, Dewey is mentioned casually as one familiar to the reader. On the whole, however, the influence of Dewey on Canadian education was more theoretical than effective until World War I. During the next two decades an increasing minority of teachers applied his ideas, but practice in the schools did not keep up with the change in thinking among influential educators. For that reason rather sudden adjustment was necessary when provincial authorities between 1935 and 1940 gave the signal for an advance by introducing elementary programs of study drastically revised to make the content more significant to the pupil.

Just as the kindergarten and activity methods of Froebel were adopted and retained in the public school systems without his basic philosophy, so the methods of Dewey and his followers were introduced without an acceptance of the new philosophy of pragmatism. Incompatibility of metaphysical assumptions, aims, values, and practices is no cause for worry among English-speaking Canadians. But the few who were willing to be disturbed by trying to understand found that pragmatism assumed nothing fixed or permanent in the precarious universe of interacting forces and perpetual change. They could no longer think of the value of such and such a subject as an independent entity. It could have value only in relation to a particular pupil in particular circumstances and to what happened when pupil, teacher, and subject interacted on one another. They could no longer assume any "eternal verities" as a prescription for virtue but would expect the most satisfactory attitudes and behavior to prove themselves in practice if given the chance. The criterion of pragmatism is "Does it work?" or "By their fruits ye shall know them."

A parallel movement which expanded rapidly in the twentieth century was the scientific movement in education. One of the Canadian pioneers was John Arbuckle, a school inspector of Prince Edward Island, who in 1849 introduced a method of testing and recording results that he hoped would give "instead of uncertain, varying opinions, authentic facts," which "when continued from year to year, become reliable statistics." The method was to ask scholars in different schools the same questions and to record all correct and incorrect responses and the percentage of correct answers; on this basis he ranked the school in comparison with other schools visited. Nearly thirty years later, at a teachers' institute in Westmoreland County, New Brunswick, a discussion on the usefulness and desirability of homework ended in a decision to make a trial for a year in two classes, one of which was to have no homework. But during the nineteenth century nearly everything in education continued to be a matter of opinion, better founded as teachers became more open-minded and better qualified to judge, but still opinion based on personal experience or approved but untested theories. The first widespread appearance of the scientific method in education in Canada came as the result of developments between 1890 and World War I. During that period the Herbartian influence was followed in the United States by the establishment of many university chairs or departments of education, by the invention of objective tests, by the development of intelligence tests from the first scale of Binet and Simon, by the working out of statistical methods, and by a new scientific approach to the study of educational psychology, history, and philosophy.

The scientific movement was reflected in educational periodicals in Canada. From its first appearance in 1912, *The School* carried such articles as "The Time Factor and the Course of Study," which cited the results of American investigations as evidence that nothing was to be gained by spending more than an optimum time per day on spelling or arithmetic and that a short recess every hour improved the achievement of younger pupils. There was a regular section in the magazine on "Educational Experiment and Comment," in which were to be found such items as evidence of the unreliability of examinations, of the great difference in value indicated by "90 per cent" in different institutions and classrooms. As might be expected, most of the articles in this field were by authors holding graduate degrees in education, which had been offered at Toronto since 1898. But interest in the movement spread to teachers, as was illustrated by an article in 1920 by an Edmonton teacher on the measurement of intelligence, which had been given wide publicity through the testing program in the American armed forces during the war. During the decade that followed, objective tests came into fairly general use for occasional purposes and were widely discussed.

In 1931 the Department of Educational Research of the Ontario College of Education was established, partly for the construction of objective measuring instruments. Twenty years later it had a staff of fifteen, extensive equipment, and spacious quarters in which additional workers were usually to be found. In 1938 the Canadian Council for Educational Research was organized by the Canadian Education Association and the Canadian Teachers' Federation. In 1942 *The School* began publishing an annual review of educational research in Canada, although the total effort was still not impressive. The British Columbia department of education established in 1946 a division of tests, standards, and research to study administrative and curricular problems, to make tests available to teachers. In that province the board of education in Vancouver had for some years employed staff for scientific study and prediction of school building requirements and similar problems. Mention has been made of national research projects under the Canadian Education Association. In 1953 the

Canadian Teachers' Federation appointed a director of educational research.

These illustrations are sufficient to show that a scientific or objective attitude had by 1953 permeated Canadian education to a noticeable degree. But it was far from dominant. Proponents of the new education had respect for objective measuring instruments but insisted that intangibles not subject to measurement were more important. "Reactionaries" kept their eyes closed to scientific findings or dismissed them with contempt as contrary to traditional beliefs or their own convictions. When an epidemic of 1918-19 caused schools to be closed for a time and a city school board refused to have teachers concentrate on "essentials" only for the rest of the year, a leading daily newspaper of Alberta declared that: "not to cut out the frills amounts, therefore, to a decision needlessly to deprive the pupils of the city of several weeks' teaching of the fundamental subjects."[16] A normal school master protested against the false assumptions, of course. But the same argument might have appeared in 1955 and have received considerable support.

From Distinctive Forms to Universal Power: 1800 - 1950

In the educational movements reviewed above one may detect the trend discussed in the previous chapter — from an emphasis on form, stability, and differentiation in the interest of alleged superiority to an emphasis on activity, change, and universality in the interest of alleged equality. This trend may be seen in statements of educational aims.

Regarding the social function of education, the *old* aim was expressed by Bishop Macdonnell in 1817:

Of all the methods that can be devised to preserve to the children, the loyal principles of their fathers, it is obvious that none can prove so effectual as implanting in their minds these principles, and conveying moral and religious instructions to them at an early age, in the emphatic language of their ancestors.[17]

Regulations for common schools in Canada West in 1845 stated that: "Teachers should neither countenance nor permit their pupils to discuss matters connected with religious or political opinions and should be careful to keep as strict a watch on their own conduct when out of school."

Contrast the *new* aim as expressed in 1870 by the Rev. Dr. Nelles, President of Victoria University:

Let education become universal and descend as an heirloom from one age to another, and there will ere long grow up an enlightened public opinion, capable of holding in check the mad ambition of kings, the schemes of mercenary politicians, and the folly of those who retard Christianity by mingling with it dogmas of their own invention.[18]

Even wider in scope was a statement by a school inspector to the teachers' association in Canada West in 1867 that Canadians "must be prepared to act in concert with other nations to regenerate and raise the sunken millions of our species . . . by education of all our classes of people."[19]

When the barriers to political freedom and economic opportunity were falling, there were bold assertions that education should have practical value for people. In 1847 Marshall d'Avray of New Brunswick declared, "The aim and end of all education ought to be preparation for the active and actual business of life." Ryerson in the section on practical education in his *Journal of Education* in 1860 quoted others who described education as the parent of material riches and as, "not only the most honest and honorable, but the surest means of amassing property."[20] At a school convention in the same year, he

urged parents, "to give their children such an education as would enable them to take care and make a proper use of property that might be left to them, or what they might make themselves by their own industry."[21] But the new aim of education for individual independence and power was given wider connotation. Ryerson in 1854 claimed that the system of education in Canada West, "developed individual independence in its highest and best sense . . . called forth self-reliance and those other virtues which adorn the human character."[22] Dawson of McGill said in 1864,

I hold to be uneducated men, those whose opportunities of training have been limited to the mere imitation of their seniors. . . . Such men may, by their physical powers, be of service to society; but in the present state of the world's progress, they are mentally and morally a dead weight upon it.[23]

The suggestion in these last two statements of a new moral aim was made explicit in other declarations. Instead of learning merely to conform to a pattern, young people were to acquire ability to discriminate. George Paxton Young wrote in 1865:

That boys and girls should hate what is mean, . . . should feel a sympathetic admiration for instances of generous self-sacrifice, is of unspeakably more consequence than that they should be able to demonstrate the propositions of Euclid or to construe Cicero or Homer.[24]

A new emphasis on universality, kindness, and tolerance was illustrated by a local superintendent in 1864:

I hope the dawn of better days is approaching when the rising generations, educated in the same schools, are taught to love and practice charity towards each other . . .

The shift in emphasis from form to power was revealed most clearly in the renunciation of mere rote memorization of textbook content and finally of all curriculum tyranny. In the 1860's reports of school inspectors everywhere harped on the theme that the object of education was not merely knowledge of subject matter but mental discipline. They advocated "more training and less stuffing," development of the "reasoning faculties," and teaching children "not only to remember but also to think." Forrester in 1867 not only stated the aim of education without reference to set content but anticipated to a degree the modern insistence on continuous development of the whole child rather than preparation for a remote future:

The real end of education is, we again repeat, the growth, the harmonious growth and legitimate direction of all the parts of the complex nature of the young, with the requisite provision for their onward, never-ending progression.[25]

With good reason in the period of pressure for efficiency, a few objected to the tyranny of the curriculum on other grounds. A correspondent wrote to Ryerson's *Journal of Education* in 1873, "Unless children can be educated in a way compatible with the preservation of their health, it were better at once to tear down our school houses."[26] In 1885, David Allison, Superintendent of Education in Nova Scotia, expressed what thoughtful men were beginning to realize, namely that curricular

materials had no eternal validity, for "all history is a protest against the folly of assuming finalities in the instruments of instruction."[27] Twenty-seven years later the final report of a committee on curriculum of the provincial education association protested against the teaching of subjects rather than of children: "Now the three R's, so called, while they are invaluable instruments of education, are not in themselves educative."[28] In the report of the Royal Commission on Education in Ontario the aims of education were stated in 1950 wholly in terms of development.

These few examples have been selected from several hundred statements of aims to summarize the tendency of new-world concepts to become acceptable to more and more people. Other examples might have been selected to illustrate the heavy emphasis on the preservation of form in the statements of a diminishing but still substantial number. Expressed aims must not be interpreted as evidence of contemporary practice, which always fell short of the intent in giving power to others and short of the hope in getting others to conform. But classroom practice, though laggard and not wholly effective, did follow the same unmistakable and continuing trend as was indicated in educational thought. The next two chapters deal with curriculum and methods as two aspects of classroom practice.

CHAPTER 23

Curriculum and Methods

The choice of content for the school curriculum was
determined by tradition, by the views people held, by the
knowledge teachers possessed, and by the possibility of testing
what the pupil learned. To an increasing degree it has been
determined also by the needs of the pupil in his immediate or
probable environment. Method was adapted to the content and
its purpose, but was limited always by the teacher's ability and
insight. Before 1850 content was much more important than
method. But as the dynamic concept of life in democratic
society prevailed over the static forms of aristocracy, method
increased in importance, especially in the elementary school.
Concurrently in educational thought the distinction between
content and method became less definite. In this chapter
content and method are considered separately; in the next
chapter they are considered together in relation to particular
subjects.

THE ELEMENTARY SCHOOL CURRICULUM

The chart on page 433 shows how the elementary school curriculum changed and expanded in schools of English-speaking Canada over the past 150 years. To some extent the subjects answered the needs of the respective periods. From 1800 to 1850 in pioneer society under aristocratic control the bare essentials of communication were sufficient for ordinary needs. To prepare pupils for democratic government after 1850, grammar was intended to train the mind to think and geography was taught to provide necessary information. Increased economic production and more liberal thought were reflected in the curriculum after 1875 in added subjects and activities. The additions suggest a somewhat fuller life, although the chief emphasis was on practical efficiency through much more arithmetic, through drawing as a technical skill, and so on. After 1900, as rural living declined and as children, with fewer home chores, learned from the home less and less about home and country living, manual training, household science, and nature study were introduced into the curriculum, partly as compensation; other subjects became less formal and added some enrichment and refinement to life. After 1925 the changes begun in 1900 became more marked, and an answer to problems of war and depression was sought through social studies to give an understanding of the world and through enterprise activities to give practice in democratic decision and co-operation.

Early Curriculum Extension

The first major curriculum revision in elementary schools was actually no more than a requirement by the newly established central authorities that all common schools should offer the advanced subjects — grammar and geography — which had formerly been taught only in private elementary schools, in the elementary grades of grammar schools, and to advanced pupils in superior common schools. Although the term "grammar school" is not as commonly used in Canada as in the United States, it would have been equally applicable here to denote a school with higher elementary grades. Marlow School in Stanstead County, Lower Canada, was distinguished in the eyes of a school visitor as having been the first in the township to teach grammar and as having been restored to prestige in 1830 under a master who taught grammar and geography "in considerable perfection." Grammar was taught to only 17 of 465 pupils in 19 schools of the Western District in Upper Canada in 1826, and geography was not even mentioned, an indication that neither the pupils nor the teachers had advanced far in their studies. The conditions of eligibility for a teacher's grant in Prince Edward Island in 1847 marked the mid-century curriculum advance: ability to teach bookkeeping, English grammar, reading, spelling, writing, and geography without the use of globes.

From 1850 to 1875 a common school in any province was fortunate to get a teacher who could handle these subjects well. In Nova Scotia in 1850 there were 384 of 887 common schools that did not attempt grammar or geography. Prince Edward Island in 1855 did have nearly 1300 of its 9500 pupils in grammar and nearly 1100 in geography, a good proportion which increased soon after; but of 505 pupils in the Acadian schools of the province there were only 54 in arithmetic, 11 in grammar, and one in geography. New Brunswick in 1861 reported all pupils in *photocopy.*

THE ELEMENTARY SCHOOL CURRICULUM
(Italics indicate subjects or activities found in relatively few schools)

extension.

1825 — 1850	1850 — 1875	1875 — 1900	1900 — 1925	1925 — 1950
		kindergarten	*kindergarten*	*kindergarten*
reading	reading	reading	reading	reading
		literature	literature	literature
writing	writing	writing	writing	writing
		composition	composition	composition
grammar	grammar	grammar	grammar	grammar
arithmetic	arithmetic	arithmetic	arithmetic	arithmetic
		bookkeeping		
geography	geography	geography	geography	social studies
		history	history	history
	object lessons	object lessons	nature study	science
	drawing	drawing	art	art
			manual training	industrial arts
			household science	home economics
	music	*music*	music	music
		physical drill	*physical training*	physical education
		physiology and temperance	*hygiene*	health
Bible verses				*religious education*
				enterprise

the three R's and more than twenty-five per cent of the pupils in grammar and geography, most of the enrolment in the higher grades. Elementary schools in New Brunswick, Nova Scotia, and British Columbia also taught British history as an advanced subject, but to a smaller proportion of pupils. Most Ontario schools taught only the three R's, supplemented by geography and grammar in the higher grades, although a few taught object lessons, drawing, and music. Nova Scotia by 1870 listed more than a third of its pupils in singing.

Further Curriculum Extension

The chief subjects added during the last quarter of the nineteenth century were composition, literature, and history, although the curriculum was enriched by the fact that more schools offered the less usual subjects of the previous period. Most of the subjects shown in the chart on this page were taught in all provinces. The first provincial course of study in British Columbia included Canadian geography in 1879-80, added Canadian history to British history in 1887, introduced physiology and hygiene in the same year, added temperance the year after, and included music, needlework, and calisthenics in 1891. The full curriculum of urban schools is illustrated by the subjects listed in a report of the secretary of the school board in Moncton, New Brunswick, in 1898: reading, spelling, recitation, composition, grammar and analysis, history, form, industrial drawing, print script, writing, arithmetic, geometry, mensuration, trigonometry, algebra, geography, minerals, plant and animal life, color, objects, temperance, teachings of science, physics, physiology, Latin, French, bookkeeping, Greek, chemistry, botany, English literature, etymology, and civics. Many of these subjects were secondary, of course, but in accordance with the

A one-room school, around 1850

combined school development in the Maritime Provinces, no distinction was made in the list.

The extension of the curriculum was greeted with the usual adverse criticism. A high school teacher of the 1870's asked in *The Ontario Teacher*, "What Subjects Should Be Taught in Our Public Schools?" He wrote in answer:

The great majority of our pupils are the sons and daughters of farmers, who intend to walk in the footsteps of their parents, and who are able, as a general thing, to attend school for only a few months in each year. . . . By forcing this extensive programme upon our youth we are inflicting an injury which will soon show itself in the abundant production of useless book-worms, and intellectual abortions.[1]

The author claimed that there were twenty-seven subjects for which time had to be found. The editor of the journal in a previous issue had made the assertion that a teacher in an ungraded school would find it necessary to teach ninety-seven different classes to cover the program. The Ontario critics neglected to

say, of course, that half of the new subjects were scheduled for post-elementary grades, or fifth-book classes, in which comparatively few pupils were enrolled. In defence of the new curriculum, Inspector McLellan of Ontario maintained in 1878 that all the subjects could be justified by their practical as well as their disciplinary value. He argued that it was not impossible for the elementary school to give the child this broader program instead of the "drudgery of barbarous routine" — reading, writing, ciphering. He contended further that improved methods would enable the children to become better arithmeticians and better readers in half the time and so to devote a correspondingly greater time to these other subjects. If for no other reason, this enriched program was necessary for national intelligence and national progress.

But there were a great many justifiable complaints in the 1880's about the excessive strain to which pupils were subjected. In New Brunswick, under the title "Overpressure in the School," the *Educational Review* said editorially:

During the past few years the question of over-pressure has, perhaps, more than any other, been urged upon the attention of school boards and educational administrators. Eminent physicians and educationists have discussed it in the journals of the day. . . . The position of the teacher (has been) complicated by the attitude assumed by parents. . . . They are often unreasonably anxious for the advancement of their children from grade to grade, and that irrespective of mental capacity and physical strength.[2]

The pressure was caused, however, not by the greater variety of subjects, which might in some cases have afforded relief, but by the requirement that more facts be memorized and further mechanical skills be mastered. The effect was stultifying on teachers and pupils alike. Bourinot wrote that under the boasted efficiency of the educational systems of 1880, the teacher was far too much of an automaton: "He is not allowed sufficient of that free volition which would enable him to develop the best qualities of his pupils and to elevate their general tone."[3] Bourinot believed that the schools should give attention to social amenities and cultivate "those graces of life which are the best endowments of youth." But the elementary school teacher, and even more the high school teacher, was prevented from doing this, and made incapable of doing it, by a philosophy that measured educational success by the number of facts memorized by pupils. The expansion of the curriculum, intended by its sponsors to liberalize education, had under these circumstances merely added to the dead weight of content.

Consideration for Children's Needs

The Froebelian revision at the beginning of the present century introduced new activities without increasing the load. Typical changes occurred in British Columbia: in 1900, nature lessons appeared on the prescribed curriculum; in 1902 manual training and domestic science were offered locally, in 1906 added as optional subjects to the curriculum, and in 1912 dignified by pertinent regulations; also in 1912 an important revision of the program gave added emphasis to creative activities, manual arts, and color work. In Alberta in 1908 a committee representative of teachers, inspectors, superintendents, and the university was appointed under the chairmanship of Dr. H. M. Tory, president of the University of Alberta, to make recommendations on curriculum revision. The committee's report, adopted by the department, recommended the extension of creative motivation from the kindergarten to all higher grades, more music and art, correlation of geography with nature study and agriculture, expansion of industrial (manual) training and home economics, active physical culture and development of habits conducive to healthful living instead of formal instruction in physiology, a liberal choice of options in the last four years of a twelve grade system, and, in Grades IX and X, practical courses in biology and physics related to agriculture instead of the formal academic courses then prescribed. Although not all of the recommendations of this advanced report were incorporated in the revised curriculum of 1912, the new elementary school subjects were given a place on the school program and the new spirit was expressed in such reforms as the abolition of examinations on hygiene. In the provinces eastward, similar changes were made. The Ontario public school syllabus of 1915 included art, music, nature study, and physical culture as regular subjects, and manual training and domestic science as optional subjects. It gave considerable emphasis in several subjects to beautifying and ennobling the pupil's life, developing a sympathetic understanding, and providing means of expression.

School equipment sold in Canada, 1860

Recent Curriculum Revisions

What Sandiford* described as the first real curriculum revision in Canada, in contrast with accretions in earlier years, occurred in the depression years. Saskatchewan set a pattern in October, 1929, and by 1937 every province had re-written its curriculum. Some provinces completed the revision in a year, some took several years. Nova Scotia published the revision and related suggestions in one handbook of 655 pages. Ontario covered Grades I to VI and subsequently Grades VII and VIII in booklets of about 150 pages each, and issued brief pamphlets on each of the secondary school subjects. British Columbia turned out voluminous publications which dwarfed all others. The new programs were based to an unprecedented degree on the concept of education as development and aimed primarily at socially desirable qualities and abilities rather than the amassing of knowledge. They raised music, art, home economics, and shop work from the status

* Professor of educational psychology and director of the Department of Educational Research, University of Toronto. See p. 462.

of optional subjects or extra-curricular activities to the importance of the traditional subjects. They placed great emphasis on health and physical education. Reflecting new educational thought in the United States under a veil of acknowledgments to Hadow in Britain, they provided for enterprises and limited activity programs. They sought to remove restrictions on teachers and pupils by providing latitude for selective emphasis and variation in methods of treatment at the teacher's discretion. These changes were limited to elementary and junior high school grades.

The innovations were not eagerly received by the large number of teachers who had clung for security to their faith in formal subject matter. But summer sessions, educational journals, supervision by converts, and pre-service professional training helped to improve understanding of the new education. By 1940 many of the older teachers and all younger teachers in the elementary schools had learned to experiment a little with education as development, and the new curricula to that extent went into effect. In keeping with the new concept, curriculum revision was regarded thereafter as a continuing process of adaptation and not as a periodic alteration of formal content. Several provinces appointed directors of curricula, and other departments made equivalent arrangements for carrying on the work.

Events in Newfoundland will serve to illustrate how the new curricula were adopted. A curriculum commission was appointed in 1933 to make a careful investigation of educational conditions throughout the country. In the following year a curriculum committee was organized. A curriculum was devised on the basis of the curriculum which had been developed for Nova Scotia. It was intended to be broad enough to provide for every type of child and every type of school. It was set forth in a teacher's handbook which included suggestions on classroom organization and methods of teaching. The aims of the eight-year elementary school program were: to give a mastery of fundamental subjects, or the tools of learning; to lay the foundation for aesthetic appreciation through instruction in art, hand-work, music, and literature; to provide a background for effective citizenship and for an appreciation of the physical world through elementary instruction in social studies and natural science; to establish effective and permanent health habits through daily instruction and practice. The new high school course attempted to provide for the three groups: those who intended to proceed to university; those who wished to complete their general education; and those who wished some introduction to vocational pursuits in the form of courses in commerce, industrial arts and household arts.

Changes in Time Allotments

In Canada, as a whole, curriculum changes were accompanied by changes in the proportions of school time spent on various subjects and activities in the elementary school as is well illustrated in the following table: *photo copy.*

APPROXIMATE PERCENTAGE OF TIME FOR SUBJECTS IN UNGRADED ELEMENTARY SCHOOLS FOR PUPILS ABOUT AGE 10 TO 12

Subject	1867 per cent	1900 per cent	1940 English per cent	1940 French per cent
Language.....	43	48	30	40
Arithmetic....	12	23	10	20
Social studies..	14	12	20	10
Science.......	3	2	10	2
Formal religious and moral instruction..	18	5	—	15
Art, music and activity subjects.....	10	10	30	13
	100	100	100	100

1867 as recommended by Forrester.
1900 as estimated by teachers in Nova Scotia.
1940 English, as recommended in Ontario.
1940 French, as recommended in Quebec.

It is probable that in 1867 the average elementary school teacher spent less time on religious instruction and activities than the redoubtable Forrester proposed for a seven-hour school day. Religious education had no regular and definite place in the curriculum of most schools after 1850, although there was a varying amount of direct and indirect teaching. By 1900, demands for efficiency had driven teachers to spend proportionately more time on the three R's against the advice of educationists. In 1940, schools in French-speaking Canada retained an emphasis on tool subjects and religious instruction, whereas in English-speaking Canada social studies, art and crafts, music, enterprises, health and physical education, and other activities took a large share of the pupil's time. Critics, including many secondary school teachers, claimed that basic subjects suffered in consequence; but others, including many elementary school teachers, maintained that the new activities were not only valuable in themselves but conducive to better achievement in tool subjects than would be possible under twentieth-century conditions by concentration on the latter alone.

THE SECONDARY SCHOOL CURRICULUM

THE SECONDARY SCHOOL CURRICULUM

(Italics indicate subjects taught in few schools or to few pupils)

1825—1850	1850 — 1875	1875 — 1900	1900 — 1925	1925 — 1950
reading	reading	reading	*reading*	
writing	writing	writing	*writing*	
grammar	grammar	grammar	grammar	
	composition	composition	composition	composition
		literature	literature	literature
Latin	Latin	Latin	Latin	Latin
Greek	*Greek*	*Greek*	*Greek*	*Greek*
	French	French	French	French
		German	*German*	*German*
				Spanish
arithmetic	arithmetic	arithmetic	arithmetic	general mathematics
algebra	algebra	algebra	algebra	algebra
geometry	geometry	geometry	geometry	geometry
practical mathematics		*trigonometry*	*trigonometry*	trigonometry
natural philosophy	*science*			general science
		chemistry	chemistry	chemistry
		physics	physics	physics
		botany	biology	*biology*
			agricultural science	agricultural science
geography	geography	geography	geography	geography
history	*history*	history	history	history
—ancient	—*ancient*	—ancient	—ancient	—ancient
	—*British*	—British	—British	—British
		—Canadian	—Canadian	—Canadian
			—general	—general
		drawing	art	art
				music
				drama
		physical training	physical training	physical education
		physiology		health
			manual training	industrial arts
			household science	home economics
bookkeeping		bookkeeping	commercial subjects	commercial subjects
			technical subjects	technical subjects

The chart on page 438 is of some value as giving an overview of the development of the secondary school curriculum in English-speaking Canada during the past 150 years. But it is an over-simplification, deceptive because it implies that there is and has been only one type of secondary school. The fact is, of course, that successive and even contemporary concepts of the function of secondary education have been so completely different that secondary schools of different types have had little in common except the name. In Chapter XI it was shown that the socially exclusive grammar schools of the early nineteenth century were supplemented by academies with broader appeal, that after 1850 a few of both persisted and eventually became private schools, that most grammar schools and academies, however, were taken over by the common school system, that some of these publicly controlled secondary schools were fused with elementary schools, that others became sharply differentiated as strictly academic institutions, and that vocational schools and courses of the twentieth century were more often kept separate at first and less often later. All the ways of thinking reflected in these developments are operative still. Some think of the secondary school as a downward extension of the university faculty of arts. Others think of it as a continuation of the common school of the people. There are also different views regarding the place, value, and function of practical subjects. And so on. As a result there were and are several secondary school curricula so different in concept that no single general statement can give an accurate summary of the conditions in any period. Even an estimate of the place and value of any one secondary school subject, may be valid for one type of secondary school but not for another.

A neat illustration of the difficulty is provided by the seemingly contradictory assertions of Marshall d'Avray, a brilliant product of old-world culture, whose words outshone his achievement as superintendent in New Brunswick. In a lecture on education in 1850 he declared that the classical education given in the schools of England was not suitable for this new country, that it was admired chiefly because of its venerable antiquity, and that even universities were tacitly admitting their past exaggeration of its value by introducing new subjects. He made an eloquent plea for study of the physical sciences, which would "make our people masters of the secrets of nature and give them powers which even now tend to elevate the moderns to a higher rank than that of the gods of antiquity."[4] Yet five years later in one of his annual reports he declared that ". . . in modern times no one man has been pre-eminent in literature, in science, at the bar, or in the pulpit who has not also been an excellent classical scholar." Here he maintained that the opponents of classical education were bound to lose an argument against the "convictions of educated men and against abler adversaries of the reverse." From d'Avray's point of view there was nothing contradictory in these assertions, since the first pertains to education of Canadians for practical leadership in the new world of the future, and the second to the education of the superior few like d'Avray, who were old-world people living in Canada and ruling her at the time.

1800-1850

SCHOOLS FOR THE SELECT

Before 1850 the traditional curriculum of classics and mathematics was taught with thoroughness and success in only a few superior institutions. The secondary and higher levels of this education were continuous. Some of the select schools were either attached to universities, like the schools at Windsor, Nova Scotia, and Fredericton, New Brunswick, or offered some work at a higher level pending the establishment of universities, as did Upper Canada College and Pictou Academy. Also efficient in teaching the traditional program were Strachan's schools at Cornwall and York, the Royal Grammar Schools at Quebec and Montreal, a few other Anglican schools in Upper and Lower Canada, and the *collèges classiques* of Quebec.

The dominant place of the traditional subjects in schools for the select minority may be seen in a summary of the weekly time-table at Upper Canada College in 1831 for grades corresponding to the senior high school: Latin, Greek, and ancient history, 16 hours; mathematics, 5 hours; French, 5 hours; other subjects 1 or 2 hours. The emphasis on French reminds us that even the select schools did not limit themselves entirely to the classics. The Reverend Burrage of the Royal Grammar School at Quebec declared his intention to teach not only Latin and Greek but "the highest order of pure and critical English literature." Pictou Academy gave attention to reasoning and science in its program of 1818:

FIRST YEAR: Latin and Greek.
SECOND YEAR: Logic, the principles of Composition and other collateral branches.
THIRD YEAR: Moral Philosophy, Mathematics and Algebra, Latin and Greek continued.
FOURTH YEAR: Natural Philosophy, Mathematics and Algebra, Latin and Greek continued.[5]

GRAMMAR SCHOOLS

Among grammar schools of intermediate rank the Midland District School in Upper Canada in 1831 had 15 of 47 pupils in the four top grades, where classics were taught, and 4 pupils studying trigonometry and algebra in the two highest grades, where Euclid also was ordinarily taught. Berthier Academy, Lower Canada,

reported a grammar school program of classics and mathematics and two higher elementary subjects, composition and geography with the use of globes, which marked it as a progressive school in 1829. Better grammar schools under educated clergymen often taught applied grammar as composition and applied mathematics as surveying, and sometimes natural philosophy. Seven *collèges classiques* before 1840 satisfied the limited demand for traditional education and introduced alternative "commercial" courses to meet the needs of those who had to make a living in business. In these better-than-average schools, at least among English-speaking Canadians, the academic program was taught to only a limited number of the pupils and with indifferent success.

In most of the so-called Latin grammar schools the traditional subjects were a complete failure. Offering only a bare program of Latin and mathematics, the schools could not have survived without subsidies to maintain the shadow of genteel education where hardly anyone wanted it. Gourlay found them in Upper Canada so lacking in patronage that most of the masters were enjoying their situations as comfortable sinecures. On the eve of the rebellion in Lower Canada the assembly cut even Burrage's salary in half.

In New Brunswick a commission reported to the legislature in 1846 that the grammar schools were inferior to many of the parish schools. Superintendent Dawson of Nova Scotia declared in 1851 that the work of the grammar schools at the secondary level was "in general defective." These and other criticisms and complaints cited in Chapter XI were evidence of the futility of a classical education for nearly all pupils under most teachers. When d'Avray found in 1856 that of 29,000 pupils in New Brunswick only 308 were in mathematics at the secondary level and only 76 in classics and natural philosophy, he thought it reason enough for advocating an adjustment of the curriculum in state-supported schools to a "more useful and practical level."

ACADEMIES

In the academies of prosperous non-conformists the traditional subjects had a secure place as part of a broader academic and semi-practical program for those who could afford it. Upper Canada Academy in 1837 was conservative in this respect: it extended mathematics into mensuration, surveying, navigation, and fluxions, and embraced also rhetoric, logic, and intellectual and moral philosophy, not to mention the few prim accomplishments offered in the female department. These offerings, with classics retained as the core, were clearly intended to give upper middle class dissenters the educational attributes for leadership and gentility approved among the aristocracy. Ryerson and his associates supplied no educational evidence to support an assertion of the Bishop of Quebec that the word "academy" was less respectable than "school." But out-and-out academies, like Stanstead with two teachers offered a remarkable variety of subjects, which changed as the teachers changed from year to year: in June, 1840 teachers Garfield and Hardy reported, in addition to all elementary subjects, Latin, algebra, rhetoric, natural philosophy, and chemistry; in December, teacher Connor alone in the male department continued the above subjects under some more impressive names like orthography and chirography, and offered also elocution, surveying, bookkeeping, logarithms, trigonometry, and mensuration of superficies and solids. Grantham Academy at St. Catharines, Upper Canada, with the usual male principal and female assistant, offered in 1829 nearly all of these subjects plus logic, natural theology, evidences of Christianity, chronology (in addition to history), natural and moral

A school desk, 1876. This familiar article of furniture remained in vogue for more than half a century.

philosophy, navigation, Greek, and Hebrew, in the male department alone. Among other subjects listed by academies in Upper Canada were physiology, drawing, sacred music, and instrumental music.

LEANING TOWARD PRACTICAL EDUCATION

The full program of secondary subjects ordinarily attempted in state-supported schools is indicated by the subjects required for a superior grant to Prince Edward Island teachers in 1847: Latin, geometry, trigonometry, mensuration, surveying, navigation, and geography with the use of globes. Nova Scotia in 1850 had twenty-five grammar schools teaching some or all of Latin, algebra, mathematics, natural philosophy, physiology, French, and Greek, and five county academies teaching the same subjects plus trigonometry, applied mathematics, and chemistry. The suggestion of a leaning towards the practical becomes clearer on examination of the enrolment in the largest of the Nova Scotia schools: of 87 pupils, 60 were studying chemistry and 20 natural philosophy, as compared with a dozen or less in different mathematical subjects and in Latin, and with only five in Greek. But that distribution showed only what happened when people could find teachers qualified in the new subjects, since the opportunities in Nova Scotia for instruction in science were then exceptional, and even there limited to only a few schools. Elsewhere, as a rule, students took what their teachers learned when they were young and claimed thereafter to be truly educative: the three R's, English grammar, book geography, Latin, Euclid, and algebra.

1850-1875

When efforts were made by provincial authorities around 1850 to provide further education for a less select group, problems were created for future generations by a momentous but perhaps inevitable step. Just as some who suddenly acquired riches used their money to purchase aristocratic accoutrements, so the *nouveaux riches* in educational opportunity found themselves entangled in a curriculum appropriate for a select minority. When superintendents of the common school systems took over the secondary schools, they were trapped by circumstances. Ryerson wanted education to have practical value: he tried to introduce instruction in agriculture and to make science an important subject, but he could not find teachers to make the innovations effective. On the other hand, educated men, and especially those who taught in secondary schools and universities, were *ipso facto* exponents of the traditional academic education. The result was that when the grammar schools were inserted between the common schools and the universities as an intermediate stage in the new educational ladder, they acquired the pupil population characteristic of the former and a curriculum adapted to the latter.

Pupils who sought an extension of their education for a better life in a workaday world among ordinary people were introduced suddenly to a curriculum distinguished by precisely the opposite characteristic. The anomaly so created was a source of dissatisfaction immediately and has been ever since.

From 1850 to 1875 the new recruits for academic secondary education garbled Latin and stumbled through algebra as bewildered human sacrifices to tradition. The preposterous incongruity of the process was recognized by classical scholars and administrators alike. George Paxton Young, inspector of grammar schools in Upper Canada, wrote in 1866:

But with the mass of girls as with . . . the Boys, the study of Latin is merely a nominal thing . . . the time they are made to squander on sapless Latin technicalities might be employed to infinitely greater advantage in studies that possess a vital interest . . .[6]

John Bennett, superintendent of New Brunswick, had written the year before:

The Grammar Schools were at one time well adapted to the circumstances of the province; I doubt very much if they are now.

We shall see in a later chapter that the schools were not efficient in preparing even a very small fraction of students for college. Yet their preoccupation with the formal content of the academic program caused them to skimp the chief ability subject, English composition, which had been introduced for the benefit of the majority.

1875-1900

Between 1875 and 1900, as the chart shows, the academic program expanded. Developments may be illustrated with reference to Ontario. There an English course alternative to the university entrance program had been introduced in 1871. Its rapid increase in popularity helped persuade the universities to accept for matriculation between 1876 and 1885 English composition and literature, modern history, modern foreign languages, and science. In response to local demands for practical work, bookkeeping was introduced and other commercial subjects were taught in a few schools at the end of the period. But the strongly entrenched academic influence was able to check the swing towards content applicable to everyday life.

The number of subjects offered in larger high schools was phenomenally large. The Saint John school board in 1873 outlined the program of the girls' high school and of the boys' high school for each of the three grades. The number of subjects ranged from fourteen in Grade I of the girls' school to nineteen in Grade II of the boys' school. In all three grades the following subjects were offered for girls: reading, writing, spelling, composition, grammar, rhetoric, drawing, arithmetic, bookkeeping, algebra, geometry, mensuration, geography, history, natural history, natural philosophy, chemistry, botany, astronomy, geology, Latin, and French. The boys had much the same program except that animal physiology was included and botany, astronomy, and geology left out; they had practical mathematics instead of mensuration alone, and Greek and German instead of rhetoric. There were twenty-six subjects in all, each with a designated textbook, and sometimes with a different textbook required in a higher grade.

But in smaller secondary schools the case was different. The chief superintendent of New Brunswick in 1890 admitted that the province had neither staff nor equipment to meet the needs of the times. He described his schools as "just about where they were nearly three generations ago," teaching classics and mathematics as if those subjects were the only two which counted in secondary education. Not that such teaching had much effect:

in 1895 less than two per cent of the school population in the province reached even the ninth grade.

1900-1925

During the first quarter of the twentieth century, there was little change in the academic curriculum, although the load of content became heavier. At the beginning of the century British Columbia added botany in the intermediate high school grade, and trigonometry, more history, and more physical science in the third or highest grade. Then in 1909 the department of education was forced to find ways of reducing the burden. In Ontario in 1913 teachers complained to the minister of education of overpressure from the same cause. Two of the usual solutions were applied by Alberta, where the length of the high school course was increased by a year in 1912 and the number of subjects to be taken concurrently was reduced in 1924, from nine to six in Grade X, from eight to six or seven in Grade XI, and from eleven to seven or eight in Grade XII. The most significant developments were the increasing emphasis on science and the appearance of practical courses. Commercial subjects became too numerous to list individually on the chart and had a much more important place in the curriculum than the mere heading implies. At the end of the period this was becoming true of technical courses also.

These developments suggest that the people had begun to express opinions on secondary education instead of leaving the curriculum to university and provincial authorities. Alberta in 1924 had a curriculum committee representative of farmers' organizations, women's organizations, labor, trade and commerce, trustees, teachers, and other groups anxious to assert themselves. The committee recommended a greater variety of subjects, a reduction in the number of subjects to be taken concurrently, promotion by subject and not by grade, more time for music and art appreciation, general science rather than science as an academic discipline in Grade IX, permission to local communities to offer courses of local interest, and, virtually, a credit system. All these ideas undermined the authority of traditional forms of secondary education. They were suggested by educators who had gone to the United States for graduate study and welcomed by people no longer convinced that the academic circle enjoyed a monopoly of wisdom. The committee recommended a choice of six high school programs: matriculation, normal school entrance, agricultural, commercial, technical, and general. But it turned out that no students wanted the general course, not many were interested in the agricultural course, only the cities could afford the commercial and the technical courses, and even the cities lost their enthusiasm for vocational education after 1929. Nevertheless the committee's recommendations mirrored the twentieth-century trend.

1925-1950

SUBSTITUTING ACTIVITY FOR FORM

In 1935 G. F. McNally, then supervisor of schools in Alberta, later deputy minister of education, and still later chancellor of the university in his province, summed up the dissatisfaction in Canada as elsewhere with the inherited academic program of the high schools:

In the light of our present knowledge, he would be a bold person who would maintain that three units of mathematics, a laboratory science, and a foreign language constitute the best curriculum that could be devised for young people who are going into business, industry, farming, garage work, housekeeping, or even teaching on the elementary level.[7]

He recommended for the lower high school grades a program that would give some meaning to education for the great majority of students who were not going to college and showed no evidence of ability to profit from academic subjects — music, art, dramatics, household economics, general shop, current history, community health, agriculture, elementary courses in business practice, geography, biology, and mechanical drawing. This proposal reflected the thinking of a high school curriculum committee that had been appointed in Alberta two years before. The committee recognized that in the machine age all people were certain to have more hours for leisure than for work, that the high schools had to develop interests which might be pleasurably pursued after graduation, and that strictly intellectual studies must be supplemented by other outlets like organized games, choral music, and drama. A glance at the chart reproduced on page 438 will show the great extent to which such thinking modified the high school program across Canada.

Revisions in all provinces affected the curriculum chiefly up to the end of Grade X, the point at which pupils, retained in school by attendance laws, left school in large numbers. The program for junior high schools introduced in British Columbia in 1927 attempted to create an educational environment suitable for most boys and girls of twelve to sixteen years of age by providing a variety of optional subjects and activities conducted in laboratories, shops, libraries, assembly halls, and gymnasiums, as well as classrooms, by teachers with sympathetic understanding of adolescents. Curricular subjects and other means were to be used for "the progressive discovery and experimental direction of pupils' interests, aptitudes, and abilities." The obligatory subjects, especially English and social studies, were to continue the integrating effect of education in the elementary school, where comprehensive content was presented by one teacher who had in mind the whole interests of the child, while the many optional subjects introduced concurrently the differentiated departments characteristic of secondary education and also provided for individual differences.

The intermediate school program introduced in Alberta for the same age group in 1937 had these and similar aims. In the pupil's timetable of 40 periods a week, 28 periods were given to obligatory courses and 12 periods to optional courses, viz:

ALBERTA INTERMEDIATE SCHOOL
CURRICULUM 1937

OBLIGATORY		OPTIONAL	
Course	*Hours*	*Course*	*Hours*
English	5	Art	2—4
Social Studies	5	Dramatics	2—4
Health and		Music	2—4
Phys. Education	3	Elem. Bookkeeping and	
Mathematics	5	Jr. Business	2—4
General Science	5	Typewriting	2—4
Supervised Study	5	Oral French	2—4
		General Shop	2—4
		Home Economics	2—4

This program was typical of the new programs introduced throughout English-speaking Canada, although dramatics as a scheduled curricular activity was exceptional. The trend away from *form* to *activity,* from imparting facts for memorization to development of appreciation and ability, was apparent even in the names that were given to some of the courses, like supervised study and oral French, and was shown clearly in the details of all courses.

GUIDANCE: A NON-FORMAL SUBJECT

Illustrative of this trend were the guidance programs developed during the period, to the fullest extent in Ontario, in the three far western provinces, and in Nova Scotia. Although group work included courses in occupations, commonly at the Grade IX level, organized content as information to be imparted and mastered had practically no place in guidance. Availability of much accurate information constantly revised was, on the other hand, essential. Of primary importance also for counsellors, and to some extent for teachers, were psychological understanding, ability to administer and interpret tests, and above all a clear perception of the function of guidance — not to direct but to enable the boy or girl to decide. Furthermore, although some space in the timetable plus the time of a designated counsellor were alloted to guidance, the program was not restricted in terms of hours or personnel, but sought to enlist the services of classroom teachers, of the psychologist or psychiatrist, and of visitors from industry and business, as seemed desirable. The lack of fixed form evoked criticism from those who saw nothing orderly and substantial in such a program. Many graduates of high schools interviewed by the Canadian Youth Commission criticized guidance for not telling them exactly what work they should choose to be sure of success. Some teachers, attached to form, made the mistake of engaging in guidance: they either gave structured courses and made decisions for students or they abandoned any attempt to deal judiciously with variables and wandered aimlessly with their students in a dreary mist.

The difficulty and the risk of futility in conducting unstructured programs caused some school systems to proceed with extreme caution in introducing guidance. The Montreal Catholic School Commission, after restricted experimentation for fifteen years, approved guidance in principle in 1944, then tried guidance interviews in Grades VII, IX, and XII, then appointed two counsellors in 1949, and only in 1950 organized a guidance service for the city with arrangements for talks to students and for various contacts with the commercial world. Both as a safeguard and as a means of advance, provincial departments of education, around 1940-45, appointed directors of guidance to advise in the establishment and operation of school programs. Ontario set up a sequence of three summer courses to train guidance personnel. Since World War II guidance has been extending in scope. In 1947 Ontario and Saskatchewan suggested some courses in guidance which might be followed in the last year of the ordinary high school program, in Grades XII and XI respectively. There was also a downward extension: the experimental outline of courses for the intermediate division in Ontario, 1950, indicated a guidance program for Grades VII, VIII, IX, and X, although "occupations" as a subject was obligatory only in Grade IX and optional in Grade X.

CONTINUING APPRAISAL AND CRITICISM

Some of the changes in senior high school courses will be mentioned in the discussion below of particular problems related to the curriculum of the secondary school. Revision characteristic of the most recent period was recommended by a committee working in Saskatchewan after 1942: changes were designed to give equal status to new and old subjects, so that even Grade XII diplomas might be obtained by the commercial and technical options; in 1948, students were enabled also to earn credits in high school by participation in activities of such organizations as glee clubs and bands.

It is noteworthy that no secondary school program at any time in English-speaking Canada has ever been generally accepted as satisfactory in the way that the elementary school program has been accepted as necessary preparation for everyday living. We have seen that the grammar schools in the first three quarters of the nineteenth century were perennial targets for attack. In 1876 the provincial board of education in Prince Edward Island said of its seventeen grammar schools that "with few exceptions they have not realized the expectations of the Board." In all provinces, there was always some evidence of complacency and pride, but more and more criticism was heard as people dared to question the allegedly beneficial effects of seemingly fruitless study. In 1943 the Survey Committee of the Canada and Newfoundland Education Association spoke for all provinces in all recent years when it admitted, with chief reference to post-primary education, that in many if not all schools considerable numbers of pupils remained in "lethargy, indifference, and indolence."

The Illusionary Ladder

Much of the difficulty stemmed from the concept of an educational ladder in which the function of each rung was to prepare the climber for mounting the next higher rung. This idea was necessary to progress in 1850 when secondary schools were opened to the graduates of common schools. Long before the end of the century it was apparent that the concept itself was unrealistic and that its effect had been to make the curriculum a lottery in which all pupils were deprived of immediate benefits for the sake of a few who would be able to profit later.

The Ontario high school inspectors declared in 1874 that the chief aim of the high schools should not be "the training of a select band of intellectual athletes for university distinctions" but to "crown the work of the public school." In Nova Scotia in 1901 the superintendent renounced the subordinate and preparatory function of the elementary school:

Although the common school course grades into the high school course, it is not designed merely as an introduction to the high school course. For such a purpose it could be much simpler and narrower.

There were then fourteen pupils in Grades I to VIII for every one in Grades IX to XI. In Ontario in 1902, Whitney stated in a political pamphlet that the public schools and high schools should each do the best they could for a boy regardless of the claims of any higher school. As for the west, D. S. Woods maintains that elementary and secondary education had never been differentiated to the same extent as in the east:

The secondary schools of Manitoba grew up as an extension of the free public school and not as an institution set apart in the beginning to maintain in some measure the idea of social status.[8]

Yet the academic distinction between elementary and secondary education was deliberately sharpened in the last quarter of the nineteenth century, and the preparatory concept of the elementary school was as embarrassing on the prairies as in the east.

The restrictive effect on the curriculum was much more serious at the secondary level when the ladder concept limited the function of the high school to preparation for college. In 1898 Superintendent Goggin of the Northwest Territories rejected the idea in emphatic terms:

The high school, except incidentally, is not a fitting school for University or College or Normal School; it is not a select school for the wealthy or well born, or the intellectually gifted. It is for all who feel the need, and believe in the benefits of education. It supplements . . . the work of the elementary school and gives a more adequate, because a broader, preparation for life.[9]

John Millar, deputy minister of education in Ontario, was no less emphatic in a pamphlet of 1901:

It should be accepted as settled, that the High Schools are not supported either entirely or mainly for the benefits of those who enter on professional pursuits or become matriculants of a university.[10]

Millar urged that the subjects of general education begun in the public schools should not be neglected in the high schools in order to provide academic disciplines essential only for the five per cent who went on to higher education. Similar views were expressed everywhere by educators employed in the provincial school systems. In the same year the superintendent in Nova Scotia supported his argument by pointing out that only one child in a hundred who entered elementary school completed the high school course.

A conference in that year, 1901, of the Queen's University Council and the Kingston school board pointed up the issue faced by the high schools. In a prepared paper John Watson argued against any options in the high school curriculum and was given strong support by the defenders of academic subjects. But W. S. Ellis, principal of Kingston Collegiate Institute, expressed in reply the views that were to prevail increasingly in the century then beginning: that the high schools must take their place as educational institutions in their own right and cease to be merely a means of preparation for university entrance examinations; that the high school curriculum should consist of a core of subjects valuable to all supplemented by optional courses, among which the university preparatory course should be only one. The issue was clear: should the high school, as an institution subsidiary to the university, offer the academic curriculum required for matriculation, or should the high school, as an extension of the elementary school, continue a curriculum related to ordinary life with the addition of options to meet the different needs of young people?

The Small Combined School

The obvious answer to these questions might have been, "Do both," if Canada in the nineteenth century had been largely urban. But it was difficult enough in the small schools of the rural areas to provide one type of secondary education, let alone two. Some of the small combined elementary and secondary schools which appeared around the middle of the nineteenth century attempted to teach the traditional subjects of the grammar schools, and they did it very badly. In Ontario, the union schools established in 1853 were required to teach Latin and were abolished as inefficient twenty years later. In New Brunswick, the superior schools set up in 1858 were not compelled to teach the traditional subjects and were reported "to stand well in the estimation of the people."

It is a fair conclusion that the small combined schools weakened the prestige of the academic curriculum, and that those who believed in the value of the traditional disciplines would have been better advised to insist that such subjects be attempted only in schools with an adequate number of capable teachers. Yet the twentieth century began with combined schools in operation everywhere, for Ontario had restored them for reasons unconnected with educational efficiency. The result throughout Canada was that the secondary school curriculum was restricted in standards and vision to the mediocre resources of rural areas.

The combined schools must be credited, however, with bringing elementary and secondary education into a close association and helping to establish the concept of secondary education as an extension of the work of the common schools. That effect remained even though these small schools were less capable of teaching the new subjects in 1950 than they had been capable in 1850 of teaching the old. Partly for that reason, regional high schools, which were replacing small rural secondary schools in 1950, had a curriculum rather closely related to ordinary life and not predominantly academic.

The One-Course Solution

Those who had unqualified faith in the educative value of academic disciplines saw no problem in prescribing a secondary school curriculum suitable for all purposes if not for all people. Their argument in the early part of the nineteenth century was based on naive acceptance of traditional courses. The student entering Upper Canada College in 1830 without a thought of proceeding to university was assured that he would be "perfectly qualified for mercantile pursuits." Later in the century, all academic subjects — even science — were justified by their power to train the mind. Near the end of the century, a balanced program of academic subjects was prescribed to ensure the many-sided interests required by all. But these incantations were backed up by more realistic measures. The humanities in particular were supported by subsidies: higher grants in the 1860's to schools qualifying as secondary by the number of students in Latin; preferred treatment to high schools qualifying as collegiate institutes in the 1870's by virtue of their having sixty boys in Latin; changes in scholarships and prizes offered by the University of Toronto in 1877 to put a premium on excellence in classics and mathematics rather than on general proficiency; a much higher value attached to foreign languages than to other subjects on matriculation examinations in the 1880's. All of these devices were used in Ontario, and the last even in Nova Scotia, where comparatively impartial views prevailed.

But in spite of these inducements, the enrolment in foreign languages fell off until Ontario devised a more compelling incentive. Preparation for the key move was made before 1890 by bringing prescribed qualifications of teachers and matriculation requirements into closer alignment. Then in 1891 the non-professional examinations for teachers and the matriculation examinations were co-ordinated and a previously existent central committee of examiners was replaced by a joint board of the University of Toronto and the provincial department of education. The impetus to language study was remarkable:

PERCENTAGE OF ONTARIO HIGH SCHOOL
STUDENTS ENROLLED

	1891	1896
In Latin	38%	63%
In German	10%	18%
In French	42%	55%

To all intents and purposes this scheme set up a single academic high school course culminating in the matriculation examinations, which the public came to regard as the one criterion of educational achievement. These events of the 1890's had a lasting effect in strengthening the prestige of academic education without raising any question about its intrinsic value. Manitoba, around 1895, also made teachers' non-professional examinations valid for matriculation, and *vice versa,* but did not require foreign languages for the former, as Ontario did for a time. In the second quarter of the twentieth century all provinces experienced difficulty in getting employers and parents to accept standards of educational achievement other than academic proficiency as measured by the university entrance examinations.

Multiple Courses

A cautious concession to the needs of an increasing majority of pupils was the introduction of an English or "commer-cial" course as an alternative to the classical or university entrance course. The alternative programs attracted growing numbers of students. In the Protestant high school of Montreal a commercial course introduced in 1870 was withdrawn in 1877. The Ontario two-course system of 1871 survived its popularity, and its adoption was seriously discussed in New Brunswick in 1882. British Columbia introduced a three-track English-commercial-classical system before 1890 and kept it for some time. Saskatchewan in 1910 offered four courses — general, teachers', university, and commercial. The multiple course plan became more realistic when vocational courses were introduced in the present century and when denser population and better transportation favored the establishment of composite schools. Since the 1930's it has been a widely accepted objective to offer five different secondary school programs — in agriculture, commercial work, home economics, academic studies, and technical subjects.

Elective Subjects and Credits

Foreign languages were optional subjects in the Nova Scotia high school curriculum drawn up in 1880-85 and again in the revision of 1892-95. In 1900 only 10 per cent of the Grade IX pupils were enrolled in French and only 15 per cent in Latin as compared with 80 per cent or more in all other subjects — English, history and geography, botany, physics, drawing, bookkeeping, arithmetic, algebra, and geometry. In the Grade XII, or senior matriculation year, all students were required to take English, British history, sanitary science, and psychology — the equivalent of English, social studies, and health, which later became the compulsory core of subjects in all provinces, plus psychology, a subject so immediately related to life that its inclusion in an academic secondary school program would be opposed by many even now. The Grade XII students had a choice of "sides" — classical or scientific and mathematical — to complete their matriculation requirements. Modern languages were optional in both of the elective programs.

This plan to provide a limited number of optional subjects was somewhat more flexible than the alternative of two structured programs. Ontario used it in addition to the alternative commercial program at the beginning of the twentieth century. Actually there was little choice open to prospective teachers and other non-matriculants in the general academic program for high school leaving at the Grade XI or junior level, since all had to take mathematics, physics, and Latin, among other subjects, and were permitted only to choose one of Greek, French, German, and chemistry. Mathematics and foreign languages were well protected still. Even in Grade XII the only optional supplement to a heavy academic program, including Latin, for others than senior matriculants was a choice of one of six combinations, three of which consisted of two foreign languages, two of science subjects, and one of French and chemistry.

Far too flexible in the view of those who upheld the traditional authority of academic disciplines was the system of credits introduced in British Columbia in 1929. One credit meant usually a forty or forty-five minute period per week throughout a school year, and 120 credits were required for a high school graduation diploma. The scheme at first provided for a core of subjects common to five different courses — matriculation, normal entrance, general, commercial, and technical. But in 1937 the defined optional courses were abolished in favor of a single high school program. The student was required merely to complete for graduation 112 credits, of which only 47 were to be obtained in "constants." This left him a wide choice of variables. Similarly

in Manitoba, where a choice of four separate courses had been offered, a unified program was introduced in 1933. For high school graduation, a student was required to obtain 20 units of credit, each unit representing a year's work in any one subject. Seven of the 20 units were left to the option of the student.

University Influence

A century ago there were many who would have thought it proper to have the secondary schools associated with universities, as the classical colleges of Quebec are associated with the universities of Laval and Montreal. In 1839, at the request of the lieutenant-governor of Upper Canada, it was suggested that the grammar schools use the curriculum and textbooks employed by the temporary university, Upper Canada College, and a further recommendation was made that the principal of the college should license all grammar school masters. But when the grammar schools came under the jurisdiction of the provincial departments of education, the only control the universities had over the secondary school curriculum was exercised through the matriculation examinations.

Typical of the early matriculation requirements was the prescription of King's College, Fredericton, in 1847 — Latin, Greek, and the rudiments of algebra and geometry. For pass junior matriculation the University of Toronto added to this nucleus: English grammar and ancient and British history in 1859; French, German, English composition and literature, and modern (Canadian) history in 1876; physics and chemistry in 1885. The University of Manitoba before 1890 required, for entrance, Greek and Latin, arithmetic, algebra and Euclid, French and English literature, and the history of Canada, England, and Rome. The sciences — botany, chemistry, and physics — were added by

1900. In 1914 Latin, like Greek, was made optional, and only one foreign language was required; ten years later requirements were broadened in other ways. In Canada generally the prescription of subjects for university entrance was still comparatively rigid in 1953. Many more elective subjects were acceptable, but the nucleus of academic disciplines still required for entrance to faculties of arts, at least, included mathematics and a foreign language. In a few cases two foreign languages were specifically required and in some other cases encouraged by option groupings. In Alberta and British Columbia the foreign language requirement could be met by study in only the last two years of high school. Western universities were more liberal than some of the eastern universities in allowing credit for courses like "modern problems" or "effective living," but music was recognized by some older institutions, as were also art, navigation, and geology in the elective list of Memorial University, Newfoundland. Apparently most members of university faculties were convinced either that a student must have studied a number of selected academic subjects to be ready, educationally, for university work, or that evidence of achievement in those subjects was proof of necessary ability.

Against the restrictive effect of university entrance requirements on the high school curriculum, education authorities sought to secure recognition of other academic subjects — chiefly between 1875 and 1900 — and, after 1925, of practical or general interest subjects as well. After the later date they also persuaded universities to accept, in some cases, the school's rating of academic achievement in lieu of external examinations. This movement, which had no great effect on the curriculum while the prescription of subjects remained, will be discussed in a later chapter. During the recent period also, changes in examinations made it possible to obtain standing by subjects in successive years. After 1950, efforts were still being made in Ontario to reduce or eliminate university demands upon middle school students. School authorities deplored the necessity of giving in the earlier grades courses whose main purpose was to introduce the elements of certain subjects that would be studied in upper school in preparation for final, external examinations. In 1952 Léon Lortie and M. E. LaZerte reported to the Canadian Education Association and the National Conference of Canadian Universities on a study of the "Articulation of High Schools and Universities." They found that:

While the high school programme, as printed and authorized, appears to offer a wide range of courses to meet individual needs and aptitudes, the actual school offerings are, in the main, restricted to university credits.

They recommended more elective courses for students proceeding to matriculation and raised the question whether it might not be possible to have a truly general high school program to the end of Grade XI at least, or even have the universities accept students who had completed "at a high level of performance any worthwhile program in the secondary school" and offer at the university introductory courses in subjects needed by a student and not previously studied. Such courses in foreign languages are now offered at the University of Manitoba.

The Demand for Practical Education

As soon as there was any demand for secondary education at all, most pupils and many of their parents wished to acquire knowledge and skills that could be applied to advantage. This spontaneous preference has always been depreciated as mundane and mercenary by educators in the Platonic tradition, who have considered it almost a religious duty to keep the curriculum unspotted by the contemporary world. A few assorted items of evidence will illustrate persistent efforts in the nineteenth century to provide or obtain instruction of a practical kind.

Typical advertisements in the *Upper Canada Gazette* announced in 1808 an opportunity for a young man to learn the practice of physic and surgery and in 1822 the availability of a private tutor in bookkeeping and land surveying. The inhabitants of York in 1831 asked that the facilities of Upper Canada College be extended to the many who wished their children to be qualified "for discharging with efficiency and respectability the Scientific and other business of Tradesmen and Mechanics."[11] The next year a teacher who voluntarily taught bookkeeping after school hours petitioned the lieutenant-governor for additional salary, but was told to have his timetable fixed by the principal and not to expect a bonus for extra work. At mid-century prominent educators and administrators who appreciated the needs of the people tried without success to provide practical education. In Quebec, says Audet, it was the dream of Etienne Parent: "Détourner la jeunesse des professions libérales déjà encombrées pour l'orienter vers les carrières toujours grandes ouvertes de l'agriculture, du commerce, et de l'industrie. . . ."[12] Marshall d'Avray in New Brunswick found the opposition from traditional forces too strong when he tried to offer subjects more useful to the people. Ryerson in Upper Canada would have been glad to accede to the repeated requests in 1848 of the *Agricultural and Canadian Journal* for an institution or courses for the education of farmers' sons "in their profession."

In educational journals and other periodicals, from about 1867, there were frequent demands for practical education. Ryerson in his reports kept hammering away:

I think the tendency of the youthful mind of our country is too much in the direction

of what are called the learned professions . . . The subjects and the teaching of the schools should be adapted to develop the resources and skilful industry of the country.[13]

The people and their representative knew this and sometimes tried to take action. The *Canada School Journal* reported in 1877 that the school commissioners of Montreal had decided to introduce telegraphy in their schools, and in 1878 that the evening classes in science and technology of Nova Scotia were filled as soon as opened. The disallowed preference of local trustees for a curriculum related to ordinary life was expressed in 1887 by J. E. Farewell, LL.B, before the Provincial Association of Public and High School Trustees of Ontario:

I venture to say that there is not a member of this Association . . . who has not felt that if more discretion was allowed trustees they would have provided for less of classical and more of a practical business education...[14]

Provincial legislators sometimes were similarly disposed. In 1899, when agricultural and industrial prospects had improved in New Brunswick, there were renewed demands in the legislature for an agricultural school, a new demand for technical education, and strong expressions of opinion that education should be made of more practical value to the "toilers," on the ground that they were the real producers of wealth.

The origin and history of vocational schools was summarized in chapter XI and something will be said in the next chapter about school subjects with more or less practical applications. By 1950, schools, courses, and subjects related to ordinary affairs had appeared in almost confusing variety. The problem in the secondary school curriculum was no longer to obtain the introduction of practical subjects but to co-ordinate the new subjects with the old. Only in populous and wealthy areas was it possible to offer a variety of

Manual Training Class, 1900

courses and subjects valid only for particular purposes. Even more searching was the question whether strictly practical or strictly academic courses and subjects were desirable in the secondary schools attended by all and supported by all.

METHODS

Textbook Assignment, 1800-1850

The acceptance of form for reality, the extremely limited aims in education, and the gross incompetence of teachers caused methods in the early nineteenth century to be incredibly crude. Most teachers were so completely dependent on the textbook that they simply assigned a portion to be memorized by a pupil and later held the textbook open in their hands while the pupil recited what he had learned. There was such a complete absence of expository teaching that John Ross, an inspector of Prince Edward Island in 1849, identified older methods as "imparting instruction without that explanation and illustration necessary for the perception of its import by the youthful mind." Outstanding teachers like Strachan earned their reputation largely because they did explain to the pupil beforehand the material he was required to learn.

In ordinary schools, however, the difference between superficiality and thoroughness was marked only by the speed at which the pupil went through the book and by the firmness with which the teacher insisted on verbal perfection. When the textbook required a pupil to do exercises not exactly like the examples provided, some early teachers simply gave the pupil a solution to copy, as did a teacher in Northumberland County, Upper Canada, in 1856. The inspector found that the pupils of this teacher could not solve problems they had presumably worked on the previous day. Even in grammar schools there was little expository teaching: in Vienna, Upper Canada, the boys sat at desks facing the wall, working on their assignments, left their seats one by one when ready to recite or show completed work to the master, and returned immediately to their places with further assignments.

There was nevertheless a growing awareness of the importance of method. Marshall d'Avray and other champions of the monitorial system pointed out that it enabled teachers to devote time to expository teaching of the older boys. Even in this contention, however, they showed their greater appreciation of difficulties in content than of difficulties in pedagogy, for they argued that a very young monitor could do as well as an experienced teacher in teaching the elements of reading and spelling — a claim that could never have been made if primary methods worthy of the name had been in vogue. Strachan's interest in methods led him to procure an outline of Lancaster's plan in 1809 and to decide that it fell short of exhibiting all the merit its author claimed, although his judgment may have been influenced by Anglican loyalty to the rival system of Bell. J. J. Perrault acquired a knowledge of Lancastrian methods and adapted them in his *Manuel pratique* into a system of instruction that he claimed would effect a great saving of time and money. At Pictou, McCullough, who was noted for his excellent teaching, showed insight into a basic purpose of method:

The duty of a teacher does not merely consist in instilling into the minds of his pupils the rudiments of knowledge but also in giving the mind itself a bias favorable to further improvement.[15]

The *Upper Canada Gazette* in 1826 reported a contest between the old methods of teaching and a new interrogative system recently invented. A teacher applying for a position in Upper Canada in 1839 claimed a discriminatory knowledge of several methods:

Insomuch as I am acquainted with the best system of analizing the mode of tuition which I have practised for five or six years, I will make the choice of that system which is best suited to the present circumstances of your school.[16]

The beginning of concern about methods was linked with a new willingness to recognize that young people have characteristics of their own that merit consideration. It is apparent that John MacNeill had his eye on the child in 1840 when he pronounced

that general system to be best, which is best suited to the age, the capacity, and the disposition of the pupil, which is calculated for exciting and sustaining the attention, and for the gradual, yet speedy development of the mental faculties and moral feelings of the children.

It was also argued in the early nineteenth century, as in the twentieth, that innovations in methods were made necessary by real or apparent changes in the attitude and behavior of young people. Guillaume Benziger in his handwritten *Guide aux Instituteurs* said that old ways might have worked with children in the past, "mais aujourd'hui que nos écoles sont remplies d'une jeunesse vive, inquiète, bouillante, nos vieux moyens sont absolument usés."[17]

Class Teaching, 1850-1875

A revolutionary change in methods began about the middle of the nineteenth century with the introduction of class teaching, made possible by the authorization of uniform textbooks and by the training of more and more teachers in the normal schools. Class teaching was linked with the so-called Socratic method, or questioning that went beyond a demand that the pupils repeat the words of a lesson they had learned. When properly carried out, this process was aptly described as the intellectual mode of teaching, which, according to the widely used *Geography Generalized* required "pupils to have a rational knowledge of everything in which they are instructed." To ensure this result the teacher himself had need of a quick intellect sensitive to the working of his pupils' minds.

For that reason, although the beginning of intellectual education dates generally from the 1850's and 1860's it was more often found — even at an earlier date — in grammar schools conducted by superior teachers. Strachan used the question and answer method; he also tried to accustom his pupils to be self-dependent and to think for themselves, and with that purpose in mind, he carried their work "beyond the meagre routine of study usually adopted in the schools."[18] The emphasis everywhere in the 1860's was on education for self-improvement. Stanbridge Academy in Lower Canada stated in its prospectus of 1860 that it would be "the aim of the teacher to induce the pupil to study, and to create habits of correct and independent thought."[19] Inspector Wood of New Brunswick gave advice typical of enlightened supervision in 1865 when he pointed out that it was futile for a teacher to ease pupils over their difficulties and allow them to proceed:

Such a teacher has, like Sisyphus, up-hill work, and a never-ending repetition of the same work. . . . The pupil is not educated by what his teacher does for him, but by what he is brought to do for himself.

One of the unfortunate results of the change from textbook study by the pupil to oral instruction by the teacher was pointed out in an address at the convention of the Provincial Teachers' Association of Nova Scotia in 1868. The speaker put great stress on having the pupils study the textbook in preparation for giving an explanation of the lesson in class. He said that time was wasted and the opportunity for educative work by the pupil destroyed if the teacher attempted to explain beforehand what was already clearly explained in the text, instead of restricting his explanations to difficulties encountered by pupils. In keeping with this counsel of perfection, which was obviously adapted to the ability of bright pupils, the speaker advised against giving any explanation when making an assignment — a practice approved in the twentieth century, when it was thought proper that below-average pupils should usurp most of the teacher's time.

As compared with the period that follows, the third quarter of the nineteenth century was characterized by extreme variation in classroom procedure. As the chief superintendent in New Brunswick put it in 1861:

In the modes of teaching there is considerable variety, as might be expected of men of different tastes, possessing various degrees of attainment, and having no professional training in common.

Convictions had become stronger that method was highly important. "All depends," said Forrester, "on the way in which this knowledge is imparted." Candidates for teachers' licences in New Brunswick in 1872 were asked to criticize the opposite opinion that the method by which knowledge was acquired was of no importance provided that the knowledge was acquired. They were asked also to illustrate and justify the principle that a pupil should never be told anything that he could be led to discover for himself. Forrester thought it a sign of confused thinking to conclude that "a great scholar or a learned man must of necessity be thoroughly educated" and believed that the educational process without direction might be "positively hurtful —

like putting a sword in the hand of a madman."[20] Outstanding teachers in the 1860's like Stewart at Maugerville, New Brunswick, were very popular with their pupils and highly regarded by their inspectors because they were skilled technicians. Stewart had worked out a plan of teaching to read, which enabled many children in the second book to read "with as much ease and correctness as the most advanced classes in many other schools." Mulholland, in a textbook published in Nova Scotia in 1864, showed the organization and order, and incidentally the learning through practice, expected in a good school:

Before beginning the lesson, the teacher should see that the slates are all clean, and, in order to secure this, each slate should have a small piece of sponge attached to it. At the commencement of the lesson, a Monitor, appointed for the purpose, should pass along each bench, carrying a small vessel filled with clean water, into which each pupil dips his sponge. On no account should the pupils be allowed to drop saliva on their slates, or to rub them with their sleeve or any other part of their dress. When the slates are thus prepared, all the pupils should be required to show their slate pencils, and, at a given signal, the work should commence. These preliminary exercises contribute very materially to form and cherish habits of cleanliness and neatness.[21]

But comparatively few teachers had the ability and training to warrant a transfer of public confidence from formal content to professional ability.

The lack of organization in many classrooms was distressing to serious visitors. Inspector Wood of New Brunswick found disorder in forming classes and dismissing school, disorder caused by pupils leaving their seats without permission and constantly interrupting the teacher by requests to be allowed to leave the room, and disorder caused by whispering and talking, which he said "should be rigidly interdicted, since pupils cannot study and chat at the same time." Questioning technique was poor. The reports of inspectors showed that most teachers asked only for verbal repetition of facts, definitions, and rules by individuals or the whole class together. In Upper Canada before 1850 a teacher at Oshawa introduced parsing in concert, and twenty years later at the central school in Hamilton memorized rules were still repeated by the whole class in a sing-song chant. Few appreciated the need of questioning to be sure that a lesson was understood and to provide the drill needed to give any permanence to knowledge or any ability to apply it.

Method as Pressure Technique, 1875-1900

The late nineteenth century might be described as the grand period of formal method. The superficial efficiency achieved by thoroughly trained teachers who remained in the profession might have seemed as near-perfect now as it did then if the twentieth century could have retained a faith in premises that seemed as solid as a rock in 1880. One had only to believe that education was achieved by getting pupils to consume great quantities of an intellectual food, called subject matter, under the direction of technicians whose practice was based on "immutable" laws of a psychology that told how the young ought to respond to such treatment. Even the partially-trained, half-educated teacher could perform wonders by conformity to the miracle-working system.

The following brief account of late-nineteenth-century methods will point out advances that were made and defects that were imperfectly covered up. It is based on a variety of sources: on books for teachers by men like Calkin in Nova Scotia, and Hughes, McLellan, Millar, and Tilley in Ontario; on normal school programs, departmental circulars for teachers, inspectors' reports, papers and articles by teachers, and other evidence.

CLASS MANAGEMENT

A marked improvement occurred in the ability of teachers to obtain and retain attention. Many relied on a timely shift to an entirely different subject as a means of relieving the strain of intensive periods of work. Many realized that the child would find school more pleasant and acquire more curricular knowledge if his teacher was cheerful, earnest, and enthusiastic. Many did not.

Equally marked improvement was shown by good teachers in ability to handle a class and to make group instruction more effective than individual teaching. The response of one pupil was used to help stimulate others. Not that the feeling in the classroom was free and easy: "Pupils should sit erect in an attitude of expectancy," said Calkin. ". . . When called on to answer a question they should rise promptly. . . . The teacher should be animated and erect but not boisterous."

Teachers were able to rely more on their own resources and to conduct oral instruction without the use of a textbook. Unfortunately they often substituted dictation of notes. Inevitably they acquired the habit of talking too much, although warned against this fault. "A wind-mill may run for hours and pump no water," said Inspector John McCormac in Prince Edward Island in 1899.

QUESTIONING AS TECHNIQUE

Considerable refinement was made in the technique of questioning. Class answering, or, the so-called simultaneous method, was used only for rules, definitions, dates, and the like, although there was a considerable bulk of such material. James L. Hughes, in his little book on *Attention,* gave an amusing illustration of the result of one teacher's reliance on class answering and entirely oral repetition. After repeating the catechism half an hour a day for four or five years, one child wrote, when finally requested to do so, the following unorthodox version:

My duty toads God is to bleed in him to fering and to loaf withold your arts withold my mine withold my sold and with my sernth to whirchp and to give thanks to put my old trast in him to call upon him to onner his old name and his world and to save him truly all the days of my life's end.[22]

Before the end of the century elliptical questions, "yes" or "no" questions, and the repetition of answers were avoided by better teachers. Many made a fetish of insisting on complete sentences since it was realized that every lesson was incidentally a lesson in composition. Considerable use was made of a consecutive distribution of questions — down one row of pupils after another — for testing purposes, although it was considered advisable to vary the order to keep the pupils alert. The best teachers preferred the promiscuous method, by which questions were thrown out to pupils indiscriminately, or to any selected pupil, even during the exposition of the lesson. Discussion of the art of questioning showed an awareness of the need of skill in handling answers of different types but made no mention of the subtle techniques now used by accomplished teachers to clear up individual difficulties without losing the attention of the rest of the class.

USE OF OBJECTIVE METHOD

There was a great advance among some teachers in the use of objective methods. A professional journal declared in 1885:

That which pre-eminently characterizes modern education is the increasing prevalence of the method of presenting truths in the concrete rather than in the abstract.[23]

But in the following issue the journal also admitted a disadvantage of all more advanced methods — that teachers may use them badly. Some teachers taught object lessons by showing an object to the class and writing on the blackboard a prepared descriptive essay for pupils to copy into their books. Some teachers had no sense at all of the concrete as opposed to the verbal. A lesson in one of the Irish National textbooks used in New Brunswick began: "The country where you, children, live in, is called Ireland." In 1870 a New Brunswick teacher gave all explanations as if the pupils did actually live where the textbook said, and an inspector found later that the children were convinced that they were living in Ireland. But trained teachers who had any gift of empathy realized that pupils often entered school not knowing their right hand from their left and that the starting point of all instruction must be the pupils' experience gained through the senses if knowledge was to result and not merely memorized words. Skilful teachers employed objective methods not merely in object lessons but in all subjects, and used incidentally such equivalents as blackboard sketches and vivid illustrations in words from their own experience. Very few were adept, but many made a plodding effort.

CRAMMING

Although one cannot be sure, it would appear that more time was spent on presentation that was thorough to the point of being ponderous, on copying and written reproduction, and on laborious reviews before examination than on lively immediate drill and recurrent practice. Evidence from various sources confirms the impression given by the following report of an Ontario inspector in 1878:

There remains to be seen whether there is that inward life of improvement in teachers and pupils, without which lasting good cannot be achieved. This to my mind is not so satisfactory as it might be. The "routine" system has not yet been eradicated. There is yet too much attention paid to cramming the memory rather than to developing the powers of the mind. The "art of teaching" has not yet attained to the position in which we hope to see it. Reading in too many of our schools is without that life and taste which should characterize it in order to make it efficient. Arithmetic is yet too much taught by rule and without a practical bearing. Grammar savors too much of textbooks, and is lacking in its practical application to Analysis and Composition. Our pupils, as a rule, are not sufficiently educated to think for themselves.[24]

Cramming was the practice most characteristic of the late nineteenth century.

It is indulged in by those teachers who have more zeal than knowledge, by those who have knowledge but not zeal, and by a third class who have neither knowledge nor zeal, and who have little business in the profession at all.

So said the editor of the public school department of the Canada Educational Monthly in 1880,[25] and the pressure was even greater in the high schools. The justification for cramming was not that there was in life any direct need of knowledge and skill in quantity but that the subjects taught under pressure had disciplinary power. Said Calkin:

Discipline is either *specific* or *general*. A study serves a specific purpose when it develops some particular faculty or power. Thus botany cultivates the power of observation chiefly; physics, the power of inductive reasoning; geometry, the power of deductive reasoning. A study serves a general disciplinary purpose when it gives tone to the mind as a whole, exercising both intellectual and emotional activities and developing an easy poise of its faculties. Such studies as language, history, and literature . . . are of this character.[26]

The precision of Calkin's confidence in the forms of subject matter was duplicated in Tilley's book for Ontario teachers, who were told to believe that intellectual discipline from the study of grammar had an indirect bearing on moral discipline also. Such faith in subjects made method the slave of content, with the result that teachers were unable to bring most children into the sunlight of "why?" as they labored in the quarries of "what?".

TOWARD REDUCTION OF PRESSURE TECHNIQUE

But questions were being asked and new approaches were sometimes tried. At the teachers' institute in Saint John, New Brunswick, in 1878 there was thorough discussion of homework, which brought out the need for careful assignments and preparatory explanations by the teacher and for co-operation of parents, some of whom still believed that they were making a sufficiently generous concession in letting their children off during school hours. At a meeting of the Toronto Teachers' Association in 1880, a teacher gave a paper on "How I manage my class." She said that a great deal of the secret of successful teaching lay in making the school hours as pleasant as possible for the children. She studied her scholars and tried by skilful suggestions to get them to propose the plans she wanted carried out for the day. She tried also to get troublesome scholars to feel that they were an object of interest to her and thus to win them from their evil ways. In Galt, Ontario, in 1881 children in the first two books spent half their time in the classroom and half their time at play under the supervision of a playroom teacher. Before the end of the century McLellan wrote in his *Applied*

Psychology that interest was essential to learning and that the separate training of the faculties was a physiological impossibility — ideas derived from John Dewey, with whom he appeared as joint author of another book on *The Psychology of Number.*

Method in the late nineteenth century was epitomized in the views of Calkin of Nova Scotia. He had a solid confidence in a science of education. Although he had the common sense to say that a method of dealing with human beings could never be as inflexible as cast-iron, he explained, with precision, the operation and value of inductive, deductive, analytical, and synthetic procedure in teaching. He was sensible in insisting that the deductive method is not suited to young children, that something better could be done than forcing children to memorize what they did not understand, and that reproduction of fact was of little value as compared with knowledge resulting from the learner's own effort. In his contentions regarding this last point Calkin differed from educators of the twentieth-century only in his greater emphasis on hard endeavor and in his unawareness of motivation. Although we should not expect him to use the twentieth-century term, even the concept of motivation seems not to have entered his mind.

The Transition to Modern Methods, 1900-1925

Prosperity in the early years of the twentieth century made it possible to improve educational methods, because people were less fearful of departure from the formulae of the past and because the provincial education authorities could insist on higher standards of education and training for teachers. But the changes of the twentieth century were also made possible by the gradual development during the preceding one hundred years of methods that were focussed on the inner response of the child. This development may be illustrated briefly by reference to psychology, to educational incentives, and to regard for individual differences of ability in pupils.

"WHOLENESS" BOTH OF CHILD AND OF SUBJECT MATTER

Canadian educators in their writing on psychology stressed the need of considering the child as a whole and of presenting a block of subject matter that the child could grasp as a significant whole before he was required to master details. Forrester in 1867 represented the child as a compound being with physical, intellectual, emotional, aesthetic, and moral attributes, but possessing unity as a person and marked differences from other children in mental endowment and temperament. Forrester advocated the teaching of outlines first — for example, in history — and was thus to an extent an early exponent of the unit method and of field theory psychology. Millar in his work on school management in 1896 also stressed the principle of "wholes, then parts." He said that a child had an idea of a house, a horse, or a man before he had a conception of the parts of any one of them. "The unit," he said, "must be the basis of instruction."[27] Some inspectors urged their teachers to recognize that children were human beings. John McCormack of Prince Edward Island in 1899 expressed the fear that education had become almost exclusively mental and suggested that teachers "make the boys and girls happy by sharing in their sports and encouraging them in their pleasures."

INCENTIVES AS DRIVING FORCES

Rewards and deprivations, praise and shame, were used throughout most of the nineteenth century with little consideration of their inner and more lasting effect.

"Burns not the Booby's breast with glowing shame,
E'en discipline dislikes the dunce to name."

These lines from the prologue of a public examination in a school in Newfoundland in 1809 show some sensitivity but also acceptance of the prevailing fashion. New Brunswick, we have seen, had a sufficiently strong aristocratic tradition to ensure the constant use of prizes. Trustees were given authority in 1816 to distribute twenty shillings in awards to the pupils who qualified by ability to repeat the Creed, the Lord's Prayer, and the Ten Commandments, and by superior achievement in other school work. In spite of discouraging results from the prizes for regular attendance in ordinary schools, a remarkable device was introduced in 1878 in the model school as an example to teachers. It was a merit book produced by an enterprising publisher, a complicated and elaborate gadget with dockets for cards of different denominations to be issued to pupils twice a day in exchange for cards previously awarded. The teacher throughout the day recorded any abatement against the pupils. Supplementary apparatus consisted of a brass cylinder on a vertical iron fan and twenty-six pieces of card money for each pupil.

In Toronto at that time parents of pupils received report cards showing the number of lessons, lessons perfect, lessons imperfect, good conduct marks, misdemeanor marks, total good marks, total bad marks, attendance, times late, and standing in class. Lieutenant-governors and other distinguished people made a habit of introducing prize giving and influencing school methods accordingly. Newspapers praised the practice, and even enlightened educators like John MacNeill in Prince Edward Island in 1838 and Egerton Ryerson much later thought it advantageous to incite a spirit of emulation in this way. The result, as pointed out by the *Canadian School Journal* in 1878 was that "nothing, indeed, seems to strike the intelligent educator from foreign lands, when visiting English or Canadian Schools, so forcibly as the extent to which prizes are given in them."[28]

But from the time of Confederation scornful criticism of such incentives was expressed more and more frequently, and positive means of encouraging achievement were explored. Forrester insisted that any incentive to excel should be used "in a way that no envious or rancorous emotions, or ambitious uncharitableness towards those who are competing with us be generated or fostered." He had no use for prizes or place-taking, urged that teachers try only to get individual pupils to do their best according to their talent, and advised that pupils be shown how to study effectively and that teachers in other ways help to make learning an intrinsically satisfying experience. Educational journals around 1880 condemned prize-giving — especially the offering of only a few prizes — and recommended methods that would help to make awards unnecessary. The *Educational Weekly* in 1885 said bluntly that the state had no right to force students to submit to classification by ability:

The business of an education system is to provide for the best and most equable development of the moral and intellectual faculties of the student, and so prepare him for life and citizenship — nothing less, nothing more. Competition is not only no essential part of this process, it is injurious to it.[29]

As might be expected, the opponents of prize-giving included Dr. Nelles of Victoria University and others interested in developing the ability of people, in contrast with those who thought of education as formal subject matter, which selected and trained leaders and gave stability to the thoughts of the many. Calkin, in his usual moderate terms, pronounced the judgment of professional educators around 1890:

As a means of influencing the members of a class generally, place-taking and prizes are of little educational value. The places of honour are within reach of only a small portion of the class and generally those who are influenced are the pupils who least need stimulating. The keen contest that is going on near the head of the class scarcely disturbs the lower half.[30]

Thereafter this was the position taken by those interested in public education for its own sake. Educators and laymen primarily interested in particular social forms advocated and continued the use of the prize incentive.

RECOGNITION OF INDIVIDUAL DIFFERENCES

At the beginning of the nineteenth century differences in the abilities and interests of people were recognized in a characteristically formal way by attributing superiority and inferiority in these as in other respects to the upper and lower social classes. Individual differences among the people generally were officially recognized by the time responsible government was established. The legislature of New Brunswick in 1847, in defining the functions of an institution to be set up for the training of teachers, stated that attention should be given especially to "the art of communicating the rudiments and elementary branches of Common School Education in a manner best suited to the capacities, ages, and conditions of each of the youth of the province."[31]

By the time of Confederation, Forrester had said about all that educators could say concerning the existence of individual differences and the necessity of adapting education to different needs. He stated that the great diversity of natural talents, so palpable to all, was to be met in part by offering a variety of subjects. He pointed out that opponents of public education used the diversity of aptitudes as a basis of their argument that not even the most skilful teacher could do justice to every child, and he showed that this objection could be met only by concentration on method and teaching skill and by attack against the narrow confines of subject matter. Yet Forrester and his contemporaries were in a position different from that of educators fifty years later. Lacking scientific measuring instruments they did not represent individuals as possessing quantitative differences of intelligence, or of mental age, but as showing qualitative differences of many kinds. Having to contend against the prestige of traditional forms of subject matter, they could do little to adapt school work to the learner.

Yet insight into qualitative differences brought the latter part of the nineteenth century closer to progressive thought in 1950 than to the scientific realism of 1925. Before the heyday of scientific method there was no preoccupation with measurement of intelligence and achievement to cause educators to overlook the differences of temperament pointed out by Forrester:

Some, again, seem to possess great sensitivity and tenderness of conscience; and others are blunt, dull, and obtuse, as if seared by a hot iron.[32]

The broader concept of individual differences prevailed before 1900. A New Brunswick examination paper in 1878 asked candidates for teachers' licences to "specify the grounds on which you consider it necessary for the Teacher carefully to observe peculiarities of disposition in pupils." A typical editorial in the *Educational Weekly* in 1885 stressed the need of preserving the individuality of the child, the need of dealing with each child according to his individual peculiarities, and the need for each teacher conscientiously to study each and every child under his control. There was no suggestion of summing a child up in one numerical rating. An illustration of the change to the narrower concept was provided by the course of study for elementary schools in British Columbia in 1900. Pupils of unequal ability or attainment were not to be required to work in the same class. Schools were to provide as many classes as necessary at the same level and to reclassify students two or three times a year or as soon as the individual interests of the pupil required such a transfer.

The scientific movement in the twentieth century confronted teachers with discouraging and irrefutable evidence that made the problems of method much more difficult. Peter Sandiford of the Ontario College of Education addressed the Saskatchewan Education Association in 1927 on the characteristics of the talented child. He pointed out that innate ability was so likely to be a determining characteristic that one could make a more accurate selection of those who would do well in advanced school subjects by taking the youngest children in any school grade than by asking teachers of the grade to make the choice. Bright children with an intelligence quotient of 140 and over had been found by Terman and his associates not only to be more successful in school subjects but also to be healthier, to possess greater maturity of character, and to show greater interest in activities that required thinking, such as conversation, and less interest in competitive games.[33]

School system struggled by reorganization of classes to reduce the educational problems implied by these findings to proportions with which the more skilful teacher might cope. Moncton around 1930 tried ungraded classes and classes for backward pupils in elementary grades, and half-yearly reclassification in both elementary and secondary grades. But these plans were only partly successful, for the gains made were usually temporary. There was greater success a little later when special programs were provided for mentally handicapped children in the elementary school, including opportunity classes for French-speaking pupils. In 1937 the city tried a hot lunch experiment to give training in home skills and manners and shortened the school day for pupils in opportunity classes to permit them to take part-time jobs. But even the new school subjects at both the elementary and secondary levels did not enable the less gifted pupils to match standards easily attained by the more gifted in almost any study or skill.

MOTIVATION

Sandiford was aware of the anti-democratic implications of the results of intelligence tests but urged teachers to keep striving to discover and develop talents in all. *The School* in 1924, commenting editorially on Thorndike's statement that pupils improved but little in general intelligence and that bright pupils would make superior progress in any subject, added these rather cryptic words of consolation: "Anyhow, it is not the subject that makes the pupil, but the pupil that makes the subject."[34]

This doctrine was one of the insubstantial corner stones of the new educational method that developed in the twentieth century. Taken with the preceding discussion of incentives, of child psychology, and of individual differences, it must serve here as an example of the significance of innumerable innovations in educational method during the present century. The most useful key to the meaning of twentieth-century method is understanding of the change from external incentives to internal motivation. All modern educational procedures have sought to stimulate a dynamic force for continuing growth and achievement in the learner himself. To do this the teacher had to think first of the child as a whole and of his special characteristics and could not be rigidly confined by subject matter requirements. In the light of these remarks and of the discussion of broader developments in previous chapters, a few scattered illustrations of methods in recent periods may be intelligible.

HIGHLIGHT ON THE CHILD

At the beginning of the century, many teachers encouraged pupils to plant and care for school gardens. A young woman graduating from Acadia University in 1907 with a keen interest in psychology became fired with enthusiasm to try pupil-centred methods of teaching and discipline, obtained permission to experiment in a city classroom, and gave up after a year. In 1911 an important new teachers' journal urged the use of the play way to make review interesting — for example, a game of sailing around North America in which the contestant had to name all waters encountered or go back to the starting point. This type of thing was an old device fifty years before, but there was a new departure in the recommendation that the teacher give help to handicapped pupils when making assignments. The journal published lists of books for home reading by high school pupils. In 1914, a comparison of practices in a graded Ontario school and in urban schools of the United States showed that Ontario teachers spent much more time on teaching and drilling the factual content and formal skills of spelling, grammar, and history, and less time on developing ability and appreciation through composition and literature. In 1924, the British Columbia course of study urged teachers to experiment with the project method and the socialized recitation. It included lists of reference books not only for teachers but for pupils. In the 1920's Alberta applied an equivalent of the unit mastery plan in the construction of textbooks and influenced classroom method accordingly. A predecessor of the Winnetka plan was studied but found too expensive. In 1924 the Dalton plan was introduced for a five years' trial in Garneau Public School, Edmonton. These few events illustrate cautious attempts and incautious failures to have children learn by doing things of their own volition and at their own rate.

In spite of accusations by uninformed critics, these changes in method did not make pupils less industrious. Demands for a reduction of the burden on pupils were made by parents, doctors, and other interested laymen. For illustration, take the discussion of homework in the Toronto *Mail and Empire*. In 1901 the school board was reported to have passed a resolution that "teachers be instructed to limit the homework to the class work already taught" — a stupid restriction on teachers who might occasionally ask their pupils to do a little investigating on their own. In 1912 the city librarian, George H. Locke, was quoted as saying that homework was "the most arid, delusive, inhuman, inconsistent thing ever perpetrated." In 1919 a columnist wrote of homework as a subduing and enslaving influence in the schools. The same year the minister of education was reported as saying in the House that homework should not be eliminated but should be limited in amount. Although teachers did find ways of reducing homework, and did so the more readily as they gave more consideration to the child and less to the subject, they were not primarily responsible for the move. Public education responds necessarily, but slowly and cautiously, to the changing attitudes of the public and to the changing conditions in society. In so doing it inevitably incurs the displeasure of the few who deplore such changes.

1925-1950

Method gained in importance during the depression. Superintendent Oulton of Saskatoon found in 1931 that results exceeding expectations were obtained from the introduction of the Winnetka plan in three primary classes. By then, in Alberta, school festivals of two or three days' duration gave children opportunity to exhibit their powers in the singing of solos, duets, action songs, and choral pieces, and in recitation and drama. In 1932 the department of education in British Columbia suggested for rural schools a re-grouping of the eight elementary grades as five divisions. Certain courses were to be taught only in alternate years and pupils at different levels were to unite in some activities. With less time usurped by formal teaching, those who needed help were to receive more attention, others were to do more work on their own, and bright pupils were to be allowed to advance more rapidly. In Ontario in 1933 some high school history classes undertook the preparation of old-time newspapers, and pupils became reporters gathering facts and side-lights on 1816, or another chosen year. This was a group project, or enterprise.

THE ENTERPRISE AS METHOD

Before World War II the enterprise, on which Donalda Dickie of Alberta was the Canadian authority, became fashionable in elementary schools across Canada. Where the enterprise was, as intended, a plan of organizing motivated group activity, it gave valuable experience in fact finding, in application of knowl-

Pupil activity in a modern school

edge and skill, in co-operation and democratic processes, and in evaluation by pupils of their own achievement. Adherents to form, however, saw nothing real in such experience. Many teachers thought of enterprises as the material objects produced in periods allotted to work with paper, paste, wood, and bits of metal. When these teachers ceased having their pupils engage in such nearly useless construction, or were told to do so, it appeared that enterprise work fell off. But in effective modern teaching the essential dynamic of enterprise teaching continued to gain strength, although the form of the enterprise might not be in evidence. The reporting by committees in social studies, the organization and management of lunch facilities in a rural school or of a dance in an urban school, the compilation of Latin phrases in common use, the operation of science clubs and French clubs, and even the inquiry and discussion set off by a seemingly casual remark in the classroom could be and often were manifestations of the spirit underlying the enterprise. The special technique continued to be effective in capable hands.

During World War II the willingness of pupils to engage in activities was exploited for patriotic reasons. Formal learning probably suffered from the diversion of the time and energy of pupils and teachers to collections and campaigns not primarily educative in their objective. Inevitably this caused some impatience to return to direct methods of getting content into pupils' heads. In one activity, the Junior Red Cross, teachers were usually successful in securing educational advantages in addition to patriotic attachment and contributions of articles and money. Pupil-participation in classroom programs and supplementary activities was positively motivated and not an escape. In Newfoundland, where the Junior Red Cross was introduced in 1936, there were over 1200 branches enrolling half of the school children on the island seven years later, and the education benefits in terms of health habits alone were considered noteworthy by L. W. Shaw, Secretary of Education.

FOCUS ON METHOD

In 1953, by virtue of more flexible curricula and some more capable teachers, and also of necessity because of stronger competition from new mass media of communication and other distractions, schools seemed likely to attach even more importance to method than before. This tendency in education was decried by many Canadians. Undoubtedly the corresponding reduction in the prestige of formal content lowered the barriers against intellectual and cultural mediocrity. But the public school systems were committed to the strengthening of the inner resources of all the people. Teachers inevitably were expected to display more and more skill in method for the benefit of all, and especially of below-average pupils, and to attach less importance to organized disciplines that challenged the few. The danger was that poorly qualified teachers might make the new method of education a fiasco.

Size of Classes

Methods of teaching have been closely related to the number of pupils per teacher. The individual assignment method kept the ratio low, the monitorial method greatly increased it, and oral class teaching established an intermediate ratio which was relatively high when teachers in graded classrooms were expected only to teach subject matter and relatively low when they were expected to give attention to all aspects of the development of individual children.

Twenty-five to fifty pupils under a single teacher were accounted too many by the superintendent in British Columbia in 1860. But much larger classes in urban schools were encouraged later by the payment of grants on the basis of average attendance. When grants were paid subsequently according to the number of teachers, the acceptable basis was

one teacher per 60 pupils in 1905, per 40 pupils in 1914, and per 35 or fewer pupils in 1929. In the Red River area around 1868 Janet Gunn taught 100 children in a school at Little Britain and managed to keep order without having to resort very often to the willow stick kept within reach of her desk. In the cities and towns of Ontario in 1880 there were 96,000 pupils enrolled in public schools and just over 1200 teachers to keep pumping facts — a ratio per teacher of nearly 80 pupils on the roll, or of about 45 pupils in average daily attendance. Inspectors complained that harassed women had sometimes to manage 80 to 100 pupils actually present in a classroom. Throughout most of Canada between 1901 and 1941 there were about 24 pupils in average daily attendance per teacher, and less than 18 in 1948. These figures are misleading, however, because of the numerous small rural schools. In Toronto in 1953 the number of pupils in an elementary school classroom was held to approximately 35, about the maximum for education which aims at the all-round development of every child.

Teaching Aids

Also linked to the development of method and to the broadening of the curriculum was the improvement of teaching aids. Textbooks were badly printed on poor paper, depressing in appearance, and sometimes unreliable in content before 1850. Then they became passably legible, then clear and dignified until 1900, then less unattractive, and finally in recent years an asset to motivated teaching. Other books were so scarce at first that the library of King's College, New Brunswick, in 1830 permitted only professors and senior administrative officials to take them out. Teachers before 1850 had often to supply all reading material at their own expense. By the time of Confederation, books were reasonably plentiful in most schools of Ontario. In the Northwest Territories in 1889 union school boards were required to purchase an unabridged dictionary, a large encyclopedia, a biographical dictionary, a gazetteer, several standard works on English literature and classical studies, and other reference books, so that libraries were more extensive than in smaller schools fifty years later. Charts and cards were used in all monitorial schools. Steel pens appeared before 1840, but were forbidden in many schools at first as a costly and dangerous new invention. Before 1900, educational periodicals carried advertisements of a "diamond point" fountain pen with a box filler, but the use of any substitute for the common steel pen was still forbidden in elementary grades. Slates were universally used in nineteenth-century schools. Even in the Red River Settlement, where in 1850 writing paper was unavailable and slate pencils so scarce that the short ends were used in reed holders, one might see "the face of the teacher in imminent danger of disfigurement from the rush of frameless slates to catch his eye."[35]

By far the most important educational invention was the blackboard. Upper Canada College in 1830 had "three wooden slates, perhaps 3 feet by 4, and painted black"[36] to take writing in chalk. Before 1850 only a few schools had blackboards; after 1860 there was hardly a school without one. They were either mounted on a stand or consisted simply of a small wall area painted black. Where teachers lacked resource or were discouraged by the poor quality of the writing surface, blackboards fell into disuse — as in New Richmond, Quebec, in the 1880's. Even then school inspectors in rural areas complained that local trustees would often do no more than paint a few spruce or hemlock boards to give a semblance of a blackboard, which was almost useless. By that time city schools had slate blackboards, and periodicals like the *Educational Review* in New Brunswick advertised "liquid slating for blackboards" to go on wood or plaster. During the twentieth century all conscientious school boards provided slate blackboards, or the modern green substitute, for the full length of at least two sides of the room. Their usefulness was again somewhat reduced in recent years by a clutter of semi-permanent notices, charts, and pictures, which elementary school teachers considered desirable.

Few schools had visual aids like maps and globes in 1850, but most schools had inadequate equipment of the kind by 1875. As early as 1860 the *Journal of Education* of Lower Canada carried a discussion of the usefulness and cost of the magic lantern as a teaching aid. The superintendent in New Brunswick in 1879 gave a paper at a teachers' institute on "The Value of Pictorial Illustrations in School Instruction" and mentioned the screen and magic lantern. Rand saw that visual aids might be used as auxiliaries to instruction, as educational instruments, and as a means of securing interest. In 1900 J. G. Hodgins suggested to Canadian historical societies that they might contribute national and patriotic pictures to schools to exert a silent but constant influence on the pupils. The characteristic school a decade or two later exhibited on its walls scenes of military heroism and portraits of royalty, and larger high schools also had stuffed birds in cases; but visual aids of a more cheerful, useful, and flexible character were still not in evidence. In 1911, however, *The School* took editorial notice of a significant development:

If the school should undertake to utilize moving pictures for purposes of education in the classroom, they would prove to be of great value, both in saving time and in making the lesson more vivid and concrete.[37]

Audio-visual aids, 1950

About 1925 films began to come into general use, and phonograph records were employed by a few teachers of French and music. Soon after, all types of audio and visual aids were accepted as valuable and were utilized increasingly by more and more teachers in the classroom.

Other materials and apparatus for instruction were used in some schools, especially after the introduction of object lessons and objective methods. In the third and fourth readers of the Irish National Series, teachers were advised "to provide themselves with specimens of all the inanimate objects mentioned in the lessons." Drawings were considered an acceptable substitute, necessary to the preservation of classroom decorum in the study of animals. David Boyle, certificated as a teacher in 1865, followed this advice so energetically that he built up as teaching aids extensive collections of Canadian birds and animals, of historical and Indian relics, and of geological and mineral specimens, and subsequently became the first provincial archaeologist in

Ontario. Teachers interested in the "kindergarten system" were informed by an advertisement in 1881 of an "instructive and entertaining geographical puzzle, consisting of dissected maps of the Dominion and of the Province of Ontario, which had been prepared for school and nursery use."[38] Apart from the "gifts" of the kindergarten, however, there was some difficulty in obtaining approval of the use of materials and equipment by pupils, even in science laboratories. In 1900 the chairman of the Protestant school board in Quebec city inspected a sand and water device for teaching geography and granted the teacher permission to use it for demonstration purposes, but only if she did not allow the pupils to handle it. Manual training, domestic science, agricultural instruction, vocational education, enterprise teaching, and various types of art work defeated objections to pupil-activity with materials, but those who held fast to the idealist-intellectual concept of education continued to think that manual operations in school were mostly a waste of time.

Summary

The elementary school curriculum has been steadily enriched, liberalized, and enlivened during the past century without extreme difficulty or major disagreements. The secondary school curriculum, on the other hand, has been expanded, contracted, supplemented, adjusted, and readjusted — and still the basic problems remain. Concurrently method gained in importance as the concept of education as development became more widely acceptable. Method was refined in the nineteenth century and given new power in the twentieth century. The comprehensive account in this chapter of changes in curriculum and method shows a trend in classroom practice parallel to the trends in ways of living and thinking. It becomes apparent that approval or disapproval of any educational practice is seldom based on specifically educational criteria and is almost always a reflection of the critic's predilections on more fundamental issues of broader significance. In the next chapter further detail on changes of content and method will be given in relation to subjects of the curriculum.

CHAPTER 24

Subjects of the Curriculum

TEACHING TO READ · SPELLING · READING AND LITERATURE · GRAMMAR AND COMPOSITION · THE FIRST FRILLS — WRITING AND MATHEMATICS · SOCIAL STUDIES · SCIENCE AND AGRICULTURE · MUSIC, ART, AND CRAFTS · HOMEMAKING, HEALTH, AND RECREATION · COMMERCIAL AND TECHNICAL SUBJECTS · THE LANGUAGES · SUMMARY

Changes in classroom practice may be shown more definitely in relation to particular subjects of instruction. This chapter records certain interesting developments in the history of most of the subjects commonly taught in elementary and secondary schools.

Teaching to Read

In the early part of the nineteenth century the alphabet method of teaching to read was universally employed. In Quebec there was a commonly used textbook by Jean Palairet entitled *La nouvelle méthode pour apprendre à bien lire et à bien orthographier.* On an introductory page the author claims that the first part of the little book, for beginners, "les conduit graduellement, d'une manière fort aisée, de la connaissance des simples lettres de l'Alphabet, à la lecture des Mots les plus longs et les plus difficiles."[1] Also of curious interest are remarks in *A New Guide to the English Tongue,* a book by Thomas Dilworth, published in Glasgow, and widely used in Nova Scotia.

Dilworth held that even the forms of language were divine creations:

Letters are the foundation of all learning . . . they are naturally divided into vowels and consonants, and again into single and double letters . . . Words consist of one or more syllables and are given to us by the all-wise God.

Needless to say, Dilworth doomed the child to learn reading in a way that would do no violence to adult concepts of the divine pattern for language.

It was difficult to persuade teachers to adopt the new phonetic (phonic) method and the even more radical "look and say" methods that appeared at the middle of the nineteenth century. On his return from abroad, Ryerson wrote scathingly in

1846 of the A - B - C method and had the phonic method introduced in the first session of the normal school. But apparently it had soon to be dropped. Twenty years later discussion at the Ontario Teachers' Association on teaching to read showed the obstinacy of men who had shut their eyes and clung to the old form of instruction. "Teach the value of sound in letters," urged a convert, Mr. McGann. "Silly," said Mr. McLelland. "Have words written as well as spelled from the beginning," advised Mr. Scarlett. "Useless," answered Mr. Brown and Mr. King. At this meeting there was a report from a committee who had visited Oswego and who recommended the adoption of the phonetic method as used there. They explained that reading and spelling were taught concurrently by presenting the regular sounds or powers of letters one or two at a time and by using cards and other devices to give the children something interesting to do. This recommendation of improved American practice aroused much indignation among members, who objected to teachers being required to learn new methods, and the report was filed with a patriotic motion for the insertion of a statement that the object lessons adopted at Oswego were British in origin and not American.

Since methods of teaching to read are of crucial importance and serve as a good index of the improvement of instruction, the practice followed by good teachers at the time of Confederation deserves close examination. In the Maritime Provinces, if not elsewhere, superior teaching may be assumed to have followed the plan approved by Forrester. The learned educator was scornful of those who compelled children to learn the meaningless and useless names of letters — a process which, he insisted, took six months to complete. But he was strong in his conviction that the alphabet had to come first. He was skeptical of the attempts

of "reforming progressive teachers" to discard the alphabet altogether until the child had made some progress in reading, and he stated flatly that "such a method can never attain the end at which it aims." Forrester had the teacher begin with the sound of letters and proceed by Pestalozzian principles from the simple to the complex and from the known to the unknown. The logic of this procedure forced him to confront the children with the same lifeless little sentences that were found in the old spellers like Webster's. The one difference was that Forrester hoped children would be able to construct for themselves such gems as: "I am up," "Is it I?", "Is he up?", "Go as I go." He made the directing of the child's first steps in reading an erudite science based on a knowledge of labials, dentals, palatals, gutturals, and nasals, and of many precise rules about the order of presentation. There is no doubt that Forrester's teachers taught the art of reading more efficiently than the schoolmasters of the early nineteenth century. But had they been able to see what the modern teacher is able to do in defiance of this rigorous logic they would have been forced to conclude that there was trickery or magic at work or that the age of miracles had been restored.

The transition to twentieth-century practice was nevertheless revealed in the controversy among advanced thinkers on whether to begin with the word instead of the letter or to begin phonics at once. Many Canadian teachers by 1870 were familiar with the comprehensive treatment of various methods by the American educator, Wickersham. But Canadians writing for educational journals were usually as conservative as Forrester in their preference for the logic of phonics. Ryerson, however, announced in 1871 that the time had come for beginning with the spoken rather than with the written word. Soon afterward, many articles on the new technique advised teachers to hold up an object before the class, to talk about it, to ask for its name, to write the word, and to ask for the name of the word. In the 1880's, normal schools instructed teachers-in-training to begin in this way with the word method, to supplement it with the phonic method, and to use for the first five or six weeks a perfectly consistent alphabet with short vowels only. In New Brunswick some of the best teachers began with lively conversation leading to the introduction first of a sentence like "Tom has a dog" and then to the idea that a sentence has parts called words. Only after considerable time spent on stories accompanied by words written on cards did the teacher come to the formation of words from letters indicating the separate sounds.

One of the last two steps in the transition was forecast late in the nineteenth century by Calkin, who insisted that nothing meaningless to the pupil should be introduced by the teacher and that the new symbols "should bring before the child the objects and incidents of his own little world." One might begin, suggested Calkin, with *A red top*. The teacher would show the top, talk about it, spin it, write *top* on the blackboard, and so on. When motivation by such means was added to improved techniques, the process of learning to read was accelerated rapidly for most children in the twentieth century. Finally it became possible for a considerable number to appreciate Rousseau's ideas, which were developed and promulgated during the present century as concepts of reading readiness and maturation. Before World War I an article in *The School* condemned the practice of rushing all pupils at reading at the same time. To profit by instruction, said the author, a pupil must first have acquired a stock of ideas, a good vocabulary, and ability to talk and listen. Another article dealt with discovery of the import-

ance of eye movements. From then on, more and more children learned to read well and to like reading, with ultimate economy of time because time was "wasted" at first.

Spelling

Standard classroom practice up to and beyond the middle of the nineteenth century was to have pupils memorize and recite orally the spelling of words in lists compiled without consideration of usefulness to the pupil in reading or written expression. Calkin gave an interesting account of the spelling exercise during the last twenty minutes of the school day in Nova Scotia:

At first came the preparation of the lesson. The pupils seated on the high benches and facing inwards studied aloud and with no uncertain sound. As they pronounced each letter and syllable of the word after this fashion — v-o vo; l-u-n lun, volun; t-a ta, volunta; r-i ri, voluntari; l-y ly, voluntarily — they swayed to and fro, keeping time in their bodily movements above the seat and below the seat with the rhythm of their voice, gathering up the syllables as they went along, and finally pronouncing the whole word. At the close of the preparation all stood in line around the room while the teacher heard the lesson. There was "going up and down," which excited much emulation, gravitating each way from about the middle of the line, the one at the foot seeming to be as proud of his position as was he at the head.[2]

In Prince Edward Island in 1849 a county inspector said that spelling was "universally taught by tasks learned by rote, generally out of the different spelling books used in school, frequently out of dictionaries." Another inspector declared that it was not unusual "to hear children literally spell columns of four or five syllables, yet unable to put together the letters of common monosyllables." The city superintendent of schools

A spelling class, around 1880

in Charlottetown complained in 1878 that children were taught to spell words as abstractions and not in their connection with other words. "A boy will spell a word correctly," he said, "when I put it to him as a word by itself, but when he has to write it in a sentence, the word is wrongly spelled." But better methods were practised by some good teachers on the island even before 1850. They used the blackboard for presenting words to younger pupils and used dictation as an exercise and as a test for older pupils. John Stark, however, had to warn teachers on the island in 1855 that the value of this "most efficacious means" of teaching orthography was lost when they failed to correct the work dictated to pupils.

In Canada West and elsewhere improved content and methods in spelling were provided at mid-century by the adoption of Sullivan's *Spelling Book Superseded* in place of the older texts. Sullivan insisted that spelling be linked to reading lessons at first, as provided for in the first three books of the Irish National Readers. Only later were pupils to study the words listed in his textbook, with the assistance of dictation exercises and rules for spelling designed to lighten the burden of memory work. Unfortunately his classification of words according to principles of orthography, orthoepy, etymology, and the like was appalling not only to pupils but to teachers as well. The *Canadian Speller*, replacing Sullivan's in the year of Confederation, followed the same pattern. But it quickly fell into disuse, and in Ontario no other spelling book was authorized immediately in its place. An *English Spelling Book*, ascribed to old Lindley Murray, but altogether different from his readers, was published in Nova Scotia in 1864. It contained comparatively light and interesting reading lessons as well as the inevitable word lists, which were somewhat more helpful in arrangement, as in the grouping of words having *ch* with the sound of *k*. The next Ontario textbook was *The Practical Speller*, used by some teachers after 1881 and authorized about sixteen years later. It was pupil-centred, by virtue of a new basis of grouping words, not by the number of letters or syllables, but by their familiar use — at home, in the parlor, in the dining room, and so on. Even in spelling, the most formal of subjects, modern education had begun.

During the last twenty years of the nineteenth century, many earnest reformers fought courageously against the incongruities and wastefulness of the conventional forms of spelling in the English language. National and provincial teachers' journals cited evidence like an announcement in the London *Times* that the extra letter in words like "favour" cost the newspaper $2500 a year. But such costs were as nothing when compared with the waste of learning effort. A. H. MacKay, who became superintendent of education in Nova Scotia, made a study in Pictou in 1880 of the time spent by pupils in school and at home on spelling. He found that spelling accounted for nearly fifty per cent of their time for the first six years, or more than forty per cent for the first eight years. At the Dominion Education Association in 1898 he read a paper that was reprinted in pamphlet form under the title, *Three Great Reforms — How May We Hasten Them?* MacKay claimed that a phonetic system of spelling by use of forty symbols for forty sounds would make it possible to teach reading in two or three weeks and to save for educative purposes nearly all of the thousands of hours wasted on irrational spelling. But those who held form to be valid against principle were not convinced even when MacKay claimed

that "the word scissors has been calculated to be capable of being spelled according to good English analogy in no less than 596,580 different ways."[3] During the twentieth century, as we have seen, efforts were directed towards the elimination of time on spelling beyond the maximum periods for efficient learning. Some relief was gained when memorization of rules, prefixes, and suffixes disappeared from the curriculum, as happened in Saskatchewan in 1913. But the drudgery of spelling continued to exact a high toll in making children averse to schooling, although adults who put a premium on docility and conformity in the young considered such time well spent.

Reading and Literature

Reading in the early nineteenth century was a mechanical exercise. As John MacNeill put it, "the child was simply taught to pronounce the words and to be able to spell them; no attention was given to the child's comprehension of what he read." Those in authority had no desire to cultivate a taste for reading among the people at large, and probably preferred that pupils should be vaguely overawed by the foreboding import of the reading lessons than that they should understand clearly what was meant. Teachers by their own limitations inevitably co-operated in the achievement of this aim. There is a story of a "school-marm" near Richmond Hill, Ontario, who started her reading class in the book of Exodus, which contained many unfamiliar words that neither she nor her pupils could pronounce, much less understand. She overcame the difficulty by telling the children that since Moses was such a good man it would be proper to substitute his name for any word they could not pronounce. When inspector John Arbuckle tried to persuade teachers in Prince Edward Island to question pupils on the meaning of a passage, he found that those who knew the meaning themselves would word their questions in such a way that "the proposition that should form the answer is embodied in the question," so that the pupil was required to guess only "Yes" or "No." Later reports of inspectors on the island up to 1892 indicated that reading in many schools was a "mere repetition of words without natural expression or any attention to punctuation." This statement might have been made of nearly all schools in Canada up to the time of Confederation at least.

The long transition from form to power, from rote knowledge of words to understanding of written language, was achieved by trying and discarding various compilations of organized subject matter — artificial divisions of language conceived by adults of analytical mind. One of these was orthoepy, or the pronunciation of words. It was taught from lists in the spelling books of words classified by position of accent, and finally in the 1880's from Ayre's *Orthoepist* and from the *High School English Word Book*. The meaning of words apart from any context was similarly taught from the same textbooks, except that the *Verbalist* was used as the counterpart of the *Orthoepist*. The books and the separated studies disappeared from public and high schools just before the end of the century. About 1850 etymology, formerly taught as a division of grammar in secondary schools, became an adjunct to reading and spelling in elementary schools under the vernacular title of "rooting." Though preposterous to pupils and beyond the capacity of teachers of limited scholarship, this exercise in sham erudition continued beyond 1883, when Connor's *Elements of English Etymology* was authorized for Ontario high schools. Connor raised etymology to a scientific study, which was tried for a while in senior high school grades and then restored to the university. By the

end of the century the pronunciation, meaning, and derivation of words had become incidental to the study of literature and composition.

As an example of the older style of teaching at its theoretical best, here is an illustration of oral work on rooting, given as a model by John Arbuckle in 1860.[4]

Q. What is the literal meaning of the word "attraction"?
A. Drawing to.
Q. From what is it derived?
A. Attract.
Q. What does the first syllable, or the prefix of that word signify?
A. "To."
Q. What was the original form?
A. "Ad."
Q. Give other forms of "ad" with examples.
A. Aspire, accede, affix, aggravate, alleviate, annihilate, append, arrogate, assimilate.
Q. Give a word signifying to draw from.
A. Abstract.
Q. How should you express "to draw together"?
A. To contract.
Q. How would you express "to draw out"?
A. Extract.
Q. How would you express "to draw under"?
A. Subtract.
Q. When a scholar is easily guided, what adjective applies?
A. Tractable.
Q. What is the contrary?
A. Intractable, or untractable.
Q. What verb expresses "to draw down"?
A. Detract.
Q. And he who detracts is guilty of —
A. Detraction.

As might be expected teachers protested that few schools had pupils able to respond in this manner to questions of the kind. But Arbuckle for a year or two continued to emphasize the value and the practicality of instruction along these lines. His later reports do not mention it.

One reason for the lingering of these formal subjects was that they, like grammar, gave the teacher a professional asset of knowledge which others did not possess. Even more important, they provided content in the acquisition of which the pupil's progress was clearly marked, since he would never pick it up out of school. In the first half of the nineteenth century even outstanding schoolmasters anxious to give a broad education could not think of literature as a school subject for the simple reason that pupils as well as teachers could presumably read, so that there appeared to be nothing to teach. When literature first descended from the universities into the senior grades of grammar schools in Canada West in the 1850's, it came in the form of the history of English literature, a subject replete with facts to be memorized and one which reduced the study of authors' works to brief extracts by way of illustration.

This barren subject was hooted out of the schools by the 1870's because it did not bring the pupil into real contact with English authors. But when longer extracts were then prescribed for high school study, teachers devoted their time in class to grammatical analyses of the writing. By the 1880's the fashion shifted somewhat to emphasize rhetorical analyses, with the result that pupils' marginal notes in old surviving textbooks consisted largely of words like "metonymy," "synechdoche," and "redundancy." At that time the amount of literature prescribed for junior matriculation into university was ordinarily two cantos of *The Lady of the Lake*, or the equivalent. Editors (or should we say "supplementers"?) of literature textbooks obligingly supplied several times the bulk in closely packed notes for memorization and reproduction on examinations. These included such solid stuff as "rules for perfect rime." By assigning this convenient content to be memorized, teachers were saved from the risk of getting nowhere with anything so intangible as understanding and appreciation.

THE LION.   41

It is observed of the lion, that his courage diminishes, and his caution and timidity are greater, as he approaches the habitations of men. Being acquainted with the power of their arms, he loses his natural fortitude to such a degree, as to be terrified at the sound of the human voice. He has been known to fly before women, and even children, and suffer himself to be driven away by them, from his lurking place in the neighbourhood of villages. His disposition is such as to admit of a certain degree of education; and it is a well-known fact, that the keepers of wild beasts frequently play with him, pull out his tongue, hold him by the teeth, and even chastise him without cause. It is dangerous, however, to provoke him too far, or to depend on his temper with too much security. The lion is found in the hottest parts of India; and in the plains of Africa, where he makes his lair or hiding place among the tall rushes, or other plants, which fringe the banks of rivers. His strength is immense. Near the Cape of Good Hope, a lion was seen to seize a heifer in his mouth, and though the legs dragged on the ground, he appeared to carry her off with the same ease that a dog does a rat, and even leaped over a ditch with her.

His favorite prey is the deer and antelope, which abound both in the plains of Africa, and the jungles of India; but there is no animal, not even man, who will not become his prey if opportunity offers.

In Scripture this animal is sometimes spoken of as an emblem of strength. Jacob compared his son Judah to a lion, to denote the future courage and power of his tribe. The devil is said to go

A page from the *Irish National Readers,* Third Book

But advanced thinkers after the 1860's conducted a persistent campaign to have the development of understanding made an objective of the schools. In Ontario, George Paxton Young around 1865 and John Seath around 1885 insisted as high school inspectors that exposition of the author's meaning was the essential work of the teacher. The *Canadian Readers,* used in elementary schools from 1867, marked a certain advance in the liberality and variety of their content, although they still retained the "useful knowledge" emphasis of their predecessors. The *Ontario Readers,* and the *Royal* series used during the 1880's and after in some other provinces, went much further in the improvement of literary quality and appeal to the interest of children. The word "literature" appeared in courses of study or in examination schedules as a subject about that time. Practice in better schools was illustrated by the report of the principal of Central School, Winnipeg, for 1877-78:

Reading, Class IV: work of Fourth Reader, corresponding to that of fifth, with all incidental information carefully elicited. Passages of a striking beauty and merit, memorized and dwelt on so as to develop refined literary tastes.

By the 1890's, largely because of the Herbartian influence, prescriptions of literature had increased to comprise whole works of authors: both Scott's *Lay of the Last Minstrel* and Goldsmith's *Citizen of the World* were prescribed for junior matriculation in Ontario in 1889. At the same time, also as a result of the Herbartian vogue, teachers acquired a new professional asset in technical skill. No longer was it necessary to teach formal content that no one else knew. The teacher could subject a poem, a story, or a play to treatment unheard of outside the classroom. Before the end of the century literature as a school subject had arrived.

Twentieth-century developments were anticipated to an extent by Calkin, who advised, before 1890, that the teacher's desk be furnished with children's magazines and books, which those who had finished assigned work should be allowed to read. In his province of Nova Scotia in 1905 the old *Royal Readers* were replaced after twenty-nine years by two new series, partly on the ground of advances made in child study. The trend was towards content more interesting to the pupil and better adapted to his level of ability. In 1914 the *Public School Manual* for Form V in Ontario stated that the object of the course in literature was "the cultivation of a taste for good literature, not by minute critical study, but by reading at home and in school."

A typical article of that time on the teaching of literature advised against any rigid method, against moralizing, and against giving facts about the poet and his age, former practices it condemned as "pedagogical iniquities"; the author urged the teacher to get the pupils into the mood for a poem as the first step in achieving the one important aim, appreciation of poetry. This illustrates the shift from the Herbartian and earlier points of view to the Froebelian and the modern. Among articles on supplementary reading from the turn of the century, one claimed that a teacher achieved more by creating a love for reading than by teaching all the facts and information in the curriculum.

What pupils read in school and outside school was a persistent cause of worry to adults who were sure about what was good and what was not. An article in the *New Dominion Monthly* in 1872 denounced "the quantity of trash, in the shape of novels, sensational newspaper stories and magazines, that is read, tainting the mind with evil, weakening its vigor and moral tone . . ."[5] Not only pupils but teachers were warned against sensational novels. One author who claimed to have observed their dire effects gave this testimony in 1881:

I tell you candidly that I would have more hope of the future of a young man who smoked tobacco, chewed the weed, and got inebriated every New Year's and Dominion Day, than I would of one who, guiltless of these habits, was an inveterate novel reader.[6]

Reading of periodicals of unobjectionable character and with some appeal to the young was made available around 1880 in the *Boy's Own Paper* and in the *Girl's Own Paper*. But the irony of all criticism then and since is that youngsters were blamed for reading what their elders' taste made it profitable to publish. When not only cheap books and magazines, but movies, radio, and television competed for the pupil's leisure hours, the school fought a losing battle when it attempted to force the young alone to read with minute care what a few adults voted excellent and the majority of adults found unpalatable. Aylesworth says that when the prescription of literature was increased greatly in Alberta in 1924, the choice of older writers esteemed by academicians caused high school students to turn away from literature in disgust. The assignment for Grade XII was two plays of Shakespeare, selections from Milton and Carlyle, and lectures by Ruskin. Modern methods and modern selection of material were adopted — often reluctantly and to an inadequate extent — to make good literature of both past and present attractive to students who should be drawn rather than driven to reading.

Reading as a skill remained as a rule mechanical until the Froebelian influence at the end of the nineteenth century emphasized the value of expression. An apparent exception was the artificial exercise known as elocution, which received attention in a number of early schools which reported use of *Enfield's Speaker* as a textbook. Elocution again came into vogue as an extra-curricular activity in the third quarter of the nineteenth century. A textbook, *The Canadian Speaker,* claimed that elocution helped to develop the ability to speak distinctly and impressively. In 1878, educational journals still carried advertisements of several such "speakers" and "reciters," including *The Prohibition Reciter* and *The Canadian Humorous Reciter*. The journals also published gems for the delectation of admiring audiences — "The Drummer Boy's Burial," "Somebody's Mother," and, in lighter vein, "School Statistics." The fact that ability to read was an accomplishment of social value when many were illiterate probably accounts in part for the continued emphasis on oral reading in school. During the interval between the two world wars more sensitive teachers began trying to motivate oral reading by arranging an audience situation. Choral reading and classroom dramatics were also a help. But the major change in recent years was greater emphasis on silent reading for comprehension and enjoyment and on remedial work to overcome disabilities and distaste for reading.

Grammar and Composition

Old-world confidence in grammar as a formal instrument and new-world reliance on the direct teaching and practice of written expression first came into conflict about the middle of the nineteenth century. Before then instruction in prose composition was unnecessary in grammar schools because pupils came from homes where good English was spoken, and futile in common schools because of the deficiencies of both teachers and pupils. On the other hand, formal grammar was taught to all secondary school pupils and to a few pupils who remained for advanced work under superior teachers in elementary schools. Although Murray and other writers lent authority to the belief that grammar was the key to good speech and writing, the terminology and structure was foreign to English; the definitions were mere words to most students, and the exercises were mechanical guesswork. Typical comments of noteworthy school inspectors at mid-century deplored the complete separation of grammar from composition of English and expressed no surprise at finding pupils able "to parse sentences grammatically in the most un-grammatical language."

The quarter century from 1850 to 1875 was the age of supremacy for English grammar, which was taught in all elementary grades but the lowest and in all secondary grades but the highest. Analy-tical parsing, which loomed large as a regular exercise, was performed in good schools according to some such formula as that recommended by Forrester, who subjects the sentence, "Milton's poems are excellent," to the following schematic treatment:[7]

WORDS	CLASS	SUBDIVISION	INFLECTION	SYNTAX
Milton's	Noun	Proper	Sing. Masc. Poss.	When two nouns, &c., the former is put in pos.
poems	Noun	Common	Plu. Neu. Nom.	Subj. of verb is put in nom. case.
are	Verb	Intransitive	Ind. Pres. Plur. 3rd person	Verb agrees with its subj. in number and person.
excellent	Adjective	Attributive	Positive	Adjectives qualify nouns.

But although Forrester advised having children analyze sentences from the first, he pointed out the "utter folly of attempting to teach grammar as an abstract science," and would have postponed any regular study of the subject until the pupil was about ten years old. The content of grammar had been made somewhat less oppressive by new textbooks; they reduced the rules of concord and government, for example, from nearly fifty to one-quarter that number. Composition was on the course of study only for secondary schools, although better teachers had pupils construct sentences on their slates or on the blackboard in connection with arithmetic or bookkeeping. But nearly all classroom time in language, apart from spelling and reading, was spent on grammar, grammar, grammar.

The result observed by numerous critics was the same everywhere. In 1894 a speaker at the Ontario Educational Association said that the average schoolboy "is, as a rule, well stocked with the mere technicalities of English grammar, but he has little facility in the correct use — either in speaking or writing — of the mother tongue." In the same year the principal of Prince of Wales College wrote:

When they [pupils from the schools] enter our classes they, as a rule, give evidence of being drilled in Parsing and Analysis of sentences, but are at a loss when they have to express their thoughts in passable English.

Seventeen years before, the author of an article in the *Canada School Journal* had declared that the teaching of English was based on the false theory "that a knowledge of the technical terms of grammar is necessary to a knowledge of the language." The *Educational Weekly* stated editorially in its first issue in 1885 that no reliance could be placed on grammar to improve ability in English:

Common experience tells us that children study grammar for years and speak as incorrectly at the end of their study as at the beginning of it, and write with nothing like correctness.

Of a syllabus on grammar issued shortly before, in Ontario, the weekly editor said that it might be useful to bright intellects but would probably lead "to much useless labor both of teacher and pupil." Yet the formal study survived for years, partly as preparation for foreign language study and partly on grounds of mental discipline. John Seath's *High School English Grammar,* published in 1887, was a worthy Canadian monument to mark the climax of grammatical study in the classroom. Comprehensive and thorough, it was weighty without being pedantic and sought by inductive presentation to achieve its avowedly disciplinary function.

But by World War I formal grammar was on the way out as a school subject. The *Ontario Teachers' Manual* of 1915 indicated that in elementary grades it was to be restricted to the "science of the sentence." The manual admitted frankly that the study did not necessarily have a direct influence on spoken language and that "no subject possesses a purely formal disciplinary value." In public schools the subject was to be made as useful as possible. It was to begin in the lower grades with incidental discussion of the relation of words and to continue as an orderly study when the child was ready for reflective thought about language. Even then it was to begin with the sentence and centre in the sentence as a unit of speech and thought, and was not to catalogue obsolete concepts of language forms under traditional categories. In the Saskatchewan curriculum in the same year grammar lost its status as a "subject for all schools" and was included as an "additional subject" only from Grade VI. In British Columbia, English grammar was dropped from the high school course in 1918. By World War II the subject survived chiefly as functional grammar subsidiary to composition in elementary schools and as an incidental to foreign language teaching in high schools. But although research by then had confirmed and reconfirmed the experience of a century that formal grammar was not helpful in improving the English of most pupils, many adults still believed in the value of the study for children. Most of the advocates thought of grammar as a

determinative of language, whereas authorities on English had come to look on grammar as a descriptive study of current and changing usage.

Since composition is concerned with ability beyond mere reproduction of verbal content, it could hardly be taught when form was supreme. John Strachan had pupils memorize the speeches of eminent British parliamentarians and deliver them in a re-enactment of debates in the House of Commons — not a useless exercise, but one clearly based on the formal concept. When first attempts were made to teach composition as a regular subject in secondary schools after 1850 and in elementary schools after about 1870, reliance was placed on auxiliary instruments. Of these, applied grammar was the chief. Another was the correction of false syntax — that is, of errors in English constructed or defaced for the purpose. Another teaching instrument was the elaborate compendium of rules for good English and of admonitions regarding faults to avoid. Many teachers had their pupils "commit" page after page of such material to memory in the hope that the authority of the textbooks would govern their use of language.

An 1867 Canadian adaptation of the mighty Bullion's *English Grammar* included examination questions which show the formal nature of this study of the "principles of composition." The first asked: "What is composition?" And the twenty-fifth began a series with the command: "Repeat the first canon and illustrate its application by an example." The teaching of actual composition by the pupil was blocked by adult belief that young people had no thoughts to express, or no thoughts worth expressing, or no thoughts they should be allowed to express. George Paxton Young said in the year of Confederation that the schools of the time gave the children "only a wretchedly scanty stock of ideas" and added that it was "of no use trying to instruct children how to say a thing when they have nothing to say."

To provide children with thoughts to express, a common device from the 1870's was to give a bare factual tabulation of information on such topics as the production of tea, or the life of Joseph, and to ask for a compilation in literary form. Other devices were stories given for reproduction, blackboard summaries of information elicited from the class after preparatory study, and use of prescribed prose literature as a source of "thought material ordinarily lacking" in the minds of pupils. As soon as practice was recognized as the means of learning to speak and write, more advanced educational thought emphasized the importance of imitation and immediate correction of the pupil's own errors. Article after article from 1875 onward pointed out that it was essential to surround the child as consistently as possible with models of good English, especially when the influence of the home and neighborhood was not conducive to good English. Rules of grammar or even of composition could not serve the same purpose. Teachers were advised that:

Nearly every School exercise, whether oral or written, may be made an exercise in Composition. The Teacher should use especial care in requiring good English from his pupils in their answers in class or at examinations.[8]

But inspectors found little improvement in the teaching of composition in many classrooms where knowledge of content in other subjects was imparted with success. Perhaps the best advice for teachers of formal outlook was given by the headmaster of an Ontario model school:

I now come to what, in my opinion, is the best means of teaching written composition in our schools. I have tried it and know its practical value. Pupils from the first book to the fifth, should copy the reading lesson, while in their seats, on their slates, and in recitation, read from their slates. I cannot put this idea too strongly.[9]

For pupils in Grades VII and VIII the writer recommended the re-writing of a given passage with substitution of synonyms for words underscored, the paraphrasing of sentences, the rendering of poetry into prose, the combining of separate statements into sentences of a specific kind, and so on. He also had pupils discuss a subject, suggest ideas, write short compositions, put their compositions on the blackboard, and criticize one another. Still more formal were the exercises provided in Dagleish's *Introductory Text-Book of English Composition,* published in Nova Scotia in 1898. The method was grammatical synthesis: "Complete the following sentences by adding substantive clauses."

But the satisfaction of some teachers in having solid material like this for themselves and their pupils was disturbed as the Froebelian movement gained converts. The new education had the audacity to invite pupils to base compositions on their own experiences. On entrance examinations in the 1890's there appeared such topics as "A Picnic" and "How I Spent the Holidays." So began motivated composition. From then the problems of new-world teachers were to get a favorable disposition towards good models, to encourage much writing, to have pupils become critical of their work. Around 1910 subjects were still assigned to pupils, but there was a choice of such subjects as "The Schoolroom Clock Makes a Speech," "Our Snowball Fight," and "Yes, I Met a Ghost." At the same time new roads to motivation were explored. One such was to have children re-tell stories in writing in order that the class might choose the best version of each scene as a basis for re-writing as a play to be performed by the pupils.

During this transition from formal grammar to ability in expression, there were always teachers a century before or behind the majority: some who won praise from the enlightened school visitor of Prince Edward Island in 1848 for having pupils relate in writing some occurrence in their life, helping them to correct their own blunders, and leaving them "to infer grammatical rules for themselves"; some who still believed even in 1950 that the speech and writing of the new generation will be governed by the rules the older generation has them memorize and, in controlled situations, apply.

The First Frills — Writing and Mathematics

At the beginning of the nineteenth century extreme conservatives still considered it a dangerous and unnecessary waste of time to teach the poor to write, and preposterous to teach arithmetic to girls. In 1850 the frills were geography and grammar. Teachers who taught these subjects were accused by irate parents of wasting pupils' time on parsing exercises which were of no help at all in cutting "the slash fornent the house" and of demoralizing them with geographical scandal like "Berlin is on the spree."[10] As the curriculum expanded, the old views were applied to new subjects. Marshall d'Avray as superintendent in New Brunswick was willing in 1855 to have common schools teach spelling, reading, writing, arithmetic, geography, and the history of the province, but considered the attempt to teach more as mischievous and impracticable:

Here is the great source of all that is imperfect in our Common School teaching; it aims at too much in the way of mere seeming, and it thoroughly teaches so little.

He added, of course, that another evil was that of demanding too much from the teacher and too little from the parent, exactly the same arguments that were used twenty, fifty, and ninety years later whenever the school experience of children of all the people was enriched. Seldom if ever was the complaint made against schools for the few.

To teach writing around 1850 most teachers simply wrote sentences for the pupils to copy. When teachers changed, pupils found strange new models confusing, and standard copy books were advocated by inspectors. But the copying method was no great handicap as compared with the inconvenient furniture and uncomfortable climatic conditions in school. Children were "often seen shivering from cold, and unable to hold a pen," and the desks and seats were "often at such inconvenient relative distances, that children could not possibly reach one from the other . . . in a sitting posture."[11] Mary Bradley in New Brunswick about 1781 learned to write before attending school by reproducing of her own accord the writing copy set for her two eldest brothers. In the 1860's and 1870's under Pestalozzian notions of "simple to complex," children were taught to make the strokes and shapes that were later combined into letters. A teacher practised this method in 1840 in a school of the county of Norfolk, Upper Canada, where "writing lessons began with the downward stroke, at an angle of 52 degrees; after the pupil could make these fairly well, then came 'pot-hooks and hangers' and next the letters."[12] Thirty-five years later, an approved system began similarly with three elements or principles, the first a straight line still slanting at precisely "52 degrees (52°) from horizontal," and the other two defined with similar exactness. Rigorous attention was paid in the later system to the pupil's position, to six steps in preparing to write, to five steps in putting away writing materials, and so on. From that time onward printing in some schools has been taught before script; shortly afterward, arm movement became a mandatory vogue until World War I; and from one decade to another various mechanical and psychological problems received attention. But no teacher of 1932 would have engaged, as did an "enthographic artist" named Phillips a century before in Upper Canada, "to teach the very worst writers to execute with facility, elegance, and despatch, in three short and easy lessons".[13]

As in learning to read, so in arithmetic trained teachers at the time of Confederation had ceased to mystify their pupils at the beginning by strange mysterious symbols. Instead they had the children count the fingers on their hands, count and arrange in groups pebbles they had gathered on the road, and perform the same manipulations on the ball-frame until they could add numbers orally. Teachers who were disciples of Stow made the transition to symbols by "picturing out" in words the difference between articles depicted on a sign-board and the articles themselves, or between written words and the things they stood for. Then the teacher wrote groups of vertical strokes on the blackboard to represent numbers, and only then did he introduce the common symbols by writing them under the corresponding groups. Good teachers also used coins for teaching the arithmetic of money, and had weights, scales, and measures for demonstration and practice before the introduction of corresponding tables. Although old-fashioned teachers might still begin with the rule, as did the teacher in our typical school of 1830,* Forrester advised his teachers to introduce multiplication, for example, by having the children count the panes in

* See p. 144.

the windows of the schoolroom, and by questioning arrive at the shorter way of getting the total number of panes in all the windows. *The Nova Scotia Arithmetic* of 1864 was written by another normal school master as a textbook to exemplify these principles of Pestalozzi and Stow. It explained at length that the conception of number in the minds of the young was always associated with objects and that pupils trained to perform arithmetical operations mentally with the aid of visible objects would be able later to perform more difficult operations mentally or in writing with the aid of objects unseen. But grading also was essential later:

In the various stages of slate arithmetic, the pupils must be thoroughly classified, if the emulative principle of their nature, through the sympathy of numbers, is to be operated on and taken advantage of.

For various reasons, many teachers did not acquire the objective technique, or did not utilize it with simple material things. Bishop Taché in Manitoba in 1877 gave an illustration of how the teaching of arithmetic might be conducted by a religious man:[14]

TEACHER: What is Arithmetic.
PUPIL: The science of numbers.
TEACHER: Give the first numbers.
PUPIL: One, two, three, four, etc.
TEACHER: Give examples of the use of numbers.
PUPIL: There is *one* God, there are two testaments, there are three persons in God.

The high school inspectors of Ontario in 1873 found "pupils too generally the slaves of rule and formula — not capable of interpreting the formulas (which ought to be banished from the *Arithmetics*), and perfectly in the dark as to the reasons of the rule." An inspector of public schools in 1879 found too many teachers still using the "foolish and inexcusable methods of the past" — having pupils learn rules and then set to work with abstract

Interest for Days

Rule. Multiply the pence of the principle by the Days and rate per Cent for a Dividend, cut off two figures on the right hand, and Divide by 365. The Quotient will be the Answer in pence

Or, 9 to 365 Days are to the interest of the given sum for a year. So are Days given to the Interest required

What is the Interest of £.240 for 120 Days at 4 per Cent per Annum.

A page from a ciphering book

numbers, and having them add columns of figures by following mechanical instructions on what to put down, what to carry, and where to draw lines.

By that date a crucial battle was raging on the subversive "unitary method," which made rules unnecessary by reducing arithmetic to a process of step by step reasoning. A pupil asked to find out the cost of a dozen oranges from the cost of five was no longer to follow mechanically the rule of three, but to work out the cost of one orange as a logical step before finding the cost of twelve. Textbooks by Hamblin Smith and by other exponents of the reasoning process were published in Toronto and greeted with blasts of criticism from die-hards. One reviewer referred to the unitary method as "this last specific for mental ineptitude." Professor M'Gregor of the McGill Normal School wrote, with reference to an exponent of the new method:

It would not be the first time that a specious adventurer had in Toronto as elsewhere, by dint of brass and the enthusiasm of his patrons, obtained a position far above what his true merits entitled him to.[15]

But Winnipeg adopted the unitary method in 1877, the textbook of Kirkland and Scott was authorized in Ontario in 1880, and the influential high school inspector, McLellan, gave the new method vigorous support. Soon reason supplanted rule throughout Canada.

Linked with the Pestalozzian movement and subsequent changes was a growing stress on mental arithmetic. Sangster's textbook of 1860 had given it prominence. McLellan in 1878 wrote two textbooks on mental arithmetic, which were authorized for the schools of Nova Scotia and Manitoba and recommended for use by teachers in Ontario.

Before the end of the century, arithmetic was being heavily stressed in the elementary schools — too heavily according to several critics. But from Prince Edward Island to Ontario there were complaints that, in spite of arduous training in the solution of complex problems, the average schoolboy was at a loss when asked to apply the first principles of the subject to practical purposes, and that he was inaccurate in simple operations. Early in the twentieth century complicated problems with no practical bearing were weeded out, more practice was given for rapidity and accuracy in simple operations, and ordinary problems were introduced at an early stage, instead of having years spent on ponderous mechanical work with lengthy numbers. Psychology gave the teacher insight into the child's first concepts of difference in number as simply greater or less. Advanced educators advised postponing arithmetic until constructive work gave the child a "sense of the need for numbering," which the objective method for all its merits failed to provide. In the revised programs of 1935-40 the child was introduced to arithmetical processes at a more leisurely pace, to simple multiplication and division in Grades III and IV and not in Grade II, as at the beginning of the century. Although the time spent on arithmetic was reduced, enterprise work in the later programs gave a new type of comprehensive and functional drill which accustomed the pupil to apply his skill without receiving a specific request from the teacher.

In the secondary schools, mathematical subjects were well established at the beginning of the nineteenth century as the only important supplement to classical studies. Just before Confederation, arithmetic was taught to nearly all pupils in the grammar schools, algebra to nearly a half, and geometry to about a third. In the last quarter of the nineteenth century mathematics rose to a position of top importance, shared only with English. In Ontario, owing to the enthusiasm of a high school inspector, McLellan, whose power and pomposity never wavered under discerning criticism, every pupil in every grade of every school was enlisted for the study of Algebra, and only five per cent escaped geometry. In all provinces the supremacy of mathematics was supported by claims that the study had unique power for mental discipline:

"When properly taught, mathematics cultivate and develop, to a high degree, the powers of memory, abstraction, and generalization . . . they familiarize the mind with the forms of strict logical inference, and impart habits of accuracy in the use of language, caution in the admission of premises, ingenuity in analysis and comparison, and power of continuity of thought."[16]

Although these claims were never substantiated, the enrolment in the separate mathematical disciplines fell only slightly in the first decades of the present century, except that geometry ceased to be taught in the lowest grade and arithmetic in higher grades. At mid-century well over ninety per cent of other than vocational course pupils studied algebra and geometry in the middle secondary grades. In Grade XIII, eighty per cent of the pupils in British Columbia, and from forty-five to sixty per cent in Ontario, were enrolled in one or more of the three mathematical subjects, including trigonometry.

A major development of the present century was the substitution of general mathematics for the separate disciplines in the lower high school grades. According to Gray, their innovation stemmed originally from the presentation in Glasgow in 1902 of a paper by John Perry who advocated the early presentation of essential notions of trigonometry, algebra, geometry, and even calculus, without theoretical proofs. The suggestion was elaborated in the following year, with emphasis on the practical applications of mathematics, by E. H. Moore in the United States, and reinforced by subsequent recommendations in Britain and the United States for integrated mathematics. In Canada, for the most part, these ideas were not applied until the curriculum revisions just before World War II. From then until 1953 nearly all pupils at about the Grade IX to X level were enrolled in general mathematics, and in the western provinces the comprehensive term, mathematics, rather than the names of the separate subjects, was largely used in courses of study for higher grades. It must be remembered, of course, that a high degree of correlation or integration is by no means guaranteed by the mere introduction of new curriculum titles like general mathematics, general science, and social studies.

If the content of general mathematics and of the separate disciplines be considered together, it is certain that no other secondary school subject, or group of subjects, has maintained a position of comparable importance in the secondary school curriculum for more than a century.

Social Studies

When geography became a subject for all pupils after 1850, it required memorization of statements regarding any part of the earth or universe. Improvements came when a few teachers made direct study of the neighborhood a starting point, as was done in Zadock Thompson's *Geography and History of Lower Canada,* and in Woodbridge's *Rudiments of Geography,* which was used in some schools of Upper Canada. A larger minority of better teachers during the 1860's used the blackboard, maps, and globes to some advantage in oral teaching. But when map geography was universally taught fifteen years later, it meant for most pupils the memorization of locations in addition to names.

From the time of Confederation, there were Canadian textbooks which made it possible to give adequate attention to the native country. But this advantage also became a curse when children were compelled to memorize all the names their elders and ancestors had sprinkled generously across the map. One sympathetic teacher of 1880 asked if it was not enough to require a pupil in Ontario to memorize the counties, county towns, townships, and other topographical nomenclature of his own province without insisting, as some teachers did, that he should also commit to memory the counties of Quebec, New Brunswick, Nova Scotia, and even of Great Britain and Ireland. Form and memory remained supreme throughout the nineteenth century. There was virtually no teaching of geography as a scientific study of environmental forces in relation to human life.

Early in the present century pupils were relieved of this burden of minute detail to be memorized. Teachers, by World War I, were advised to aim only at giving a general knowledge for the ordinary purposes of life and to accustom pupils to looking up particulars in works of reference when the need arose. The superintendent of schools in Edmonton in 1912 said that school geography had changed so completely that it "begins and ends in the doings of men" and that anything apart from the theatre of action was no longer of interest. Before World War II elementary school geography had merged with history into social studies. In the secondary school, geography was seeking reinstatement, but as a science and not merely as some organized descriptive facts. It had not attained parity with history as a senior high school subject in 1950.

Curiously enough, geography suffered in any close association with history. The first edition of Calkin's *Geography and History of Nova Scotia* gave much greater prominence to geography, whereas an edition dated 1911 reversed the order of subjects in the title and devoted the first eighty-six pages to history before adding twenty-five pages on geography at the end. Similarly, in the present century, social studies came to consist almost entirely of history in Grades VII and VIII in Ontario. The reason for this must surely be the influence of conservative thought interested in preserving respect for traditional forms. Such thought looked with favor on geography as long as its content was presented as static and fixed, but not when the aim became understanding of current change. For this reason, and for such other reasons as the Herbartian influence and the growth of nationalism, history gained in importance. Whereas the only history regularly taught around 1860 was ancient history in secondary schools, both British and Canadian history appeared in all schools after Confederation, and, with the addition of content relating to the mediaeval and modern period in other countries, history courses spread through all school grades but the lowest around the turn of the century.

Canadian history ranked a poor second to British history in the 1870's, partly because patriotism still meant loyalty to Britain and partly because textbooks in British history were more readily available. Teachers in Ontario were advised in the regulations of 1878 to give only oral instruction in Canadian history without use of a textbook by the pupils. Some Ontario teachers for their own use acquired Archer's *History of Canada,* which was authorized in New Brunswick. The lack of a textbook might have restricted memory work to "leading facts" as the regulations advised, but in the 1880's the authorization of a public school history of England and Canada provided the usual source of information to cram. The inculcation of a primary and a secondary patriotism then imposed a double burden of national history on English-speaking children.

The place of British and Canadian history in schools was determined less by educational considerations than by the fear that an opposition party might exploit the susceptibility of voters to cries of disloyalty. In Ontario the requirement of British history for high school entrance was _rescinded_, apparently at the almost unanimous request of "the most experienced teachers and inspectors," but was suddenly and almost immediately restored in December, 1893, when an election was in prospect.[17] Even at the middle of the twentieth century in Ontario, pupils had four years of British and Canadian history in Grades VII to X, so that the large numbers who left school with an education incomplete in other respects were bound to have had enough of those subjects at least. The more articulate were

known to declare that they had had enough of both to last them for the rest of their lives.

There was a tendency, nevertheless, to give increasing attention to Canadian history. In British Columbia in 1925 Canadian history replaced British and European history as a Grade XII subject for senior matriculation. In Alberta in the previous year general history, including both ancient and British, had been made preparatory to Canadian history in the senior high school. At the same time in that province the aims of history teaching were broadened. World history was to lead young Canadians away from narrow nationalism and imperialism towards an international outlook. There were also to be courses in civics and in economics to give a better understanding of contemporary problems. The whole program in history was intended to expand the imagination and engender worthy personal and social ideals.

The depression of the 1930's helped to destroy much of the remaining faith in formal content. When a *Reader in Canadian Civics* was introduced in Ontario, the Minister of Education expressed the desire that teachers be allowed a large measure of discretion in methods of presentation and that civics should not be made a subject of departmental examinations. In the western provinces history was studied to an increasing extent topically in relation to modern problems. In class, material was presented more often by students as a committee report. Extreme emphasis was given to the dynamic concept of the new education by H. C. Newland, supervisor of schools in Alberta:

If a course in Social Studies defines the goals of social endeavor, that is, sets forth the social purpose of education, and if it is definitely stated that the aim of education is the preparation for a new social order, based on justice for the common man, and if we apply science to the solution of social problems, we shall have a curriculum which will in a considerable measure discard the tradition of book learning, and of culture *in vacuo;* all learning and all education will have a direct bearing on the social purpose which is to be achieved. There will also be a very close relation between the activities of the classroom, and the economic activities outside of the classroom.[18]

But the immediate issues of totalitarianism and war made it unrealistic soon after to talk of education for social justice in democracy. Formal teaching of history survived as one bulwark of the democratic form of society already achieved. In eastern Canada, history as a formal subject was never seriously threatened at a higher level than Grade VI. In French-speaking Canada, history textbooks continued to be used from the lowest grade.

Science and Agriculture

In most elementary schools the first semblance of science teaching appeared about 1850 — chiefly in the form of useful knowledge extracts in the readers and sometimes in the form of object lessons. From 1875 to 1900 readers became more literary and less scientific, and object lessons more widespread. From 1900 until 1935 nature study was a required subject in most schools. Thereafter the scope of science in Grades VII and VIII was extended to manufactured articles in everyday use, like electrical appliances, although later programs of study in Ontario restricted attention again to the world of nature. The teaching of science has always been limited, even more than instruction in other subjects, by a lack of qualified teachers. In 1850 there were virtually no teachers who had any knowledge of science, and in 1950 elementary school teachers of all subjects could not be expected to explain even practical

applications of rapidly developing and changing theory.

But even in the early days some elementary schools taught a wonderland type of science. An American textbook found in the Maritime Provinces at mid-century was Mary A. Swift's *First Lessons on Natural Philosophy for Children.* It gave questions and pat answers:

Is the sun useful to us? It is very useful. In what way is it useful? It gives us light, so that we can see, and it makes us warm . . .

The youthful pilgrim was directed through a difficult morass of terminology on astronomy, on the properties of matter, like cohesion, impenetrability, and inertia, and on everything in the universe — all defined with the precision of certainty by his confident guide. Then he read and learned at the end what he thought of it all:

Is Philosophy a useful study? It is a very useful, and a very pleasant study, too. What good does it do children to learn it? It explains so many things . . .

Here the author led the child to see God as the one who had given everything in the world the form that his textbook ascribed to it.

Textbooks of this kind indicate more clearly than any other source the essential difference between the nineteenth and twentieth centuries in the teaching of science and other content subjects. Some of the books, including the one described, were not wholly unlike those of today in use of a style to appeal to children. Peter Parley's *Geography for Beginners,* an American textbook frequently used in Canada at mid-century, began with an attractive narrative to take the reader on a journey:

You will perceive that Thomas, as he goes along, sees a variety of objects, such as a carriage, a man on horseback, cattle in the fields, trees, and houses.

Geography textbooks often extended their content into broader fields of science. Calkin's *Geography and History of Nova Scotia* introduced such excursions in a pleasant way:

Children, you have seen a heavy fall of rain. Did all the water sink immediately into the earth? *No.* Did it remain standing on the ground like a great pond? *No, it ran in brooks . . .*

But Calkin, like other textbook authors, piled up masses of fact, including not only mileage tables which might be expected to remain constant, but data on production, population, and the value of real estate in various towns, which even in the nineteenth century were inevitably subject to change. It is more than likely that teachers required pupils to learn even this information. The characteristic of the nineteenth-century teacher was his faith in curriculum content as authoritative and permanent truth, and his consequent insistence that pupils accept it and memorize it just as it was in print. This point of view delayed the introduction of scientific study.

Hence an Ontario inspector of 1871 might have been speaking of the elementary schools throughout Canada when he reported that "the great Book of Nature is yet a sealed volume" and that memory was confounded with mind. A teacher in the 1880's "was sharply reprimanded by his board of trustees for 'wasting the time' of his small school by getting his pupils to make lists of the sorts of common forest trees, and give the names of the wild birds and animals they saw on their way to and from school."[19] Science, apart from the verbal summarizing of object lessons, was again of the wonderland type when it was introduced by some teachers towards the end of the century. A series in the *Educational Weekly* in 1885 on "The Fairy Land of Science" had high appeal to the imagination:

What is this little green tip peeping out of the ground under the snowy covering? It is a young snow-drop plant. Can you tell me why it grows? Where it finds its food? What makes it spread out its leaves and add to its stalk day by day? What fairies are at work here?[20]

This romantic treatment of nature by women, who had very largely taken over from men the teaching of the elementary school, ushered in Froebelian nature study a few years later. It was probably the only type of "science" that could be introduced as a substitute for the factual compilations of geography, physiology, and object lessons. Nature study with feminine overtones may have been one of the reasons that girls liked school much better than boys did in the twentieth century.

Some outstanding teachers of secondary schools gave instruction in science early in the nineteenth century. But when Ryerson listed science as a grammar school subject in the 1850's, there were virtually no teachers who could do more than have pupils read and memorize scientific content in the fifth book of the National Readers. In the 1860's George Paxton Young, as inspector of grammar schools, tried without success to have teachers limit the content to be learned, in order to give pupils practice in observation and reasoning. In the 1870's there was effective teaching of science as a factual subject, with the accent on chemistry. But the problem was still to discover a new type of instruction that would give pupils an appreciation of scientific method. In 1872 the annual report of the superintendent in Ontario declared that one of the first lessons a pupil must learn from science was "not to trust in authority but to demand proof for each assertion." This was a complete reversal

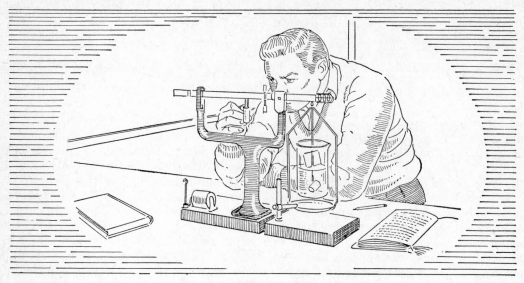

An experiment in physics, 1950

of the duties previously emphasized in school and out.

During the 1880's science laboratories were set up in better schools. Although experiments were conducted by teachers only at first, pupils were permitted increasingly from the 1890's onward to perform experiments themselves. By then the emphasis had shifted from chemistry to physics and was beginning to shift also from content to method. The advance during the last three decades of the nineteenth century was achieved against academic opposition. In Ontario until 1885 science was recognized as a subject for high school graduation into teaching and other pursuits but not for university entrance. Only in 1885-86 did the University of Toronto concede a place to physics and chemistry on the pass matriculation examination. Even ten years later, science subjects were allowed only one examination paper each, valued at 75 marks a paper, whereas foreign languages had two examination papers each at 150 marks a paper. Pressure for the advancement of

science teaching in the schools came from teachers, from the education authorities of the provincial school systems, from university professors of science, and from educated people in ordinary pursuits. In the Maritime Provinces between 1887 and World War I a summer school of science was supported by teachers, with grant assistance from provincial departments in later years. The first intensive two weeks' program included courses on zoology, botany, mineralogy, chemistry, physics, uranology, and physiology, and excursions for observation. Only by such means was a place won for the new subject against the reluctant forces of tradition.

By the time of World War I science had become a subject of first-rate importance in the secondary schools of most provinces, although in the Protestant schools of Quebec it remained at a disadvantage until the 1930's, when laboratories were installed in a considerable number of schools. In Quebec, in the French-language secondary schools the traditional program left little room for science even then, although Roman Catholic high schools for English-speaking pupils have given the subject more adequate attention in recent years. In the English-speaking provinces from the 1930's the usual practice was to offer general science in the first years of high school for the benefit particularly of those who left school at an early age. In the senior grades, physics and chemistry were then taught as academic disciplines for most pupils, and biology as an elective for some in the final year.

In spite of efforts to introduce agricultural science in one form or another after 1850, there was very little teaching of agriculture in rural elementary or secondary schools before World War I. In eastern Canada, Nova Scotia appointed a lecturer in agriculture at the normal college in 1885, established a College of Agriculture near the normal college in 1899, encouraged school gardens and offered summer training to teachers after about 1905, and appointed a director of rural science schools in 1913. In western Canada, the Northwest Territories added agriculture to the curriculum in 1890. Saskatchewan introduced in the high schools in 1910 a special agricultural course which dealt with the soil and its treatment, plant life and products, farm and garden crops, animal life and products, farm management, construction and mechanics, and experimental work. In 1915 the province appointed two directors of school agriculture. Alberta in 1913 made agriculture a compulsory subject in the teachers' course, introduced plant and soil science in Grades VII and VIII, and established three agricultural high schools. These schools were designed to teach practical farming to prepare pupils for university work in agricultural science and other fields, and to give immediate service to farmers by demonstration, experiment, and consultation. In nearly all provinces an impetus was given to agricultural in-

struction in 1913 by the grants of the federal government.

At the elementary and junior high school level, instruction in agriculture during the next forty years was an extension of nature study, intended to arouse interest in scientific principles underlying practical agriculture. A sentimental or propaganda value appeared also to have been attached to agriculture in the elementary schools, especially in Nova Scotia, where much was done to foster a love of rural life. In 1915 more than 230 schools of the province conducted 57 local fairs. During the 1920's, helping teachers distinguished for rural-mindedness and leadership ability were appointed under L. A. De Wolfe, director of rural science schools or, subsequently, director of rural education. Practical education in agriculture at the Grade VIII-IX level was offered, however, in special schools of French-speaking Quebec. But in English-speaking Canada even at the secondary level most instruction in agriculture was more in the nature of general education with rural bias than strictly vocational. Agriculture or agricultural science was offered in rural high schools instead of the usual science after World War I. Ontario established a few agricultural high schools similar in purpose to those of Alberta. When regional composite high schools increased in number through most of Canada during and after World War II, students in the agricultural option were given shop work or home economics related to the farm, in addition to agricultural science.

Perhaps because of possible applications to agriculture, perhaps because school study of natural life was more in harmony with old world views than emphasis on man's growing power through physics and chemistry, biology or simply botany was made a subject for middle school or junior matriculation in some provinces for a time between 1885 and

A rural school garden, 1904

1910. But Ontario dropped the arrangement early, and British Columbia later, in the period. After World War I botany was encountered by most pupils only in the elementary school or as elementary or general science in the lowest high school grades. In Ontario the industrial development after World War II confirmed the suitability of physics and chemistry as the major scientific subjects for most high school pupils.

Music, Art, and Crafts

Music was heard in the elementary schools when the good nature, enthusiasm, and ability of the teacher made it possible for the children to sing. Even in the pioneer days there were occasionally teachers who had these qualities. At Omemee, Upper Canada, in 1837, the common school teacher was an old soldier who had been a band master and who could play any instrument that happened to be at hand — violin, cornet, clarinet, flute, or bagpipes; the pupils encouraged him to use his talents and acquired a

liking for music, if nothing else. After 1850 education authorities tried to make singing a regular part of the common school program. Normal schools acquired tuning forks, books, and sheets for teaching John Hullah's system of vocal music. In 1870 a new campaign was begun, and outlines of instruction in music throughout the elementary grades appeared in courses of study. But teachers were still inadequately prepared, and only cities under vigorous superintendents were able to show real progress. Hughes in Toronto engaged a supervising teacher to teach pupils and teachers, organized an elaborate program, introduced the tonic sol-fa system, beat down opposition, secured the interest and co-operation of teachers, and was able soon to demonstrate that at least some schools of Canada were not far behind those of other countries in vocal music. School commissioners in Montreal began experimentation with the sol-fa system. Educationists wrote earnestly about the value of school music to refresh the mind, to counteract the hard ambition of commercial society, to stimulate and regulate the emotions, and to prepare for church worship. Skilled teachers spoke and wrote on the teaching of music, but most teachers did little or nothing.

The spread of music throughout the elementary schools was accomplished largely between 1910 and 1930 as a result of more adequate teacher education and summer school instruction in music teaching. Candidates for elementary school teaching were encouraged to acquire skill in music by changes in the regulations: in British Columbia, in 1926, music might be substituted for geometry or for one of the sciences as a subject for normal school entrance; in Ontario, in 1928, music was made an option for ancient history among subjects required for middle school (Grades XI and XII) standing. But in the high schools the appearance and expansion of music dated chiefly from the 1930's. In Ontario the proportion of high schools offering music was negligible in 1936 but over seventy per cent five years later. Instrumental music was also added to singing. In 1950, music was a regular classroom activity for all pupils in kindergarten and the elementary grades, for many throughout the junior high school grades, and for a few pupils in senior high school. Music appreciation gained equally in effectiveness after the 1920's. Graduates of well-staffed schools had a lively and continuing appreciation of good music formerly possessed by very few.

Arts and crafts were taught in the nineteenth century in schools for young ladies and in schools set up as private ventures. One of the latter in Kingston, offered in 1816 drawing of various types — "ornamental, natural history, architecture, landscape, etc." — for an entrance fee of half a dollar and half a dollar per lesson. A lifetime later, in New Brunswick, the Saint John Academy of Art in 1887 advertised instruction in oil and water-color painting, in free-hand and mechanical drawing, and in pottery painting, during the day or evening, and instruction in oil painting by mail. Halfway between the dates of these typical examples of private enterprise, concerted efforts were made by Ryerson and other superintendents to encourage instruction in drawing in the common schools. In Nova Scotia, the *Journal of Education* in 1867 urged teachers to obtain and put to use drawing materials made available by the Council of Public Instruction. It explained the abstract method of learning to draw and then to combine straight and curved lines. This was the ordinary method based on Pestalozzian theory and in accordance also with the contemporary practice of analyzing authoritative forms for synthetic reproduction by the pupil. In the concrete method the teacher was advised to have youngsters make drawings of pictures of objects rather than of the objects themselves, although there was "no harm in having them attempt to draw cats, horses, fowls, dogs," and other animals. Drawing from pictures was represented as easier and more interesting, drawing from memory as difficult but correspondingly valuable as a discipline. To apply these notions, teachers were urged to make constant use of the blackboard for giving instruction and for practice by the pupils.

After 1870, drawing became a regular subject in elementary schools. The *Canada School Journal* reported in 1877 that it had been made compulsory in all schools of Quebec. But on the whole, throughout Canada, it received little attention except in city schools. The instruction there centred in rigid drawing techniques until the end of the century and then turned, under the Froebelian influence, to color painting. Even then, the interest of pupils was limited by the choice of subjects like flowers, which had no appeal for boys, and by insistence on approved techniques, which were even discouraging to many of the girls. But around 1940 such revolutionary changes appeared as encouragement of a free choice of subjects, provision of a variety of solid media in addition to materials for drawing and painting, and the offering of instruction as needed rather than in preparatory courses. When interest had been thus established by expressive and creative activity, it became possible to make appreciation of art a force in living rather than a summary of canons and examples soon to be forgotten from misuse. By 1950 the results were beginning to appear in the better taste displayed in the homes of recent graduates from many schools. By 1950, art was everywhere an activity for all: throughout the elementary grades for all children, usually an option with music in the junior high school grades, and chiefly as a technical school elective in higher grades.

Although craft work became associated with art, similar creative activity developed also from manual training. When first introduced at the beginning of the twentieth century, manual training was often called by its Scandinavian name, "sloyd," since it followed a plan developed in Finland and Sweden by educators who sought to apply the principles of Pestalozzi, and to some extent of Froebel, in the teaching of simple woodwork. Instructors believed that manual training produced intellectual and moral qualities not easily obtained through other studies, that it cultivated habits of industry and self-reliance and encouraged neatness and accuracy in addition to giving manual skill. Typical of the articles made by sloyd pupils was the wooden paper knife with a carved handle. But before being permitted to make any such article, the boy had to master the use of various tools under disciplinary instruction which often destroyed initial interest. Only as the Froebelian influence prevailed over the Pestalozzian, was creative work permitted from an early stage. In spite of efforts to provide woodworking in consolidated and smaller schools, it was still restricted almost entirely to manual training centres in cities and large towns. Elsewhere, paper cutting, cardboard construction, and raffia work served for "hand and eye training."

After about the time of World War I, however, manual training appears to have acquired motivation and new life through a more practical and utilitarian emphasis. This was frankly advocated by Fletcher Peacock, who as director of manual training in New Brunswick after 1911 succeeded in getting many school systems to introduce the work. An illustration in a 1916 circular of the Ontario Department of Education showed a teacher and his pupils engaged in the construction of a small building. The later tendency outside New Brunswick, however, was to regard all hand work in school as an aspect of general education. From the 1930's onward, manual training was broadened into industrial arts conducted in the general shops of larger schools at the junior high school level. Motivation was secured through opportunity for creative construction. In all elementary schools, including the smallest, constructive work incidental to enterprises gave pupils experience in art, crafts, and other work akin to industrial arts.

Homemaking, Health, and Recreation

In the early days, sewing was taught to girls of lower economic status in schools of the charity type. Convent schools for girls sometimes taught other housekeeping skills. To St. John's, Newfoundland, in 1833, at the invitation of the Roman Catholic bishop, there came a community of Presentation Nuns, who set up a school in the back room of a tavern named "The Rising Sun" and there taught young girls of poor families to spin, weave, knit, sew, and cook. But most girls up to the end of the nineteenth century learned to do housework under the mother's direction at home. During the first two or three decades of the twentieth century, household science was formal in nature and was taught in laboratory-like rooms of many graded schools. In the second decade provincial directors of household science were appointed and efforts were made to have the subject taught in rural schools also. From the 1930's onward, up-to-date schools had large rooms divided into areas representing various rooms of a house for practice in homemaking under the guidance of the teacher. In Quebec *écoles ménagères* gave girls in residence a complete preparation for marriage and motherhood through comprehensive experience in homemaking, which included even designing and weaving materials for the model apartment. Elsewhere in the best schools the girls shared in the planning of home economics programs and gained not only skills and knowledge but continuing interest in making home life more pleasant aesthetically and more satisfying in other ways. Like industrial arts, home economics for most of the pupils was offered chiefly in Grades VII to X.

When health teaching began in the last quarter of the nineteenth century,* teachers were instructed not to use textbooks but to give "familiar lectures," to which Ontario pupils in the top grades of the elementary school were to be "made to listen." Hygiene, defined as the science of health, was not only a formal and burdensome subject, but frightening propaganda, taught with little regard for its accuracy and no sensitivity whatever to the effect on the pupil's mind. Even a medical doctor, formerly chairman of the Toronto public school board, stressed the need of teaching that would "aid children in escaping the terrible consequences

* See p. 363.

of habits which to their uninstructed minds appear to be entirely harmless," including "the secret vice of self-abuse," which he said was "sure ultimately to lead to imbecility, if not to dethronement of reason."[21] In the *Educational Review* of New Brunswick in 1888, a reprinted article, "Teaching Gone Mad," cited examination questions like "How can it be proved that nicotine is a poison?" In *The School* in 1910, G. A. Cornish gave an interesting evaluation of the type of teaching which was only then disappearing:

The subject of physiology first found a place in the course of study throughout Canada as a result of the efforts of temperance societies . . . At this stage the effects of alcohol were presented in a grim light, accompanied by charts of diseased stomachs, livers and brains, painted in the most lurid colours. It was considered that these facts would have the same effect on boys tempted to take a first glass as the old-time sermons on hell-fire and brimstone had (or were supposed to have) on a former generation when tempted to do evil . . . Altogether, there was a good deal of downright hypocrisy and dishonesty in the subject as taught. Dry, uninteresting facts, presented in a dogmatic manner, were more liable to irritate than impress the pupil, and, as a total result, the effect morally and intellectually was not wholesome.[22]

Yet the teaching of physiology persisted — in British Columbia until 1920. Five years later that province substituted a prescribed course in health education, including physical exercises previously introduced, and a detailed course in hygiene.

After the 1920's, however, an entirely different approach began to be used. Health was treated as a positive state of well-being, not to be gained by having pupils memorize technical names of the bones of the arms and legs, but to be encouraged by cheerful incidental teaching and fostered also by the whole environment of the school. In the lower

A domestic science class, about 1914

elementary grades children became aware of healthful and less healthful practices in their imaginary trips to other lands. In the secondary schools of Ontario the new point of view was exhibited particularly by teachers who graduated from the course in physical and health education of the University of Toronto. British Columbia in 1950 introduced in junior and senior high schools courses in "Effective Living," which included units on physical fitness, the healthful community, and other aspects of health. The whole program was the very antithesis of nineteenth-century subjects. Comprehensive rather than particular, and related to the daily process of living and not to a formal structure of facts and alleged facts, it was designed to give pupils the help they needed rather than the training that their elders found it satisfying to impose.

Recreational and cultural activities were conducted in exceptional schools before 1850, occasionally in most secondary schools from 1850 to 1900, and increasingly in all schools thereafter. In the early period recitations at public examinations and at close of term were the most usual exercises. Around 1880 outstanding schools provided for a surprising variety of extra-curricular and supplementary activities, as may be seen in Kedy's account of life at Pictou Academy in Nova Scotia. Under A. H. MacKay, who was principal of the school from 1873 to 1879, students were offered, in addition to their academic courses, special classes in elocution, art, and music. There were also various clubs for students such as the Pictou Academic Choral Club, the Entomological Club, the Botanical Club, the Debating Society, and the Typographical Club. Journalism was a student activity of considerable importance. During the session 1881-82 a "Kritosophian Society" was formed in opposition to the Debating Society, and each before long issued a paper. These two societies united in 1883 and in December published *The Pictou Academy Debating Society Gazette*. The Typographical Club issued a bulletin of their own. In 1884, journalistic

A modern home economics room (Westdale Secondary School, Hamilton, Ontario)

efforts were pooled to produce a paper in magazine form called "The Academy." Dr. MacKay was very much interested in the sciences and did much to encourage scientific study and investigation. A Pictou Academy Scientific Association was instituted in 1882, and several scientific organizations were set up later as offshoots of this association. A Pictou Academy School of Music was opened to the public in 1886. Although gymnastics did not form part of the curriculum, the students of Pictou Academy had their own athletic clubs, for playing football, cricket, baseball, and lacrosse.

During the present century, extra-curricular activities became less academic as they were extended in scope to provide opportunities for all pupils in all schools. Theatrical performances of a farcical nature for sheer amusement had been tolerated in aristocratic grammar schools, as in Upper Canada College around 1830; but in later secondary schools, attended by strict middle-class Protestants and controlled by authorities who disapproved of

frivolity, public extra-curricular activities had become more restricted and serious in tone. The later change occurred chiefly after World War I. Dramatic production became a curricular subject in Alberta and an incidental curricular activity in most schools everywhere. Organized sport became a prestige occupation for students and staff and a means of attracting publicity and popular approval. In the second quarter of the twentieth century the distinction between curricular and extra-curricular activities was breaking down, if only because demands on the time of teachers and pupils gave little preference to the former in secondary schools.

Commercial and Technical Subjects

There was always some teaching of bookkeeping. After the introduction of provincial programs of study it was taught in some elementary schools before 1880, to many pupils in higher elementary grades and most pupils in lower secondary grades from then until World War I, and thereafter chiefly to high school pupils taking a commercial option. Other commercial subjects, appearing about 1890, were taught most extensively in Ontario, Quebec, and British Columbia until World War II, when expansion occurred in other provinces. The chief of these subjects were stenography and typewriting, but, especially in comprehensive commercial courses after World War I, many additional subjects appeared, including commercial geography, law, economics, history, banking and correspondence, business forms, office routine, filing, and salesmanship. Enrolment in commercial courses increased rapidly in the 1920's, fell during the depression, and then rose again.

Much research and experimentation has been done in connection with commercial education, not only regarding suitability of subject matter and efficiency of method, but also on the history of commercial education in Canada. From the wealth of information available, here are two or three interesting sidelights on concepts of the cultural and practical values of the study.

A teacher named Thorn who offered his services as a commercial tutor through an advertisement in the *Quebec Gazette* in 1818 described the work as

a delicate and difficult office, and which ought to be sustained either by a man of superior genius or by one who, like himself, has a full initiation into the theory of numbers, added to extensive and varied Counting house Practice.[23]

Bookkeeping was countenanced or supported as a subject of general education value in the nineteenth century. One inspector of schools in British Columbia in 1895 pointed out that bookkeeping afforded the opportunity of "giving instruction in penmanship, spelling, arithmetic and neatness"; a colleague of his felt that bookkeeping should be postponed until

the pupils had acquired these attainments, and that instruction in it should be held out as a reward to those who had proved themselves in this way ready to profit from the privilege. The former, a Froebelian, saw educative value in a practical subject; the latter, with Pestalozzian convictions and Hegelian leanings, thought that educative discipline should precede comprehensive application in practical life.

During the present century, although commercial subjects were represented as part of general education at the secondary school level, reliance was placed on the requirement of academic subjects in addition in order to inculcate cultural values. Events in higher education were more pertinent to the issue involved.

Universities were reluctant to admit the academic respectability of commercial education. The University of Toronto offered a course in commerce in 1901, but for a diploma and not a degree. In 1909 the Department of Commerce and Finance was established in the Faculty of Arts, and a course was instituted leading to the Bachelor of Arts degree. In Montreal the School for Higher Commercial Studies was founded in 1907. Degrees in commerce were first conferred in Quebec. The number of such degrees granted by universities in different parts of Canada shows how commercial studies grew to recognized status:

	1920	1922	1924	1934
Quebec	8	39	40	58
Ontario	—	7	24	88
Maritime Provinces	—	—	2	26
Western Provinces	—	—	9	69
Totals	8	46	75	241

The effect on secondary education of university attitudes and practice in commercial education was slight as compared with the influence of traditional departments in the faculty of arts. Before World War II, only the University of Toronto appears to have defined admission requirements attainable by students pursuing a commercial course in high school. The university courses, although carrying credit towards certification as a chartered accountant, were not vocational at the mundane level of typewriting or stenography. Yet the granting by universities of degrees in a work-a-day field like commerce made it less easy to deny the general educational value of practical subjects in high school even for those who were seeking university entrance.

Drawing, a little carpentry, and other practical skills were taught as technical subjects after 1872 in evening classes maintained with government assistance by the Council of Arts and Manufactures in Quebec. After 1884, technical subjects related to coal-mining were offered in colliery towns of Nova Scotia in evening schools supported by the provincial government. Evening classes in technical subjects organized by the city of Toronto in 1891 were taken over by the school board in 1904. In that year extension classes in technical subjects were offered by Dalhousie and King's universities. Comprehensive programs of technical education were first provided when technical schools were opened in Montreal, Quebec, and Winnipeg in 1911. In Alberta in 1913, when a provincial director of technical education was appointed, a pre-vocational school at Calgary was set up with the aim of developing industrial intelligence and adaptability. Expansion was rapid after the federal government had offered financial assistance to agricultural and technical education.* A few of the many courses offered in larger technical schools of 1950 were: machine shop, sheet metal, woodworking, automobile mechanics, print-

* See pp. 208 and 344.

ing, mechanical drafting, electronics, and plastics in the industrial department; home economics; and commercial art.

The general education value of technical subjects was often limited by the narrow qualifications of some instructors and by mechanical methods of instruction that required only the imitating of a manual operation or the following of step-by-step instructions in job sheets. On the other hand, the director of vocational training in New Brunswick maintained in 1943 that a fatal mistake had been made by vocational educators who did not "dissociate their work clearly from that of general purpose education," with the result that "the old-line school man dominated the situation and the so-called vocational courses became academic."[24] He maintained that vocational education had succeeded only where its dominant aim was openly and frankly to train for profitable employment.

Yet the depression of the 1930's had been a disillusioning experience in provinces where technical schools had been established. Aylesworth says that the Calgary Technical High School, which opened in 1929, had been expected to provide suitable school work for those who found academic subjects too difficult, and by giving vocational training to solve problems of unemployment. Bitter failure in the latter objective caused doubt regarding the former. There was evidence that those who were not good workers in academic subjects were likely to be equally incapable of good work in more practical fields, and there were assertions by many industrial employers that they had to give the same preliminary training to all beginners whether their previous education had been practical or academic. In 1950 no final answer on the purpose and place of technical education had been found. A few believed that practical subjects might be taught in such a way as to motivate school work even for pupils who failed to respond in purely intellectual studies, and to secure the values of liberal education by broadening the content of the subjects themselves to include study of their social significance and related ethical problems. This obviously required teachers of exceptional quality. The ordinary view was that vocational pupils should be required to study certain academic subjects as a cultural supplement. But pupils often showed neither interest nor ability in the latter, and a study made in 1951 in Toronto technical schools indicated that academic subjects accounted for a large proportion of failures and drop-outs.

The Languages

Although the relative importance of classical languages declined as other secondary school subjects increased in number, a larger percentage of young people in eastern Canada were taught Latin between 1900 and 1950 than in the corresponding period a century before. In Grade X in the coastal provinces of Nova Scotia and British Columbia, one-quarter and one-fifth of the pupils respectively were enrolled in Latin in 1948; in the Prairie Provinces from one-sixth to one-seventh; and in Ontario one-half. Ontario's 40,000 students in Latin classes of all grades — almost one-half of the enrolment in academic schools and almost one-third of the enrolment in all secondary schools — must surely have come close to establishing a record in the post-war world. This could not be attributed to any exceptional demand for language study among students, for classical and modern languages were the subjects valued least by high school graduates who replied to the questions of the Canadian Youth Commission. It was the result rather of a continuing operation of forces described in the previous chapter, which in Ontario virtually compelled the election of two foreign languages in Grades

X to XII of the academic program. Enrolment in French in Grade X was twice to four times as high as in Latin in the provinces mentioned, except Ontario. Much smaller numbers were enrolled in German, fewer still in Spanish, and only a few score in Greek and Italian.

As might be expected, the content of the Latin curriculum changed comparatively little. When the Anglican Bishop of Quebec visited Strachan's school in Cornwall in 1809, he found that the boys were deficient in prosody and that the elegant and pleasing ode they had construed abounded in false quantities. Most pupils and many teachers in 1950 would not have been enlightened by this criticism. Though accustomed to drill on the quantities of vowels, and in senior forms to the scansion of difficult metres, they would hardly have ventured to compose Latin, as did the students of scholarly masters of old. But the fashion in authors persisted. At Kingston in 1829, pupils in the three highest grades read Caesar first, then Ovid, and finally Cicero. The four boys in the top grade were reported as able to translate with freedom and fluency and to construe and translate literally — not to mention their study of prosody for a "proper and just pronunciation" and their practice in turning English prose and poetry into Latin "at stated times in the year." In the same year at Berthier Academy in Lower Canada, Caesar, Virgil, and Cicero were read. Ovid, Virgil, and Horace were studied in Pictou Academy in 1857. In Ontario high schools from the 1870's until World War II, Caesar and Virgil held sway for junior matriculation, with reinforcement from Cicero and Horace in the upper school. Then at the junior level there was a reversion to Nepos, Livy, and Ovid, who were favorites of teachers in days of old. A pupil or teacher in New Brunswick had a *Cornelii Nepotis Vitae Excellentium Imperatorum,* published in 1797, with text and translation in parallel columns, the latter offered as an aid to boys not able to read without help. Such aids were not unknown in later days, although the vernacular was printed separately for easier concealment when masters became more strict.

Boys in the early part of the nineteenth century spent most of their time preparing to recite grammar lessons in their beginning years and preparing to construe, or parse, when they read Latin authors later. When they had mastered an assignment, or when called on to perform, they went to the master individually or in small groups to recite. There had been a time when even the explanatory text of the grammar was written in Latin. A transitional text, printed in 1805 and apparently used in New Brunswick, gave explanations, examples, and prose passages, in both Latin and English. Whatever actual composition of Latin prose and verse was accomplished in some early schools, such creative activity was less in evidence later, even in the *collèges classiques*. In English-speaking Canada after 1850 Latin for most pupils consisted of forms to memorize, relationships to perplex, and translations with no real meaning. But the challenge of the new education was met to a degree after World War I by a classical counter-reformation. Alberta in 1924 tried to encourage reading rather than deciphering by the removal of Caesar, Virgil, and Cicero from the curriculum of lower grades, advocated a modified form of the direct method, and added the study of Roman social institutions. The effectiveness of the changes may be judged from Aylesworth's remark that the latter did not appear in examination questions and received corresponding inattention. In most provinces, soon afterward, there were somewhat more successful efforts to restore humanistic value to the study of Latin by illustrated textbooks related to aspects of Roman

life other than Caesar's campaigns in Gaul and by other classroom and after-school activities to arouse and sustain interest. Even so, the study which had once been the hallmark of culture for the few seemed an anomaly in high schools for all.

But entrenched academic authority had saved the classics from persistent attacks in the past. A grammar school trustee of Clinton County, Upper Canada, claimed in 1868 that pupils were forced into classical studies only to earn grants for their school and that "under the like inducements and urgency, they would all study Syrian and Sanskrit."[25] The same complaints were made in Quebec, where it was said in 1879 that "classes of boys and girls, against the openly expressed wish of parents, are dragged by main force through *hic haec hoc* and *amo amas amat* to save appearances and a grant of some $50 from the Superior Education Fund." Educational journals at that time published article after article against compulsory Latin. One answered the mental discipline claim by the argument of the Right Honorable Robert Lowe of England that more difficult languages like Russian or Chinese would serve the purpose better, since the former required a separate grammar for every word and the latter used 30,000 different characters for as many words. A teacher contributor was sure that the classics could not "satisfy the demands of our busy practical times" and an editor was equally positive that the study of Latin could not "among a democratic people retain the prestige it has in older countries."[26] These and all later contentions, classical scholars were able to refute by requiring Latin in high school and so recruiting students for the classics courses in college. University graduates in academic fields not useful for other employment frequently turned to teaching and became staunch advocates of the subjects in which they were trained. The operation of this cycle sustained the teaching of Latin.

French was offered in many private schools and academies and in some grammar schools of English-speaking Canada in the early days. Since ability to speak the second language had a special usefulness in this country, the direct method was used in schools for the upper classes if an accomplished teacher was available. An advertisement of a boarding and day school for young ladies opened by the Misses Brown in Toronto in 1844 announced their intention of having the pupils study the French language "in order that it may be generally spoken in school." But after 1850, when teachers of secondary schools, like most of their pupils, came from a middle-class environment, almost none of them had had the opportunity to acquire fluency in French conversation. Textbooks were of little help. A straightforward little book on *The Elements of French and English Conversation,* published in New York in 1823 and used in Nova Scotia, gave vocabularies followed by sentences in French and in English but no indication of the French pronunciation. Hence the study of French, as the school population expanded, became grammatical and artificial. The proportion of secondary school pupils studying the language increased steadily: in Ontario from 30 per cent in 1860, to 40 per cent in 1880, to 60 per cent in 1900, and, in academic schools, to 80 per cent in 1920, and 90 per cent in 1945. But the achievements were not so definite. From Confederation to World War I, pupils in larger schools under university trained teachers were given strenuous mental exercise and temporary ability to work out accurate translations. But attempts thereafter to introduce direct method teaching were still unsuccessful, and Alberta compromised in 1924 by aiming only at an ability to read and write with facility.

12, 13.]   NASAL VOWEL SOUNDS.   7

3. ð.—Intermediate between u in ‘hum’ and o in ‘sot.’ Best obtained by uttering ó above with mouth slightly more open and tongue slightly less drawn backward.

Ex. : Mort, sotte, encore, robe, Rome, porte, hômme, école.

[ARTIC.—Mouth slightly more open than for ô, tongue less drawn back (§ 6), and less *rounding* (§ 7, 3). *Narrow.*]

NASAL VOWEL SOUNDS.

12. Principles of Formation. 1. In ordinary breathing, the soft palate (terminated by the uvula) hangs loosely down and the breath passes freely through nose or mouth, or through both. 2. In uttering ordinary vowels (as **a, o,** etc.), the soft palate presses backwards and upwards, closing the nose passage entirely. 3. If, however, a vowel is uttered with the soft palate hanging loosely, as in ordinary breathing, the breath escapes through both nose and mouth at once. The resonance of the air in the nose passages gives a new value to the vowel, which is said to be *nasalized* and is called a *nasal* vowel.

NOTE.—The process of nasalization may be well observed before a mirror while uttering the vowel *à* (§8, 1), which, if repeated with the soft palate hanging loosely, gives the corresponding nasal, as in ‘blanc,’ ‘blanche.’ The nasalization may be made more conspicuous by stopping the nostrils.

13.   *ã, ẽ, œ̃, õ.*

1. *ã.*—Is the nasal corresponding to *à* (pas, §8, 1).

Ex. Plan, plante, enfant, danse, an.

2. *ẽ.*—Is the nasal corresponding to *è* (père, §10, 4).

Ex . Fin, prince, pin, lapin, jardin.

3. *œ̃.*—Is the nasal corresponding to *œ* (leur, §10, 5).

Ex. Un, brun, lundi, tribun, commun.

4. *õ.*—Is the nasal corresponding to *ò* (mort, §11, 3).

Ex. On, monde, non, bonté, front.

N.B.—Avoid carefully the final sound of words like English ‘sang,’ ‘long.’

[ARTIC.—Position of tongue, etc., etc., as for *à* (§8, 1), *è* (§10, 4), *œ* (§10, 5), *ò* (§11, 3), respectively. *Soft palate hanging loosely.*]

A page from The High School French Grammar *by Fraser and Squair. This late nineteenth-century textbook was authorized for use in the schools of Ontario and widely used for a long time. Although the first 29 pages gave a very thorough treatment of pronunciation, oral French was neglected in class and attention was concentrated on the following 350 pages of grammatical material.*

The teaching of French, even more than of other subjects, suffered from the imposition of an academic program on small rural schools. In the 1930's at a large convention of teachers in New Brunswick there was debate on whether an attempt should be made to use the French pronunciation of words in classroom instruction. Even in the 1950's French was being taught in a very large number of one-room schools by teachers whose faulty knowledge had been acquired from three years' instruction in schools of the same type. The effect, as observed by Nova

Scotia educators among others, was a farcical transmission of pseudo-French which could hardly escape deterioration in the recurring cycles of inadequate teacher education.

Recent improvement in the teaching of oral French in larger schools was achieved by teachers with a thorough university education in French and in modern methods of instruction. A majority of the highly qualified teachers were women, who could afford to spend some time in the French-speaking environments of Quebec and France. In some classrooms, therefore, the resources of early upper-class schools were restored and improved. One of the difficulties remaining was that most of the pupils had no real occasion during school days or later to speak the French language, so that motivation was

lacking and loss of skill immediate. Moreover, teachers were bothered and pupils confused by the incongruity of direct method instruction and the academic requirement of ability in grammar and translation, which was needed to pass examinations and which was all that most teachers were able to impart.

Language instruction had stronger motivation in French-speaking Canada. The use of Latin by the church imparted a present reality to the traditional study, which suffered no loss of prestige in the *collèges classiques*. Since the position of French is secure, there is now no hesitancy about teaching English as a second language to large numbers of pupils at the upper elementary level as well as in the secondary schools. Ability to speak English has economic value in urban Quebec.

Summary

Thought applied to method has resulted in an amazing improvement in teaching to read. Spelling continued to usurp an inordinate amount of the pupil's time. Other instruction in English until 1875 aimed at imparting formal skills and knowledge of a specialized nature. Only thereafter was a direct effort made to teach young people to express their thoughts and to appreciate literature, and not until recent years was emphasis transferred from oral reading to reading comprehension. Objective methods made arithmetic intelligible to beginners after 1850, and the supplanting of rules by reasoning made the subject an intellectual exercise after 1875. Geography was made a burden by multitudes of facts before 1900 and has not yet been fully revived as a scientific study. History gained additional time at the expense of geography in the last sixty years. Social studies during the last quarter century have been taught in some modern elementary schools and high schools of the west to give an understanding of the world. Science won out against entrenched academic opposition as a high school subject in the last quarter of the nineteenth century and has contributed to the importance of method as compared with content. Although Canada was an agricultural country, little progress was made in the teaching of agriculture until after World War I; then some rural elementary schools were given an agricultural orientation and more recently regional high schools have given a definite place to agricultural subjects. Music, art, and crafts, in which nineteenth-century instruction was restricted and formal, have been taught in the twentieth century for active participation and lively appreciation. Education in homemaking and health has been similarly transformed. Extra-curricular activities have changed with the changes in social environment and high school population. Commercial and technical subjects since World War I have gained an important place in the secondary school curriculum, but there is still dispute about their value and function. Although it is difficult to maintain the traditional importance of foreign languages in secondary schools for all, it is probable that Latin is taught to more pupils in Canada than in other countries. The deficiencies of foreign language instruction given by teachers with little knowledge to pupils with little interest, are more obvious in the teaching of French, although, under fully qualified teachers, students might escape confusion if the objective were defined as either oral or reading or grammatical ability. In French-speaking Canada the teaching of both Latin and English has better motivation.

The above are a few salient facts and implications of facts related to the teaching of particular subjects. The next chapter will attempt to evaluate the results achieved.

CHAPTER 25

Standards and Examinations

This chapter deals with changes in educational standards, real and imaginary, and with the development of the chief instrument of appraisal, written examinations.

STANDARDS

There was never a time when critics did not complain that educational standards had fallen. In Canada the evidence of improvement over any period of fifty years since 1825 is as clear and irrefutable in education as in means of transportation. Yet in 1884 the Bishop of Niagara could look back thirty years and say:

I can testify that the pupils in our common schools of those days could spell, read, write, cipher, and understand geography better than they do now.[1]

In Prince Edward Island fifteen years later a contributor to a periodical gave similar testimony:

I cling to the belief that in some of the best of the old schools the elementary branches of education were taught with greater efficiency than in our better equipped schools of the present day.[2]

Since no one today, regardless of his views on modern education, would deny the advances made in the latter half of the nineteenth century, such utterances must be attributed to nostalgia for the seemingly brighter days of departed youth, to admiration for everything associated with one's success in life, and to continuing faith in forms which a younger generation seemed no longer to respect. We must discount on similar grounds much severe criticism of contemporary schools in all periods.

1800-1850

By any more recent standard, however, education in the first half of the nineteenth century deserved the scathing remarks made by nearly every observer. Most children attended school irregularly for a few short terms in uncomfortable buildings without equipment, and there committed to memory under the compulsion of ignorant, untrained, and inadequately supervised teachers some of the content in such few poor textbooks as their indifferent parents were willing to provide. The minority who fared better was smaller than the minority who fared worse. "An English education is, I have no doubt, superior to anything colonial," wrote Mrs. O'Brien in 1836, and enlightened Canadians had to admit that colonial education could hardly have been more deficient.

In Upper Canada in 1830 the United Presbytery stated that education generally was "in a deplorable condition." Lord Durham reported in 1839:

Nor can even wealthy land-owners prevent their children from growing up ignorant and boorish, and from occupying a far lower mental, moral, and social position than they themselves fill. . . . Even in the most thickly peopled districts there are but few Schools, and those of a very inferior character; while the more remote settlements are almost entirely without any.[3]

In Lower Canada, according to an article in the *Quebec Gazette* in 1819, only one adult in eight could read, and fewer still could write or do arithmetic. In 1831,

when more schools were being established, a member of the legislature said of the teachers receiving government money in his constituency:

Out of twelve there are nine capable of teaching Writing; of the same twelve six are capable of teaching Arithmetic; and of these six only three are capable of teaching more than the first Rules.[4]

As for the Maritime Provinces, G. R. Young represented about half the children as growing up "entirely destitute of education." A report of a committee in New Brunswick in 1844 mentioned a school newly built with a ceiling six feet high, another in a wretched hut with a few stones piled in the corner to form a fireplace, another in the kitchen of the teacher's dwelling, and another with fifteen broken panes of glass in the sashes. Teachers taught what they fancied, parents were apathetic, and pupils used a miscellany of books which together "would present a catalogue of nearly every elemental work published during the last 70 years."* For an inspector's visit in 1845 a teacher selected as a reading lesson the seventh chapter of Revelation, beginning "And after these things I saw four angels standing on the four corners of the earth, holding the four winds of the earth." When asked by the inspector to explain this passage, the teacher was unable to tell the children to whom "I" referred, what John saw, or what the angels were said to be doing.

Many commentators attributed the deficiencies of the schools to "the total indifference which many evince about educating their children," as a letter to the *Acadian Recorder* of Halifax put it in 1821[5]; to the half-educated populace, as MacNeill of Prince Edward Island said in 1841; to toleration of "cheap unqualified

* Warner, J. E. (208) pp 208-210.

teachers," according to a legislative committee witness in Lower Canada in 1831; to the impatience of parents to put their children to work to help them lay up money, according to an interested layman in Upper Canada. The *Kingston Gazette* in that province published in 1810 one of the earliest of many exhortations to parents that they try to improve themselves educationally as a step towards improving their children.

1850-1875

Articles on a related theme appeared in the *Journal of Education* in Lower Canada from 1857, its first year of publication, onward. There were many discussions of ways in which both parents and teachers could work together or, more bluntly, of the duty of parents to support the work of the teacher. When public interest was strengthened by the free school campaigns and reinforced by strong direction from central authorities, the achievement of Canadian schools improved. A definite curriculum was taught by men and women whose average educational and professional qualifications rose steadily though slowly. Supervision was more regular, and textbooks and other equipment were better and more plentiful. Yet the marked improvement during the period left standards still very low. An article in the *Ontario Teacher* in 1873 represented the state of education as "ominous and humiliating" even then:

Take, if you will, any ten young men or women, at random, who have taken a regular and ordinary course at a Public School, and how many of them will you find intelligent, fluent, and correct in reading, speaking, and writing? Not more than one. Hardly that.[6]

He should have conceded, however, that a large majority in the province left school by that time with some mechanical ability in elementary subjects.

In Quebec, conditions were much less satisfactory. Inspectors' reports at the end of the period indicated that only about two out of five pupils could read with tolerable accuracy and fewer still with any fluency. Only $9.50 per annum per pupil in average attendance, was spent on education — about three-quarters of the Ontario expenditure, which was miserly enough. In New Brunswick, typical remarks of inspectors around 1860 indicated that pupils left school with careless habits in reading and with insufficient practice in other basic skills. One report measured the limited improvement by the quality of services obtained at bargain rates:

The teachers, at present, being generally illiterate females, are neither zealous nor attentive; and consequently unimpressed with a sense of the important duties of teaching. The conduct and habits of the teachers, otherwise, may bear a safe comparison with those of former years.[7]

As for Nova Scotia, out of a population of 284,000 persons over five years of age in 1861, 81,000 could not read a printed page and nearly 115,000 could not write their names. The great advances made under free schools, shortly afterward, were needed to overcome gross deficiencies and could not immediately achieve qualitatively higher standards. In Prince Edward Island before the Act of 1877, people showed little or no interest in education, and standards were correspondingly low. The normal school had of necessity to concentrate on the teaching of content because of the ignorance of those who came for teacher training, and the consequent failure to improve methods of instruction made the problem persistent. Teachers in most schools continued to drive their charges through the book at the rate of so many pages a day, with the result that not one pupil in five understood the meaning of what he read. So said a school visitor newly appointed to Prince County in 1874. He described this so-called education as "a delusion, a sham, a perfect absurdity."

1875-1900

Ontario in the last quarter of the nineteenth century showed what could be done by getting every child in school for a few years, by enforcing regulations for minimum efficiency, and by obtaining as teachers docile young men and women who had had at least a bare minimum of secondary education and a little professional training, by prescribing exactly what should be taught and how it should be taught, by having all teachers work under the supervision of men with high professional qualifications, and by subjecting the whole process of education to the pressure of external examinations. Ontario pupils in the elementary schools of 1890 were able to reproduce accurately an exceptionally large number of prescribed facts, to repeat from memory an unusual quantity of approved verbal content in prose and poetry, and to make a good showing in the performance of mechanical skills in spelling, reading, arithmetic, and grammar. Those who survived the grind and the selective examinations and went on to do advanced work under better educated teachers showed equal proficiency in content requiring more intellectual ability, although power to memorize was still the greatest asset. Critics said that in spite of the complacent pride of the provincial department of education, the school system showed a specious efficiency without having solid merit. But the Ontario system was envied and copied by other provinces, especially in the west.

Quebec continued to labor under handicaps. In a panel of seventeen jurors in 1877, according to the Montreal *Star,* only four could write their names. Teaching was regarded by the French-speaking population as a function of the church and by the English-speaking people as the despised occupation of men unfit for success in commerce. Improvements were effected before 1900, but slowly. In the Maritime Provinces educational standards in this period ranked between those of the larger provinces. But the *Educational Review* of New Brunswick found reason for moderate satisfaction when, in 1887, it looked at conditions in Newfoundland. There, in a population numbering less than 200,000, over 50,000 above the age of ten were reported as unable either to read or write. The superintendent of Methodist schools claimed that this estimate was made by counting as literate only those discovered to be so by enumerators and including in the illiterates all others of whom they had no knowledge. But in an ensuing controversy the critics had the stronger case. They claimed that the teachers were so poor and so poorly paid that they could not afford to educate themselves and were therefore without resources to educate children.

1900-1925

A great advance was made before and after the turn of the century. The percentage of illiterates in the population over ten years of age fell throughout Canada from 13.8 per cent in 1891 to 3.4 per cent in 1931, and in Newfoundland to 16.2 per cent in 1921. Other provinces caught up with Ontario. The Montreal *Star* said editorially on St. Patrick's day, 1904:

That educationally the Province of Ontario is not maintaining the relative position it held a generation ago is not only admitted but strongly asserted by many of its prominent educators.

There had probably been no absolute decline of standards within the province. The impression that education was deteriorating was created by more open criticism of the schools, since there was some truth in an allegation of 1905 that those in authority had been accustomed to "beslobber the educational system of Ontario with praise, to regard it as the one perfect thing in an imperfect world," and to treat any criticism as treason. In any case, those who were new-world minded counted as great steps forward the more liberal curriculum of 1904, the spread of Froebelian methods, and the adoption in 1907 of much higher minimum qualifications for teachers. Similar developments occurred elsewhere in Canada.

But those who had a narrow concept of the function of the school intensified their attacks on the newer education during the period of reform. The Toronto *News* from 1900 onward made a practice of canvassing the opinions of business men and publishing the perennial complaints that handwriting was illegible, arithmetic inaccurate, discipline lax, all because the energy of pupils and teachers was dissipated on too many unnecessary subjects. The Victoria *Colonist* discovered similar opinions and attributed them to the same cause:

Business men who employ our graduates tell us that they are sadly lacking in the simplest and most commonplace things, and their knowledge is superficial and inaccurate, and they lack the perseverance which habits of thoroughness would foster.[8]

A few educators seemed to agree. The inspector of schools in Barrie, Ontario, informed an audience in Los Angeles early in the century that letters from teachers in the two countries required "the largest mantle of all sorts of charity" to cover their defects and made him fear sometimes that education had "sacrificed the essentials for the sake of the veneering." Later, when the superior skill of new teachers was utilized to develop the ability of pupils and not to step up pres-

sure on pupils to memorize content, the editor of *The School* in 1912 felt obliged to admit that old-fashioned pedagogues could claim "with some show of reason that we are making education too easy for the child." He admitted also that many people had an erroneous impression that the three R's had been taught more effectively before.

The criticism of education early in the twentieth century demonstrated chiefly that controversy regarding standards is mostly disagreement regarding criteria. One of the critics in the *News* proved unintentionally that educators were foolish to allow schools to be judged by their efficiency in teaching fundamental skills as a preparation for employment and economic advance:

What does a capitalist — and what American does not dream of becoming a capitalist — want with spelling? He can pay for any number of humbler beings to do his spelling for him. No one is going to challenge the spelling of a man who can write out a big cheque.[9]

In the previous year, 1901, when others were denouncing newer subjects as frills, W. S. Ellis, principal of the collegiate institute in Kingston, Ontario, gave a reverse twist to criticism of unnecessary subject matter:

In my opinion the subjects that lead to waste of energy and waste of time in schools are chiefly grammar, especially the endless, tedious analysis and parsing; arithmetic in the unsystematized manner in which the examination requirements compel the teaching of it; history that deals with minute unimportant events, or even with great happenings whose surroundings and importance children cannot understand; the geography which consists of learning of countries and capitals, islands and capes, boundaries and governments; foreign languages as far as the greater part of the alleged prose exercises are concerned.[10]

1925-1950

The point of view expressed by Ellis and its positive corollary established a new criterion of standards in the second quarter of the twentieth century, and especially after 1935. In breadth of knowledge, in variety of skills, in lively interests, and in the proportion of young people educated in such enrichments of life, standards were raised far above any previous level. Such was the judgment of those whose life work had kept them closely in touch with the younger generation from decade to decade. After fifty years experience in the classroom, J. H. Mills, a distinguished Ontario teacher of the classics, declared when he retired in 1939 that boys and girls then did more thinking and showed a wider knowledge and understanding of religion, politics, and world affairs than the young people of half a century before. Statistical and other evidence in every province demonstrated conclusively that from 1935 onward (as compared with 1910 or before) pupils attended school more willingly, more regularly, and longer, under much better qualified teachers. Public education had enlarged its achievements against the handicaps and distractions of war, depression, and commercialized entertainment.

It was not possible, of course, to maintain, for large numbers, the standards formerly set for the few survivors of repeated examinations. High school teachers of academic subjects protested against the lowering of barriers when they were obliged to teach students of ordinary ability. Aylesworth in a master's thesis of 1936 pointed out that although courses in French, Latin, and history had been shortened twelve years before, the high school program of Alberta was still too burdensome and too academic for the average student. The implications of secondary education for all were not merely quantitative:

The social level of our high school population has changed; 67% of the students do not belong to that social class which considers high school and more advanced education a matter of social necessity. Many of our students have neither the native ability, nor the desire to master abstract or academic subjects. There has also been a change in the student attitude towards high school work. The average student sees no adequate reason why he should spend the evening in home study, when such a feast of entertainment has been spread before him, as the picture show, the automobile, the radio, all of which are infinitely more attractive than study after five hours a day of school work.[11]

A visible manifestation of the influence of this new student body on secondary education was the greater amount of time devoted to sports and school entertainments. Yet there was no reason to believe that the percentage of brilliant students dwindled, or that they failed to attain the highest standards of academic proficiency, although some of the bright relapsed into boredom while teachers labored the obvious in their efforts to penetrate non-academic minds.

At mid-century there was some intensification of the usual complaints about the teaching of the three R's in elementary schools. A minor reaction towards emphasis on formal subject matter was made inevitable by the shortage of good teachers and the certification of candidates with inferior educational and professional qualifications and mediocre ability. Trustworthy evidence showed no significant decline or advance in basic skills in spite of the greater proportion of time spent on newer subjects. Whether a return to more time and drill on fundamental subjects would effect sustained improvement was doubtful. Schools competing with television took a risk when they substituted stricter discipline for the keen interest in school engendered by some less apparently useful activities.

EXAMINATIONS

Oral Examinations

Before Confederation, school examinations were conducted orally. They were called private if a class or an individual was examined without fanfare by an inspector or other person with authority, and public if an open invitation was issued to parents and others to attend. Private oral examinations were used also as a basis of awarding licences to teachers and often as a basis of admission to a higher institution. In 1830 entrance to King's College in New Brunswick was obtained by matriculation at a public examination followed by private examination of the individual by the president. Admission to grammar schools in Upper Canada from 1853 to 1873 was secured through a private examination by the principal of the grammar school, who was under pressure to pass all candidates to bolster his school's share of the grants. Reliance was placed on public examinations to demonstrate the efficiency of the school. The unpopular grammar schools were required by law in 1819 in Upper Canada to conduct annual public examinations for this purpose.

Public examinations in important secondary schools were pretentious affairs. John Strachan at Cornwall put on a demonstration lasting up to five hours, invited "all the respectable people within thirty miles," and gave them dinner. When he moved to York, Strachan regularly contrived to have the lieutenant-governor present and took advantage of the opportunity for propaganda by having his student "poet laureate" intermingle, in a rhyming prologue, lofty sentiments, fulsome praise, and a plea for a university. The program and exhibits encountered in public examinations are described in the Newfoundland *Gazette's* account of the examinations in Phillips' School at St. John's in 1809:

The various performances of the pupils in the several branches of useful learning, the uncommon cleanliness of their respective Copy and Arithmetic Books, the admirable execution of their writing specimens; together with a correct recitation of their exercises of Arts and Sciences, Grammar and Arithmetic, as well as the animated and impressive delivery of their various elocutionary exercises, reflected on them the highest credit, and drew from the feelings of the audience repeated effusions of general applause.[12]

Public and private examinations in common schools, when held at all, were simple and sometimes farcical in character. A popular equivalent was the spelling match. Trustees who examined schools preferred, because of their own limitations, to keep to spelling: Newfield cites an occasion in the Red River area when a trustee stumped the class with the word "pekilar" and threatened to dismiss the teacher, who saved the reputation of the school and his own situation by asking to see the word in writing. In schools under Church of England supervision, the clergy made an effort to lend dignity to the occasion. A typical report of the Reverend Cridge on Vancouver Island around 1860 begins: "The sixth annual examination of this school took place 16 July ultimo at which 53 pupils were present:

and 15 boys received prizes, the donation of his Excellency the Governor."[13]

High importance was attached to public examinations in the early days. In 1789 the *Quebec Gazette* reported that the school of the Reverend Mr. Keith was examined by the Bishop of Nova Scotia and that Mr. Jones's school was examined in the presence of a very numerous and respectable assembly of magistrates, of clergy of the Anglican, Presbyterian, and Roman Catholic churches, and of the principal ladies and gentlemen of the city. The pupils of Mr. Jones's school received the "universal applause of the spectators." Among the many subsequent advertisements, one of 1808 announced the yearly literary exercise of the students of the little seminary at Quebec: the examination of classes was to be conducted during the afternoons of Friday and Saturday; a *"plaidoyer,"* or court-room defence oration, was to be presented by students of rhetoric; prizes were to be distributed; and the public was invited. In a report of 1830 the school commissioners of Stanstead were at pains to explain their reasons for not holding a public examination at Merrill's Hill School, which was closed because of the illness of the mistress.

Although peculiarly suited to old-world conditions and temperament, public examinations survived the introduction of written examinations in some places. They were permitted and even required by regulations up to the beginning of the present century. It was a duty of Ontario public school teachers in 1887 to hold quarterly public examinations and to give due notice to trustees, to school visitors, and through pupils to parents and guardians. School law in New Brunswick provided for an examination day to give parents an opportunity to see for themselves what progress their children were making. Professional opinion in the 1880's was opposed to the continuance of the practice as being essentially a show put

on by teachers for the satisfaction of their own vanity. At the turn of the century, however, examination day was still a major event in the schools of Moncton. Robinson described one such event in these words:

The classes were called up. Reviews were conducted in all school subjects: grammar, history, geography, mental arithmetic. Exercises were written on the slates and these passed to admiring parents. Then, of course, there was the spelling match when the excited visitors followed the progress of the contest with bated breath but very thankful the words were being given to the pupils and not to themselves. After this came lessons from the "readers," some recitations, and, perhaps, a few songs or even a dialogue. But an attempt really was made to examine the children in the work of the term.[14]

During the twentieth century, examination days or their equivalent became more and more of an entertainment. When parents attended the schools to see a performance by pupils, the program was usually a play or a concert or a demonstration of physical education. Other successors to the public examinations after World War I were commencement exercises and parents' nights conducted by home and school associations.

Written Examinations

Written examinations were introduced for entrance to university before 1850, for teachers' certificates around 1860, and for pupils within the school systems around 1870. By that last date they were hailed as a great educational invention, equivalent to the free enterprise system in business, stimulating effort and giving driving power to the educational process. A distinguished champion of written examinations was George Paxton Young, a Scotsman, an inspector of grammar schools, a university professor, and in the 1870's chairman of the central committee of examiners in Ontario. Young was largely responsible for the introduction of a system of payment by results, which from 1876 to 1882 in Ontario made financial aid from the province to high schools largely dependent on the number of pupils who passed an intermediate examination after a year or two of attendance. The working of such a system had already been demonstrated in England, where grants had been made dependent on inspectors' examinations fifteen years before. The effect was, of course, to narrow all school effort to the cramming of content most likely to be tested in the subjects prescribed for examination. The system also caused teachers to concentrate on the average and slightly below-average pupils, with whom their efforts would pay dividends through a larger percentage of passes, and to neglect other students — the bright because they would pass anyway, and the dull because they were hopeless or at best a poor risk in terms of expenditure of time. But payment by results undoubtedly did lash both teachers and pupils to work harder at drill and review in order to avoid failure.

As judged by that criterion, the high schools of Ontario improved greatly under the new stimulus. All but a few outstanding exceptions had been in a sorry state in 1872. In that year the smallest were required to employ two teachers of secondary subjects, and the next year all entrants were screened by a uniform written entrance examination. Even so, most of the high schools had little success in getting pupils through the intermediate examination, when it became a basis for payment of grants in 1876. Then, under full pressure of payment by results, teachers and pupils began rapidly to measure up to the requirements. Whereas at the beginning a very few efficient schools earned nearly the whole of the grant, the number of passes achieved by other schools rose so amazingly that the value of a suc-

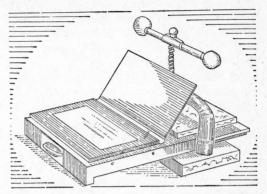

"The Patent Papyrograph", advertised as a device for making 500 or more copies of examination papers, 1877

cessful candidate dropped in two years from $57 to $9. The latter figure was close to the average that would have been earned if all pupils in the province passed.

One reason for this amazing improvement in efficiency was that trustees were aroused from lethargy. When their school failed to earn grants, their immediate response in several places was to blame the senior master and to dismiss him. This happened in Lindsay, where the master, working with only one assistant and with meagre resources grudgingly supplied by the trustees, had a commendable record in graduating fifty-five future members of professions during a five-year period. When he failed in 1879 to attract capable students in competition with schools more adequately staffed, and was unsuccessful in getting any of his pupils through the intermediate examination, the board fired him. Dismissal for the same cause was also the fate of the headmaster of Walkerton High School. He had worked for three years single-handed and for five years with one assistant; during this time he had increased the attendance of pupils from seventeen to nearly one hundred, graduated sixty-nine teachers, four law students, and seven university matriculants, of whom three were awarded scholarships. Yet he too was unfortunate in a single year on the intermediate examinations and for this reason was turned loose by his employers.

No doubt some of the teachers dismissed were lazy or inefficient. But nearly all were shrewd enough to take advantage of every new means that was offered to get results. Teachers' professional journals were filled with sample examination papers, model answers, and advertisements of little books containing notes on various subjects, the memorization of which would ensure success on the examinations. History teaching became the application of a system of mnemonics and the teaching of literature little more. Perth Collegiate Institute offered $10 to every pupil successful on the intermediate examination. The *Canada Educational Monthly* stated editorially in 1881:

As matters now stand, the High School Master who does not deliberately coach his pupils for their examinations, study the peculiarities of the examiners, get up old examination papers, and train for the examinations and the examinations alone, may be an honest man, but he is a Quixotic fool so far as his temporal interests are concerned.[15]

Lists of questions likely to be asked on examinations were openly published and advance copies of actual examination papers were offered for sale confidentially by at least one enterprising individual. He was reported to have done an extensive business in examination papers for Second Class teachers' certificates, the equivalent of the intermediate examination, before being brought to trial in 1881.

Experience with payment by results in Ontario proved that it is possible to raise standards quickly if the criterion is defined as mastery of prescribed content. But there was a storm of protest against the sacrifice of all other educational values for the attainment of this end. In 1883 payment by results was abandoned in the province.

Similar pressure was brought to bear in some other provinces. In British Columbia the superintendent in his report for 1877 warned teachers that failure to get pupils through examinations would be regarded in future as inefficiency in imparting instruction. Rand, as superintendent of education in New Brunswick, introduced in 1879 a system of payment by results under which schools were graded by the percentage of pupils in the various elementary subjects who passed examination by an inspector. The teachers whose schools earned a high rating received a bonus grant.

High School Entrance Examinations

As a rule, pupils were admitted to the secondary schools before 1850 without examination, then by oral and subsequently by written examinations conducted by some secondary schools, then in the last quarter of the nineteenth century by written examinations uniform for a whole province, and increasingly during the present century on the recommendation of the elementary school. The purpose of the written entrance examination was to improve the standard of work in secondary schools by keeping out pupils of mediocre ability. As McLellan said after the introduction in 1873 of a written high school entrance examination in Ontario:

Boys and girls possessing a mere smattering of the elements of a public school education had been allowed to swarm into the High Schools to swell the average attendance, and increase the grant from the public treasury. The consequence was that the character of the public schools was greatly impaired, while many of the high schools, far from doing the work for which they were designed, might be said to have a local habitation and a name, but nothing more.[16]

Examinations near the end of the nineteenth century were highly competitive. In 1876, the first year of the entrance examination in British Columbia, only 68 of 160 candidates passed, although the ratio was very much better in the case of a few good schools. Halifax High School around 1878 conducted an examination on the basis of which scholarships, or free places, were awarded to some 20 pupils from five elementary schools; in that year the qualifying standard was raised from 65 per cent to 75 per cent of the possible marks, presumably to keep the number of entrants down. In Ontario around 1900 less than 60 per cent of the candidates passed the entrance examinations, although only about half of the senior fourth book pupils tried. In Saskatchewan 55 per cent of the candidates passed in 1908, as compared with 80 per cent twenty years later. The pressure of the entrance examination on senior elementary school pupils was greater at first because the examinations were conducted twice a year. This was so in the Northwest Territories until 1899, in Ontario until 1891, and in British Columbia until 1910.

Teachers competed with one another in driving as many pupils as possible through the entrance examination at the earliest possible age. M. W. Althouse, whose son became Chief Director of Education in Ontario, recalled one of his own achievements in the 1880's:

With other foolish young teachers, I plead guilty to getting a little lady into High School a few weeks before she attained her ninth year. *She broke down in health before her third year* in that institution, and never was able to go further in secondary education.[17]

The practice of granting admission to high schools on the basis of recommendation was begun in Ontario in 1904, in Saskatchewan in 1917, in British Columbia in 1918. At first the operation of this plan was carefully restricted; for example, in British Columbia only pupils from elementary schools in larger cities were thus admitted. But the basis of recommendation was broadened, and the percentage of failures among the decreasing number who wrote the entrance examination was also reduced. In Ontario, entrance boards were permitted in 1924 to grant a "dunce's certificate" to pupils who had succeeded in reaching the age of sixteen when they failed the examination. By 1950 virtually all pupils from the elementary schools were accepted by the high schools, a development made inevitable by the extension of the years of compulsory school attendance after World War I. Saskatchewan abolished departmental examinations in Grade VIII in 1932 and Ontario eliminated the last vestige of entrance examinations in 1950. Where schools were reorganized on the 6 - 3 - 3 plan, there was no place for a high school entrance examination.

A brief synopsis of events in New Brunswick will illustrate the usual chronological sequence of changes in high school entrance requirements. In 1861 the superintendent deplored the admissions of pupils with too slender attainments to grammar schools, only three of which had any admission requirements. A later superintendent in 1896 said that the arrangement then of leaving examinations for admission to high schools in the hands of local officials led neither to uniformity nor efficiency. A departmental high school entrance examination was introduced belatedly in the following year. It provided eight tests, each of one hour's duration, in the elementary subjects. In the last year of World War I, pupils with satisfactory standing in Grade VIII were granted their high school entrance if they assisted in farm work at seeding time. In the fall of 1935, regulations permitted the granting of entrance standing to superior students by recommendation. In 1939 the Department of Education abolished the provincial high school entrance examination.

Other High School Examinations

The same movement towards centralization from the time of Confederation to the end of the nineteenth century and towards decentralization or abolition thereafter occurred in connection with numerous other examinations written by high school pupils at various levels. These annual tests included the examinations by which teachers obtained non-professional or academic standing for First, Second, or Third Class certificates. They included also leaving examinations for those who did not complete all years of the high school course and other inventions like the intermediate examination. By the 1890's nearly all of these examinations had been brought under the control of provincial departments of education or at least of some central body that set external examinations for the schools. Even in Newfoundland a council of higher education, appointed in 1893, introduced examinations to be written by pupils in schools of all denominations in each of the Grades from VI to XII. With regular tests also set by teachers during the year, life for the students became just one examination after another. At the normal school in Prince Edward Island in 1875 formal examinations were written six times during the year, so that the school visitor said: "One examination is no sooner over than the preparation for another begins."

Ontario reduced the number and the frequency of examinations in the 1890's, began gradually after 1904 to exempt students in approved high schools from external examinations in certain subjects for teachers' qualifications, and introduced recommendation as a substitute for complete lower school standing in 1923 and for middle school standing in 1932. Manitoba in 1921 discontinued departmental examinations for promotion at the end of Grades IX and X. Saskatchewan in 1934 introduced recommendation in accredited high schools, in place of external examinations, for promotion from Grades XI to XII. Alberta in 1920 experimented with leaving promotion from Grade VIII in the hands of teachers in larger schools, restored the examination in 1924, and again after 1930 reintroduced the privilege of recommendation and gradually extended it to all schools. Newfoundland in 1936 abolished the external examinations for Grades VI and VII and from 1937 to 1940 had external examinations for Grades VIII and XI only. For many years Newfoundland papers were set and examined in England, but from 1931 the Grade XI examination was conducted by the Common Examining Board of the Maritime Provinces and Newfoundland, and other examinations were administered by Newfoundland itself.

University Entrance Examinations

Examinations for university entrance before 1890 had commonly to be written at the university itself and often in the Fall rather than in June. In Upper Canada these examinations clearly revealed the low standards prevailing in secondary schools after children of ordinary people were admitted in the 1850's; and before high pressure was applied to improve efficiency twenty years later. In 1860 there was lively controversy between Egerton Ryerson, superintendent of education, and Daniel Wilson, professor of English and later president of the University of Toronto. In giving evidence before a select committee of the House of Assembly, both admitted that matriculation standards had been lowered. Wilson claimed that the examinations had to be made easy to permit any students from the grammar schools to pass:

In truth, Gentlemen, if our Examinations were to be strict, and *bona fide,* as we had resolved they should, we might just as well have literally nailed up the University door . . .[18]

Ryerson countered by pointing out that the universities of the province had been responsible for the education of a good proportion of the grammar school masters and marvelled that men like Wilson should have the face to make the assertions they did regarding the work of their own graduates. Whatever the cause of low standards, some of the pass matriculation papers suggest that standing could be obtained by a little formal knowledge. Here are the first three of six questions which appeared on the examination in English grammar and composition in 1862.

1. How many genders are recognized in grammar? To which gender do we refer inanimate things?

2. How many cases has an English noun? What is meant by the possessive case? In what variety of ways is the possessive expressed?

3. In what variety of ways may adjectives take the signs of the comparative and superlative? Give instances.

A junior matriculation examination of the University of New Brunswick in English grammar and composition for 1899 shows that higher standards at the end of the nineteenth century meant memorization of a greater bulk of more erudite forms. The paper is almost wholly etymological. Questions asked for the meanings of "beck," "garth," etc., for the Teutonic equivalents of "flower," "purchase," etc., for modern English equivalents of "wanhope," "book-hoard," etc. Other questions revealed plainly that the examiner was interested only in the candidate's ability to reproduce the content of the prescribed textbook. They asked what Meiklejohn was writing about when he cited certain words as examples, for a note on "Latin of the Second Period," and for

such curious facts as why Edward the Confessor was so called.

During the nineteenth century, standards for university entrance were raised quantitatively by an increase in the number of subjects required. An advertisement of the entrance requirements to King's College, Windsor, Nova Scotia, was published in the Quebec *Gazette* for December, 1802:

No Students will be admitted who have not a competent knowledge of the Greek and Latin languages, and it will be required in particular, that they should be able to construe Virgil and Horace, the Gospels in the Greek Testaments, Homer's Iliad, and Xenephon's Cyropaedia, Memorabilia, or some other book of Greek Prose, that they be capable of translating English into Latin, and of making Latin verses.

Though standards may have been high, the area of knowledge was small. In contrast, the requirement for junior matriculation in Ontario in 1915 was a total of twelve papers — two in Latin, two in English, two in History, two in Mathematics, and two in each of any two of Greek, German, French, or Experimental Science. After 1900 there was a tendency to reduce somewhat the number of papers and to allow a somewhat freer choice of options. Ontario in 1922 and British Columbia in 1926 introduced the practice of granting credit for individual subjects as written, instead of requiring a candidate to write a complete set of papers at one time and to obtain a stipulated average on the whole.

In 1953 there were provincial departmental examinations in the last two years of high school only, except that: (1) in Newfoundland, Prince Edward Island, and Nova Scotia such examinations were set and marked by the Atlantic Provinces Examination Board; (2) Ontario had departmental examinations for Grade XIII only; (3) other departmental examinations, not obligatory in all cases, were conducted in Newfoundland (Grade IX), in Prince Edward Island (Grades VIII, X), in Quebec (Roman Catholic Grades VII, IX, X and Protestant Grades VII, IX), Manitoba (Grade IX), Saskatchewan (Grades VIII, IX, X), and Alberta (Grades VII - X); (4) exemption from departmental examination was granted to pupils with good standing in accredited schools in Nova Scotia, Manitoba, Saskatchewan, and British Columbia, although not as formerly in New Brunswick, Ontario, and Alberta; (5) in the last three provinces, nevertheless, local responsibility for examinations giving high school graduation diplomas had been increased in one way or another; and (6) this concise statement is subject to several minor qualifications.* In spite of some apparent reversals in policy, the tendency towards decentralization of examinations is clearly marked.

Examination Standards

Although it is not possible to accept numerical marks as a reliable measure of achievement at different times, consideration of some of the characteristics of earlier examinations will give a sounder basis for judgment. The usual requirement before the end of World War I was a comparatively low passing mark on individual subjects plus a rather high average on all subjects combined. The passing grade on the notorious intermediate examination in Ontario was 20 per cent in each subject and 40 per cent in each of four groups of subjects. Before 1912 the passing grades for junior matriculation in the province were 33-1/3 per cent and 50 per cent, and after 1912 they were 40

* For complete information see Manning, W. G.: *Department of Education Examinations in the Schools of Canadian Provinces*. Unpublished master's thesis, University of Saskatchewan, 1954. Procurable on loan from the Canadian Education Association.

per cent and 60 per cent; more than three-quarters of the candidates were successful in 1904, less than two-thirds in 1913. In Nova Scotia from 1893 to 1906 candidates for Grade XI standing were required to make 25 marks on each paper and were permitted to write six, seven, or eight papers to make up the required minimum total of 400; in 1907 they were required to write English and any other five papers, and to make 30 per cent on the individual papers and 50 per cent on the six papers combined. British Columbia before and after 1900 used 30 per cent and 60 per cent, and then 33-1/3 per cent and 50 per cent respectively as the passing grades. While these dual standards of subject and aggregate percentage marks prevailed, supplemental examinations were provided for partially successful candidates. When credit by subjects was introduced around 1925, the usual passing grade throughout Canada became 50 per cent on any subject.

Tendencies since World War I have been towards the requirement of fewer subjects for examination and towards a higher percentage of passes on all examinations. In British Columbia the number of entrance examination papers was increased from five to nine during the nineteenth century and was reduced again to five in 1922. In Ontario between 1910 and 1950 the proportion of passes rose from 46 per cent to 80 per cent in upper school science, and also rose appreciably in other subjects. From the evidence as a whole one might conclude that, if there was any constancy in the meaning of percentage marks, standards were raised in terms of temporary knowledge and skill but reduced in terms of the native ability required for comprehensive examinations.

Unfortunately, methods of setting and marking examinations were not conducive to consistent results. In the 1880's the Ontario Department of Education and the

University of Toronto were criticized for employing examiners "not sufficiently wise, conscientious, and experienced." Papers touched on only a few points that occurred first to the examiners' minds, or went beyond the prescribed limits of the subjects, or repeated the same questions year after year, or contained errors and ambiguities. Critics said that there were papers so eccentric that a candidate who was expected by his teachers to make eighty per cent would not make five. Even in 1927, Anderson found in Manitoba wide fluctuation in the Grade XI passing standard from year to year and from subject to subject, viz.:[19]

Percentage of Failures

	1924	1925	1926
Literature	14.8	27.4	
History	20.2		37.2
Physics	38.	25.2	

The scientific movement and the study of measurement in the present century called attention forcibly to weaknesses in the validity and reliability of examinations, with the result that much greater care was exercised later in the setting and marking of papers. In most subjects the remaining external examinations for high school leaving or university entrance gave in 1950 a reasonably fair and accurate measure of the pupils' achievement. But as Paton* found, there are still grave discrepancies between marks obtained on external examinations in English literature and ratings by teachers of candidates' appreciation of literature. In several subjects the achievement of new aims such as the development of desirable attitudes, interests, and more general abilities could not be measured, or could not be measured with the same accuracy as could factual recall or specific skills.

* Paton, J. M.: *Examinations in English;* unpublished doctoral thesis, University of Toronto, 1948.

The institution of two levels of matriculation, though of respectable British origin, was used to cover up educational deficiencies in Canada. Before Confederation it was common for students from weaker grammar schools to obtain even junior matriculation standing in preparatory classes of institutions attached to the universities. Later, many high schools were considered capable of preparing for junior matriculation but not senior matriculation. Although Canadian vanity preferred to regard the latter as the equivalent of the first year at college, there was equally good reason for counting it as the last year of secondary education, which small inferior high schools in a sparsely settled country could not adequately provide. In many provinces Grade XI, instead of the standard North American Grade XII, is still represented as the level of ordinary high school graduation. In Ontario between 1875 and 1885 there was agitation to let the high schools do all the work of preparation for university, and there were related proposals to do away with junior matriculation and with Upper Canada College, which was still looked on by some as the only school fully capable of senior secondary work. After 1931 all who entered the University of Toronto had to have honor (or senior) matriculation standing, a step which may be interpreted either as a raising of standards or as a recognition that high schools were more capable of doing senior work.

The regrettable and inconvenient differences in standards throughout Canada were recognized in 1892 by Principal Adams of Bishop's College. He recommended to the Dominion Education Association a common standard of junior matriculation but unwittingly demonstrated the impracticability of his own proposal by stipulating that Greek should be an obligatory subject for admission to faculties of arts. Half a century later, failure of Canadians to agree, as Amer-

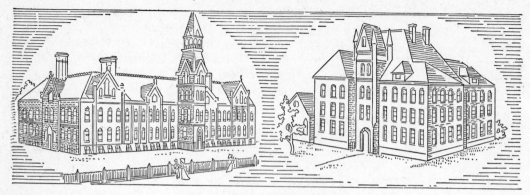

Schools of the 1890's

icans had agreed, on a uniform terminology and grade level for university entrance, caused much inconvenience and confusion.

Limitations of Examinations

To the extent that education was identified with the mastery of formal content, examinations gave a good measure of educational standards. A fairly accurate numerical rating could be assigned to answers according to the number of facts reproduced in approved phraseology or the fidelity with which the recognized steps in a problem were followed. Reliable results could be achieved by tests on the content of books like the *Common School Compendium* of 1885, which gave a large collection of facts stated so concisely that no such imponderables as understanding, imagination, or judgment were called into question. Fairly reliable results were also achieved by listing the questions that might be asked on examinations, as was done when teachers were examined for certificates in Quebec, provided that the answers were taught or provided in textbooks in equally definite form. That the latter precaution at least was taken in the nineteenth century is clear from a study of examination papers. Consider the following questions from

five different papers for First Class licences in New Brunswick in 1894.

Classify the Mental Powers. Give the order of their development. Show what use a knowledge of this is to the educator. (Teaching and School Management).

Specify the various provisions relating to school grounds. (School System)

Enumerate and describe the principle (*sic*) tissues of the body, giving the function of each. (Physiology and Hygiene)

What were (1) the political and (2) the private reasons for the murder of Caesar? (English Literature)

What hurts the brain? (Domestic Economy)

These questions leave no doubt that acceptable answers, and the only acceptable answers, had been reduced to definite form, so that no judgment was called for from either the candidate or the examiners.

Unfortunately, examinations ceased to be an equally accurate measure of achievement when the development of more general powers became the objective of education. In 1912 G. M. Jones sent out to 127 Ontario teachers nine compositions considered of unequal merit, asked the teachers to mark them, and received thirty-five sets of marks. There was a variation of forty per cent in the average total marks of each of the teachers and a variation of from 30 to 100 marks in the grades awarded to the various compositions. During the next two decades educational journals discussed various types of objective tests and the reliability and validity of examinations in various subjects. Alberta teachers in the 1920's were asked by the department of education to use a number of standardized achievement tests. Partly because of the new critical attitude towards examinations, schools from the 1930's onward put an increasing emphasis on evaluation of pupil's day-to-day efforts. At mid-century a considerable minority of teachers were clearly aware of the usefulness of examinations for definite and limited purposes and also of their limitations in evaluating the achievement of broader objectives.

Those who preferred to regard education as a simple process to be measured by mastery of form looked with irritation and impatience at twentieth-century uncertainty regarding examinations. In Newfoundland in 1940, when only forty-six per cent of the pupils passed the Grade XI examinations, the teachers' association demanded and obtained the restoration of a Grade X examination. Prince of Wales College in Prince Edward Island failed fifty-three per cent of the Grade IX candidates for admission during the nine-year period 1929-37, although no alternative educational opportunity for further education was open to rejected candidates. The retention of highly selective examinations at a low grade level in these provinces was clearly regarded as a necessity to maintain educational standards. Yet elsewhere in Canada selective tests had been abandoned in order to raise the educational level of the majority. Long before, Bishop Strachan of Upper Canada had been anxious to make further educational opportunities available to any pupil of outstanding talent, and Bishop Anderson of the Red River area admitted to his collegiate school, without fees, boys of exceptional ability from the parochial school. Any statement regarding the improvement or deterioration of educational standards can be valid only in relation to one of two concepts of the purpose of public education — to select and advance the gifted, or to do the most for all.

In 1884 an Ontario inspector expressed a belief commonly held without question at the time, that "there can be no greater injury done a pupil than to advance him to a class before he has been properly prepared for it." In the application of this principle the casualties on promotion examinations were sometimes incredibly high. The same inspector reported the following results for the town of Morrisburg:[20]

Number of Pupils

On the roll		Writing examinations	Promoted
Book II	61	52	2
Book III	112	101	16
Book IV	35	32	6

Perhaps not wholly disassociated from over-exacting standards were irregularities in the enforcement of admission standards to higher schools. In 1888 the inspector of schools at Gananoque insisted on recruiting students for the newly opened model school there by admitting several candidates who had failed their non-professional examinations. In correspondence with the county board he maintained:

> You would do well to allow me to have my way here, for I can assure you that I know more about *some* things than you do . . . I would dread the anger of Gananoque if we left the school with [only] one teacher-in-training.[21]

Broader Criteria

In his history of Prince Edward Island, Warburton quoted a letter dated 1821:

The children here thrive uncommonly in infancy and in general are as big and stout at twelve months old as those in Scotland at fifteen or sixteen. As their bodies grow faster in youth than there, so the vigour and strength of their minds appear to grow in proportion. I was told by a teacher from Scotland that the children here would learn as much in school in three months as they would do at home in twelve. At the age of ten years they have the freedom of speech, and the fortitude and boldness of a Scottish boy of twenty.[22]

Although these statements must be heavily discounted, they show an awareness more than a century ago that there are more lively criteria of education than the weight of knowledge imparted. It seems unlikely that education in the early part of the nineteenth century could have done much to develop more general powers. As a relevant item of interest, here is an extract from a composition written in the early days and transcribed as accurately as possible from handwriting difficult to decipher:

But to my story, the first I observed of the storm was about 6 oclock a very bright filask apeared in the east but unacompaned with thundre which sup suprised me the more when in a fiew minutes a very bright flash opened to my view the church & yard as plain a day, acompanied by a heavy clap of thunder. This being so with litle wind at the present & the other flach in a different direction shows that the cloud must have traveled at an amasing rate.[23]

The author was head boy at Grantham Academy in 1832, but he may have written the essay at an early age. If that is so, it appears that some progressive teacher encouraged him to give expression to his imagination and judgment before he had mastered essentials. Or perhaps spelling and sentence structure left much to be desired in the days of oral spelling and formal grammar.

When judged by broader criteria the last quarter of the nineteenth century was particularly deficient. The schools crushed most initiative under a heavy burden of curricular content. If the repeated protests of the medical profession had any significance, the pressure was injurious also to both the physical and mental health of pupils and teachers. Much evidence suggests that ordinary standards were low, in spite of the exceptional attainments of a very few. For all the boasted insistence on accuracy, faulty grammar and spelling and the results of careless editing appeared in educational publications far more frequently than now. Much newspaper writing was affected and stilted:

When Mr. Jones falls in love he "becomes a victim to the tender passion;" when he marries he "is united in the holy bonds of matrimony." Mrs. Jones is not now his wife, but "his lady." The worthy couple do not live in rooms in a certain place but they "occupy apartments in a certain locality."[24]

Educators realized the deficiencies of school graduates in language ability and all the more general powers. The superintendent of education in New Brunswick wrote in 1889:

One thing seems to be plain, and that is, that we are not accomplishing all we should accomplish in the direction of providing our pupils with a practical education. In too many cases boys and girls graduate from our advanced and high schools who are unable to grapple with many everyday problems, often unable to express themselves in good English.

There were frequent complaints about "the loose modes of expression prevailing in ordinary conversation, the slip-shod composition of the majority of letters." Yet for all the concentration on basic skills a critic attributed the inability of high school students in English to "an almost total lack of training in elementary and practical branches and an elaborate expansion of the aesthetic and impractical." In spite of the deficiencies of formal

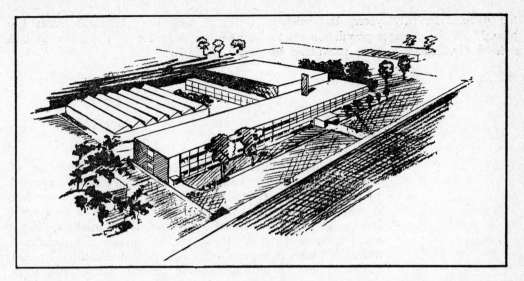

George Harvey Vocational School, York Township, Ontario. An excellent example of modern school architecture (Based on drawing courtesy John B. Parkin Associates, Architects)

schooling in Quebec, the French-speaking members of the legislature seemed to Principal Grant in 1880 to be better educated than the English-speaking members and certainly to be superior in precision and elegance of language.

When the new century opened, instructors at higher levels complained, as they always did and probably always will, that students could neither use nor understand the English language. John Seath said in 1903:

Every now and then University dignitaries say to me: 'What is the matter with the High School? We are all the time getting matriculants ignorant of the elements of English, not to speak of the elements of the languages.'[25]

In spite of the great advance that had been made in fifty years, reading habits and aesthetic tastes near the end of the nineteenth century left much to be desired. Only a small proportion of the people had the education, leisure, and means to read good books. One cannot forebear quoting a few words from a picturesque editorial in the *Canada School Journal* for May, 1884.

The malignity of Satan has never devised anything worse for youth than the Dime Novel, Nickel Library, and the rest of the foul brood . . . a far more awful scourge to our race than leprosy, cholera, and yellow fever combined . . . This Jesse James and Buffalo Bill literature is allowed to cross our lines without objection, although it is destroying our first born and steeping many a home in woe.

In 1893 the *Dominion Illustrated Monthly* published its contribution to perennial complaints on the public preference for trash in reading material. The next year members of the Ontario Educational Association were told that it was not enough to give ninety-five per cent of the population a bare grounding in the three R's and to leave them without an understanding of history or appreciation of literature.

By the change in philosophy and improvements in method already noted, and by strengthening the inner resources of pupils and teachers in ways to be discussed below, the twentieth century set out to raise standards in terms of the broader values of education which previously had been neglected in schools for the people. In fifty years, the schools brought all the younger population up to a level of mediocrity more provoking to those of superior attainments than the former acquiescence of the many in cultural obscurity.

Summary

Perennial complaints about an alleged deterioration of education have never within the past century been supported by objective evidence covering any considerable area or period. A consideration, period by period, of such factors as general knowledge and professional qualifications of teachers, length and regularity of pupils' attendance, and quality of instructional materials makes it impossible to believe that education has not improved steadily by any criterion generally acceptable. Even the percentage of marks required to pass examinations has been raised, although the number of examinations has been reduced. A larger number of candidates attempt the educational hurdles and a higher percentage than formerly pass, so that not even a pedagogical genius could possibly have raised the academic ability of the majority in 1950 to a level displayed by a selected minority in 1900. The reliability of examinations as a measuring instrument was greatly improved as the oral examinations of 1825 were supplanted by the written examinations of 1875. Both the reliability and validity were improved in the present century when more searching criticism led to a humbler attitude in the use of examinations and in the interpretation of examination results. Although no means exists of measuring with precision and irrefutable certainty just what schools in different periods were able to achieve, changes in education were made and practices were retained or discarded in most cases to give a more liberal and effective education to more children. There is abundant evidence to show that by any broader criterion, such as ability to use the native language, the schools did very little for most children until almost the end of the nineteenth century.

CHAPTER 26

Discipline and Ethics

THE ETHICAL AIM · DISCIPLINE BY CORPORAL PUNISHMENT · OTHER FORMS
OF PUNISHMENT · POSITIVE METHODS OF CONTROL · CHARACTER EDUCATION
· PERENNIAL CRITICISM · AN APPRAISAL · SUMMARY

All aspects of education are interrelated. Aims, curriculum, methods, types of discipline, and qualifications of teachers are all affected by one another, and all help to determine the nature and quality of the educational product. But in this chapter attention is focussed on the interaction of two closely related factors — school discipline and education for ethical development.

The Ethical Aim

"The highest aim of education is the formation of character," wrote John Millar in his *School Management* of 1896. Most educators and interested laymen in Canada and elsewhere, before and after, have been in agreement. Sixty-one citizens of Quebec in 1768 introduced their petition for the employment of a schoolmaster by the premise "that as the want of Education is the General Cause of the Depravity of Youth everywhere, it is nowhere more so than in this city." Early in the nineteenth century, patrons of a school in St. John's heard in the prologue to a public examination the function of learning:

She prompts the sacred duties of mankind,
Gives fear to God from whom all blessings
   spring,
To parents reverence — honor to the King;
To laws obedience, Magistrates respect,
Britain's just rights and honor to protect.[1]

The University of New Brunswick, declared Governor Douglas, would serve "to train men to virtuous and well educated, accomplished manhood . . . to enable them to live to an old age with consciences devoid of strain and conduct devoid of censure."[2] The first of nine aims enunciated by the Royal Commission on Education in Ontario for the schools of the province in 1950 was "to develop capacity to apprehend and practise basic virtues." In French-speaking

Canada the emphasis on character education has been even stronger: *l'Enseignement Secondaire* in recent decades published frequent articles under such titles as *Agents de la formation du caractère* and *Pour former des citoyens canadiens français.*

But if there was always agreement regarding the importance of the ethical objective, there was increasing disagreement on the basis of good character and on the type of discipline and education desirable. The old world aimed directly at overt profession of prescribed beliefs, at conformity to an approved pattern of behavior, and at limitation of self-reliance. To ensure acquiescence it found fear of punishment necessary and deemed it proper. The increasing number of exponents of a new-world philosophy aimed less at acceptance of truths than at the pursuit of truth, not so much at obedience as at initiative, not at submission as an inferior person but at growth in power and independence.

The old-world concept was dualistic in keeping spirituality apart from the business of life. A characteristic statement appeared in an article on *Public School Ethics* in 1905:

There is a lack of reverence among your boys and girls. . . . There is a laxity in obeying parents and others placed in authority. . . . Teach a boy to believe in God first and then in himself. Do not reverse this. Self-reliance is a good thing, but reliance in the Supreme Being is better for his spiritual nature.[3]

New-world ethics and education, on the other hand, developed in the nineteenth century in close association with economic, political, and social life. Exponents of the new point of view thought of ethical education in relation to ordinary affairs. Accepting the common assumption that education enabled a young man to succeed, they tried to make school work more conducive to business enterprise.

But being unable to disassociate virtue from any activity, they became later less tolerant of the pursuit of economic gain. J. M. Harper in 1895 classed as a pedagogic fallacy the notion that education should help people make money:

The purpose of a school or even college education is not to enable people to get on in the world but rather to make it a little less important than it is at present whether they get on or not.[4]

After World War I, J. R. Tuck of the Camrose Normal School repudiated preparation for economic competition as an educational aim. He decried encouragement to exploit one's neighbor and the excessive use of a traditional type of literature which glorified fame achieved by individuals in some magical way. School studies, he said, should imbue pupils with a spirit of service.

During the depression of the 1930's, progressive, or child-centred, education became definitely social in its emphasis. As commercial and industrial organizations increased in size, more young people became employees and fewer had use for the qualities needed in a business of their own. After World War II, those associated with successful economic enterprises showed some preference for a return to old-world ethical training in public schools attended by the large numbers who were likely to be employed in routine work. But in spite of confusing shifts in their social backing, the two types of ethical development remained sharply differentiated in educational thought.

Although old-world educators were insistent on specific moral and religious instruction, they assigned to the school only a limited responsibility for character formation. But early nineteenth-century exponents of the new education, like David Paige and Horace Mann in the United States and Robert Owen in England, had the utmost confidence in the power of education to promote virtue and cause evil to wither away. Ryerson claimed in 1858 that scarcely one of the many delinquents who passed through the courts was or ever had been a regular pupil of the schools. Fifteen years later the inspector of schools in Hamilton, Ontario, declared:

Let me repeat once more that school houses are cheaper than jails — teachers than officers of justice; moreover they stand towards each other in an inverse ratio. . . . The education of the masses, in connection with the moral and religious training of youth, constitutes the only efficient means of drying up the sources of crime.[5]

The minister of education in the province in 1881 stated that morality as taught in the schools made it seven times less likely that the educated would reach prison than the illiterate. But Goldwin Smith in 1873 warned teachers that "it is only to a very limited extent that the school can be expected to contend against the general bent and bias of society."[6]

In the twentieth century, educators of the new persuasion sought to overcome this difficulty by bringing education into closer harmony with ordinary life, not only to increase the effectiveness of the school but also to influence the "bent and bias of society." Their opponents continued to believe that the school should play only a supporting role to the church and home in teaching the ethics of social stability.

Discipline by Corporal Punishment

In the social environment of the early nineteenth century it was inevitable that discipline by punishment, which included corporal punishment, should be almost universally practised and approved. As Johnson says in his study of school discipline in Canada:

To a large extent, it has been the social and religious views of the time which have helped to determine the nature of school discipline . . . Under theological auspices the doctrine of original sin cast over childhood and the schools a shadow not to be dispelled until this century.[7]

The prevailing educational belief was that punishment and fear of punishment could eliminate the child's will as a factor in education, and that the exaction of obedience to the direction of others caused children to be "trained up in the way they should go, so that when they are old they shall not depart from it."[8]

To demonstrate even the superficial and immediate working of this premise, teachers had to resort to drastic measures. Pupils could be made to memorize and recite meaningless words and to acknowledge unintelligible but obviously repressive concepts of right and wrong only if the alternative was sure to be more unpleasant. Presbyterian children, who were flogged if they failed to master the Shorter Catechism, are said to have envied their friends in other denominations who escaped this curricular enrichment of lash or toil. But even the common burdens of secular content shared by all pupils were so repulsive to eager young minds, and most teachers were so lacking in understanding and skill, that credence may be placed in the following reconstruction, made in 1880, of schools a generation or two before:

Let us not forget to throw in the appropriate accompaniments around the various figures — the old, defaced armchair from whose upright post hangs the ominous walking-stick, or cat-o'-nine-tails — the ever-ready ferule on the writing table — the mysterious, carefully locked desk, from which comes out, on the great occasions when revolt or insurrection threatens, the murderous rawhide, and which childish curiosity and terror have made the dread abode of a thousand other untold horrors — the old pine desks ranged around the wall, bespattered with the ink, stained

Old-fashioned discipline

with the tears, and curiously carved with the jack-knives of youthful genius — here, in one corner, an urchin half-dead with no groundless terror, blubbering over his blotted copy-book — there, in another, a trembling, cowering culprit awaiting the swift-coming vengeance for some morning misdemeanour — yonder, a third, in dire disgrace, conspicuously perched upon table or bench, with one foot in his hand, a stick in his mouth, and the terrible dunce's cap on his head; while through the crevices of dust and cobweb which line the seven-by-nine window-pane, may be seen a fourth, ploughing his way through wintry drifts to the nearest grove, to replenish the master's armory and prepare, for aught he knows, a rod for his own back.[9]

There is little if any exaggeration in this. The birch or blue-beech rod, the round ruler called a ferule, and the rawhide strap called the taws were standard educational aids. An old-time Niagara teacher hit a pupil over the head with a ferule, knocked him senseless, and revived him in a snow bank. In his grammar school at Brockville, the Reverend Rossington Elms used the rod without stint if the boys neglected to learn their lessons. At Scarboro, Upper Canada, an ingenious teacher suspended a culprit from the ceiling by a thumb in a way that forced him to keep an uncomfortable balance with one foot touching the floor. Teachers who were hard and callous usually succeeded in reducing children to subservience and in so attaining one of the major objectives in character education for the many. Pupils occasionally rebelled. Percival observed that it was no unknown occurrence in Lower Canada for a teacher to be tossed out through a window. Hughes said that in some schools of Upper Canada when a pupil escaped punishment by dodging the master, his fellow pupils would stand up and cheer him on. Perhaps rebellion gave education for leadership. Teachers who lacked stern qualities were unable to keep order and had to give up. The school visitor in Stanstead County, Lower Canada, reported in 1830:

About the first of Janry our first Teacher abandoned this School in despair of Being able to Govern it. When it was resumed by Mr. Lampshire who also chose to loose his time and abandon it.[10]

Objections to corporal punishment began to come from parents as soon as they themselves had any experience of a more generous and kindly way of life. On their behalf a contributor to the *Acadian Magazine* protested even in 1826 against cruel and unjust masters like a crabbed old clergyman who displayed his arrogance and vanity in stupid jokes at which the terrified pupils were obliged to laugh. Before 1850 enlightened educators like John MacNeill of Prince Edward Island saw that corporal punishment was a cloak for educational deficiency:

The most incompetent teachers are those who punish their Scholars the most. . . . I find those schools to be best conducted where the discipline is mild, but decisive and firm.

John Ross, another discerning inspector of the province, saw the effect of harsh discipline on character:

No punishment should be retributive, or vindictive, or have a tendency to degrade or render the child ridiculous or contemptible in the eyes of his schoolmates, as it often induces recklessness and renewal of the crime by way of retaliation.

In the New Brunswick Regulations for 1863 teachers were enjoined "to exercise such discipline as would be pursued by a judicious parent in his family"; thirty years later the model parent was described as kind no less than firm, and teachers were warned to avoid even the appearance of indiscretion in the corporal punishment of pupils. Central authorities in all provinces issued similar regulations in the last half of the nineteenth century and recommended mildness rather than severity. Before 1880 corporal punishment was condemned in most educational literature. A Toronto principal wrote that it failed in its purpose and degraded the teacher. The superintendent of education in New Brunswick issued in 1877 a circular filled with adverse opinions of educators who were opposed to corporal punishment and who would tolerate its use only as a last resort.

Yet the use of corporal punishment and related practices of an objectionable nature were never entirely eliminated. In 1868 in Nova Scotia there was a complaint against a woman teacher who pulled the ears of pupils severely, whacked them with a ferule, smote them on both sides of the head with a book, and kept them constantly on edge with threats of worse to come. In Halifax in 1878 a teacher was charged with assault and fined, although the board paid the fine. In Ontario a few years later a pupil died as the result of corporal punishment. In Quebec City around 1880 a school principal used to stand at the school door and apply the taws on the legs of the boys. Although he felt privileged to delay the opening of school until he had finished shopping in the morning, he whipped the boys when they came late. The principal of the high school in Victoria, British Columbia, was dismissed in 1899 for punishing a boy too severely. When Ontario in 1884 issued instructions to inspectors to impress on teachers and school boards that the better a teacher's qualifications, the less often would he have to resort to punishment, teachers objected, saying that parents and administrators were not required, as they were, to keep order in large classes with obstreperous boys who had never learned to respond to any treatment except a blow.

In the old days it had been recognized as a duty of parents to support the teacher and not to side with their children against them. But later in the nineteenth century, court decisions usually went against the teacher when injury occurred as a result of corporal punishment in school. In the twentieth century however, the courts nearly always supported the

Punishment by use of the strap, 1870

teacher, probably because the infliction of corporal punishment was much less frequent and was unlikely to be used by well-qualified teachers without exceptional justification.

This reduction in the incidence of corporal punishment became clearly marked around 1900, and thereafter the trend continued. Hughes said in 1905 that there was not one blow "for every hundred in the corresponding number of classes thirty years ago."[11] In Toronto in 1933 about eleven per cent of the principals and thirty-eight per cent of the teachers had found no occasion to use corporal punishment during the year. In Ottawa, before World War I, about three pupils per school per day received the strap, whereas on the eve of World War II the number had dropped to one per day although the schools were considerably larger. Johnson found in 1950 that the strap was still used occasionally by most school principals in British Columbia. At that time, according to the Canadian Institute of Public Opinion, about three in five of the adult population in Ontario

approved of teachers' being allowed to administer such punishment, but that less than half as many approved in Quebec.

Nevertheless there were twentieth-century champions of the old-world point of view. In 1905 the principal of Parkdale Collegiate Institute stated with some measure of pride that corporal punishment was still used in lower high school forms. He said that he had boys who begged him to whip them — rather than suspend them. His remarks to an interviewer revealed the attitudes of an earlier generation:

We are feeding boys on sugar and water and do not give them enough of the rough side. . . . We are raising a lot of silly fish. . . . Chicago is another city of that kind and we are introducing into the city a lot of American twaddle.[12]

He admitted however that his school did not whip girls but simply sent them home. Even after World War II an exceptional principal of an elementary school in a less desirable neighborhood of Toronto made the corridors ring five or ten times a day with the shrieks of his victims. A vocational school teacher of the city in 1953 used the strap when work was not completed after a scheduled number of warnings and claimed, perhaps with reason, that many pupils had been trained at home to respond only to violent treatment.

Other Forms of Punishment

In the period 1850 to 1900 punishment continued to be the chief means of control, but ridicule, reprimand, impositions, detentions, isolations, deprival of privileges, and suspension were used as substitutes for the rod. Although the chief reason was a change of social attitudes, a contributory factor was an increase in the number of women teachers. They constituted only a small minority before 1850 but outnumbered men in New Brunswick before 1860 and in other provinces ten or fifteen years later. When women teachers in Ontario early in the twentieth century were almost three times as numerous as men teachers, newspaper editors and others commented on the deleterious effect of this female predominance on character education.

According to Johnson, shame and ridicule were approved as more humane than corporal punishment when introduced in monitorial schools and were commonly used until about 1880. The imposition of "double tasks" was used without misgiving by excellent teachers like Strachan early in the nineteenth century. Teachers continued to impose additional school work and the writing of lines as penalties until after World War I, but the manual on *School Management* published by the Ontario Department of Education in 1927 condemned the practice as causing pupils to dislike school work. Detentions survived even longer but became less frequent in the second quarter of the twentieth century. Reprimands were regarded as a reasonable and unobjectionable

means of control by most teachers in the nineteenth century, although Forrester insisted that any reproof of individual pupils should be private, and Calkin went on to say that reproofs in class should be directed against the fault and not against the offender. Reprimands were generally disapproved early in the twentieth century as ineffective and injudicious, since they made for bad pupil-teacher relations, caused a dislike of school, and so led to further disciplinary problems without having the advantage even of checking immediate disorder. Authority to expel was conferred on school boards by legislation in Upper Canada in 1844. The threat of expulsion was made to loom large in the regulations, and doubtless in the minds of pupils. A report of 1860 on the schools of Vancouver Island mentioned that a pupil was expelled for immoral conduct. Temporary suspension by the principal was generally approved after 1850 as more desirable than mere chastisement.

The latter half of the nineteenth century was characterized by a new spirit of kindness in school discipline but also by caution in its application. The general regulations in Upper Canada in 1855 made it the duty of teachers to treat pupils "with kindness combined with firmness, and to aim at governing them by their affection and reason, rather than by harshness and severity." The statement of an inspector in Upper Canada in 1866 gives a clear impression of the classroom atmosphere considered desirable:

Good discipline implies order, punctuality, silence, cheerful obedience, respectful attention, and steady patient working.

There was some concern in Canada about making "the punishment fit the crime"; Forrester urged that corrective measures be adapted to the nature of the offence and also to the character of the offender. A curiosity from the adolescent age of science was a suggestion in Bain's

Education as a Science, which was published in Toronto in 1879:

It is in graduated artificial inflictions, operating directly on the nerves, by means of electricity, that we may look for the physical punishments of the future that are to displace floggings and muscular torture.

Before 1900, regulations showed a clear intention to protect children from recognizable harm, but not to permit them to escape punishment. Regulations in the Northwest Territories of 1889 made it the duty of the teacher to punish children for misbehavior, non-attendance, and disobedience, but "in such manner as trustees may permit or direct." Calkin echoed the widely used admonition: "The teacher should aim at such discipline in his school as would be exercised by a kind and judicious parent over his children." He admitted the need for punishment on occasion, but not the "rigorous forms of punishment which characterized the sterner ages of the past."[13] The practice of teachers faced with immediate difficulties in the classroom did not keep up with the attitudes and ideas of educational authorities. Teachers were driven to use the newer punishments more frequently and injudiciously, and corporal punishment less rarely, than the professional books advised.

Since many teachers in 1875 were young, poorly trained and limited in ability, discipline was often lacking entirely. One inspector of Prince Edward Island gave the following as a true picture of the manner in which some teachers attempted to maintain order:

We must have less noise, scholars. You are the worst set of children I ever saw. Sit down, Mary. John, didn't I tell you not to whisper. Susan, what are you doing? Sarah, I've told you twenty times that you must not look out of the window, and you don't mind one word I say. Peter, didn't I tell you I should punish you if you did that again? You'll get it by and by. Thomas, what are you out of your seat for? If you do not mind better I shall punish you.[14]

These fussy, petulant orders, said the inspector, fell on the ears of heedless incorrigibles as idly as the sound of the wind; the disorder and disobedience continued unabated, and the louder and oftener the orders were issued or repeated, the more ineffectual they became.

In the present century confidence in all forms of punishment began gradually to weaken. In 1929 J. G. Althouse, subsequently Dean of the Ontario College of Education and Chief Director of Education in Ontario, questioned the value of the general detention room, which he said seemed likely "to follow the dunce's cap and the taws into the limbo of obsolete machinery of discipline."[15] Two types of punishment escaped censure even by mental hygienists — deprivation of privileges and isolation. The former was used as a major punishment in the Toronto Model School in the 1880's. The latter was generally approved by education authorities, including the Roman Catholic committee in Quebec, with the proviso, of course, that extreme measures should be avoided. Johnson found, however, that isolation was seldom used in school discipline. By 1950, capable teachers made only infrequent use of any type of punishment, and some had abandoned the use of punishment entirely.

By the same token, faith in rules and prohibitions was undermined in the twentieth century. Except in monitorial schools moderation was shown in drawing up rules during the first half of the nineteenth century. The London District trustees of Upper Canada contented themselves with three rules and regulations in 1834:

1. Punctuality, regularity, and strict attention to studies are enforced.
2. No talking, laughing, whispering, or leaving of seats is allowed.
3. Hours of school from 9 a.m. to 4 p.m. with an hour's intermission at noon.[16]

Between 1850 and 1890, however, education authorities showed a naïve faith in the value of formulating multitudinous duties of pupils. It would appear from the publications of departments of education in Ontario and New Brunswick that the two provinces were engaged in a rule-making contest. Ontario arrived at a total of thirteen in 1878 and seventeen in 1891. The first of the thirteen in the former year covered considerable ground:

Pupils must come to school clean and neat in their persons and clothes. They must avoid idleness, profanity, falsehood, and deceit, quarrelling and fighting, cruelty to dumb animals; be kind and courteous to each other, obedient to their instructors, diligent in their studies, and conform to the rules of their school.[17]

In 1892, however, New Brunswick simplified its rules, and four years later Ontario went even further and cut the list to only three. In the twentieth century the Roman Catholic committee in Quebec stated the principle that rules should be well defined and not overloaded. In recent decades it has been held that rules should be few, general, formulated in collaboration with pupils, and strictly enforced. But it is no longer considered desirable to have precise rules such as those which formerly required immobility and silence. Even before 1900 some teachers questioned the value of keeping pupils quiet at all times, and a generation later the director of Protestant education in Quebec expressed definite disapproval of demands that pupils remain still for lengthy periods. For the new education something more flexible than rules was needed to give direction.

Positive Methods of Control

From the introduction of the monitorial system early in the nineteenth century there was a development of positive means of control, sometimes defined as preventive discipline. The chief of these in the early days was the use of prizes and awards which, as we saw, were subsequently condemned. Bain saw the futility of promising rewards which had no immediate meaning to the young:

To talk to them about riches, honors, and a good conscience is in vain. A half-holiday is more to them than the prospect of becoming head of a business.[18]

A much more effective method, recommended by virtually every nineteenth-century educator from Lancaster to Herbart, was simply to keep pupils busy. New Brunswick in 1863 made it the duty of the teacher "to afford full employment to each scholar during the school hours, and so vary the exercises and tasks as to sustain the attention." Other positive means of maintaining good order were stressed by Forrester, who recommended that the teacher establish his position of control in the school in nine ways: by making a good impression at the outset, by thorough organization, by vigilant supervision, by having a short code of regulations, by careful registration of progress and of conduct, by making love a force for order, by securing the sympathy of the school, by awakening public interest, and by setting a good example.

A revolutionary advance in positive methods of control came with the belated recognition that pupils were living human beings with thoughts and feelings of their own. Canadian educators, influenced by Rousseau, Pestalozzi, and Froebel, were at least verbally aware of the child as the forgotten factor in education. But up to the 1870's more sympathy for children in school was shown by the medical profession than by teachers or educational administrators. In the British Columbia regulations of 1879 the one duty of the teacher that seemed to be based on consideration of the pupils was that

Concentrated attention in junior grade, around 1950

no one should be admitted, after having contracted a communicable disease, without a certificate from a doctor. The regulations in Ontario for the previous year did require assistant teachers "to render study pleasant" by introducing variety, but went no further. The new point of view was shown in the Ontario regulations of 1901, which made it a duty of teachers:

> To give assiduous attention to the health and comfort of the pupils, to the cleanliness, temperature, and ventilation of the school room . . . and to report . . . any infectious or contagious disease in the school, or the unsanitary conditions of outhouses and surroundings.

In his work on *School Management* published a few years before, Millar had emphasized the need of attractive school surroundings and attention to the physical comfort of pupils. A clause in the School Law of New Brunswick in 1922 that teachers should have a care to the health and comfort of the pupils in school could hardly have provoked comment then, but it would have been startling fifty years before.

After about 1890, advanced thinkers considered more than these bodily needs of pupils. That year James L. Hughes of Toronto wrote a *Personal Letter to a Young Teacher,* in which he insisted that "the child is the power; knowledge is not power." Although he had no patience with lack of definite control by the teacher, or anything less than precise obedience in the pupil, Hughes urged his teacher never to be satisfied "so long as one of your pupils has to be restrained by any external coercive agency." By the 1920's the new point of view had developed to the point where there was official recognition of the possibility of limited student government. The Quebec Catholic School Regulations of 1926 recommended student government to develop a sense of collective responsibility and to make external control by the teacher less necessary. From the 1930's onward, at least some measure of student government was the approved practice in secondary schools of all provinces. Typical of new concepts related to child-centred control was a statement in the *Journal of Education,* Nova Scotia, in 1933 that laziness was "the inevitable reaction to tasks imposed by another will." Enterprise was seen as a means of reducing problems of discipline, since children engaged in strongly motivated group activities were unlikely to cause or tolerate disturbing interference. In September, 1942, *The School* published an issue with articles on discipline by educators from Montreal to Saskatoon: all recommended in one way or another consideration of the pupils' problems and development through experience of self-direction and responsibility. At mid-century there was increasing concern about negative attitudes of pupils towards school — with the thought not of making school work easier but of strengthening earnestness of purpose in pursuit of educational goals. A report of the Canadian Research Committee on Practical Education indicated that drop-outs from school occurred more often because of such negative attitudes than from any other single cause. By the date of the publication of the report in 1950, industry and business had begun to show a lead in improving personal relations with and among employees. At least a few educators were interested in the potentialities of similar measures in education.

Associated with this later approach to discipline was the mental health movement. Soon after World War I the National Committee for Mental Hygiene engaged in activities for the improvement of teacher-pupil relations. Around 1935, prominent members urged a review of teacher-training programs to see what could be done to get teachers to take more interest in children as individual people. Thereafter larger school systems gave increasing attention to children's problems through an extension of vocational guidance, through the appointment of school psychologists, and through the establish-

ment of child guidance clinics. In 1948 the National Committee for School Health Research published a booklet of case studies to illustrate mental health procedures in dealing with problems of individual pupils. Far from attempting to suppress objectionable behavior by punishment, the method of mental health was to seek the cause of such behavior in the maladjustment, insecurity, fears, and other afflictions of problem pupils. But since mental hygienists were opposed to strong emphasis in school on subject matter, on competition, on examinations, on burdensome work, and on authoritative pronouncements by the teacher, the new movement encountered strong opposition.

Character Education

CLOSE SUPERVISION

In character education the early nineteenth century relied heavily on close supervision even at the higher educational level. At King's College, New Brunswick, in 1830 it was intended that all students should have a tutor, who would

assist and direct the private studies of their pupils, inspect their religious and moral conduct, control their expenses, and regulate those parts of their education and behaviour which are not within the province of the Professors.[19]

There were strict instructions regarding conduct and compulsory attendance at church and chapel, and rules against visiting any place of amusement without special permission. Obviously this reliance on supervision was based on an assumption that observation or violation of a rule was of more importance than the development of ability to make moral decisions, or that the establishment of habit was more likely to lead to acceptable conduct than instruction or educative experience. Regulations continued in later years to be particularly stringent in controlling the conduct of teachers-in-training. Ontario regulations in 1878 required students in normal schools "to lead orderly and regular lives, to be in their respective lodgings every night before half past nine o'clock, and to attend their respective places of worship with strict regularity." A new normal school built that year in Truro, Nova Scotia, had doors "near each end of the main building, one in the front, and one in the rear, for the students, male students entering at one end and female at the other."[20] The west was no more liberal, for in Manitoba, in 1882, teachers in training were required to place themselves under the care of a clergyman in the city and to live only in approved boarding houses. At the Toronto Normal School in 1884 there were rules "enforcing the avoidance of all personal intercourse even after the hours spent in receiving instruction."[21] Nothing could be more indicative of the type of character training pupils in the schools were likely to receive nor of the degree of confidence older school pupils were likely to place in their teachers' views on human behavior.

It is a reasonable surmise that the retention of close supervision of teachers in training in the twentieth century had unfortunate consequences in urban schools. Such regulation was undoubtedly necessary to reassure parents of young women in the rural areas from which a large proportion of the candidates for teaching were drawn. In Nova Scotia in 1950 rural opposition to placing a normal school in the city of Halifax expressed the same fear of moral corruption as it had almost a century before. But when teachers of rural origin and restricted training took positions in city schools, their attitudes must have seemed strange and unrealistic to some of the younger generation of urban outlook. Only in the second quarter of the present century, as a rule, did

teachers of rural origin living in the city acquire to a notable extent the characteristics regarded as human by city people. Not only in education but in other social services the dominance of rural attitudes proved an obstacle to communication. Much of the hypocrisy which distinguished middle-aged people from younger people in 1950 may have stemmed from early conclusions that the ethics exemplified and expounded by teachers had nothing to do with life.

FORMAL INSTRUCTION

As a supplement to close supervision, or to intimidation at a lower social level, reliance was placed also on formal instruction as a means of influencing behavior. Most of this instruction was religious verbalism. Durham reported that teachers in Lower Canada in the 1830's were unable to do more than teach children to say the catechism by rote, and that when children held a book in their hands their reading was no more than a repetition of words they had committed to memory. In English-speaking Canada, children read moral tales and expositions of morality in their textbooks and copied moral precepts as writing exercises. But not until after Confederation, when some efficiency in teaching had been achieved, were all-out attempts made to control conduct by organized courses of instruction.

Egerton Ryerson was responsible for a major effort of the kind. Having given approval for many years to weekly lessons in school on Christian conduct, he wrote a textbook entitled *First Lessons in Christian Morals*. In view of his position as superintendent of education, it is not surprising that the textbook was authorized by the Council of Public Instruction in Ontario. Nor is it surprising, after an examination of the contents of the volume, that the textbook was withdrawn and the course in Christian morals dropped from the program of studies after a short trial in the 1870's. Here is an extract from the fifth lesson, dealing with duties of children to their parents:

22. *What do you understand by this duty to your Parents?* I understand three things. First — I am to love my parents, as those to whom I am more indebted than to any other human beings; to whom I owe my existence, who fed me, clothed me, cared for me day and night when I could not talk, or walk, or help myself; who have often denied themselves of rest, and labored much that they might provide for me and educate me. Secondly — I am to obey my parents; that is, I am to do promptly and willingly whatever they direct me, without asking the why or wherefore of the command. Thirdly — I am to honor, or reverence my parents, which includes not only love and obedience, but that respect and deference which are due to those who are superior in age and wisdom, as well as in authority, and which I owe to my parents more than to any other persons.

23. *Do the Scriptures pronounce any punishment upon undutiful children?* Yes; the punishment of death was commanded by God, under the Jewish law.

As if these required responses of the child were not enough, Ryerson adds a footnote to the effect that "the experience of all ages and countries testifies the fact that disobedience to parents in youth is followed by disgrace and misfortune in manhood and old age," and supplements this observation with a further two pages of notes on filial obligations.

PROMOTION OF SPECIAL CAUSES

When compulsory attendance laws made the public schools the one sure means of reaching everyone, willing or not, zealots in every cause saw their opportunity. The temperance forces were quick to advocate a new course for the school curriculum. Some of their efforts were local. In Kingston, Ontario, in 1885 they exerted pressure on the board of education to introduce the teaching of temperance in the schools. The wily trustees left the matter as unfinished business for the next year's board, which managed in turn to evade the issue. But in 1887 the Women's Christian Temperance Union got permission to give temperance lessons once a week in one school, and later in the same year the board of education instructed all teachers to give weekly lectures to pupils on the subject. Shortly afterward, temperance was linked with hygiene in courses of instruction prescribed by provinces. In 1892 Mrs. J. P. Noyes of Cowansville, Quebec, carried the message to top education officials throughout Canada at the convention of the Dominion Education Association. She insisted that "scientific temperance" must be taught with the same thoroughness as other subjects:

Statistics tell us that at least three-fourths of all crimes committed are directly traceable to alcoholic indulgence, yet our legislators in their blindness and madness hug the hydra-headed monster who is destroying the Canadian people.[22]

As we have seen, the spirit and content of the instruction was not precisely scientific, and the courses were curtailed and abandoned early in the twentieth century. Later the issue was revived. During and after World War II some provincial governments were persuaded to appoint directors of temperance education. But either because faith in formal courses had dwindled, or for other reasons that may be surmised, the effect on classroom teaching was much less obtrusive than sixty years before.

The teaching of citizenship is another field in which formal courses were widely adopted after many years of agitation. In 1872 the *Journal of Education* in Lower Canada discussed the question whether citizenship should be taught in school. A paper given by a teacher before the

Toronto Teachers' Association and published in 1880 urged the imparting of knowledge of the duties of citizenship, including "an acquaintance with Social Law and the Functions of Government." In 1887 the *Educational Review* of New Brunswick asked readers to consider the need for teaching civics to make intelligent citizens and to develop patriotism. In 1920 in Ottawa a conference promoted by the leadership of the National Council on Education took the form of a National Council on Character Education in Relation to Canadian Citizenship. Sufficient educational wisdom was in evidence at the conference to give precedence to the better education and professional training of teachers as a primary means, but there were cautious statements about the need of character education and the possible value of a textbook in civics. During the next two decades textbooks and courses in civics were introduced in public school systems, but with increasing skepticism as to their value.

At the end of the nineteenth century John Millar, deputy minister of education in Ontario, expressed views that were subsequently accepted by an increasing number of professional educators. He pointed out that "no human agency is beset by more plausible nostrums than the public schools," that "the question as to how ethical training may best be given in our schools is a pedagogical and not a theological one," and that "morality cannot be taught by a textbook any more than football or swimming."[23] There were also positive objections to the teaching of morals under classroom pressure. A contributor to the *Educational Review* in New Brunswick wrote in 1892:

Further, our examination system, with the consequent glorification of prize winners, is largely responsible for a race of intellectual prigs. One fears lest formal instruction in ethics may produce a host of moral prigs.[24]

In the same year a course in manners and morals was introduced to replace religious instruction in schools of the Northwest Territories, but in 1907 such instruction was made incidental to the teaching of other subjects, and in 1921 it was dropped from the printed course of study. Yet many laymen retained their faith in the intrinsic and functional value of content imparted to serve an ethical purpose. In 1950 the Royal Commission on Education in Ontario recommended for high schools the introduction of a course in ethics as an alternative to religious instruction.

INCIDENTAL TEACHING

A number of distinguished educators in the nineteenth century put their confidence in the incidental teaching of ethical values. George Paxton Young believed that ethical instruction could be given "most naturally, most impressively, and with the greatest likelihood of abiding effect in connection with the study by the pupils of the work of good English authors."[25] This Herbartian view, extended to include history, was generally accepted and widely applied at the end of the century. Even later, when faith was shaken in Herbart's convincing logic regarding the ethical potentialities of ordinary instruction, there was continued confidence, and no reason for lack of confidence, that much could be accomplished in this incidental way. Goldwin Smith, who believed that common school education must be secular, was insistent nevertheless that there was a moral element in education. An influential monograph on education in Nova Scotia in 1914 stated that there was seldom need for separate lessons in moral education but that much could be accomplished if the teacher was ready to take advantages of opportunities as they occurred.

EXAMPLE OF THE TEACHER

Again there was a sharp distinction between the two points of view when it was realized that the teacher's example and influence were likely to carry more weight than the repetition of moral precepts. In 1864 David Mills, a local superintendent of Upper Canada, expressed the opinion that "a really well qualified teacher not only develops the intellect, but in a great measure forms the character of the pupils." John Millar in 1901 said bluntly that "the only way to secure the best ethical training in our schools is to secure better teachers."[26] Millar's great concern was that teachers should have the respect of pupils, the confidence of the parents, the co-operation of the principal, and the support of the trustees, that there should be harmony among the staff, and, in short, a school and community environment favorable to effective operation of the teacher's good influence.

In contrast to this new-world point of view was the insistence of others that the teacher be a paragon of all virtues. Provincial regulations respecting the duties of teachers, following those published in Upper Canada in 1850, formed a cumulative thesaurus of every pure and noble quality. The teacher was expected to exhibit to his pupils and to demand from them a saintly perfection not encountered outside the schoolroom. Here again was the perennial conflict between content and method, between those who paid deference to every form of virtue and those who were willing to be much less definite in order to establish contact and achieve effective communication. When the course in Christian morals was dropped in Ontario, the teacher was told in 1877 that pupils would "insensibly learn his ways" and that his deportment must be "not only consistent with the ordinary proprieties of life but also characterized by a high moral code." The question was whether the definition of "moral" took precedence over the pupil's inner acceptance of the ways to which he felt obliged to conform in school.

When attention was first given to the pupil's response, those who thought in terms of authority and punishment showed a common-sense negative attitude. The public school board of Kingston, Ontario, in 1866 condemned the use of pupils as spies to report the names of offenders to teachers. When positive measures were taken in relation to pupil behavior, methods at first were strongly directive. Forrester, who closely followed the lead of his master Stow, explained in 1867 how the teacher could utilize incidents that he observed in the playground for moral instruction. If a boy were seen to steal and pocket the favorite marble of another, no notice was to be taken of the incident at the time. But later, when the children were seated in the gallery, the teacher was to recount the story of the theft without naming the culprit. He was to elicit from the pupils suggestions of suitable punishment for crimes like this, then to remind them that God sees and punishes all, then to appeal on behalf of the nameless offender for mercy on the grounds that this was a first offence. Finally the girls in the class were to cry out: "Forgive him, forgive him." Said Forrester:

Now, mark the natural effect upon all parties; the guilty is condemned by his fellows — the milder feelings are brought into play, and all have been exercised in the principles of truth and justice.[27]

Perhaps because they thought this procedure to be too highly charged with old-fashioned religious emotion, or perhaps because they failed to appreciate its power, education authorities preferred to have teachers concentrate on the pupils' observance of proprieties and to trust that an outward pattern of good conduct would work wonders within. The Northwest

Territories in 1885 issued typical directives to teachers: "Maintain a regular supervision of the pupils in the playground, repress the use of improper language, and have a care that games are honorably played, and generally have a care out of school over the deportment of the pupils while absent from their homes." Evidently the administrators were chiefly concerned about immediate overt behavior for which school authorities might be held responsible. On the other hand, Calkin, as an educator, continued in Forrester's tradition and urged teachers to use the occurrences of the day in the schoolroom and playground not only for moral lessons but to develop moral judgment and the ability of the child to govern himself.

SELF-DIRECTED PRACTICE

The transition, in pupil-centred character education, from externally directed to self-directed practice may be illustrated by the institution of school savings banks. One of the first school banks, in Dartmouth, Nova Scotia, was described in a report of 1888. Its sponsors claimed that the encouragement of deposits by pupils gave sound practical training in thrift, self-restraint, and industrious habits. In 1906 the Dominion Penny Bank Act provided for the incorporation of school banks and for the entrusting of funds to the Receiver-General. A Penny Bank of Toronto was incorporated under this act. Every Monday morning a short time was devoted in the classroom to receiving deposits of pupils, some of whom were given practice also in counting cash. Such banks continued to be popular in many parts of Canada until after World War I.

In modern schools, reliance in character education was placed on practice increasingly self-directed. The experience of the pupil in the school environment as a whole was considered to be more important and more reliable than any single factor. The entire school program, including extra-curricular activities, the influence not only of the teacher but of pupils on one another, and the interaction of many forces were judged to be effective in the aggregate, whereas confidence in any separated subject, distinct person, formulated code, or allotted period was felt to be unjustified. An illustration of the new approach appeared in the program for junior high schools in British Columbia in 1927. There was to be "an enlarged and extended background of experiences":

Increased opportunities both for the development of leadership and for learning social co-operation and democratic citizenship. This should be effected through (1) an adequate programme of extra-curricular activities and (2) participation in such school duties as, under guidance, it may be possible for the pupil to assume.[28]

In modern education there is a tendency for all factors formerly differentiated to coalesce — competition and submission blended in group co-operation, selfishness and self-sacrifice in more active pursuit of a common good. Hence student government was not distinctly a disciplinary measure, but equally a means of character education. In Northern Vocational School, one of the large secondary schools of Toronto, the student council by 1935 had assumed wide responsibility. It had much to do with the planning and management of social events and school sports, conducted opening exercises in the auditorium, and looked after such disciplinary problems as smoking, bad language, and unbecoming conduct in halls and washrooms. From the newer point of view responsibility developed by such practice was more valuable in itself, and likely to be far more effective in terms of citizenship or ethical conduct, than any course of instruction or the dominating influence of any teacher. From the older point of view the training was formless and dangerous.

The most modern, or the most radical, type of character education was related to mental health. In 1898, New Brunswick teachers read in the *Educational Review* an article "On the Teaching of Morals" by J. E. Wells of Toronto, who had been editor of the *Canadian Baptist* and previously of the *Educational Journal*. Wells stated that any true teaching of the kind must always be inductive, that it must begin with a problem for the pupils to discuss, and that there must be "no authoritative decision," not even from the Bible. He believed that there was need of an ethical principle — the Golden Rule — acceptable because in its very nature it must commend itself, and not thrust on the pupil because it was scripturally authoritative. As an example of a problem for discussion, he cited the case of a respectable church-going lady who saw an article in a shop priced at fifty cents; she knew it to be worth twenty times the sum, purchased it, and boasted of the purchase to her friends. The students were asked to consider whether this transaction was honest and to give reasons for their answers. The procedure recommended by Mr. Wells was only a step or two away from the practice followed in classes in human relations in Forest Hill Village, Ontario, half a century later. In this later mental health experiment the problems raised were the pupils' own, and extreme care was taken to avoid any pronouncement by the teacher as to the correct solution or the identification of right or wrong behavior. Not all communities in Canada in 1950 were prepared to tolerate refusal by instructors to impress on the young the authority of certain forms of behavior.

Nevertheless a considerable advance had been made — whether dangerous or not — away from authoritative teaching and towards the development of power to make and carry out moral decisions. A report on "Objectives of Education" prepared by a committee appointed by the Board of Education in Toronto in 1946 included aims which carried more than a suggestion of this purpose:

> To develop in the child a sense of purpose which will serve as a guide for living . . . to develop in the child confidence, ability to make decisions, and willingness to accept the consequences of his decisions . . . to develop the ability to think clearly, critically, and constructively . . . to develop in the child a sense of his responsibility for the welfare of his home, his school, his community, and his country . . . to develop a faith in the democratic way of life.

Perennial Criticism

There has always been pessimism in some quarters regarding the ethics of the younger generation. In every period of history, contemporary problems have appeared to be unique in their difficulty and young people to be lacking in respect for the old and in modesty of speech and behavior. Peter the Hermit in 1274 A.D. is said to have had just that opinion. Some felt the same way six hundred and eighty years later. Yet if we look back a century from 1950 we shall see that in earlier decades conditions were more scandalous and critics no less severe than in any recent years.

In 1862 in Ontario Ryerson wrote of the "great evil of youthful demoralization" in cities and towns and of an increasing class of children "without the sphere of any influence secular or religious."[29] In New Brunswick in the same year two men teachers lost their licences when they were charged with seduction and bastardy, two women teachers because they had given birth to illegitimate children, and another teacher for drunkenness, altering a certificate from Third to Second Class, and forging the signatures of trustees to school returns. In Toronto "the

Good," Goldwin Smith testified in the 1870's:

I have seen a whole party of schoolboys, mere children, waiting for a street car, go into a neighboring tavern to get their nip; and you will find cigars in the mouths of mannequins not much bigger than a monkey.[30]

In 1887 Archbishop Cleary of Kingston, Ontario, was reported as saying:

Modesty is not one of the things taught in our public schools; on the contrary, girls at these schools learn to be boisterous, immodest, screaming, kicking creatures, such as was (sic) never seen even among pagans. Our public schools are destroyers of modesty, an abomination, and a disgrace.[31]

In 1902 a storm developed when someone complained to Sir Oliver Mowat of the rudeness of boys and girls in many of the public schools and suggested that impoliteness and want of deference were encouraged by some teachers. As a result of a note from the lieutenant-governor, the librarian of the education department for two or three years collected newspaper clippings reporting criminal charges against children and criticisms of their behavior. Phrases or sentences from a few of the items will show that young people had not been made perfect by the early years of the twentieth century:

The City of Toronto Fire Department complains that youths and boys are in the habit of playfully breaking the glass on the call boxes . . . Islington lad stole bovine and offered it at a bargain . . . Thomas Jones, aged 15, admits passing false orders . . . The number of petty thefts by small boys continually occurring in the neighborhood of Winchester street school . . . To receive their sentence on a charge of robbing the residence — the boys range from eleven to eighteen years of age . . . Three boys go to jail — purse snatcher punished . . . Several youths convicted of stealing this morning . . . Three boys charged with highway robbery . . . Sold small articles and practised

stealing as a side line — a lad of 13 . . . Young criminals sentenced — four boys had committed twenty-six burglaries . . . Four boys caught — charged with breaking . . . Boy of 13 carried on systematic pilfering — selling needles as a blind, his thefts of purses and chatelaines have been many . . . Costello gang disposed of — overcoat thieves caught — about a dozen young men hardly any of whom were over twenty years of age. Most of them were bright and of respectable appearance . . . Corporal punishment — is its disuse a mistake? . . . Ontario children good — few criminally disposed — kindness is best cure for crime . . . Boys congregate from 8 o'clock till 10 — their talk is often obscene and vulgar . . . Riotous conduct of a band of pupils in a streetcar — whistling and violent horseplay . . . Why children run away from school — effect of flogging . . . Church of England conference comes to a decision — biblical instruction should be given in schools.

Religious education as a means of improving conduct was repeatedly advocated, and its value for that purpose was always challenged by some outspoken educator. In the 1870's a high school inspector addressed a convention of Ontario teachers on the subject. He said that criticism of the younger generation had created something like an educational scare among the public, some of whom were demanding religious instruction in the schools, apparently because of their failure to distinguish between religion and morality. The inspector pointed out that a man's morals were to be judged by his conduct, that conduct was a result of habit, and that habits were formed by what a child did. As far as the school was concerned, the important factors were the everyday work and discipline and the example of the teacher. It was frequently stated that the virtually secular public school gave merely intellectual education. This was again emphatically denied in 1898 before the Ontario Educational Association. The speaker said that quite apart from any modicum of religious instruction the whole exercises of the school were moral as well as intellectual. Millar and others declared repeatedly on pedagogical grounds that religious instruction in schools could no more be expected to control conduct than formal courses in morals. Subsequently this contention was supported by scientific evidence, including the result of a doctoral study made after religious education was introduced in Ontario during World War II.

An Appraisal

Yet in appraising the result of character education it seems reasonable to assume that formal instruction was efficacious among those whose home training and background were conducive to its acceptance. No less reasonable is the corollary that the new education in responsibility was effective among those whose parents and early associates had put into practice an equally strong faith in the operation of principle. Ethical development was hampered when young people were confused by the contradictions of old-world and new-world teach-

ing and also by the failure of either the one or the other to take effect.

A half century ago there was less travel than today; people had fewer amusements and perhaps more leisure time; the newspaper, the theatre, professional sports, and the excitement of rapid travel did not engage the time and attention of the average boy and girl as they do today.

The above words were written, not in 1953, but forty years before, when the changes described had just begun. They appeared in *The School** as an editorial commenting on a belief that the Bible was not read as much as formerly. Yet in spite of much greater changes in the world and the devastating moral effect of wars and depression, and in spite of conflicts in faith and ideas, the schools by one means or another succeeded in graduating young people who would stand comparison in the aggregate with any previous generation. There was strong support for belief that those who were worse by the old-world criteria were fewer than those who were better by the new.

* Vol. I, no. 6, p. 373.

Summary

In discipline and character education, as in every aspect of school teaching and school administration, the trend has been away from the exercise of external authority and towards the encouragement of co-operation — away from formulae and rules and towards development of inner power. First the harsher forms of punishment were abandoned; then gradually the educational value of all punishments began to be questioned, although punitive action had still to be taken occasionally to put an immediate if temporary stop to intolerable behavior. A growing number of teachers began before 1900 to rely increasingly on positive or preventive discipline, and later some began cautiously to utilize inherent factors of control which operate when human beings do things together for purposes they value. Every step in this direction was regarded by others as dangerously subversive.

Similarly, in character education, an increasing number lost faith in the teaching of formal content, although others continued to advocate courses in citizenship or ethics. The new method was an attempt to instil constructive attitudes and behavior in action, not in words, and through experience, not by direct teaching. The new objectives were of a type that may be illustrated by responsibility and the operation of the Golden Rule. There was as much opposition to this concept of character as there was to the methods employed. The lack of form and structure caused critics to believe and say that the behavior of the young and the work of the schools were both deteriorating.

An appraisal reveals, however, that such criticism was never lacking, and that conditions from any point of view were no better in the past. From the modern point of view, of course, both the schools and young people are much better than ever before.

CHAPTER 27

The Teacher

QUALIFICATIONS, STATUS AND REMUNERATION: BEFORE 1850 · 1850-1890 ·
1890-1950 · LEVELLING · ECONOMIC SECURITY · CERTIFICATION ·
SUPPLY AND RECRUITMENT · HUMILITY AND HUMILIATION

The qualifications and status of teachers have improved
greatly since 1800, in spite of the conflicting forces of the old
world and the new. The history of the development is not simple, for conditions, policies, and agencies changed from time
to time, sometimes favoring and sometimes discouraging higher
standards. For example, certification was introduced to require
more than the majority demanded, but it appears to have
legalized at times what only a minority would tolerate. Again,
the influx of women into teaching first drove out the worst
men and then many of the best. This chapter deals with all
factors affecting the status of the teacher except teacher education, which is reserved for the chapter which follows.

If there is one indisputable axiom in education, it is this:
"As is the teacher, so is the school." Administrative organization,
buildings, curricula, and textbooks are appurtenances that undoubtedly affect instruction. Principals and supervisors have
contributory influence. But the quality of education depends
directly and immediately on the quality of the teacher. The
implications of this truth were forcefully expressed by Inspector
McCormac of Prince Edward Island towards the end of the
nineteenth century:

There is no more important calling than that of the teacher,
and therefore no quacks should be permitted to remain in the
profession. The mission of the teacher cannot be measured, nor can
the interests that cluster around him be transient. His power in
shaping the future of his pupils is almost infinite, for it is a fact that
children in school study the teacher more than they study arithmetic,

545

language, orthography, and it is far more important that they learn the right things of their teacher than that they learn much more their books. If the teacher be true, all is well; but if the teacher be weak and false, he can damn the child to a degradation of heart and conscience, which will be aggravated instead of alleviated by the learning he received. In a political campaign may be evolved a great railway scheme; on the reception of a book may depend a literary reputation; but on the smile or frown of a teacher may tremble a human destiny.

Before 1850

IN PATERNALISTIC SCHOOLS

Teachers in the paternalistic schools of the eighteenth and early nineteenth centuries had to give evidence of some qualifications, however humble, in terms of approved faith, loyalty, and a modicum of knowledge. Such teachers were regarded by the authorities as trustworthy inferiors and were paid considerably more than those who were employed locally in schools of the people. Most of them were men of mediocre spirit and ability, narrow-minded and inoffensive. But occasionally men of superior attainments found their way into teaching. Audet mentions two outstanding teachers who were employed under the Royal Institution in Quebec.

One of these was Charles Desrosiers who was driven from France at the time of the French Revolution. He became an officer in the British Navy and there acquired experience and knowledge which he put to good account later when teaching school. He taught not only the ordinary school subjects but also navigation and geography, in which he had skill and knowledge of a very practical type. He was versatile in other ways, for among the subjects taught at his school at Cap-Santé he mentions Protestant religious knowledge for English-speaking children and Roman Catholic religious knowledge for French-Canadians, along with the catechisms of the churches of England and Rome. The other teacher mentioned by Audet was Donald McDermid, who came to Canada at the end of the eighteenth century, taught for a few years in schools of Upper Canada, entered the ship-rigging business and eventually lost his money, suffered a further loss of property during the war of 1812, became an officer in the army and was wounded, held several different jobs in the auxiliary services for which an able-bodied man was not required, and again about 1814 turned to school teaching, this time in the province of Lower Canada.

Teachers brought out from England by the paternalistic authorities were tempted to take some advantage of a status slightly higher than that of the settled population. Spragge, of the Central School at York, was charged with unpunctual and irregular attendance, as were several teachers of the Royal Institution. One of the latter, at Argenteuil around 1822, was absent for fourteen months over a three-year period and during his absence employed a farmer's daughter as a substitute at four dollars a month plus board. Some of these teachers were reprimanded or dismissed for excessively heavy drinking and for inflicting extremely harsh punishments. To cite an early instance, the schoolmaster appointed to instruct orphan children and other poor children in Halifax was dismissed in 1762 for drunkenness and other irregularities. But on the whole, teachers in the paternalistic schools were, by the standards of the time, virtuous men and women with some aptitude for teaching, and those who were members of religious orders or conscious of a religious mission were also zealous in their work.

IN THE SCHOOLS OF THE PEOPLE

Much inferior on all counts were the great majority of teachers in common schools of the people before 1850. In the first stage of democratic educational development it was inevitable that the populace should be satisfied with almost anyone who would take charge of a school. Neither trustees nor parents had the discrimination, the resources, or the will to procure the services of capable men. With few exceptions, the early common school teachers were a sorry lot: "ignorant and immoral persons, old soldiers, idlers of all descriptions, notorious for habits of drunkenness"; "old men who had a mere smattering of learning and who were very incompetent instructors"; "not infrequently men of dissolute habits"; "shipwrecked characters, who, to keep body and soul together, were compelled to teach." Such were the descriptions of three contemporary historians and critics and one later essayist in the Maritime Provinces.

Said Haliburton, in *The Old Judge*:

When a man fails in his trade, or is too lazy to work he resorts to teaching as a livelihood, and the school-house, like the asylum for the poor, receives all those who are, from misfortune or incapacity, unable to provide for themselves.[1]

Even in 1853 the superintendent of education in New Brunswick admitted that "if a man could get no other work or was incompetent, he tramped the country in search of a school." In Lower Canada and Upper Canada contemporary censure of common school teachers was only slightly less severe: they were "ignorant," "the lame and the lazy," and "generally men who were unable or unwilling to do any other kind of work."

Anecdotes regarding individual teachers confirm and add color to the more general impression. The first teacher in the Bon Accord settlement, near Fergus, Upper Canada, would often fall asleep and slumber on until the pupils roused him with the request that he hear their lessons and let them go home. A farmer-teacher in Prince Edward Island, who worked in the fields from dawn until school time, went to sleep with a warning to his pupils: "Wait till I get up in the evening, I'll give it to you fellows."

Although little evidence of scandal involving teachers has been permitted to survive, mention of one colorful incident will relieve the somewhat bleached appearance of the pedagogical character. An Upper Canada teacher named Goff was unable to collect his government money because of a charge made against him by one, Samuel Smith. Goff protested not his innocence — but the injustice of being accused by Smith of asking the latter's "wife to come to bed with me when boarding at his house without the least shadow of seduction or prosecution or proof." He made counter charges that Smith was an incendiary and that Smith had been compelled to marry the wife in question.[*] That was in 1835.

To show that there were exceptions on the bright side of the scale, one may point to a school built that same year in Lower Canada that acquired as teachers, soon after it was erected, a man with a college education and his wife. In the following year a newly opened school in Fergus, in Upper Canada, obtained a teacher named McQueen who remained for twenty-two years and turned out "many a good scholar." But the bad examples are easier to find.

* Educational Papers, U.C. (72), 1835, no. 484.

"BOARDING 'ROUND"

One of the indignities that kept more sensitive men out of teaching was the common requirement that teachers accept part of their pay in board, which was provided by the parents of pupils in succession. Contracts often indicated washing and mending as services to be provided for the teacher in addition to food and lodging. Sometimes parents of pupils would also bargain to do work on the teacher's farm or to take care of his stock in lieu of paying fees. Any of these services received by a teacher meant a reduction from his meagre pay, whereas the teacher might be required to do extra work gratuitously.

A schoolmaster in the county of Victoria, Upper Canada, in 1834 was boarded in only two houses near the school, where he did the chores of a hired man in the morning and evening. Another in Prince Edward Island was expected merely to rock the cradle, to make pap for the baby, and to cut firewood. Women teachers handy with the needle were welcome guests. A Nova Scotia contract of an exceptionally dignified and enlightened type stipulated that the children of families with whom the teacher boarded should have the advantage of his instruction during the evenings. But the usual lot of the boarding teacher, according to the principal of the New Brunswick Training School in 1854, was poor fare and indifferent lodging in home surroundings where ignorant adults and unruly children gave no opportunity for reading or intellectual conversation.

Conscientious teachers complained that their authority in school was undermined by unavoidable familiarity with pupils in their homes and that they were put in a position of degrading dependence by being shuffled from family to family. John Thomas of Lunenburg, Nova Scotia, was fed only Indian meal without milk or sweetening by some families and slept on straw beds where "mice, fleas, and bugs could be felt at all hours of the night." When he woke up he often found two or three mice crushed to death by the weight of his body. A teacher named Kerr in Upper Canada rebelled in more than one community against home conditions and slept on two benches in the cold schoolhouse. Many abandoned teaching because of the treatment received. But according to the inspector of Northumberland County, Upper Canada, in 1856, teachers interested only in making an easy living did not object to boarding around and welcomed the opportunities so provided for smoking, snuff-taking, and joke-telling as an excuse for not preparing the school work of the following day. Sometimes there was embarrassment and a bit of fun if a family forgot to make arrangements for the coming of the teacher, as when two daughters came home late one night and found their bed occupied by a slumbering dominie.

"Boarding around" disappeared in most of Upper Canada and in better districts elsewhere in the 1860's. Although Superintendent d'Avray of New Brunswick had insisted, before then, that superior school teachers be paid in cash to elevate them professionally, the boarding of common school teachers persisted after Confederation. In Quebec the practice was finally abolished in 1882.

PAY: IN PATERNALISTIC AND COMMON SCHOOLS

The remuneration paid to lay teachers has reflected fairly accurately the esteem in which they were held. To compare salaries in different periods it is necessary to compensate for various factors. Supplements like the privilege of collecting fees and the provision in some way for housing or board were common before 1850. Also to be considered in the early period were the scarcity of money and the possible nuisance of being paid in

A certificate to enable a teacher to collect the government allowance,
Upper Canada, 1829 (Public Archives of Canada)

kind. A most important factor was the cost of domestic food, simple clothing, and ordinary shelter, since elementary school teachers until the end of the nineteenth century seldom had a surplus for anything more.

In estimating the value of higher salaries paid to secondary school teachers and some others before 1850, one should remember also that many things that are now cheap — like tea, oranges, and means of transportation — were then expensive luxuries, whereas land and labor were then cheap and are now dear. For convenient comparison in the following discussion, the probable equivalent in dollars of the total remuneration received by the teacher is given in brackets, with a factor to indicate the approximate value of the dollars as compared with those of 1950 for purchasing the bare necessities of life. For example, if it is stated that a teacher in 1830 received £12.10.0 government money ($125 x 4), the meaning is that the teacher probably received, in addition to his $50 in government money, the equivalent of another $50 as board for six months and about $25 in fees — a total of $125 at a time when bare necessities cost about one-quarter as much as in 1950. It will help a little to keep in mind that the median salary for all teachers in English-speaking Canada in 1950 was close to $2000 for ten months' work.

Paternalistic schools in the Maritime Provinces before 1800 tried to get teachers for £20 a year but usually had to raise £40 with minor supplements ($250 x 2). In 1775 a weekly supply of foodstuffs for a small family — say, three pounds of meat, ten and one-half pounds of bread, a pound of butter, half a pound of sugar and seven quarts of milk — would have cost about $2.75 if all items were purchased. Badly off as the schoolmaster was, day laborers were said to earn only half as much, and women servants only a tenth as much, with board added in the latter case. A Church of England clergyman received three times as much as a schoolmaster and a high government official about twice as much as a clergyman.

Half a century later salaries in paternalistic schools were better and living costs lower. Teachers in Lower Canada employed by the Royal Institution in 1818 received salaries of £60 ($240 x 4). Although they claimed that this amount was "not sufficient to support the smallest family" unless supplemented by tuition fees, it was more than twice as much as common school teachers received from the government in Upper Canada. A man and wife in Newfoundland received £140 ($600 x 3) in 1828. The British and Canadian monitorial school in Quebec in 1841 paid its English master £96 ($400 x 4), its French master £30, and the teacher of a girls' department £40. As master of a Church of England school favored by the aristocratic government, Spragge at York, Upper Canada, received £150 salary plus £40 for a house ($760 x 4). Teachers in quasi-paternalistic schools supported by the governments of Vancouver Island and British Columbia around 1855-65 got £200 to £250 from all sources (say, $800 x 3).

In schools of the people before the introduction of local taxation the teacher received a small and precarious income. He could be sure of the government money — usually about £15 or £20 — if he and the trustees observed the law. But he could not be sure of the amount to be raised locally by subscription and fees. New Brunswick legislation requiring local expenditure as a condition of receiving the grant was sometimes circumvented by getting the teacher to accept half or less of the declared local salary, or to take payment in kind at an inflated evaluation. Including the value of wretched board, the collections, from all sources, of a man teaching common school anywhere in Canada in 1845 might range from £30 to £50 ($120 x 4 to $200 x 4) for six months' hire. In Prince Edward Island the average salary in 1840 was said to be as high as £45. In New Brunswick a man usually received £20 in money and about £10 in value in board and services. In Lower Canada around 1840 a teacher with twenty scholars might collect up to two shillings a month from only ten of them, since the local board could insist on free tuition for ten; and if the fee did not reduce attendance to less than the minimum of twenty scholars required for his £20 grant, he might expect about £26 altogether in cash, or £36 ($144 x 4) including the value of his board.

A few additional figures will give more meaning to these estimates of salaries. In Cobourg, Upper Canada, in 1845 skilled workmen made about $1.50 to $2.00 a day, laborers 50 cents a day and board, domestic servants $3.00 to $4.00 a month. The cost of the weekly food bill itemized above would have been about $1.30, or less than half the earlier amount; and one family of six is said to have obtained abundant board for $6.00 a week. Under the circumstances, a man teaching six or seven months a year in Upper Canada for $150 and board, or $200 (x 4) without board, could survive even without other work.

SECONDARY SCHOOL SALARIES

Secondary school masters before 1850 were in an altogether different and superior position. Top status was enjoyed by those brought out from England to take charge of the high-ranking grammar schools. In 1829, the Reverend R. R. Burrage of the Royal Grammar School at Quebec drew from the government £200 plus the high allowance of £100 for a schoolhouse and collected about £90 in fees. After paying £45 to an assistant, he probably had nearly £300 ($1200 x 4) for his own use. At the next lower level, clergymen headmasters of the district grammar schools in Upper Canada received only £100 from the government but could make much more from fees and from charges for the board of pupils. The net earnings of the master of the Midland District school in 1829, after payment of an assistant and some other expenses, were nearly £250 ($1000 x 4). In secondary schools which lost their exclusive Church of England and socially superior character, the master received very much less, especially in small schools of the Maritime Provinces that became merely superior schools of the people. An indication of some of the factors that determined salaries is given in the following data for Lower Canada in 1831:[2]

Salary of the master of a Royal Grammar School	£200
Salary of the master in St. Andrew's School	£135
Salaries paid by Monitorial School Societies	£60 - £90
Ordinary salary paid in county schools	£18

St. Andrews was a secondary school, but Presbyterian. Note the comparatively good salary paid in paternalistic elementary schools and the pittance received by ordinary teachers. Assistant masters in secondary schools received about £40 to £50 ($200 x 4). If the school was large enough to have several teachers, a senior classics master was either the head or enjoyed a status superior to the mathematics master, as the latter did in relation to instructors in other subjects.

The teacher was a "master" in traditional secondary schools and paternalistic elementary schools of the early nineteenth century. In schools under public control he was called "teacher" — a designation of work and not a recognition of humble authority. But in schools that reflect the old aristocratic concept of society there are "masters" still.

1850-1890

After the middle of the nineteenth century, the qualifications of elementary school teachers were gradually raised by the increasingly higher standards imposed by central authorities and by the slowly growing appreciation of education shown by a better educated people. Improvement was retarded, however, when the chief source of teacher supply became young women narrowly educated in the relatively poor rural schools. Up to 1890 the low cost of bare living persisted in spite of temporary fluctuations, so that salaries may be compared directly with those of the previous period. But one must remember that the school year lengthened to ten months or more and that supplements like board and tuition fees disappeared. The salaries mentioned hereafter constituted the sole income of the teacher.

Most men teachers during the period received between $250 and $450, most women between $150 and $300 (x 4). Before Confederation, in the more favored localities there was an upward swing to near the top of these ranges, but no general advance thereafter. A few men — mostly principals in larger centres — received close to $1500 (x 4). In less favored districts salaries were appallingly low. An inspector in the province of Quebec reported in 1877:

I have 97 female teachers, and the magnificent number of 1 male teacher, in 20 municipalities. 76 female teachers receive from $64 to $72 salary; 21 a little over $100. I have done deploring, or rather I. will deplore no more, the fate of most of these young ladies, for I know by experience that they are the direct authoressess of their own misfortune, and that because they take situations at the lowest price.[3]

There was a marked discrepancy in salaries between the east coast and the west. In New Brunswick Superintendent Fisher wrote in 1858:

It is an evil that must not be concealed and cannot be but deplored, that to a great extent in this Province, pauperism and Parish School teachers have multiplied and diminished together.

Around 1870 the average salary in his province was less than $115 (x 4) whereas in British Columbia it was close to $700 (x 2). Board in the western province was high — $20 a month around Victoria and Vancouver, $40 a month in the interior. In 1874 a floor of $50 a month was placed under the teachers' salaries in British Columbia, with a bonus of $10 a month where living costs were high, and bonuses of from $10 to $30 a month where the average attendance was more than 20 and not more than 50 pupils. Since unskilled laborers could earn $50 a month and board, even these salaries were attractive only to women. In middle western Manitoba the average salary of all teachers around 1885 was about $475 (x 4). Average salaries in rural schools there were about 20% higher than Ontario rural salaries for men and more than 75% higher than Ontario rural salaries for women.

Secondary school teachers' salaries were higher, and markedly so in larger centres and schools, where a sharp distinction between elementary and secondary education could be maintained and where to a considerable degree gentility continued to be associated with scholarship. The differential was highest where common school teaching was held in the lowest

esteem. In the grammar school of Saint John, New Brunswick, in 1857 the English master was paid £150 ($600 x 4), the classical master £250 ($1000 x 4), and the principal £290 ($1160 x 4). In the high school at Quebec, teachers were paid from $300 to $600 and the principal $1000 (x 4) in the 1880's — not much, but vastly more than rural elementary school teachers. School reports for the city of Halifax show that around 1877 four men were appointed to the high school staff at salaries of $1600, $1400, $1200, and $600; in contrast, salaries of one man and three women appointed to an elementary school of the city were $650 for the former and $360, $310, and $280 each for the latter.

While the denominational system continued in the middle west there were large discrepancies in salaries. The effect of the entrance examination and of other factors which restored distinctive characteristics to secondary education may be illustrated by reference to Ontario. In 1872 the average salary in secondary schools was $594, about 65%* higher than the average of men teachers in elementary schools; in 1882, secondary school teachers averaged $764, or nearly 85 per cent more than men in the elementary schools. Admittedly the salaries of the latter were kept down by the influx of women; yet in 1892 when it had become established practice for women to graduate from university and teach in high schools, secondary school teachers averaged $926, or 120% more than men teachers in the elementary schools.

1890-1950

By the end of the nineteenth century teachers' salaries had begun to move upward, but so had the cost of living and wages in other occupations. In elementary schools of Ontario, men averaged about $400 (x 3) and women about $300 (x 3), and on the whole salaries were about 20% lower in the Maritime Provinces and about 20% higher in the west. But weekly wages in Ontario had risen by 1903 to about $10 for unskilled and beginning labor, to $12 for telephone operators and the like, to $20 for skilled labor in ordinary trades, and to $25 or $30 for special skills like watchmaking and glass-blowing. Ontario elementary school teachers' salaries increased steadily to about double the 1900 average by 1914 and doubled again during the inflation at the end of World War I to $1644 (x 3/2) and $1117 for women by 1922. These averages fell to an apparent low of $1332 (x 2) and $1041 respectively in 1936 and recovered to $2803 and $2267 in 1950. Comparable changes took place in other provinces although sometimes the recovery after the depression was slow. The following advertisement shows the value attached to educational services by one municipality under war-time conditions when labor was at a premium:[4]

High School teacher for Shelburne Academy, for school year 1942-43. Principal subjects History, Physics, Chemistry, Geometry, Trigonometry. Salary $750. Apply to Town Clerk, Shelburne.

Median salaries of teachers in all schools in 1950 were:

NEWFOUNDLAND	$ 966
PRINCE EDWARD ISLAND	1083
NOVA SCOTIA	1569
NEW BRUNSWICK	1341
ONTARIO	2109
MANITOBA	1689
SASKATCHEWAN	1580
ALBERTA	2279
BRITISH COLUMBIA	2668

The median for these nine provinces was $1965.

Levelling

As the distinction between elementary and secondary education became less clearly marked, differences in salaries were correspondingly reduced. On the whole in English-speaking Canada, secondary school teachers were paid about twice as much as elementary school teachers in 1900 and about 50% more than elementary school teachers in 1950. In some large cities in the later year — notably in Ottawa, which had separate boards for elementary and secondary schools — the difference was greater; but in Toronto and Vancouver, where the average of all teachers was highest, the difference was less. Indeed, there was a tendency for boards to adopt single salary schedules for all teachers, so that differences in the averages of several cities were the result only of the higher average professional qualifications and longer average service of secondary school teachers. As we shall see later, changes in teacher education in some provinces were tending to cause even this distinction to disappear. Fully qualified experienced teachers in many urban centres in 1950 could earn a maximum of $5500 to $6000 regardless of the grade level of the pupils they were instructing.

SALARIES FOR EDUCATIONAL CIVIL SERVANTS

The effect of levelling may be observed also in the salaries paid to chief civil servants in departments of education. Ryerson in Ontario at the time of Confederation retained from the old regime a sufficient appreciation of the value of leadership to accept a salary of $4000 (x 4). When a minister of education was appointed, this amount was transferred to him and the salary of the deputy as top civil servant became $3000 (x 4) in 1880 but only $2300 (x 3) in the last decade of the century. The prestige of the permanent head of the department was partially restored by salaries of $3333 (x 3) in 1910, $5400 (x 3/2) in 1920, $6000 (x 2) in 1930, $7500 (x 2) in 1940, and from $10,000 to $14,000 in years following 1950. Individual educators were able to resist the tendency of free enterprise democracy to pay low salaries to civil servants, as when Superintendent Goggin obtained and retained a salary of $3000 (x 3) in the Northwest Territories in the 1890's, and when Superintendent Munroe received a salary of $7500 (x 2) in Nova Scotia in the 1930's. New Brunswick put a low value on the services of its early superintendents, whose total allowances of $1000 (x 4) in the 1850's were less than the salaries of senior masters at King's College and less than half the salary of the principal of that college. The salary of the superintendent or deputy minister then improved in New Brunswick to $1600 (x 4) in 1875 and remained at about that level of purchasing power — $2000 (x 3) in 1900 and $6260 in 1950.

The reduction in advantage formerly enjoyed is even more marked in the case of teacher training and supervisory personnel employed by central authorities. The salary of £300 ($1200 x 4) received by a professor, or assistant master, at the McGill Normal School in 1857 gave him a social position relatively superior to that of his counterpart today. Senior masters in Ontario normal schools were paid about four or five times the average salaries of men teachers around 1880, and only a little more than twice as much by 1950. In the School of Pedagogy at Toronto in 1893 lecturers received $2500 (x 3½) a year. The total income of high school inspectors was well over three times the average salary of secondary school teachers in 1880 but dropped to twice the teachers' average by World War I. Cutting salaries of supervisory staff in education was apparently considered good politics towards the end of the nineteenth-century. In 1878 the premier of Quebec in a speech at St. Hyacinthe admitted that teachers received less than women who scrubbed

floors in the provincial legislature and promised to find more money for teachers by reducing the amount given to inspectors. He boasted that his government had already reduced the salary of the provincial superintendent to $3000 (x 4). When the estimates appeared later, however, the allotment for school inspection was, as before, $30,000.

Since 1880 the highest salaries of principals of elementary and secondary schools also dropped in relation to the average salaries of teachers, but rose in relation to the salaries of departmental employees. The change in the latter ratio was probably the result of urban advance. In the 1880's the chief education officer in Toronto received $2500 (x 4) — no more than a high school inspector or principal of a normal school. By 1950 superintendents employed by capital cities and other large cities of most provinces received more than deputy ministers or other chief officers of the respective provincial departments of education. In Ontario in the 1920's the prescribed qualifications of elementary school inspectors were so high and the salaries, then paid by the counties, so low that few would apply for appointment. After 1930, inspectors in the counties were paid by the province but in 1953 they were financially at a marked disadvantage in comparison with their colleagues employed by urban boards.

RELATIONSHIP OF URBAN AND RURAL TEACHERS

Since 1850 there has been a marked difference between the status of urban and of rural teachers. Average salaries in cities, about twice as high as average rural salaries before Confederation, became nearly three times as high by 1900, partly because of the large number of poorly qualified women available for employment at low rates in rural districts. In the present century the difference has become less. Salaries of men in the province of

Quebec increased between 1901 and 1918 less than 60 per cent in towns and more than 130 per cent in the country. In 1950 the median salary of teachers in all provinces except Quebec was not quite 70 per cent higher in cities than in one-room rural schools. But the salaries of men teachers alone were still more than twice as high in cities as in the small rural schools, where cheapness was the major consideration.

The difference in salaries of men and women in 1950 was therefore slight in rural areas, where the salary level of all was low, but still about 50 per cent in cities where the highest salaries were paid. Nevertheless old-world discrimination between the sexes was being slowly wiped out. Women received less than 60 per cent as much as men around 1860, about 75 per cent as much in 1900, and about 80 per cent as much in 1950. The discrepancy was less as a rule in the west than in the east and most persistent in the province of Quebec, where the average salary of Roman Catholic teachers in rural elementary schools increased only from $112 in 1901 to $194 in 1918, while the corresponding salaries of men in such schools increased from $221 to $513. In contrast, Ontario salaries of rural elementary school teachers increased during the same years from $262 to $609 for women and from $359 to $743 for men. Data for Ontario also indicate that during the second quarter of the present century the discrepancy between salaries of men and women in secondary schools was being reduced. There has been a recent trend, besides, towards somewhat greater equality in the numbers of men and women teachers. Women outnumbered men more than four to one in 1901 and five to one in 1919, but less than three to one in 1939 and 1950. The proportion was about equal at the time of Confederation and heavily weighted on the male side in the early nineteenth century.

MEN AND WOMEN: PROPORTIONATE RELATIONSHIPS TO TEACHING

The preponderance of women then in the profession was deplored on educational grounds. Said Goggin in 1904:

We used to have men and women in charge of our public schools. Now we have boys and girls — mainly girls . . . boys from twelve years of age upwards need a man's guidance and control to develop them properly.[5]

President Burwash of the University of Toronto in the following year set ten years of age as the upper limit for a boy to be under a woman teacher and urged that the teaching staff be improved "not so much in scholarship, as in maturity and strength."[6] Newspapers echoed professional lamentation in the more picturesque language of journalism:

Teaching, once a stern masculinity whose symbol was the blue beech gad, has become a Tennysonian feminine idyll whose motto is moral suasion.[7]

Governments in the aristocratic period tried to resist the employment of women as teachers, except in schools for girls and young children. In New Brunswick in 1833 women were given only half the government grant and half the local equivalent required for men. In 1837 this distinction was removed, but the number of women teachers was limited to three in each parish. But prosperity and the difficulty of securing men made it impossible to enforce such restrictions. Nova Scotia authorized the employment of women in common schools in 1838 and in academies in 1845. Soon thereafter farmers were welcoming this opportunity of having their daughters employed, even at low salaries. In Quebec it was "not an unheard of plan to elect a committee pledged in favor of one neighbor's daughter for the one term, another for the second, and some other spinster for the third."[8] New Brunswick in

1900 again paid higher grants for men teachers than for women in a vain effort to stem the tide. In Ontario in the last two decades of the nineteenth century, the large number of available daughters of farmers contributed to a decline in rural school salaries.

But even in the west, to which many men teachers had migrated, the professional or continuing teacher before World War I was discouraged by the competition of a succession of young women who took a school in a rural area, found a suitor, and married. Central authorities reduced this competition by raising academic and professional standards until World War II, but they subsequently capitulated, as if accepting the argument that more years of service could be obtained from a young woman teacher if the required qualifications were low enough to encourage her to begin teaching at the earliest age at which the law would permit her to work. Inevitably the competition of women on equal terms has tended to make teaching unattractive financially to capable men. The effect has been greater because of the temporary employment of large numbers of young women more likely to be interested in marriage than in raising the status of the profession.

Economic Security

Uncertainty regarding payment and other difficulties made the lot of the early teacher even less attractive than the low salaries suggest. Sometimes the government money was withheld. Kimmings of Lachine began teaching in 1810, but was told at the end of the year that his salary could not be paid further back than November. James Conolly, a common school teacher of the 1820's in a remote section of Haldimand County, Upper Canada, did not see a published request for complete school returns and failed to comply; the government assumed that he

had left the country, distributed all the money alloted to schools, and could give him no recompense. Often the local contribution in the form of fees or subscriptions was not forthcoming. In Upper Canada, in 1822, a petitioner stated that he had given up his farm to take a teaching position at a promised £50 a year and had later found the inhabitants too poor to pay him.

Teachers found it difficult to appeal against summary discharge. A school visitor recommended the dismissal, as incompetent, of Angelique and Julie Délâge, two teachers of Cap-Santé; the attorney general gave his opinion that the government could act on this advice by withholding their money, provided the decision was "concurred in by the Resident Member of the Assembly of the County," who in this case was the school visitor. After the middle of the nineteenth century regular contracts and defined responsibilities of various parties eliminated the most flagrant abuses, but niggardly bargaining, unfair impositions on the teacher, and lack of security left teachers with good reasons for uniting to protect their interests.

TEACHERS' ASSOCIATIONS

The *Journal of the Legislative Assembly* in Prince Edward Island mentioned in 1840 a Society of Schoolmasters who had written to the special committee of the legislature regarding difficulties arising from insecurity of tenure. The committee was sufficiently impressed with the desirability of retaining the services of a teacher that they suggested discontinuance of the grant for two years in the case of a dismissal without cause. Another record of an early association of teachers is preserved in a neat little printed booklet of 1846 entitled *Règlement de l'Association des Instituteurs de Montréal*. It indicates that the objects of the members were self-improvement, the better service of education to society, and a higher status for teachers. A similar association for the district of Quebec was incorporated by act of parliament in 1849. After 1857 the associations of teachers in the two cities were linked with the newly founded normal schools. These and other local organizations formed in both Canada East and Canada West in the 1850's, including teachers' institutes, were designed almost wholly for professional improvement, although a few members urged political action to obtain better salaries. Similarly, the first provincial organizations were educational in character. The Teachers' Association of Canada West, established in 1861, became thirty years later, after several changes of name, the Ontario Educational Association, which continued in operation even after teachers' federations were formed in the twentieth century to improve the economic status of the profession. Other nineteenth-century organizations were the Provincial Association of Protestant Teachers of Quebec, founded in 1864, and the Teachers' Federation of Prince Edward Island, founded in 1880, both of which were still active in 1950, and the Educational Association of Nova Scotia and the Teachers' Institute of New Brunswick, both established about 1863.

An early attempt to organize a teachers' union was initiated at a meeting of teachers of Perth County, Ontario, in 1886. The avowed aims were to encourage the organization of other unions, to seek legislation of advantage to teachers, and, more specifically, to secure sickness and unemployment benefits and control over admission to the teaching profession. The proposed program was denounced in the press, and even in educational periodicals, although some of the latter gave it lukewarm support. "After organization, will striking and boycott be in order?" asked the New England *Journal of Education*. The teachers were asked to remember the high ideals of their profession and not to weaken the schools even to obtain redress for their grievances, which were admittedly serious in the extreme. The union did not actually operate as such, and a revived demand for aggressive action around 1900 met an even colder reception. Nevertheless a committee of the Ontario Educational Association, set up in 1905, recommended the organization of an Ontario Teachers' Union to set qualifications for teaching, to establish a teachers' register, to devise a superannuation scheme, and to foster by discipline of members and other means a high esteem for the teaching profession. An Ontario Teachers' Alliance, affiliated to an extent with the O.E.A., was founded in 1907.

Most of the present provincial federations of teachers, however, were formed within a short period at the end of World War I. The organizations in the western provinces were the first to appear and the first to employ full-time staff for vigorous and persistent action. The British Columbia Teachers' Federation originated in Vancouver at a meeting of delegates from six local associations, held its first annual convention in 1917, and had a paid-up membership of 1600 by 1921-22. The Alberta Teachers' Association, at first called the Alberta Teachers' Alliance, sprang in 1917 from an older-type educational association, which subsequently disappeared. At the beginning the A.T.A. was resisted by a minister of education who was opposed to the increasing strength of unions; but the Liberal government was defeated in 1921 and the Alliance under strong leadership made gains resulting in greater security of tenure for teachers. A Saskatchewan Teachers' Alliance, formed in 1916, united with other organizations to become the Saskatchewan Teachers' Federation in 1933. The Manitoba Teachers' Society, organized in 1918 as the Manitoba Teachers' Federation, enrolled three-quarters of the teachers in the province by 1930.

The Federation of Women Teachers' Associations of Ontario was organized in 1918, the Ontario Secondary School Teachers' Federation in 1919, and the Ontario Public School Men Teachers' Federation in 1920; these three federations and two others — *L'Association de l'Enseignement Français de l'Ontario* and the Ontario English Catholic Teachers' Association, organized in 1939 and 1944 respectively — were affiliated in the Ontario Teachers' Federation by legislative enactment in 1944. In addition to the older associations in Quebec, there have recently been French-speaking and English-speaking Roman Catholic federations, including the comprehensive *Corporation générale des instituteurs et institutrices catholiques de la province de Québec;* but aggressive policies analagous to those of federations in other provinces were opposed by the government after World War II. The New Brunswick Teachers' Association arose in 1918 from the institute previously mentioned, as did the Nova Scotia Teachers' Union in 1920 from a provincial educational association. In Newfoundland, a convention met in 1890 to form the Newfoundland Teachers' Association, a constitution for which was drawn up in 1898. Other conventions were held in the present century, and in 1924 a permanent secretary was appointed, although less than half of the teachers in the province were members in the depression year 1936. The Canadian Teachers' Federation, organized in 1919, included by 1927 all provincial associations except those of the Roman Catholics in Quebec.

The provincial associations of teachers have done much since World War I to maintain and improve the economic status of the teacher. As an illustration of the changes that occurred in conditions of employment, consider the development of security of tenure in British Columbia. The first step in 1879 was to require thirty days' notice by the teacher or the board

when resignation or dismissal occurred during the term. In 1905 the same notice was required even at the end of the term. After 1922, dismissal, except for gross misconduct, was not effective until the end of the half-year term; after 1925, a teacher might appeal against dismissal to the Council of Public Instruction; and after 1933 there was provision in such cases for a board of reference. By 1940 teachers in the other western provinces and Ontario had this same right of appeal to a board of reference in case of allegedly unjust dismissal. Throughout Canada, whether by law or by custom, teachers were dismissed by most boards only for cause — that is, on grounds that their continued employment would be detrimental to the school — and annual appointment of teachers was being supplanted by contracts of a continuing type.

Teachers' associations have made it their business to insist on the observance by members of good ethics in dealing with boards and in relations with other teachers. They have also in recent years extended their activities for the professional growth of teachers and for the improvement of education by conducting study groups, research, and conventions, and by assuming much responsibility in the construction of new curricula. After experiencing the weakness of voluntary organizations during the depression, most of the associations sought to strengthen their position by legislation requiring membership of all certificated members of the profession. By 1944 Alberta, Saskatchewan, Manitoba, Ontario, New Brunswick, and Prince Edward Island had in operation plans of automatic membership which made virtually all teachers fee-paying members of their provincial organization.

PENSIONS

The status of teaching was improved when the promise of superannuation benefits helped to retain teachers in the profession and to reward faithful service. The Royal Institution in Quebec paid generous pensions to at least four teachers in the 1820's, but the practice ceased when the paternalistic agency, soon afterwards, lost its favored position. In the early part of the nineteenth century many petitions from incapacitated teachers and widows of teachers illustrated the prospect of dire poverty faced by those who survived the period of remunerative employment. Superannuation schemes were introduced in Canada West in 1854 and in Canada East three years later, but they were so inadequately financed that in the former province the average annual pension was only $26.54 in 1860 and in the latter the rate of payment per year of service had fallen from $4.00 to $1.75 by 1867.

Quebec in 1880 introduced a plan under which teachers contributed two per cent of their salaries and the government contributed $1000 plus one per cent of the school fund; although no minimum pension was guaranteed, a half-pension was provided for widows and the amount of the pension could be increased by increased contributions from the teacher. Ontario teachers in the following year asked the Minister of Education for the last two privileges, but they received a reply characteristic of nineteenth-century thought: the minister was against making pensions compulsory, especially for women, and was also against giving a higher pension to those who remained for more than twenty-five years of service, for fear that teachers who had outlived their usefulness would continue teaching in order to get a larger pension. From 1885 to 1917 no superannuation plan was supported by the government of Ontario. In Newfoundland a Teachers' Pension Fund on an actuarial basis was established in 1892 to provide $100 a year at age 60; teachers contributed for twenty years before the first pensions were paid in 1912, so that the fund was in a strong position from the first and resulted in teachers gaining an unusually favorable superannuation scheme.

In Ontario in 1917 and in all other provinces before 1940, new or revised pension plans gave a degree of security to teachers. Unfortunately they were not actuarially sound and could rely only on fixed contributions from the provincial governments. On some of the superannuation funds, like those of Ontario and Alberta, there was a heavy drain of immediate payments. The British Columbia plan of 1929 tried to avoid this handicap but assumed other liabilities, which in 1940 forced a reconstruction on an actuarial basis with provision for periodic evaluations of its financial position. Soon afterward, the province of Quebec set an example in providing for the payment from consolidated revenue of sums needed in addition to the contributions of teachers. After World War II, revisions of the Ontario scheme provided in the same way for equally liberal pensions. In 1950, although superannuation plans of other provinces were not generally as favorable as those of Central Canada, the old-age security of the teacher, in all provinces, was sufficiently definite that the Canadian Education Association sought to devise a scheme that would permit the teacher to move from one province to another without loss of pension benefits.

Certification

The chief means employed by central authorities during the nineteenth century for raising the qualifications and the status of teachers was related to the issuing of licences to teach. The regulations became more exacting in two ways. At first the central authorities permitted local authorities or intermediate agencies to issue certificates at discretion; then they defined qualifications that candidates should have; then they took over the setting and later the marking of written examinations on which certificates were based; simultaneously they began themselves to issue higher certificates and subsequently all certificates — the whole evolution being completed as a rule between 1820 and 1900. Again, between 1840 and 1940, as opportunities were presented, the central authorities raised the requirements for certification and stopped the issuing of certificates of a lower grade. Improvement was effected by requiring local authorities to employ certificated teachers and often by paying larger grants either to the school board or to the teacher when the latter held a certificate of higher grade. Hence a purpose was served in the nineteenth century by issuing from three to five grades of certificate in each province to elementary school teachers alone. But during the present century, as incentive grants were reduced and higher minimum standards for certification secured, the retention of several grades of certificate tended to become instead an easy means of descent to lower standards when local authorities rebelled at the increasing cost of fully qualified personnel.

CERTIFICATION BY LOCAL AUTHORITY

The chief requirements to be met by an applicant for a licence in the old days were of a distinctly formal nature: for a time in the eighteenth century that he be a member of the Church of England, and after 1816 in Upper Canada that he be a British subject. Inevitably such formal requirements had the effect of condoning favoritism or excessive latitude in granting certificates to those who possessed the designated qualification. "Our expectations have been defeated," said Acting Governor Campbell of New Brunswick regarding parish school legislation of 1816, "by the appointment of improper and incompetent schoolmasters." In Prince Edward Island in 1834 a member of the legislative assembly urged "that no candidate be admitted to an examination unless he can produce a testimonial of his sobriety and correct moral habits signed by at least four of the most respectable inhabitants of the district in which he is to teach." In Lower Canada two years later a member deplored the "too great facility" with which teaching diplomas were issued to persons who showed need of attending school not as teachers but as pupils. District or county boards, charged with the examination of teachers in Upper Canada after 1820 and in New Brunswick after 1837, were usually more capable and impartial than local trustees but they could hardly make a good choice from candidates lacking any real qualifications. People who appreciated the difficulty saw that the selection and certification of teachers must be linked to a plan of teacher education. New Brunswick after 1847 had a board of examiners in connection with the newly established training school and tried unsuccessfully to enforce the attendance of all teachers for a short period. In a Halifax periodical, *The Provincial,* in 1853, a contributor wrote:

The art of public teaching in this province should ere long assume a more elevated tone, and be acknowledged as a profession in the same manner as law, physic, or divinity; for the furtherance of which a public institution should be established for the study of those requisites of a good teacher which all will acknowledge are so earnestly called for.[9]

CERTIFICATION BY THE CENTRAL AUTHORITY

Between 1850 and 1900 teacher education and certification by the central authority became the rule, although not all who secured a licence were trained. The written examination as a test of knowledge became a chief means of selection.

That the examination sometimes demanded no more than the memorization of prescribed formal content is suggested by practice in the 1860's in Canada East, where the Council of Education approved the main questions that might be asked of a candidate in sixteen content subjects and in pedagogy. But the required content, especially for higher certificates, soon attained much bulk, as may be seen by the prescriptions for the five grades of licence in Nova Scotia in 1867:

GRADE E: geography of Nova Scotia, general geography, teaching, school management, arithmetic, English, and grammar

GRADE D: the above plus British history, algebra, English analysis, and English composition

GRADE C: the above plus bookkeeping, plane geometry, and prosody

GRADE B: the above plus outlines of universal history, natural philosophy, chemistry of common things, practical mathematics, and navigation

GRADE A: the above plus history of Greece, history of Rome, ancient geography, solid geometry, Latin, and Greek.[10]

Knowledge of the above content was measured in Nova Scotia by a provincial board that had just been set up to conduct uniform examinations and issue certificates valid anywhere in the province. A candidate was required to earn an average of at least 50 per cent and to have no mark on any one paper further below 25 than his average was above 50. Those who failed within limits to obtain a higher certificate were granted the next lower certificate. The results for 1868 tabulated in the *Journal of Education* were:

GRADE OF CERTIFICATE	CANDIDATES FOR	CERTIFICATES GRANTED
A	1	0
B	78	31
C	210	76
D	178	107
E	38	78
	505	292

From this it would appear at first glance that there were plenty of applicants for admission to teaching and that the examiners could afford to be strict in their selection. But as we shall see later, preparatory courses for teaching were offered in high schools and foisted on more candidates than would otherwise have chosen to write such examinations. In 1880, however, minimum standards were raised by dropping the grade E licence.

RAISING THE STANDARDS

Such raising of standards for certificates was general in the last third of the nineteenth century, although storms of protest arose when central authorities made it more difficult to obtain certificates. In Ontario the normal school entrant of 1869 could not have passed the high school entrance examination of 1877, and all teachers by the later date had at least a year or two in high school. Twenty years later the minister of education pointed to other evidence of improvement: women were required to reach the age of eighteen, instead of sixteen, before being eligible for a certificate, and three times as many teachers in service were normal school graduates. Even in the west, where teachers were scarce, standards were stiffened around 1890 to protect qualified teachers who had come out from the east to pursue teaching as a career. The usual plan in the latter part of the nineteenth century was to permit a teacher to begin service with limited qualifications and a low grade certificate and to encourage inservice improvement by offering higher certificates when superior academic and professional qualifications were attained.

Attempts were made occasionally to grade teachers by performance and either to make the grading public or to use it as a basis of payment. As early as 1834-35 the board of education in the London District of Upper Canada rated its schools according to the merit of teachers:[11]

Year	Schools Graded				Total
	1st	2nd	3rd	4th	
1834	1	2	35	50	88
1835	8	11	58	36	113

But in spite of the upgrading, which seemed to show that the plan was successful in effecting improvement, there were complaints from teachers, and especially from those with large classes, about the unequal distribution of public money on this basis. In New Brunswick it was decided to base provincial aid to the teachers after 1876 partly on their efficiency as judged by inspectors. In Prince Edward Island, from 1886 to 1892, inspectors listed in public reports the names of teachers judged to be doing the best work. In the Northwest Territories about 1886 the Third Class certificate given to any normal school graduate was upgraded by the inspector's report to a Second Class for a "good" rating and to a First Class for an "excellent" rating. But shortly afterward, written examinations were introduced to determine First, Second, or Third Class non-professional standing, and the inspector's report simply gave the teacher the corresponding professional standing needed for a certificate. Discrimination among teachers on any basis other than standards attainable by further study or longer service appears to have been abandoned after a short trial.

During the present century, progress was made by dropping lower grades of certificates and getting a larger proportion of teachers to qualify for the higher certificates. Nova Scotia raised the minimum grade of academic standing from IX to X in 1926, and to XI in 1932. British Columbia abandoned Third Class certificates in 1922 and Second Class certificates in 1935, and concurrently raised the minimum academic qualifications to Grade XII standing in 1930 and Grade XIII in 1935. In fifty years the distribution of public school teachers in two provinces by grade of certificate changed as follows:

Number of Teachers Holding Certificates

	Year	First Class	Second Class	Third Class
Ontario:	1900	575	3742	3819
	1950	10,950	2935	28
P.E.I.:	1900	120	349	117
	1951	248	384	16

Another factor was the introduction of still higher certificates, like the "academic" licence that appeared in Nova Scotia in 1896. British Columbia introduced an academic certificate in 1901 and required university graduation as a qualification for the certificate in 1918. Many teachers also procured certificates as specialists in various fields. In several provinces teachers began service with interim certificates, which were ordinarily made permanent after two years of successful experience; but during the 1930's further in-service training, usually at summer schools, was commonly required for permanent certification. As a result, teachers in 1940 had qualifications incomparably superior to those acceptable at the beginning of the century.

Supply and Recruitment

Unfortunately there is another side to this record of progress. It has never been possible to procure an adequate supply of candidates with high qualifications for teaching, except when economic conditions have made it difficult to find employment in other fields. This fact and the chief reasons for it were recognized more than a century ago. The Bishop of Montreal pointed out to the governor in 1838 that only "the poorest types" could be obtained as teachers for the money available. In the Maritime Provinces a member of the assembly said in 1840 that teachers were so hard to find that trustees sometimes were "obliged to wait in the market place when an immigrant vessel arrived and ask if there were anyone qualified and willing to take charge of a school in the country." An Englishman who had come to Upper Canada before 1840 declared:[12]

Were it not that I am encouraged by two or three respectable families, I would as soon be found thieving as teaching school here.

A government report in New Brunswick in 1842 said:

No man unless degraded will take charge of a school in a remote settlement where the inhabitants are generally poor and illiterate and amongst whom he must board and lodge.

This points to an educational problem inherent in democracy. The common school teacher was employed by common people who had little education or appreciation of education. In contrast, the grammar school master served a section of the population who valued what he had to offer, and the master of a paternalistic school worked for employers who gave him some prestige as their agent.

The low respect for education among the people was a handicap that might have been fully overcome by the schools in a few generations had it not been for cleavages and inequalities in society that were exploited as easy ways of keeping education cheap. Women, debarred from other employment, formed a great reservoir of teaching personnel; and when the flood-gates were opened about 1850, no man could sell superior educational services in competition against them. Then, when industrial progress gave the means to attract into teaching the sons and daughters of families at a higher social level, the more prolific and less prosperous rural areas sent out their sons and daughters to underbid all others even in the city market. As a result, in spite of urbanization and greatly increased appreciation of education by the people, teaching continued to be regarded as employment suitable for women and for men of inferior ability. After World War I, new opportunities for women in other fields operated as a partial corrective. But the standards and values of rural society associated with teaching still prevented the recruitment of personnel from the higher levels of urban society. On one occasion at least, a city looked for an escape from dependence on rural areas: in 1880 the Toronto Public School Board proposed to use its own schools as model schools for a preliminary year of training, after which successful candidates were to be sent to normal school to acquire Second Class certificates. Subsequently the term "county and city model schools" replaced "county model school" in the Ontario regulations.

In Alberta only 50 per cent of the students at Edmonton Normal School came from farm homes in 1932-33, but the proportion increased to 64 per cent in 1937-38 and to 80 per cent in 1943-44. At the Calgary Normal School the year before, students reported the occupations of their parents as follows: farmers, 56%; laborers, 13%; business men, 9%; clerical workers, 7%; skilled laborers, 7% professional men, 1%; miscellaneous, 7%. Between 1930 and 1943 the percentage of normal school students of British origin dropped from 50 to 35. Finally, in the early years of the war, tests showed a marked decline in the number of more able students preparing to be teachers. In Nova Scotia in 1950 it was found that a comparatively large proportion of students at the normal college came from agricultural or mining areas where the people were poor, and that only a very small number of students came from some prosperous agricultural areas and from the urban centres of Halifax and Halifax County.

Local influence in rural areas has been persistently opposed to high qualifications for teachers. Among the reasons for taking away the power of licensing from trustees was their willingness to qualify anyone as a teacher in order to obtain the grant. Even district boards showed some partiality, which was reduced around 1850 by the introduction of written examinations, further reduced around 1875 by having boards composed of professional educators, and eliminated around 1900 by the abolition of all licensing boards except the provincial body. But through the provincial legislatures, rural voters continued to block the attempts of departmental officials to raise the requirements for minimum certificates and the prestige of teaching. Professional educators and laymen interested in the improvement of education have urged for a century that recurrent problems of teacher supply be overcome by raising qualifications to a level that will command the respect of young men and women with professional aspirations. But governments and provincial departments of education, under contrary pressure, have done less than they conveniently might have done when teachers were in over-supply. As a result, teaching lacked the prestige to hold its own against other occupations in times of prosperity, so that standards had then to be lowered to appeal to the less capable as an emergency measure. The "emergency" by 1953 had lasted for a decade, with the certainty that the shortage of teachers would become more critical as the number of pupils increased, and with no relief failing economic recession.

Central authorities, especially that of Ontario, showed weakness in continuing to issue low-grade certificates wholesale when an adequate number of better-qualified teachers might have been obtained at a reasonable cost to school boards. The model schools of Ontario were described by a professional journal in 1880 as "fifty-two mills or teacher manufactories that bid fair to swamp, by their over-production of an article which is now a drug on the market, the profession of teaching in this province."[13] Five years later an-

other educational periodical complained that for the lower positions in both public and high schools the number of available teachers was greatly in excess of the number required, that "from twenty to fifty applicants for one position was no uncommon number," and that annual swarms of new candidates underbid and drove out experienced teachers. The major difficulty arose from the fallacious assumption that it is possible to give easy access to a profession and require practitioners to improve their qualifications later. The pretence was that beginners should be permitted to teach not longer than three years on a Third Class certificate and that they should then spend a year or two at high school and six months at normal school to acquire Second Class certificates. Actually three-quarters of them dropped out of teaching by the end of the three-year period and many of the rest sought and obtained permission to continue teaching on Third Class certificates. In 1879 the department granted extensions or permits to teach to 356 of 362 applicants. Although the number the next year was much smaller, a deputation of teachers in January, 1881, protested against the practice to the minister of education, who was reported to have replied diplomatically. Below the level of Third Class certificates, the regulations of 1878 provided for monitor's and assistant's certificates valid only for a year but renewable without much difficulty.

The first acute shortages of qualified teachers in the present century occurred in the rapidly developing middle west and generally throughout Canada before the end of World War I. In Manitoba, around 1912, from 200 to 300 permits to unqualified persons were issued annually. In Saskatchewan the number of permits rose from 187 in 1906 to 915 in 1911 and to about 1400 in 1914, in spite of a steady increase in the number trained in normal school and in spite of the offering of

Third Class certificates on easy terms — Grade IX standing and ten weeks' training as the initial requirement. Yet towns were able to entice First Class teachers from Ontario. The province of Alberta, faced with similar difficulties, advertised for teachers in other provinces and in the British Isles, and in 1913 admitted to normal school graduates of accredited high schools and universities in the United States on condition that they pass special examinations in history, geography, and civics. In 1919 a Manitoba commission reported on the teacher shortage throughout Canada and the United States. It pointed out that too many teachers had qualifications of the lowest grade, that the proportion of men was declining, and that the value placed on the services of teachers outside cities was less than the amount received by agricultural laborers, section men, clerks, stenographers, dressmakers, milliners, and experienced telephone operators. Asked what steps had been taken or were contemplated to obtain teachers, three provincial departments indicated the adoption of minimum salaries and four departments reported higher grants to improve salaries. The shortage was overcome in a few years with the assistance of newly-formed teachers' associations.

The depression of the 1930's caused a surplus of teachers, since many former teachers again sought positions in the schools. Standards were raised to require at least an extra year of pre-service education. British Columbia and Alberta in 1931 set limits on the number of students to be admitted to normal schools and in 1932 raised the tuition fees. These and other measures calculated under conditions of financial stringency to discourage attendance at training institutions were successful in causing a drop in enrolments. Had the depression been followed by a protracted period of moderate prosperity, it is probable that the status of teaching would have been enhanced and that the higher minimum standards would have attracted candidates of superior quality. Some improvement was effected, but the advance was reversed after two years of war.

By the fall of 1941 recruitment for the armed services and the attraction of more remunerative employment in war industries had so decreased the supply of teachers that it was impossible to find qualified personnel willing to accept employment in schools of more remote and less desirable districts. Had the districts lacked doctors or lawyers, it is unlikely that provincial governments would have authorized recourse to unqualified substitutes. But to have schools with no older person in charge was too flagrant evidence of neglect of the young, and ministers of education issued letters of permit that enabled trustees who could not find a qualified teacher to employ what was presumably the best person they could find. This cheap solution proved so popular that the number of permit holders multiplied — to 1950 by 1944 in Saskatchewan, where there were then about 4500 qualified teachers. Permits were granted to candidates with lower and lower qualifications — in Manitoba to untrained graduates from Grade XII at the beginning of the war, and to untrained graduates from Grade XI in 1942. Students with inferior qualifications were admitted to normal schools. British Columbia in 1942 accepted applicants if they had only one grade XIII subject. Alberta in 1943 admitted students without a high school diploma. In Ontario, the qualifications required of prospective teachers were progressively lowered, from eight upper school papers in 1940, to seven in 1943, and to five in 1944; and after 1948 such conditional students were no longer required to make up the deficiencies in their qualifications.

Emergency short courses of "training" were offered in summer sessions, when schools were closed and practice teaching was impossible, not only to those who were qualified for admission to normal school, but sooner or later to others with incomplete or inferior qualifications. Assurances that candidates of low attainments would be forced by regulations later to improve their qualifications were no more reliable than the empty promises regarding Third Class teachers in the nineteenth century. Manitoba found that two-thirds of those who entered emergency summer courses with Grade XII standing did complete their training but that only one-third of those who entered with Grade XI standing were willing to take time off to acquire full qualifications and return to teaching. To retain the services of the latter, it was provided in 1951 that a fraction of the Grade XII work given in a summer session should be accepted for entrance to the normal school year. From 1944 to 1956 Ontario intermittently offered emergency summer sessions on a somewhat similar plan and disinterred the Second Class certificate, the demise of which had been a cause of congratulation twenty years before.

This depressing account of retreat in teachers' qualifications might be extended to include other expedients and to cover all provinces, but enough has been said to show that the loss in quantity and quality of educational personnel was extremely serious. There was, however, a brighter side. In cities and populous areas and in larger high schools, which were accustomed to employ teachers with high qualifications, teachers with high qualifications continued to be employed. In fact there was never a serious over-all shortage of high school teachers, who by virtue of the requirement of four or five years of university education were placed on a par with members of other professions. It appeared certain, however, that even in urban centres the qualifications of elementary school teachers would be ad-

versely affected in the future, because a large proportion of all such teachers would continue to receive their early education in rural schools where teachers with reduced qualifications were most likely to be employed. An encouraging factor was the resistance of teachers' associations and the reluctance of departmental officials when further concessions were sought. Most important, the certificate structure of 1940 was maintained on paper almost intact, so that regularly trained and certificated teachers were nearly as well prepared as formerly. Some believed that the status of teaching could be maintained if those who from inability or indifference were content with inferior preparation were called monitors rather than teachers. But the probability was that the North American levelling process would make the introduction and retention of any such distinction impossible. Secondary school teachers in Ontario in 1953 were fighting to keep their identity separate from that of elementary school teachers, whose professional status was being undermined. But under twentieth-century conditions the prestige of the whole teaching profession was bound to be determined ultimately by the standards of admission to the profession at the lowest level.

In the immediate future, however, the demand for high school teachers will be so great that they will be in a favored position. The tidal wave of a school population suddenly increased by the higher birthrate will break into the secondary schools before 1960, at a time when the supply of university graduates will be far from sufficient to augment the teaching staffs. During the 1960's the universities will provide more graduates if they are able then to accommodate a much larger number of students. But the school population will continue to multiply and the need for teachers will remain acute for many years.

Humility and Humiliation

Traditionally the teacher, or at least the teacher at the elementary level, has been a lowly person. It means little to say that he was usually a slave in ancient Greece and Rome, since doctors and business executives were also often slaves. But even in North America in more recent times, Benjamin Franklin accurately reflected the common assessment of the teacher's work when he argued that his proposed academy would educate young men of ability for important callings and at the same time prepare others of a "lesser sort" to serve as schoolmasters. When schools for all were established in the nineteenth century, there were insurmountable obstacles to any immediate improvement in the teacher's lot — the poverty of the common people whose children were to be taught, the low value attached to education by the uneducated majority, the limiting effect of distances in a sparsely settled country, and above all, the poor esteem in which children were held. When youngsters were many and the chances of survival were adverse, parental sacrifice to provide lengthy education for the first comers was a poor risk and subsequent investments of the kind were not economically feasible. Hence the teacher was one who kept the child from immediately productive work with no certain promise that his intangible offerings would serve any solid purpose later.

Although these handicaps had been largely overcome by 1950, older concepts of teaching and old ways of dealing with teachers persisted — perhaps not wholly of necessity, but partly, one suspects, to recruit for teaching those likely to be amenable to old-world views. For example, in teaching, very great importance has been attached to keeping minimum salaries a little above the subsistence level and not much attention has been paid to the illiberality of long-term incentives. In efforts to interest young people in teaching, verbal appeals have ascended at times to a lofty plane but policy in action has disclosed a preference for the lowly and mediocre in circumstances and ability. Petty bribes were offered to bring into the fold those least able to refuse them immediately and least likely to rebel at such treatment later.

Partly because the need for normal schools was not appreciated, it became the practice from the first to offer living allowances to induce students to attend; in Canada West such allowances were offered after 1847 and in Canada East after 1857. In New Brunswick the provincial board of education was empowered in 1858 to offer an allowance not exceeding £6 ($24 x 4) to any one teacher for expenses during his ten weeks at training school. Since the instruction in the ten weeks' session was largely of a general character, it is not surprising that nearly half of the graduates that the principal of the Saint John school was able to trace had taken employment in some other profession. After nearly half a century of comparable inducements, teachers in New Brunswick with higher qualifications were getting out of teaching as fast as they could, while large numbers of low-level candidates were hired and licensed to take over classrooms for a while. "Easy come, easy go" was a rule that applied even more disastrously to the occupation of teaching than to the handling of money, for the easy-comers forced the going of those whose training had been hardest. Said Superintendent J. R. Inch in 1901:

The time has come when some remedy must be found for this growing evil; otherwise every effort which has been made to raise the standards of efficiency in the schools . . . will be rendered abortive.

Twenty-five years before in Prince Edward Island, when 110 teachers withdrew from the profession in Queen's County alone, the annual report of the department of education had declared:

To remedy this evil the teaching profession must be raised, and sufficient inducement offered to men of culture and talent to enter it.

But gifts or loans to teachers-in-training were still used as inducements in the present century. New Brunswick offered loans from 1921 until 1926, when improved salaries and pensions made them unnecessary. Alberta also offered loans to bring students into normal school before the depression increased the supply of teachers. Subsequent reforms in the western province raised the prestige and dignity of teacher education, but when the supply of teachers was reduced as an effect of the war, rural pressure forced the government to offer gifts of money to those who would take a short-cut to certification.

Those who thought of teaching as a career had to be prepared to accept treatment which in other ways was less than generous. At Portneuf, Lower Canada, in 1822, local regulations required the teacher to make up, during a one-month holiday, time lost by his absence from school throughout the year. Thirty or forty years later many teachers were still required

to perform the duties of caretakers, a nuisance that was also a detriment to professional prestige.

Enough has been said of indignities in conditions of work and in financial matters and of the extremely strict supervision of the lives of teachers-in-training. Even in the Victorian age, people expected the teacher to observe proprieties not always exhibited by themselves. Education authorities counselled perfection, but one experienced teacher gave more flexible advice on being sociable in the wicked world without becoming too familiar and losing dignity and self respect:

If you ever have occasion to go into a hotel, walk in; don't sneak in . . . Smoke boldly, moderately, and above all genteely, for we may say that such habits are relieved of half their vice in losing what is gross about them, and people will think none the worse of you.[14]

By 1950, seventy years later, a larger proportion of the public had no objection to teachers' being like other people in their social life. Concurrently, one would hope, teachers acquired a more appropriate distinction by virtue of professional knowledge and skill. The development of a basis for such respect is the subject of the next chapter. The summary of this chapter is included with that of Chapter 28.

CHAPTER 28

Teacher Education

PRE-SERVICE EDUCATION: BEFORE 1850 · 1850-1875 · 1875-1900 ·
1900-1940 · 1940-1953 · CHANGING EMPHASIS IN TEACHER EDUCATION ·
PRACTICE TEACHING · THE PREPARATION OF HIGH SCHOOL TEACHERS

IN-SERVICE EDUCATION: INSTITUTES AND ASSOCIATIONS · SUPERVISION ·
SUMMER SCHOOLS · PROFESSIONAL READING · POST-GRADUATE COURSES ·
PERSONAL QUALIFICATIONS · SUMMARY

There are at least six important aspects of a teacher's education: home and social life from an early age; general education in school and college; acquisition of content to be taught; pre-service professional education; teaching experience; and in-service, further education. Attention is directed in this chapter chiefly to pre-service and in-service education of a professional character, but not because the other aspects are less important. For an historical overview, pre-service education is discussed in relation to successive periods. Separate accounts are given of a few important developments and also of in-service training of different types.

PRE-SERVICE EDUCATION

Before 1850

The qualifications of elementary school teachers remained at an exceedingly low level in the early period largely because teacher education was confined to the cramped circle of the elementary school.

The pupil usually became a teacher without receiving a broader education in secondary school or college. He also acquired from his own elementary school experience firmly rooted ideas of pedagogical procedure without any subsequent corrective in the shape either of professional in-

569

struction or of some better example. The common school teacher was therefore inevitably trained to teach as he had been taught. Since a very large proportion of the common schools were very bad, little improvement was possible.

But around 1830, academies, especially in English-speaking Lower Canada, enrolled students who were willing to take more than a bare common school education in preparation for teaching. The better academies not only extended the knowledge of future teachers but set an example of teaching methods superior to those encountered in ordinary common schools. Georgeville school in Stanstead County, Lower Canada, received high praise for its work in preparing teachers. A report of May, 1830, stated:

[The school] hath flourished from its commencement to its close, the schollars evincing the greatest emulation as well as the greatest proficiency in their Several Studies. Several left the School the first of the Year last and became Teachers in this and the adjoining Towns and twelve or fifteen females have left the first of this month for the same purpose . . .[1]

After a summer term beginning July 8th, the school received another glowing report in November:

It has now Several Young Gentlemen well qualified who intend to take Schools in this county the ensuing Winter. While Several females who have been absent Teaching this Summer are now about re-entering this School and Extend their studies through the winter — This is undoubtedly the first School in the Eastern Townships and the system of Teaching is well adapted to the qualifying of Elementary Teachers.[2]

The alternating of teaching experience and further education in complementary seasons by the young men and women suggests seriousness of professional purpose. Among French-language schools in Lower Canada a superior school for girls at St. Eustache was described by Dr.

Meilleur in 1825 as "une véritable école normale." At Boulardarie in Nova Scotia in 1839 an academy opened by a Mr. and Mrs. Munro was an early exemplar in North America of the "training system" of David Stow.

There were several early attempts to introduce teacher training of a more formal character. During the French régime the Ursuline nuns gave training to novices for the work of teaching, and the Sisters of the Congregation of Notre Dame in the mother house at Montreal organized a special class to prepare sisters for teaching. The Frères Charon, or Hospital Brothers, tried, though without success, to provide training for teachers to be sent out to rural parishes.

Early in the nineteenth century, monitorial schools trained teachers to follow the prescribed system. In the *Quebec Gazette* in 1816 and 1817 the Canadian Committee for Promoting Education advertised for young men to attend the Lancastrian school in the city "for the purpose of being instructed in the method of teaching there introduced" and so qualifying as teachers and causing the method to spread throughout Canada. One of the objectives of the British and Canadian School Society, founded in Montreal in 1822, was to "train up and qualify young persons of both sexes to supply well instructed teachers."[3] The government made grants to the society for the purpose and also a grant in 1831 to Lancaster himself, who was then in Montreal. Lancaster was voted £100 for the support of a school and additional grants of £5 each for not more than ten persons "whom he shall instruct and qualify for teaching and managing a school, according to the method and system followed by him."[4] The Royal Institution sometimes required men seeking employment as teachers to take some training in the Madras system at the school in Quebec. J. F. Perrault in 1830 offered free instruction at his school in Quebec to anyone wishing to qualify for teaching in a French elementary school. Although a few teachers were trained in the monitorial method, the system could not be applied in less populous areas, a fact that soon became obvious.

In 1836 in Lower Canada an act was passed to establish two normal schools, for which a generous budget was provided. On behalf of the committee in charge of the Montreal school, the Abbé Holmes went to Europe and brought back two instructors, one from Scotland and one from France. But the school had only three students when it opened and lost its students and its grants during the rebellion. Religious differences hindered the opening of the second school in Quebec. Nevertheless, grants provided by the Act of 1836 did result in the training of some sixteen women teachers in the convents of the Ursulines and of the Sisters of the Congregation. After their arrival in Montreal in 1837, the Brothers of the Christian Schools prepared a considerable number of young men for teaching. In response to a suggestion of Dr. Meilleur, the classical college at St. Hyacinthe also attempted to give courses in methods of teaching, but apparently with little success. In Upper Canada in 1836 the report to the assembly of Dr. Charles Duncombe recommended the establishment of four teacher training schools, three for men and one for women, but nothing was done immediately. The Act of 1841 did provide for township and county model schools, but these schools made little impression and soon disappeared.

In Newfoundland some of the teachers of outlying schools of the Newfoundland Society were men who had received instruction at the central school in St. John's and who continued to work under the supervision of staff members of the central school. The Methodists in Newfoundland also established a central or training school for teachers in 1850.

1850-1875

ESTABLISHING TEACHER TRAINING

The first permanent establishment in Canada of institutions designed specifically for teacher training occurred when the developmental concept of education and the importance of method first began to gain acceptance. Those who could see no purpose in education but the teaching of formal content opposed the establishment of normal schools as an unnecessary duplication of other institutions for teaching post-elementary subjects. Partly because the content concept was still supreme, and partly because the students entering normal schools had very little knowledge, the teacher training courses at first were almost wholly academic in character. Only those who understood the potentialities of education and wanted the people to acquire control over their own lives fully appreciated the value of method. Marshall d'Avray, who had been the first principal of the first training school in New Brunswick, admitted in 1856 that he had seldom encountered students with a desire to become better teachers, although some were prepared to make heroic sacrifices to become better scholars. The knowledge concept of education was still strong even among advocates of normal schools, among whom in 1853 was an inspector in Kamouraska, Canada East, who wanted teachers trained in order that they might acquire "the best systems of instruction, the difficult art of educating children and of leading them, step by step, from the bare elements of knowledge to its more advanced branches."[5]

Content outweighed method by virtue also of the importance attached to particular forms of religious teaching. In Canada West in 1858, the staunch Anglican sceptic, Angus Dallas, attacked the normal school as "an expensive fraud." In

Canada East, denominational cleavage was partly responsible for the failure of the Act of 1836 and for a delay which postponed the establishment of normal schools for ten years after the opening of the normal school in Canada West. Although the Roman Catholic Church was no laggard in the preparation of teachers, the supreme value placed on religious instruction made method relatively less important than content, at least to the extent that clergy teaching in the schools were not required to attend regular courses for certification even when such courses became obligatory for laymen.

Largely through the efforts of provincial superintendents of education, normal or training schools for teachers were established in Canada West and in New Brunswick in 1847, in Nova Scotia in 1855, in Prince Edward Island in 1856, and in Canada East in 1857. That the campaign for the new institutions was taken seriously by both sides may be illustrated by the resignation of William Dawson from the superintendency in Nova Scotia when a bill for the establishment of a normal school failed to pass the assembly in 1852-53.

THE FIRST NORMAL SCHOOL

A candidate seeking admission to the normal school in Upper Canada in 1847 had to be at least sixteen years of age, to produce a certificate of good moral character signed by a clergyman, and to have ability in reading, writing, and arithmetic. To be exempt from fees and to secure an allowance for board, he had to declare his intention of devoting himself to the profession of teaching. Twenty students presented themselves at the opening of the normal school in November, 1847, but the number soon increased to fifty-four. At the opening of the second session in May, 1848, there were one hundred and eighteen students in attendance, including twenty women, since a "female department" had by then been established.

The program of the first Canadian normal school was inordinately heavy. Lecture hours were from nine till one, from two till five, and from six till eight. The headmaster spent five hours a day lecturing on the philosophy of grammar and parsing, on mathematical, physical, and political geography, on the art of reading, on linear drawing, on lessons, on reasoning, on history, and on trigonometry for land surveying. His assistant spent four hours a day, in the afternoon and evening, lecturing on geometry, algebra, arithmetic, various branches of physics, and agricultural chemistry. These were regular subjects scheduled for five days a week. There was also "repetition" on Saturdays from nine to twelve, and apparently in off hours time was found also for "miscellaneous subjects" — music, the mode of teaching writing, writing from dictation, exercises in composition, orthography, derivations of words, and the philosophy of education. Students also attended a model school for an hour a day for observation and practice teaching. Only because there were two divisions, junior and senior, in the normal school, and because some of the lectures were for one division or the other, did the teachers in training have even an occasional spare period during the forty-eight-hour week of lectures.

A student in attendance at the Toronto Normal School in 1853 wrote a letter which gives a spirited account of his experiences in the halls of learning and in a city boarding-house:

We met at the School Rooms on Monday and heard the Laws of the Institution, had a Lesson pointed out for us for Wednesday — and that you may know something of the amount of labour that is required of us I will give you an account of the number, and also the length of them — History 18 Pages — Arithmetic 17 — Geography 8 — Algebra 6

Normal and Model School, Toronto, 1852

— in all 49 Pages — this is pretty good for the first Lesson, I think — We were also told that we would not receive more than 3/9 or 2/6 per week instead of 5/ — in consequence of which I think there will some of the Students leave — We now number in all Male & Female 149 — they are here from 16 to 40 years of age, and some regular green ones I can tell you. . . .

I have been to School to day and I can tell you that we have got to work and no mistake — we are obliged to go to School at 6½ in the morning and stay till 7½, then have 1½ Hours for Breakfast and recreation, or Studies if we choose to deprive ourselves of exercise — go again at 9 and leave again at 12, then 2 Hours for Dinner etc. back at 2 and Home again at 5 — and we cannot leave our Boarding Houses after 9½ without permission from our head Teacher — cannot speak, Bow or Winck at one of the Female Students — nor Spit about the School Rooms or even Premices occupied by the Buildings. Now if we violate the least of the Rules given (and some are hard to keep) or fail of being at the Rooms at the time the Role is called we are *Expelled* without farther ceremony — and it can be done if we are not able to keep up with our several Classes — a

Lady was expelled for this — she saw a young Man while in the Lecture Room poke his slate Pencil against a Lady by the side of whom she was sitting, to call her attention for some purpose — it was found out — the Boy was expelled for the offence, and the Lady for seeing it and not informing against him — I can give you but a vague Idea of the strictness with which we are governed — I shall not intentionally violate any Law — but I may do so inadvertantly, and if such should be the case I should expect no clemency. . . .

The Mistress says I must take a Bed-fellow or pay extra, but I am done having a Male Roommate — I have a small Room and a narrow Bed and I shall neither have a Roommate or pay extra — she says we must also pay extra for Washing, but I also told her I would not do that atol, she says I am a hard case to deal with as I will stick for my rights — I also kicked up a little fuss about our Meet Potatoes & Bread and made her bring on bettern — I told her where I lived our dogs would not smell of the Meat she sot before us — and the Swine would run from the Potatoes & Bread, this was at dinner, before the whole of the Boarders — some bit their Lips, others held their Breath

— but none spoke — after dinner they concluded I should be presented with a Medal but it has not yet come — I asked the Misses if she wished me to leave — she said, no, sure she would sooner part with any of the Gents than me —[6]

COURSES OF STUDY — THE BURDEN OF LEARNING

The length of the session in early normal schools varied: in New Brunswick it was ten weeks at first, with four sessions a year, then twelve weeks, and after 1865 forty weeks, although not consistently so; in Prince Edward Island it was three months; in Nova Scotia and Canada West, it became five months; and in Canada East it was ten months from the beginning. Admission standards were exceedingly low: the required proficiency in reading, spelling, writing, and arithmetic was that which might be attained by a twentieth-century pupil in Grade VI, plus a smattering of grammar and perhaps of geography. Students might remain or return for further sessions to obtain higher certificates — a First Class instead of a Second Class after an extra half-year in Canada West, a Model School or an Academy certificate instead of an Elementary after a second and a third year respectively in Canada East.

In short sessions, as D'Avray pointed out, the pressure was intolerable because of the "great unfitness" of the candidates and the amount of knowledge which they were required by the regulations to absorb. The cramming at Toronto persisted: a gentleman who sent his three daughters to the model school of the Toronto normal school and one of them to the normal school itself wrote in 1868:

The "Model" is a model for examining. There girls are stuffed with more algebra than common sense, and far more than they ever have occasion for. The "Normal" is even worse. There each pupil has no less than twenty-one books to swallow . . . They are taught too much in too short a time, and the mental and physical sufferings some of them have to endure while studying them I too well know.[7]

The normal school must therefore be charged with part of the blame for slave-driving teachers who made life miserable for their pupils and themselves in the decades following Confederation. In 1881 Joseph Workman, M.D., of Toronto addressed the Ontario Educational Association on "The Morbid Results of Persistent Mental Overwork." He stated that the proportion of deaths from consumption among teachers was more than twice as high as among skilled workmen and four times as high as among doctors, that the number of women teachers admitted to asylums for the insane was disproportionately high, and that a reduction would have to be made in the quantity of knowledge teachers were required to memorize and to force on their pupils if the health of both was to be preserved. His paper of about 12,000 words would itself have taxed the endurance of a later audience.

In other provinces the courses of studies followed by normal schools covered the same wide range of content subjects. In Canada East the Act of 1856 defined the program for two French-language normal schools, Laval at Quebec and Jacques Cartier at Montreal, and for the English-language normal school at McGill. Study of the "art of teaching" was made a primary objective, but the course was also to include, among other studies:

Religious Instruction — Methodical Reading — Elocution — Recitation — French and English Grammar — Literary History, both General and Particular — Sacred History — The Histories of England, France, and Canada — Geography — Arithmetic in all its branches — Bookkeeping — Algebra — the Elements of Geometry — Mensuration — Astronomy — Natural Philosophy and Chemistry — Natural History — Agriculture — Horticulture — Linear Drawing — Singing.

Original Normal School Building (right) and Model School (left), Truro, 1855

To teach this program to forty students attending the opening session at McGill, William Dawson, principal of the normal school and of the university, had a relatively adequate staff of two full-time professors and several associate professors for special subjects. At the training school in Saint John, New Brunswick, about the same time, the principal and two assistants gave instruction in school management and the art of teaching and in content subjects, which included spelling, reading, grammar, penmanship, dictation, geography, history, arithmetic, algebra, geometry, mensuration, trigonometry, etymology, vocal music, land surveying, navigation, and bookkeeping. Teachers and would-be teachers entering the training school around 1850 were described as very bad readers and very bad grammarians, utterly ignorant of geography and able only with the greatest difficulty to express their thoughts in writing. Yet they completed this prodigious program in twelve weeks and emerged with an education and a certificate. Such a pedagogical feat could not have been accomplished if the training had been anything more than a transfer of formal content without time-consuming intellectual activity other than memorization.

PROFESSIONAL CONTENT

But by the time of Confederation, method had gained the ascendancy in the better normal schools, which by then had proved their worth. In Nova Scotia, inspector after inspector sent in laudatory reports on the work of normal school graduates. Inspector Miller of Halifax offered a typical comment:

Perhaps no feature in our educational system strikes one more forcibly than the contrast both in discipline and advancement between the schools taught by trained and untrained teachers.[8]

The principal of the normal school in Nova Scotia was Alexander Forrester, who was convinced that such institutions should "adhere rigidly to their own proper work, the manufacture or the training of teachers." He was able to give some attention to methods and practice, and to psychol-

J. B. Calkin

ogy, history of education, school law, and school management as professional subjects, although not to the extent he thought desirable. At Toronto by 1869 about as much time was devoted to method as to content. Principal J. H. Sangster, in a pamphlet of that year, said that every lecture at the normal school was designed not only to give information but to "serve as a model of the method in which the same subject is to be discussed before a class of children."

By 1875 an influential minority of teachers in all provinces had received professional training. In New Brunswick a partially successful attempt was made from the first to bring all teachers to the training school, and in 1868 two-thirds of the teachers had received at least a short course but could hardly be said to have had a professional education. In Ontario less than a quarter of the teachers were normal school graduates in 1875, but they had received at least half a year's training, largely professional in nature.

Selected questions from the normal school examination for First Class certificates in 1874 will show that graduates were expected to have an understanding of education and the techniques of instruction:

What is comprehended in the expression "A well educated person?"

Show the importance to the Teacher of some knowledge of the law of thought; and state what methods you would adopt to cultivate the thinking powers of your pupils.

Upon what foundations may the obedience of children be most securely based, and what expedients would you employ to secure it?

How would you deal with the following cases:
(a) Inattention has become habitual in a Class.
(b) A boy's spirit has been crushed at home.
(c) The girls are boisterous and rude.

Candidates for Second Class certificates in 1873 answered questions of comparable difficulty — for example:

State the arguments for and against giving prizes.

Discuss the comparative advantages of relative and absolute marking.

Describe your method of dealing with pupils who have formed the habit of coming late.

Teacher education had at least set a professional goal.

1875-1900

By 1875, an important transition in teacher education had taken place. It had become the rule for those who intended to teach in elementary schools to acquire some secondary education. There were three important results. First, the qualifications of beginning teachers in terms of general education were higher to the extent of attendance at high school for a year or two, and the qualifications of continuing teachers were often raised to a much higher level. Second, the sharp social and intellectual distinction between elementary and secondary education was blurred. Third, the transfer to the high schools of responsibility for imparting knowledge left the normal schools free to concentrate on professional education.

ONTARIO'S MODEL SCHOOL TRAINING SCHEME

Unfortunately the money was not found to provide pre-service normal school training for all teachers even at the end of the nineteenth century. Ontario opened two additional normal schools, one at Ottawa in 1875 and one in London in 1900. But teachers began their careers after a year or two at high school and about three months' training in the fall of the year at one of the fifty or more county model schools. These were simply elementary schools in which the principal held a First Class certificate and in which three assistant teachers had Second Class or higher certificates, or in other words were normal-school trained. In the model schools, student teachers received a brief apprenticeship and a little instruction, reinforced by lectures from the local inspector. After teaching for a year or more, those who had serious professional aspirations attended high school for another year or two, unless they had previously attained a higher academic level, and then went to normal school for five months' professional training. In this way they obtained a Second Class certificate; and similarly after attaining academic standing equivalent to senior matriculation, or still higher, they might, by further normal school training, obtain a First Class certificate. This scheme would have had merit in giving protracted and intermittent teacher education if it had worked for the majority of teachers in the manner described. Actually, however, two-thirds of those who entered the model schools ceased teaching by the end of the three-year period during which their

Third Class certificates were valid or obtained a renewal of their Third Class certificates, as they could do at first by petition and after 1885 by re-writing the Third Class non-professional examinations. Even if such a teacher failed to make the required average of 50 per cent, but did make the required minimum on each subject — as little as 25 per cent in several cases — the beneficent examiners would add a bonus of 200 marks to the total earned if the teacher's inspector so recommended on the basis of teaching ability.

This coaxing-in and nursing-along of candidates with minimum qualifications discouraged teachers of ability and ambition. The renewal of Third Class certificates by examination was hailed by the department of education as an advance because women without resources or desire for improvement were spared the humiliation of petitioning for an extension. But it was only too clear to teachers seeking a professional career that everything about the model school system was governed by cheapness, most notably the low cost of providing such training and the low salaries for which teachers could be made available by maintaining an over-supply of the least expensive variety. As Althouse says, "the effect of the model schools upon the status of the profession was devastating." They "succeeded only in handing over the vast majority of the schools to the half-trained and immature."[9]

Although spokesmen for the provincial government claimed from the first that the model school plan "met with a large measure of popular favor," and could point at the end of the century to a larger proportion of teachers who were normal-school trained, educational journals and other spokesmen for teachers found little to praise and much to criticize. The principals were too busy to give proper attention to students, the assistants violated in their teaching the pedagogy imparted in lectures, the practice teaching was artificial, and the students, being forced to cram, graduated with the notion that it was their business to see that pupils in school were placed under similar compulsion. When such faults appeared in model schools, there was little chance for the operation of counteracting influences, whereas in normal schools, at least some members of the staff were sure to stand for other ideas and practices.

TEACHER TRAINING IN HIGH SCHOOLS

In other provinces, high schools rather than model schools were used to offer the local and inferior type of teacher education. In Nova Scotia until 1893 professional subjects were included in the regular high school program and taught at the expense of an alternative group of matriculation subjects, so that students with no thought of becoming teachers wrote departmental examinations on teaching, on school law, and on temperance and hygiene. In 1893 the high school course of study was made wholly academic, and the examinations for Minimum Professional Qualifications were separated from the high school graduation examinations. But until 1926 a high school student by writing the Minimum Professional Qualifications examinations could get a professional certificate one grade lower than he might have obtained after a year at normal school, and, up to 1933, temporary licences were issued to applicants without training.

In the sparsely settled west the first high schools to be established were utilized almost immediately to prepare elementary school teachers. In Manitoba, where the first teacher training was provided by the Roman Catholic section of the provincial board at St. Boniface in 1882, the Protestant section of the board opened a high school at Winnipeg in the same year and made it a teacher training centre two years later. In the Northwest

Territories, where union schools combining elementary and secondary grades were introduced in 1888, an attempt was made at first to have every union school maintain a teacher training department. But since the teaching of academic subjects suffered, the number of such departments was limited in 1890 to four centres in the Alberta district and two in the Saskatchewan district. After 1893 teacher training was offered only in one centre, Regina, where a territorial normal school was set up under a special inspector of schools. Superintendent Goggin tried to make training at Regina obligatory, but regulations of 1896 made it necessary only for First and Second Class certificates and provided for the granting of Third Class certificates to candidates prepared in local union schools. In British Columbia, where the first high school was opened in 1874, a few students who were preparing to be teachers were awarded allowances of $100 each and given practice one day in five in Victoria elementary schools. In 1895, while high school training was still the only type of teacher education in the province, the trustees of Victoria tried a supplementary pupil-teacher system, under which one pupil-teacher was placed in each graded school.

ACADEMIC TRAINING FOR TEACHING

Where high schools were competitors of normal schools in giving professional training, the normal schools were sometimes compelled to give academic and general education in competition with the high schools. In Nova Scotia and New Brunswick students were admitted to normal school at various levels, the lowest of which required only Grade IX standing. It is not surprising, therefore, that in New Brunswick an inquiry at the end of the century showed that four-fifths of the time at the normal school was still spent on academic work. In fact, students even then could raise their academic status by attendance at more than one normal school session. In Prince Edward Island in 1876 a parliamentary committee found that the normal school had ceased to give adequate attention to methods. A solution was sought by combining the normal school in 1879 with Prince of Wales College, where the student might complete his academic preparation before writing an examination which gave admission to the normal school department. In Quebec, where entrants were found to have a very imperfect foundation of academic education, up to three years of normal school training was offered until 1885, when the third-year course was dropped. In Ontario, the high schools relieved the normal schools of the need to teach academic work up to the junior matriculation level required for Second Class certificates. But at the highest level — that is, in the course for a First Class professional certificate — the normal schools still spent most of the time on content. This anomaly was under strong attack around 1880, on the ground that collegiate institutes were by then quite capable of handling advanced academic subjects. After 1891 all teacher training institutions in Ontario centred their attention on professional education.

Teachers in all provinces, by 1900, were required to have had some education beyond the elementary level — at a secondary school, at a training school, or at both, but were not necessarily required in all provinces to have had actual professional training. The Ontario model school system did make such training obligatory after 1877. Mention has been made of the attempt in the Northwest Territories, after 1894, to require training at Regina in spite of the difficulties of travel over great distances; after 1890 some training was demanded for teaching in the eastern area bordering Manitoba. In Quebec, where certification could

still be obtained by writing examinations, efforts were made before the end of the century to require normal school attendance. But, actually, in all provinces before 1900 a large proportion of elementary school teachers had no more than two years' secondary education, and either no professional training at all or no such training at the normal school level.

CURRICULUM

The curricula of normal schools in the late nineteenth century differed considerably in printed descriptions and probably even more in practice. In Ontario, around 1880, candidates for Second Class certificates heard lectures on the principles of education, which instructors were supposed to apply and demonstrate in relation to particular subjects. Occasionally students and graduates complained that the lectures were either impossible to follow or excessively boring and wholly unrelated to practice. Students also received instruction in school law but spent more time on school subjects. There was a special need for instruction in music, drawing, domestic economy, and other "frills," likely to be taught only where a teacher of higher qualifications was employed. Additional subjects and activities were added to normal school programs through the period. At Truro, Nova Scotia, a department of drawing was introduced in 1878, a department of elocution and music in 1888, and a department of manual training in 1893. The curriculum in 1894 included psychology, general principles of education, history of education, and methods of teaching the different subjects — in addition, of course, to content subjects. The professional subjects required of First Class teachers in the Northwest Territories in the 1890's were philosophy of education, psychology, school organization, management, and law, and history of education.

1900-1940

INCREASED FACILITIES

From the beginning of the twentieth century the number of normal schools began to increase. In British Columbia in 1901 the Vancouver school board offered facilities in a high school for a provincial normal school, which opened that year. The province erected a building for the Vancouver normal school in 1908 and opened a second normal school in Victoria in 1915. In Alberta, although teacher training was given in Calgary and Edmonton early in the century, normal schools as such began operations at Calgary in 1906, at Camrose in 1912, and at Edmonton in 1919. In Saskatchewan, in addition to the institution already established at Regina, normal schools were set up at Saskatoon in 1912 and at Moose Jaw in 1927. In Manitoba, there were normal schools not only in Winnipeg as before, but at several other places for a short time early in the century, and at Brandon after 1914. Some of the normal schools in the middle west had to wait a few years before acquiring buildings of their own. They were unable for some time to prepare all teachers needed for the rapidly expanding country: in Saskatchewan two-thirds of the licences were issued to teachers from other provinces in 1906, and about one quarter of the licences in 1916, but by 1926 the province was training more teachers than the schools could absorb.

Ontario opened a third normal school in London in 1900 and built four others at Hamilton, Peterborough, Stratford, and North Bay immediately after the county model school plan was abandoned for ordinary purposes in 1907. To prepare teachers for schools in which French was used as the initial language of instruction, model schools were set up at the same time, but were made less necessary by the opening of the University of Ottawa Normal School in 1927, and were discontinued eight years later. Between 1891 and 1919, and to a limited extent thereafter, the province trained First Class teachers in other institutions which will be described below in connection with the professional education of teachers for secondary schools.

To train women teachers for the Roman Catholic elementary schools of Quebec, normal schools were established by various religious orders early in the twentieth century: by the Ursulines at Rimouski in 1906 and at Three Rivers in 1908; by the Sisters of the Good Shepherd at Chicoutimi in 1907; by the Nuns of the Assumption at Nicolet in 1907; by the Sisters of the Holy Names of Jesus and Mary at Valleyfield in 1908; by the Grey Nuns at Hull in 1910; and by the Sisters of the Congregation of Notre Dame at Joliette in 1911. By 1931 there were eighteen, and by 1950 forty, of these convent normal schools for girls. For teaching as laymen, boys continued to be trained in the two long-established normal schools at Montreal and Quebec. In 1931, scholasticates, training religious to teach, were recognized as normal schools, and fifteen scholasticates were in receipt of provincial grants in 1950. The normal schools of French-speaking Canada, especially those for girls, offered not only professional training, but academic content elsewhere taught in high schools, so that the length of the courses ranged from two to four years. For the training of Protestant teachers in Quebec, the McGill Normal School was replaced in 1907 by the School for Teachers of Macdonald College at St. Anne de Bellevue. Each of the three Maritime Provinces continued to operate one provincial normal school — at Fredericton, Truro, and Charlottetown respectively. In Newfoundland, the department offered teacher training to a few candidates after 1921, built a normal school in 1923-24, shared the building with University

Memorial College in 1925, closed the normal school in 1933, and in 1934 set up a new course in professional training at the College.

LENGTHENED TRAINING PERIOD

Between 1900 and 1940 the minimum qualifications for admission to training school were raised in most provinces from one or two years to four or five years of secondary education. During the same period the length of pre-service professional training increased from around four months to about nine months. Saskatchewan, which had a ten weeks' session for Third Class certificates and a sixteen weeks' session for First and Second Class certificates before 1919, introduced a thirty-three weeks' session that year and extended it to thirty-eight weeks in 1926. Ontario, after three years' experience with an optional second-year normal course, in 1933-34 required a second year of attendance by recent graduates after an interval of service. Teachers regarded the year as wasted and the plan as a device to reduce the teacher surplus. The department dropped it. At the beginning of World War II, the shortest period of pre-service teacher education in any of the English-speaking provinces led to a Second Class certificate in Prince Edward Island — Grade X standing obtained at Prince of Wales College plus a further year in which the work was partly academic and partly professional. A further year of academic work led to a First Class certificate. At the other extreme, Ontario and British Columbia required Grade XIII plus a full year of professional courses. In most other provinces Grade XII plus one year was the minimum requirement.

These standards of 1940, the peak of Canadian achievement in raising the minimum pre-service qualifications of teachers, were low in comparison with requirements in comparable countries. The required period of teacher education after secondary school graduation was two years in England, three years in Scotland, and from two to four years in practically the whole of the United States. Superintendent H. H. Shaw of Prince Edward Island, when pleading in 1938 for the minimum requirements mentioned above, made a request that would have seemed moderate to educators of the nineteenth century:

It is unreasonable to expect that teachers who are only one grade in advance of their best pupils can cope with the difficulties that arise in instruction or discipline, and no teacher should be licensed who has not had at least two years study in advance of the classes he must teach.

Yet the advance in four decades had been real, for up to 1906 along the west coast, and longer still near the east coast, rural schools had been staffed by untrained Third Class teachers, whose efforts in the classroom were described by the superintendent in Prince Edward Island in 1914 in these words:

Young, inexperienced, untrained, without sufficient knowledge of the subjects they attempt to teach, much less of how to teach them, with no idea of how to organize classes, no confidence in themselves nor power to govern others, they expend their whole energy in vain efforts to maintain some appearance of authority and discipline.

In contrast, the teacher of 1940 with a high school education and a regular course of training was very much better prepared.

1940-1950

As indicated in the previous chapter, the change in teachers' qualifications that attracted most attention at mid-century was the breach in minimum requirements. Even apart from letters of permit and temporary licences, standards for certification had been lowered or were still low. Conditions in 1950 were summarized by M. E. LaZerte:

In Newfoundland, a candidate with junior matriculation standing may qualify in one summer session for a Third Class certificate, valid in all grades of the school system. In Catholic Quebec, girls who have completed Grade 9 may qualify in two years for the Elementary Diploma, valid as a teaching licence in Grades 1 to 7. In the three Maritime Provinces, one year of professional training following Grade 11 gives certification valid in all grades; in Manitoba and Saskatchewan, senior matriculation standing with one year of professional training leads to certification valid to Grades 9 and 10 respectively. In Ontario, Alberta, and British Columbia, limited certification to Grades 10, 9, and 6, respectively, is given after a year of professional training based on general education that is a little below senior matriculation level.[10]

Nevertheless an evolution in teacher education was under way. We have seen that normal school courses, by the beginning of the present century, had become largely professional in character, with chief emphasis on special methods or techniques related to the teaching of particular subjects. Before World War I such additions to the elementary curriculum as household science, manual training, art, and nature study made it necessary in professional education to give attention to the content of these subjects, especially since few teachers in training had attended larger urban schools in which new subjects were introduced first and taught most effectively. The need to stress content in normal schools diminished yet again as admission requirements demanded longer attendance at secondary schools. But for elementary school teaching the usefulness of additional years at high school depended on the nature of the secondary education received. The strictly academic curriculum taught at the beginning of the century in all secondary schools, and still taught at mid-century

in small rural secondary schools or departments, was of direct use only to the teacher of a combined elementary-secondary school. The broader curriculum of larger high schools in later years, being more closely related to ordinary activities of everyday life, was an asset to all teachers of elementary grades.

For this reason, teacher education has been improved by the determined efforts of provincial departments of education since 1940 to replace small rural secondary schools with well-staffed regional high schools. Improvement has come also from the persistent pressure of departments of education for more flexible university entrance requirements, which make it possible for high schools to offer general education better adapted to the needs of the teacher. But the arrangement whereby the final year of the high school program in Canada — Grade XII or Grade XIII — is considered the equivalent of first year pass Arts in university makes it almost inevitable that the curriculum of that final year shall be preponderantly if not exclusively academic. For this reason, the introduction in Ontario in 1953 of a two-year program of teacher education following graduation from high school at the Grade XII level, as an alternative to the one-year program following graduation at the Grade XIII level, promised more effective preparation of the elementary school teacher, not only in terms of professional courses, but in general education as well.

TREND TOWARDS PROFESSIONAL
TRAINING IN UNIVERSITIES

The need for more than a year of professional education, pointed out in the recommendations of a Canadian Education Association committee in 1949, was apparent to educators across Canada. One reason was that the normal schools in the traditional one-year program were constrained to concentrate attention on spe-

Faculty of Education, University of Alberta

cial methods and techniques and to give correspondingly little attention to educational psychology, philosophy of education, and other content of a more general character. In a sample of nine training schools for elementary school teachers, distributed across Canada, it was found in 1949 that a median of twenty hours a week in a thirty-eight week year was devoted to courses of instruction, and that most of this time was taken up by some fifteen to twenty separate courses related to particular subjects of the elementary school curriculum. This excessive burden of formal instruction on content and special techniques showed that the normal school programs still retained their nineteenth-century characteristics.

To raise the professional level of teacher education, the province of Alberta in 1945 ceased to operate normal schools and transferred responsibility for teacher education to the University of Alberta. A four-year program following senior matriculation and leading to a Bachelor of Education degree was instituted for teachers of all grades, although elementary school teachers were expected to attend for only the first two years before beginning to teach and to complete degree requirements later by summer sessions. The man chiefly responsible for the success of this innovation was Dean M. E. LaZerte of the Faculty of Education, University of Alberta. Through no fault of his, an alternative one-year "emergency" program was offered as a pre-service alternative because of the teacher shortage. But in spite of such difficulties, the new plan achieved several objectives generally regarded as desirable: it gave all future teachers the experience of university life together with students who were preparing for other professions; it gave pre-service general and professional education at the university level; it helped to raise the status of elementary school teaching and brought elementary and secondary school teachers into closer association; and it encouraged teachers to improve their qualifications, since all further education during service carried credit towards full professional status and a university degree.

These and other advantages made it appear likely that the plan introduced in Alberta would set a new Canadian pattern of teacher education. Saskatchewan in 1946 adopted a similar Bachelor of Education program, although one year's training at normal school was retained as a first requirement for elementary school teachers. In 1950, a commission on teacher education in Nova Scotia recommended that three universities of the province offer a four-year B.Ed. program but accept as the second or pre-service year for elementary school teachers a course in one professional school. No action was taken on this recommendation, partly because there are obvious difficulties where several universities are in competition, especially if the total population of a province is small. In British Columbia, where there is one provincial university, as in Alberta and Saskatchewan, the minister of education announced in April, 1952, that the university would take over the responsibility for all teacher education in the following year. Defeat of the government in an intervening election nullified this promise.* In Quebec, however, McGill University introduced the four-year Bachelor of Education program in the fall of 1953. In one other province, Newfoundland, teacher education was offered only by the university, but not on the same terms as elsewhere in Canada.

In other provinces, normal schools continued in operation, although in New Brunswick and Ontario the name "teachers' college" was adopted, as if to begin the type of evolution that had occurred in the United States half a century before. Manitoba, by acquisition of an existing building, set up a residential normal school at Winnipeg. But there were indications in 1953 of a future shift towards university responsibility even in Ontario, where training for teachers in institutions for

* The present government subsequently announced that the change would take place in 1956.

that exclusive purpose seemed to be most strongly entrenched. The elementary school option in the training year for high school teachers at the Ontario College of Education was attracting many students. The University of Toronto had introduced a Bachelor of Education degree at the graduate level. The Public School Men Teachers' Association had published a request for university teacher education leading to an undergraduate degree. The provincial department of education could hardly avoid seeking university entrance or undergraduate credit for the two-year teachers' college program, which was partly professional in character. No overt move was likely to succeed, however, until much later in the century.

Changing Emphasis in Teacher Education

The emphasis in teacher education was almost wholly on content before 1860 and thereafter chiefly on method related to particular subjects and grades, with some shift towards general method from about 1890. About the end of the nineteenth century, also, educational psychology gained in importance. Finally, in recent years, there have been some signs of attention to sociology, or to a philosophy of education related to the social environment. In other words, the emphasis in teacher education has been successively: first, on knowledge of content; second, on methods of instruction; third, but only to an increasing extent and not predominantly, on an understanding of the pupil; and fourth, but only slightly as yet, on an understanding of the world in which education must play its part.

Of these innovations in teacher education, the introduction of psychology was the most significant, because it marked the transition from education as knowledge to education as development, and because it first gave to teachers some

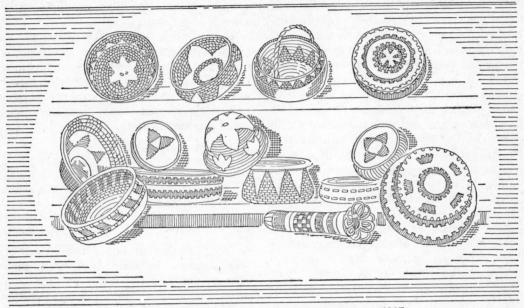

Baskets made by Normal School students, Toronto, 1907

professional understanding instead of mere technical skills. One of the first teacher-training institutions to give attention to the new science was the New Brunswick Normal School. In that school, in the 1870's, and in the second session of the year, a course was given on the nature of the being to be educated, and in the third session a course on psychology as a basis of method. In Ontario at this time occasional lectures on psychology were given to teachers by George Paxton Young and others. In 1877, the minister of education mentioned in his report the possibility of a course of lectures for normal school students on the psychological principles underlying method. Two years later a teachers' association requested the department of education to take such action. In 1883 the principal of the Toronto Normal School in his lectures "entered more fully" into the subject of psychology. Said the minister:

Psychology has hitherto had no place — or a very insignificant place — in our course for teachers, though it is admitted to be the basis of all true principles of education. But, with judicious teaching, it will soon, I hope, be made one of the most interesting of studies, as it certainly is one of the most useful, whether regarded as a means of intellectual discipline, or as the solid groundwork in the professional training of teachers.

The value of psychology in giving teachers a basis for professional judgment was recognized. McLellan, author of *Applied Psychology*, published in 1889, and a high school inspector in Ontario, recommended that teachers acquire a number of books on education but warned them to accept no statement on method which they themselves could not justify on psychological principles. Even more pointedly, another school inspector declared in 1879 that one purpose of teacher education should be "the tracing of method to the psychological and physical conditions in youth that have suggested its adoption, in order that [the teacher] may be made acquainted with principles capable of adaptation to various circumstances, and not mistake a mere slavish imitation of form or manner for the possession of knowledge of the real art of teaching."[11] But very few had such insight then, and the limitation of professional courses to one year in Canada made it impractical to have teachers in training rely on psychological understanding; instead they must learn to use the techniques and methods recommended by their instructors at training institutions.

At the end of the nineteenth century, textbooks used in teacher education usually gave an exposition of psychology which began with the human soul, directed attention to consciousness, and identified such psychic elements as knowing, feeling, and willing. Books recommended to candidates for graduate degrees in pedagogy at the University of Toronto early in the twentieth century included those of Wundt and Titchener, whose psychology was of this structural type. But McLellan in his *Applied Psychology* of 1889 was frankly indebted to John Dewey. Another book published in Toronto twenty years later — *Introductory Educational Psychology* by Sinclair and Tracy — instructed the student to perform experiments and asked questions on what was observed. On the whole it called on the reader to exercise thought and judgment instead of giving authoritative answers to be memorized; and it was modern enough to include chapters on "Reconstruction of Experience" and "Child Study." Other educational psychology textbooks used in teacher education before 1920 included works of G. Stanley Hall, William James, J. R. Angell, E. A. Kirkpatrick, E. L. Thorndike, C. H. Judd, William McDougall, and Peter Sandiford. McDougall's "purposive" psychology emphasized the importance of motives in human behavior, whereas Sandiford and others set forth with somewhat discouraging detachment the effects of heredity and the means of measurement. But some of the above authors and several others centred their attention on the child's growth and development.

The relative importance attached to psychology and to other professional courses is indicated in Ontario regulations of 1896, which state the number of marks assigned to examination subjects at the end of the normal school course for Second Class certificates:

Psychology and science of education	200 marks
History of education	150 marks
School management	150 marks
Methods of teaching (4 papers — 100 x 4)	400 marks
Practice teaching	400 marks

A large number of books were used or recommended in connection with such courses. Some of the books on classroom management, like one by James Currie, published in Great Britain and prescribed in Ontario for Third Class teachers in the 1870's, were so thorough and ponderous that their appearance on book lists and shelves must have been less useful than impressive. Another British book by James Saunders, re-published around 1880 in Toronto, was lighter and more practical, pithy in content and pointed in style. Baldwin's *School Management,* comprehensive enough, was authorized in the 1890's for use in county model schools and normal schools of Ontario. Although history of education was the chief means of relating education to society, books on educational sociology or something akin to it were recommended in teacher education at the First Class level. Giddings' *Elements of Sociology* and Mackenzie's *Social Philosophy* appeared on an Ontario list in 1908.

Practice Teaching

Most founders of normal schools recognized that practice teaching was essential, and teachers in training throughout the ensuing century declared that classroom practice was the most valuable part of the program. Unfortunately, however, the old faith in short cuts to learning led to reliance on artificial substitutes for actual experience. Fear of departure from controlled forms of instruction and penny-wise economy of time and money made it difficult later to abandon the old devices entirely. At the training school in New Brunswick around 1860, one of the students at the end of the day would teach a lesson to the rest of the group, two of whom were designated to criticize the performance. Women students had no other type of practice, since they were kept in isolation from the other sex and practised the art of instruction only on themselves — hardly a realistic preparation for a future career inside the classroom and without. Even in 1885 Principal Kirkland of the Toronto Normal School was obliged to announce to his students:

You will occasionally be required to teach a class of normal school students, who are expected to put themselves in the attitude of children. I am fully aware of the want of naturalness in this practice.[12]

This make-believe teaching exercise was still used in some convent normal schools and possibly elsewhere in 1950.

Model schools for demonstration, observation, and practice were attached to most normal schools almost immediately — at Toronto in 1848 and at Vancouver in 1902, only one year after the opening of their respective normal schools. Although model schools were attached to the normal schools of Quebec, including the McGill school of which Dawson was principal, the eminent Nova Scotian had not favored such an adjunct to the normal school he proposed for his own province. Events there show how even practice teaching arrangements can be hampered by extraneous forces and prejudices.

A probable reason for Dawson's negative attitude regarding a model school for Nova Scotia was his anxiety to locate the normal school in a rural environment, on grounds that living would be cheaper and temptation weaker than in the city. With remarkable perspicacity, the editor of *The Provincial* pointed out in 1852 that a rural location would make it impossible to provide adequately for practice teaching and, incidentally, that a young person without the firmness of moral purpose to withstand the seductions of a centre like Halifax ought not to be an instructor of youth. But legislation of 1854 stipulated that the normal school should be built in Truro and that the town schools be used for practice teaching. Apparently there was a designated model school for some years after 1857, when Forrester was principal, and again between 1887 and 1900. When a new normal school was erected in 1877, it was reported that the town of Truro was to put up $10,000 for a model school, probably only a gesture to justify the retention of the normal school there. In 1893, the time allotted to practice teaching was doubled. But even so, most practice lessons, more than forty years later, were still ten-minute exercises of students appearing one after another before a single class to apply special techniques previously expounded in lectures by the normal school staff. Like other schemes inherited from the nineteenth century, this plan had the merit of relating practice to theory but the defect of not relating practice to life. The plan was retained because inadequate facilities made it impossible to provide real classroom experience.

Although model schools served a good purpose in their time, they, too, were abandoned when it became easy to find good ordinary schools in the vicinity of the training institution. The older normal schools of Ontario, at Toronto and Ottawa, had attached model schools, which were used less and less but retained until World War II; the normal schools built in the present century used ordinary schools in their vicinity for practice. A convenient compromise in Calgary in 1905 was the housing of one of the city schools in the normal school building. Apart from unnecessary expense, reasons for closing model schools were that they could not provide the increasing amount of practice considered desirable and that their classroom conditions were somewhat unusual.

A difficulty resulting from the use of city schools for practice teaching was that teachers in training had no experience in ungraded one-room schools, the type of institution in which the majority were to begin their teaching careers. In 1877 in New Brunswick, Superintendent Rand called attention to the arrangements made in the new normal school building for practice teaching in ungraded classes — equipment with desks adjustable for height "so that such portions of the several grades of pupils in all the departments as the Principal of the Normal School may find necessary, may be assembled in their respective school room, and for any period, without difficulty or disorder."[13] Typical of the nineteenth century, this plan employed a mechanical contrivance and arbitrary organization to produce the form but not the reality of an ungraded school. Even in 1919 such an arrangement was suggested as an expedient by the principal of Saskatoon Normal School, G. M. Weir, who tried unsuccessfully in the following year to obtain transportation to rural schools by bus for teachers-in-training.

Not until the second quarter of the present century were rural schools widely used to provide experience for rural school teaching. The innovation was due not so much to improvements in transportation, as to the greater willingness to give up control over the form of practice and to relax supervision generally, for students had often to be located at a distance from the normal school for a week or more at a time. In 1950 an ingenious plan in operation at the Nova Scotia Normal College gave half of the students practice in schools near their homes for two weeks before the Easter vacation, and the other half for two weeks after the vacation. Ontario had a similar plan.

In all professional schools the programs of practice teaching in 1950 differed in two respects from those of the nineteenth century. In the first place, the amount of practice was very much greater. In the second place, the practice as far as possible was continuous, with the student remaining in one classroom, or with one teacher for at least a week, or engaged in teaching a single unit of work to the same students for three or four weeks. At the Ontario College of Education, students preparing for high school teaching spent alternate weeks during most of the academic year in the practice schools and remained with the one critic teacher for the entire week. In the second year of the B.Ed. program in Alberta students spent half-days for observation and practice, five days a week, for three periods of three weeks each.

These changes in practice teaching have not taken place to the same extent by any means in all professional schools, but there has been almost everywhere a trend in these directions. The reader not professionally interested in the details of teacher education may nevertheless be impressed by the general significance of this development. In no other type of education has the pragmatic method gained as definite acceptance as in pre-service practice teaching. The need for teaching experience was in 1950 unquestioned, and no amount of formal instruction was upheld as an equivalent. Virtually everyone engaged in teacher education was no less firmly convinced that the practice had to be realistic. There was less concern than formerly about organizing and controlling practice to ensure the learning of defined skills, and more concern about giving full, comprehensive, and genuine, if sometimes unpredictable, experience. One difficulty encountered in the new undergraduate programs of teacher education was the provision of adequate practice teaching, which was almost sure to interfere with course work, the only basis of academic credit. It was too soon to ask credit towards a degree for practical experience, no matter how the educative value might compare with the value obtained from formal instruction.

The Preparation of High School Teachers

When secondary education was sharply differentiated from elementary education in the early part of the nineteenth century, the few secondary school teachers were men with a good academic education. Of thirty-eight masters appointed to district grammar schools in Upper Canada between 1807 and 1830, twenty-two were clergymen. From about mid-century onward, however, when the secondary school clientele lost its social distinction, and when secondary grades were added to elementary grades in combined schools, a lower level of academic attainment was perforce made acceptable for teachers of secondary education. In Canada West standards were kept up as a minimum to the equivalent of honor matriculation, and university graduation was required for headmasters from 1865. The differentiation of elementary and secondary education by means of the entrance examination and the abolition of union schools enabled Ontario in the last three decades of the century to maintain fairly high academic requirements for the secondary school teacher. Small combined schools elsewhere were sometimes taught by teachers with academic qualifications barely adequate for instructing elementary grades. On the whole, however, if the term "secondary" is applied only to schools with some claim to the title, secondary school teachers were required up to the end of World War I to have at least the academic qualifications of an elementary school teacher with a First Class certificate — roughly the equivalent of honor or senior matriculation. Thereafter, for a certificate valid in any true high school, a teacher had to have a university degree, as most teachers in schools of repute had had since the opening of the first Latin grammar schools.

PROGRESS TOWARDS PROFESSIONAL TRAINING

The higher academic qualifications of secondary school teachers delayed the introduction of professional training for secondary school teaching. In the traditional subjects of classics and mathematics there was a traditional routine of instruction that every teacher learned during his last years of schooling, so that training in method seemed unnecessary. At the higher academic level, moreover, respect for scholarship was so exclusive that it was impossible to think of teacher education or any education as anything but the imparting of content. It was therefore taken as an insult to the universities that graduates should be asked to submit to further instruction, and even more so if candidates without a degree were to be admitted on equal terms to the same professional courses.

In an early attempt to provide training for secondary school teachers, a model grammar school was opened in Toronto in 1858. Masters of other grammar schools were invited to come and observe its method of operation, and between 1861 and 1863 some teacher education was offered. But the provincial expenditure on the school was judged to be of benefit chiefly to pupils attending from Toronto and the vicinity, and the school was closed in 1863. Twenty years later, the minister of education proposed having a course of lectures offered by the department to prepare candidates for high school teaching, but abandoned the plan when objectors said that the graduates would rightly consider the requirement of attendance an indignity and a useless nuisance. In 1885 a compromise plan designated certain collegiate institutes — ultimately five altogether — as training institutes, at which graduates might at their discretion receive in the fall fourteen weeks' apprenticeship of observation and practice teaching reinforced by demonstration lessons and a number of lectures. In 1890 the training institutes were replaced by the Ontario School of Pedagogy, where fourteen weeks' instruction was offered in psychology, science of education, history of education, school organization and management, and methods of teaching each subject in the high school program. In 1897 the short course at Toronto was supplanted by a full year of professional education, from the beginning of October to the end of May, at a new institution, the Ontario Normal College, in Hamilton.

At this point in the Ontario development, training for high school teachers became obligatory. Throughout Canada most of the trained teachers in secondary schools in 1900 were men and women who had attended a normal school to obtain a professional certificate and who had later improved their academic qualifications. Their colleagues without training were university graduates, or undergraduates with partial credit, who were exempted from professional education by virtue of their academic attainments. The usual requirements for high school teaching at the end of the century were either a First Class professional certificate or a bachelor's degree. The continued acceptance of the latter may be illustrated by regulations in Nova Scotia, after World War I, permitting graduates to attend a shorter

normal school course, or, more strikingly, by regulations in New Brunswick, after World War II, permitting graduates to obtain teachers' licences by writing examinations without the benefit of any professional training. There was some difficulty, especially in less populous provinces, in providing courses related to teaching in secondary grades. Even in Ontario, the School of Pedagogy and its successors until the end of World War I were attended by candidates for First Class certificates valid either in elementary schools or in high schools. In British Columbia, when university graduates towards the end of World War I began attending the normal schools, the unsuitability of a course centred on elementary school teaching was apparent.

PROFESSIONAL COURSES IN UNIVERSITIES

To provide appropriate training for high school teachers, universities introduced professional courses, a first step of far-reaching significance in raising the prestige of teaching. Bishop's University at Lennoxville, Quebec, set up a training department for high school teachers in 1898. Then in 1907, when the Protestant normal school of Quebec was transferred to Macdonald College, responsibility for the training of high school teachers was assumed by McGill University — not a revolutionary step in this case since the normal school had formerly been affiliated with McGill, but unprecedented in that the new function was assumed by the university proper. In the same year in Ontario, the work of the Ontario Normal College was taken over by two faculties of education, at Queen's University and at the University of Toronto. Then in 1920 the Ontario College of Education at the University of Toronto assumed sole responsibility for the preparation of high school teachers and admitted only university graduates to its course of professional training. After 1923 the University of British Columbia gave professional courses to graduates, who at first received part of their training at normal school but subsequently spent the full year at the university. In Saskatchewan in 1928, in Alberta in 1929, and in Manitoba in 1935 professional training for high school teachers was introduced at the provincial universities in a faculty or college of education. At mid-century there were faculties or departments of education to prepare high school teachers in one university of each province from Ontario westward, in two English-language universities of Quebec, in two universities of New Brunswick, and in three universities of Nova Scotia.

The pattern of high school teacher education established in Ontario after 1897, and later elsewhere, was one year's professional training after university graduation. At McGill, courses in education at first were taken during the third and fourth undergraduate years. Similarly when the department of education in Nova Scotia made arrangements with universities in 1926 to offer courses in education for certification, the professional work until 1932 was taken concurrently with academic work for graduation in arts or science. Subsequently, however, a year of post-graduate training was required, as it was also at McGill and other universities. This arrangement, although desirable on the whole, left a wide discrepancy in the education required for secondary school teaching as contrasted with the requirements for elementary school teaching, so that Canada in relation to other countries ranked as high in the former as low in the latter. The difference was even greater where specialist certificates for high school teaching were obtained by graduates of honors courses. In Ontario, during the 1880's, at least some teachers in collegiate institutes were required to have "specialist's" standing, which after the 1890's meant university graduation with

honors, so that since World War I many secondary school teachers have had Grade XIII plus four university years in Arts and one of professional preparation, or eighteen years of education, whereas four or five years less education was accepted as sufficient for teaching in the elementary school. At the beginning of the twentieth century Nova Scotia and British Columbia also had "academic" certificates, which were obtained by high school teachers with superior qualifications, and at mid-century Nova Scotia, Manitoba, Saskatchewan, and British Columbia, like Ontario, had academic, specialist's, or advanced certificates for high school teachers who had seventeen or eighteen years' education instead of the sixteen or seventeen years needed for the ordinary high school certificate.

The recent introduction of the undergraduate Bachelor of Education program marked a possible reversal of the above trend, for qualifications as a high school teacher could be acquired in the four years required for the new degree. The older alternative of a first degree in arts remained, however, and was in most provinces strongly entrenched. The shortage of teachers, which had yet to be felt acutely at the high school level, caused rumors of a reversion in Nova Scotia to courses in education during the undergraduate years in arts. This would obviously be a retrograde step unless credit towards a Bachelor of Arts degree could be granted for an adequate program of professional education, with the result that candidates for elementary school teaching might be attracted also. But university reluctance to allow credit for professional courses was the cause of setting up an undergraduate Bachelor of Education degree instead of a Bachelor of Arts in education in accordance with the American pattern. The conflict was between those who wanted strong academic emphasis in education for high school teaching, and degree credit for that alone, and those who wanted all teachers to have adequate general and professional education at university. The chances were that the levelling process would produce the latter result in time, but not immediately in parts of Canada where traditional distinctions were cherished.

In the Roman Catholic system of Quebec, an initial attempt failed in 1857 to have the Laval normal school affiliated with the university, as was done at McGill for the Protestant system; but the council of the university was consulted regarding appointments to the normal school staff. In the present century a department of education was set up in the faculty of arts at Laval University, and a faculty of education was established at the University of Montreal — the latter including the *Institut des Soeurs de la Congrégation de Notre Dame* and the *Institut pédagogique Saint-Georges*. At mid-century, preparation for teaching in classical colleges was offered at the universities and at *l'Ecole Normale Secondaire de Montréal* in courses of two or more years after the baccalaureate. The requirements for a *licence en pédagogie* from Laval, a certificate valid for teaching up to Grade XII, were eighteen years of teacher education — a baccalaureate at the Grade XII level and three years at the university. Preparation for teaching in complementary and superior schools was offered in normal schools, where qualifications for teaching in secondary grades could be obtained in courses of two to four years terminating at the Grade XIII to XV level.

IN-SERVICE EDUCATION

The licensing of teachers with very low qualifications had one good effect: it established a custom of in-service improvement. But in-service education became common only after 1850, when central authorities set definite requirements for higher certificates and awakened, through the normal schools, an interest in professional growth. Of major importance, for teachers who interrupted their teaching careers for the purpose, was the program of further education at secondary schools, normal schools, and universities. But to avoid repetition of what has been said in connection with pre-service education, attention in this section will be confined to professional improvement during actual service.

Institutes and Associations

From the 1850's onward, much good work was done by local associations of teachers and teachers' institutes. In Canada West, institutes were set up by the central authority in 1850: a grant of £25 was made available to each institute, meetings were held over a period of from two to five days, and the assembled teachers listened to lectures by a visiting normal school master and saw a few model lessons. But the teachers failed to participate with any enthusiasm in follow-up discussions, probably because the initiative had come from above and not from the teachers themselves. After a further trial in the following year, the plan was abandoned. Teachers were ready enough to set up voluntary associations, which were fairly numerous by 1860. Through these organizations they exchanged ideas on classroom work and showed an active interest in the educational affairs of the province.

In Nova Scotia, also, one teachers' institute was conducted in 1850, and twelve institutes in 1851; during the two years

230 teachers attended. In New Brunswick, Superintendent Fisher spoke with approval of institutes in Maine and Nova Scotia, and five counties in 1859 established institutes in response to his suggestion. At the meetings, which were sometimes held quarterly, papers were read and discussed. There were nine organized institutes in 1863, when a provincial institute was first set up. The institute plan was adopted in other provinces: in British Columbia at the suggestion of Superintendent Jessop a first institute was organized in Victoria in 1874; in the Northwest Territories under Superintendent Goggin over ninety per cent of the teachers in the 1890's were reported to have attended institutes conducted by inspectors between April and June.

Most institutes in the last quarter of the nineteenth century were directed from above. In Quebec, where voluntary associations of teachers had been formed earlier, as they had been in Ontario, institutes were held for one week in the summer for about fifteen years after 1884, and arrangements were made for the normal school staff to take part. In Ontario the central authority organized and financed institutes and required teachers to attend. In 1884 it took the further step of appointing a departmental official, J. A. McLellan, as director of teachers' institutes. From the departmental point of view the institutes were a valuable means of reinforcing the meagre training received in the model schools, but Althouse says that the proceedings were regarded with indifference, if not hostility, by the teachers, who had no responsibility for their operation, no share in planning the programs, and no choice but to attend. The department set the days on which the institutes were held, and in 1896 showed its unconcern about the wishes of the teachers by designating Friday and Saturday as the two days for institute meetings. Although there were few teachers as yet

whose educational philosophy recognized the need of some self-determination and responsibility for the pupil, it was apparently no longer possible to gain the active co-operation of the teachers themselves by arbitrary orders from constituted authority. Departmental officials secured the presence of teachers at institutes but no lively or continuing interest either from the young transients with Third Class certificates or from serious members of the profession.

Undoubtedly the low attainments and indifference of many teachers made it difficult for central authorities to refrain from compulsion. In British Columbia in the 1880's all teachers were forced to undergo periodic re-examination, at first annually regardless of the grade of certificate held, and subsequently at longer intervals for holders of higher certificates. Teachers resented this treatment, of course; but Superintendent Pope could not tolerate the "drone" or "educational fossil" who refused to study and improve his ability as a teacher. There were disadvantages as well as advantages in leaving in-service activities to voluntary initiative. In 1880 the West Middlesex Teachers' Association in Ontario was a lively local organization, which drew to its meetings an average attendance of 90 from the 112 teachers in the area and circulated professional books from its library. But one of the volumes sent out — *The Pupil-Teacher's Handbook*, published in England three years before — contained formulae more likely to appeal to the lazy teacher than to stimulate professional growth. The teacher was instructed to begin the teaching of reading by lessons on the letters of the alphabet. In the first lesson he was to:

(1) Select one of the capital letters formed by right lines only, e.g. L. Draw the letter in the simplest manner on a blackboard in front of the class, and name it distinctly.

(2) Let the children copy the letter on their slates, naming it as they do so.

These mechanical directions for use of an antiquated method were on a par with the busy-work included in some professional journals preferred by overworked teachers of ungraded schools in the twentieth century.

Yet voluntary professional activities proved more educative in the long run. We have seen how provincial educational associations of the late nineteenth century developed into teachers' federations, which in most provinces took over the responsibility for institutes and conventions for professional improvement. The Alberta Teachers' Association around 1950 conducted fifteen or twenty local conventions in the autumn and brought speakers from distant points to supplement discussion groups and other activities. In the nineteenth century, Ontario teachers objected to departmental bureaucracy but gained virtually no representation on the reorganized Educational Council of the province in 1896. A half-century later the Ontario Teachers' Federation helped to organize and continued to sponsor an Ontario Association for Curriculum Development as one of its many activities for the improvement of education.

Supervision

Most inspection in the nineteenth century was, as the minister of education in Ontario admitted in 1892, "more for examination than instruction." Around mid-century, inspector's reports often resembled the following appraisal of a school in Prince Edward Island in 1856:

This school continues in the most backward state imaginable; teacher very incapable of performing the duties of his office; a change very necessary.

Percival in *Across the Years* quotes the 1877 report of a Quebec inspector who spent nearly the whole of his time examining and rating the individual pupils with meticulous care in order finally to allocate prizes. A contrasting report of 1946 showed that the inspector looked into every aspect of the school and its work, including among many other items "the manner and address of the teacher, the quality and modulation of her voice, her choice of words and the clarity and coherence of her manner of speaking."[14] But too much effort was still being expended on appraisal and too little on encouragement and help. As explained in a previous chapter, a major change for the better took place after about 1870, when inspection by laymen gave place to supervision under a regular staff of qualified former teachers. In 1907 in Ontario a special course for public school inspectors was set up in the two faculties of education. Candidates wrote examinations in four appropriate fields, including the supervision of instruction in all subjects of the elementary school. Subsequently graduate courses in pedagogy were required. Supervision as a means of in-service education was improved still further in this way. But the value of supervision as in-service education depended on the individual supervisor. John MacNeill in Prince Edward Island in 1841 was helpfully instructive. He advised the teacher not to depend on "any peculiarity of external arrangement."

I was careful not to trammel him by too minute a system of martinet arrangements. Beyond general instructions I left a good deal to his own tastes, judgment and good discretion . . . no formal enactments, however precise, will render a school efficient when the teacher is wanting in right spirit and good sense.

MacNeill's desire to give scope to the good teacher and his distrust of restrictive forms would have made him feel more at home a century later.

Summer Schools

The most important device for in-service education of teachers has been the summer school. We have seen that summer courses for teachers were offered in some academies around 1830 and short summer courses in teachers' institutes after 1850. But only in the last quarter of the nineteenth century were summer courses of the present type proposed and occasionally offered. In 1878 the *Canada School Journal* pointed out that in some parts of the United States "summer normal classes" were organized by teachers to prepare themselves for teaching certain subjects, and invited Canadian teachers to use the columns of the journal to discuss the advisability of such classes in Canada. In that year, two summer schools were announced in Ontario, one to be held in the Thousand Islands, where teachers attending lectures would be charged only for board, and one of five weeks' duration at Victoria College, Cobourg, where at a cost of $30 lectures in experimental chemistry and determinative mineralogy were to be offered for high school teachers. The need for the instruction of teachers in new subjects was from the first a major reason for summer schools. Mention has been made of the science summer school in the Maritime Provinces. In 1887 a letter to the editor of the *Educational Review* of New Brunswick made a plea for the establishment of summer schools in English literature, modern languages, music, and drawing. The following year Queen's University introduced summer instruction in Arts and some professional subjects. Before the end of the century Ontario teachers could obtain special certificates in drawing and music by attendance at summer sessions.

But the widespread use of summer sessions dates from the educational awakening, the introduction of new subjects and methods, and the raising of teachers' qualifications in the present century before World War I. In 1905 the first summer school for teachers was conducted by the University of Toronto, and about the same time McGill offered a summer school in French. In 1911, Quebec teachers were offered a summer course in methods of teaching French; and in 1916, Ontario teachers could enroll in summer sessions at the University of Toronto as candidates for the degree of Bachelor of Arts. The requirements of teachers were met chiefly, however, by summer schools of provincial departments of education. In 1913 *The School* pointed out that the variety of summer courses offered that year by the Ontario department left no excuse for the reproach that Canadian teachers did not use summer schools to improve their qualifications, as did teachers in the United States. Departmental circulars of 1915 and 1916 gave notice to teachers that regulations would be enforced regarding special qualifications which had been obtainable at free summer sessions for some years in art, physical culture, and commercial subjects. Altogether at that time there were summer courses leading to a score of special certificates in agriculture, home economics, farm mechanics, manual training, vocal music, kindergarten-primary, auxiliary class work, and other fields.

In the west, also, the summer school movement became prominent at the time of World War I. In 1911, inspectors in Alberta asked for a summer school in the new subjects of the curriculum. In 1913 on the campus of the University of Alberta the department of education conducted a first summer session at which courses were offered in agriculture, school gardening, nature study, manual training, woodwork, methods in art, design, drawing and painting, household art, household science, and physical training. In the same year, because of an influx of settlers to the Peace River area of the province, a summer school was held there for fourteen Roman Catholic teachers, of whom eleven were religious sisters. The University of Alberta in 1919 opened a summer session that was carried on jointly with the department of education until both were taken over by the faculty of education in 1944. In Saskatchewan a joint departmental and university summer school was established in 1916. In Manitoba and British Columbia the departmental summer schools were opened in 1911 and 1914, and the university summer schools in 1923 and 1920, respectively.

At the beginning of World War II there were departmental and university summer schools, in some cases united, in all provinces of Canada except Prince Edward Island, and in some provinces several additional summer schools or divisions of schools, including those of four universities in Ontario. In Quebec, Laval University offered courses in French language, literature, culture, and philosophy, Macdonald College offered courses leading to higher certificates, and two other schools offered educative experience in oral French. Two universities and the department of education conducted summer schools in New Brunswick. At Halifax the comprehensive Nova Scotia Summer School was conducted by the department but employed university and other personnel. Altogether these summer schools in all parts of Canada offered a great variety of professional and academic courses attended by many thousands of teachers. Summer school activity was curtailed somewhat during the war years but revived later.

Professional Reading

Although professional books were available in limited numbers before 1880 and in unlimited variety after 1920, reliance on prescriptions of reading for teachers was most noticeable between those dates.

Ontario built up its teachers' libraries, recommended in 1885 a reading course to cover a three-year period, and revived flagging interest at the end of the century by issuing a certificate for each book read and a diploma at the end of the course. The Northwest Territories early in the present century published a list of books to be read by teachers and awarded professional certificates on the basis of such reading. The first graduate degrees in education were obtained before 1900 by examination after courses of reading without instruction.

The first professional journals were published and distributed gratis by provincial superintendents as one instrument in the mid-nineteenth-century campaign to awaken interest in education and improve the schools. Ryerson's *Journal of Education* was published regularly for thirty years, from 1848 to 1877. In Quebec from 1857 until 1879 the *Journal de l'Instruction publique* was issued in two languages, nominally as one publication, although the English-language version was made up largely of material copied from American periodicals. After an interval not devoid of other periodicals in the French language, the department of education published and distributed to schools from 1898 *l'Enseignement Primaire*. Meanwhile *The Educational Record* began publication in 1881 as a departmental journal for Protestant education. In Nova Scotia, a *Journal of Education* was published from 1851 to 1853, in 1858 and 1859, and regularly after 1866, although it sometimes appeared only twice a year until 1931, when it became a regular periodical offering professional reading for teachers. The *Educational Review* was first published in Saint John, New Brunswick, in 1887 as an educational journal "for the Atlantic Provinces of Canada," with leading educators from the three provinces as editors. It placed emphasis at first on science and nature study.

In the thirty year period from 1875 to 1905, half a dozen lively educational periodicals were published as independent commercial ventures in Ontario, including *The Canada Educational Monthly* (1879-1903), *The Canada School Journal* (1877-1887), *The Educational Weekly* (1885-1887), and *The Educational Journal* (1887-1897). *The Canada School Journal* claimed in 1879 to have a circulation of more than six thousand. The success and comparative longevity of these publications suggest that teachers were sufficiently interested in professional reading to pay for the privilege, although allowance must be made for the sales appeal of examination papers with answers and other teaching aid materials which abounded in some of the journals. Some of the journals were put out by book publishers largely as a means of advertising the many textbooks and condensed summaries sold to teachers and pupils in the era of fact-cramming, so that much of the circulation of the journals may have been "controlled," or free. Yet the need of a professional journal in the continuing education of the teacher was clearly recognized at the end of the century. In 1899 an inspector in Prince Edward Island wrote:

To improve the matter of instruction the teacher must think more, prepare more, read more. A good educational periodical is as necessary to the teacher as the market reports are to the merchant or trader.

In the same year a predecessor of the *Western School Journal* appeared in Manitoba.

In the twentieth century Ontario continued the free-enterprise tradition by avoiding publication of an official journal. From 1912 to 1947 *The School* was published by the Ontario College of Education with only a limited subsidy, so that it depended very largely on sales to teachers to keep up a paid circulation, which sometimes exceeded eight thousand when it had at least a few readers in every province of Canada. In order to encourage subscriptions, *The School* gave teachers practical articles relating to their particular subjects and fields of work but included also general articles for in-service education of a broader and more professional character. About half of the provincial departments of education at mid-century continued to publish periodicals of an official nature. The trend after World War I was towards publication by teachers' federations of educational periodicals, and by the time of World War II to include in these periodicals articles of a professional character.

Post-graduate Courses

Partly because of the large number of transients, but chiefly because of the continuing low standards for elementary school teaching, the proportion of teachers with university degrees in Canada has been smaller than in Britain or the United States. At the beginning of World War II, only one province, British Columbia, had 30 per cent of its teaching staff with degrees; Ontario, Manitoba, and Nova Scotia had less than 20 per cent; Alberta and Saskatchewan less than 15 per cent; New Brunswick less than 10 per cent; and Prince Edward Island less than 5 per cent. Most of the graduates, of course, were high school teachers, nearly all of whom had not only a bachelor's degree but a subsequent year of teacher education at a university. Graduate work in education in Canada ordinarily extends beyond that level. A substantial and increasing number of teachers who hold one university degree — and especially of elementary teachers so qualified — continue their professional education at the graduate level.

The University of Toronto in 1894 established the degrees of Bachelor of Pedagogy and Doctor of Pedagogy. The requirements for admission to the B.Paed. program were a degree from a British University and a professional certificate of the highest grade for elementary school teaching or of a type valid only in high schools. One qualification for admission to the D.Paed. course was a B.Paed. degree; but at first, high school specialists with ten years experience might enter the D.Paed. program directly without qualifying for the B.Paed. Books were recommended for reading courses in psychology, science of education, history of education, and management, including methods in optional subjects and criticism of methods. Four students were examined in pedagogy in 1895 and the first doctor's degree was conferred in 1898. From 1907 until 1919, students had the alternative of registering for pedagogy degrees at Queen's University. Only after 1908 were courses offered, and attendance was optional until 1919. Summer courses were offered from 1915, at Queen's and Toronto in alternate years, until 1920, and from then onward at Toronto only. The requirements and content after 1908 became more professional in nature.

Nothing could refute more conclusively the contention that educational standards have deteriorated, or that education has become easier, than the changes in requirements for graduate degrees in pedagogy or education. At the beginning of the century a candidate could procure even a doctor's degree with no greater effort than was required to read a few books and write a thesis that would no more than satisfy the term work requirements in one or two of the twelve course units required by the University of Toronto in 1952. Even in the 1920's, the B.Paed. could be obtained by two summers' attendance and by writing examinations that could be passed by the memorization of notes. In the 1930's, the two summers for the B.Paed. became three, and course requirements for the D.Paed. were increased by one-third; in the 1940's a division of the courses into units to give a wider choice of options had the effect again of making the content more intensive and difficult; in the 1950's, when degrees in education replaced degrees in pedagogy, course requirements for the doctorate were increased again by one-half, and requirements for the M.Ed. were set to include one-third more content than for the B.Paed.; and concurrently during the thirty years the standards demanded in the doctoral thesis were made correspondingly more exacting.

During the present century many of the universities offering the year of professional education for certification established a graduate Bachelor of Education degree, for which requirements varied widely. The University of Alberta in 1922 introduced the B.Ed. as a graduate degree requiring two years' work under a committee of graduate studies. Several universities also began to confer the degree of Master of Arts in education, as did Manitoba in 1929. The degree of Master of Education was also established at the University of Manitoba in 1935. The University of Toronto, having extensive resources in its School of Graduate Studies and in the Ontario College of Education as the only faculty of education in a large province, was able at mid-century to offer advanced graduate work for the degrees of Doctor of Philosophy and of Doctor of Education.

Personal Qualifications

From early in the nineteenth century onward it was recognized increasingly that the good teacher would have assets other than knowledge, ability to instruct, and strength to keep order. A letter in the *Kingston Gazette* in 1815 said that in teachers for Upper Canada classical learning was of less value than respectability. In 1840 in New Brunswick, Alfred Reade,

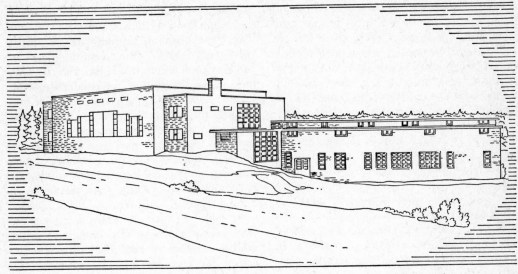

Upper Miramichi Regional High School, 1951, Boiestown, New Brunswick

secretary and son-in-law of the lieutenant-governor, declared that in a teacher "honesty, sobriety, and morality are essential . . . but a certain amount of mental and intellectual power must be considered equally indispensable."[15] Marshall d'Avray in the same province fifteen years later was skeptical of the assumption that one who had mastered higher subjects like mathematics and ancient languages would be superior as a teacher, and expressed a preference for one "who to moderate requirements adds general intelligence, and an at once fluent and precise style of telling what he knows." Perhaps following a lead, a local inspector of schools wrote in 1857, with regard to superior licences: "My experience leads me to conclude that a knowledge of mathematics should not be the test qualification."[16] He said that he knew several Second Class teachers, without high academic qualifications, whose schools were among the very best.

Others saw the need for reinforcing minimum qualifications by scholarship of a more liberal type. William McPhail, school visitor of Prince Edward Island, said in 1811 that the accomplished teacher must have a definite knowledge of what he taught and of how to teach it, but must also have "that general knowledge which will enable the teacher to stand above his subject, and survey it in its relation to others, and furnish wealth of illustration and give weight of character."[17] The same view was expressed more often near the end of the century when literature became a school subject and the appreciation of literature was a revolutionary new aim. In the *Educational Review* of New Brunswick in 1888 a writer admitted that there was need for some teaching of facts about the history of English literature but protested against bare, formal instruction as likely of itself to do more harm than good. He asserted boldly that a student should "leave school or college with an avidity for reading," but saw no way of achieving such an objective except by discovering "educated and cultured teachers."

Cheap schemes of teacher education failed to attract or produce people who measured up to any such standard. In 1878 the fifty masters of model schools in Ontario pointed out the deficiencies of those who entered the short training course, and the editor of the *Canada Educational Monthly* summed up these deficiencies by referring to the candidates collectively as "veal." But if intellectual excellence and maturity were too expensive, others saw promise of professional qualifications in virtues less dependent on exceptional ability and prolonged study. A woman teacher in a model school, Miss Riddell of Madoc, Ontario, emphasized the importance of a good disposition. In a paper read to a local teachers' association in 1879 she said:

A teacher who is kind, active, and full of tact may and will gain an almost unlimited influence over the minds and feelings of his pupils and lead them cheerfully onward and upward in the paths of knowledge.[18]

In the last two of thirteen lectures used in county model schools at that time to metamorphose candidates for Third Class certificates, it was laid down that the good teacher should be honest, candid, truthful, well-informed, purposeful, calm, firm, energetic, methodical, persistent, polite, genial, sympathetic, consistent, and a pattern of gentleness, kindness, forbearance, and true politeness. A contemporary definition of teacher power summarized the qualities and abilities needed as the power of arresting attention, the faculty of setting pupils to work for themselves, cheerfulness, and forbearance. Millar of Ontario in 1896 listed eleven attributes of the good teacher: physical health and vigor, scholarship, professional attainments, personal magnetism, executive ability, tact, common sense, vigilance, heart power, will power, and moral character.

It is evident, then, that by the end of the nineteenth century the ideal teacher was expected to exhibit a combination of masculine and feminine virtues not unlike the desiderata sometimes set forth with unrestrained generosity today. The Royal Commission on Education in Ontario in 1950 felt that the qualities of the teacher should include, in addition to scholarship and professional skill, "a high standard of physical and mental health, superior intelligence, a deep and abiding religious faith, a mature and stable personality, and a willingness and ability to mingle and co-operate with his fellows . . . a general culture . . . aesthetics to appreciate beauty,"[19] and much more. Such demands are not exaggerated in relation to the extreme difficulty of education for the development of all kinds of children in every possible way. But the multifarious qualities listed above have not always been compatible, and hopes of developing some of the more important have been inconsistent with methods of teacher recruiting and teacher education. The Toronto Normal School was attacked for many years by educational journals for bringing in teachers to "fritter away their time" on a course that was an "unmitigated sham," taught by a staff distinguished only for "superannuated incompetence" and calculated to shut out the young people who were "looking forward to a life of freedom."[20]

In the mid twentieth-century some believed that a liberal type of teacher education on a university campus would attract many who would otherwise be repelled, and help to give all teachers a greater breadth of outlook and a more generous endowment of other qualities.

An example of the type of teacher respected in his community at the end of the nineteenth century will show that no excessive emphasis was then placed by most people on the newer abilities expected in a teacher, and that approval was given to form — to the outward pattern of the teacher's life and to the quan-

A modern elementary school in New Toronto (John B. Parkin Associates, Architects)

tity of measurable matter absorbed by the pupil. Samuel W. Irons was appointed principal of Victoria School in Moncton in 1890. He is depicted by A. S. Robinson in a history of the schools of that city as tall, gaunt, slightly stooped, and adorned with a Vandyke beard. On Sundays Mr. Irons went to the Presbyterian Church, where he was an elder, appropriately dressed in a long black Prince Albert suit and carrying a cane. Although school-teaching was his profession, he had also the reputation of being an excellent business man and a shrewd investor. He was a great reader, took a keen interest in current events, had definite political views, loved to play cards, and was an enthusiastic member of the Independent Order of Odd Fellows. At school he taught the highest elementary grade, where the success of a teacher was rated by his ability to produce a "medalist" — a pupil who led the county in the high school entrance examination. Mr. Irons quite openly directed his teaching efforts towards the attainment of this goal. Robinson remarks that in doing so,

He necessarily gave his classes such doses of good old-fashioned drill that many of his pupils acquired a substantial percentage of the information and skills in spite of all they could do to the contrary.[21]

If others managed to escape the effect, their ignorance did not show up among the great majority who left school at an early age.

A description of the teacher preferred fifty years later may be put together from the views of 135 Ontario high school teachers in 1949. In their opinion the successful high school teacher was distinguished above all for personal qualities — for ability to maintain good relations with pupils, for interest in pupils as individuals, for readiness to enter wholeheartedly into the work of the school, including its extra-curricular activities, and for fairness and good judgment. The superior teacher, of course, was also able to control a class and to show teaching skill in the classroom. But those were expected abilities and not the distinguishing marks of excellence. The same might be said regarding the assets rated last of all by the principals — scholarship and ability to get pupils through examinations. It was not that a low value was attached to academic attainment in Ontario high schools, but that the teacher had to be much more than a well-informed drill-master if the school as a whole was to exert a positive interest for good on all young people of the community. Many of the teachers might have preferred to select and educate the academically gifted by classroom work alone, and to escape responsibility for the rest. But the function of the school and teacher was no longer so simple.

Advanced thought regarding teacher education in the twentieth century characteristically placed limited reliance on particular aspects and insisted that the whole be considered as well as the parts. In 1926 F. M. Quance pointed out that "teacher training must be thought of as beginning from the earliest years of the individual."[22] He argued that personal qualifications were acquired from the home, the school, and the community environment over a long period. For the same reason, from the time of World War II, many educators regarded teacher selection as a continuous process and believed that the quality of teachers could most effectively be raised by professional requirements likely to appeal to the parents, teachers, and young people of better homes and schools.

Summary

These last two chapters have brought us to the crucial problem in public education — how to get good teachers.

During the aristocratic period the solution was realistic. To teach the few who would become leaders in society, good scholars were employed at salaries that gave them a position of dignity. To teach the many in larger centres, men and women of sound faith were selected and enabled in their humbler sphere to command a little respect. Although the limited operation of the plan left most children in utter ignorance, the recruitment and education of teachers were consistent with social values of the time.

During the transition, before 1850, to elementary schools of the people, the number of teachers increased but the quality deteriorated. The people had neither the education nor the means to demand good teachers for their children. Those who took charge of the schools had less solid faith and knowledge without the compensation of more ability and understanding. Having attended only wretched common schools themselves, they kept schools equally wretched. A new class of people with money and with no great respect for traditional secondary schools sent their children to better educated teachers in superior academies and private schools.

Between 1850 and 1875, central authorities brought the academic qualifications of all elementary school teachers up to a very low minimum standard, encouraged a few teachers to acquire more knowledge, and gave an increasing number of teachers some training in normal schools. In spite of skepticism and hostility at the beginning of the period, method and professional education conclusively demonstrated their value in the obviously superior classrooms of trained teachers.

Between 1875 and 1900, several developments previously under way became clearly marked. Professional education was made obligatory as preparation for teaching, although in some provinces candidates at two extreme levels escaped — those with a university degree because they were few enough to claim exemption, and those with very little education because they asked little for their services. Country girls, willing to acquire minimum qualifications and to teach for a pittance while they waited for husbands, kept standards and salaries down. But all teachers received some high school education, so that the separation of elementary and secondary school teaching was no longer complete.

From 1900 to 1940 the length and quality of teacher education improved greatly at both high school and normal school. Even so, the requirements for elementary and secondary school certificates remained wide apart. Towards the end of the period, however, when it was possible to select candidates with good personal qualifications and to demand more adequate general and professional education, there was a good prospect that the status of elementary school teaching could be raised to the level of other professions.

The shortage of teachers caused by full employment during World War II, and subsequently by the high birth rate, resulted in a lowering of standards and a danger of reversion to fact-dispensing and the rest of the lifeless routine that teachers without ability or insight are able to conduct. Fortunately, however, an encouraging start had been made by 1955 in the reorganization of teacher education to attract better candidates and to give them a better preparation for teaching. Those who scorned short cuts to a certificate and who continued their pre-service education while in service acquired a new breadth of professional understanding as the foundation for constant improvement of teaching practice.

The Years Ahead

We have looked at education as it was in Canada during the French regime and the first half-century of British rule. We have traced the development of public school systems over the past 125 years. We have considered also the concomitant changes in educational philosophy and method. In all of this we have observed the increasing strength of concepts and practices that would give all Canadians without distinction more power over education and, through education, over their own lives.

The persistent movement of public education in this direction has been and still is regarded by interested people with mixed feelings. To many in the present century it has been the inspiring march of progress. To others it has been more like a reckless sortie from the fortress of established values.

How can we say what the future of Canadian education will be? If world events, conditions in Canada, and the experience and thoughts of people demonstrate human limitations and the imminence of disaster, there will almost certainly be a return in education to older ways. The schools will give the majority less of what they want; they will give higher priority to the education of a selected few and to the strengthening of institutions, including academic disciplines, which command respect and sup-

port authority. But if there is no serious check to North American optimism and progress, we may expect further changes in public education to encourage active participation and more wide-spread assumption of responsibility. In either event, however, the reaction or advance in Canada is not likely to be drastic. Conflicting points of view will continue to make their influence felt.

It is desirable that this should be so — that differences should persist and that divergent forces should continue to operate. There has been too much insistence in the modern world that such forces must be resolved, or that thesis and antithesis must be supplanted by a clearly defined synthesis. Canada's major contribution in these dangerous times is a demonstration that people do not need to be unified or immersed in a melting pot to live even in one country together. Laments that there is no distinctive Canadian nationality or culture are themselves lamentable. We should be proud that we do not need to establish one characteristic pattern.

Our best hope for the future, therefore, is that Canadian education will not lose its seemingly contradictory advantages — neither those which some regard as obstacles nor those which appear to others as rash concessions to ignorance. The secondary school curriculum, for example, has apparently been fossilized by the influence of the traditional liberal arts point of view in universities; or it has seemingly been vitiated by adaptations to the so-called needs of the stupid and lazy. Yet without the goal and standards of university entrance the high schools might have driven their pupils in futile circles; and without the infusion of new life from other sources the high school program might have failed to move most pupils at all. The combination of these two forces has left secondary education with perennial problems, but has left it nevertheless with some shape and some vitality. The working of both forces in the future promises to be more effective than any consistent and one-sided theory in reducing the deficiencies and increasing the value of the schools.

Disregarding world factors beyond our immediate frame of reference and control, we may look to a bright future for Canadian education. Achievements during the short period of our history have been encouraging, to say the least. They should be even more impressive during the next stage of Canadian development. New understanding is being gained from psychological and sociological studies. New generations of better educated parents have a keener and more enlightened interest in the educative process. It is reasonable to expect that they will become more insistent on teachers of higher and higher ability. With such teachers we need not worry very much about what type of educational thought and practice is better or in what direction education is likely to move. Better teachers, better young people, and better parents will give the only convincing answer to these constantly recurring questions.

Bibliography

Listed below are works and materials quoted in the text and indicated by numbers in the references on pages 616 to 622. Also listed are other publications found particularly useful, including several general histories.

1. ADAMSON, JOHN W.: *A Short History of English Education*. Cambridge: University Press, 1919.
2. ALTHOUSE, J. G.: *The Ontario Teacher*. Unpublished doctoral thesis, University of Toronto, 1929.
3. ALTHOUSE, J. G.: *Structure and Aims of Canadian Education*. Toronto: W. J. Gage and Co. Ltd., 1949.
4. ANGLIN, F. A.: *Catholic Education in Canada in Its Relation to the Civil Authority*. Pamphlet. Toronto, 1910.
5. ANSPACH, LEWIS: *A History of the Island of Newfoundland*. London, 1827.
6. AUDET, LOUIS-PHILIPPE: *Le Système Scolaire de la Province de Quebec*. Vols. I-IV. Quebec: Les Presses Universitaires Laval, 1951-52.
7. AYLESWORTH, N. M.: *A History of the High School Courses of Study for Alberta*. Unpublished master's thesis, University of Alberta, 1936.
8. BANNISTER, J. A.: *Early Educational History of Norfolk County*. Toronto: University of Toronto Press, 1926.
9. BARNARD, H. C.: *The French Tradition in Education*. Cambridge: University Press, 1922.
10. BARNARD, H. C.: *A Short History of English Education*, from 1760 to 1944. London: University of London Press, 1947.
11. BELL, W. N.: *The Development of the Ontario High School*. Toronto: University of Toronto Press, 1918.
12. BINGAY, JAMES: *History of Education in Nova Scotia*. Kingston: The Jackson Press, 1919.
13. BIRCHENOUGH, CHARLES: *History of Elementary Education in England and Wales*. London: University Tutorial Press, 1938.
14. BLACK, N. F.: *History of Saskatchewan and the Old North West*. Regina: North West Historical Company, 1913.
15. BOARD OF EDUCATION, GREAT BRITAIN: *Special Reports on Educational Subjects*. Vol. IV. London, 1901.
16. BOARD OF EDUCATION, TORONTO: *Centennial Story*. Toronto: Thomas Nelson and Sons, 1950.
17. BOLGER, J. A.: *A Comparative Study of the Educational Traditions of New England with Those of French Canada*. Unpublished master's thesis, McGill University, 1942.

18. BOUCHER DE LA BRUERE, P. B.: *Le Conseil de L'Instruction Publique et le Comité Catholique*. Montreal: Le Devoir, 1918.

19. BOURINOT, J. G.: *The Intellectual Development of the Canadian People*. Toronto, 1881.

20. BOVEY, WILFRED: *Canadien*. Toronto, J. M. Dent and Sons, 1933.

21. BOYD, WILLIAM: *The History of Western Education*. London: A. and C. Black, Ltd., 1921.

22. BRACQ, J. C.: *The Evolution of French Canada*. New York: The Macmillan Co., 1924.

23. BRADLEY, MARY: *Life of Mrs. Mary Bradley*. Boston, 1849.

24. BRADY, ALEXANDER: *Canada*. London: Ernest Benn Ltd., 1932.

25. BROWN, C. A.: *Elementary School Supervision in Ontario*. Unpublished doctoral thesis, University of Toronto, 1948.

26. BROWN, GEORGE W.: *Building the Canadian Nation*, Toronto: J.M. Dent and Sons, Ltd., 1942.

27. BROWN, G. W.: *Readings in Canadian History*. Toronto: J. M. Dent and Sons, Ltd., 1940.

28. BRUCE, GRAHAM: *Business Education in British Columbia*. Unpublished master's thesis, University of British Columbia, 1941.

29. BURGOYNE, LOLA M.: *A History of the Home and School Movement in Ontario*. Brampton: Charters Publishing Co. Ltd. n.d.

30. BURT, A. L.: *The Old Province of Quebec*. Toronto: The Ryerson Press, 1933.

31. CALDER, D. G. S.: *An Outline History of the Department of Education, Province of Saskatchewan, 1884-1951*. Typescript.

32. CALKIN, J. B.: *Notes on Education*. Truro, N.S., 1888.

33. CALKIN, J. B.: *Old Time Customs*. Halifax: A. and W. MacKinlay, 1918.

34. CAMERON, M. A.: *Property Taxation and School Finance in Canada*. Toronto: Canadian Education Association, 1945.

35. CAMPBELL, DUNCAN: *History of Prince Edward Island*. Charlottetown, P.E.I., 1875.

36. CAMPBELL, G. C.: *The History of Nova Scotia*. Toronto: The Ryerson Press, 1948.

37. CAMPBELL, J. D.: *The Arithmetic of the Elementary Schools of Ontario*. Unpublished doctoral thesis, University of Toronto, 1943.

38. CANADA, BUREAU OF STATISTICS: *Biennial (Annual) Survey of Education in Canada*. From 1921 to 1946-48 (Parts I and II). Ottawa: Queen's Printer.

39. CANADA, BUREAU OF STATISTICS: *The Canada Year Book*. Most years from 1910. Ottawa: Queen's Printer.

40. CANADA, BUREAU OF STATISTICS: *Historical Statistical Survey of Education in Canada*. Ottawa: King's Printer, 1921.

41. CANADA, BUREAU OF STATISTICS: *The Organization and Administration of Public Education in Canada*. Ottawa: Queen's Printer, 1952.

42. CANADA, DEPARTMENT OF LABOUR, TECHNICAL EDUCATION BRANCH: *Vocational Education*. Bulletin No. 28. Ottawa: King's Printer, 1928.

43. *The Canada Educational Monthly*, 1879-1903, and *The Educational Monthly of Canada*, 1903-1905. Toronto, Ontario.

44. CANADA, PUBLIC ARCHIVES: Reports, various years. Ottawa: Queen's Printer.

45. *The Canada School Journal*, 1877 - 1887. Toronto, Ontario.

46. CANADIAN EDUCATION ASSOCIATION: *Canadian Education*. From 1946. Toronto.

47. CANADIAN EDUCATION ASSOCIATION: *Proceedings*. Records under various names from 1892.

48. CANADIAN EDUCATION ASSOCIATION: *Recommendations concerning the Status of the Teaching Profession*. Toronto, 1949.

49. CANADIAN EDUCATION ASSOCIATION: *The Status of the Teaching Profession*. Toronto, 1948.

50. CARELESS, J. M. S.: *Canada: a Story of Challenge*. Cambridge: University Press, 1953.

51. CARROLL, JOHN ROGERS: *Public School Education in Nova Scotia - 1870 to 1935*. Unpublished master's thesis, Dalhousie University, 1950.

52. CHAUVEAU, M.: *L'Instruction publique au Canada*. Quebec, 1876.

53. CHURCH, E. J. M.: *An Evaluation of Pre-school Institutions in Canada*. Unpublished doctoral thesis, University of Toronto, 1950.

54. CLARK, S. D.: *The Social Development of Canada*. Toronto: University of Toronto Press, 1942.

55. COLBY, C. W.: *Canadian Types of the Old Regime*. New York: Henry Holt and Co., 1908.

56. COLEMAN, H. T. J.: *Public Education in Upper Canada*. New York: Teachers College, Columbia University, 1907.

57. COPP, HAROLD W.: *The History of Physical Education and Health in the Elementary and Secondary Schools of Ontario, Canada*. Unpublished master's thesis, University of Michigan, 1933.

58. CREIGHTON, D. G.: *Dominion of the North*. Boston: Houghton Mifflin Co., 1944.

59. CROAL, A. G.: *The History of the Teaching of Science in Ontario*. Unpublished doctoral thesis, University of Toronto, 1940.

60. CROCKETT, J. E.: *Origin and Establishment of Free Schools in Nova Scotia*. Unpublished master's thesis, Dalhousie University, 1940.

61. CUBBERLEY, E. P.: *The History of Education*. New York: Houghton Mifflin Co., 1920.

62. CURTIS, S. J.: *History of Education in Great Britain*. London: University Tutorial Press, 1948.

63. DAWSON, J. W.: *Fifty Years of Work in Canada*. London, 1901.

64. DAWSON, J. W.: *On Some Points in the History and Prospects of Protestant Education in Lower Canada*. Pamphlet. Montreal, 1864.

65. DAWSON, R. MacG: *The Government of Canada*. Toronto: University of Toronto Press, 1949.

66. DENNY, J. D.: *The Organization of Public Education in Saskatchewan*. Unpublished doctoral thesis, University of Toronto, 1930.

67. DEPARTMENT OF PUBLIC RECORDS AND ARCHIVES, ONTARIO: various materials indicated specifically in the references.

68. DONALDSON, HELEN: *A Descriptive Bibliography of Manuscripts, Pamphlets and Books on Education in Upper Canada, Particularly for the Years 1791 to 1841*. Unpublished master's thesis, University of Toronto, 1953.

69. DOUGHTY, A. G.: *Quebec of Yester-year*. Toronto: Thomas Nelson and Sons, 1932.

70. DOUGHTY, A. G. AND McARTHUR, D. A.: *Documents Relating to the Constitutional History of Canada, 1791 — 1818*. Ottawa: King's Printer, 1914.

71. DOUGLAS, JAMES: *New England and New France*. New York: G. P. Putnam and Sons, 1913.

72. *Educational Papers, Upper Canada, 1791 — 1841*. In Records of the Provincial and Civil Secretaries. Public Archives, Ottawa.

73. *The Educational Record*. From 1882. Quebec: The Protestant Committee of the Council of Education.

74. *The Educational Review*, 1887—. Saint. John, N.B.

75. *The Educational Weekly*, 1885 — 1887. Toronto, Ontario.

76. ENGLISH, J. F. K.: *The Combined Junior-Senior High School*. Unpublished master's thesis, University of British Columbia, 1933.

77. FITCH, J. H.: *A Century of Educational Progress in New Brunswick, 1800 to 1900*. Unpublished doctoral thesis, University of Toronto, 1930.

78. FOGHT, H. W.: *A Survey of Education*. Regina: King's Printer, 1918.

79. FORRESTER, ALEXANDER: *The Teacher's Text Book*. Halifax, N.S., 1867.

80. GAITSKELL, C. D.: *Art Education in the Province of Ontario*. Toronto: The Ryerson Press, 1948.

81. GARNEAU, F.-X.: *Histoire du Canada*. Revised by Hector Garneau. Paris: Libraire Félix Alcan, 1913.

82. GARRIOCH, A. C.: *First Furrows*. Winnipeg, 1923.

83. GESNER, ABRAHAM: *New Brunswick: with Notes for Emigrants*. London, 1847.

84. GLAZER, W. A.: *The Development and Status of Correspondence Instruction*. Unpublished master's thesis, University of Manitoba, 1942.

85. GLINZ, L. A.: *The Development of Public Secondary Education in Manitoba*. Abstract of doctoral dissertation, Stanford University, California, 1930-31.

86. GOLDSTICK, I.: *Modern Languages in the Ontario High School*. Unpublished doctoral thesis, University of Toronto, 1928.

87. GORESKY, ISIDORE: *The Beginning and Growth of the Alberta School System*. Unpublished master's thesis, University of Alberta, 1944.

88. GOSSELIN, A. E.: *L'Instruction au Canada sous le Régime Français*. Quebec: Laflamme et Proulx, 1911.

89. GOURLAY, J. L.: *History of the Ottawa Valley*. 1896.

90. GRAY, W. B.: *The Teaching of Mathematics in Ontario*. Unpublished doctoral thesis, University of Toronto, 1948.

91. GREEN, G. H. E.: *The Development of the Curriculum in the Secondary Schools of British Columbia*. Unpublished doctoral thesis, University of Toronto, 1944.

92. GROULX, LIONEL: *L'Enseignement Français au Canada*. Vol. 1: Montreal — Librairie d'Action Canadienne-Française Ltée, 1931—33. Vol. II: Montreal — Librairie Granger Frères Ltée.

93. GUILLET, E. C.: *Early Life in Upper Canada*. Toronto: Ontario Publishing Co. Ltd., 1933.

94. HALIBURTON, T. C.: *The Old Judge*. London, 1849. 2 vols.

95. HANNAY, JAMES: *The History of Acadia*. St. John, N.B., 1879.

96. HANNAY, J. H.: *History of New Brunswick*. St. John, N.B.: John A. Bowes, 1909.

97. HARDY, J. H.: *Teacher's Organizations in Ontario*. Unpublished doctoral thesis, University of Toronto, 1939.

98. HARVEY, D.C.: articles in the Journal of Education, N.S. (114) — Jan., March, May 1934; Jan., March, Sept. 1935, April 1936.

99. HAUCK, A. A.: *Some Educational Factors Affecting the Relations between Canada and the United States*. Easton, Pa., 1932.

100. *Health Education and Medical Services in Canadian Schools*. Ottawa: Dominion Bureau of Statistics, 1941.

101. HEWSON, JOHN C.: *The History of Commercial Education in Canada*. Unpublished master's thesis, University of Alberta, 1940.

102. HICKMAN, G. A.: *The History of Education in Newfoundland*. Unpublished master's thesis, Acadia University, 1941.

103. HODGINS, J. G.: *Documentary History of Education in Upper Canada, 1792 — 1876.* 28 vols. Toronto: Warwick Bros. and Rutter, 1894 — 1904.

104. HODGINS, J. H.: *The Establishment of Schools and Colleges in Ontario, 1792 — 1910.* 3 vols. Toronto: King's Printer, 1910.

105. HODGINS, J. G.: *Historical and Other Papers and Documents of Ontario, 1792 — 1876.* 6 vols. Toronto: King's Printer, 1911.

106. HODGINS, J. G.: *The Legislation and History of Separate Schools in Upper Canada.* Toronto: William Briggs, 1897.

107. HODGINS, J. G.: *Ryerson Memorial Volume.* Toronto, 1889.

108. HOPKINS, J. C. (ed): *Canada, an Encyclopedia of the Country,* Vol. III. Toronto, 1888-1889. Contains articles on the history of education in seven provinces and in the Northwest Territories.

109. HUGHES, KATHERINE: *Father Lacombe.* Toronto: William Briggs, 1914.

110. INNIS, H. A.: *Select Documents in Canadian History.* Vol. I. Toronto: University of Toronto Press, 1929.

111. JOBLIN, E. E. M.: *The Education of the Indians of Western Ontario.* Toronto: Ontario College of Education, Department of Educational Research, 1947.

112. JOHNSON, F. H.: *Changing Concepts of Discipline and Pupil-Teacher Relations in Canadian Schools.* Unpublished doctoral thesis, University of Toronto, 1952.

113. *The Journal of Education for Lower Canada.* Montreal, 1857 — 1879.

114. *The Journal of Education, Nova Scotia.* Intermittently from 1851 and regularly from 1866. Halifax, N.S.

115. *The Journal of Education for Upper Canada, 1848 — 1877.* Toronto, Ontario.

116. KARR, W. J.: *The Training of Teachers in Ontario.* Ottawa: R. J. Taylor, 1916.

117. KEDY, CLAUDE J. W.: *Pictou Academy.* Unpublished master's thesis, Mount Allison University, Sackville, N. B., 1933.

118. KELSO, J. J.: *Early History of the Humane and Children's Movement in Ontario.* Toronto: King's Printer, 1911.

119. LAHONTAN, BARON DE: *New Voyages in North America.* Edited by R. G. Thwaites. Chicago, 1905.

120. LAIDLAW, A. F.: *Theodore Harding Rand.* Pamphlet. Nova Scotia Historical Society, 1944. (Reprint from the Journal of Education, Nova Scotia)

121. LANGLEY, G. J.: *The Programmes of Study Authorized for Use in the Northwest Territories . . . and Saskatchewan.* Unpublished master's thesis, University of Saskatchewan, 1944.

122. LANGLEY, G. J.: *Saskatchewan's Separate School System.* Unpublished doctoral thesis, Columbia University, 1951.

123. LAPP, D. A.: *The Schools of Kingston.* Unpublished master's thesis, Queen's University, Kingston, 1937.

124. LAZERTE, M. E.: *Teacher Education in Canada.* Toronto: W. J. Gage and Co., Ltd., 1951.

125. LEGRESLEY, OMER: *L'Enseignement du Français en Acadia, 1604-1926.* Doctoral thesis, University of Paris. Mamers, France, 1926.

126. LESCARBOT, MARK: *Nova Francia.* Translated by P. Erondelle. New York: Harper and Bros., 1928.

127. *Letters from Nova Scotia and New Brunswick.* Edinburgh, 1829.

128. LEWIS, A. C.: *Contracts and Tenure of Canadian Teachers.* Unpublished doctoral thesis, University of Toronto, 1940.

129. Logan, E. D.: *Educational Achievements in Nova Scotia 1840-1865.* Unpublished master's thesis, Dalhousie University, 1936.

130. Lortie and LaZerte: *Articulation of High Schools and Universities,* Unpublished report, Canadian Education Association, 1952.

131. Lower, A. R. M.: *Colony to Nation.* Toronto: Longmans, Green and Co., 1946.

132. *Lower Canada, Schools, 1768-1856.* In Records of the Provincial and Civil Secretaries. Public Archives, Ottawa.

133. Lucas, C. P. (ed): *Lord Durham's Report.* Vols. I-III. Oxford: The Clarendon Press, 1912.

134. Lynam, Josephine B.: *Educational Institutions in New Brunswick, 1830-1871.* Unpublished master's thesis, McGill University, Montreal, 1947.

135. Lysecki, J. E. L.: *Education in Manitoba — North of 53.* Unpublished master's thesis, University of Manitoba, 1936.

136. MacBeth, R. G.: *The Selkirk Settlers in Real Life.* Toronto, 1897.

137. McCutcheon, J. M.: *Public Education in Ontario.* Toronto, 1941.

138. Macdougall, J. I.: *Recent Developments in Teacher Education in Western Canada.* Unpublished doctoral thesis, University of Toronto, 1953.

139. McIlwraith, J. N.: *Sir Frederick Haldimand.* In the Makers of Canada Series (Anniversary Edition), Vol. III. London and Toronto: Oxford University Press, 1926.

140. McInnes, Edgar: *Canada a Political and Social History.* New York: Rinehart and Co., 1947.

141. McIntyre, W. A.: "Sixty Years of Education in Manitoba". In the *Western School Journal,* April, 1930, pp. 134-144.

142. Mackenzie, W. L.: *Catechism of Education.* York, Upper Canada, 1830.

143. MacKinnon & Warburton (editors): *Past and Present of Prince Edward Island.* Charlottetown: B. F. Bowen and Co., about 1910.

144. MacLaurin, D. L.: *The History of Education in the Crown Colonies of Vancouver Island and British Columbia and in the Province of British Columbia.* Unpublished doctoral thesis. University of Washington, 1936.

145. MacNaughton, Katherine F. C.: *The Development of the Theory and Practice of Education in New Brunswick.* Fredericton: University of New Brunswick, 1947.

146. Madill, A. J.: *A History of Agricultural Education in Ontario.* Toronto: University of Toronto Press, 1930.

147. Magnan, C. J.: *L'Instruction Publique dans la Province de Quebec.* Quebec, 1932.

148. *Manual of the System of Primary Instruction.* British and Foreign School Society, 1843.

149. Martyn, H. G.: *Grammar in the Elementary Schools.* Toronto: The Ryerson Press, 1932.

150. Matthews, H. R.: *Education in Prince Edward Island.* Unpublished master's thesis, Mount Allison University, Sackville, N.B., 1938.

151. Matthews, W. D. E.: *The History of the Religious Factors in Ontario Elementary Education.* Unpublished doctoral thesis, University of Toronto, 1950.

152. Meilleur, J. B.: *Mémorial de l'Education du Bas-Canada.* Quebec, 1876.

153. Middleton, J. E.: *The Romance of Ontario.* Toronto: W. J. Gage and Co., Ltd., 1940.

154. Millar, John: *School Management.* Toronto, 1896.

155. Miller, J. C.: *National Government and Education in Federated Democracies, Dominion of Canada.* Philadelphia, 1940.

156. MILLER, S. A.: *A Comparative Study of Supervision*. Unpublished doctoral thesis, University of Toronto, 1946.

157. MOMBOURQUETTE, F. A.: *Administration of Bilingual Schools, with Special Reference to the Province of Nova Scotia*. Unpublished master's thesis, University of Toronto, 1948.

158. MOORE, ANDREW: *Educational Administration in Manitoba*. Unpublished doctoral thesis, University of Toronto, 1944.

159. MURRAY, A. M. S.: *History of Education in New Brunswick*. Unpublished master's thesis, Mount Allison University, Sackville, N.B., 1933.

160. NEWFIELD, G. M.: *The Development of Manitoba Schools Prior to 1870*. Unpublished master's thesis, University of Manitoba, 1937.

161. NOVA SCOTIA, DEPARTMENT OF EDUCATION: *Monograph on the Curricula of Public Schools of Nova Scotia*. Halifax, 1914.

162. Ontario Educational Association, Proceedings. Records under various names from 1873.

163. ONTARIO HISTORICAL SOCIETY: Papers and Records. Vols. XXVI, XXVII, and XXVIII. Toronto: Ontario Historical Society, 1930-1932.

164. *The Ontario Teacher*, 1873-1875. Strathroy, Ontario.

165. Pamphlets, Public Archives, Ottawa. Designated by number as in the Catalogue of Pamphlets in the Public Archives of Canada, by Magdalen Casey, Vols. I and II.

166. PARKMAN, FRANCIS: *Montcalm and Wolfe*. Boston: Little, Brown and Co., 1913.

167. PARKMAN, FRANCIS: *The Old Regime in Canada*. Part IV. Boston: Little, Brown, and Co., 1908.

168. PARMELEE, G. W., AND SUTHERLAND, J. C.: *Education in the Province of Quebec*. Quebec: Department of Public Instruction, 1914.

169. PEDLEY, CHARLES: *The History of Newfoundland*. London, 1863.

170. PENROSE, G. H.: *The Educational Significance of the Home and School Movement*. Unpublished master's thesis, McGill University, 1946.

171. PERCIVAL, W. P.: *Across the Years*. Montreal: Gazette Printing Co. Ltd., 1946.

172. PHILLIPS, C. E.: *The Teaching of English in Ontario*. Unpublished doctoral thesis, University of Toronto, 1935.

173. PROWSE, D. W.: *A History of Newfoundland*. London, 1895.

174. PUTNAM, J. H.: *Egerton Ryerson and Education in Upper Canada*. Toronto: William Briggs, 1912.

175. PUTNAM, J. M.: *Teacher Training in Nova Scotia*. Unpublished master's thesis, Acadia University, 1943.

176. RAND, T. H., (ed.): *The Educational Circular*. Numbers I to XIV. Fredericton: Education Office, 1875-1882.

177. RENNIE, H. L.: *History of Education in the Eastern Townships*. Unpublished master's thesis, Bishop's University, Lennoxville, P. Q., 1930.

178. Reports issued annually (from about 1850 in eastern Canada) and other publications of provincial departments of education, including school acts, regulations, courses of study, etc.

179. REXFORD, O. B.: *Teacher Training in the Province of Quebec*. Unpublished master's thesis, McGill University, 1936.

180. ROBBINS, J. E.: *Youth Figured Out*. Ottawa: Canadian Youth Commission, n.d.

181. ROBINSON, A. S.: *A History of the Public Schools of the Moncton and Shediac Districts.* Unpublished master's thesis, Mount Allison University, Sackville, N.B., 1943.

X 182. ROSS, G. W.: *The School System of Ontario: Its History and Distinctive Characteristics.* New York: D. Appleton and Co., 1896.

183. ROWE, FRED W.: *The History of Education in Newfoundland.* Toronto: The Ryerson Press, 1952.

184. ROY, R. P. EGIDE: *La Formation de Régime Scolaire Canadien-Francais.* Quebec, 1924.

X 185. ROYAL COMMISSION ON EDUCATION IN ONTARIO: *Report.* Toronto: King's Printer, 1951.

186. Royal Institution for the Advancement of Learning — Letter Books, 1820-1849. Microfilm, eight reels.

187. SANDHAM, ALFRED: *Villa-Marie, Sketch of Montreal, Past and Present.* Montreal, 1870.

188. *The School*, 1912-1945. Toronto, Ontario.

189. SHAW, L. W.: *Education in Newfoundland with Special Emphasis on Recent Developments.* Unpublished master's thesis, Mount Allison University, Sackville, N.B., 1943.

190. SHEANE, G. K.: *The History and Development of the Curriculum of the Elementary Schools in Alberta.* Unpublished doctoral thesis, University of Toronto, 1948.

191. SHORTT, ADAM, AND DOUGHTY, A. G. (editors): *Canada and Its Provinces.* 22 vols. and index. Toronto: Glasgow, Brook and Co., 1914. Contains articles on the history of education in nine provinces.

192. SHORTT, ADAM, AND DOUGHTY, A. G.: *Documents Relating to the Constitutional History of Canada. 1759-1791.* Ottawa: King's Printer, 1918.

193. SIMMS, E. F.: *A History of Public Education in Manitoba from 1870 to 1890, Inclusive.* Unpublished master's thesis, University of Manitoba, 1944.

194. SISSONS, C. B.: *Bilingual Schools in Canada.* Toronto: J. M. Dent and Sons, Ltd., 1917.

195. SMITH, FRANK: *A History of English Elementary Education, 1760-1902.* London: University of London Press, 1931.

196. SMITH, W. L.: *The Pioneers of Old Ontario.* In the Makers of Canada Series. Toronto: X George N. Morang, 1923.

197. SPRAGGE, G. W.: *Monitorial Schools in the Canadas, 1810-1845.* Unpublished doctoral thesis, University of Toronto, 1935.

198. STANSELL, SIDNEY S. S.: *The Rise of Elementary Education in Alberta.* Unpublished master's thesis, Stanford University, California, 1934.

199. TANSER, H. A.: *Settlement of Negroes in Kent County.* Unpublished doctoral thesis, University of Toronto, 1939.

200. THIBEAU, PATRICK W.: *Education in Nova Scotia before 1811.* Doctoral thesis, Catholic University of America, Washington, D.C., 1922.

201. THOMAS, J. M.: *A Study of Teacher's Retirement Schemes in Canada.* Unpublished doctoral thesis, University of Toronto, 1942.

202. THWAITES, R. G. (ed.): *Jesuit Relations and Allied Documents, 1610-1791.* 73 vols. Cleveland, 1896-1901.

203. UNITED STATES BUREAU OF EDUCATION: Bulletin ,1919, No. 49 (on the language issue).

204. VALLERY, H. J.: *A History of Indian Education in Canada.* Unpublished master's thesis, Queen's University, 1942.

X 205. WAGNER, EDITH: *Education as Revealed in Family Papers, Ontario 1800-1900.* Unpublished master's thesis, University of Toronto, 1954.

206. WAITE, W. H.: *The History of Elementary and Secondary Education in Saskatchewan.* Unpublished master's thesis, University of Manitoba, Winnipeg, 1936.

207. WARBURTON, A. B.: *A History of Prince Edward Island.* St. John, N. B.: Barnes and Co., 1923.

208. WARNER, J. E.: *History of Secondary Education in New Brunswick.* Unpublished master's thesis, University of New Brunswick, Fredericton, N.B., 1944.

209. WEIR, G. M.: *The Separate School Question in Canada.* Toronto: The Ryerson Press, 1934.

210. WESTWATER, ROBERT: *A Study of the Work in Canada and Newfoundland of Canadian Legion Educational Services.* Unpublished doctoral thesis, University of Toronto, 1949.

211. WHITE, E. T.: *Public School Textbooks in Ontario.* London, Ontario: The Chas. Chapman Co., 1922.

212. WILLOUGHBY, J.: *Progress of Education in Nova Scotia during Fifty Years.* Halifax, 1884.

211. WITTKE, CARL: *A History of Canada.* Toronto: McClelland and Stewart, Ltd., 1935.

214. WOODLEY, ELSIE C.: *The History of Education in the Province of Quebec.* Unpublished master's thesis, McGill University, 1932.

215. WRONG, GEORGE M.: *A Canadian Manor and Its Seigneurs.* Toronto: The Macmillan Co., 1926.

216. WRONG, GEORGE M.: *The Canadians.* Toronto: The Macmillan Co., 1938.

217. YOUNG, G. R.: *Colonial Literature, Science, and Education.* Halifax, 1842. 3 vols.

Among the many useful materials not included in the above bibliography are school text-books, textbooks on education (with a few exceptions), later educational periodicals, other periodicals and newspapers, and local histories and records. For further bibliographies see the following:

Smith, A. H. et al.: *A Bibliography of Canadian Education.* Bulletin No. 10, Department of Educational Research, University of Toronto, 1938.

Humanities Research Council: *Canadian Graduate Theses in the Humanities and Social Sciences,* 1921-1946. Ottawa: King's Printer, 1951.

———: *Graduate Theses in Education.* Mimeographed. Toronto: Canadian Education Association, 1952.

Bibliographies of recent works are published periodically in the Biennial Survey (38), and in: National Library of Canada: *Canadian Theses — a List of Theses Accepted by Canadian Universities,* Ottawa: Queen's Printer, 1953.

References

Sources of most longer quotations are indicated below. The numbers in brackets refer to publications so listed in the bibliography. The many quotations obviously taken from annual reports of provincial departments of education or other provincial government publications are not annotated, unless they are copied from a secondary source. An attempt has been made to make the text self-explanatory and to reduce the need for numerical references. It is obviously not possible in a general work to give credit specifically for all information and ideas.

Below the references by number to quotations a list has been given, where practicable, of items in the bibliography useful in relation to the period or topic covered in the chapter.

CHAPTER ONE

Specific Reference:

1. Thwaites (191) vol. XXIII, p. 291
2. Douglas (71) pp. 363-366
3. Thwaites (191) vol. LII, p. 47
4. Boyd (21) p. 296
5. Barnard (9) p. 42
6. Barnard (9) p. 49
7. Parkman (167) pp. 441-442
8. Colby (55) pp. 328-329
9. Colby (55) pp. 327-328
10. Clark (54) pp. 71-72
11. Clark (54) p. 71
12. Garneau (81) vol. I, p. 234
13. Barnard (9) p. 293
14. Barnard (9) p. 48
15. Barnard (9) p. 292
16. Gosselin, A. E. (191) XVI, pp. 363-364
17. Douglas (71) pp. 387-388
18. Thwaites (191) vol. LVII, p. 61
19. Thwaites (191) vol. LII, p. 99
20. Clark (54) p. 73
21. Drummond, Lewis (191) vol. II, p. 421
22. Bracq (22) p. 30
23. Woodley (214) p. 24
24. Parkman (167) pp. 414-415

General Reference:

For social history, including education, Bracq (22), Brown (26 and 27), Burt (30), Clark (54), Colby (55), Douglas (71), Doughty (69), Drummond (191, vol. II), Lower (131), McInnis (140), Parkman (167), Sandham (187), Wittke (213), and Wrong (215 and 216).

For educational history, Audet (6, vol. II), Gosselin (88 and 191, vol. XVI), the chief authority, Roy (184), and Woodley (214).

For the French tradition in education, Barnard (9); for convenient source material, *Jesuit Relations* (202) and Lahontan (119) and quotations in Brown (27), Clark (54), Colby (55), Douglas (71), Gosselin (88 and 191, vol. XVI), and Parkman (167).

CHAPTER TWO

Specific Reference:

1. Hannay (95) pp. 304-305
2. Raymond, W. O. (191) vol. XIII, p. 55
3. Campbell (36) p. 118
4. Bingay (12) pp. 2-3

The authors of the other two dissertations are Le Gresley and Thibeau.

General Reference:

For social history, including education: most references of chapter I and Campbell (36), Hannay (95), MacMechan (191, vol. XIII), Macphail (191, vol. XIII), Parkman (166), and Raymond (191, vol. XIII).

For convenient source matgay (12), Hay (191, vol. XIV), MacKay (191, vol. XIV), Le Gresley (125) and Thibeau (200), of whom the last two are much the most useful.

For convenient source material, the works mentioned under chapter I and also Lescarbot (126).

CHAPTER THREE

Specific Reference:

1. Adamson (1) p. 191
2. Cubberley (61) pp. 449-450
3. Smith (195) p. 56

General Reference:

For educational history, Adamson (1), Barnard (10), Birchenough (13), Curtis (62), and Smith (195).

CHAPTER FOUR

Specific Reference:

1. Pedley (169) pp. 51, 197
2. Prowse (173) p. 119
3. Pedley (169) p. 191
4. *Ibid.* p. 156
5. Prowse (173) pp. 376-377
6. *Ibid.* p. 218
7. Rowe (183) pp. 18-19
8. *Ibid.* p. 52

General Reference:

For social history, Pedley (169), and Prowse (173); for educational history, Hickman (102) and Rowe (183).

CHAPTER FIVE

Specific Reference:

1. Hannay (96) pp. 152-153
2. MacKay, A. H. (191) vol. XIV, p. 515
3. Matthews (150) p. 10
4. Hannay (96) pp. 206-208

5. Fitch (77) p. 9
6. Thibeau (200) p. 93
7. *Ibid.* p. 50
8. Bingay (12) p. 20
9. Thibeau (200) p. 93
10. Bingay (12) p. 22
11. Thibeau (200) p. 85

General Reference:

For social history: of Nova Scotia, Campbell (36); of New Brunswick, Hannay (96); of Prince Edward Island, Warburton (207); generally, Brown (27) and books listed for chapter II.

For educational history: of Nova Scotia, Bingay (12), Le Gresley (125), MacKay (191, vol. XIV); of New Brunswick, Fitch (77), Hay (191, vol. XIV), MacNaughton (145); of Prince Edward Island, MacKay (191, vol. XIV), Matthews (150); of Cape Breton, Harvey (98) Sept., 1935; of an outstanding school, Pictou Academy, Kedy (117). Convenient source material has been published by Harvey (98).

CHAPTER SIX

Specific Reference:

1. Lower (131), p. 158
2. Shortt and Doughty (192) p. 191
3. Dawson (65)
4. Woodley (214) p. 48
5. Audet (6) vol. III, pp. 10-11 footnote
6. Boucher de la Bruère (18) p. 203, Desrosiers (191) vol. XVI, p. 409 and Parmelee (191) vol. XVI, pp. 452-453
7. Woodley (214) pp. 52-56
8. Audet (6) vol. III, pp. 118-127, 204, 304-313
9. Desrosiers (191) *loc cit.*
10. Royal Institution (186) reel 1, 144
11. Groulx (92) vol. I, pp. 14, 37-58
12. Desrosiers (191) vol. XVI, p. 404
13. Shortt and Doughty (192) pp. 907-908
14. Lucas (133) vol. III, p. 243

15. Lucas (133) vol. II, p. 31
16. McIlwraith (139) pp. 191-192
17. Lucas (133) vol. II, p. 32
18. Shortt and Doughty (192) p. 500
19. Lucas (133) vol. II, p. 30
20. *Ibid.* p. 39

General Reference:

For social history, Bourinot (19), Burt (30), Doughty (69), Lower (131), Wrong (216).

For educational history, Audet (6), Boucher de la Bruère (18), Buller (133, vol. III), Desrosiers (191, vol. XVI), Groulx (92), Magnan (147), Parmelee (191, vol. XVI), Rexford (179), Roy (184), Woodley (214). For convenient source material, Shortt and Doughty (192) and Lucas (133); in the Public Archives of Canada see especially the collection of manuscripts, L. C. Schools, (132), and also the *Quebec Gazette.*

CHAPTER SEVEN

Specific Reference:

1. Ontario Historical Society (163) vol. XXVI, pp. 555-556
2. Smith (196) p. 313
3. Hodgins (104) vol. III, p. 3
4. Hodgins (103) vol. I, p. 62
5. *Ibid.,* vol. III, p. 263
6. *Ibid.,* vol. I, p. 268
7. *Ibid.,* vol. III, p. 158
8. *Ibid.,* vol. VI, p. 132
9. *Ibid.,* vol. VI, p. 20
10. *Ibid.,* vol. II, p. 73
11. *Ibid.,* vol. II, p. 292
12. *Ibid.,* vol. I, p. 32
13. *Ibid.,* vol. I, p. 33
14. *Ibid.,* vol. I, p. 130
15. *Ibid.,* vol. I, p. 109
16. Coleman (56) p. 97
17. *Educational Papers, U.C.* (73), no. 104
18. Bannister (8) pp. 52-53
19. *Educational Papers, U.C.* (73) no. 64

General Reference:

For social history: Guillet (93), Innis (110), Middleton (153), Smith, W. L. (196).

For educational history: Bannister (8), Bell (11), Coleman (55), McCutcheon (137), Pakenham (191, vol. XVIII), and Putnam (174). For convenient source material: on education, Hodgins (103, 104, and 105) and, in the Public Archives of Canada, *Educational Papers, U.C.* (73), as listed by Donaldson (68); on social conditions the Papers and Records of the Ontario Historical Society (163) and also early newspapers.

CHAPTER EIGHT

Specific Reference:

1. Manual (148) pp. 29-30
2. Murray (159) pp. 9-10
3. *L. C. Schools* (132), 1830
4. Simms (193) p. 5
5. Harvey (98) May, 1934, p. 469
6. *Ibid.*, pp. 478-479
7. Woodley (214) p. 64

General Reference:

For monitorial schools: Murray (159), and Spragge (197). For early school legislation, see references of chapters IV, V, VI, and VII. For an estimate of the state of education, material must be sought chiefly in journals of the legislatures and in other documents in the archives.

CHAPTER NINE

Specific Reference:

1. Hodgins (103) vol. II, p. 37
2. *Ibid.* p. 271
3. Quoted in the introduction to Sullivan's *Spelling Book Superseded,* one of the Irish National textbooks.
4. Martyn (149) pp. 11-12
   The above scene and parts of the other lessons are based on a play written and produced about twenty-five years ago by the late W. E. MacPherson, Professor of the History of Education, University of Toronto, and by the author.

General Reference:

For classroom conditions and methods of teaching: Bannister (8), Calkin (33), Campbell (37), Hodgins (104, vols. I-II), Martyn (149), Percival (171), Phillips (172), White (211).

CHAPTER TEN

Specific Reference:

1. Simms (193) p. 17
2. Newfield (160) p. 38
3. Garriock (82) pp. 120-121
4. Goresky (87) p. 1
5. Hughes (109) p. 88
6. MacLaurin (144) pp. 41-42
7. *Ibid.* pp. 67-68

General Reference:

For Manitoba: Newfield (160), Simms (193); for Saskatchewan and Alberta: Black (14), Goresky (87); for British Columbia: MacLaurin (144), Robinson (191, vol. XXII).

CHAPTER ELEVEN

Specific Reference:

1. Lower (131) p. 524
2. McNaughton (145) p. 6
3. Gesner (83) p. 322
4. *Canada Educational Monthly,* (43) II, p. 366

CHAPTER TWELVE

Specific Reference:

1. Suggested by a table in Waite (206) p. 159
2. Feb. 26th
3. Lysecki (135) p. 25
4. Murray (159) pp. 42-43

CHAPTER THIRTEEN

Specific Reference:

1. *Educational Papers, U.C.* (73) no. 405
2. MacLaurin (144) pp. 198-199
3. *Ibid., loc. cit.*
4. *Canada Educational Monthly* (43) vol. III, pp. 387-389
5. Bourinot (19) p. 47

General Reference:

For this and most of the following chapters no short list of references is possible because there are few historical studies of a topical nature on Canadian education. The material in this chapter is based partly on general histories of education in the various provinces, already mentioned, but chiefly on primary sources, including annual reports on education and other publications of provincial governments, periodicals, newspapers, pamphlets, and documents in the archives. Later statistical data may be secured from publications of the Dominion Bureau of Statistics.

CHAPTER FOURTEEN

Specific Reference:

1. Hickman (102) p. 29
2. Vol. II, p. 81 (*C.S.J.*)
3. Bolger (17) pp. 172, 211-214
4. *Canada School Journal* (45) III, page 90
5. Simms (193) pp. 7-11

General Reference:

Histories of education in nine provinces up to the beginning of World War I may be found in *Canada and Its Provinces* (191). There are a few published histories covering later as well as the early years: for Newfoundland, Rowe (183); for New Brunswick, McNaughton (145); for Roman Catholic Quebec, Audet (6) and for Protestant Quebec, Percival (171); for Ontario, McCutcheon (137). Unpublished or not conveniently available are: Matthews (150) for Prince Edward Island; Bingay (12) for Nova Scotia; Newfield (160), Simms (193), Glinz (85), and Lysecki (135) for Manitoba; Calder (31) for Saskatchewan; Goresky (87) for Alberta; MacLaurin (144) for British Columbia.

CHAPTER FIFTEEN

Specific Reference:

1. Feb. 25, 1830
2. *L. C. Schools* (132) vol. XIV, p. 125
3. Pamphlet (165) II, 2212 and Ross (182) pp. 26-27
4. *Educational Papers, U.C.* (73) no. 557
5. *L. C. Schools* (132) vol. IV
6. *Canada Educational Monthly* (43) vol. II, pp. 169, 209
7. *C.E.M.* (43) vol. I, p. 185
8. Lucas (133) vol. III, p. 263
9. *L. C. Schools* (132) vol. XII
10. P. 27
11. Rowe (183) p. 121
12. Quoted in the *Canada School Journal* (45) vol. I, p. 12
13. *C.S.J.* (45) vol. III, p. 89
14. November 9th
15. *C.E.M.* (43) vol. II, p. 184
16. Audet (6) vol. IV, p. 224
17. Murray (159) p. 16
18. Pamphlet (165) I, 2706
19. See *C.E.M.* (43) vol. II, pp. 177-179, 233, 268, 271 and vol. III, p. 94
20. Dawson (64) p. 72
21. Althouse (2) p. 66
22. *C.E.M.* (43) vol. II, p. 334 and also pp. 297-298, 139-145, 365-367
23. *Educational Weekly* (75) Dec. 17, 1885

CHAPTER SIXTEEN

Specific Reference:

1. Hickman (102), p. 29
2. Mss. p. 215 in *L. C. Schools* (132) vol. XIV
3. Woodley (214) p. 79
4. Calkin (33) p. 42
5. *Canada School Journal* (45) vol. III, pp. 126-127
6. Calder (31) p. 12
7. Bingay (12) p. 78
8. *Centennial Story* (16) pp. 69, 96
9. Fitch (77) pp. 67-68
10. Lynam (134) p. 128
11. Murray (159) p. 44
12. Laidlaw (120) p. 6
13. Lynam (134) pp. 167-168
14. *Centennial Story* (16) pp. 100-102

15. *C.S.J.* (45) vol. III, p. 141
16. Robinson (181) pp. 120-123
17. Murray (159) p. 32
18. *Centennial Story* (16) p. 22
19. January 31, 1852
20. MacLaurin (144) p. 66-67
21. Bingay (12) p. 64
22. *C.S.J.* (45) vol. IV, p. 77
23. Robinson (181) pp. 51-52
24. Quoted by Dunkin, pp. 148-149 — *L. C. Schools* (132) vol. XIV
25. Cameron (34) p. 49
26. Groulx (92) pp. 51-52
27. Foght: *A Survey of Education* (78) p. 22
28. *Canada Educational Monthly* (43) vol. II, pp. 284-286
29. Penrose (170) p. 9
30. *C.S.J.* (45) vol. III. p. 127

CHAPTER SEVENTEEN

Specific Reference:

1. *Educational Papers, U.C.* (73) no. 96
2. Parkman quoted by Woodley (214) p. 30
3. Newfield (160) p. 21
4. Hickman (102) p. 4
5. *E.P.U.C.* (73) no. 253
6. Clark (54) p. 192
7. *E.P.U.C.* (73) no. 402
8. Rennie (177) pp. 94-96
9. Goresky (87) pp. 66-67
10. Hickman (102) pp. 40-41
11. *L. C. Schools* (132) vol. XIII
12. *Ibid.*
13. Archives, Bishop's Palace, Quebec, *C.I.R.* vol. I, p. 29
14. Hodgins (106) pp. 37-39. A similar attitude was expressed in 1852 (May 22) by the Roman Catholic *Mirror*, which declared that in sparsely settled districts of Upper Canada there could be no objection to the teaching in schools of secular content without religious content.
15. Pamphlet (165) I, 2391
16. *Canada Educational Monthly* (43) vol. I, p. 149
17. *Kingston Daily News*, Nov. 16, 1887
18. Page 493

19. Hodgins (106) p. ix. Ryerson, in the *Report of the Superintendent of Education* for 1852 (p. 25), said that "the law has to do with individuals and individual rights, not with religious persuasions or ecclesiastical authorities." He argued that a denominational system "annihilates individual right of choice."
20. Hodgins (106) p. 105
21. Lapp (123) pp. 153-154
22. Woodley (214) p. 95
23. Weir (209) p. 28
24. *C.E.M.* (43) vol. III, pp. 253-254
25. Extracts quoted by Simms (193) pp. 92-94
26. Statutes of Canada, 38 Victoria, chapter 49, quoted by Waite (206) p. 43
27. Weir (209) p. 68
28. Sheane (190) p. 26
29. Anglin (4) pp. 14-15
30. Pamphlet I, 3015
31. MacNaughton (145) p. 196
32. MacLaurin (144) p. 28
33. *Ibid* p. 55
34. *Ibid* pp. 45-46
35. Warner (208) p. 241
36. Hodgins (103) vol. X, p. 301
37. *Ibid.* vol. VII, p. 165. The separate school controversy caused many people to oppose any religious instruction in school. The Toronto *Globe* in 1855 (June 25) declared that religious education must be left to the home and the church and that the schools should be made entirely public and unsectarian. The same year in his annual report (p. 11) even Ryerson admitted that if there were renewed agitation for further concessions to the denominational point of view it would be better "to abolish the separate school law altogether" and to keep religious instruction separate from secular instruction.

38. *The Ontario Teacher* (164) 1873, p. 68
39. Millar (154) p. 50
40. *Ibid.* p. 52
41. *C.E.M.* (43) vol. III, pp. 321-327
42. Lucas (133) vol. III, p. 275
43. Hickman (102) p. 30
44. Pamphlet (165) I, 1498
45. *Ibid.* I, 4187

General Reference:

On separate schools: Weir (209). On religious education: Matthews (151).

CHAPTER EIGHTEEN

Specific Reference:

1. *Educational Papers, U.C.* (73) no. 709
2. Lysecki (135) pp. 46, 56
3. Sissons (194) p. 81
4. Bulletin No. 49, p. 4
5. *Kosmos,* 1885, p. 216
6. MacNaughton (145) pp. 24-25
7. *Educational Weekly* (76) vol. I, p. 55
8. *Ibid., loc. cit.*
9. Hodgins (103) vol. I, p. 3
10. Public Archives, Canada — Q Series, 410 (2) p. 307, U. C. 1838
11. Murray (159) p. 14
12. Q Series 410 (2) pp. 296-297, U. C. 1838
13. *E.P.U.C.* (73) no. 464
14. *E.P.U.C.* (73) no. 636
15. Copp (57) pp. 24-25
16. *Canada Educational Monthly* (43) vol. III, p. 250
17. Pamphlet (165) II, 5285
18. *C.E.M.* (43) vol. II, pp. 100, 101

General Reference:

On federal government activities: Miller (155). On the education of Indians: Vallery (204).

CHAPTER NINETEEN

Specific Reference:

1. Lynam (134) pp. 209-210
2. (45) Vol. II, pp. 103-104

3. Vol. I, p. 473
4. Percival (171) p. 39
5. *Canada Educational Monthly* (43) vol. II, p. 107
6. Clark (54) p. 264
7. Hodgins (103) vol. VI, p. 294
8. Kelso (118) p. 13

CHAPTER TWENTY

Specific Reference:

1. Warner (209) p. 122
2. March, 1852
3. May, 1851
4. Issues published in 1848, p. 57
5. *Canada Educational Monthly* (43) vol. II, p. 480
6. *Ibid.* vol. I, p. 276
7. *Ibid.* vol. III, p. 425
8. Pamphlet (165) II, 678
9. *Educational Review,* N.B. (75) vol. I
10. Vol. VII, p. 144
11. Report of a Select Committee of the Legislature, U.C., on Upper Canada Academy, 9th February, 1837
12. MacNaughton (145) p. 140
13. Pamphlet (165) I, 3632
14. *C.E.M.* (43) vol. I, p. 551
15. *Ibid.* vol, I, p. 483
16. Percival (171) p. 185
17. *C.E.M.* (43) vol. I, p. 202

CHAPTER TWENTY-ONE

Specific Reference:

1. Pamphlet (165) I, 1876
2. *Journal of Education,* N.S. (114) April, 1867
3. Clark (54) p. 184
4. Pamphlet (165) I, 2706
5. *Catechism of Education,* pamphlet of 1830
6. *Canada School Journal* (45) vol. IV, p. 128
7. *Canada Educational Monthly* (43) vol. I, p. 507
8. *Canadian Magazine,* July 1893, pp. 363-364
9. Bourinot (19) p. 10
10. Strachan Papers (67, 205), March 31, 1802
11. Gesner (83) pp. 330-331
12. Calkin (33) p. 60
13. Clark (54) p. 384

14. *Ibid.,* p. 158
15. *Ibid.,* p. 187
16. Public Archives, Canada, G Series, vol. XVI
17. MacNaughton (145) p. 77
18. Clark (54) p. 392
19. *Ibid.,* p. 468
20. Woodley (214) p. 46
21. *C.S.J.* (45) vol. I, p. 97
22. Strachan Papers (67, 205), July 20, 1808
23. *Journal of Education,* N.S. (114) April, 1867

CHAPTER TWENTY-TWO

Specific Reference:

1. *Journal of Education,* U.C. (115) 1848, p. 337
2. Forrester (79) p. 434
3. *Proceedings,* Dominion Education Association (47), 1892, p. 249
4. Forrester (79) p. 434
5. *Ibid.,* p. 461
6. *Canada Educational Monthly* (43) vol. I, p. 30
7. *Lectures on Teaching,* p. 217
8. *C.E.M.* (43) vol. II, p. 105
9. *Ibid.,* p. 329
10. June 16th
11. *Canada School Journal* (45) vol. I, pp. 24-25
12. December
13. *C.S.J.* (45) vol. II, p. 74
14. Langley (121) p. 124
15. *Minutes,* O.T.A. (162) 1884, p. 46
16. *The School* (188) vol. VII, p. 451
17. Hodgins (103) vol. V, p. 307
18. *Ibid.,* vol. XXII, pp. 133-134
19. *J. of E.,* U.C. (115) 1867, p. 197
20. *Ibid.,* 1860, p. 10
21. *Ibid.,* 1860, p. 34
22. Hodgins (103) vol. XI, p. 171
23. *J. of E.,* U.C. (115) 1864, p. 19
24. Hodgins (103) vol. XIX, p. 100
25. Forrester (79) p. 12
26. *J. of E.,* U.C. (115) 1873, p. 124
27. *Minutes,* O.T.A. (162) 1885, p. 31

28. *The School* (188) vol. I, p. 260

CHAPTER TWENTY-THREE

Specific Reference:

1. *The Ontario Teacher* (164) vol. I, p. 323
2. November, 1887
3. Bourinot (19) p. 43
4. Warner (208) p. 211
5. Kedy (117) pp. 7-8
6. Hodgins (103) vol. XX, pp. 112-113
7. *The School* (188) *vol.* XXIII, p. 377
8. Hewson (101) p. 120
9. Aylesworth (7) p. 11
10. Pamphlet (165) II, 2622
11. *Educational Papers,* U.C. (73) no. 328
12. Audet (6) vol. I, p. 52
13. Hodgins (103) vol. XX, p. 156
14. *Minutes* of the association, pamphlet, p. 5
15. Harvey (98) March, 1935, p. 132
16. John Steele Papers (67, 205), Nov. 27, 1839
17. *L. C. Schools* (132) vol. XVI
18. *Toronto of Old* by Henry Scadding 1873, p. 161
19. Rennie (177) p. 54
20. Forrester (79) p. 13
21. *The Nova Scotia Arithmetic*
22. Page 85
23. *The Educational Weekly* (75) Jan. 1. 1885
24. Report (178) Appendix, p. 26
25. *Canada Educational Monthly* (43) vol. II, p. 528
26. Calkin (32) p. 32
27. Millar (154) p. 217
28. *Canada School Journal* (45) vol. III, p. 102
29. December 10th
30. Calkin (32) p. 85
31. Lynam (134) p. 226
32. Forrester (79) p. 214
33. *The School* (188) vol. XV, pp. 860-866
34. *Ibid.,* vol. XII, p. 612
35. Newfield (160) p. 57
36. *Colonial Advocate* (67) Dec. 16, 1830

37. *The School* (188) vol. I, p. 161
38. *C.E.M.* (43) vol. III, p. 192

General Reference:

Curriculum development in Saskatchewan: Langley (121). Elementary school curriculum development in Alberta: Sheane (190).

CHAPTER TWENTY-FOUR

Specific Reference:

1. Audet (6) vol. IV, pp. 227-228
2. Calkin (33) p. 47
3. *Proceedings, Dominion Educational Association* (47), 1898, p. 335
4. Bound records, Department
5. Page 198
6. *Canada Educational Monthly* (43) vol. III, p. 207
7. Forrester (79) p. 378
8. *Canada School Journal* (45) vol. I, p. 65
9. *C.E.M.* (43) vol. III, p. 216
10. Hodgins (107), p. 115
11. Report (178) P.E.I., 1846
12. Hodgins (104) vol. II, p. 110
13. *The Courier,* U.C., March 14, 1832
14. Pamphlet (165) I, 4187
15. *C.E.M.* (43) vol. II, p. 151 cf. vol. I, p. 122
16. Hodgins (103) vol. XXIII, p. 165
17. *Minutes* O.E.A. (162) 1894, pp. 168-175
18. Aylesworth (7) pp. 77-78
19. Mss. of M. W. Althouse
20. January 1st
21. *C.E.M.* (43) vol. II, pp. 256-258
22. *The School* (188) vol. I, p. 192
23. August 22nd
24. *Educational Review,* N. B. (74) Oct. 1943
25. Pamphlet (165) I, 3520
26. *C.S.J.* (45) vol. IV, p. 65; *C.E.M.* (43) vol. I, p. 273; *C.S.J.* (45) vol. III, p. 70; *E.W.* (75) Jan. 29, 1885

General Reference:

Arithmetic: Campbell (37). English: Phillips (172). Mathematics: Gray (90). Modern languages: Goldstick (86). Science: Croal (59).

CHAPTER TWENTY-FIVE

Specific Reference:

1. *The Globe,* Toronto, Feb. 9, 1884
2. Matthews (150) p. 9
3. Hodgins (103) vol. III, p. 241
4. Woodley (214) p. 66
5. December 19th
6. *The Ontario Teacher* (164) vol. I, p. 232
7. Murray (159) pp. 39-40
8. *Educational Monthly of Canada* (43) Jan., 1905
9. *The News,* Toronto, Dec. 2, 1902
10. Pamphlet (165) II, 2523
11. Aylesworth (7) pp. 62-63
12. Hickman (102) p. 14
13. MacLaurin (144) p. 38
14. Robinson (181) p. 91
15. *C.E.M.* (43) vol. III, p. 237
16. *Canada School Journal* (45) vol. III, p. 90
17. Mss.
18. Hodgins (103) vol. XV, p. 214
19. Glinz (85) p. 53
20. Cartwright Papers (67) 1884, p. 205
21. Reynolds Papers (67) 1888, p. 205
22. Warburton (207) p. 358
23. Merritt Papers (67)
24. *C.E.M.* (43) vol. II, p. 325
25. Ontario Educational Association, *Proceedings* (162), 1903, p. 71

CHAPTER TWENTY-SIX

Specific Reference:

1. Hickman (102) p. 14
2. Lynam (134) p. 71
3. *Educational Monthly of Canada* (43) March, 1905
4. *Proceedings,* Dominion Educational Association (47) 1895

5. *The Ontario Teacher* (164) vol I, p. 156
6. *Minutes,* O.T.A., (162) 1873
7. Johnson (112) p. 13
8. For example, Hodgins (103) vol. X, p. 6
9. *C.E.M.* (43) vol. II, p. 242
10. *L. C. Schools,* 1830
11. *E.M.C.* (43) Nov. 1905
12. *Ibid.*
13. Calkin (32) p. 291
14. Bound records in the Department of Education, P.E.I., vol. II, p. 86
15. *The School* (188) vol. XVII, Jan. 1929
16. *Educational Papers,* U.C. (73) no. 444
17. Regulations
18. Quoted in *C.E.M.* (43) vol. I, p. 325
19. Lynam (134) p. 73
20. *Canada School Journal* (45) vol. III, pp. 141-142
21. Pamphlet (165) II, 669
22. *Proceedings,* D.E.A. (47) 1892, p. 233
23. Millar (154) p. 61 and pamphlet (165) II, 2622
24. *Educational Review,* N. B. (74) Dec., 1892
25. Hodgins (103) vol. XX, pp. 119-120
26. Pamphlet (165) II, 2622
27. Forrester (79) pp. 500-501
28. MacLaurin (144) pp. 277-279
29. Hodgins (106) pp. 150-151
30. *Minutes* O.T.A. (162) 1873
31. Kingston *Daily News,* Nov. 16, 1887

General Reference:

Discipline: Johnson (112).

CHAPTER TWENTY-SEVEN

Specific Reference:

1. Haliburton (94) pp. 128-129
2. Canada, Public Archives, Report, (44) 1900
3. *Canada Educational Monthly* (43) vol. II, pp. 123-124
4. Putnam (175) p. 68
5. *Proceedings,* Dominion Educational Association, (47) 1904 p. 39
6. *Proceedings,* Ontario Educational Association, (162) 1905, p. 80
7. Toronto *News,* 1903
8. Percival (171) p. 63
9. *The Provincial,* Halifax, Feb., 1853
10. Hickman (102) pp. 25-26
11. *E.P.U.C.* (73) nos. 497-499
12. Althouse (2) p. 18
13. *C.E.M.* (43) vol. II, pp. 139-145
14. *C.E.M.* (43) vol. III, p. 202 ff.

General Reference:

For the status of the teacher: in Ontario, historically, Althouse (2); in Canada, 1948, C.E.A. report (49).

CHAPTER TWENTY-EIGHT

Specific Reference:

1. *L. C. Schools* (132) 1830
2. *Ibid.*
3. Pamphlet (165) I, 1205
4. Woodley (214) pp. 67-68
5. Rexford (179) p. 77
6. Mss.
7. Clarke Papers (67, 205) March 15, 1868
8. Putnam (175) p. 22
9. Althouse (2) pp. 120, 160
10. LaZerte (124) pp. 29-30
11. *C.E.M.* (43) vol. I, pp. 156-158
12. *Educational Weekly* (75) Feb. 5, 1887, p. 87
13. *Canada School Journal* (45) vol. I, pp. 47-48
14. Percival (171) pp. 128-138
15. Lynam (134) pp. 126-127
16. Murray (159) p. 40
17. Records in the Department of Education, P.E.I., 1871
18. *Canada Educational Monthly* (43) vol. I, p. 502
19. Report (185) p. 564
20. Althouse (2) pp. 173-174
21. Robinson (18) pp. 35-36
22. Langley (121) p. 138

General Reference:

On teacher education: LaZerte (124), C.E.A. Report (48), Putnam (175), Rexford (179).

Index